Husserl, Kant and Transcendental Phenomenology

Husserl, Kant and Transcendental Phenomenology

Edited by
Iulian Apostolescu and Claudia Serban

DE GRUYTER

ISBN 978-3-11-056304-7
e-ISBN (PDF) 978-3-11-056428-0
e-ISBN (EPUB) 978-3-11-056296-5

Library of Congress Control Number: 2020933360

Bibliographic information published by the Deutsche Nationalbibliothek
The Deutsche Nationalbibliothek lists this publication in the Deutsche Nationalbibliografie;
Detailed bibliographic data are available in the Internet at http://dnb.dnb.de.

© 2022 Walter de Gruyter GmbH, Berlin/Boston
This volume is text- and page-identical with the hardback published in 2020.
Cover image: Bishop Board 2 - Gabriel Embeha (2018)
Print and binding: CPI books GmbH, Leck

www.degruyter.com

Table of Contents

Claudia Serban and Iulian Apostolescu
Husserl, Kant, and Transcendental Phenomenology
    Editors' Introduction —— 1

Section I: The Transcendantal and the A priori

Veronica Cibotaru
The Meaning of the Transcendental in the Philosophies of Kant and Husserl —— 23

Susi Ferrarello
The Ethics of the Transcendental —— 41

John Rogove
The Phenomenological *a priori* as Husserlian Solution to the Problem of Kant's "Transcendental Psychologism" —— 57

Elena Partene
On the Naturalization of the Transcendental —— 83

Claudia Serban
Kant, Husserl, and the Aim of a "Transcendental Anthropology" —— 101

Section II: The Ego and the Sphere of Otherness

Inga Römer
Transcendental Apperception and Temporalization
    Husserl on Kant —— 127

Vincent Gérard
"The Ego beside Itself"
    On Birth, Sleep, and Death from Kant's *Anthropology from a Pragmatic Point of View* to Husserl's *Late Manuscripts on Time-Constitution* —— 143

Corijn van Mazijk
Kant and Husserl on Overcoming Skeptical Idealism through Transcendental Idealism —— 163

Antoine Grandjean
"Pure Ego and Nothing More" —— 189

Irene Breuer
Towards a Phenomenological Metaphysics
　　The Contingent Core of the ego and of all Eidetic Forms —— 213

Raymond Kassis
The Transcendental Grounding of the Experience of the Other (*Fremderfahrung*) in Husserl's Phenomenology —— 235

Section III: Aesthetic, Logic, Science, Ethics

Julien Farges
Aesthetic, Intuition, Experience
　　Husserl's Redefinition of the Transcendental Aesthetic —— 259

Daniele De Santis
Synthesis and Identity
　　Husserl on Kant's Contribution to the History of Philosophy —— 279

Bernardo Ainbinder
Questions of Genesis as Questions of Validity
　　Husserl's New Approach to an Old Kantian Problem —— 303

Dale Allen Hobbs, Jr.
Philosophical Scientists and Scientific Philosophers
　　Kant and Husserl on the Philosophical Foundations of the Natural Sciences —— 333

Dominique Pradelle
A Phenomenological Critique of Kantian Ethics —— 359

Section IV: Transcendental Philosophy in Debate

Alexander Schnell
Is There a "Copernican" or an "Anti-Copernican" Revolution in Phenomenology? —— 391

Garrett Zantow Bredeson
Back to Fichte?
    Natorp's Doubts about Husserl's Transcendental Phenomenology —— 411

Ovidiu Stanciu
"An Explosive Thought:" Kant, Fink, and the Cosmic Concept of the World —— 439

Yusuke Ikeda
Eugen Fink's Transcendental Phenomenology of the World
    Its Proximity and Distance in Relation to Kant and the Late Husserl —— 455

Steven Crowell
Amphibian Dreams
    Karsten Harries and the Phenomenology of 'Human' Reason —— 479

Natalie Depraz
Husserlian Phenomenology in the Light of Microphenomenology —— 505

Index of Persons —— 523

Subject Index —— 527

Claudia Serban and Iulian Apostolescu
Husserl, Kant, and Transcendental Phenomenology

Editors' Introduction

From Kantian criticism to Husserlian phenomenology, transcendental philosophy has proven to be undeniably resilient and, at the same time, has seen a controversial reception. The aim of this volume is to inquire into the profound meaning of this motif by contrasting the Kantian and phenomenological versions of transcendental philosophy on several crucial points.

Far from being unanimously accepted by his students and contemporary philosophers of different orientations, the transcendental turn in Husserl's phenomenology has always been a source of divided interpretations among scholars. Thus, the deep significance and necessity of this turn have been continually interrogated: what is the precise content and nature of the transcendental, and what does it mean vis-à-vis Husserl's relationship to Kant? To what extent does phenomenology square with idealism, insofar as it redefines transcendental subjectivity and uncovers the realm of intersubjectivity? How does it reshape the project of a transcendental aesthetic or logic, as well as the foundation of the sciences or ethics? In short, what is it that distinguishes the "baroque" (Moran 2002, p. 51) form of transcendental philosophy advocated by Husserl from the Kantian one?

The contributions gathered here approach these issues both historically and systematically by means of a thorough engagement with the available literature in Kant and Husserl studies, while also taking into account some indispensable recent publications (such as that of *Husserliana*, volume XLII: *Die Grenzprobleme der Phänomenologie*, 2014). Following the latest research trends in the field of transcendental phenomenology (Mohanty 1997; Crowell 2001 and 2013; Luft 2011; Fabbianelli and Luft 2014; Luft 2018; Heinämaa, Hartimo, Miettinen, 2014; Staiti 2014; Gardner, Grist 2015; Honenberger 2016; Kim, Hoeltzel 2016; Engelland 2017; Zahavi 2017), the present volume offers a range of in-depth analyses that aim at elucidating and evaluating some of the essential features of transcendental philosophy, as well as some of the important debates that its reception has generated in German Idealism, Neo-Kantianism, and in the subsequent phenomenological tradition. Without pretending to accomplish the task of a systematic confrontation between Husserl's phenomenology and the main lines of Kant's transcendental strategy (which might be impossible, if we follow Luft 2018, p. 47), this collection of works authored by both junior and senior researchers provides a complex and nuanced picture of the challenges and possibilities opened up by the transcendental problematic.

The Transcendental and the A Priori

This volume brings together twenty-three contributions arranged into four sections. The first section deals primarily with the significance and scope of the transcendental from a perspective that presents itself from the outset as both historical and systematic.

In "The Meaning of the Transcendental in the Philosophies of Kant and Husserl," Veronica Cibotaru highlights the discrepancy between the two uses of the transcendental: while Kant introduces and develops the notion in an attempt to ensure the possibility of metaphysics, Husserl mobilizes it within his endeavor to provide a deeper understanding of the relationship between the subject and the world. Nevertheless, these uses display one common feature: both of these appeals to the transcendental manifest the imperative of the infinite as a fundamental structure of subjectivity. Following this path, Cibotaru engages several key questions: for instance, she refutes the perspective according to which the meaning of the transcendental in Kant's philosophy is primarily defined as reflecting knowledge or self-knowledge of human reason and subjectivity, and argues that transcendental philosophy is more specifically preoccupied with the grounding of the concepts of pure reason, with their possibility and legitimacy. Thus, it is the foundation of the sciences – and eventually, of metaphysics itself – that is at stake in transcendental philosophy: it is for this reason that its elaboration by Kant takes the shape of a critical project. In contrast, for Husserl, the meaning and scope of the transcendental is quite obviously no longer determined by the concern for the possibility of a metaphysics. Yet this does not imply any relinquishing of interest in the general problem of foundation, insofar as for Husserl the grounding of knowledge in general, and of a pure logic or of sciences in particular, is a major and constant active preoccupation. From this perspective, phenomenology itself has a critical significance, in the Kantian sense of the term: with its development marking the turn to transcendental idealism, Husserl aims at a radical foundation of knowledge in general and of science in particular, a foundation that simultaneously disclaims the epistemological pretensions of psychology and the unchallenged hegemony of the natural sciences. This radical foundation finds its privileged methodological tool in phenomenological reduction, whose reshaping and new interpretation as transcendental only accentuates this constant concern for a grounding.

In "The Ethics of the Transcendental," Susi Ferrarello points out the distinctive characteristics of a thought which aims at elucidating the link between Being and meaning, while also investigating its ethical implications and the kind of meaning-giving activity it involves. The author initially retraces the historical path that leads to Kant's philosophical use of the transcendental through Calov and Baumgarten and states that it is only with Kant that we truly face a shift from an ontological to an epistemological way of explaining the transcendental, and a new orientation towards subjectivity in the determination of the object. Importantly, if Husserl attempts to overcome the anthropological limitation of Kant's account of the transcendental, he also joins Kant in considering *time* to be that which ultimately explains the interconnection between Being and meaning. Nevertheless, if the productive function of time bridges Being and meaning for Husserl as well, the anthropological and psychological dimension of time is bracketed through phenomenological reduction, thus reaching into a deeper realm of subjectivity. Where, then, might the ethical quality of transcendental philosophy come from? This ethical dimension comes into view precisely in connection with the search for meaning experienced as a crisis of meaning demanding a subjective commitment to truth and to moral imperatives. For this reason, Husserl is ultimately able to speak of a "transcendental humanity" (Husserl 1973, Hua XV, p. 24) as a concrete intersubjective community which decides to assume an ethical stance within its common lifeworld through a radical epoché that separates it from the point of view of the natural attitude.

In "The Phenomenological *A Priori* as the Husserlian Solution to the Problem of Kant's 'Transcendental Psychologism,'" John Rogove turns our attention to and analyzes Husserl's critique of the Kantian doctrine of the faculties, frequently accused of harboring naturalistic and empiricist metaphysical presuppositions. Furthermore, the author highlights the affinity between Husserl's denunciation of Kant's "transcendental psychologism" and the critique of Foucault, formulated in terms of a "*doublet empirico-transcendantal,*" which claims that critical philosophy inevitably results in anthropology. The phenomenological attempt to ensure the de-anthropologization of the *a priori* leads Husserl to the discovery of a new kind of necessity, neither solely empirical nor merely formal, namely, the material *a priori*. This radical divergence in the interpretation of the *a priori* appears to lie at the very heart of the difference between Kant's and Husserl's versions of transcendental philosophy. The latter's corollary is the assertion of the intuitive givenness of the *a priori* – whether subjective or objective – whereas Kant had maintained that everything pertaining to the transcendental ego cannot be given in intuition or in any experience whatsoever. The critical gap between form and content, or between epistemology and ontology, is thus considerably narrowed. In a nutshell, Rogove proposes an interpretation of Husserl's phenomenology which revolves around a joint de-subjectivation of the transcendental and of the *a priori*, entailing an inevitable distanciation from psychology and anthropology.

In her contribution, "On the Naturalization of the Transcendental," Elena Partene reevaluates Husserl's criticism of Kant's conception of transcendental structures, wondering whether one might be justified in interpreting Kant's transcendental theory as a form of naturalism. By means of a minute analysis of this approach, she attempts to formulate an answer to the phenomenologist's accusations from a Kantian point of view. Drawing upon the consequences of the idea of an epigenesis of pure reason, she additionally proposes a defense of the Kantian account of human or subjective finitude. In his joint disapproval of Kant's psychologism and anthropologism, Husserl equally reproaches the author of the *Critiques* for his conception of the faculties of the *Gemüt*, for the resulting account of the *a priori*, and for the epistemological limitations that come with the standpoint of the finite rational human being, which cannot therefore be conceived of as an exemplary intellect. Confronting this criticism, Partene stresses the fact that Kant introduces the idea of an "epigenesis of pure reason" precisely in order to avoid any naturalization of the transcendental and to prevent the temptation to consider it as a nature, as a psychological *datum*, or as something innate to the human mind. From a transcendental point of view, everything is acquired, and the transcendental structures of experience and knowledge are acquired in an original sense. This also means, as the author states, following Grandjean (2009), that everything that pertains to the transcendental is characterized by a certain facticity: a *non-innate, non-psychological facticity*. However, it is with respect to "the central thesis of finitude" that Partene identifies "the real point of contention between Kant and Husserl:" Kant's philosophy asserts an irreducible finitude which expresses the posteriority of the subject with respect to being; thus, being finite means being confronted with something radically exterior or with an irreducible form of otherness.

With "Kant, Husserl, and the Aim of a 'Transcendental Anthropology,'" Claudia Serban reconsiders the question of the facticity specific to the transcendental. She examines the manner in which both Kant and Husserl have conceived of and developed an anthropological counterpart to transcendental philosophy, going so far as to propose the aporetic and presumably oxymoronic idea of a "transcendental anthropology." Serban argues that it is the necessity of developing a transcendental egology for the purpose of incorporating certain fundamental aspects of the empirical (psychological and worldly) dimension of subjective life that expresses itself in these anthropological projects. In following this path, transcendental philosophy is no longer obligated to choose between subscribing to an "anthropological prohibition" (denounced in Blumenberg

2006, pp. 60, 61, 91, etc.) or accepting the "anthropologization" of the transcendental that was vigorously disavowed by Husserl. It is not only the core of philosophical anthropology and of its concept of humanity that might be reshaped in this way, but also the sense and the contents of the transcendental itself. Following Foucault's diagnosis of the "anthropologico-critical repetition" (Foucault 2008a, p. 52; Foucault 2008b, p. 83), Serban shows that it is precisely the firm rejection of any form of scientific psychology and the new articulation of the relationship between internal and external experience that leads Kant to develop his pragmatic anthropology as a genuine means of replacing psychology (whether rational or empirical). Thus, Kant's anthropological inquiry responds to a postcritical necessity and proves that instead of adhering to an anthropological prohibition, the *Critique* issues a call for an anthropology. The same can be argued for Husserl himself, given that while the famous 1931 conference on "Phenomenology and Anthropology" stresses the separation of the two disciplines, the research manuscripts from the same period thoroughly explore and develop that which the conference had already designated as their "intrinsic affinity (*innere Affinität*)" (Husserl 1989, Hua XXVII, p. 181; Husserl 1997, p. 500): in this way, it becomes possible to envision a legitimate phenomenological, and thus properly transcendental, anthropology.

The Ego and the Sphere of Otherness

Complementing the results of these inaugural analyses, the second section of the volume approaches the crucial problem of the ego: how has the view of subjectivity evolved between critical philosophy and transcendental phenomenology? Do Kant and Husserl speak of a transcendental "I" in the same sense, and does their adherence to transcendental idealism carry the same significance? Moreover, how do they conceive of the sphere of otherness – whether intersubjective or worldly?

In "Transcendental Apperception and Temporalization: Husserl on Kant," Inga Römer examines Husserl's reappropriation of Kant's idea of transcendental apperception and his interpretation of the transcendental deduction of the categories. In view of the contrasting accounts of these crucial topics in critical philosophy offered by Hegel, Cohen, and Heidegger, Römer insists upon the reasons for which, in Husserl's eyes, Kant's deductions have an anthropological and, thus, ultimately skeptical character that needs to be overcome by a more rigorously scientific transcendental philosophy, which would benefit from the fruitful methodological tool of phenomenological reduction. Drawing upon the unpublished manuscript A VI 30 (most likely written in 1926) and the late *C*-

Manuscripts, Römer extends the classical analyses of Iso Kern (1964), Klaus Held (1966), and Eduard Marbach (1974) in order to show that Husserl's final answer to the problem of a phenomenological transcendental apperception (which leaves behind what he denounces as "the mythology of the transcendental apperception" in Kant) lies in his conception of the ultimate, most fundamental layer of time-constitution. Yet the temporalization characterized by anonymity and drive-intentionality is not so much the "highest point" of transcendental phenomenology (as transcendental apperception was for Kant), but rather the "lowest," or the deepest, pre-personal dimension of subjective life.

With "'The Ego beside Itself': On Birth, Sleep, and Death from Kant's *Anthropology from a Pragmatic Point of View* to Husserl's *Late Manuscripts on Time-Constitution*," by Vincent Gérard, the volume embarks upon an exploration of the C-Manuscripts from a different perspective in order to contrast Kant's account of subjectivity with that of Husserl. The frame of reference for this comparison is no longer that of the "Transcendental Analytic," but rather that of the 1798 *Anthropology*, which is simply pragmatic or empirical without explicitly assuming a transcendental significance. It is in this context that the author of the *Critiques* analyzes the empirical processes that affect self-consciousness and discusses the traditional analogy between sleep and death. Gérard's claim is that in the analysis of sleep, birth, and death found in the *C-Manuscripts* (mainly in the *C8 Manuscript* from 1929 that the Freiburg phenomenologist considered to be "the best elucidation of the idea of limit," Husserl 2006, Hua Mat. VIII, p. 159), Husserl makes transcendental use of Kant's non-transcendental anthropology. The transcendental reconsideration of the borderline empirical phenomena of subjective life is accomplished by considering and deepening the structure of the living present: from this perspective, birth designates a past present which does not send us back to any anterior genesis, or the limit-case of the impoverishment of the living present, while death appears as the borderline case of the dreamless sleep, or as a "final sleep" where waking up is impossible. This undertaking can be regarded as an illustration of the way in which anthropological concepts or descriptions call for their own transcendental transposition or interpretation in late Husserl.

In "Kant and Husserl on Overcoming Skeptical Idealism through Transcendental Idealism," Corijn van Mazijk examines the compatibility between transcendental idealism and a form of realism that we find both in critical philosophy and in Husserl's phenomenology. This subtle position, which overcomes a simplistic contradiction between idealism and realism, goes hand-in-hand with a redefinition of the norm for the real, which is now to be found within the scope of possible experience and not in the ideal of absolute mind-independence. In other words, as the author puts it, "for an object to be real does not mean, as with transcendental realism, that it exists radically independently from us." From the standpoint of transcendental idealism, objects are to be considered as *transcendentally* inseparable from us: as a transcendental condition of objectivity, subjectivity is required in order for objects to exist at all. Thus, at this level, it is their common rejection of transcendental realism that serves as a ground for an essential proximity between Kant and Husserl. This reading is tested and reinforced by taking into account the polemical relationship of both philosophers to Descartes, their common aim of overcoming skepticism, and their subtle treatment of the hypothesis of a thing existing beyond our cognition or of a world beyond ours. In this way, Van Mazijk's analysis substantially clarifies the realism-idealism debate, which still animates the reception of both Kant and Husserl, and establishes a proximity between the two, which might counterbalance their well-known and no less radical divergences.

But what is the nature and content of the ego from which objects might ultimately derive their sense of reality? Does Husserl's view on subjectivity join Kant's analysis of the "I think" or of internal experience? In "'Pure Ego and Nothing More,'" focusing on the *Ideas I*, Antoine Grandjean examines the phenomenologist's conception of an ego which is nothing beyond its own acts. Proceeding from the natural life of the ego towards the transcendental, Husserl progressively unveils the egoity of consciousness as the other side of its intentionality, as the irreducible identity of conscious intentional life. The purity of this ego, which differs from all forms of the psychic ego – as it is characterized as the mere identity of conscious life –, contributes specifically to our understanding of the transcendental meaning of egoity. As the pole of identity of all flowing, temporal, lived experiences, the "I" itself is no lived experience; and yet, it is more than nothing, since it is that which is omnipresent and permanent where everything else is in flux. Therefore, as Grandjean insists, "its qualitative emptiness is the other side of a never-ending description." He also convincingly argues (against Marbach 1974) that one should not too hastily assign the function of unifying the stream of lived experiences to the ego: as already granted by the *Logical Investigations*, the temporal flow of consciousness has no need of an external principle in order to synthesize its unity. In turn, the ego indicates an identity, discovered through reflection, inscribed within all of the acts belonging to a life of consciousness unitary in itself. Thus, with respect to individual lived experiences, the ego is characterized as a form of transcendence-in-immanence. Consequently, Grandjean can claim that it is the discovery of the intentional sense of immanence that led phenomenology to both idealism and transcendental egology.

The pure ego of the *Ideas I* is a prepersonal ego characterized by its radical poverty and emptiness. Nevertheless, it is well-known that this vacuity has been challenged and revised by Husserl, as early as in the analyses of the personal, habitual ego provided in *Ideas II*, as well as in the genetic and monadological developments of his phenomenology. In "Towards a Phenomenological Metaphysics: The Contingent Core of the Ego and of All Eidetic Forms," Irene Breuer retraces the significant transformations of both eidetic and transcendental phenomenology which have resulted from these evolutions of Husserlian egology and highlights the remarkable emergence of a renewed, phenomenological metaphysics to which they ultimately lead. But how is it that transcendental philosophy and metaphysics have managed to cross paths again? At the time of the composition of *Ideas I*, transcendental phenomenology subscribes to an eidetic method which assigns it the rank of "first philosophy" concerned with the invariant structure inherent to all possible factual realities. In contrast, metaphysics understood as a rational investigation of factual actuality acquires the status of a "second philosophy" that presupposes eidetic phenomenology as the primordial science of possibilities. However, the specific facticity of the ego requires particular treatment not only on methodological grounds (in order to account for the task of eidetic variation), but also insofar as it opens up a new dimension of analysis, that of originary primal facts taken up by a renewed metaphysics. Hence, at the end of the path leading from transcendental philosophy, understood as an eidetic science, to phenomenological metaphysics based on originally given primal facts, the order of foundation is revised: phenomenological metaphysics – a metaphysics of apodictically given primal facts that cannot be subject to modalization (*cf.* Tengelyi 2014), substantially different from the Kantian figure of metaphysics – does indeed underlie transcendental phenomenology.

The connection between the factual "I" and the *eidos ego* obtained through self-variation appears to be an exception to the law that commonly governs the relationship between matter and essence. In "The Transcendental Grounding of the Experience of the Other (*Fremderfahrung*) in Husserl's Phenomenology," Raymond Kassis revisits this question while examining the manner in which transcendental phenomenology manages to chase away the specter of solipsism. How can the transcendental reduced ego, deprived of any natural commerce with transcendent beings, encounter the specific otherness of the *alter ego*? The response to this difficulty, which engages the intersubjectively objective unity of the world, entails significant implications for transcendental egology. In his critical reading of the available accounts of the experience of otherness, Husserl considers that both analogical reasoning (Erdmann) and recourse to empathy (Lipps) presuppose a more original manner in which the other is given in reference to the specific structure of self-experience. Indeed, the possibility of imaginative self-variation discloses the path of access to the otherness of the *alter ego*, insofar as it manifests an *eidos ego* or a realm of egological possibilities prior to any factual, existing "I." Consequently, the structure of the intersubjective community is that of a mutual implication (*Ineinander*), which is a primal fact (*Urfaktum*) as much as egological facticity is. It is on this basis that the objective unity of the world, threatened by the menace of solipsism, is eventually grounded: the ultimate subject of constitution being understood as an egological community, the world possesses an intersubjective unity for every real and possible ego.

Aesthetic, Logic, Science, Ethics

The third section of this volume further explores the confrontation between the Kantian and Husserlian versions of transcendental philosophy by approaching certain key issues, such as the scope of a transcendental aesthetic and transcendental logic, the breadth of a transcendental foundation of the empirical sciences, and the phenomenological elaboration of ethics.

In "Aesthetic, Intuition, Experience: Husserl's Redefinition of the Transcendental Aesthetic," Julien Farges examines the complex revision of the task and range of a transcendental aesthetic in Husserl's phenomenology. Committed to the structural elucidation of the subjective processes within which empirical and intuitive objectity is constituted prior to any idealizing activity, the revised transcendental aesthetic relies upon an understanding of intuition that goes beyond mere sensibility and does not preclude the intuitive givenness of categorial determinations. Moreover, it implies a radically non-Kantian aesthetization of causality, or its integration into the aesthetic frame, along with time and space, in the service of the development of a "real logic." Thus, by broadening the range of intuition and introducing the synthesis itself as the *Urform* of consciousness within the transcendental aesthetic, Husserl performs a proper phenomenological subversion of Kant's distinction between the aesthetic and the analytic, the latter being specifically called upon to give an account of the constitution of the scientific world by highlighting the acts of idealization that underlie it. Consequently, the Kantian tripartition of sensibility, understanding, and reason not only finds itself reduced to the duality of the intuitive and the discursive, of the given and the constructed, or to that of experience and thought, but the phenomenological task is also reformulated as the disclosure of the genetic continuity that exists between the two realms. Furthermore, Farges shows that this reorganization of Kant's topology is strikingly akin to the objections that Schopenhauer had raised against the author of the *Critiques* a century earlier.

In "Synthesis and Identity: Husserl on Kant's Contribution to the History of Philosophy," Daniele De Santis takes us back to Husserl's reading and use of the

Kantian articulation of the relationship between synthesis and identity. This inquiry shows that the phenomenologist repeatedly insists on the great importance of Kant's notion of synthesis, while also stressing its particular fruitfulness for an accurate understanding and definition of intentionality. Furthermore, an examination of Husserl's lectures on the history of philosophy confirms that he had fully grasped the significance of the perennial problem of determining the identity of being as it had first manifested itself in Greek thought. From this standpoint, Kant's contribution to the history of philosophy consists in his transcendental development of the notion of synthesis in order to address properly the perennial problem of identity and to oppose its Humean dissolution. While praising Kant's "profound doctrine of synthesis [*tiefsinnige Lehre von der Synthesis*]" (Husserl 1956, Hua VII, p. 237), Husserl also criticizes Brentano's shortcomings, and subsequently stresses the necessity of placing the Kantian insight at the very heart of the idea of an "intentional relation," for without synthesis there is no intentionality, and without the identity ensured through synthesis there is no intentional object (Husserl 1962, Hua IX, pp. 420-427). However, this also means that it is only when it is interpreted specifically as *intentional* synthesis that the Kantian outcome can be properly appreciated and used within the realm of phenomenology.

With "Questions of Genesis as Questions of Validity: Husserl's New Approach to an Old Kantian Problem," Bernardo Ainbinder extends the confrontation whose native ground is to be found in Kant's "Transcendental Analytic." Why did Husserl contest and refuse the Kantian exclusion of that which pertains to genesis (the subjective deduction of the categories, for instance) from the domain of transcendental inquiry? Can genetic analysis be transcendentally motivated, given that it leads to the unveiling of prepersonal cognitive mechanisms (like instincts, drives, or passive associations)? Ainbinder shows that it is Husserl's appeal to a concrete form of subjectivity that grounds a transcendental perspective in which questions of genesis and questions of validity are legitimately and intricately connected. He also opposes the interpretation according to which the phenomenologist's genetic investigations are motivated by a naturalistic assumption and are independent from the transcendental question concerning validity. Far from orchestrating a relapse into a kind of naturalism incompatible with the transcendental inquiry, Husserl retraces the genesis of intentional rational behavior in cognitive subjects and shows, with his recourse to teleology, that cognition is rooted in a tendency towards self-coherence and self-preservation that pervades living beings. Thus, the contingent factual conditions of organisms capable of cognition may gain a form of transcendental necessity, insofar as they contribute to the determination of the norms of knowledge. In this way, phenomenology integrates the outcome of Kant's "Analytic of Teleological Judgment" into transcendental philosophy and manages to overcome successfully the separation between the formal "I think" and the bodily concrete and mundane "I." However, this does not imply a naturalization of the realm of rationality, but rather a disclosure of the roots of rational normativity within the contingent concrete mechanisms of embodied biological life, which significantly reshapes the very way in which we account for the transcendental.

In "Philosophical Scientists and Scientific Philosophers: Kant and Husserl on the Philosophical Foundations of the Natural Sciences," Dale Allen Hobbs explores and contrasts the conceptions of the relationship between science and transcendental philosophy elaborated by the author of the *Critiques* and by the author of the *Crisis*. If the two converge in assigning a foundational role to transcendental philosophy, they disagree about the precise nature of this role and therefore about the nature and scope of science itself. For Kant, transcendental philosophy is the foundation of all genuine science, insofar as it alone is capable of attaining the synthetic *a priori* truths that are necessary for the application of apodictic knowledge to the natural world. Nevertheless, this philosophical rigor is responsible for certain limitations in Kant's view of science, namely, for the denial of the status of science proper to several disciplines (such as chemistry, geology, biology – not to speak of psychology or the social sciences), given that they lack the type of rigid adherence to the truly apodictic truths of transcendental philosophy that characterizes physics. While Husserl similarly claims that any genuine science must be rooted in transcendental philosophy and endorses Kant's criteria for scientificity (systematicity, the presence of grounding relations, and apodictic certainty), his conception of the natural sciences is nevertheless a less restrictive one. Especially in Husserl's later work, the phenomenological focus on the *lifeworld* – the world of our everyday interests and experiences – requires and ultimately makes possible a closer connection between science and the concerns of our prescientific lives. Thus, the phenomenologist does not limit the scope of science to the purely mathematical elements of physics, but rather broadens the category of natural sciences and admits the possibility of scientific investigation into several regions of our ordinary experience. The validity of a science does not come from the mathematization of the real that it accomplishes, but rather from the fact of its having its roots firmly planted within the soil of the lifeworld.

In "A Phenomenological Critique of Kantian Ethics," Dominique Pradelle extends his previous work on the "anti-Copernican revolution" specific to Husserlian phenomenology (Pradelle 2012, frequently referred to and quoted in this volume) by asking whether the anti-Copernican principle might also be applicable to the ethical realm, and if so, to what extent. While Kant and Husserl share the goal of refuting ethical skepticism in its various forms and agree that moral laws cannot be reduced to any kind of factual legality (whether psychological, sociological, ethnological, historical, etc.), their understanding of the practical *a priori* diverges significantly. First of all, in contrast to Kant, the phenomenologist expresses a Platonic preference for the primacy of theoretical reason and therefore tolerates or even requires recourse to reason within the practical sphere in the form of an intuition or insight (*Einsicht*) into practical norms: thus, ethics becomes "a matter of discernment or perceptiveness." Furthermore, ethics must be built – and this is a particular illustration of the relationship of grounding or *Fundierung* – "from the bottom up," as an *Ethik von unten*, in reference to the moral being's capacity for feeling and desiring. Thus, what is true in the perceptual and theoretical order is confirmed within the practical realm: the moral sense is grounded in a practical sensibility that must necessarily belong to any ethical subject, even God. This illustrates both the "essential neutralization of the distinction between God and the finite subject, infinity and finitude" (in Pradelle's wording) and the universal validity of the *Fundierung* relation within Husserl's phenomenology, whose anti-Copernican revolution, accordingly, suffers no exception in the practical field.

Transcendental Philosophy in Debate

The fourth and final section of the volume, which groups together a significant number of papers, presents and examines a few of the many debates in which transcendental philosophy has been engaged since its Kantian elaboration. The first inevitable *quaestio disputata*, raised by the contribution of Alexander Schnell, "Is There a 'Copernican' or an 'Anti-Copernican' Revolution in Phenomenology?," consists in discussing and challenging the very thesis that guides the understanding of the relationship between Kantian critical philosophy and Husserlian transcendental phenomenology found in Pradelle's contribution and previous work (see Pradelle 2012): namely, the view that opposes Kant's "Copernican revolution" to the "anti-Copernican revolution" accomplished by Husserl himself. Schnell attempts to deconstruct this apparent antinomy that separates the two transcendental projects by arguing for the necessity of going "beyond" or rather "beneath" the Copernican revolution, that is, below the subject and the object as given poles or terms of a constitutive relation. From this perspective, Husserl's endeavor appears to be a *radicalization* of the Copernican revolution. Indeed, if the anti-Copernican move seeks to avoid the perils of an anthropologization of the subject, it nevertheless risks ultimately depriving the subject of its constitutive power by condemning it to being a mere "transcendental mirror of its transcendent correlates" (Pradelle 2012, p. 365). On the other hand, going "beyond" the Copernican revolution, as envisioned by Pradelle himself, implies the disclosure of the anonymous or a-subjective structures of experience that equally precede and determine the subject and the object. It is this very task which, in Schnell's account, is taken up by his own project of a "constructive" or "generative" phenomenology that exhibits the transcendental field at work beneath the immanent field of consciousness (Schnell 2015), thus arguing for a constructive circularity between transcendental constitution and ontological grounding.

With Garrett Zantow Bredeson's contribution, "Back to Fichte? Natorp's Doubts about Husserl's Transcendental Phenomenology," we move to the field of certain remarkable historical debates inspired by the reception of transcendental philosophy. As Bredeson maintains, it is in the light of their contrasted appropriations of Kant's legacy that the divergences between Neo-Kantians (Natorp or Cassirer, in the lineage of Cohen) and phenomenologists (Husserl or Heidegger) have to be examined. Natorp does indeed share Cohen's insurmountable reticence to follow Fichte in asserting the absolute primacy of a subjective grounding of cognition, and considers, accordingly, that the approach to that which pertains to subjectivity can only be *re*constructive. This position is far from being without influence on the methodological development of early phenomenology, that of Husserl as well as that of Reinach. It is well known that Husserl's *Logical Investigations* resonate with Natorp in rejecting the psychological talk about "activities" of consciousness (Husserl 1984, Hua XIX/1, p. 393) and in stating that there is no room for the pure "I" within the stream of lived experience. However, in Natorp's eyes, Husserl's insistence upon subjective operations and accomplishments (reflected, for instance, in his preference for Kant's 1781 version of the transcendental deduction) was forceful enough to suggest a perilous proximity to Fichte. This suspicion was rightfully amplified after the publication of *Ideas I*, where the commitment to the given and to intuitive givenness could only broaden the gap between Husserl's phenomenology and Natorp's reconstructive psychology. Nevertheless, to some extent, Natorp had always considered that phenomenology's program of research was a genuinely Kantian project. What is more, as Bredeson points out, Reinach had emphasized the distance that separated the Neo-Kantian refutation of the given from the phenomenological bottom-up approach inaugurated by Husserl in an even more radical manner.

Another major player in the confrontation between phenomenology and Neo-Kantianism was Eugen Fink, Husserl's brilliant assistant. The following two contributions attempt more precisely to situate Fink within the landscape of the reception of transcendental philosophy – be it Kantian or Husserlian. In "'An Explosive Thought': Kant, Fink, and the Cosmic Concept of the World," Ovidiu Stanciu stresses the major importance of Fink's engagement with Kantian philosophy and shows that it is under the aegis of Kant that Fink accomplished the transformation of the phenomenological inquiry into a cosmological philosophy and his breakthrough towards the question of the world as the ultimate level of analysis of the constitution of meaning. In his profound reading of the "Transcendental Dialectic," Fink held Kant to be the "true discoverer of the problem of the world" (Fink 1985, p. 112) while also considering that the treatment of this problem within critical philosophy had remained insufficient. If Kant's indisputable merit consisted in dismissing the traditional vision of totality and, accordingly, the cumulative concept of the world, the subjectivistic principle of the critical solution was inacceptable in Fink's view: unveiling the "a-ontic nature of the world" and its irreducibility to an aggregate of beings does not automatically transform it into a subjective Idea. This consequence must, in fact, be referred to its hidden ontological presuppositions: namely, to the tacit hegemony of an ontology of the thing and to the secret complicity between the reification of mundane totality and its theologization – shortcomings that the phenomenological approach to the world will have had to overcome.

With "Eugen Fink's Transcendental Phenomenology of the World: Its Proximity and Distance in relation to Kant and to the Late Husserl," Yusuke Ikeda provides us with the hallmarks of Fink's phenomenological approach to the world, while also arguing that this endeavor legitimately belongs to the field of transcendental phenomenology. In contrast with researchers who claim that Fink's philosophy is neither transcendental nor strictly phenomenological and who emphasize its proximity to Hegelian speculative dialectics, Ikeda proposes reading it as a radicalization of the late Husserl's phenomenological inquiry into the problem of the "pregiven world." Indeed, while praising Kant for the discovery of the "cosmological difference" between innerwordly beings and the world itself, Fink can only deplore a certain loss or even oblivion of the genuine cosmological problem in Hegel. This problem is phenomenologically handled by Fink as one of "world-consciousness," leading to an interrogation of the pregivenness of the world. Although Fink considers that the modalities of world-consciousness are not reducible to intentionality, this does not imply a dismissal of phenomenological description and a relapse into speculation. Instead, it is upon the trail of Heidegger that Fink attempts to be "more phenomenological" than Husserl himself, by deepening rather than abandoning the transcendental orientation of inquiry into the pregivenness of the world.

In "Amphibian Dreams: Karsten Harries and the Phenomenology of 'Human' Reason," the discussion of the work of Karsten Harries gives Steven Crowell the opportunity to revisit the meaning of the transcendental profile which was adopted by phenomenology quite early in its history. In denouncing the "antinomies" of transcendental philosophy, Harries considers that phenomenology cannot efficiently dissolve or prevent these aporetic results, but is rather condemned to reproduce them: in Husserl, in the form of the "paradox of human subjectivity" which brings the medieval doctrine of the "double truth" up to date, and in Heidegger, as an inescapable "antinomy of Being" (Harries 2012, p. 10). Crowell's goal, then, is to defend phenomenology against such accusations. In order to do so, he interprets phenomenology as a "transcendental empiricism" whose purpose is to remain true to the meaning found in experience, leaving aside the traditional motivations that animated the Kantian transcendental endeavor and adopting an entirely different method: while critical philosophy employs transcendental arguments (like that of the transcendental deduction) in order to establish the conditions of possibility of experience *a priori*, phenomenology employs a transcendental reduction, or a peculiar reflection that unveils the meaning of the entities given in our experience. Thus, phenomenologically, and quite apart from any antinomy, Being and meaning depend on subjectivity, as the latter alone defines the normative space of true significations; and from this perspective, "reason is originally reason-giving," or norm-responsive. In this defense of transcendental phenomenology, Crowell will moreover insist upon the distance that separates phenomenological empiricism from traditional foundationalism.

It is this very profile of phenomenology as a transcendental empiricism that is adopted by Natalie Depraz in "Husserlian Phenomenology in the Light of Microphenomenology." She stresses anew the fact that, from Kantian philosophy to transcendental phenomenology, while subjectivity does indeed remain the provider of meaning for the object, we move from the formal conditions of the possibility of experience, which themselves cannot be experienced, to a transcendental experience in which the subject constitutes the intentional meaning of given objects. If the task of transcendental phenomenology itself is to uncover the subjective operations responsible for the objectivation process, the recent project of a microphenomenology (inaugurated by Pierre Vermersch and taken up by Depraz herself), far from representing a naturalization attempt, can be regarded as a radicalization of the transcendental orientation of Husserlian phenomenology insofar as it performs a significant shift of its descriptive focus towards the irreplaceable singularity of embodied and situated lived experiences that a mere generic or structural description cannot grasp. But the philosophical interest of microphenomenology is also directed towards the manner in which it enforces the claim of a mutual renewal of psychology by phenomenology, and vice versa. As Depraz demonstrates in her discussion of telling cases of introspection and attention, Husserl himself was largely open to the salutary and constructive influence of contemporary debates in psychology, whose major actors were Wundt, Külpe, Titchener, and Lipps. While asserting its capacity to be informed by the richness of psychological analysis, the phenomenological legacy of Husserl reaffirms the vital connection between transcendental and empirical analysis, which justifies interpreting it as a transcendental empiricism.

Over the course of these in-depth analyses, some constant features that can be regarded as decisive emerge. Thus, the specific way of defining the boundaries of experience, of intuition, or of the *a priori*, engages the vital yet problematic connection between transcendental elucidation and empirical description. The account of the living body and the status conferred upon the givenness of the world determine access to otherness and the functional role of the *alter ego*. The oscillation between a formal and ultimately vacuous figure of subjectivity and a concrete, bodily, and historically situated subject deeply affects the configurations that might be formed at the nexus of transcendental philosophy, psychology, and anthropology; and so does one's stance towards finitude (leading either to its exacerbation or to its neutralization) and towards anthropologism (regarded either as fatal or as susceptible to a transcendental repetition or conversion). For any transcendental endeavor, the resistance to naturalism and the refusal of a naturalization of philosophy is the correlate of its refutation of skepticism and of its concern for a foundation – whether epistemological or ontological. Finally, its relationship to metaphysics appears inevitable, even as we move towards a phenomenological metaphysics substantially different from that of Kant.

The thematic organization of the contributions does not exhaust their multiple affinities and mutual resonances; the present volume is likely to offer several different reading paths. For instance, Römer's contribution can be paired with those of De Santis and Schnell; Grandjean's or Schnell's with that of Bredeson; and Depraz's with that of Kassis or Hobbs. By providing accounts and interpretations that are not always convergent and which occasionally contrast with each other, this collection has the virtue of identifying a range of problems as well as of reshaping and sometimes even softening a number of false or apparent alternatives. The goal of such thorough discussions is not only to demonstrate once again the interrogative force of the transcendental problematic, but also to show that Kant's and Husserl's legacies are inseparable when it comes to an evaluation of the significance and contemporary relevance of transcendental phenomenology.

Acknowledgments

The editors are grateful to all authors for their generous participation and engagement in this project, and to Christoph Schirmer, Tim Vogel, and Anett Rehner at Walter de Gruyter for their support and patience during the preparation of the manuscript. We are profoundly thankful to John Rogove for contributing to this volume not only in the form of a paper, but also in the form of translating two other chapters into English and rereading a third one. We are also indebted to Jonathan Lewis, Shawn Loht, and Yuliya Tsutserova for various stylistic suggestions and remarks pertaining to the introduction. Special thanks are furthermore due to the editors of the journal *Meta: Research in Hermeneutics, Phenomenology, and Practical Philosophy* for the permission to include new versions of articles initially published in the issue *Husserl and Kant: The Transcendental-Phenomenological Project* (Vol. VIII, n°2, December 2016. Guest Editor: Iulian Apostolescu).

Bibliography

Blumenberg, Hans (2006): *Beschreibung des Menschen*. Frankfurt am Main: Suhrkamp Verlag.
Crowell, Steven (2001): *Husserl, Heidegger, and the Space of Meaning: Paths Toward Trancendental Phenomenology*. Evanston, IL: Northwestern University Press.
Crowell, Steven (2013): *Normativity and Phenomenology in Husserl and Heidegger*. Cambridge: Cambridge University Press.
Depraz, Natalie, Varela, Francisco, Vermersch, Pierre (2003): *On Becoming Aware: A Pragmatics of Experiencing*. Boston/Amsterdam/New York: Benjamins Press.
Engelland, Chad (2017): *Heidegger's Shadow: Kant, Husserl, and the Transcendental Turn*. New York: Routledge.
Fabbianelli, Faustino, Luft, Sebastian (Eds.) (2014): *Husserl und die klassische deutsche Philosophie*. Dordrecht: Springer.
Fink, Eugen (1985): *Einleitung in die Philosophie*. Würzburg: Königshausen und Neumann.
Foucault, Michel (2008): "Introduction à l'*Anthropologie*". In: *Emmanuel Kant: Anthropologie du point de vue pragmatique*. Paris: Vrin, pp. 11–79.
Foucault, Michel (2008): *Introduction to Kant's* Anthropology. Trans. Robert Nigro and Kate Briggs. Los Angeles: Semiotext(e).
Gardner, Sebastian, Grist, Matthew (Eds.) (2015): *The Transcendental Turn*. Oxford: Oxford University Press.
Grandjean, Antoine (2009): *Critique et réflexion. Essai sur le discours kantien*. Paris: Vrin.
Harries, Karsten (2012): *Wahrheit: Die Architektur der Welt*. München: Wilhelm Fink Verlag.
Heinämaa, Sara, Hartimo, Mirja, Miettinen, Timo (Eds.) (2014): *Phenomenology and the Transcendental*. New York: Routledge.

Held, Klaus (1966): *Lebendige Gegenwart. Die Frage nach der Seinsweise des transzendentalen Ich bei Edmund Husserl, entwickelt am Leitfaden der Zeitproblematik*. Phaenomenologica, vol. 23. The Hague: Martinus Nijhoff.

Honenberger, Phillip (Ed.) (2016): *Naturalism and Philosophical Anthropology: Nature, Life, and the Human between Transcendental and Empirical Perspectives*. London: Palgrave Macmillan.

Husserl, Edmund (1956): *Erste Philosophie (1923/1924). Erster Teil. Kritische Ideengeschichte*. Ed. Rudolf Boehm. *Husserliana*, vol. VII. The Hague: Martinus Nijhoff.

Husserl, Edmund (1962): *Phänomenologische Psychologie. Vorlesungen Sommersemester 1925. Husserliana*, vol. IX. Ed. Walter Biemel. The Hague: Martinus Nijhoff.

Husserl, Edmund (1973): *Zur Phänomenologie der Intersubjektivität. Texte aus dem Nachlass. Dritter Teil. 1929-35. Husserliana*, vol. XV. Ed. Iso Kern. The Hague: Martinus Nijhoff.

Husserl, Edmund (1984): *Logische Untersuchungen. Husserliana*, vol. XIX/1. Ed. Ursula Panzer. The Hague: Martinus Nijhoff.

Husserl, Edmund (1989): "Phänomenologie und Anthropologie". In: *Aufsätze und Vorträge (1922–1937). Husserliana*, vol. XXVII. Ed. Thomas Nenon and Hans Rainer Sepp. Dordrecht/Boston/London: Kluwer Academic Publishers.

Husserl, Edmund (1997): *Psychological and Transcendental Phenomenology and Confrontation with Heidegger (1927-1931)*. Trans. Thomas Sheehan and Richard E. Palmer. Dordrecht: Springer.

Husserl, Edmund (2006): *Späte Texte über Zeitkonstitution (1929-1934). Die C-Manuskripte. Husserliana Materialien*, vol. VIII. Ed. Dieter Lohmar. Dordrecht: Springer.

Kern, Iso (1964): *Husserl und Kant. Eine Untersuchung über Husserls Verhältnis zu Kant und zum Neukantianismus*. Phaenomenologica, vol. 16. The Hague: Martinus Nijhoff.

Kim, Halla, & Hoeltzel, Steven (Eds.) (2016): *Transcendental Inquiry: Its History, Methods and Critiques*. London: Palgrave Macmillan.

Luft, Sebastian (2011): *Subjectivity and Lifeworld in Transcendental Phenomenology*. Evanston, IL: Northwestern University Press.

Luft, Sebastian (2018): "Kant, Neo-Kantianism, and Phenomenology". In Dan Zahavi (Ed.): *The Oxford Handbook of the History of Phenomenology*. Oxford: Oxford University Press, pp. 45-67.

Marbach, Eduard (1974): *Das Problem des Ich in der Phänomenologie Husserls*. Phaenomenologica, vol. 59. The Hague: Martinus Nijhoff.

Mohanty, Jitendra Nath (1997): *Phenomenology: Between Essentialism and Transcendental Philosophy*. Evanston, IL: Northwestern University Press.

Moran, Dermot (2002): "Making Sense: Husserl's Phenomenology as Transcendental Idealism". In Jeff Malpas (Ed.): *From Kant to Davidson: Philosophy and the Idea of the Transcendental*. London: Routledge, pp. 48-74.

Pradelle, Dominique (2012): *Par-delà la révolution copernicienne. Sujet transcendantal et facultés chez Kant et Husserl*. Paris: Presses universitaires de France.

Schnell, Alexander (2015): *La déhiscence du sens*. Paris: Hermann.

Schnell, Alexander (2018): "Phenomenology and German Idealism". In Dan Zahavi (Ed.): *The Oxford Handbook of the History of Phenomenology*. Oxford: Oxford University Press, pp. 68-87.

Staiti, Andrea (2014): *Husserl's Transcendental Phenomenology: Nature, Spirit, and Life*. Cambridge: Cambridge University Press.

Tengelyi, László (2014): *Welt und Unendlichkeit. Zum Problem phänomenologischer Metaphysik.* Freiburg/München: Karl Alber.
Vermersch, Pierre (2012): *Explicitation et phénoménologie.* Paris: Presses universitaires de France.
Zahavi, Dan (2017): *Husserl's Legacy: Phenomenology, Metaphysics, and Transcendental Philosophy.* Oxford: Oxford University Press.

Section I: The Transcendantal and the A priori

Veronica Cibotaru
The Meaning of the Transcendental in the Philosophies of Kant and Husserl

Abstract: The aim of this chapter is to study the meaning of the concept of 'transcendental' in the philosophies of Kant and Husserl by focusing on the motives that led these two thinkers to introduce this notion into their systems. We will show that they are guided by two different motives. While Kant introduces the concept of transcendental because he aims to save the possibility of metaphysics, Husserl reengages it in his quest for a deeper understanding of the relationship between the subject and the world. Nevertheless, I aim to show that these two different uses of 'transcendental' share one common feature: they both account for the imperative of the infinite as a fundamental structure of subjectivity.[1]

The philosophies of Kant and Husserl represent two poles of the history of the concept of the transcendental, which are the object of the present study. Kant is the first modern philosopher to use the concept as a paradigmatic one and Husserl, by introducing a new philosophical method, a method that continues to inspire philosophers today, takes it over in order to give it new life.[2]

My aim in this chapter is to examine the meaning of this concept in the thought of these two thinkers and its role in their philosophies. In particular, I will be concerned with why Kant introduced the concept of the transcendental in the first place, to which problems he aimed to respond, and why Husserl took it over in its phenomenology, even though he remained far removed from Kantian philosophy. Thus, my aim will be to find a common ground for the use of this concept, notwithstanding the considerable differences between the problems

---

[1] I express all my gratitude to Mary L. Edwards (Teacher in Philosophy, School of English, Communication and Philosophy, Cardiff University) for her corrections and useful comments on a previous draft of this paper.
[2] Subsequently, other philosophers also used this notion of the transcendental. Thus, Gilles Deleuze speaks of a transcendental empiricism. However, this concept does not play the same fundamental role as in the phenomenology of Husserl. For more details, see Depraz 2011. The rather recent publication of a Polish book dedicated to the concept of the transcendental from Kant to Wittgenstein is a testimony of the fertility of this concept far beyond the limits of Kantian or Husserlian philosophy and, more generally, beyond those of phenomenology; see Parzutowicza & Soina 2011.

which led each of these thinkers to adopt the concept of the transcendental. This common ground lays, as we will argue, in the act of unveiling and accounting for an infinite task of reason, even if this task is not understood in the same way by both thinkers.

One can already observe that the concept of transcendental is in neither Kant's work nor Husserl's phenomenology an independent noun, but rather an adjective. Originally, though, the concept was used as a substantive (*transcendentalis*; *transcendentalia* in its plural form) and designated, in the thought of Thomas Aquinas and other medieval thinkers (such as Henry of Ghent, Eckhart, Duns Scotus), as a property attributed to every being as being and one which is convertible with other transcendental properties, or has at least a specific relationship to them (Goris & Aertsen 2016).[3] The fact that the concept of the transcendental is used as an adjective both by Kant and Husserl makes the meaning of this concept more difficult to grasp; it does not designate something concrete, but rather can characterize different things.

1 The Meaning of the Transcendental in Kant's Philosophy

The first thing that the concept of the transcendental characterizes in the *Critique of Pure Reason* is a kind of knowledge. Thus, Kant writes in the second version of the *Introduction* to the first *Critique*: "I call all cognition transcendental that is occupied not so much with objects but rather with *our mode of cognition* of objects *insofar as this is to be possible a priori*" (Kant 1787, B 25; Kant 1998, p. 149).[4] We can already distinguish two elements that characterize the concept of the transcendental as transcendental knowledge. First, a transition from the objects

---

[3] Goris and Aertsen show in their article that the concept of *transcendentalis* appears only in the 15th–16th century to designate that which medieval thinkers called *transcendentia*, probably in order not to confuse transcategorial properties of every being with a transcendent, non-sensible being.

Kant refers to the medieval doctrine of the *transcendentalia* in paragraph 12 of the *Transcendental Analytics* (Kant 1787, B 113). Interestingly enough, he refers to it as to the "transcendental philosophy of the ancients," implying by this that he does not consider his philosophy the *first* transcendental one, but as a *new* one (Kant 1998, p. 216).

[4] In the original German version (B-edition), Kant adds "*überhaupt*" (meaning "in general") to "occupied," implying by it that transcendental knowledge is occupied with the possibility of our *a priori* knowledge *in general* and not with some specific *a priori* principles of our knowledge. It is thus occupied with the general *modus operandi* of our *a priori* knowledge.

to the knowledge of objects. What is at stake, according to this passage, is not a direct knowledge about objects but a knowledge about our own knowledge mode, and second, that the knowledge mode about which there should be knowledge is *a priori*.

In addition, Kant also says: "A *system* of such concepts would be called *transcendental philosophy*" (Kant 1787, B 25; Kant 1998, p. 149). In order to understand what the expression "such concepts" refers to, one must read the 1781 version of this text (Kant 1781, A 11–12; Kant 1998, p. 133), where Kant defines transcendental knowledge somehow differently. It reads as follows: "I call all cognition *transcendental* that is occupied not so much with objects but rather with our *a priori* concepts of objects in general." The concepts that shall constitute the subject of transcendental philosophy are therefore our *a priori* concepts of objects, and their study will explicate our mode of *a priori* knowledge.

In the metaphysics lecture *Mrongovius*, which Kant delivered in 1782/1783, transcendental philosophy is also characterized as "a kind of self-cognition," which "concerns not the object, but the subject" (Kant 1983, AK. XXIX, p. 756; Kant 1997, p. 116), so in that sense it concerns not objects as such but our way of knowing them. Could we say that it is precisely this reflective knowledge, this self-knowledge, that determines the meaning of the transcendental in the Kantian thought? If this is the case, then we could not understand in what sense Kant distinguishes himself from his predecessors, since Descartes speaks already about the principles of human knowledge in his in Latin work *Principia philosophiae*,[5] just as Wolff analyses these same principles of human knowledge in his *Ontologia*.[6] Moreover, these principles are, in the Cartesian philosophy as in the Wolffian, *a priori* principles, just as the *a priori* concepts which, following Kant, ground the fundamental principles of knowledge. It thus becomes clear that this reflective knowledge cannot by itself determine the specific meaning of the transcendental theme in the Kantian thought, unless we accept the fact that Kant uses a new concept to express an old idea. This seems quite improbable if we consider Kant's habit of not using new words where ancient terms already exist.

In order to better understand this issue, I propose to consider a text which is generally accepted as the first Kantian text where the critical question, or its first formulation, is expressed. It is the famous letter which Kant wrote to his pupil Marcus Herz on February 21, 1772. It is one of the few texts which allows us to

---

5 The title of the first part of the *Principia philosophiae* (1644) is indeed "*De principiis cognitionis humanae.*"
6 The complete title of the *Ontologia* (1730) is "*Philosophia prima sive ontologia methodo scientifica pertractata qua omnis cognitionis humanae principia continentur.*"

find a transition from the Kantian pre-critical period, specifically from the last work which appeared in this period, the *Inaugural Dissertation De mundi sensibilis atque intelligibilis*, published in 1770. Marcus Herz published his *Considerations from the Speculative World Wisdom* in 1771 as a commentary to the *Dissertation* of Kant, but Herz's work also contained an important critique on the work of Kant. Kant probably read this critique, since he received the *Considerations* as a present from Herz himself (Watkins 2001). The question we can raise now is, in what measure did this critique influence the Kantian formulation of the critical problem? Furthermore, why does Kant not mention (at least explicitly), in his letter of February 21, 1772, Herz' *Considerations*, since the question which he there treats resonates with Herz's critique?

Herz's critique is positioned against evidence used to argue that intellectual representations grant us access to their objects. He refers specifically to paragraph 23 of the *Dissertation*, where Kant argues that the method of philosophy as metaphysics lays in the use of the pure intellect.[7] Herz writes: "We want to be convinced that a God must necessarily exist, not that it is necessary for us to think him; that our soul *according to its nature* is incapable of mortality, not that it *appears to us as such*" (Watkins 2001, p. 72, own translation). In this passage, Herz expresses very well the requirement of the correspondence between thinking and the object of thought. Indeed, how can we be sure that an object does not exist necessarily *only* in our thinking, and that his properties do not *only* appear to us as such? How can we thus be certain of the correspondence between thinking and being?

In Kant's letter to Herz one can recognize this questioning, which puts into doubt the unlimited scope of reason, although formulated in a new way and within the context of a wider problematic. Right at the beginning of his letter, Kant mentions a project of his bearing the title, "The limits of sensibility and reason." Thus, we see here that the critical problem of the limit appears already, even though it is not yet clear which concrete meaning it has for Kant. This work was supposed to have two parts, a theoretical one and a practical one and, interestingly, the theoretical part should have consisted of two sections: "General phenomenology" and "Metaphysics." Surprisingly enough, Kant almost never again uses the concept of phenomenology in his critical works (with the exception of the *Metaphysical Foundations of Natural Sciences* and the *Opus post-*

---

7 "Verum in Philosophia pura, qualis est Metaphysica, in qua *usus intellectus* circa principia est *realis*."

umum),⁸ although, as we already know, the concept of phenomenon plays a central role in his critical system. The reason probably lies in the fact that he no longer opposes a sensible world (*mundus sensibilis*), i.e. a world of phenomena, with its specific laws, to an intelligible world (*mundus intelligibilis*), as he does in his pre-critical period.⁹

With the project of developing this new philosophy, Kant poses for himself a new problem: namely, that which concerns the second section of the theoretical part of this philosophy, i.e. metaphysics. He writes: "I noticed that I still lacked something essential [...] which in fact constitutes the key to the whole secret of metaphysics, hitherto still hidden from itself" (Kant 1910, AK. X, p. 130; Kant 1999, p. 132–133). We can see here the radical scope of this project: what is at stake, indeed, in this new philosophy is the discovery of a new metaphysics, a metaphysics which has always been there, yet in a hidden form. The key to it, this essential element which still misses, lies in the question: "What is the ground of the relation of that in us which we call 'representation' to the object?" (Kant 1910, AK. X, p. 130; Kant 1999, p. 133). At first sight, one could see here the first formulation of the critical question, namely, the possibility of *a priori* synthetic judgments. This would suppose, however, that we forget that this question is indeed essential, but only in relationship to the problem of a new metaphysics, as it already appears from this letter. This last question is precisely an echo of Herz's question, which does not ask about the general relationship between representations and the object, but about the certitude of the existence of God or the immortality of the soul, which are precisely metaphysical questions.

After considering the question of the possibility of correspondence between our representations, as far as they are not empirical representations and thus do not come from experience, Kant writes this important passage:

> As I was searching in such ways for the sources of intellectual knowledge, without which one cannot determine the nature and limits of metaphysics, I divided this science into its naturally distinct parts, and I sought to reduce transcendental philosophy (that is to say, all

---

8 Thus, the fourth and last chapter of the *Metaphysical Foundations of Natural Sciences* is called "Metaphysical Foundations of Phenomenology." Lambert is one of the first to use the concept of phenomenology in the fourth part of his *Neues Organon* (1764). Phenomenology is presented in this work as a logic and a science of appearance, with the aim of going beyond it. For more details, see the work of Fanfalone 1997.
9 As Kant argues in the *Prolegomena to Any Future Metaphysics*, paragraph 34, there is no intelligible world, only a sensible one. That is why later, in the second part of the introduction of the *Critique of Judgment*, Kant asserts that, although phenomena and noumena have two different domains (*Gebiet*), with two different laws, they have yet the same ground (*Boden*), namely the sensible world.

> the concepts belonging to completely pure reason) to a certain number of categories, but not like Aristotle, who, in his ten predicaments, placed them side by side as he found them in a purely chance juxtaposition. On the contrary, I arranged them according to the way they classify themselves by their own nature, following a few fundamental laws of the understanding. (Kant 1910, AK. X, p. 132; Kant 1999, p. 134)

We can find here three important elements. First of all, one question arises: what is the relationship between the quest for the sources of intellectual knowledge, i.e. non-empirical knowledge, and the problem of the correspondence between the representation and the object? Indeed, it is clear that such a relationship exists for Kant, since the expression "in that way" refers to the analysis of the question of the correspondence between a representation and its object. This reference is to be understood in the context of the preceding paragraph. In this paragraph, which closes his reflections on the correspondence between representation and object, Kant rejects the solutions of Plato, Malebranche, and Crusius. All three presuppose, in different modes, a divine source for our pure, non-empirical concepts of understanding. Kant rejects these solutions as "the greatest absurdity one could hit upon" (Kant 1910, AK. X, p. 131; Kant 1999, p. 134). On the contrary, he reinterprets the quest for the sources of our intellectual knowledge as the quest for a source for our pure concepts of understanding, which have in themselves enough evidence in order to guarantee the correspondence between concepts and objects, without requiring us to make use of a *deus ex machina*. Kant tells us here something about the quest for this source. In fact, it appears to us through a transcendental philosophy. This philosophy consists of "all the concepts of pure reason," as Kant argues here; but it is more than the sum of these concepts. This philosophy shows us the "principles of understanding," which provide a systematic connection between these concepts, and finally traces them to a source which Kant calls later, in the transcendental deduction, the synthetic unity of apperception. Consequently, it becomes clear from this letter, written nine years before the publication of the *Critique of Pure Reason*, that the concept of the transcendental does not mean a mere reflexive knowledge of concepts or principles of our pure understanding. The concept of transcendental implies here a way of understanding the ground of the concepts of pure reason or, to use a critical concept, a way of understanding the possibility and legitimacy of concepts of pure reason – and, later in the first *Critique*, the more general understanding of the possibility of our *a priori* knowledge.[10]

---

[10] We see here that Kant does not distinguish yet the understanding from the reason, as in the *Critique of Pure Reason*.

Finally, it becomes clear through this 1772 passage that the transcendental in Kantian thought is closely connected with the quest for a new metaphysics and with the critical task of determining the nature and limits of this new metaphysics (since, as Kant asserts, we cannot determine its nature and limits without it.)[11]

This is a first meaning, a first layer so to speak, of the concept of the transcendental in Kant's thought. This concept is broadened and specified in every section and chapter of the *Critique*: transcendental Aesthetic, Logic, Dialectic, transcendental Theory of Elements and of Method. On this level, however, we find two important features of Kant's conception of the transcendental: first, the quest for the sources of the possibility of our knowledge in the nature of our reason, and second, an intimate bond between the notion of the transcendental and the possibility of metaphysics. As what concerns the first *Critique*, it displays this relationship between the transcendental theme and metaphysics in an equivocal way, since the status of transcendental philosophy oscillates between, on one side, a propaedeutic to metaphysics and, on the other, a part of metaphysics itself. Thus, Kant writes in the "Architectonic of pure reason:" "Now the philosophy of pure reason is either propaedeutic (preparation), which investigates the faculty of reason in regard to all pure *a priori* cognition, and is called critique, or, second, the system of pure reason (science), the whole (true as well as apparent) philosophical cognition from pure reason in systematic interconnection, and is called metaphysics" (Kant 1781/1787, A 841/B 869; Kant 1998, p. 696). Since transcendental knowledge is the knowledge of the conditions and possibility of our knowledge *a priori*, according to the Kantian definition in the introduction of the *Critique of Pure Reason*, which we have already seen, this critical philosophy, "which investigates the faculty of reason in regard to all pure *a priori* cognition," shall be a transcendental philosophy. It is not yet a science as such, but a propaedeutic to metaphysics as science. However, Kant writes a bit further on: "Metaphysics in this narrower sense[12] consists of *transcendental philosophy* and the *physiology* of pure reason. The former considers only the *understanding* and reason itself in a system of all concepts and principles that are related to objects in general, without assuming objects that *would*

---

11 Thus, Wilhelm Teichner writes in his *Kants Transzendentalphilosophie*: "Philosophy as a science is necessarily transcendental philosophy, and as such necessarily critical philosophy" (Teichner 1978, p. 69, our translation from German: *"Philosophie als Wissenschaft ist notwendig Transzendentalphilosophie, und als diese notwendig kritische Philosophie."*) According to George di Giovanni, Kant has not determined the limits of metaphysics as such but only the limits of dogmatic metaphysics (Di Giovanni 1992, p. 441).
12 Metaphysics of nature, as opposed to metaphysics of morals.

be given (Ontologia)" (Kant 1781/1787, A 845/B 873; Kant 1998, p. 698). As we see in this section, Kant speaks about transcendental philosophy as a part of metaphysics which shall be named ontology; moreover, he speaks about a system, juxtaposed to the critique of pure reason, which is only a propaedeutic and which at the same time seems already to be a form of transcendental philosophy.[13] It appears thus that the meaning of transcendental philosophy oscillates in the first *Critique* between the status of a propaedeutic and that of a science, i.e. between the status of a critique and that of metaphysics understood as *metaphysica generalis*.

In any case, it is possible to find a new distinctive element in the *Critique of Pure Reason*, which is not present in the letter to Marcus Herz and which determines the meaning of the concept of the transcendental within critical philosophy: it is the central role which Kant assigns in the first *Critique* to sensibility. "Transcendental Aesthetic," i.e. the transcendental doctrine of sensibility, provides the entrance to the *Critique of pure reason*. This is quite remarkable, when we think that the aim of the critical project, as it clearly appears already in the letter to Marcus Herz, is the realization of a new metaphysics; or how could metaphysics be possible without a pure thinking, which goes and thinks beyond the boundaries of sensibility?

This pure thinking, which manifests itself in two capacities, understanding and reason (in its restrained sense as a faculty of principles), is unfolded in the first *Critique* through its double radical difference: firstly, through the necessary relationship of the concepts of understanding with the pure forms of our sensibility, i.e. space and time, and secondly, through the necessary relationship of space and time to sensations, of which they are only the forms.[14] The theme of pure thought is developed in the first *Critique* in relationship with its double alterity: first, with the alterity of sensibility, which is radically different from thinking, since it is a receptive faculty, to which all concepts of our understanding are necessarily bound; second, through this relationship to sensibility, it is also bound to sensation, which constitutes the matter of space and time, which are for this reason pure but also mere forms of sensibility. In this sense, although the concept of the transcendental in Kantian critical thought implies understanding of the inherent possibility and legitimacy of our knowledge structures, it does not mean confinement within the sphere of our subjective

---

[13] For the relationship between Kantian transcendental philosophy and ontology, see Baum 2012.

[14] Kant names the sensation the matter of the phenomenon, and space and time its form (Kant 1781, A 20).

knowledge structures, but it implies, on the contrary, an opening to what lays outside of this sphere through sensation.[15]

Interestingly enough, metaphysics finds its first ground in this opening, since it receives its first orientation through the concept of *noumenon*, a pure being of thought as a limitation of sensibility. The unveiling of the transcendental structures of our knowledge, which have a necessary relationship to empirical sensibility, opens, paradoxically, a noumenal field, precisely that of metaphysics in its true sense.[16] The latter does not, however, constitute an ontological realm in itself, but its necessity (and, at the same time, legitimacy) arises precisely through the limitation of sensibility. Indeed, what makes possible a metaphysics understood as knowledge of the supersensible is the field of *noumena*, of which we cannot know anything but to which we can neither deny the possibility. This is how, even if metaphysics in its true sense is not possible as theoretical knowledge, its possibility is opened by the necessary orientation of the understanding towards the *noumenon*, and realized, as Kant argues in his work *What Progress has Metaphysics Made in Germany since the Time of Leibniz and Wolff?*, through the practical knowledge of moral reason as well as the ideas of reason (God, immortality). These ideas reinforce the possibility of the final aim of moral reason, i.e. the realization of the highest good in this world.

Transcendental philosophy leads thus finally to the "foundation of metaphysics" and makes possible through this investigation what Kant calls in the "Architectonics of Pure Reason" "philosophy in a genuine sense," a philosophy which "relates everything to wisdom, but through the path of science" (Kant 1781/1787, A 850/B 878; Kant 1998, p. 700–701). This conception of philosophy remains a constant in Kantian thought. We find it even in the *Opus Postumum*

---

[15] The relationship of sensations to subjectivity is ambiguous, since sensations are in a double way subjective: subjective in a general way, since they are the result of the apprehension of a knowing subject which has specific sensorial organs, and subjective in an individual way, since I cannot fully grasp the sensation of another subject. At the same time, sensation is not fully constituted by subjectivity. Sensations *give* us something to know, even if it is only raw material which must be organized by the knowledge structures of transcendental subjectivity. If sensations are not fully immanent to the subjective sphere but sit, on the contrary, at the limits of this sphere, what causes them ultimately? Kant's answer on this point remains ambiguous, since it might seem from some passages of his works, but also from the logic of his system, that it is precisely the thing in itself which causes the sensation, by affecting the subject. However, at the same time, this would mean knowing something about this thing in itself beforehand, which is impossible according to Kant.

[16] Namely, that of special metaphysics, which, contrary to general, ontological metaphysics, is the only form of metaphysics which fully aims at the realm of the supersensible, as Kant argues in his work *What Progress has Metaphysics Made in Germany since the Time of Leibniz and Wolff?*

(Kant 1936, AK. XXI, p. 7), where science is considered as the means and wisdom as the aim of philosophy. The latter, however, remains an ideal, something unreachable for human beings.[17]

2 Husserl's View of the Transcendental

If we consider now the context in which Husserl introduced the concept of the transcendental into his philosophy, we see right away that the question which moved him is very different from the Kantian problematic. Indeed, what is important for Husserl is not the possibility of metaphysics. It is possible to think that Husserl's research orientation is opposed to Kant's, since at the beginning of the *Logical Investigations*, where we find the very first articulation of phenomenology, Husserl describes his project as being a part of the "pure phenomenology of lived experiences (*Erlebnisse*)" (Husserl 1968, Hua XIX/1, p. 2; Husserl 1970, p. 166) which requires "freedom from metaphysical [...] presuppositions" (Husserl 1968, Hua XIX/1, p. 22; Husserl 1970, p. 179).[18] But even here there is a similar element, since Husserl is also concerned with grounding problems, i.e. with the grounding of pure logic as a science and with the grounding of knowledge in general.

Husserl introduces in a systematic way the notion of a transcendental phenomenology only in 1913, in the *Ideas I*. But the path that leads to this notion begins much earlier, in 1903, two years after the publication of the *Logical Investigations*. In 1903, Husserl writes a review of Theodor Elsenhans' article "The Relationship of Logic to Psychology (*Das Verhältnis der Logik zur Psychologie*)," published in 1897 in the *Journal for Philosophy and Philosophical Critique* (*Zeitschrift für Philosophie und philosophische Kritik*). Husserl refers to this review in the foreword to the *Logical Investigations*, which he wrote in 1913, at the same time as the publication of the *Ideas I*. In this foreword, he writes:

> As regards the Second Volume of the new edition, the hesitant Introduction, so little true to the essential sense and method of the actually written *Investigations*, was radically revised. I felt its defects immediately after its appearance, and also found immediate occasion (in a review in the *Archiv für systematische Philosophie* XI (1903), pp. 397sq.) to object to my misleading account of phenomenology as descriptive psychology". (Husserl 1968, Hua XVIII, p. XII; Husserl 1970, p. 6)

---

17 We find this definition of philosophy also in the third part of the introduction of the *Logic of Jäsche*.
18 For the question of whether the *Logical Investigations* are really metaphysically neutral or not, see Benoist 1997, p. 207–214, and Zahavi 2001.

In this passage, Husserl refers openly to his rewriting of the introduction to the second part of the *Logical Investigations*, which in its first version did not express correctly the essential meaning and method of the *Investigations*. The reason of this inadequate expression is Husserl's own "misleading account of phenomenology as descriptive psychology." This account is misleading because it can give the impression that phenomenology is an empirical science, and it is precisely this designation that Husserl criticizes in his review of 1903. We see thus that the problem which led Husserl to transcendental phenomenology lays very deep, since it concerns the meaning and method of phenomenology as a science and philosophical discipline.

From this excerpt of Husserl's review, we can see how far he pushes the essential meaning of his phenomenological investigation, even though the passage still situates this meaning in the narrow context of logic and the investigation of its phenomenological grounds:

> However, exactly from these pre-critical objectifications – with their divisions between I's and non-I's, between "own" and "foreign" I; with their interpretative lodgings of immediate data of consciousness as "psychical activities and states" in the own I and their interpretative extrapolations outside of the I of physical things and states, of "foreign" persons, experiences, etc. – from such pre-critical objectifications, do I say, arise the difficulties of the metaphysical problem of the possibility of knowledge, which presupposes on its part an elucidation of knowledge as such, apart from all metaphysical intentions. This elucidation requires a phenomenology of knowledge. It has to fix and to analyze knowledge experiences, in which lays the origin of logical ideas, by keeping far away every interpretation which goes beyond their real content – and thus to bring to the evidence the "actual" meaning of logical ideas and their general essence. (Husserl 1979, Hua XXII, p. 206, my translation)

The first thing which strikes us when reading this text is the implicit Kantian motive of a critical philosophy. The text is clearly structured around the opposition between "pre-critical objectifications" and phenomenology, which is implicitly critical. This opposition shows us that Husserl is searching for a radically new foundation for phenomenology, a foundation that distinguishes itself from the foundations of other sciences and so also from psychology. A second contradistinction between two opposing poles appears in this text as well. We have, on the one hand, the *interpretation* of those pre-critical objectifications ("with their interpretative lodgings" / "with their interpretative extrapolations") and, on the other hand, the "immediate data of consciousness" and the "real content" of "knowledge experiences." Although the meaning of this real content and of these immediate data of consciousness remains here still undetermined (they acquire a clearer meaning only after the transcendental reduction), we can already see that they shall determine the new foundation of phenomenology. The method of phenomenology shall thus be that of a pure seeing, free of every interpretation, since through interpretation we cannot see anymore the pure given and the real content of our experiences. The phenomenological method is thus a recourse to the pure given. This is why phenomenology cannot be a psychology, since psychology, as a natural science, provides specific questions, conceptual tools, and hypotheses and remains thus in the sphere of the interpretation of our experiences. But there is a question remaining, namely, that of knowing through which concrete methods phenomenology can achieve this "given in its most strict sense," this "experience such as it is in itself" free from every interpretation.

We find an answer to this question in Husserl's lecture from 1906/1907, *Introduction to Logic and Theory of Knowledge*, § 35. In this text, Husserl asks himself what the difference is between natural sciences and phenomenology. The difference lays in a "nuance" and yet it is "the true Archimedean point of philosophy (*der wahrhaft archimedische Punkt*)" (Husserl 1984, Hua XXIV, p. 211; Husserl 2008, p. 206). The point of departure of the phenomenological method, its πρότερον πρὸς ημᾶς, is what Husserl calls "the natural consciousness." Natural consciousness is opposed to phenomenological consciousness, which is for Husserl also the philosophical consciousness. This natural consciousness can express itself through individual experiences, to which Husserl here seems to assign an essential reflexive character. Thus, an external perception can become a lived experience (*Erlebnis*) through reflection on my perception as such. The experience is an inner experience "in relationship to me." It is on the ground of these experiences that Husserl introduces a concept which is the *modus operandi* of the phenomenological method and which later leads to transcendental phenomenology. It is the concept of the phenomenological reduction (which he does not yet designate as transcendental),[19] which operates on the ground of individual experience, but is not identical to it.[20] He describes it as follows:

---

[19] According to Iso Kern (Kern 1964, p. 31, n.1) and Jean-François Lavigne (Lavigne 2005, pp. 532–533), Husserl first uses the notion of transcendental in a manuscript of 1908 (Manuscript B II 1, 27). Lavigne insists on the fact that Husserl does not recuperate this Kantian concept under the influence of Kantian philosophy, but the development of his *own* phenomenology leads him to the adopting of this concept, in order to show however the *limited* Kantian understanding of the genuine meaning of the transcendental theme (Lavigne 2005, pp. 529–537). On this point, Lavigne clearly disagrees with Walter Biemel's view on Husserl's relationship to Kant ("*Einleitung des Herausgebers*," In: Husserl 1958, Hua II; Husserl 1973).

[20] Thus, Husserl asserts at the end of this paragraph that that which the investigator "contemplates" (*schaut*) through the phenomenological reduction is *de* facto "the individual lived experience (*individuelles Erlebnis*)" (Husserl 1984, Hua XXIV, p. 214; Husserl 2008, p. 209). However, phenomenological reduction does not limit itself to the simple individual experience, insofar as it brackets every existence position, that is, also the position of my existence in the world, as

Now, let us perform the phenomenological reduction step by step. This ego belongs in the sphere of what is questionable, of transcendence. I form no opinion about it. I change the positing of a judgment just carried out into a positing phenomenon.

[...] I suspend the believing without any decision, either affirming or denying. I then have the I-phenomenon. Naturally, the suspending is further connected to all of the I's natural relationships, to my birth, to my parents, to my physical surroundings, to the whole world with objective time and objective space. Insofar as such things come to my consciousness, I keep on performing the reduction, or suspension. (Husserl 1984, Hua XXIV, p. 212–213; Husserl 2008, pp. 207–208)

We see that this phenomenological reduction, which gives philosophy a "wholly new dimension" and an "entirely new point of departure" (Husserl 1958, Hua II, p. 24; Husserl 1973, p. 19),[21] as he asserts in his lessons of 1907 on *The Idea of Phenomenology*, is grounded on the disconnection from a natural belief, which Husserl also dubs belief in the transcendence.[22] This disconnection, which Husserl also calls suspension, is accomplished *gradually*, moving from belief in my own existence to the belief of the existence of my own history and environment and finally reaching belief in the existence of the whole world. Thus, phenomenological reduction does not reduce the content of experience in itself, nor does it reduce the essential form of experience, since it is still able to grasp the transcendent form of our experiences. What it really reduces is the mode of experience, i.e. it makes us pass from a transcendent to an immanent mode. The reduction is achieved by bracketing our belief in a world which is transcendent to the immanent sphere of our subjectivity. And it is precisely this immanent mode that constitutes one of the essential differences between the natural reflective experience and the experience of the phenomenological reduction, although the latter operates on the ground of the former, as a first step towards the immanent sphere of subjectivity.

What led Husserl to introduce the concept of transcendental reduction and to deepen, by doing so, the meaning of this phenomenological reduction? Interestingly enough, from these lessons until the publication of the *Ideas I*, Husserl

---

subject to my experience. Phenomenological reduction brings to the individual experience this famous "nuance" of which Husserl speaks previously in this same paragraph.
21 Husserl insists several times in these lectures on this new dimension of philosophy, which, however, is "essentially connected with the old dimensions" (Husserl 1958, Hua II, p. 25; Husserl 1973, p. 21).
22 Husserl also calls the phenomenological reduction "Copernican conversion (*Kopernikanische Wendung*)" in his letter to Pannwitz of April 14, 1937 (Husserl 1994, Hua Dok. III/7, p. 227). On the relationship between Husserl's phenomenology and the (originary) Kantian concept of a Copernican revolution, see Pradelle 2012.

orients his phenomenological investigation towards the problems of the world, of the natural belief in the existence of the world, of its meaning and the importance of bracketing it through phenomenological reduction by means of the phenomenological method. Thus, he asks himself in the 10th paragraph of *Basic Problems of Phenomenology*, a lecture given in 1910–1911: "For now, we leave undecided what questions of a philosophical character this thetic evidence, this general evidence of the fact of the world as such, poses to us" (Husserl 1973, Hua XIII, p. 133–134; Husserl 2006, p. 24). According to my interpretation, this research orientation is important for the introduction of the transcendental theme in *Ideas I*. Although, from a methodological point of view, the transcendental-phenomenological reduction is not essentially different from the phenomenological reduction that Husserl describes in his lecture on logic and theory of knowledge, the relationship of the I to the world after the reduction is much more deeply problematized and acquires a central meaning for the transcendental-phenomenological reduction.[23] This manifests itself with clarity in a posthumous note to *Ideas I*:

> So the precedent question will be answered, what can still remain, when, through that phenomenological epoché we put out of scope the universe, as we conceive of him first, as the totality of being in general. There remains or better said there opens itself for the first time through this epoché the absolute region of being, that of the absolute or "transcendental" subjectivity – not a partial region of the total region of reality named universe. It is on the contrary fundamentally separated from it and all its special regions. However it is not at all separated in the sense of a limitation, as if it would be bound in a complementary way with the world, as if it would build with it a global whole. The world is in itself a totality which, according to its meaning, does not allow an extension. And yet it will show itself, that the region of the absolute or transcendental subjectivity "bears in itself," namely through real and possible "intentional constitution" the real universe, with other words all possible real worlds and all worlds of every extended meaning, in a special, wholly unique way. Only by

---

[23] Let us remark that other interpretive frameworks for this transcendental turning point in Husserl's phenomenology are possible. Thus, according to Roman Ingarden, it is the quest for an absolute fundament of every knowledge which led Husserl to the reduction to transcendental subjectivity, as he argues it in his work *On the Motives which led Husserl to Transcendental Idealism*. However, Ingarden reproaches Husserl for attributing an unjustified ontological and metaphysical scope to what in itself is a mere epistemological act, arriving thus at an unjustified idealism. In the same perspective, Jean-François Lavigne considers that a (ontologically) non-idealist transcendental phenomenology is possible. Moreover, its possibility becomes clear in the "analysis of the logical structure of the establishment of the phenomenological transcendental idealism in the *Ideas I*" (Lavigne 2009, p. 307, my translation). Thus, according to Lavigne, the possibility of a non-idealist phenomenology which is still transcendental lays in the very premise of Husserl's early phenomenology.

understanding this the singular meaning of the described phenomenological epoché will be understood. (Husserl 1976, Hua III/2, pp. 590–591, my translation)

This text contains two important elements for our topic. First of all, it tells us that the phenomenological epoché, i.e. phenomenological reduction, opens a new sphere of being, namely, the sphere of the transcendental subjectivity. Secondly, it lets us know that transcendental subjectivity paradoxically bears the world in itself, although the world is already a totality and does not allow any "extension," even that of the transcendental subjectivity. Through this reduction, a very specific relationship between subjectivity and world is unveiled, a relationship that cannot be understood as taking place within the world or as being exterior to the world. An important part of the meaning of the Husserlian concept of the transcendental consists in this relationship, since transcendental subjectivity, through which the transcendental realm arises, constitutes the meaning of the world. But how should we understand this relationship? Does it mean that the world acquires new meaning through the manifestation of its relationship to transcendental subjectivity? Do we see the world differently through transcendental reduction? Does transcendental reduction allow us to grasp something more about the world than what we already see through the natural attitude?

In order to answer these questions, it can be useful to consider a later Husserlian work or, better, a work-complex, namely, the *The Crisis of European Sciences and Transcendental Phenomenology*. Here, Husserl gives a more concrete meaning to the relationship between transcendental subjectivity and the world. Transcendental subjectivity constitutes the world as an infinite horizon or, as Husserl also says, as an "open infinity (*offene Endlosigkeit*)" (Husserl 1993, Hua XXIX, p. 200, own translation).[24] Only through the philosophical act of reduction are we capable of grasping this infinite horizon that goes beyond our environment.[25] Transcendental reduction gains in that way a new nuance: it is not a mere descriptive method, but a task of philosophy. We can ask ourselves, why is it then so important to grasp this constitutive relationship between subjectivity and world? Indeed, in my natural attitude, I remain imprisoned inside my envi-

---

24 Here the theme of intersubjectivity is of course crucial.
25 Thus, Husserl writes: "The openly endless horizon in which he <man> lives is not disclosed; his ends, his activity, his trade and traffic, his personal, social, national, and mythical motivation—all this moves within the sphere of his finitely surveyable surrounding world. Here there are no infinite tasks" (Husserl 1976, Hua VI, p. 324; Husserl 1970, p. 279). Husserl also speaks in this text (the *Vienna Lecture*, Appendix 1 to the *Crisis*) about the practical attitude, which characterizes this environment, by opposition with the theoretical attitude of philosophy, through which the world appears to us in its infinity.

ronment, in which the world as such remains very vaguely present in the background. Through transcendental reduction, I become fully aware of the infinite horizon of the world and thus of the essential meaning of the world.[26]

It is here that we finally find resonance with the Kantian conception of transcendence. Even if the Kantian conception was originally an answer, as we have seen, to a different problem, eventually the notion of the transcendental allows Kant to think something crucial, which we can see only through the critical investigation of our subjectivity, namely the essential end[27] of human reason, which extends itself to the unconditional and the infinite (Kant 1781/1787, A 839–840/B 867–868; Kant 1998, p. 695).[28] For both Kant and Husserl, the transcendental motive does not lock us inside the sphere of our subjectivity. By aiming beyond the finitude of our sensible knowledge mode or of our surrounding world in the case of Kant,[29] as well as beyond the finitude of our natural attitude in the case of Husserl, the transcendental opens us to the imperative of the infinite, an infinite that according to both authors we can find only inside of ourselves, as transcendental subjects, and not in the world.

---

[26] In connection with this point, Emmanuel Housset has an interesting interpretation of the transcendental constitution of the world: the constitution of the world makes us conscious of our responsibility towards the meaning of the world, since it cannot exist without our subjective and intersubjective constitutive act. This meaning implies precisely a dimension of infinity (Housset 2000).

Let us remark that the infinity of the world does not have here a spatial or temporal meaning, this last belonging to the way natural sciences (or more precisely, modern physics) might conceptualize the universe, but which remains an abstract geometrical conception and is not original but derived from the original world experiencing mode of the transcendental subject, as Husserl argues in the *Crisis*.

[27] Understood in the Kantian sense of *Zweck*.

[28] Kantian transcendental philosophy is in that sense "a quest to a language of the essential (*quête du langage de l'essentiel*)" (Marty 1980, p. 533). That is why the philosopher is the one who "puts forward the essential ends of human reason," following the words of François Marty (Marty 2010, p. 284, own translation). The act of philosophy is here to be understood in its cosmic and not scholastic sense.

[29] Thus, transcendental philosophy is not a mere subjectivist philosophy but shows the paradox of the human subject "in its distance from itself to itself (*distance de soi à soi*)", a distance which remains infinite (Grandjean 2009, p. 227).

Bibliography

Baum, Manfred (2012): *Ontologie und Transzendentalphilosophie bei Kant* in *Metaphysik-Ästhetik-Ethik, Beiträge zur Interpretation der Philosophie Kants*. Würzburg: Königshausen & Neumann.
Benoist, Jocelyn (1997): *Phénoménologie, sémantique, ontologie, Husserl et la tradition logique autrichienne*. Paris: Presses universitaires de France.
Depraz, Natalie (2011): "L'empirisme transcendantal de Deleuze à Husserl". In: *Revue germanique internationale*, vol. 13, pp. 125–148.
Descartes, René (2009): *Principles of Philosophy*. SMK Books.
Di Giovanni, George (1992): "The First Twenty Years of Critique: The Spinoza Connection". In: *The Cambridge Companion to Kant*. Cambridge: Cambridge University Press, pp. 417–448.
Fanfalone, Gilbert (1997): *La phenomenologie restrictive de Jean-Henri Lambert*, Ph.D thesis, defended at the university of Nice Sophia-Antipolis, France, in 1997. http://www.sudoc.fr/043854028, visited on 14/03/2018.
Grandjean, Antoine (2009): *Critique et réflexion, Essai sur le discours kantien*. Paris: Vrin.
Goris, Wouter & Aertsen, Jan (2016): "Medieval Theories of Transcendentals". In: *The Stanford Encyclopedia of Philosophy* (Winter 2016 Edition). Ed. Edward N. Zalta. URL <https://plato.stanford.edu/archives/win2016/entries/transcendentals-medieval/>. visited on 14/03/2018.
Housset, Emmanuel (2000): *Husserl et l'énigme du monde*. Paris: Seuil.
Husserl, Edmund (1954): *Die Krisis der europäischen Wissenschaften und die transzendentale Phänomenologie. Eine Einleitung in die phänomenologische Philosophie*. Husserliana, vol. VI. Ed. Walter Biemel. The Hague: Martinus Nijhoff.
Husserl, Edmund (1958): *Die Idee der Phänomenologie. Fünf Vorlesungen*. Husserliana, vol. II. Ed. Walter Biemel. The Hague: Martinus Nijhoff.
Husserl, Edmund (1970): *Logical Investigations*, II, I. Trans. John N. Findlay (from the second edition of the *Logical Investigations*). London & New York: Routledge.
Husserl, Edmund (1970): *The Crisis of European Sciences and Transcendental Phenomenology*. Trans. David Carr. Evanston: Northwestern University Press.
Husserl, Edmund (1973): *The Idea of Phenomenology*. Trans. William P. Alston & George Nakhnikian. The Hague: Martinus Nijhoff.
Husserl, Edmund (1976): *Ideen zu einer reinen Phänomenologie und phänomenologischen Philosophie. Ergänzende Texte (1912–1929)*. Husserliana, vol. III/2. The Hague: Martinus Nijhoff.
Husserl, Edmund (1979): *Aufsätze und Rezensionen (1890–1910)*. Husserliana, vol. XXII. The Hague: Martinus Nijhoff.
Husserl, Edmund (1993): *Die Krisis der europäischen Wissenschaften und die transzendentale Phänomenologie. Ergänzungsband. Texte aus dem Nachlass*. Husserliana, vol. XXIX. Dordrecht: Kluwer Academic Publishers.
Husserl, Edmund (1994): *Briefwechsel: Wissenschaftler Korrespondenz*. Husserliana Dokumente, vol. III/7. Dordrecht: Kluwer Academic Publishers.
Husserl, Edmund (2006): *The Basic Problems of Phenomenology, from the Lectures, Wintersemester 1910/1911*. Trans. Ingo Farin & James G. Hart. Dordrecht: Springer.

Husserl, Edmund (2008): *Introduction to Logic and Theory of Knowledge, Lectures 1906/07*. Trans. Claire Ortiz Hill, Dordrecht: Springer.
Kern, Iso (1964): *Kant und Husserl*. The Hague: Nijhoff.
Kant, Immanuel (1952): *Critique of Judgment*. Trans. J.C. Meredith. Oxford: Clarendon Press.
Kant, Immanuel (1983): *What Progress has Metaphysics Made in Germany since the Time of Leibniz and Wolff?* Trans. T. B. Humphrey. OPAL Publishing Corporation.
Kant, Immanuel (1992): *Lectures on Logic*. Trans. J. Michael Young. Cambridge: Cambridge University Press.
Kant, Immanuel (1997): *Metaphysik Mrongovius*. In: *Lectures on Metaphysics*. Trans. Karl Ameriks and Steve Naragon. Cambridge: Cambridge University Press.
Kant, Immanuel (1998): *Critique of Pure Reason*. Trans. Paul Guyer & Allen W. Wood. Cambridge: Cambridge University Press.
Kant, Immanuel (1999): *Correspondence*. Trans. Arnulf Zweig. Cambridge: Cambridge University Press.
Kant, Immanuel (2004): *Prolegomena to any Future Science*. Trans. Gary Hatfield. Cambridge: Cambridge University Press.
Kant, Immanuel (2004): *Metaphysical Foundations of Natural Sciences*. Trans. M. Friedmann. Cambridge: Cambridge University Press.
Kant, Immanuel (2014): *Dissertation on the Form and Principles of the Sensible and the Intelligible World*. CreateSpace Independent Publishing Platform.
Ingarden, Roman (2012): *On the Motives which Led Husserl to Transcendental Idealism*. Trans. A. Hannibalsson. The Hague: Martinus Nijhoff.
Lambert, Johann (1965): *Neues Organon (New Organon)*. Hildesheim: Georg Olms.
Lavigne, Jean-François (2005): *Husserl et la naissance de la phénoménologie 1900–1913*. Paris: Presses universitaires de France.
Lavigne, Jean-François (2009): *Accéder au transcendental? Réduction et Idéalisme transcendantal dans les Idées I de Husserl*. Paris: Vrin.
Marty, François (1980): *La naissance de la métaphysique chez Kant*. Paris: Beauchesne.
Marty, François (2010): "Le concept cosmique de la philosophie". In: *Lectures de Kant*. Eds. Michaël Foessel & Pierre Osmo. Paris: Ellipses, pp. 281–293.
Parszutowicz, Przemysław & Maciej, Soin (Eds.) (2011): *Idea transcendentalizmu. Od Kanta do Wittgensteina* [*The Idea of transcendentalism from Kant to Wittgenstein*]. Warsaw: Ifis.
Pradelle, Dominique (2012): *Par-delà la révolution copernicienne. Sujet transcendental et facultés chez Kant et Husserl*. Paris: Presses universitaires de France.
Teichner, Wilhelm (1978): *Kants Transzendentalphilosophie*. Freiburg/Munich: Karl Alber.
Watkins, Eric (2001): "The 'Critical Turn': Kant and Herz from 1770 to 1772". In: *Kant und die Berliner Aufklärung, Akten des IX. Internationalen Kant-Kongresses*, Gerhardt Volker, Horstmann Rolf-Peter, Schumacher Peter (Eds.) Vol. II. Berlin: Walter de Gruyter, p. 69–77.
Wolff, Christian (2011): "Philosophia Prima Sive Ontologia". In: *Gesammelte Werke*. Hildesheim: Georg Olms.
Zahavi, Dan (2001): "A propos de la neutralité métaphysique des *Recherches logiques*". In: *Revue philosophique de Louvain*, vol. 99, pp. 715–736.

Susi Ferrarello
The Ethics of the Transcendental

Abstract: In this paper I will investigate the ethical implications that Kant's and Husserl's notions of the transcendental exert on the meaning-giving activity of one's life. Hence, the paper will focus first on how Kant arrived at his view of the transcendental as a bridge between being and meaning; second, the paper will show the Kantian heritage in Husserl and describe how Husserl's interpretation of the transcendental facilitates an understanding of it as fully based on the ethical commitment expressed by the epoché and reduction. The aim of this comparison is first to clarify whether or not Kant's and Husserl's philosophical use of the transcendental invites an individualistic ethical attitude in relation to the constitution of meanings within the life-world; second, the goal is to see if our affective, emotional, in one word *interpretive* answer, to the transcendental rule triggers in humans a way to interpret reality that emphasizes the separation more than the interconnectedness of reality itself.

Introduction

In this paper I will investigate the ethical implications of Kant's and Husserl's notions of the transcendental as means to enable the meaning-giving activity that one exercises in its life-world.[1] Both in Kant and Husserl transcendental knowledge seems to point to the traditional role of bridging meaning and being as the transcendental represents the condition of possibility for something to be known by human beings. The way in which we assign meanings to the Being of our lives (our own body, our deeds, feelings etc.) seems to be affected by the way in which we conceive the condition of possibility for knowing objects, that is, the way in which we explain the transcendental itself.

The transcendental represents the condition of the possibility to perceive and explain objects as units of meanings arising from the indistinct flow of being in lived experience. As Kant writes, "experience itself, and therefore the object of experience would be impossible without a connection of this kind" (Kant 1781/1787, A 783/B 811). It is by means of this bridge that the manifold of

---

[1] In Castoriadis (Castoriadis 1986) and Foucault (Paden 1987) for example, we can see how essential unquestioned meanings, such as nature or humanity, shape the way in which we conceive of ourselves within the life-world. I believe that something similar happens with the notion of the transcendental.

https://doi.org/10.1515/9783110564280-003

reality is given to us in the form of individual objects. "The object is viewed as that which prevents our modes of knowledge from being haphazard or arbitrary [...]. For in so far as they relate to an object, they must necessarily agree with one another, that is, must possess that unity which constitutes the concept of an object" (Kant 1781, A 104–5).

In the paper I will discuss the kind of ethics that this notion of the transcendental invites and what kind of meaning-activity is generated from this way of conceiving of the transcendental. Hence, the paper will be divided into two parts. The first part will focus on how Kant arrived at his view of the transcendental; to this end I will discuss several passages from the first edition of the *Critique of Pure Reason* (1781) and from Kant's *Reflexionen* (1782) in order to describe the bridging function of the transcendental. In the second part, I will briefly show the Kantian heritage in Husserl and describe how Husserl's interpretation of the transcendental facilitates a certain ethical understanding of the transcendental as fully based on the ethical commitment expressed by the epoché and reduction. The aim of this comparison is to clarify whether or not Kant's and Husserl's philosophical use of "transcendental" invites an individualistic ethical attitude in relation to the constitution of meanings within the life-world.

1 The History of the Transcendental and Kant

This section will focus on Kant's notion of the transcendental and on those who, according to Sgarbi (2011)[2], mainly influenced Kant: Calov, Baumgarten, and Lambert. In particular, the goal of this section is to explain how Kant approaches the problem of radical heterogeneity between being and meaning through the notion of transcendental.

Through Calov Kant addressed the question that he raised in *De Mundi Sensibilis Atque Intelligibilis* (1770): "how is it possible for several substances to coalesce into one thing (*unum*), and upon what conditions it depends that this one thing is not a part of something else?" (Kant 1905, AK. II, p. 389). Calov's notion of *ens qua ens* (being as a being)[3] led Kant to deduce that the manifold of being

---

[2] There are four possible sources for the notion of the transcendental in Kant according to the *Kant-Forschung:* 1) *Schulmetaphysik* (see in reference to this source: Schmidt 1873; Gideon 1903; Leisegang 1915, pp. 403–421; Knittermeyer 1920; Knittermeyer 1924a; Knittermeyer 1924b; Martin 1951; Vaihinger 1992. For an exhaustive *status quaestionis* see Hinske 1970); 2) Chr. Wolff: in reference to this, see Tommasi 2000; Tommasi 2003; 3) A. G. Baumgarten: see Hinske 1968; Hinske 1970; 4) J. H. Lambert: see Angelelli 1972; Angelelli 1975.

[3] On the subject of metaphysics in Calov, see Sgarbi 2009, pp. 381–398.

coalesces in one thing due to the intrinsic property of that being; the manifold of being is originally one. The *ens*, according to Calov, is that which does not imply any contradiction (Calov 1640, p. 176); contradictions belong to the realm of thinking and intellection while the *ens* is a *primum cognitum*[4] whose primary properties cannot interfere with thinking since what is known is a *primum concretum*. What Calov deduces from this assumption is first that the *ens qua ens* is a *realitas objectiva* which exemplifies itself as an *objectum* in front of the *subjectum* (Calov 1640, pp. 182–183); second, that the *ens* is the first *cognoscibile* because transcendental affections converge around this core and take the form of an object of knowledge.[5] Therefore, Calov considers the transcendental as that which allows the transition from Being to a known object: transcendentals are the *concreta* and affective means that make Being knowable. Nevertheless, while for Calov's description of the transcendental, the *cognoscibile* refers to an objective reality, for Kant the way in which the transcendental shapes this reality is affected by the subject of apprehension.

The second relevant influence on Kant's idea of transcendental is Baumgarten. Kant's *Reflexion 3765* is in fact a comment on Baumgarten's *Metaphysica*, § 89. In this commentary, Kant states that transcendentals are concepts applicable to all things and, similarly to Baumgarten, he considers transcendentals the *ratio sufficiens* for affections. Yet, Kant disagrees in that the latter considers this *ratio* to be not distinguishable from the essence. For Baumgarten, in fact, the ontological and epistemological layers are inseparable, whereas in Kant the transcendentals seem to be an epistemological means to determine Being. Hence, for Kant, the essence is the condition for the possibility of the determination of a manifold as real (*wirklich*, metaphysical condition) and as understandable (transcendental condition). At the end of 1760, in fact, Kant began to identify 'transcendental' with 'essential,' in opposition to 'metaphysical' with 'real,' following Baumgarten only in part.

In fact, according to Kant, the transcendentals are defined as the means through which it is possible to conceive of everything, not only being.[6] The shift from an ontological to a logical and epistemological way of explaining the transcendental shows, according to Hinske (1970), that Kant's description of transcendental unity was closer to Lambert's than to Baumgarten's. In fact, in the first edition of the *Critique*, Baumgarten's idea of transcendental unity, ex-

---

[4] On the *primum cognitum*, see Blackwell 2004, pp. 287–308.
[5] Calov was the first to introduce the science of gnostology and of noology into the System of metaphysics. The former deals with the knowable qua knowable, the latter with the first principles of knowledge.
[6] See Kant 1998, AK. XVII, p. 287.

pressed in § 37 as the "inseparability *per se* of the essential determinations," does not bear any relation to Kant's conception of the transcendental. In *Reflexion 4402*, line 78 (1771), Kant states: "everything is considered in a transcendental sense (*transcendentaliter*), it is conceived respective to the essence, while in a metaphysical sense, it is conceived in an absolute (*absolute*) and universal (*universaliter*) way" (Kant 1905, AK. XVII, p. 533). The opposition between "transcendental" and "metaphysical" is interpreted here in such a way that the former, the transcendental, is used to indicate the essential determination as in the fragment 4025 (1769), while the latter, the metaphysical, points to the logical determination as in *Reflexion 5738* (Kant 1905, AK. XVII, p. 389).[7]

Hence, in *Reflexion 5738*, line 91, Kant states: "the determination of a thing for its essence (as a thing) is transcendental;" and in *Reflexion 5741*, line 92, he states that "the transcendental properties of a thing are those with which the concept of a thing in general is related in an essential way" (Kant 1905, AK. XVIII, p. 341). Also, *Reflexion 4806*, line 93 establishes that what determines the transcendental is an essential unity, which, as he explains further in *Reflexion 4807*, is given to us in a form of understanding that connects metaphysics to logic and the transcendental to ontology (Kant 1905, AK. XVII, p. 734). "The *ens realissimum* is the transcendental idea. It can never be thought *in concreto*, but precedes all judging *in concreto* [...]. [O]ntology is nothing other than a transcendental logic" (Kant 1905, AK. XVII, p. 734).[8]

By the time Kant finishes writing the first edition of the *Critique*, he describes the transcendental according to three primary and distinctive features:
1. The transcendental entails a connection of the manifold in the *unum* which pertains to understanding;
2. This reciprocal connection of the manifold pertains to judgment;
3. The connection of the manifold in the whole is due to an agreement of the manifold with the rule (*Reflexion 4028*, Kant 1905, AK. XXVII, p. 390).

While the first two points bear directly on human faculties, the latter implies the presence of an ontological bridge, which Kant calls *rule*, that connects the manifold of being to human understanding under the form of units of meaning. The next section will be dedicated to explaining how this rule solves the problem of

---

[7] In that sense, Hinske seems to be right to notice that Kant was freeing himself from Wolff's cosmogonic view of the transcendental and getting closer and closer to Baumgarten in his way of limiting the definition of 'transcendental' to '*essentialia*,' hence detracting the advantage of the metaphysics.

[8] For a further discussion of these passages, see Sgarbi 2011.

the radical heterogeneity between being and meaning, transcendental essence and metaphysical meaning.

2 The Kantian Bridge

In Kant, the word *rule* refers to the schema that explains how Being can be determined into concepts and accordingly into units of meanings. Differently from Smith (1918), Woods (1970) considers Kant's attempt to explain the Schematism as capable of solving the problem of homogeneity or radical heterogeneity of being and meaning – we could summarize the problem in these terms: if being *per se* is radically different from meaning, how can it be given to us in units of meanings?[9] Kant resolves that the chaos of the manifold is subsumed under the universal of the epistemological thought through intuitions:

> In all subsumption of an object under a concept the representation of the object must be homogeneous with the concept; in other words the concept must contain something which is represented in the object that is to be subsumed under it. This, in fact, is what is meant by the expression "an object is contained under a concept." Thus, the empirical concept of a plate is homogeneous with the pure geometrical concept of a circle. The roundness which is thought in the latter can be intuited in the former. (Kant 1781/1787, A 137/B 176)

As shown in this passage, Kant explains the problem of radical heterogeneity or homogeneity of being through the system of grouping made possible by intuitions. In contrast to thinking or just being, intuition is a complex bridging function of the human mind which triggers, according to Kant, a synthetic affective activity that explains how different essences can be thought together:

> The formative synthesis through which we construct a triangle in imagination is precisely the same as that which we exercise in the apprehension of an appearance in making for ourselves an empirical concept of it. (Kant 1781/1787, A 224/B 271)

Taken in itself, an intuition is a bare sensible representation devoid of cognitive content. Yet, since our mind groups together intuitions that share similar contents, (then) an intuition happens to become a vehicle for contents in itself.

---

9 However, it is true, as Philstroem (2002, p. 188) remarked, that the transcendental can hold a psychological component which can influence the ethical layer of our apprehension and lead to deceptive and misleading choices, for example, our wish to be immortal can thus find a theoretical foundation. From this point of view, for example, our wish to be immortal can trick us into a consistent transcendental illusion.

As Pendlebury (1995, p. 10) remarks, this grouping activity takes place because of a specific disposition of the human mind to respond to the data that affect our perception. Kant calls this activity formative synthesis. The affective quality attached to the formative synthesis demands each *concretum* become part of a whole that human beings understand as *abstractum*.

> The concept dog signifies a rule (i.e. a schema) according to which my imagination can delineate the figure of a four-footed animal in a general manner, without limitation to any singular figure such as experience or any possible image that I can represent *in concreto*, actually present. (Kant 1781/1787, A 141/B 180)

The rule, which Kant calls schema, describes both a transcendental (essential) and a metaphysical (logical) way of delineating an image in a concrete moment; the concreteness of that moment is made apparent through time and imagination. You do not know what a cat is unless you know which images count as the same cat at different times. Rules, in fact, are schemata which generate images that attach to the sensation we call intuition; these images differ from each other because of the affective impression with which affections shape the mind in a given unit of time. In that sense, a schema is what makes the regulatory function of the pure concepts acceptable.

> The schema of substance is the permanence of the real in time, that is, the representation of the real as a substrate of empirical determination of time in general and so as abiding while all else changes. (Kant 1781, A 143)

In that sense, a schema of permanence is "the permanence of the real in time, " which means that time is the image of the sensed which operates on both a metaphysical (logical) and transcendental (essential) level. On the metaphysical level the schema is an image of time that demands that the apprehension of impressions (the manifold) be translated in different degrees of representation of being proportional to the intensity of affections (as they present themselves according to the inner sense). On the transcendental (essential) level, the schema temporalizes the manifold in a productive affective way according to permanence, succession, and reciprocity. It is this affective productive level that makes us capable of using categories whose content, that is the passive impressions of the manifold, would be understandable for us.

This rule involves a specific attitude of human beings by which they recognize the affective impression of time and interpret it in discrete moments of appearances. Despite the fact that we do not know exactly in what form being is in itself, our mind is such that we make sense of it through discrete units of meanings that do not fully capture the actual complexity of its web.

3 The Kantian Heritage in Husserl

In several places Husserl acknowledges the influence that Kant had on his work, although in a very critical way. For example:

> Kant's oeuvre contains gold in rich abundance. But one must break it and melt it in the fire of radical critique in order to bring out this content. (Husserl 1986, Hua XXV, p. 206)

According to Crowell (2013, p. 13), Husserl's merit consists in breaking the concreteness of being and overcoming the anthropological flaw of Kant's philosophy. In fact, according to Crowell, while Kant's use of the transcendental schema is grounded in human sensibility, Husserl's use of epoché and reduction[10] commits the transcendentals to ethical transparency. By 'transparency,' Crowell means "in Moran's terms, an avowal [...] that expresses commitments [...] to something that transcends any description of my psychological state" (Crowell 2013, p. 90). This form of commitment is ethical for three main reasons: first, it involves an actual choice based on personal values; secondly, it invites human beings to the ethical effort to overcome the biases of one's own understanding; third, it fosters the awareness that an individual can have of its own limitations. From an ethical point of view, Husserl seems to take a step forward with respect to Kant's way of conceiving the 'transcendental.' Indeed, an ethical commitment to a transparent knowledge (i.e., unbiased knowledge) invites individuals to fully grasp the intersubjective essence of their lived-experiences.

4 *Abstracta* and *Concreta*, Ought and Should

Differently from Stapelton (1983), Crowell argues that for Husserl the transcendental question is a question of *being* a *meaning*, in the sense that the transcendental exists as a unit of validity or *Seinsgeltung* (2013, p. 23). In Husserl, the reduction which is the act through which we bring (*duco*) the meanings of a perception or experience back (*re*) to a specific point of view is ethically and emotionally motivated by the need to recover the *Seinsgeltung* of the world (Cro-

---

[10] To remind the reader, epoché and reduction are two phenomenological devices introduced by Husserl in order to suspend the natural way in which we look at reality. While the epoché entails that we suspend the attitude through which we take reality for granted as a network of meanings that stand there for us, reduction leads the phenomenological actor to assume a questioning attitude toward suspended reality, and it is thanks to this attitude that one has the chance to grasp the essential, unshakable truth of what is experienced.

well 2013, p. 24). Therefore, this transcendental act which presents the possibility for us to know the world finds its roots in an ethical commitment and an emotional need for meanings and values (Crowell 2013, p. 26). Hence, while Crowell considers the ontology of meaning as the normative connection between being and meaning, Stapelton regards this gap as a logico-ontological one (Crowell 2013, p. 25). I believe that, as in Woods' interpretation of Kant, Husserl's explanation of the 'foundation' of being as a unit of validity cannot be regarded as merely epistemological, because it is not only categorial activity that determines the sensuous data of material being: Being itself determines its own matter. The condition for the possibility of objects' existence lies in their necessary correlation to other objects (Stapleton, cited in Crowell 2013, p. 25).

Constitution is a logical phenomenon that is "unintelligible from a worldly perspective since worldly concepts presuppose [...] an ontological concept of reality" (Crowell 2013, p. 11). "The logical pieces integrate the *concreta* in the emotional (as *Gemüt*) animation and understanding of the *concreta* itself" (Crowell 2013, p. 116). Hence, the concreteness of being, the *Washeit* as Scheler named it (Scheler 1973, pp. 157-158), is "what is to be found in the very own being of an *individuum* as the 'What' of an *individuum*" (Husserl 1976, Hua III/1, p. 8; Husserl 1983, p. 16). It is the emotional 'answer' that individualizes concrete data, and simultaneously the *Seinsgültigkeit* (Husserl 1984, Hua XIX/1, p. 15; Husserl 2001b, p. 16) that pre-exists any possible concrete body. As Husserl writes: "*Esse* and *percipi* fall together" (Husserl 1966, Hua XI, p. 15; Husserl 2001a, p. 51), but this does not mean that they are the same. The essence is a *Sollen* and a *Müssen* – *being* and *being correctly perceived*; it is not only "the being but is something connected to the being" (Husserl 1988, Hua XXVIII, p. 340). Logical and ontological moments coexist.

The transcendental being constitutes the condition for the possibility of being as a unity; this being is an ought, that is, a necessity that is given to us in a co-founded unity. The being, in fact, regulates the direction of the logical inference and its consequent meaning-giving activity. In this unity, meaning and being, *abstracta* and *concreta* are co-founded around time. For Husserl, similarly to Kant, our sense of time obeys a rule that is tightly connected to affections because time spontaneously produces affective images to which we give emotional and then cognitive interpretations. In human beings the rule of time holds a productive function which transforms the interconnection of the parts into wholes of meaning. Breaking from the seeming concreteness of this being enables us to discover this implicit interconnection as it is given through time; it is in time that we acknowledge the meaning of what is given through the worth that the given holds for us.

It is this value – which comes through an abiding by the ought – that bridges the ontological nature of the concreteness of being with its emotional and epistemological way of ordering its sense within a meaningful unit. Therefore, the totality of life belongs to the essence of the transcendental subject: that is, a generative unitary life is motivated through and in that. This unity of temporality, of objective temporality in which the world and the subject determine themselves, is one unit of motivation of evolution (Husserl 2014, Hua XLII, p. 445).

The main point I meant to argue in this paper is that our affective, emotional, in one word, *interpretive* answer to time resolves into a specifically ethical choice that is based on implied values, expressed through a meaning-giving activity, and practiced through acts in the life-world. When we actively assign meaning to the life-world, we tend to *dissect the concreteness of Being into units of meanings and forget about the interconnectedness of this unit*. I think that Husserl's epoché and reduction can be useful devices to overcome this human bias and encourage an intersubjective worldview in which its parts are interconnected with each other.

5 The Ethical Access to Transcendental Concreteness

To summarize briefly the previous sections, according to Husserl and Kant, time is what explains the interconnection between Being and meaning because of the interpretive answer we give to its flow. This connection is made visible to us through imagination which provides images that convey in an understandable way the impressions with which time affects human minds. Both for Kant and Husserl the transcendental depends on the way in which human minds are affected by and react to the rule of time. These human faculties shape the way in which we know things; for Husserl, differently from Kant, we can overcome human biases and penetrate the concreteness of Being that stands at the very origin of the interconnection of being and meaning, parts and whole, *concreta* and *abstracta*, through epoché and reduction. I agree with Moran (2011) and Crowell (2013) when they recognize that the epoché possesses an ethical quality because of the personal commitment to the truth that it involves. The epoché, in fact, is for Husserl "a methodological device that allows us to suspend one's participation in the belief characteristic of the natural attitude, the belief, that world and its objects exist" (Drummond 2008, p. 68) in order to facilitate our change of attitude from a natural to a theoretical one. In effecting an epoché, we begin questioning our normal beliefs and make ourselves available for digging deeper into the meaning of being as it presents itself to us. This enables us to grasp and react to our previously unrecognized limiting assumptions and assume a critical scientific attitude, both cognitively and emotionally. The ethical layer of the epoché relies upon the fact that we recognize the crisis of meaning in which we are living and commit ourselves to a search for truer meanings belonging to that portion of being (Husserl 1954, Hua VI, first part.). In that sense, Husserl specifically mentions the researcher's enacting of an *ethical epoché* in order to emphasize the emotional responsibility involved in the act of suspension (see Husserl 1954, Hua VI, p. 485 or p. 349). Once we commit to the epoché, we can never be the same again in the sense of naively returning to the natural flow of life in which we were previously living.

6 The Ethics of the Transcendental and Transcendental Humanity

Similarly to the relationship between parts and wholes, *concreta* and *abstracta*, meanings and beings, we as human beings are *concreta* whose Being falls together with the *percipi* – with the *abstractum* of being perceived by others. The word *individuum*, the Latin for "indivisible," can lead us to the idea that our lives belong to separate units of meanings (if and when one finds some meaning in life), which seems to imply that we are doomed entirely to a life of ultimate solitude and disconnection from others. However, if we take a closer look at transcendental unity as it appears in Kant and Husserl, we can see how even though it synthesizes meanings into units, these units are nevertheless formed around the rule of time as it is expressed through a flow of interconnected being-time given to us in moments of affections that are interpreted by our mind according to a human 'rule.' Around the rule of time we build units of sense that bridge together Being and meaning as givens that acquire value for us. It often seems that in acquiring these units of meaning we neglect the flow in which they, and we ourselves as human beings, are placed.

The rule of necessity of being, to put it in Kant's terms, or of the *Seinsgeltung* (unit of validity), to use Husserl's words, might lead us to assume an affectively biased attitude that blinds us to the interconnectedness of being. Hence, the fact that transcendental conditions determine being in units of meaning should not lead us to the false understanding that these units are separate once and for all or that the Being of our own life is solipsistically encased in ontological categories; it is in fact the transcendental conditions of being that show how the schema is characterized by permanence, succession, and reciprocity through time.

The temporalization of the manifold is a productive function of affective rules that demand the productions of percepted sensuous appearances. These appearances are a necessity stemming from the structure of our mind, yet the necessary indivisibility with which they appear to us should not be taken as an ontological necessity.

According to Husserl, transcendental humanity (Husserl 1973, Hua XV, p. 24), as a whole, is that community of living beings who, through effecting the epoché, decide to assume an ethical attitude in recognizing their interconnectedness with each other (Husserl 2012, Hua Mat. IX, p. 188). Each part of this whole has a goal that can be determined through its permanence in time. The absolute universal will that lives in all transcendental subjectivities and which makes possible the individual-concrete being of the total transcendental subjectivity is both a universal and a transcendental will.

In the ongoing awakening of subjects, there is an ongoing reconstituting of the whole, but always through a multiplicity of individual monads, in a field in which there are always both sleeping and awakening monads. The totality of monads, a total monadic unity, is an infinite ascending process and this is necessarily a constant process in the development of sleeping monads into awakening ones; and it is a development toward a world that is always reconstituting itself in monads such that those that constitute them insofar as they are awake are not all of them. But the totality is always involved in a foundational way. And this constitution of the world is the constitution of an always-higher minded humanity, which is hopefully aware of its proper and true being. In this way the constitution assumes the form of a whole that freely determines itself, having as its scope the knowledge and form of its perfection (Husserl 1973, Hua XV, p. 410).

The part 'demands' the whole – something uniform awakens something else that is uniform, which is not yet at all constituted as a unity explicitly for itself; and it does not demand the whole by a pure and simple awakening, but rather by a co-connected 'expectation,' by the demand as coexisting, as co-belonging to the unity. Even the force of this apperceptive expectation increases with the number of "'instances' – or with habit, which amounts to the same thing" (Husserl 1966, Hua XI, p. 190; Husserl 2001a, p. 240).

As shown in these lines, human beings are in fact defined by Husserl as organic functioning elements (Husserl 2012, Hua Mat. IX, p. 170 and 176) which do not refer solely to their own monads but are parts of a larger whole of interrelated monads in ongoing contact with each other as part of an inclusive whole. My genetic and lower life is not primordially mine because it is made of passive matter which my psychical ego cannot fully make mine through any act of recognition and ownership; it is the awakening of my ego that makes that life mine. The intimate space which that awakening unfolds makes my own functioning and validating system part of other systems through the recognition of that interconnected whole. For Husserl, individuals are units of goals, values, and certitudes (Husserl 2012, Hua Mat. IX, p. 171) that relate to each other in a social community. I can grasp the interconnection of my space of intimacy with other spaces through my habitual I which can sediment layers that allow the reflecting I to grasp its own being. Human beings are *concreta* that relate to the whole of society as parts to a whole, and these parts are a whole in turn. They can function independently of the whole-society, but as they explicate their task they form a whole with the society to which they belong. Hence the individual is not an isolated monad in society. Everyone is responsible for what part of herself she brings into 'one single universal coherence.' The goals and the values that move each personal subject to action are inevitably interconnected to the values of others.

Conclusions

Through this analysis of Kant's and Husserl's notion of transcendental, a few similarities and differences have emerged between the two. Mainly, for both philosophers the notion of the transcendental is connected to the productive function of time in which Being determines itself through meaning. Nevertheless, in Husserl, differently from Kant, the biased psychological way in which humans interpret and use this bridge is parenthesized by the epoché, which represents an ethical commitment through which human beings recognize their biases and commit themselves to a more and more objective way to observe and assign a meaning to Being. In both Husserl and Kant, the human bias regarding the transcendentals consists in a way of interpreting Being that dissects its sensuous flow into distinct units of meanings which ultimately impact the way in which human beings tend to conceive of themselves and their lives as distinct units. Instead of perceiving themselves as intersubjective and co-constituted Being participating in the flow of life, humans tend to consider themselves as part of a separated constellation that cuts them off from the apparent interconnectedness of Being. The epoché, as Husserl showed us, can be used as a theoretical and ethical device to broaden the human view on transcendentals. The ethical outcome that an epoché of this kind would involve is to overcome the sense of separatedness between parts and the whole and increase the awareness of the flow of interconnectedness from which human Being and its meanings stem. This awareness might contribute to enriching human social life and facilitating the meaning-giving activity that humans are called to exert in their lives.

Bibliography

Angelelli, Ignacio (1972): "On the Origins of Kant's 'Transcendental'". In: *Kant-Studien*, vol. 63, pp. 117–122.
Angelelli, Ignacio (1975): "On 'Transcendental' Again". In: *Kant-Studien*, vol. 66, pp. 116–120.
Baumgarten, Alexander Gottlieb (2011): *Metaphysica*. Berlin: Olms Verlag.
Bennett, Jonathan (1974): *Kant's Dialectic*. Cambridge: Cambridge University Press.
Blackwell, Constance (2004): "The Vocabulary for Natural Philosophy. The *de primo cognito* question. A preliminary Exploration: Zimara, Toletus, Pereira and Zabarella". In: *Lexiques et Glossaires Philosophiques de la Renaissance*. Ed. Jacqueline Hamesse and Marta Fattori. Louvain-la-Neuve: Fédération internationale des Instituts d'études médiévales, pp. 287–308.
Calov, Abraham (1640): *Metaphysica divina, pars generalis*. Rostock: Rostochii Sumptu Hallervordiano.
Castoriadis, Cornelius (1986): "The Nature and Value of Equality". Trans. David A. Curtis. In: *Philosophy and Social Criticism*, vol. 11, n° 4, pp. 373–390.
Crowell, Steven (2013): *Normativity and Phenomenology in Husserl and Heidegger*. Cambridge: Cambridge University Press.
Drummond, John (2008): *Historical Dictionary of Husserl's Philosophy*. Chicago, Lanham, MD: Scarecrow Press.
Gideon, Abraham (1903): *Der Begriff Transzendental in Kants Kritik der reinen Vernunft*. Marburg: Friedrich.
Henckmann, Wolfhart (1998): *Max Scheler*. München: Beck Verlag.
Hinske, Norbert (1968): "Die historischen Vorlagen der kantischen Transzendentalphilosophie". In: *Archiv für Begriffsgeschichte*, vol. 12, pp. 86–113.
Hinske, Nobert (1970): *Kants Weg zur Transzendentalphilosophie. Der dreißigjährige Kant*. Stuttgart: Kohlhammer.
Husserl, Edmund (1954): *Die Krisis der europäischen Wissenschaften und die transzendentale Phänomenologie. Eine Einleitung in die phänomenologische Philosophie*. Husserliana, vol. VI. Ed. W. Biemel. The Hague: Martinus Nijhoff.
Husserl, Edmund (1966): *Analysen zur passiven Synthesis. Aus Vorlesungs- und Forschungsmanuskripten 1918–1926*. Husserliana, vol. XI. Ed. M. Fleischer. The Hague: Martinus Nijhoff.
Husserl, Edmund (1970): *Crisis of European Sciences and Transcendental Phenomenology*. Trans. D. Carr. Evanston, IL: Northwestern University Press.
Husserl, Edmund (1976): *Ideen zu einer reinen Phänomenologie und phänomenologischen Philosophie. First Book: Allgemeine Einführung in die Phänomenologie*. Husserliana, vol. III/1. Ed. Karl Schuhmann. The Hague: Martinus Nijhoff.
Husserl, Edmund (1983): *Ideas Pertaining to a Pure Phenomenology and to a Phenomenological Philosophy. First Book: General Introduction to a Pure Phenomenology*. Trans. Fred Kersten. The Hague: Martinus Nijhoff.
Husserl, Edmund (1973): *Zur Phänomenologie der Intersubjektivität. Texte aus dem Nachlass. Dritter Teil. 1929–35*. Husserliana, vol. XV. Ed. I. Kern. The Hague: Martinus Nijhoff.
Husserl, Edmund (1984): *Logische Untersuchungen. Zweiter Teil. Untersuchungen zur Phänomenologie und Theorie der Erkenntnis*. Husserliana, vol. XIX. Ed. U. Panzer. The Hague: Martinus Nijhoff.

Husserl, Edmund (1986): *Aufsätze und Vorträge 1911–1921. Husserliana*, vol. XXV. Ed. T. Nenon and H. R. Sepp. The Hague, Netherlands: Martinus Nijhoff.
Husserl, Edmund (1988): *Vorlesungen über Ethik und Wertlehre 1908–1914. Husserliana*, vol. XXVIII. Ed. U. Melle. The Hague: Kluwer Academic Publishers.
Husserl, Edmund (2001a): *Analyses concerning Active and Passive Syntheses*. Trans. A. J. Steinbock. Dordrecht: Kluwer Academic Publishers.
Husserl, Edmund (2001b): *Logical Investigations*. Trans. J. N. Findlay and ed. D. Moran. London, New York: Routledge.
Husserl, Edmund (2012): *Einleitung in die Philosophie. Vorlesungen 1916–1919. Husserliana Materialien*, vol. IX. Ed. H. Jacobs. Dordrecht: Springer.
Husserl, Edmund (2014): *Grenzprobleme der Phänomenologie. Analysen des Unbewusstseins und der Instinkte. Metaphysik. Späte Ethik (Texte aus dem Nachlass 1908–1937). Husserliana*, vol. XLII. Ed. R. Sowa & Th. Vongehr. New York: Springer.
Kant, Immanuel (1781): *Kritik der reinen Vernunft*. 1st (A) edition. Riga: J. F. Hartknoch. 2nd (B) ed: 1787.
Kant, Immanuel (1882): *Reflexionen Kants zur kritischen Philosophie. Aus Kants handschriftlichen Aufzeichnungen*. Leipzig: Fues's Verlag.
Kant, Immanuel (1902): *Kants gesammelte Schriften*. Preussischen Akademie der Wissenschaften (vols 1–22), Deutschen Akademie der Wissenschaften (vol. 23), Akademie der Wissenschaften zu Göttingen (vols 24–9). Berlin: Walter de Gruyter. (AK.)
Kant, Immanuel (1986): *Latin Writings, Translations, Commentaries, and Notes*. Trans. Lewis White Beck in collaboration with Mary Gregor, Ralf Meerbote, John Reuscher. New York: Peter Lang.
Kant, Immanuel (1998): *Reflexionen zur Metaphysik. Aus Kants handschriftlichen Aufzeichnungen*. Leipzig: Fues's Verlag.
Kant, Immanuel (2007): *Critique of Pure Reason*. Trans. N. Kemp Smith. New York: Palgrave Macmillan.
Knittermeyer, Hinrich (1920): *Der Terminus 'transzendental' in seiner historischen Entwickelung bis zu Kant*. Marburg: Hamel.
Knittermeyer, Hinrich (1924a): "Transzendent und Transzendental". In: *Paul Natorp zum 70. Geburtstage von Schilern und Freunden gewidmet*. Ed. Ernst Cassirer. Berlin/Leipzig: Walter de Gruyter, pp. 195–214.
Knittermeyer, Hinrich (1924b): "Transzendentalphilosophie und Theologie. Eine kritische Erinnerung zum 22. April 1924". In: *Die christliche Welt*, vol. 38, pp. 220–226.
Leisegang, Hans (1915): "Ober die Behandlung des scholastischen Satzes: 'Quodlibet ens est unum, verum, bonum seu perfectum,' und seine Bedeutung in Kants *Kritik der reinen Vernunft*". In: *Kant-Studien*, vol. 20, pp. 403–421.
Martin, Gottfried (1951): *Immanuel Kant. Ontologie und Wissenschaftstheorie*. Köln: Kölner Universitätsverlag.
Moran, Dermont (2011): "Edmund Husserl' phenomenology of habituality and habitus". In: *Journal for the British Society of Phenomenology*, vol. 42, pp. 53–77.
Paden, Roger (1987): "Foucault's Anti-Humanism". In: *Human Studies*, vol. 10, n° 1, pp. 123-141.
Pendlebury, Michael (1995): "Making Sense of Kant's Schematism". In: *Philosophy and Phenomenological Research*, vol. 55, n° 4, pp. 777-797.
Smith, Kemp (1918): *A Commentary to Kant's Critique of Pure Reason*. London: Macmillan,

Sgarbi, Marco (2011): "The Historical Genesis of the Kantian Concept of 'Transcendental'". In: *Archiv Für Begriffsgeschichte*, vol. 53, pp. 97-117.
Sgarbi, Marco (2009): "*Unus, Verus, Bonus* et Calovius. L'oggetto della metafisica in A. Calov". In: *Medioevo*, pp. 381–398.
Stapleton, Timothy (1983): *Husserl and Heidegger. The Question of a Phenomenological Beginning*. Albany: State University of New York.
Tommasi, Valerio (2000): *Philosophia transcendentalis. La questione antepredicativa e l'analogia tra la Scolastica e Kant*. Firenze: Casa Editrice Leo S. Olschki.
Tommasi, Valerio (2003): "Kant di fronte alla tradizione del 'trascendentale': stato della ricerca e prospettive alia luce di un nuovo particolare". In: *Studi Kantiani*, vol. 16, pp. 53–66.
Vaihinger, Hans (1992): *Kommentar zu Kants Kritik der reinen Vernunft*. Stuttgart: Union Deutsche Verlagsgesellschaft.
Woods, Allen (1970): *Kant's Moral Religion*. Ithaca, NY: Cornell University Press.

John Rogove
The Phenomenological *a priori* as Husserlian Solution to the Problem of Kant's "Transcendental Psychologism"

Abstract: In this chapter we first propose an analysis of the Husserlian critique of the Kantian doctrine of the faculties (and of their transcendental division into sensibility and understanding in the first *Critique*) and of the premises of a "transcendental psychologism" such as they are found in Kant, but in terms of the genesis of this doctrine in the empirical division of the faculties in the *Anthropology*, relying on critiques proposed by Foucault and D. Pradelle. By underscoring the radical differences between Kant and Husserl, we critique the notion according to which Husserlian phenomenology is a Kantian-inspired "philosophy of the subject." We then propose an analysis of this critique in terms of a mereological reading of Husserl's understanding of the *a priori* in such a way as to examine and radicalize that de-anthropologization of the a priori that is carried out or made possible by Husserl. Our hypothesis is that this overcoming of the Kantian model, which is bogged down by naturalistic and empiricist metaphysical presuppositions, requires both an overcoming of classical hylomorphism in favor of the mereology of immanence and the transition to an a-subjective phenomenology required in turn by an extension of this interpretative model to Husserl's "transcendental turn."

It was once a common error among doxographers and historians of philosophy to situate Husserl in particular, and the phenomenological movement he founded in general, directly downstream of Kant and the Kantian moment in the history of philosophy, a natural heir to what, retrospectively, were seen as the historical premises of the long tradition of what was to become a "philosophy of the subject." This latter was quite naturally thought to be the continuation or the radicalization of Kant's "Copernican revolution," which turned the question of knowledge back toward the subject as a transcendental condition of the possibility of knowledge, no longer centering the question around descriptions of what *is*, of the whole, or of the absolute, but rather around a description of the subject as a transcendental function of representation, and of the very idea of the object as relative to the structures of that functioning. In the retroprojected light, especially, of later French phenomenologically-inspired philosophy, and of the specifically Anglo-American reception-phenomenon known as "Continental philosophy," the continuity or at least the "family resemblances" uniting Kantian Criticism and Husserlian phenomenology seemed sufficient to identify them as a single "species" (or at least a "genus") of philosophizing, in terms both of their methodology and their concerns.[1] The *philosopheme* that seemed to unite them is what appears to be their common concern with representation and its transcendental conditions, with a description of the world uniquely with respect to its phenomenal aspects, with how it appears *for* a subject, to the pointed exclusion of what either one of them variously termed "metaphysics."

But whereas the term "metaphysics" in both cases designates something inaccessible to experience and something which then, by definition, cannot be the object of science, what the two philosophers understand by "science," and consequently by "experience," and finally, therefore, also by "metaphysics" leads them to entirely different commitments and claims. The misunderstanding or underestimation of the extent to which this is the case is what has led to these readings of Husserl's phenomenology as an absolute subjective idealism, or even as a sort of solipsistic or relativistic representationalism.[2] For indeed, while both philosophies are called "transcendental," and both can, with certain reservations, be understood to be a sort of "idealism," what Kant understands or at least assumes by these terms embodies, for Husserl, the cardinal philosophical sin against which he established the basic principles upon which he erected the rest of his subsequent philosophy: the sin of "psychologism," or what is even worse, of "transcendental psychologism."

---

[1] *Cf.*, for example, Paul Ricœur's reading of Husserl as a sort of radicalization of Kant (e.g., Ricœur 1955, pp. 44–67; Ricœur 1967, pp. 183–196, both reprinted in Ricœur 1986, pp. 227–250 and pp. 7–20; or Ricœur 1950, which is his commentary on Husserl's *Ideen I*). *Cf.* also Derrida 1962, pp. 146–155.
[2] The type of doxography that sees phenomenology as a sort of radical continuation of Kantianism is generally the same type that sees Husserl only in the retro-projected light of the so-called "post-modern" philosophy which has supposedly issued from it and for which phenomenology is supposed to be the matrix. It is in large part thanks to a resurgence of interest in the early Husserl, and of philosophical practices among both phenomenologists and so-called analytic philosophers that ceased to read Husserl in light of later "Continental" trends, but rather in light of the early post-Brentanian problematics from which his conceptuality actually emerged and which were held in common with early analytic philosophy, that this type of misreading has been largely overcome. Which is to say, Husserl is no longer read as the last, preparatory, stage in the overcoming of the Cartesian-Kantian axis by Heidegger, Levinas, or Derrida, but is read in and for himself.

While it is in a sense anachronistic to attribute to Kant psychologism (or, for that matter, antipsychologism), since this concept as a polemical trope only arises posthumously concerning his work,³ the attribution remains pertinent insofar as the claim is not that Kant was explicitly a partisan of psychologism as a thesis, but that his premises are those of psychologism. On the one hand, independently of whether we attribute a form of psychologism to Kant, it is indisputable that Husserl (as well as Frege) understood their own antipsychologism to be fundamentally directed at Kant, to whom they attributed the paternity of contemporary psychologism.⁴ Husserlian phenomenology sets itself up from the outset as an antidote to what we might call the philosophy of the relativity of knowledge to a "conceptual scheme." Davidson describes this thesis in terms of a dualism between total scheme and uninterpreted content (Davidson 2006, pp. 201–202). The latter, which designates reality "as it is in itself," is relative, with respect to our ability to know it, to the former, our conceptual scheme (Davidson 2006, pp. 196–197). Now, the "conceptual scheme" thesis is precisely the one according to which "intuitions without concepts are blind" (Ferraris 2004, p. 74).⁵ To this Kantian philosophy of the schematizing construction of categorial forms, Husserl opposes his philosophy of the intuitive givenness of these forms. In so doing, he rehabilitates the possibility of ontology and of access to the "things themselves," the banishment of which Kant had previously taken, as a good Humean, to be the condition of all scientific philosophizing.⁶

In this paper, we intend to present and to elaborate on the phenomenological critique of this notion of a "transcendental psychologism" such as it is

---

3 J. F. Herbart, in 1816, considered Kant's doctrine of the faculties to be psychologistic in nature, insofar as it sets them up as both natural entities (which are nevertheless hypotheses to which we have no direct cognitive access) and as the markers of an absolute dependence of all knowledge on the nature or activity of the human subject, leading directly to subjectivistic idealism and/or to solipsism (*cf.* Herbart 1816/1891). See on this point especially Bonnet 2015.
4 On the question of the legitimacy of the Husserlian and Fregean attribution of a proto-psychologism to Kant, see Ehrsam 2015.
5 *Cf.* more generally Ferraris 2004, pp. 73–87, "Conceptual schemes and phenomena."
6 See on this point Bouriau 2000, pp. 80–81: "The Husserlian problematic initially seems to have a Kantian epistemological flavor to it" since it seeks to guarantee the objectivity of knowledge. "Only, the way in which Husserl conceives the objectivity of knowledge is from the very beginning of his work essentially distinct from Kant [...], since the forms or conditions of possibility of knowing are no longer dissociated from the objects of knowledge themselves [...]. Husserl's goal is to reach *absolute, given* forms in their indubitable self-evidence, as well as the correlations among these forms. Kant, as we know, conceived of the forms of knowledge, on the one hand as not objective in themselves (insofar as they do not refer to a given matter), and on the other hand [...] as constitutive of the human subject, and as immanent and relative to its faculties." *Cf.* Pradelle 2012, pp. 10–14.

found in Kant. Enrolling Michel Foucault, whose commentary on Kant's *Anthropology* (Foucault 2008) purports to demonstrate the dependence of the latter's doctrine of the faculties on an empirically derived picture of human nature, we also enlist Jean Cavaillès and Dominique Pradelle, whose recent work (Pradelle 2012) has likewise sought to emphasize the clarity and radicality of the Husserlian departure from Kant's supposed psychologism. In our Husserlian reading of Kant's doctrine of the faculties and of the possibility, nature, and extent of *a priori* knowledge as the root of the latter's psychologism and of what constitutes the gulf separating Criticism from phenomenology, we will then propose a radicalization of this critique in terms of precisely that which separates Husserl's doctrine of the *a priori* from Kant's, namely, the material *a priori* and the specific formal ontology that underpins its possibility.

1 Husserl's Anti-representationalism: an anti-Kantian Thesis, Intentionality, Expounded by an un-Kantian Method, the Reduction

Indeed, it is the question of ontology, and of logic, that can be said to constitute the heart of the divergence between Kantian Criticism and Husserlian phenomenology. The "critical" gesture, which is "critical" towards traditional metaphysics, especially the ontology of Leibniz and Wolf, consists essentially in a severing of logic (and of a theory of representation) from ontology: for Kant, the categories of formal logic no longer correspond to the necessary categories of being, as they did for Aristotle, but rather simply to those of the (human) understanding. In Kant's eyes, this gesture would seem to be a step in the direction of the edification of a theory of knowledge that is rigorous and scientific precisely in that it unties logic and the theory of representation (logic being the theory of how representations are properly combined) from metaphysics, and thereby constitutes a step in the direction of a science of knowledge that recognizes the *sui generis* character of the mind. Kant thought and meant thereby to sidestep the pitfall of the sort of psychologistic reductionism we find him criticizing when he seeks to dissociate the *a priori* science of logic, which provides the rules for the functioning of the understanding, from the empirical sciences of anthropology or psychology,[7] and we might be (and some have been) tempted to see in

---

[7] See for example both the second preface to the 1st *Critique* (Kant 1787, BVIII-BIX) and the introduction to the *Logic* (Kant 1923, AK. IX, pp. 13–16). Logic, Kant says in the most basic defi-

this separation, which motivates and is coextensive with Kant's separation of the phenomenon from the *Ding an sich*, a precursor to the phenomenological reduction. What, indeed, is Husserl up to in the reduction if not an isolation of the *Weltthesis*, of the positive and natural assertion that entities *are* in such and such a way, from the way in which they are necessarily represented, from the inner logic of their simple appearing? However, it is in Kant's case precisely this separation, and moreover the conditions or terms of this separation, that pose an unbridgeable gap between transcendental criticism and phenomenological description; indeed, it is just this separation that, from a Husserlian perspective, causes Kant to fall, backwards as it were, into the anthropologistic psychologism he sought to avoid by this very means.

For Husserl, the goal of the reduction is not to isolate our representations from the pretensions to know things themselves (*Dinge an sich*), but rather to attend methodically to the things themselves (*Sachen selbst*) such as to allow them to be what they are; and the method in this attention is meant to allow this to occur through a radical and systematic neutralization of the prejudices (*Vorurteile*) and presuppositions (*Voraussetzungen*) that prevent this from occurring. However, if such specifically cognitive phenomena as "prejudices" and "presuppositions" are what get in the way of the things themselves being what they are, such that the methodical removal or neutralization of these phenomena is what allows this being to occur, this indicates that some *collapsus* has taken place in the distinction between being and appearing; and indeed, it is precisely in this *collapsus* that the definitional core of Husserl's method consists – and from which the rest follows, almost analytically as it were. Husserl calls this core the "principle of principles" – *viz.*, the principle according to which the ultimate arbiter of truth, of any thesis or assertion, can only be the adequate constitution of the object in question in an intuition, in its complete *givenness* –, and reduction is nothing more than its methodical application, *i.e.*, the methodical elimination of anything that had previously been thought or asserted about the phenomenon or attributed to it which does not appear in or with it in a necessary (or a possible) way.

But what ultimately justifies or grounds the principle of principles as a methodological starting point and is, as such, phenomenology's true heart and point of departure, is the tautology according to which all consciousness is intentional, *i.e.*, that it is always consciousness *of* something. Negatively put, we can say that this tautology consists in the observation that it is absurd or nonsensical to

---

nition he gives of it (Kant 1923, AK. IX, pp. 11–13), is both the form of the understanding abstracted from its content and the rules governing its use.

posit objects that cannot in principle appear, *i.e.*, that cannot be objects. What follows analytically from this, then, is that things themselves can therefore be constituted in an adequate intuition and rigorously described. This constitution and description become, then, not the hallmark or dogmatic invocation of an unexperienceable metaphysics, but the very content of a rigorous account of experience itself. The ultimate methodological criterion for this intuitive constitution is, in its most basic form, the eidetic variation that allows us to see which sorts of things can appear together and which sort of things cannot, and which sorts of phenomena cannot *not* appear together. For example, it is by trying simultaneously to presentify red and green covering the same surface that I learn that these phenomena cannot be combined in the same way that, say, red and rough can be combined. It is by trying to fulfill the intention meant by the signification "greenish red," the signification "square circle," or the signification "square in the key of b-flat" that I learn that it is an *a priori* truth that the elements of a given region of experience or of diverse regions given in these significations cannot be combined in themselves. And it is here that we arrive at one of the fundamental fruits of this method such as it distinguishes itself radically from the Kantian doctrine of knowledge: for Husserl, necessity, that is, the necessary connections and exclusions among things, can be constituted as an experiential (i.e., intentional) object.[8] It is the radical attentiveness to things themselves, which the idea of intentionality alone permits, that shows me that it is just as necessary that a color be extended as are the truths of formal logic. And indeed, since the concept of extension is in no way contained analytically in the concept of color, and vice versa, this truth, *a priori* as it is, must be taken to be a synthetic one. It is this type of synthetic *a priori* truth, the sort that are only accessible through phenomenological observation, that Husserl calls the material *a priori*.

At the heart of the difference between Kant and Husserl, then, lies a radical divergence in their respective understandings of the *a priori*. This divergence is radical, as we have shown, because whereas for Kant for something to be *a priori* means for it to be prior to all possible experience, according to Husserl the *a priori* refers to the sort of universal and necessary truths we can also find *in* experience, *i.e.* of which we can have direct intuitive experience. Now, the question of what can be known *a priori*, which is central to both Kant's and Husserl's reflec-

---

[8] Nowhere is this radical divergence clearer than when compared to the "Transcendental Deduction" (Kant 1787, B130-B169): "All combination [...] is an act of the understanding. [...] We cannot represent to ourselves anything as combined in the object which we have not ourselves previously combined [...]. [C]ombination [...] cannot be given through the objects. Being an act of the self-activity of the subject, it cannot be executed save by the subject itself" (Kant 1787, B 130).

tion, is analytically identical to the question of what consciousness can grasp adequately, of what it fundamentally "*has;*" but this way of putting the matter is already phenomenological, since it is a way of formulating the question of what consciousness can "access" and what is "given" to it that collapses or "*reduces*" their difference – insofar precisely as this difference itself is neither given nor accessible, and must as such be excluded by phenomenological reduction as an unconstitutable metaphysical hypothesis or presupposition. So there is a structural solidarity among the various methodological *moments* that underpin, or rather constitute, phenomenology, insofar as *consciousness as intentionality*, the *principle of principles*, and the various stages of *reduction* all mutually imply one another, and it is in the context of this structure of mutual implication as a whole that it can be said that the *a priori appears* or is given. For Kant, on the other hand, the *a priori* cannot, by definition, be given in experience but rather conditions experience, which is in its turn and by definition *a posteriori* or contingent. So whereas for Husserl, since necessary connections among objects (or species of object)[9] can be adequately constituted, the *a priori* can and must be an object of experience, lest it violate the principle of principles, for Kant the *a priori* is, independently of any possible experience, defined as being independent of any possible experience. In both cases, the *a priori* is defined as that which is the case universally and necessarily; but for Kant, these qualities mean that it is independent of and, indeed *prior to* any *possible* experience. But this is in turn because Kant has inherited the Humean division of all types of relations into either "relations of ideas" or "matters of facts," the first being purely logical relations, derived from the principle of non-contradiction, on the basis of which all abstract thought must operate, and which is the site of all conceivable necessity (and so the source of all thoughts of necessity), and the second being purely contingent empirical events given through the sensory intuitions Hume calls impressions. The Kantian criteria for that in which the

---

[9] Kit Fine, in his article "Part-Whole" (Fine 1995), problematizes what he sees as Husserl's failure to differentiate between relations of dependence and independence between *objects* or between *species* or *genera* of objects. However, Fine makes no attempt to explain or justify why this is a problem. He merely attempts to formalize Husserl's mereological laws of dependence and independence on the basis of such a distinction which is not found in Husserl. It seems to us that Fine sees this as problematic and thinks it critical to introduce this distinction precisely insofar as he has overlooked the critical importance of eidetic intuition for the very idea of this mereology of the material *a priori:* indeed, it is *only* insofar as individual objects or aspects are seen *as* members of a species – *i.e.*, that they are seen *in* their specific or generic aspect or *as* concrete examples of a species – that it is possible for them to be seen as enjoying mereological relations of this sort. It would seem then that there is an atomistic presupposition, or at least aftertaste, to this concern.

distinction between *a priori* and *a posteriori* knowledge consists simply reproduces this Humean distinction (which was in itself simply a radicalization of already existing empiricist theories of knowledge) according to which *a priori* knowledge can only bear on the *form* and not the content of knowledge. The *a priori*, being implicitly identified with the formal and thereby, as per the Humean distinction, identifiable with the logico-grammatical structures of the human understanding called categories or with the pure form of our sensory faculties insofar as their contents are ready for use by the understanding, is thereby also *excluded*, *a priori* as it were, from the domain of experience – i.e., from the domain of possible intentional objects for consciousness. The die has already been cast, so to speak, before the content of possible experiencing has even been attended to, certain types of experience having been declared *a priori* impossible – i.e., the appearing of just the sort of necessity that forms the supposed object of the very statements that exclude their appearing. And it is precisely the absurdity of this situation, from a phenomenological point of view, that is denounced by Husserl when he points out the manifest absurdity of the very idea of positing a realm of "things in themselves" separate in principle from that of the "phenomena" (Husserl 1956, Hua VII, "Beilagen", pp. 401–406, *et passim*). As the phenomenological starting point of intentionality and its subsequent dynamic methodical unfolding in the reduction demonstrate, the only appropriate starting point for a rigorous examination and explication of experience and of what can possibly appear in it must originate in the hypothesis (which is not a hypothesis in the sense of being a metaphysical presupposition, because its very *essence* is to be given in experience) of the identity of that which *is*, i.e., that which *can* be an object, and that which can, in principle, appear.

From a phenomenological point of view, then, a certain number of the core principles of Kant's "transcendental" method constitute stumbling blocks on the road to the realization of his promise to replace "dogmatic" metaphysical speculation with a rigorous account of what sort of knowledge can be legitimately accessed in and through given conscious experience. Moreover, these core theses of Kant's – the distinction between phenomenon and *Ding an sich* or noumenon, the distinction between *intellectus ectypus* and *intellectus archetypus*, or the *a priori* separation of the faculties of sensibility and understanding, which is concomitant to the separation, just discussed, of the *a priori* from the experientially constitutable – are precisely what implicitly make his transcendental criticism a transcendental psychologism. D. Pradelle has demonstrated (Pradelle 2012, pp. 86–114) the extent to which the Kantian distinction between the *intellectus archetypus* and the *intellectus ectypus* cannot help but lead to a transcendental psychologism of the faculties, of the sort denounced by Foucault in his commentary on Kant's *Anthropology*.[10] This distinction is the "Copernican" idea according to which the sorts of truths to which human consciousness has access have a validity that is only relative to the type of understanding with which the human species happens to be endowed, while positing the regulative possibility of a non-human intellect which knows not just the phenomena but the things as they are in themselves. This would implicitly relegate the laws and structures according to which phenomena manifest themselves to a domain that is strictly relative to the real acts of constitution that belong to the contingent *anthropos*. Pradelle has shown, moreover, that the transcendental division of all possible experience into the active synthetic judgments of understanding and the passive receptivity of the senses, and the identification of the subject with the faculty of the understanding and with the purely formal aspects of the faculty of sensibility, is implicitly derivative of the pre-phenomenological natural attitude – *i.e.*, it is dependent on *Voraussetzungen* that violate the "principle of principles."

2 Kant's Implicit Empirical Inspiration and Presuppositions

Moreover, these *Voraussetzungen*, Foucault convincingly shows in his complementary dissertation, are implicitly derivative of the empirical science of anthropology, and more specifically of the collection of more or less rhapsodical empirical reflections, observations and opinions contained in Kant's thirty year-long course on anthropology. Where Husserl speaks of Kant's "transcendental psychologism," Foucault speaks of a "*doublet empirico-transcendantal*"[11] in which the embryonic positive science of anthropology forms the grounding and transcendental foundation for a critique of knowledge, a foundation that was to replace, in Kant's system, the pre-critical "dogmatic" metaphysical systems. While Foucault sees fit to distinguish Kant's properly critical thought (one which deals with thinking in its possibility) from its transformation into an implicitly anthropological thought (one which takes a positive science of man as its point of departure and ultimate horizon), his thesis is that this transformation occurred

---

10 On the differences between Husserl's critique of Kant's anthropologism and Foucault's critique, and the missed alliance of the two, see Rogove 2014.
11 *Cf.* Foucault's *Les mots et les choses* (Foucault 1966, pp. 328–354), which was the published form taken by his "Introduction à l'*Anthropologie* de Kant," which he refrained from publishing, and of which he considered it a more fully elaborated version. For the history of these texts, see the editors' introduction to the latter (Foucault 2008, p. 7).

not *despite* but *by means of* Kant's transcendental turn. Whereas the former asks the question of the condition of possibility of knowledge as such, the latter proports to have discovered these conditions of possibility in a series of positive empirical theses, or rather presuppositions, concerning the finite human faculties. Kant's "Copernican Revolution" banishes any talk of "absolute" knowledge by re-centering the very idea of knowledge around "man" as a real and finite subject, through the elaboration of a science remade in his image and to his measure. By making the transcendental condition of knowledge the equivalent of the concrete, finite faculties of the human subject, Kant limits the notion of the *a priori* to a purely formal *a priori*, and also limits thereby all effective knowledge to merely *a posteriori*, empirical and positive knowledge. In his commentary, Foucault traces the evolution of Kant's thought, which he suspects to have been anthropologistic from the start. He shows not only that the structure and presentation of the three *Critiques* corresponds to the implicit structure of the *Anthropology*, where the same picture of the human subject is presented as being empirically determined, but he also examines how the *Critiques* were written in parallel to Kant's evolving lecture notes in which he exposed his anthropological doctrine (Foucault 2008, pp. 41–61, *et passim*). He shows how the "Architectonic of Pure Reason" announces the replacement of traditional metaphysics by anthropology (Foucault 2008, pp. 46–52, *et passim*), an anthropology which is the culmination of all the Cartesian- and Lockean-type treatises on "man" and "human nature."[12]

Likewise, Jean Cavaillès points out that Kant's *Logic* reproduces the terms and the conceptuality of that great "Cartesian-type treatise on man," the Port-Royal *Logic* of Arnauld and Nicole, by which Kant is, for Cavaillès, visibly inspired. Indeed, despite Kant's protestations that it is absurd to derive logic from psychology, his categories seem to be a calque of the Port-Royal conception according to which the notion of "logic" is equivalent to that of the rules, or regularities, governing the understanding – *i.e.*, it is simply a prescriptive way of giving the manner in which mental representations can be combined and divided; which is to say: it provides the laws governing a particular region of nature, namely the mind (Cavaillès 1997, pp. 17–20; Arnauld & Nicole 1992). Kant's ultimate strategy for avoiding the reduction of logic to psychology is to pose the question of knowledge in *de juris* terms rather than in the *de facto* terms of empirical psychological operations; but this is exactly, from a Husserlian point of

---

[12] For a full demonstration, on which the present article relies, of the anthropologistic presuppositons on which Kant's *Logic* and "Architectonic of Pure Reason" rest, see Foucault 2008 and Rogove 2014.

view, where he confines himself, *a priori*, to a mere description of the workings of the human understanding, whose laws have no universal validity.[13] To simply assert the normative validity of *a priori* necessity is not sufficient, from a rigorous phenomenological point of view, to guarantee the absolute validity of that necessity. This is all the more obviously the case once we have taken into consideration, along with Foucault and Pradelle, the implicit epistemic priority Kant gives to the type of cognition that is presupposed by the natural and empirical sciences. If it is only sense data and not eidetic idealities that can be intuitively given, then these norms according to which thought "*must*" function have only a practical and not a theoretical validity, since they can never constitute the *object* of consciousness, but only a regressive *construction* erected on the basis of the empirical *fact* of thought, which it takes as its point of departure. Insofar as this normativity is simply a formal characteristic of human reason rather than the object of an adequate intuition, it remains implicitly dependent on all the non-given dogmatic metaphysical hypotheses which were denounced by Husserl and whose genealogy in the empirical Foucault and Pradelle have traced: it leads, or is even identical to, the psychologistic misconception according to which "all truth resides in the judgment" (Husserl 1975, Hua XVIII, § 49, p. 180) or is a characteristic of the subjective phenomenon that is the act of judging, rather than residing in the object of the judgment. Logic, for Husserl, cannot be a normative science – or, at the very least, its normative character must be derivative of its theoretical character, and it can only possess this normative

---

[13] In addition to his *Anthropology*, the psychologistic presuppositions in the background of Kant's critical philosophy can perhaps be most clearly discerned in his *Vorlesung über Logik* (Kant 1966, AK. XXIV), his lectures on logic spanning a thirty-year period from the pre-critical years to the end of his life, where Kant explicitly and on numerous occasions places his philosophy under the sign of Locke. He variously characterizes Locke's *Essay Concerning the Human Understanding* as being the first example of a "critical" as opposed to a dogmatic approach to the subject (Kant 1966, AK. XXIV, p. 37); or as being "still dogmatic," except insofar as it had the merit of initiating the division of the powers of the soul into the appropriate faculties (Kant 1966, AK. XXIV, p. 32). Kant presents Locke as the one who blazed the trail on which he finds himself, which is no longer "dogmatic" but "critical," and which consists in no longer philosophizing "objectively" as Wolf had, but rather "subjectively," asking the question of the "*genesis* and the origin of concepts" (Kant 1966, AK. XXIV, p. 338). He nevertheless characterizes Locke as having "treated philosophy psychologically, *i.e.*, as an analysis [*Zergliederung*] of the *human powers* of cognition" (Kant 1966, AK. XXIV, p. 804); indeed, he criticizes not Locke's drawing of the categories of the human understanding from experience, but his reduction of the very normative *content* of logic itself to this origin, as if they were empirical discoveries, which is a "metaphysical" error – which is to say, Kant's main criticism of Locke is precisely that Locke failed to pose the question of logical validity in *de juris* rather than *de facto* terms (Kant 1966, AK. XXIV, p. 701).

character with respect to its practical application as a "technology" (Husserl 1975, Hua XVIII, § 16, pp. 59–62; Husserl 1970, pp. 38–39). It is neither *de jure* (normative) nor *de facto* (empirical), but *eidetic: i.e.*, both *descriptive* and having universal and necessary validity. This universal and necessary validity does not have a hypothetical character because it can be grasped adequately as an intentional object and as a *theoretical* object, and not simply as a formal-transcendental analysis of "necessary" human comportment. This is possible because, for Husserl, logical propositions indeed are *given* in intuition:

> Logical *data* [*logischen Gegebenheiten*] are also in their own way given in experience [*Erfahrungsgegebenheiten*], identifiable and examinable objects [...]. And this "experience" (with its variants such as memory, such as "possible" experience, etc.), like any other experience functions as a basis for the formation of descriptive concepts and for the fulfillment of descriptive knowledge, and especially of knowledge of essences. (Husserl 1974, Hua XVII, p. 45; Husserl 1969, p. 42, trans. modified)
>
> [...] the "true", the "consequent", the "non-contradictory", which are obtained through intuition [*Einsicht*] appear [...] on the objective side [of judgments]. (Husserl 1974, Hua XVII, p. 47; Husserl 1969, p. 43, trans. modified)

So indeed, in opposition to both Kant and to the empiricists on which he draws, we see that for phenomenology the "necessary" character of the object of necessary propositions is directly constituted in the intuition, just as sense *data* are. For Husserl, logical essences are given through *founded intuitions* – but in a way that is no different from that in which material-sensible essences are: they are founded like any intuition of essence on a concrete instantiation taken as an example through an ideation that gives its *eidos* as an ideal object. And in the case of the *logical* eidetic object, it is founded on a categorial state-of-affairs rather than on a sensory given.

Hence, then, the essential necessity, in phenomenology, of a transcendental reduction that puts the *eidos* of the subject-object relationship into relief with no reference to any causal relationship with any "metaphysical" (i.e., in this case, natural or empirical) entity that is not itself *given* in and as a part of that relationship. In this sense, Husserl's phenomenology takes more seriously than Kantian Criticism does the purportedly Kantian "bracketing" of dogmatic, metaphysical theses and claims.

As opposed to phenomenological reduction, which aims to clarify the essential structures of manifestation as such and independently of any metaphysical doctrine – including those concerning human nature and human understanding –, the Kantian critique develops its doctrine of the categories of understanding and of sensibility as belonging essentially to the *subject*, rather than to the things themselves, which can never be given; in trying to have the world in view, the subject is always running up against its own nature and its own categories, which are nothing else than those of "man." The transformation of the transcendental illusion into the anthropological illusion is thus, from a phenomenological perspective, the very premise of the Copernican Revolution. In this sense, the Kantian project is to be situated in a straight line from the Galilean and Cartesian decision which was to subordinate any knowledge of consciousness to the new empirical sciences of nature; for this decision was made at the cost of problematizing the relation between "mind" and "world," between phenomenal interiority and the external effectivity of nature, which was to haunt philosophy ever thereafter. It is important to keep in mind that the result of this metaphysical substruction has been not only the project aiming to naturalize consciousness, or even to eliminate it purely and simply and in favor of its reabsorption without remainder into the causal *nexus* of an extended physical substance, but also what has often been presented as an ineffable egology of purely private experiences which, while being irreducibly "mine," are on the other hand resistant to conceptualization and deprived of any real efficacity.[14]

Hence this tenaciously held erroneous opinion concerning phenomenology, according to which the "consciousness" that is its "object" is one and the same as this "mind" opposed to "nature," or according to which it is the real site of sensations or regularities that might or might not be the *sign* or *causal result* of the things in themselves as they are in the world. However, the whole point of transcendental reduction in phenomenology is to avoid this "*dédoublement empirico-transcendantal*" diagnosed by Foucault: by putting itself as well as the world between brackets, the phenomenological subject suspends any positive thesis concerning its own nature just as it does concerning the real, objective world. It is, then, a consciousness that is not simply a subject manifesting itself to itself. All intentional content, as soon as it is grasped or thematized as such, gives us by that very act access to intentionality's subjective constituting pole, which is an inseparable moment of the whole of intentionality in just as absolute a way as color is inseparable from extension or tone from pitch. In this sense, the phenomenological method is reminiscent on at least this point of Descartes's, for whom any intentional state, even the most radical doubt, reveals the subject to itself. But like Kant, Descartes remains a prisoner to the natural attitude insofar as he substantivizes the subject by confusing transcendental and empirical ego,

---

[14] For a notorious example of the first, see Dennett 1991; for a less obvious and more subtle example of the second, see Thomas Nagel's famous essay "What's it like to be a bat?" (Nagel 1974), reprinted in Nagel 1979. For the inverted agreement between the seemingly opposed Dennett and Nagel concerning the ineffability of supposedly "epiphenomenal" *qualia* to become clear, see Dennett 1991, pp. 369–411.

thus opening the door at once to its naturalization and to the misreading of phenomenology as a solipsistic egology. But in the cases of both Descartes and Kant, as Pradelle has shown (Pradelle 2012, pp. 30–35, *et passim*), the subject, whether it is explicitly substantialized or whether it is simply a function that is formally deduced from that of which it is the condition, is always implicitly tributary to the natural attitude – in other words, it is dependent or founded upon *Voraussetzungen* that violate the principle of principles. For Kant, the transcendental "I" is simply the correlate of the transcendental object "x," which is itself nothing more than an impredicable *etwas* without any assignable attributes; as such, this "I" is not predicable or representable either. But if, as Husserl thinks, the transcendent *Ding an sich* is an absurdity and even an *a priori Widersinn* or contradiction (like "square circle" or "greenish red," since the very notion of a "thing" cannot be separated from the possibility of being experienced as such, at least in principle), the same must be the case for its formally deduced subjective correlate. Moreover, if this transcendent object is, as is the case, a spontaneous thesis of the natural attitude which is hypostasized and doubled back into an absurd metaphysical hypothesis, then the idea of the transcendental subject that is its correlate and which possesses the same transcendence with respect to any possible experience as its just-as-inexperienceable objective correlate does is also a metaphysical extraction from this same natural attitude. The Kantian transcendental ego cannot be fulfilled intuitively and as such remains a metaphysical hypothesis: it is a regressive construction erected on the basis of the fact of objectivity. As Pradelle points out (Pradelle 2012, pp. 53–54), while this subject is not explicitly a "substrate" as it is for Descartes, it is nevertheless a metaphysical "substruction:" it is the result of deduction, of discursive reasoning that is as such purely conceptual and not intuitive.

3 Two Mereologies for an Ontology: from Naturalistic Metaphysical Theses to a Coherentization of Appearing

But not only, as Foucault's and Pradelle's close Husserlian or quasi-Husserlian readings enable us to see, are the faculties of the Kantian transcendental subject simply a transposition of those that anthropology attributes to the empirical soul; the very *a priori* distinction made by Kant between the subjective faculties of sensibility and understanding seems not to come from any rigorous phenomenological analysis of the modes of manifestation of things, but rather to be imported directly from the aforementioned Humean categories of "relations of ideas" and "matters of fact." Indeed, Husserl underscores that Kant's "*kopernikaniche Umwälzung*" had already been carried out by Hume, who had made knowledge relative to finite human *Möglichkeit* rather than the inverse (Husserl 1956, Hua VII, pp. 353–354). But this Humean skeptical "reduction" is, from a phenomenological point of view, dogmatic insofar as it seeks simply to replace a certain number of our most self-evident eidetic intuitions, such as our intuitions of logico-mathematical principles, with a series of non-given hypotheses so as to reduce these self-evident intuitions to a hypothetical anthropological positivity. Thus, "mystical abstractions" such as "custom," "human nature," "sense organs," and "stimulus" are allowed and even required to take the central place of the "given" that is thereby refused to our actually given experience, reducing these experiences to simply "psychological" effects (Husserl 1973, Hua II, pp. 17–26; Husserl 1999, pp. 15–21). The Kantian categories of the understanding are then largely simply a refinement of the psychological-subjective representational "grid" in which the "relations of ideas" consist and which are in turn implicitly derivative of these supposedly deeper anthropological categories. And this *a priori* division, as we have already pointed out above, is implicitly determinative of the Kantian criterion for *a priori* and *a posteriori* knowledge, which also means that this determination is itself made according to this Kantian criterion for *apriority*, making this criterion both circular and in violation of the principle of principles. *I.e.*, it is defined, independently of any possible experience, as being independent of any possible experience, requiring us to interpret the types of material and logical necessity that present themselves through intuitive experience in terms other than those by which they give themselves, to explain them away dogmatically rather than taking them seriously phenomenologically.

While the phenomenological criteria for apriority is formally the same as the Kantian criteria – *i.e.*, universality and necessity, Husserl obviously does not draw the same conclusions with respect to the extra-experiential analyticity of this necessity. Indeed, the fundamental phenomenological ideas that are the "principle of principles" (the imperative of intuitive givenness) and its methodological complement and extension, the reduction, by means of an eidetic variation, of all that cannot be given intuitively, demand that this necessity in turn offer itself up to the intuitive gaze, "in person" and not simply as a transcendental deduction from empiricity. So, if the Kantian criteria for the *a priori* are dependent on the supposedly *a priori*, crypto-empirical, hypothetico-metaphysical division of the faculties into sensibility and understanding, it has then to be through an immanent examination of the phenomenological *a priori* itself as it presents itself in its own spontaneity that the alternative criteria can be discovered and elaborated, and it is then only on the basis of these authentically phenomenological criteria for the *a priori* that the phenomenological subject itself can be adequately characterized and accurately described.

As already established, it seems that Kant's basic error lies in his empiricist assumption that experience "such as it is in itself," *i.e.*, before any active intervention of the subject and as a raw, unprocessed given, is a chaotic sensory manifold, and that the "categories" are to be found in the subject and belong to it alone (Kant 1787, § 24, B 150–153). Moreover, Kant makes the possibility of my representations' relating to objects conditional on imaginative syntheses which in turn depend on the hypothetical unity of consciousness itself (consciousness itself being implicitly defined, as we have seen time and time again, as the substrate and bearer of the qualities called categories, qualities which the unexperienceable thing-in-itself that is the transcendental ego bears as *phenomenal* qualities, in just the same way as the unknowable things-in-themselves can only be inferentially known through the phenomenal qualities of which they are the hypothetical substrate). The very premise of this chain of conditions, as we have seen, is profoundly and fundamentally anti-phenomenological and is, from Husserl's point of view, a material *Widersinn*. This is because it remains phenomenologically blind to the basic (eidetic) fact of consciousness, *i.e.*, that it is always consciousness *of* something, and so not only is "unexperienceable object" a *Widersinn*, but "consciousness without subject and object" is also a material *Widersinn*. But this, then, can only be determined on the basis of an eidetic variation carried out on consciousness itself. It becomes clear then that in order to complete the Husserlian critique of the Kantian doctrine of the *a priori* and of the faculties (which reveal themselves to be two aspects of the same error), it is necessary to attend eidetically to the thing itself, *i.e.*, to the objects such as they present themselves necessarily to consciousness. Only then does it become possible to determine the sort of eidetic, rather than metaphysical, relation that the subject has to these objects, and what sort of necessity is at work in their appearing.

The eidetic reduction consists in an experimental testing of the limits of what is representable, or, put in a way that cannot be misinterpreted in terms of a simple examination of the empirical powers (*facultates* – *Vermögen*) of the real human subject, of what can coherently and cohesively appear. Husserl characterizes the structure according to which this necessary appearing occurs, in ontological terms[15] in the third *Logical Investigation*, in terms of a mereology

---

15 The third *Logical Investigation*'s presentation of the material *a priori* laws of combination and separation in *ontological* terms is not, as is sometimes claimed, an alternative to the phenomenological status of these laws, but rather to their merely *psychological* status. Indeed, the collapsing of the distinction between phenomenological and ontological being, as we have seen,

of dependent and independent parts of given wholes. As we have already stated above, the eidetic variation consists then in a revealing or clarifying of the necessities according to which certain types of object must appear together, can appear together, or cannot appear together, such as, respectively, color and extension, redness and circularity, or redness and greenness. These necessities are precisely revelatory of the site at which ontology and phenomenology collapse into one another and become, or rather reveal how they always already are, identical. This is because we simply do not know what it would mean for it to be possible for a point to be both red and green – or for there to be a type of object that cannot *in principle* be an object *for* a consciousness. The very idea of such an object is meaningless, not because of any grammatical contradiction, since, from the point of view of both formal logic and empirical grammar, the sentences which describe these states of affairs are perfectly correct and coherent. It just so happens that the states of affairs or types of objects to which they refer are impossibilities. But they are not *empirical* impossibilities – such empirical impossibilities, such as objects violating the law of gravity or a chemical component other than H2O having the same phenomenal properties as what we call "water," are always provisional hypotheses and subject to permanent

---

the very premise of phenomenological reduction, the breakthrough that Husserl's third *Logical Investigation* represents, exists with respect to prior work done on what we might call a "proto-theory" of the material *a priori* laws of combination and separability that had been done in the 19th century mostly by empirical psychologists (but also legal theorists) and on which Husserl was building. In addition to Brentano's work on essential parts of psychological representations, his student Carl Stumpf's *Tonpsychologie* (Stumpf 1883–1890) and *Über den psychologischen Ursprung der Raumvorstellung* (Stumpf 1873) had a decisive influence on Husserl's mereology. However, Brentano's and Stumpf's descriptions were still ensconced in the psychologistic and naturalistic methodological and metaphysical presuppositions proper to empirical psychology at the time, and Husserl's breakthrough largely consisted in de-psychologizing these combinatory laws by means of the reduction. The mereology of the *Logical Investigations*, which is an ontology of any possible being (which, thanks to the phenomenological method, can be described as identical to any possible phenomenon), is thereby not simply a description of anthropologically contingent psychological laws.

More generally, Husserl's struggle against atomistic ontologies is to be understood as a part of the post-Brentanian ontologies and psychologies of the time, one of the most notable being the *Gestalt* movement. *Cf.* von Ehrenfels 1890, pp. 249–292, at the movement's beginnings, and, for an overview of the movement in its synthetic fullness, Köhler 1947, especially the critique, in many ways parallel to Stumpf's critique of mechanistic and atomistic theories, of behavioristic theories in psychology proposed in chapter 1. For a full synthetic picture of the entire evolution of this mereological movement from empirical psychology and legal theory to Leśniewskian and Ajdukiewiczian logic by way of Husserlian ontology, see Smith (ed.) 1982, especially Smith & Mulligan 1982, and Simons 1982.

empirical control and possible experimental contradiction. The essential eidetic characteristic of these merely empirical impossibilities is that it is possible to *imagine* their converse – it is (phenomeno-)logically possible to imagine a possible world in which these laws would not hold or would be replaced by other laws, and this eidetic possibility is precisely what makes it possible for the empirical scientist to carry out experiments: she knows what to look for, and can, at least passively and theoretically, anticipate the possibility of contrary results to the ones expected or obtained up until the present. On the contrary, the types of eidetic, phenomenological impossibilities in which the above-mentioned *material* a priori consist are indeed deprived of meaning or possibility in any possible world – we are incapable of imagining them having any meaning, *i.e.*, any possibility, whatsoever, and therefore of assigning any possible meaning to a hypothetical empirical horizon of expectation. And, most importantly, this horizon of expectation is not a subjective horizon, *i.e.*, the work of our active awareness of what to expect or of what we happen to think is likely to occur or is likely to become of the phenomena we have, but it is rather an *objective* horizon in that it is the absolute sum of possible determinations of these phenomena. But unlike the Kantian transcendent thing in itself as the hypothetical absolute x that is likewise the sum of all objective determinations inhering in an object independently of our knowledge of those determinations (a knowledge or system of representations which is precisely that *to which* it is transcendent), this *phenomenologically* absolute thing itself is the sum of all possible determinations inhering in the phenomena's possibilities of self-presentation. The meaning of which they are deprived or with which they are endowed is nothing more than the set of their inherent ontological possibilities.

But additionally and above all, not only is it the case that we do not even know *what it would mean* for there to be color without extension, we moreover do not even know what it would mean for this meaninglessness or this impossibility *to be only an impossibility for us*, *i.e.*, for the type of empirical being that we are; and this is in turn because of the already stated eidetic fact that the very idea of an object that cannot in principle be an object for a subject is a *Widersinn* – a contradiction or an absurdity – of the same order as the other *a priori* material impossibilities. And this "transcendental" material *a priori* principle is nothing more than the negation of the metaphysical hypothesis according to which things can somehow *be* outside of the realm of any possible appearing. It is by this very same token, then, a phenomenological absurdity to attribute the sort of absolute and unconditioned necessity that we experience directly and self-evidently in eidetic intuition to a mysterious and unexperienceable causal connection to hypothetically constructed faculties of the human animal.[16]

Thus, it cannot – in phenomenological descriptions of these eidetic necessities that are "internal," as it were, to consciousness or to the field of appearing, and of which logico-mathematical type necessities are a species – be a question of simple "subjective descriptions," because "beyond the results obtained and the subjective constitution in which they are progressively realized, an *intentional* subjectivity, in which the elements that are being constituted as synthetic unities […] must be explored – *a subjectivity to which we have no access as long as we are simply turned toward the 'I think'*" (Husserl 1974, Hua XVII, p. 39; Husserl 1969, p. 44, trans. modified, our emphasis). Nowhere do we see more clearly the solidarity between the respective doctrines of the *a priori* on the one hand and that concerning the articulation between subjective judgments and the structure of experience on the other. Indeed, for Kant, what we find is an attribution of the necessity of necessary judgments to the form of the judgment itself rather than to its content. As J. Cavaillès again emphasizes concerning this structure that Kant attributes to logic as a whole: "science is, for Kant, the product of certain faculties, understanding, and reason; Logic can only be defined subsequently [*postérieurement*] to the positing of the faculties, even though it is supposed to direct them" (Cavaillès 1997, pp. 17–18). General logic, which is what Kant calls formal logic, is therefore just a codification of the structures that are supposed to govern the operations of the knowing subject, *i.e.* the faculties of judgment and reason, and *can* be nothing more than a formalization of the *a posteriori* structures of experience, and it is in this "can," this possibility, that the specter of the "*dédoublement empirico-transcendantal*" incessantly haunts – structurally and essentially haunts, as it were – the Kantian understanding of the relation between consciousness, on the one hand, and logical necessity, on the other.

And indeed, this is not simply a meta-logical problem, because what is at stake is the very *content* of the science of logic – the question of what this science is *about*. As we have seen, Kant's "normativist" and formalist strategy for guaranteeing the objectivity of the "content" of the science of logic fails to meet the Husserlian criterion for any scientific object, namely that consciousness should be able to constitute it as a speculative and descriptive object in itself, and that its necessity should not simply be transcendentally deduced from the empirical fact of the human understanding's functioning. The consequence of

---

16 *Cf.* Kant 1787, B 144–146: the connection, for Kant, between the nature or fundamental determinations of the given, on the one hand, and the categories of the understanding according to which the subject has no choice but to understand that given, on the other, remains a complete mystery.

the empirico-Kantian dogma according to which all *a priori* necessity is to be found in the pure structures of the subject, whereas all epistemic *content* is to be found in the *a posteriori* happenings of sensory experience, is that logic is *both* hermetically separated off from ontology *and* reducible to a mere empty formalization of the empirical structures of our understanding: it becomes a science of representations, differing from psychology only in that it has been formalized, made completely empty of all content. And it is precisely this content that would constitute the science of being. But this "being," for Kant, is dispersed, chaotic, and above all *atomistic*, and it is only in attending to the science of representations that he proposes that we find the site of all that is unified and necessary. The ultimate consequence of this is an atomistic ontology of the type we find in Wittgenstein's *Tractatus Logico-Philosophicus* and in the radical empiricism of the logical positivists. Here, we see just those aspects of Kant's system that were criticized by Husserl made explicit and taken to their coherent conclusion: all necessity becomes "grammatical" in that the only *a priori* possible must come from the representationally inevitable rules that compose the mind, which is, in turn, nothing more than the empirical psyche.

The problem with this view may be represented as follows. If this psyche's internal mental representations are the site of all necessity (1), and everything outside of this immanence is *a posteriori* and contingent (2), the first consequence of (1 & 2) is that this psyche which is the site of all necessity is itself a contingent thing in "nature" (3), since it cannot be internal to itself; and the consequence of (1, 2 & 3) is that the *relation* between consciousness and that *of which* it is consciousness is itself contingent and atomistic. Consciousness is simply another thing in a world governed entirely by relations among separable, independent parts, and the sort of necessity that obtains in the relations among inseparable, non-independent parts is nothing more than an accidental property inhering in this contingent part of the world. This is vividly illustrated by the fact that Kant thought of the faculties, precisely, as *Stücke* – *i.e.*, he thought of them as relating to one another and to the whole of the psyche or of consciousness (which he of course confuses) in an independent, separable, atomistic way.[17] For Husserl, on the contrary, they are all non-independent moments of the whole that is conscious experience.[18] The same eidetic variation that gives to

---

17 "According to Husserl, sensibility, on the one hand, and understanding, on the other, are not strictly separate, but rather intertwined with each other, or even better, what we are dealing with here is not so much two distinct zones, but rather two aspects of a single, deeper unity" (Kern 1964, p. 62, our translation).

18 *Cf.*, for example, Husserl's numerous demonstrations of the non-independent existence of sense data, which, even if they are not purely and simply an artificial hypothetical theoretical

us the separability and non-separability of objects must then be applied to the whole of the field of consciousness or of appearing itself, and it is this move that brings us back, as it were, to phenomenology's point of departure: the eidetic unity of intentionality. Having begun from the seemingly banal, tautological thesis that consciousness is always consciousness *of* something, we find this material *a priori* truth confirmed through the systematic application of the eidetic and transcendental stages of the reduction – *i.e.*, through the application of the eidetic reduction to intentional consciousness itself, whereby it becomes self-evident that a subject without an object is nonsense and *vice versa*, subject and object, or ego and world being two inseparable moments of the concrete intuited whole that is appearing or phenomenality in general. In this way, phenomenology can complete itself and ground itself only once it becomes clear that the transcendental stage of phenomenological reduction is nothing more than an application of eidetic reduction to the field of consciousness, which becomes thereby identical to appearing or to phenomenality itself – a move which can only follow from the bracketing of any Kantian idea of faculties.[19]

Thus also, by putting between parentheses Kant's hypothesized faculties and attending solely and methodically to the appearing things themselves, does Husserl remain faithful here as well to phenomenology's "principle of principles." Rather than positing hypothetical entities that *do not appear* (the subject or ego as separable part, and the faculties of this subject as in turn separable parts of this subject or ego), Husserlian phenomenological description allows the thing itself, which here is the field of consciousness itself, to appear along with all of its essentially inseparable component parts or moments. In this way, *it is the mereological analogy with other material* a priori *truths that enables us to see how the phenomenological exposition of what consciousness is avoids cir-*

---

construction of empiricism, can only become an object for consciousness insofar as they are abstract, non-independent moments of the concrete wholes that are authentically given in experience (see the fifth *Logical Investigation*, §§ 11, 20, 23, 25; and the sixth *Logical Investigation*, §§ 40 – 46), or his discussions of *Abschattungen*, the adumbrations synthesized by *phantasia*, which allow for example for me to "see" the back-side of a lamp as I walk around it, and which alone allow for the perception of objects, thus indicating the role of *phantasia* as absolutely *inseparable* from simple perception, and *vice-versa*. For our analysis of Husserl's argument in favor of the incoherence of the sort of "raw sense data" that empiricism takes to be the most fundamental building-block of experience, *cf.* Rogove 2018.

19 A full development of the idea according to which the transcendental reduction is an application to consciousness itself of the eidetic reduction, which is itself to be understood as a mereological variation, is the object of our doctoral thesis, *Une science sans présupposés? Intuition eidétique et structure méréologique entre réduction phénoménologique et réductionnisme logico-empiriste*, Université Paris-Sorbonne, 2016.

cularity. Indeed, it is on this condition alone that the entirety of the phenomenological method can be justified, since it is on this condition alone that this method's founding thesis – *viz.*, that consciousness is intentional, along with the non-metaphysical realism that this implies – can itself be understood to be a synthetic, rather than an analytic, proposition. And only in this way can it be said that phenomenological description brings *real knowledge* that is both *a priori* and non-trivial, thus underscoring the chasm that separates its method and its philosophical spirit from Kant's empiricist presuppositions. The apparent striking similarities between Kant and Husserl turn out, upon deeper examination and excavation, to be just that – mere appearances, and not in the phenomenological sense of appearance, but in the non-phenomenological sense, which is to say, in the sense that this apparent similarity belongs to the same *Vorurteilen* that phenomenology proposes to remove.

* * *

As Foucault lamented in a 1978 interview, the reception of Husserl in France guaranteed the insertion of his thought into a Cartesiano-Kantian matrix that made French phenomenology ever thereafter an anthropologistic "philosophy of the subject," whereas, he insists, phenomenology's founding problematic had always been the question of the foundation of logic (Foucault 2013; *cf.* Rogove 2014, pp. 58–59). As we have shown, recent work has gone in the direction of taking up this very same logical and ontological thread from Husserl's earlier, supposedly "pre-transcendental" work and following it carefully, seeing it along through its coherence and consequences, never ceding to any "external" Sirens singing the song of much received intellectual history to the tune of phenomenology's reputedly Kantian heritage and subjectivist posterity, and letting this thread methodically and rigorously unravel the artifice of any such hastily constructed resemblance. From another point of view, it is a matter of being more Kantian than Kant himself – *i.e.*, of reducing and eliminating Kant's residual naturalistic, empiricist presuppositions, of radicalizing and prying open whatever distance he had established between his own work and what Foucault called "all of the Cartesian-Lockean type 'treatises on man'" that had inspired him and at whose pinnacle he stood. However, as we have seen, this *mise en évidence* of the distance that separates Husserl from Kant comes with the price of radicalizing phenomenological method itself, a radicalization that translates to its *desubjectivation*. This in turn may or may not entail a transformation of the very idea we have of what phenomenology is. What it is *not*, at any rate, is an egological study of an ineffable interiority or a subjectivist idealism of any kind. It is not a solipsistic representationalism, nor is it a naturalistic study of the real psychological properties of the human mind. If it is to avoid these pitfalls, it must separate itself as radically as possible from the same sorts of presuppositions that prevented Kantianism from thinking and seeing phenomenologically.

Bibliography

Arnauld, Antoine & Nicole Pierre (1992) [1662]: *La logique ou l'art de penser*. Paris: Gallimard.
Bonnet, Christian (2015): "La querelle du psychologisme: Fries, Herbart et Beneke", in Gyemant 2015, pp. 61–76.
Bouriau, Christophe (2000): *Lectures de Kant*. Paris: Presses universitaires de France.
Cavaillès, Jean (1997): *Sur la logique et la théorie de la science*. Paris: Vrin.
Davidson, Donald (2006): "On the Very Idea of a Conceptual Scheme" (1974), reprinted in *The Essential Davidson*. Oxford: Oxford University Press, pp. 196–208.
Dennett, Daniel (1991): *Consciousness Explained*. Boston: Little, Brown & Co.
Derrida, Jacques (1962): "Introduction". In: E. Husserl: *L'origine de la géométrie*. Trans. J. Derrida. Paris: Presses universitaires de France.
Von Ehrenfels, Christian (1890): "Über Gestaltqualitäten". In: *Vierteljahrsschrift für wissenschaftliche Philosophie*, vol. 14, p. 249–292.
Ehrsam, Raphaël (2015): "Kant, un psychologisme destinal?", in Gyemant 2015, pp. 43–60.
Ferraris, Maurizio (2004): *Goodbye Kant! Cosa resta oggi della Critica della ragion pura*. Milan: Tascabili Bompiani.
Fine, Kit (1995): "Part-Whole". In: *Cambridge Companion to Husserl*. Eds. B. Smith & D. W. Smith. Cambridge: Cambridge University Press, pp. 463–485.
Foucault, Michel (1966): *Les mots et les choses*. Paris: Gallimard.
Foucault, Michel (2008): "Introduction à l'*Anthropologie*". In: I. Kant: *Anthropologie du point de vue pragmatique*. Trans. M. Foucault. Paris: Vrin.
Foucault, Michel (2013): "Considérations sur le marxisme, la phénoménologie et le pouvoir. Entretien avec Colin Gordon et Paul Patton". In: *Cités*, vol. 52, pp. 101–126.
Gyemant, Maria (Ed.) (2015): *Psychologie et psychologisme*. Paris: Vrin.
Herbart, Johann Friedrich (1816): *Lehrbuch zur Psychologie*. Königsberg: Unzer.
Herbart, Johann Friedrich (1891): *A Textbook in Psychology*. Trans. M. K. Smith. New York: Appleton.
Husserl, Edmund (1950): *Idées directrices pour une phénoménologie et une philosophie phénoménologique pures*, tome premier : *Introduction générale à la phénoménologie*. Trans. and commentary P. Ricœur. Paris: Gallimard.
Husserl, Edmund (1956): *Erste Philosophie, Erster Teil: Kritische Ideengeschichte*. Husserliana, vol. VII. Ed. Rudolf Boehm. The Hague: Martinus Nijhoff.
Husserl, Edmund (1969): *Formal and Transcendental Logic*. Trans. D. Cairns. The Hague: Martinus Nijhoff.
Husserl, Edmund (1970): *Logical Investigations*. Trans. J.N. Findlay. London: Routledge.
Husserl, Edmund (1973): *Die Idee der Phänomenologie*. Husserliana, vol. II. Ed. Walter Biemel. The Hague: Martinus Nijhoff.
Husserl, Edmund (1974): *Formale und transzendentale Logik*. Husserliana, vol. XVII. Ed. Paul Janssen. The Hague: Martinus Nijhoff.

Husserl, Edmund (1975): *Logische Untersuchungen*, Erster Band: *Prolegomena zur reinen Logik*. Husserliana, vol. XVIII. Ed. Elmar Holenstein. The Hague: Martinus Nijhoff.

Husserl, Edmund (1976): *Ideen zu einer reinen Phänomenologie und phänomenologischen Philosophie*. Erstes Buch. Husserliana, vol. III/1. Ed. Karl Schuhmann. The Hague: Martinus Nijhoff.

Husserl, Edmund (1984): *Logische Untersuchungen. Untersuchungen zur Phänomenologie und Theorie der Erkenntnis*. Husserliana, vol. XIX. Ed. Ursula Panzer. The Hague: Martinus Nijhoff.

Husserl, Edmund (1993): *Ideas Pertaining to a Pure Phenomenology and to a Phenomenological Philosophy. First Book: General Introduction to a Pure Phenomenology*. Trans. F. Kersten. Dordrecht: Kluwer Academic Publishers.

Husserl, Edmund (1999): *The Idea of Phenomenology*. Trans. L. Hardy. Dordrecht: Kluwer Academic Publishers.

Jansen, Julia (2015): "Transcendental Philosophy and the Problem of Necessity in a Contingent World". In: *Metodo. International Studies in Phenomenology and Philosophy*, Special Issue, n° 1, chapter 1.

Kant, Immanuel (1904): *Kritik der reinen Vernunft. Kants gesammelte Schriften*, AK., vol. III. Berlin: Walter de Gruyter.

Kant, Immanuel (1923): *Logik. Kants gesammelte Schriften*, AK., vol. IX. Berlin: Walter de Gruyter.

Kant, Immanuel (1966): *Vorlesung über Logik. Kants gesammelte Schriften*, AK., vol. XXIV. Berlin: Walter de Gruyter.

Kant, Immanuel (1993): *Lectures on Logic*. Trans. M. Young. Cambridge: Cambridge University Press.

Kant, Immanuel (2007): *Critique of Pure Reason*. Trans. N. Kemp Smith. New York: Palgrave Macmillan.

Kern, Iso (1964): *Husserl und Kant*. The Hague: Martinus Nijhoff.

Köhler, Wolfgang (1947): *Gestalt Psychology: An Introduction to New Concepts in Modern Psychology*. New York: Signet Books.

Nagel, Thomas (1974): "What Is It Like to Be a Bat?". In: *Philosophical Review*, vol. 83 (October), pp. 435–450.

Nagel, Thomas (1979): *Mortal Questions*. Cambridge: Cambridge University Press.

Pradelle, Dominique (2012): *Par-delà la révolution copernicienne. Sujet transcendantal et facultés chez Kant et Husserl*. Paris: Presses universitaires de France.

Ricœur, Paul (1955): "Kant et Husserl". In: *Kant-Studien*, vol. 46, n° 1–4, pp. 44–67.

Ricœur, Paul (1967): "Appendice consacré à Husserl". In: E. Bréhier: *Histoire de la philosophie allemande*, 2nd ed. Paris: Vrin, pp. 183–196.

Ricœur, Paul (1986): *À l'école de la phénoménologie*. Paris: Vrin.

Rogove, John (2014): "La phénoménologie manquée de Foucault: Husserl et le contre-modèle de l'anthropologisme kantien". In: *Philosophie*, vol. 123, pp. 58–67.

Rogove, John (2018): "Husserl entre hylémorphisme traditionnel et *a priori* matériel: vers l'abolition phénoménologique de la notion de «matière»". In: *Phénoménologies de la matière*. Eds. P.-J. Renaudie & C.V. Spaak. Paris: Editions du CNRS.

Simons, Peter (1982): "Three Essays in Formal Ontology". In: *Parts and Moments. Studies in Logic and Formal Ontology*. Ed. B. Smith. Munich: Philosophia Verlag, pp. 111–260.

Smith, Barry (Ed.) (1982): *Parts and Moments. Studies in Logic and Formal Ontology.* Munich: Philosophia Verlag.
Smith, Barry & Mulligan, Kevin (1982): "Pieces of a Theory". In: *Parts and Moments. Studies in Logic and Formal Ontology.* Ed. B. Smith. Munich: Philosophia Verlag, pp. 15–109.
Stumpf, Carl (1873): *Über den psychologischen Ursprung der Raumvorstellung.* Leipzig: Hirzel Verlag.
Stumpf, Carl (1883–90): *Tonpsychologie.* Leipzig: Hirzel Verlag.

Elena Partene
On the Naturalization of the Transcendental

Abstract: The relationship between Husserl and Kant is as much a story about continuities as it is about new beginnings. Despite their shared transcendental standpoint, many disagreements remain between them regarding their conceptions of transcendental subjectivity. This chapter focuses on Husserl's criticism of Kant's conception of transcendental structures, which implies that Kant's transcendental theory is a form of naturalism. In particular, this chapter examines the relevance of Husserl's reproach from a Kantian point of view and attempts to address the question whether it is possible to find, amidst the themes raised in the *Critique of Pure Reason*, an answer to Husserl's accusations. I argue that by drawing the consequences of the explicit idea of an epigenesis of pure reason and of the implicit idea of subjective finitude, it is possible to provide a response to Husserl's critiques. It is in fact the creativity of Kant's philosophy that enabled him in some ways to anticipate the objections that Husserl later raised against his work.

While transcendental phenomenology, as defined by Husserl, fits within and claims an indisputable Kantian filiation, it is equally true that, according to Husserl, Kantian transcendental philosophy remains unfinished, confined within a criticized naturalism from which Kant ultimately fails to depart. In the end, Kant remains hostage to Humean psychological empiricism despite having refuted it. More precisely, Husserl's charge that Kant naturalizes the transcendental can be divided into two criticisms: one of Kantian psychologism, and another of Kantian anthropologism. The mainspring of these criticisms touches upon two different aspects of Kant's philosophy. The first reproaches Kant for having taken a mind (*Gemüt*) composed of faculties that are nothing more than psychological functions as the norm of objective knowledge and for having reduced the *a priori* to an innate structure. The second criticism denounces the fact that synthesis is conceived of in relation to the finitude of the Kantian subject, defined in contrast to an *intellectus archetypus*.

This chapter intends to go back to these Husserlian criticisms and reconsider their pertinence from a Kantian point of view: are these accusations against Kant's philosophy effective? Is it possible to defend Kant against Husserl?

With regard to the first point, it is necessary to recall Kant's insistence on the distinction between *a priori* and innateness: Kant introduces the concept of an "epigenesis of pure reason" (Kant 1902, AK. III, p. 128; Kant 1998, p. 265) precisely to avoid a conception of the transcendental as a nature "*mentibus nostris ingenita*" (Descartes 1996 I, p. 145).

As concerns the second point, it is important to distinguish finiteness and finitude: while the first is in fact an anthropological concept that denotes human mortality and subjection to need, finitude is a metaphysical concept that accounts for the limitation of knowledge and does so for the requirement of transcending the *datum*.

Instead of the incompleteness or the thoughtlessness of the Kantian conception of the transcendental, emphasis will be placed here on the irreducible difference that remains, despite their numerous and evident proximities, between Husserlian phenomenology, which defines the reduction within an infinite horizon, and Kant's philosophy, which asserts an irreducible finitude that is nothing but the posteriority of the subject with respect to being.

1 The Criticism of Psychologism: The Epigenesis of Pure Reason

One of the most essential and recurring criticisms that Husserl levels against Kant is that of psychologism. Kant's assertion that the object must conform to the cognitive structures of the subject, and not the other way around, implies that the object of knowledge is dependent on human nature, since, according to Husserl, the faculties constituting objectivity have a psychological meaning.

> Kant abhorred the foundation of theory of thought on psychology, understood as the empirical science of psychic faculties. This is perfectly legitimate. However, a kind of psychologism also seems to be in his doctrine of forms. To the nature of human understanding – obviously not that of the individual human being [...], but of humankind in general – belong specific functional forms whose legality is such that it has a general validity that belongs to every human as such. Hume would say in the same way: to the essence of the human nature belong the laws of habit, and these are the source of the factual sciences [...]. When Kant introduces principles of experience-formation common to every human in place of the principle of habit – obviously different, but just as subjective – is it such a fundamental difference? Is the Copernican reversal, according to which any unity of experience is adjusted to thought, not already present in the Humean doctrine? (Husserl 1956, Hua VII, p. 354, quoted by Pradelle 2012, p. 78, our translation)

This naturalist interpretation of Kantian philosophy is not new. Serban notes that from 1915 onwards, Husserl criticizes Kant precisely on this point: "The dogmatic presuppositions act in a particularly regrettable way on the subjective side: the human subject is constantly understood as the subject of psychological faculties" (Husserl 1956, Hua VII, p. 401, quoted by Serban 2017, pp. 198–199, our translation). According to Husserl, Kant's transcendental philosophy remains unfinished because it is bound to the naturalism that Kant so strongly criticizes but ultimately fails to escape. In fact, Kant himself remains a prisoner of the very idea of Hume's psychological empiricism that his concept of the transcendental aimed to refute, simply because the subjective structures on which experience depends are a part of human nature. The categories are a fact, i.e., a metaphysical *datum* that belongs to the characterization of the human being. Each human is so constituted as to possess these structures constitutive of objectivity: transcendental structures are an integral part of human nature. This leads to subjectivism because the object becomes dependent on human subjectivity even if this subjectivity is not the result of personal idiosyncrasy, but rather of human nature. We are still looking at a universal, but an anthropological universal. Why does this matter? What difference does it make whether the transcendental is innate or not? The difference is considerable, because it completely destroys the very goal of grounding an objective knowledge. The object of knowledge is such for me; it is also such for others, but only *insofar as they are human* and therefore share the same nature. However, we cannot say that the object is such objectively. In the end, *doing without an ontological touchstone while maintaining transcendence as a thesis, i.e., while refusing to adopt the phenomenological thesis of a total transcendental constitution, irremediably leads to subjectivism.*

Far from being a naive and superficial reading of Kant, this question raised by Husserl is truly perspicacious, first of all because it seems that transcendental structures can only be innate, seeing as they do not derive from experience. Otherwise, how could we imagine that something that does not come 'from the outside,' to put it simply, does not come 'from the inside' either? An ability either comes from within or without, but there is no third possibility.

In addition, this critical reading also corresponds to a more ambitious reading of Kant's notion of the transcendental, conceived of as endowed with a certain facticity precisely because it is transcendental, that is, because it is a regressive condition of knowledge, but absolutely unrepresentable. Indeed, transcendental legality refers to an activity of the subject, which cannot be objectified. The categories define an activity of the subject, but this activity is never fully captured. In other words, on the side of the subject, we have a legislation that is active but which cannot be objectified, and on the opposite side we have an object, but deprived of any activity. Therefore, we could summarize Kant's doctrine of knowledge as a combination of a non-acting objectivity and a non-objectifiable activity. Now, if this activity cannot be objectified, can we say that the transcendental itself is a kind of fact? Is there a facticity of the transcendental? This is one of Grandjean's theses: in *Critique et Réflexion*, he states that "the transcendental, brought out by the fact that it conditions, [is] itself an irreducible fact" (Grandjean 2009, p. 180, our translation). The fact of science is explained by transcendental principles, which also belong to the realm of facts, and which, by virtue of this facticity, cannot be explained – in the Leibnizian sense. Instead, they must simply be acknowledged, as the very first facts beyond which we cannot go, and which, consequently, cannot be created or derived from a superior principle. However, we can clearly see the problem raised by this thesis: if the transcendental is a fact that cannot be created, then how can we avoid the criticism of naturalism? This thesis, which reveals the truth of the transcendental, is even more susceptible to Husserl's criticism, whose finesse and extreme relevance are even better highlighted. Pradelle, justifying Husserl's criticism, asks the following legitimate question about the Kantian transcendental subject: "Can the latter be something other than a pre-constituted subject, thought of as a center of dispositions, functions and invariant properties? Consequently, can the investigation of the categories of being in general in the transcendental logic do anything other than determine them under the guiding principle of the universal structures of a pre-constituted, finite subject?" (Pradelle 2012, pp. 78–79, our translation). Are the categories a psychological *datum* that characterizes human nature as such?

Therefore, if knowledge is built in a new way on the grounds of transcendental structures, what meaning should we ascribe to Kant's conception of the transcendental? One of the possible responses to this question, and to Husserl's naturalist interpretation, may be to insist on the Kantian criticism of innatism, which reveals the refusal to define the transcendental as a *datum* in the human mind. One of the canonical texts on this point is found at the very end of the Analytic of concepts[1]:

> Now there are only two ways in which a necessary agreement of experience with the concepts of its objects can be thought: either the experience makes these concepts possible or these concepts make the experience possible. The first is not the case with the categories (nor with pure sensible intuition); for they are *a priori* concepts, hence independent of experience (the assertion of an empirical origin would be a sort of *generatio aequivoca*). Consequently, only the second way remains (as it were a system of the epigenesis of pure reason): namely that the categories contain the grounds of the possibility of all experience in

---

[1] On this passage, see also the interpretation of Callanan 2013.

general from the side of the understanding. But more about how they make experience possible, and which principles of its possibility they yield in their application to appearances, will be taught in the following chapter on the transcendental use of the power of judgment. If someone still wanted to propose a middle way between the only two, already named ways, namely, that the categories were neither self-thought *a priori* first principles of our cognition nor drawn from experience, but were rather subjective predispositions for thinking, implanted in us along with our existence by our author in such a way that their use would agree exactly with the laws of nature along which experience runs (a kind of preformation-system of pure reason), then (besides the fact that on such a hypothesis no end can be seen to how far one might drive the presupposition of predetermined predispositions for future judgments) this would be decisive against the supposed middle way: that in such a case the categories would lack the necessity that is essential to their concept. (Kant 1902, AK. III, p. 128; Kant 1998, pp. 264–265)

The aim here is to reject both the metaphysics of innateness (Descartes, but most of all Leibniz) and the empiricism of the adventitious. The innatist paradigm corresponds indeed to preformation, and we are bound to recognize that it accords very well with Leibnizian thought, who also made use of this biological metaphor. Our mind is not a blank slate; rather, as in a marble block, there are veins that pre-trace a form. This form is virtually present in the entity, but it is brought to actualization through work. However, even in this complexified theory of innatism as preformation, the question remains as to what justifies the truth of what is innate. In Leibniz, as in Descartes, we need the summoning of a third authority, namely God. Even though the seeds of truth need to be actualized, that they are truth is due to the fact that God sowed them in us. Consequently, the relationship between thought and object, in the innatist theories, is ultimately founded in God and therefore is not grounded in itself.

Conversely, the philosophical paradigm that corresponds to the model of *generatio aequivoca* is empiricism. Equivocal generation refers to a model where the progenitor is heterogeneous to the product as, for instance, when insects are born from the putrefaction of tree leaves. In the same vein, empiricism claims to derive *a priori* concepts from sensible impressions. Yet, deriving the *a priori* from the *a posteriori* comes down to overstepping a heterogeneity, exactly as in equivocal generation. If we exclude these two possibilities, which are preformation and equivocal generation, only epigenesis remains, which refers to the development of an embryo though the successive formation of new parts, implying the concurrence of external causes. The epigenetic stands in opposition to the genetic, which means precisely development starting from internal and pre-existent *data*. What does all this mean when applied to the categories? It means that they are not innate seeds, or pre-constituted seeds, inborn in our minds, nor do they derive from experience. The fact that categories do not derive from experience has already been shown, as they were defined both as pure (of purely rational composition) and as *a priori* (of purely rational provenance). But the fact that the categories are not innate, that is, do not belong by nature to our understanding, is more difficult to understand immediately. What does Kant mean? Because the sensible and intellectual forms are considered to result from an epigenesis, they cannot be part of the pre-constituted nature of a subject. The transcendental structures are not preformed, but they are not derived from experience either. They are indeed acquired, but originally. This acquisition means that they have not always been there, but the fact that their acquisition is original indicates that it has always already taken place. They are immediately implemented, but do not precede their implementation. It is in this subtle in-between that we must consider the genesis of the categories and the subject's transcendental functions. They are at the crossroads between experience and thought, and they even demonstrate the intrinsic and essential relationship between experience and thought.

Of course, one might object that Leibniz's innatism stated precisely the same idea: experience was an opportunity to actualize innate ideas, but they did not derive from it.[2] Are the categories to be considered according to this dichotomy of potentiality and actuality, which is not contrary to innatism, but is one of its forms? Are the categories always already there, as a potentiality, but requiring experience to be actualized? No: according to Kant, experience is not just the opportunity, because there are only empirical objects, there is no object but through experience; *experience is not simply an opportunity to encounter the object, it is what creates objectivity.* The transcendental is constitutive of experience, but at the same time, the transcendental – and knowledge – only have a meaning when applied to experience.[3] And not only is experience not simply an opportunity for an actualization, but there is also no actualization through work or effort in Kant's view, precisely because acquisition is *original*, that is, *immedi-*

---

2 This is the general interpretation proposed by A. Vanzo in "Leibniz on innate ideas and Kant on the origin of categories" (Vanzo 2018).

3 J. Callanan also insists on this point: "For Leibniz, the role of sensible experience is at most that of a possible enabling condition for the realization of contents determined by the predispositions of our rational capacities alone. Such a conception makes space for the possibility of an application of those rational capacities through alternative enabling conditions (such as the intuitional capacities of a different kind of being) – on such a conception, human sensibility is merely a sufficient but not necessary condition for the realization of the outputs of our rational capacities. Kant's discursivity thesis on the other hand entails that the contribution of sensibility is not a mere enabling condition for concept-application. Sensibility must instead be thought of as co-determining the possible 'sense and significance' [*Sinn und Bedeutung*] of our *a priori* concepts in combination with the contribution of the understanding. An *a priori* concept's application conditions, i.e. sensible intuition, provide strict limits for any possible application of the categories" (Callanan 2013, pp. 14–15).

ate. Consequently, the acquisition of transcendental structures cannot be viewed as an actualization, and the models of the original acquisition or epigenesis cannot be equated to any innatist theory. Therefore, Kant's theory of knowledge cannot be assimilated, as Husserl suggested, to a naturalism or a psychologism. From a transcendental point of view, indeed, everything is taken for granted: the *a priori* is not a pregiven nature that falls to human beings. Categories are originally and spontaneously produced by the understanding, which means that they are not more innate than empirical. Therefore, if there is a certain facticity about the transcendental – in the sense of a primary fact that cannot be derived from anterior reasons –, this does not mean that it is what characterizes human nature. In other words, Kant suggests a *non-innate facticity*. In Descartes's philosophy, metaphysical facticity goes hand in hand with an innatist theory, so that the truth, instilled in our minds by God, is inherently contingent, even though it appears necessary to me. Innatism is the best way to consider the metaphysical contingency of truth, because the necessary depends on divine will. Kant, on the other hand, while refusing any innatist scheme, suggests a superior contingency with what we could call the "possibilisation" of experience, that is, the transcendental conception. Here, the fact is neither given nor pregiven: it is originally produced. Now, if the categories are not *mentibus nostris ingenitae*, it means that they are not preformed and hence that Kant's transcendentalism is not a psychologism.

But if Kant rejects the innatist model, why does he use it to conceptualize the base from which emerge the conceptual and sensible forms, and in particular, as he states in his response to Eberhard, space? Let us examine the text: "That way arises the formal intuition that we call space, as a representation originally acquired (of the form of external objects in general), whose ground (as mere receptivity) is nevertheless innate"; or previously, after having said that space and time, as well as categories, are originally acquired: "There must indeed be a ground for it in the subject, however, which makes it possible that these representations can arise in this and no other manner, and be related to objects which are not yet given, and this ground at least is innate" (Kant 1902, AK. VIII, pp. 221–222; Kant 2002, p. 312). Here, Kant proffers the paradoxical concept of a transcendental innateness. What does this mean? The transcendental, as we saw, is the opposite of the innate, because innatism is a way to define a content immanent to a being. The eternal truths are classically innate. But, in Kant's philosophy, it is not a question of truths, because the transcendental does not start from an ontological position and does not have a positive content. Therefore, what does this transcendental innateness mean? *Innatus* means what is in me natively: it refers to an immanent field. Now, what is innate in Kant's texts? Neither contents, as in Descartes or Leibniz, nor truths; rather, innatism refers here to original forms: the innate forms involved in the representation, and in particular, space. And at this point, this form is not yet, strictly speaking, a form, in which contents could lie, but it is a pure field of relations. Space in its first meaning – as innate – refers, indeed, to the primordiality of the relation to alterity. In other words, and very strangely, *Kant calls innate that by which I relate to something else.* What is innate is my relation to the other. The innate does not refer to what lies in my immanent field, but to that by which I relate to transcendence. Indeed, space, understood as that which ensures the encounter with otherness, is intended to open the subject to what is other than itself. This is the reason why the ultimate transcendental forms do not express the naturalism of the innate or an empirical facticity, but rather refer to that by which the subject has a relation to transcendence. The innate is, paradoxically, in Kant's views, what projects me towards the outside. This is the ecstatic structure of transcendental which is innate in Kant's philosophy. Indeed, the context is still that of the relationship between representation and object. Innateness responds precisely to this question. The innate does not fall under the category of truths, or even of faculties, but rather of subjective functions that constitute the object. Thus, the innate is never thematized as positive content, but qualifies precisely this relationship of representation to the object. What is innate is the relation to the object, not the content that we should then put in relation with it. It is the relationship that is primary and which reveals the ecstatic essence of the transcendental, which, consequently, is precisely not an essence. Kantian transcendentalism is not a subjectivism, neither in the sense that it could make the object relative to human nature, nor in the sense that it could repatriate everything within the immanent sphere of subjectivity, precisely because only the relation to the object is innate: the transcendental is the *Beziehung auf etwas anderes*, the relation to something other than me; it is, therefore, what projects the subject away from him or herself. The subject is not given from the beginning in Kant's philosophy, but is thought of fundamentally as a relation to the object. Consequently, we cannot say that ultimately the transcendental subject is "a human being," but it is a relation to something. The French commentator J. Moreau sums up this idea superbly:

> This immediate connection to the object, naively represented as the reception of a form in the empiricist theories of knowledge, is fundamentally required by cognitive reflection, which presupposes being as an object in general, correlative to the pure subject, to the transcendental ego. The latter cannot be set, indeed, in an absolute interiority; there is being beyond him; the transcendental subjectivity is open to being. But this ontological openness is manifested at the level of our sensible faculty by the form of the outer sense: the thinking subject in us does not possess an original intuition; it is not able to give itself objects, to make things exist [*entsehen lassen*]; it can only, from received impressions, put them in

front of him as objects [*entgegenstehen lassen*] in a horizon of exteriority that corresponds to the form of sensible intuition. Exteriority, always present to the imagination and the outer sense, indeed cannot be regarded as subsisting *per se*, because it is nothing but the infinite emptiness, a pure diversity of parts that reciprocally exclude each other; it can only exist for a subject who is capable of receiving impressions, and it is characterized, in opposition to the received impressions, as the general form of receptivity; but in this very form, the receptive subject is confirmed to be nothing but a finite being, which is overtaken by the reality. If the external objects, the things that we see in space, appear to us as being outside of us (*extra nos*), this indicates that something exists apart from us (*praeter nos*), something that appears to our consciousness, to our sensible faculty, but that our mind does not create. (Moreau 1984, pp. 19–20, our translation)

Space and the transcendental object are two instances of the *außer uns*, as Kant writes in a variant of the first edition of the *Critique:*

> But since the expression outside us carries with it an unavoidable ambiguity, since it sometimes signifies something that, as a thing in itself, exists distinct from us and sometimes merely something that belongs to outer appearance, then in order to escape uncertainty and use this concept in the latter significance – in which it is taken in the proper psychological question about the reality of our outer intuition – we will distinguish empirically external objects from those that might be called "external" in the transcendental sense, by directly calling them "things that are to be encountered in space." (Kant 1902, AK. IV, p. 234; Kant 1998, p. 428)

But if it is necessary to avoid confusion between these two meanings of "outside us," this ambiguity is not necessarily fortuitous or merely one of language: it expresses a profound correlation between space and the transcendental object. As Moreau says, borrowing an expression from Heimsoeth, the *extra nos* reveals the *praeter nos*. Space, as presupposed by the succession of our internal states and thus escaping idealism, refers to a transcendence that we cannot know – by definition, because it escapes the phenomenal sphere –, but the *praeter nos*, the 'apart from us,' must necessarily be presupposed. Indeed, if space still refers to external *representations*, idealism cannot be refuted; now, if it is refuted, it is because space opens onto a transcendence. The text of the second edition confirms this: "for outer sense is already in itself a relation of intuition to something actual outside me; and its reality" (Kant 1998, p. 121), Kant says. The authority of the "outside of us" is valid within the refutation of idealism only if it refers to the "apart from us," that is, to the alterity of immanence. "The paradox of idealism is cleared up, the transcendental ambiguity is resolved, once it is recognized that the *extra nos* refers to the *praeter nos*, that exteriority is the trace of transcendence" (Moreau 1984, p. 21, our translation).

But if space refers to a transcendence, it is necessary to pluralize again the meaning of space. Indeed, neither space objectified as a container, nor space as an *a priori* form of the intuition, whereby objects are outside of one another, reveals such a relation to transcendence. Therefore, we have to say that there is a third meaning of space that is the radical ground of the two other ones and which Kant qualifies as innate in his response to Eberhard and also mentions in a letter to Rehberg:

> This insight of the necessary synthesis of inner sense with outer sense, even in the determination of the time of our existence, seems to me of aid in proving the objective reality of our representations of outer things (as against psychological idealism) though I am not able to pursue this idea farther at the moment. (Kant 1902, AK. XI, p. 448; Kant 1967, p. 168)

Space is not even yet an *a priori* form of intuition here: it seems to be an innate *a priori* intuition. However, once again – and we understand better now – to what does this innateness refer? To a *Beziehung auf etwas anderes*, a relation to something that is not me. *The only thing which is innate for Kant is precisely not a thing, but a relation: the relation to alterity.* So, the ultimate meaning of space is this relation. We see very well here that original space is no longer even a form, in which there would be a content, but a relation to something. Space, in its most original signification, rather than indicating the exteriority of things from one another, *partes extra partes*, is exteriority as such. As Moreau puts it, in space "the relation of our finite consciousness towards what transcends it is expressed; and if space appears to us as infinite, it is because the ontological distance between our mind and the absolute that dominates it is also infinite; exteriority without limits is the image of the transcendence of being" (Moreau 1984, p. 37, our translation).

2 The Critique of Anthropologism: Kantian Finitude

What is more, Husserl's critique of anthropologism reflects, in our view, a misconception of Kantian finitude. As such, it is important to distinguish between finiteness and finitude: while the former refers in fact to an anthropological concept that denotes human mortality and subjection to need, the latter, finitude, is a metaphysical concept that accounts for the limitation of knowledge and for the claim of transcending the *datum*. Finiteness therefore means that, though I am in the world, I am not the world: I am not all, but one part, and external nature is like my inorganic body. By contrast, finitude only appears when the *datum* is insufficient, or in other words, when the subject transcends the *datum*. This transcendence corresponds to the imperious requirement of a manifestation of what the *datum* cannot manifest. Finiteness of need expresses the fact that I am not everything (all of empirical reality), while finitude of need expresses the fact that constituted reality is not everything. It is therefore precisely this transgression of what is constituted that brings this constituted reality out. It is this transcendence of need that unveils the immanence of the world. This implies, therefore, that reality stands out as reality from the requirement, peculiar to the finite subject, of an impossible givenness – impossibility which is the mark of the reality *per se*.

More generally, what Husserl has in common with Kant is the fact that he rejects any dogmatic form of ontology and neutralizes all ontological positions. Indeed, the starting point of phenomenology is the process of reduction: we start with the epoché as an inaugural act, from which emerges the criterion of originary presentive intuition, which is to say, the phenomenological evidence:

> Enough now with absurd theories. No conceivable theory can make us err with respect to the principle of all principles: that every originary presentive intuition is a legitimizing source of cognition, that everything originally (so to speak, in its "personal" actuality) offered to us in "intuition" is to be accepted simply as what it is presented as being, but also only within the limits in which it is presented there. (Husserl 1976, Hua III/1, p. 43; Husserl 1983, p. 44)

In Husserl's philosophy, the phenomenon is being itself. In phenomenology, the phenomenon is a phenomenon of something. As the name suggests, phenomenology means that we reach being by reaching the phenomenon: it is the idea of transcendence within immanence. Is this the same phenomenalism that we find in Kant's philosophy? This paper argues otherwise. Indeed, Husserl first practiced a methodological epoché by means of which we describe the way that things appear to us. For the natural attitude, indeed, things exist independently of consciousness. This naivety can only appear as such from the viewpoint of the epoché. This is why the epoché mainly has a methodological function: that of bracketing the world and suspending the assumption of being independent of consciousness. However, and this marks one of the peculiarities of Husserlian philosophy, we go surreptitiously from this methodological epoché, by which we describe how things appear to us, to a transcendental constitution, that is, to the claim that the being of things is relative to consciousness.

> One recognizes that all that exists for the pure ego becomes constituted in him himself; furthermore, that every kind of being – including every kind characterized as, in any sense, transcendent – has its own particular constitution. Transcendency in every form is an immanent existential characteristic, constituted within the ego. Every imaginable sense, every imaginable being, whether the latter is called immanent or transcendent, falls within the

domain of transcendental subjectivity, as the subjectivity that constitutes sense and being. (Husserl 1950, Hua I, p. 117; Husserl 1982, pp. 83–84)

The notion of being existing independently of consciousness is devoid of sense. But what explains this transition from a phenomenological approach to a transcendental approach in Husserl's thought? How do we go from a methodological epoché to the thesis that the whole being of things results from consciousness? In reality, this seems to be *a leap, which remains phenomenologically unjustified*, or a surreptitious metaphysical thesis, with which being totally shifts to the phenomenal sphere. We therefore understand why Husserl's position differs from Kant's, despite its also being transcendental and even though it entails accomplishing Kant's transcendentalism: for Kant, we *think* being independently of the phenomenon, even if we do not *know* it. The Husserlian neutralization (defined as the suspension of any ontology) is therefore infinite because nothing can escape the phenomenal sphere. The phenomenological approach implies the possibility of a complete resumption of my experience: in theory, nothing can escape the light of consciousness, not even consciousness itself. It is in this sense that neutralization is infinite in Husserl's philosophy. The illusion of phenomenology, read with the Kantian conception in mind, is the illusion of infinity, that is, the omission that neutralization implies finitude, so that any neutralization is limited. As Kant puts it, the territory falls within a domain[4]: there is a sphere of immanence, but there is also the necessity to think what transcends this sphere. Husserl, on the other hand, claims to encompass everything within this sphere of territorial immanence.

Let us then return to Kant's conception, based on his definition of the transcendental, and unpack the central thesis of finitude, for herein lies the real point of contention between Kant and Husserl, and perhaps even the profundity of the Kantian thesis, which seems to have escaped Husserl's attention.

The status of the transcendental implies first of all a "genetic" point of view, which is not intended to trace a genesis of the transcendental, but rather signals the status of representation as secondary in relation to being. How can we characterize this "secondariness" of representation, which is based on the transcendental? It is characterized by what we might refer to as a "secondariness of the *a priori*," as paradoxical as this expression may sound. This secondariness defines the status of representation as a condition. Indeed, as its etymology (re-presentation) suggests, representation is always second: *the immanent meaning of representation is to be thought in relation to transcendence*. If not, there is only

---

[4] On this comparison, see Kant 1902, *Critique of Judgment*, AK. V, p. 174; Kant 1987, p. 13.

a globalizing immanence of which representation constitutes only a part. Representation in itself implies transcendence. This is the meaning of finitude, the defining characteristic of the Kantian subject: I refer to something that I am not. The essence of representation is precisely to refer to something. There is a relationship that goes from representation to reality but not the other way around: we cannot go from being to representation, but we can go from representation to being. There is no self-givenness (*Selbstgebung*), because this would imply that I could be the origin of givenness: if I had access to being directly, I would have no receptivity, and the simple fact of thinking being would give me access to it. Yet, thought does not create its objects, since an *intellectus archetypus* would produce the ideal essences of things. There is a secondariness, a posteriority with respect to being: *this is the only ontological thesis, whose significance is precisely to remove ontology*. The secondariness, the "afterwards" of the representation concerns neither time nor accident, but rather essence: the representation is neither co-extensive with being, nor contemporary with the origin. The *a priori* of secondariness implies the corollary of the neutralization of being: nothing can be said concerning being because we are limited to the element of representation. Thus, it is only from this standpoint that something can be said or thought about the world.

This *a priori* secondariness that is the essence of representation implies the two aspects proper to human existence: finitude and transcendence. Finitude implies the receptive and irremediably passive structure of representation constitutive of subjectivity; transcendence, which is its corollary (to be finite means that there is something exterior to me), indicates that the sense of representation is to include a relationship to something. The transcendental is the authority that neutralizes both immanence and transitivity because it cancels any determination of a relationship between reality and representation. As soon as we begin with the *a priori* fact of representation (*fact* that rejects any *right* to ontology), transcendental philosophy must unfold as an analytic of representation, which will take the form, in Kant, of an analytic of the faculties involved in the representative process. It is now clearer why the Kantian position is something unseen in the history of modern philosophy. The transcendental rejects the idea of an original givenness (contra Husserl and phenomenology), the *intuitus originarius*, as well as the idea of original production (against the classical metaphysics and German idealism), the *intellectus archetypus*.

What does this *a priori* secondariness imply? On the one hand, a receptivity, structured by sensible forms; on the other hand, an activity, producing intellectual forms. It is the second perspective, a structural one, that we will adopt on the transcendental: the intra-transcendental difference implies not only an *a priori* secondariness of representation, but also a structural duality. This second perspective is as paradoxical as the first one: just like the secondariness is nonetheless *a priori*, now the duality is nonetheless structural. Why "nonetheless?" Because commonly, the "two" comes after the "one." This is not the case here, however. Indeed, the transcendental entails a radical duality as a condition of representation: the duality of a *logos*, the categories, and an *alogon*, that is, space and time defined by their alogic nature. Why are space and time resistant to any logic? On the one hand, space rejects the principle of indiscernibles; on the other hand, time rejects the principle of contradiction. Time is contradiction in action: it brings into existence the contradictories. That is why, from the beginning, the condition of simultaneity has been placed in the principle of contradiction: the same thing cannot be and not be at the same time in the same respect. Plato handled this issue in the fourth book of *The Republic* with the tale of the spinning top. As for the Kantian conception of space, it calls the Leibnizian principle of indiscernibles into question, given that space is not reducible to conceptual relations between substances. This is shown by the paradox of symmetrical objects: space distinguishes entities, the left glove is not exchangeable with the right glove, even though they have the same *logos*, the same definition; for Leibniz, on the contrary, space was not able to distinguish beings: every difference was considered to be conceptual. If two entities occupy a different place, they are conceptually different; inversely, if an entity has the same conceptual properties as another, they are identical, the same entity. Space and time do not bring any real distinction, they are mere logical relations, extrinsic properties of things. On the contrary, for Kant, space is a source of distinctions and, because it is irreducible to conceptual relations, it contradicts the impossibility of indiscernibles claimed by the Leibnizian principle.

The fact that the object entails an irreducible duality between a logical root and an extra-logical one represents the revolution carried out by Kant in the history of the concept of the object, and it is certainly well known. However, as Heidegger puts it, the well known is often the least known, and we must recognize that the consequences of this idea have not always been drawn, either by Husserl or (subsequently) by Heidegger. It is possible to think indeed that the struggle of interpretations that Kant's philosophy has received is directly derived from this internal duality of the object. To show this, we should briefly consider, besides Husserl's interpretation, the other main hermeneutic schools of Kantian philosophy: the Neo-Kantian Marburg school and the Heideggerian interpretation. We will see that, against all odds, all three share the same perspective on Kant because they underestimate this irreducible duality. Indeed, the discussion between Cohen and Heidegger is almost virtually present in the Kantian thematization of objectivity, so that we can say that the debate is in reality intrinsic to the specificity of Kantianism while at the same time missing the latter in its comprehensiveness and as a whole. These two hermeneutic schools originate in the criticism of German idealism, which restored ontology and claimed the equivalence between *logos* and being. This rehabilitation of metaphysics is made by moving from an ontology of nature as it existed in 17th century, before Kantian criticism, to an ontology of freedom, but in both cases what is implied is the equivalence of thought and being. If we reject this equivalence, as Neo-Kantianism and Heidegger did, we promote one of the two poles unilaterally: the transcendental *logos* for the Neo-Kantians, who interpret the Kantian doctrine as a theory of knowledge, reducing the importance of the Transcendental Aesthetic and understanding space as an objectified mathematical space; or the transcendental *alogon* for Heidegger, who gives primacy to time (the less objectifiable form) and reduces the role of Transcendental Logic, prioritizing the first edition of the *Critique of Pure Reason*.

The two main directions of interpreting Kant's philosophy are burdened by a double undervaluation:
- Undervaluation of the *logos* and priority given to time by Heidegger.
- Undervaluation of the *alogon* by the Neo-Kantians and the identification of space with its mathematical objectivation.

On the one hand, the transcendental is understood as the objectifying synthesis of science, endlessly; and the thing-in-itself is seen as a horizon towards which science moves without ever reaching it. On the other hand, Heidegger insists on the analytical inclusion of transcendence within finitude. These two hermeneutic lines are both textually grounded, and both allow us to ascribe a comprehensive significance to the Kantian project; therefore, they are equally challenging. Such being the case, where does this antinomy come from? It is possible to think it is due to a common fault, i.e., to the fact that neither interpretation fully appreciates the heterogeneity of the two sources present in the object. In each case, the issue that both the Neo-Kantians and Heidegger have to face is finding the underlying unity of the two roots: logic in Cohen's interpretation, time and imagination in Heidegger's. This interpretative commonality appears very clearly in the moments of concession that are to be found in Heidegger, as, for example, here:

> Although one cannot defend the attempt of the so-called "Marburg school" to interpret space and time as "categories" in the logical sense and to reduce the transcendental aesthetic to logic, one must admit that the attempt is inspired by a legitimate motive. This motive arises from the conviction, certainly never clearly justified, that the transcendental aesthetic taken by itself can never constitute the whole of that which lies in it as a possibility. However, from the specific "syn" character of pure intuition it does not follow that this intuition is dependent on the synthesis of the understanding. On the contrary, the correct in-

terpretation of this "syn" character leads to the conclusion that pure intuition originates in the pure imagination. Moreover, the reduction of transcendental aesthetic to logic becomes all the more questionable when it is shown that the specific object of transcendental logic, pure thought, is itself rooted in the transcendental imagination. (Heidegger 1991, GA 3, p. 145; Heidegger 1962, p. 152)

The legitimacy of the interpretation proposed by the Marburg school, regardless of its errors of content, consists in the form of its attempt, namely, to establish which source of knowledge is primary. If the answer given by Cohen is incorrect for Heidegger, it remains true that the question is correctly asked and totally legitimate. The conviction that we can regress to an "origin" or a common "root" of the two poles of knowledge is shared by both hermeneutic schools.[5] Only their answers differ, the text clearly says so, but the legitimate question we should pose to Kant's text is the following: what is the primordial root? Now, what we would like to defend is precisely that the profound meaning of the Kantian transcendental is that which cannot be traced back to an original unity: the transcendental is the affirmation of an insurmountable heterogeneity. Missing this irreducible duality necessarily leads one to pose antinomic interpretations that emphasize either *logos* or time.

Why did these important interpreters and historians of Kantian philosophy miss this point? Precisely because their interpretation focuses on the *Critique of Pure Reason*, that is, on the objectifying process of knowledge, which consists in the accord between the two transcendental poles and thus lets us think that if this accord exists, we need a ground for it, that is, an inherent unity. Husserl's interpretation of Kant has the same presupposition. The irreducible duality between the two sources can only appear in their dissension and inadequacy, that is, in their non-constitutive yet reflective moment. It is in the third *Critique* that this inadequacy appears most clearly; the *Critique of Pure Reason*, on the contrary, conceals it and presents a "pacified" scenario of the transcendental. Therefore, if neither the Neo-Kantians nor Heidegger nor Husserl emphasizes the fundamental heterogeneity that the transcendental articulates, it is because their interpretation prioritizes the *Critique of Pure Reason*, where heterogeneity is pacified. The radical sense of the transcendental, which has been missed by those hermeneutic lines, is *the absence of a unified ground*. The ground in Kant's philosophy takes the form of an original dissension. Kantian philosophy is a "tragic" philosophy because it is haunted by an irreconcilable duality. And it

---

5 D. Pradelle also remarks on this point in *Par-delà la révolution copernicienne. Sujet transcendantal et facultés chez Kant et Husserl* (Pradelle 2012).

is because there is such an irreconcilable duality, dissension, and irreducibility that there is a necessity to think of a bridge (*Übergang*).

* * *

Therefore, however insightful Husserl's critique of Kant may be, this paper has attempted to express a possible Kantian rebuttal – or at least to identify some possible leads that would allow him a right of reply to Husserl's accusation of being trapped within psychologism and anthropologism. We tried to show that Kant has essentially anticipated this critique and that he has avoided this double pitfall through his conception of the transcendental, for the Kantian transcendental is neither an innate nature nor an openness to infinity. It is rather the claim of a radical finitude that is not to be understood as anthropological mortality, but as the metaphysical posteriority of subjectivity with respect to being, which means that the human subject is necessarily a subject who needs experience.

Bibliography

Callanan, John (2013): "Kant on Nativism, Scepticism and Necessity". In: *Kantian Review*, vol. 18, n° 1, pp. 1–27.
Descartes, René (1996): *Oeuvres Complètes*, 13 vol. Edited by Adam-Tannery. Paris: Vrin.
Grandjean, Antoine (2009): *Critique et Réflexion. Essai sur le discours kantien*. Paris: Vrin.
Heidegger, Martin (1962): *Kant and the Problem of Metaphysics*. Trans. James S. Churchill. Bloomington: Indiana University Press.
Heidegger, Martin (1991): *Kant und das Problem der Metaphysik. Gesamtausgabe*, vol. 3. Ed. Friedrich-Wilhelm von Herrmann. Frankfurt am Main: Vittorio Klostermann.
Husserl, Edmund (1950): *Cartesianische Meditationen und Pariser Vorträge. Husserliana*, vol. I. Ed. S. Strasser. The Hague: Martinus Nijhoff.
Husserl, Edmund (1976): *Ideen zu einer reinen Phänomenologie und phänomenologischen Philosophie*. First Book: *Allgemeine Einführung in die Phänomenologie. Husserliana*, vol. III/1. Ed. Karl Schuhmann. The Hague: Martinus Nijhoff.
Husserl, Edmund (1982): *Cartesian Meditations*. Trans. Dorion Cairns. The Hague: Martinus Nijhoff.
Husserl, Edmund (1983): *Ideas Pertaining to a Pure Phenomenology and to a Phenomenological Philosophy*, volume I. Trans. Fred Kersten. The Hague/Boston/Lancaster: Martinus Nijhoff.
Kant, Immanuel (1902–): *Gesammelte Schriften*. Edited by the Prussian Academy of Sciences. Berlin: Walter de Gruyter.
Kant, Immanuel (1998): *Critique of Pure Reason*. Trans. Paul Guyer and Allen W. Wood. Cambridge: Cambridge University Press.

Kant, Immanuel (2002): *Theoretical Philosophy After 1781*. Ed. Henry Allison and Peter Heath. Trans. Gary Hatfield, Michael Friedman, Henry Allison, and Peter Heath. Cambridge: Cambridge University Press.

Kant, Immanuel (1967): *Philosophical Correspondence 1759–1799*. Ed. and Trans. Arnulf Zweig. Chicago: The University of Chicago Press.

Kant, Immanuel (1987): *Critique of Judgment*. Trans. Werner S. Pluhar. Indianapolis/Cambridge: Hackett Publishing Company.

Moreau, Joseph (1984): "De l'ambiguïté transcendantale". In: *La problématique kantienne*. Ed. Joseph Moreau. Paris: Vrin, pp. 1–17.

Moreau, Joseph (1984): "Le temps, la succession et le sens interne". In: *La problématique kantienne*. Ed. Joseph Moreau. Paris: Vrin, pp. 184–199.

Pradelle, Dominique (2012): *Par-delà la révolution copernicienne. Sujet transcendantal et facultés chez Kant et Husserl*. Paris: Presses universitaires de France.

Serban, Claudia (2017): "*A priori*, nécessité, facticité, *ego:* Husserl critique de Kant". In: *Kant et les empirismes*. Ed. Antoine Grandjean. Paris: Classiques Garnier, pp. 195–212.

Vanzo, Alberto (2018): "Leibniz on Innate Ideas and Kant on the Origin of Categories". In: *Archive für Geschichte der Philosophie*, vol. 100, n° 1, pp. 19–45.

Claudia Serban
Kant, Husserl, and the Aim of a "Transcendental Anthropology"

> "Ich und Menschheit, das ist eben nicht ein Nebeneinander, sondern ein Ineinander, so vor allem transzendental und absolut verstanden."
> (Husserl 1989, Hua XXVII, p. 235)

Abstract: This chapter deals with the question of whether transcendental philosophy should inevitably have to choose between subscribing to an "anthropological prohibition" (denounced by Blumenberg) or accepting an "anthropologization" of the transcendental (disavowed by Husserl). While examining the relationship between transcendental philosophy and anthropology both in Kant and Husserl, a special emphasis is placed upon their common idea of a "transcendental anthropology." The project of such an anthropology addresses the necessity of developing the transcendental egology in several directions in order to incorporate and re-elaborate certain fundamental aspects of the empirical – psychological or worldly – dimension of subjective life. Thus, it is not only the core of a philosophical anthropology and of its concept of humanity that might be reshaped, but also the meaning and scope of the transcendental itself.

Does transcendental philosophy necessarily lead either to an "anthropological prohibition" (like the one identified by Blumenberg in his reading of Husserl and Heidegger[1]) or to an "anthropologization" of the transcendental (such as the one that Husserl had denounced in Kant)? Is this alternative truly a dead end? It is this two-layered question that will be handled here, in respect to both Kant and Husserl.

1 From Empirical Egology to Transcendental Anthropology

Without a doubt, the accusation of "transcendental anthropologism" that Husserl directed against the author of the *Critiques* has some truth to it. As one

---

[1] See Blumenberg 2006, pp. 60, 61, 91.

https://doi.org/10.1515/9783110564280-006

reads in his *Reflections on Anthropology* – and more precisely, in "Reflection 875" stemming (according to Adickes) from 1776–1778, a period during which the critical enterprise was in full development –, Kant was willing to admit that "[e]verything that obtains its rule not on objective, but on subjective grounds [...] pertains to anthropology" (Kant 1913, AK. XV, p. 384). In this sense, the meaning of the transcendental according to Kant does indeed contain an anthropological element. Nevertheless, in understanding this element as the subjective constitution of the "rational finite being" that we are, the author of the *Critiques* had openly hesitated to admit that transcendental philosophy had a properly anthropological *ground*. The human being and its reason do not entirely coincide: as Blumenberg put it (with his characteristically sharp irony), for Kant, in a way, "[t]he human being is the cheap, popular edition of reason [*Der Mensch ist die verbilligte Volksausgabe der Vernunft*]" (Blumenberg 2006, p. 501). But might one paraphrase this statement and say that anthropology is the cheap, popular edition of transcendental philosophy?

The relationship between transcendental philosophy and anthropology in Kant has attracted the attention of scholars for a long time. In more recent research, one of the works particularly worthy of mention is the interpretation of Foucault (developed in the 60s, but made fully accessible to the public only in 2008), in the "Introduction" accompanying his translation of Kant's *Anthropology from a Pragmatic Point of View*. In this "Introduction," Foucault makes the henceforth famous claim of an "anthropologico-critical repetition" and considers that the *Anthropology* "says nothing *other* than what is said in the *Critique*" and is "only [...] possible [...] from the standpoint of the *Critique* having already reached its end, having already led to the realization of transcendental philosophy" (Foucault 2008a, pp. 52 and 54; Foucault 2008b, pp. 83 and 87).[2] On the other hand, in his imposing work on Kant's *Anthropology*, Reinhard Brandt has expressed reservation with regard to such a tendency to minimize the distance between (pragmatic) anthropology and transcendental philosophy, and even considered that "as a piece of popular philosophy, anthropology, empirical

---

[2] Another relevant contribution in French literature is that of Alain Renaut, in the "Presentation" of his new translation of Kant's *Anthropology* and in a paper published in 1997. Renaut insists both upon the fact that the *Anthropology* is "impossible to situate (*insituable*)" within critical philosophy and that the question of the human progressively reveals itself for Kant as "the center of the system" (Renaut 1997, p. 57; Renaut 1993, p. 5), while also highlighting the reasons for which pragmatic anthropology is "the veritable inheritor of rational psychology" (Renaut 1993, p. 32).

or pragmatic, does not belong to philosophy in a strict sense" (Brandt 1996, p. 26).[3]

As a preamble to our inquiry, this tacit depreciation of Kant's anthropology on account of its "popular" character, often reiterated in Kantian literature, deserves to be taken seriously. First of all, what serves as a basis for the popular character of the *Anthropology* in the opinion of its author? Importantly, while stressing the systematic character of his enterprise, Kant also insists, in the "Foreword" to his work, on the "reference to examples which can be found by every reader" (Kant 1907, AK. VII, p. 121; Kant 2006, p. 5). This use of examples, which can cause Kant's *Anthropology* to appear irremediably obsolete, excessively boring, or filled with prejudices unacceptable in the eyes of contemporary readers, can be understood in different ways. One can either see it as a proof of a kind of anthropology that is mostly literary in its sources (as Reinhard Brandt does), or pay more attention to its subtle swaying between third- and first-person speech. It is too seldom observed that in his *Anthropology* Kant makes room for descriptions of genuine experience, sometimes (not very often, it is true) even given in first-person speech. Such is the case with the quite exceptional passages in which he recalls his childhood dream of drowning (§ 37) or describes the episode of his sea-sickness during the crossing from Pillau to Königsberg (§ 29),[4] passages that can each be read as a consequence and application of the egological point of departure of his inquiry, according to which self-consciousness and the possession of the representation of the "I" are the distinctive landmarks for approaching the human being (§ 1).

And yet, one should not too hastily conclude that Kant is conflating anthropology and autobiography, or that his *Anthropology* consists mainly of a collection of anecdotes: as he puts it in his famous 1773 Letter to Marcus Herz, in which he describes the intention of his *Anthropology* lecture and distances himself from the current practice of the discipline: "my plan is quite unique. [...] I shall seek to discuss phenomena and their laws rather than the foundations of the possibility of modifying human nature in general" (Kant 1969, AK. X, p. 145; Kant 1999, p. 141).[5] Thus, the aim of the *Anthropology* is to display and describe a legality of experience – a legality wider or, in any case, distinct from that prescribed by the nature of our understanding. In this respect, I fully share Reinhard Brandt's opinion of seeing in this statement of intention the expression of a "phenomenological attitude" (Brandt 1996, p. 31, note 1), or the sentiment of Ber-

---

[3] See also Louden 2000, p. 66.
[4] First-person descriptions are also to be found, for instance, in §§ 85 and 88.
[5] The English translation was modified here in accordance with the German original.

nard Vandewalle when he writes that "Kantian anthropology equally attests an interest for the concrete forms of human existence that finds a certain echo in contemporary phenomenologies" (Vandewalle 1997, p. 185).

Nevertheless, Kant's practice and idea of anthropology goes further than this original alliance between an empirical egology and a descriptive (proto-)phenomenology. As a postcritical work, the *Anthropology From a Pragmatic Point of View* (and the "Didactic" in particular) is not simply rich in passages that mobilize the results of the first *Critique* and allow one to speak, as did Foucault, of an "anthropologico-critical repetition;" what is more, the proximity between transcendental philosophy and its anthropological extension can appear to be predetermined from the very beginning. At least this is what the fascinating and tricky *hapax* mention of an "*Anthropologia transcendentalis*" in the famous "Reflection on Anthropology n° 903," stemming from 1776–78 (Kant 1913, AK. XV, pp. 394–395), seems to suggest. This peculiar "Reflection" deals with the case of the "science egoist," or the scholar who, as a prisoner of his research domain, resembles a Cyclops who lacks a "second eye:" namely, the eye or the specific gaze provided by "the reflexive knowledge of human reason." And it is precisely this "reflexive self-knowledge of understanding and reason" that Kant depicts as "*Anthropologia transcendentalis*." Of course, one should not take this expression too literally: a reticence like that of Reinhard Brandt, who considers that "Kant has never – not in a lecture, not in a writing – elaborated this transcendental anthropology as a discipline, or even mentioned such a discipline," is more than legitimate. Indeed, in its pragmatic version, anthropology "is not a part of critical philosophy, or of transcendental philosophy" (Brandt 1996, p. 26).[6] However, it is still significant that Kant speaks of a "transcendental anthropology" while plainly referring to the "plan of the critique of pure reason," in other words, that this expression should designate precisely the task of a self-knowledge of reason – of a reason that knows itself *as human*; and it is equally significant that, in this context, it should be so tempting to replace "*anthropologia*" with "*philosophia*" and conceive of a form of coincidence between anthropology and transcendental philosophy. Here, we once again stumble upon Blumenberg's ironic sentence according to which, for Kant, the human being is

---

[6] See also, from the same author, the *Kritischer Kommentar zu Kants* Anthropologie in pragmatischer Hinsicht (Brandt 1999, pp. 7–20).
   A different view, and closer to our perspective, is expressed by Claudia M. Schmidt, in her paper "Kant's Transcendental, Empirical, Pragmatic, and Moral Anthropology" (Schmidt 2007), who distinguishes different anthropological projects in Kant and considers the 1798 work to be the result of their joint elaboration.

"the cheap, popular edition of reason;" however, in this context anthropology is not necessarily interpreted as "popular" (or "mundane") in a pejorative sense.

As we shall see further on, an equally remarkable occurrence of "transcendental anthropology" is to be found in Husserl, where it is explicitly present only as the designation of a subgroup of work manuscripts, and yet not entirely disconnected from the research program of transcendental phenomenology. Let us also briefly remark that another important affinity between the anthropology developed by Kant subsequent to (or even in parallel with) his critical philosophy and Husserl's transcendental phenomenology consists in their common reticence towards what one might call, in terms that are closer to contemporary debates, the "naturalization of consciousness." In this regard, the passage from the 1773 Letter to Marcus Herz quoted above continues as follows: "Hence the subtle and, in my view, eternally futile inquiries as to the manner in which bodily organs are connected with thought I omit entirely" (Kant 1969, AK. X, p. 145; Kant 1999, p. 141). Quite similarly, the Preface to the *Anthropology* will state, with regard to the naturalist or physiological explanation of human behavior, that "every reasoning led in this direction is unproductive" (Kant 1907, AK. VII, p. 119; Kant 2006, p. 3). Both transcendental philosophy and (postcritical or pragmatic) anthropology reject the physiological approach to consciousness and trade the aim of causal explanation for that of phenomenological description: thus, quite predictably, Kant could only be an ally in Husserl's combat against naturalism.

2 Psychology, Anthropology, and Transcendental Philosophy

Yet, in his *Crisis of European Sciences*, § 57, Husserl reproaches Kant for the "fateful separation [*verhängnisvolle Trennung*]" he had established between transcendental philosophy and psychology and pleads instead for the "transformation [of psychology] into a universal transcendental philosophy" (Husserl 1954, Hua VI, pp. 201 and 207; Husserl 1970, pp. 198 and 203). Such a transformation, which Husserl envisions accomplishing in his latest work, would manifestly transgress a Kantian prohibition. For this reason, the fate of psychology within transcendental philosophy has a profound impact on the particular status of anthropology, given that the meaning of anthropology is as highly dependent upon the division between the empirical and the transcendental as that of psychology, and confronts us with a certain account of the empirical subject as well.

Husserl's uncompromising dissatisfaction with Kant's version of transcendental philosophy is well known: in spite of his sustained combat against dogmatism, Kant has presumably failed to complete his critical enterprise and remained prisoner of certain serious dogmatic presuppositions. In particular, while limiting the validity of our categorial framework to objects given to our sensibility, he had acquiesced to the subjection of our knowledge to a double restriction, phenomenal and anthropological. Husserl also finds it "rather surprising that, since Kant, transcendental philosophy has not really profited from psychology," and even asks himself, focusing on Kant's critical enterprise, "why did it not work out a better psychology" (Husserl 1954, Hua VI, p. 205; Husserl 1970, p. 201). By aiming at grounding and developing "the relationship between transcendental psychology and transcendental phenomenology as an authentic way to a pure self-knowledge," the last sequence of the *Crisis* openly confirms that Husserl not only believed in the possibility of a pure self-knowledge – and consequently, of a pure (apriorical or eidetic) psychology –, but even envisioned a form of psychology intimately related to transcendental philosophy "in virtue of the alliance of difference and identity [*Verschwisterung der Verschiedenheit und Identität*] [...] between the psychological ego (the human ego, that is, made worldly in the spatiotemporal world) and the transcendental ego" (Husserl 1954, Hua VI, p. 209; Husserl 1970, p. 205).

By re-establishing an "indissoluble inner alliance [*unlösliche innere Verschwisterung*]" (Husserl 1954, Hua VI, p. 210; Husserl 1970, p. 206) between transcendental philosophy and psychology in this fashion, the phenomenologist is well aware of transgressing a Kantian prohibition. But he considers that his project of an apriorical psychology that is ultimately transcendental does not fall under this prohibition, which is only directed against dogmatic rational psychology and empirical psychology of introspection.[7] Husserl's manifold protestations against the fate to which Kant condemns psychology (by decreeing that it can only be empirical, and thus non-scientific, and that a presumably pure psychology would necessarily be dialectic) nevertheless suggest that he might not have fully grasped the meaning and the ultimate implications of this profound reti-

---

7 As the "Introduction" to the 1925 lecture on *Phenomenological Psychology* clearly states: "In previous times admittedly, *a priori* psychology was much discussed, namely, in the Leibnizian-Wolffian school of the eighteenth century. Kant's critique put an end to that. But this psychology was ontological-metaphysical. It was not a psychology which like this new one was purely intuitive and descriptive and yet at the same time *a priori*, which therefore, beginning with intuitive concrete instances ascended to intuitive necessities and universalities" (Husserl 1962, Hua IX, p. 39; Husserl 1977, p. 28).

cence. In this respect, one could indeed agree with Blumenberg, when he writes the following:

> In his *pathos* of a new beginning of philosophy directed against its decay into psychologism, Husserl disdained the historical results as being that which had made this decay possible. This concerns first of all his relation to Kant. Had he not done so, he couldn't have entrusted to self-experience all the profit that phenomenology has to rely on. One has to admit that phenomenology would have paid a high price for being lectured by Kant. (Blumenberg 2006, p. 162)

This quote points to the Kantian lesson which Husserl would not have been able to take advantage of, in Blumenberg's view: namely, that of questioning the rights of internal experience with respect to self-knowledge. As is well known, for Kant, this interrogation reaches its climax in the "Refutation of Idealism," which was inserted into the "Analytic of Principles" in 1787. By means of this "Refutation," it is shown that internal and external experience are not equally fundamental and profitable for knowledge, and that the presupposed primacy and superiority of internal experience must, in fact, be reversed. And it is precisely this inversion that is responsible for the definitive destitution of psychology, rational or empirical, and for the alternative proposal of a pragmatic (or postcritical) anthropology destined to restore balance to the relationship between the "inner" and the "outer man."

Of course, the way the *Critique of Pure Reason* defuses the surreptitious identification of the unity of thought with the object of internal intuition, or myself as given in time, is equally responsible for the destitution of psychology. As a result, "the whole of rational psychology, as a science transcending all the powers of human reason, collapses" (Kant 1903 (A 382), AK. IV, p. 217; Kant 1998, p. 432).[8] The "Preface" to the *First Metaphysical Principles of the Science of Nature*, published between the two editions of the first *Critique*, is equally severe towards empirical psychology, stating that it "can never become anything more than an historical doctrine of nature, and, as such, a natural doctrine of inner sense which is as systematic as possible, that is, a natural description of the soul, but never a science of the soul, nor even, indeed, an experimental psychological doctrine," given that "mathematics is not applicable to the phenomena of inner sense and their laws" (Kant 1903, AK. IV, p. 471; Kant 2004, p. 7). However, it is precisely the firm rejection of any form of scientific psychology and the new articulation of the relationship between internal and external expe-

---

[8] See also Kant 1903 (A 361), AK. IV, p. 227; Kant 1998, p. 422.

rience that leads Kant to develop his pragmatic anthropology as a genuine means of replacing (rational or empirical) psychology.[9]

3 The Anthropological Clause

Undoubtedly, Husserl was not willing to follow Kant in his condemnation of psychology. He even considered that the author of the *Critiques* not only failed to reform psychology in accordance with transcendental philosophy, but also surreptitiously maintained a significant residue of former, precritical psychology within transcendental philosophy itself, by submitting it to an anthropological restriction evident in the clause "for us humans." Indeed, this clause unavoidably weakens the status of the *a priori* (of the universal, non-empirical features of our knowledge and experience), by entailing what Husserl denounces as its illegitimate anthropologization. For the phenomenologist, such an anthropologization is unfounded and misleading, insofar as the *a priori* does not solely pertain to the form that the cognizing subjectivity prescribes to the object, but is grounded in the very content of knowledge, in the essential features of the cognized type of object. Thus, the *a priori* is valid for any kind of subjectivity, be it human or not, and it is only on this condition that it can be regarded as truly necessary, in the sense of a necessity – namely, that of the essence of the object – which does not depend upon any facticity. The *a priori* that takes root in such an essence imposes itself upon every cognizing subjectivity: this is the meaning of the clause "even for God" (Husserl 1976, Hua III/1, pp. 350–351) that Husserl substitutes for the Kantian clause "for finite rational beings like us" or "for us humans." In doing so, the phenomenologist firmly rejects the hypothesis of an intellect with logical laws other than our own, for such an hypothesis would inevitably lead to assigning a merely anthropological validity to the form of our knowledge. In a 1908 research manuscript that bears the title "Against Kant's Anthropological Theory" (where the target, accordingly, is not the anthropology subsequently developed by the author of the *Critiques*, but rather the anthropological restriction that weighs upon his transcendental philosophy), Husserl denounces the fact that Kant "confounds the necessity and generality of the human fact with the necessity and generality pertaining to the content of the evidence and which is the opposite of any fact;" more precisely, "he confounds the gen-

---

[9] The sharp separation between pragmatic anthropology and psychology is also stressed by Kant in a *Reflection* from the 1780s: "Pragmatic anthropology should not be psychology" (Kant 1913, "Reflection 1502a," AK. XV, p. 801). See also Wilson 2006, pp. 20–33; Louden 2000, pp. 63–66.

eral constraint derived from the human specificity (from a fact) [...] with the necessity apprehended in the evidence of 'it cannot be otherwise'" (Husserl 1956, Hua VII, pp. 358–359). Indeed, for Husserl, the step taken by Fries in 1807 with his *Neue oder anthropologische Kritik der Vernunft* had been largely prefigured by Kant himself, who had already engaged in the anthropologization of the transcendental. Thus, Husserl holds the critical enterprise responsible for a genuine "shift to relativism and anthropologism [*Wendung zum Relativismus und Anthropologismus*]" (Husserl 1956, Hua VII, p. 354).

However, the anthropological restriction that the phenomenologist diagnoses in Kant's transcendental philosophy goes even further. Husserl deplores the ambiguous status of the Kantian faculties, which he considers to be merely psychological powers whose transcendental genesis remains unclear, and for him this constitutes an irrefutable proof of Kant's clear affiliation with a subtle form of psychologism.[10] While challenging the thoroughgoing necessity of what pertains to the subjective faculties – to their structures and accomplishments –, Kant presumably amalgamated "the factual and the apriorical" in his transcendental considerations, and in doing so, he had been guilty of disregarding the true nature of the "phenomenological *a priori*" (Husserl 1956, Hua VII, p. 390). The ultimate reason for this confusion is promptly revealed by Husserl in very clear terms: "Because he understands inner perception in this empiricist, psychological sense, [...] Kant gets involved in his mythical concept-formation" (Husserl 1954, Hua VI, p. 117; Husserl 1970, p. 115). The all-too-narrow scope and meaning that the author of the *Critique* prescribes to internal perception does not allow him truly to overcome the psychology of his time and condemns him to endorse its shortcomings.

Yet, with this severe diagnosis, the Husserl of the *Crisis* does not intend – as he did when he made psychology rhyme with psychologism – to plead for a firm separation between transcendental philosophy and psychology, but, quite the contrary, to deplore the inconveniences of such a separation and stress the "indissoluble inner alliance [*unlösliche innere Verschwisterung*]" (Husserl 1954, Hua VI, p. 210; Husserl 1970, p. 206) of these twin disciplines, an alliance which reflects that of the transcendental and the psychological "I." Consequently, unlike what one might be led to believe, it is not the presence of a psychological residue that ultimately disqualifies Kant's transcendental philosophy in Hus-

---

[10] According to the *Crisis of European Sciences*, the "faculties", "functions," or transcendental-subjective "formations" presupposed by the critical discourse are only "mythical constructions" that reveal the "obscurities of the Kantian philosophy" and which in their literal meaning "poin[t] to something subjective, but a mode of the subjective which we are in principle unable to make intuitive to ourselves" (Husserl 1954, Hua VI, p. 116; Husserl 1970, p. 114).

serl's eyes, but rather the absence, within critical philosophy, of a renewed psychology made compatible with the transcendental enterprise, an absence which is fundamentally motivated by the distrust of internal experience. This once again proves that the profound reasons for the divorce which Kant had proclaimed between the transcendental and the psychological "I" were never considered to be consistent enough and were therefore never ratified by Husserl.

4 From the Inner to the Outer Man

In the preceding paragraphs, I have already brought up the new kind of relationship that the first *Critique*, and especially the 1787 edition, institutes between interiority and exteriority. In this regard, I will presently attempt to show – and, in my opinion, this is a point that illustrates remarkably well Foucault's idea of the "anthropologico-critical repetition" (Foucault 2008a, p. 52; Foucault 2008b, p. 83) – that the same kind of relationship is to be found, in Kant's anthropology, between what he calls the "inner man" and the "outer man." This should not only justify and explain Kant's reticence towards a rehabilitation of psychology within transcendental – critical or postcritical – philosophy, but also allow one to solve some of the difficulties and paradoxes legitimately pointed out by scholars. First and foremost, such is the case with the program of the *Anthropology From A Pragmatic Point of View* and its realization: if the inaugural characterization of anthropology as "knowledge of the world [*Weltkenntnis*]" (Kant 1907, AK. VII, p. 120; Kant 2006, p. 4),[11] contained in the "Foreword," is taken seriously, one would be quite surprised to acknowledge, as Foucault has emphasized, that "the majority of the analyses, and virtually all those which appear in the first part of the book, are undertaken not in the cosmopolitical dimension of the *Welt*, but that other – interior – dimension of the *Gemüt*" (Foucault 2008a, p. 34; Foucault 2008b, p. 55). Of course, the *Gemüt* is not the *Seele*, and is irreducible to a psychological interiority; yet, one could still remain under the impression that the 1798 *Anthropology* gives up on keeping its initial promise to study the human being as a citizen of the world.

Is this impression truly justified? I would say, quite the contrary – and this clarification should contribute to a dissipation of this apparent contradiction to a certain extent –, that the stake of the *Anthropology* consists precisely in revealing the conditioning of the "inner man" by the "outer man." Importantly, it is for this reason that its development rests upon an inner experience which is conditioned

---

11 *Cf.* also "Reflection 1482" (Kant 1913, AK. XV, p. 659).

by outer experience, or upon a self-experience that is conditioned by the experience of the world (and of humans as beings-in-the-world). Far from proposing a description of interiority, the "Anthropological Didactic" places the inner man and the outer man on the same level and categorically refuses any privilege to self-experience. Furthermore, on more than one occasion, Kant expresses his reticence towards the presumed richness of introspection or superiority of inner experience: such is the case, for instance, with § 4, in which he deals with self-observation (*Selbstbeobachtung*) and confesses that "the real purpose of this section concerns the warning mentioned above, namely not to concern oneself in the least with spying and, as it where, the affected composition of an inner history of the involuntary course of one's thoughts and feelings," explained a bit further on thusly: "For the situation with these inner experiences is not as it is with external experiences or objects in space, where the objects appear next to each other and *permanently* fixed. Inner sense sees the relations or its determinations only in time, hence in flux, where the stability of observation necessary for experience does not occur" (Kant 1907, AK. VII, pp. 133 and 134; Kant 2006, pp. 22 and 22–23). It is the very argument of the "Refutation of Idealism" that Kant recalls here: inner experience cannot provide us with the representation of permanence, and therefore is profoundly dependent upon outer experience.

But then, how can anthropology present itself as an empirical egology, as seen previously, and orchestrate such a superimposition of the description of the human over the description of the "I" from the very beginning – from the first paragraph, where the dignity of the human being is rooted in the fact of having "the I in its representation?" Let us not forget that this egological starting point is immediately exposed to potential deviations implied within this very capacity of saying "I;" indeed, § 2 provides us with a presentation of the different forms of egoism: logical, aesthetic, and moral. Consequently, even if the egological problematic as such "does not really belong to anthropology," according to the famous "Remark" of § 7 (Kant 1907, AK. VII, p. 142; Kant 2006, p. 33), questioning the status and the value of the "I" is an efficient means of delimiting the domain of anthropology with respect to both psychology and that which, within transcendental philosophy, pertains to logic. While recalling the division of apperception into pure and empirical, in order similarly to divide self-consciousness into intuiting and reflecting consciousness, Kant clearly draws a line of demarcation: "In psychology we investigate ourselves according to our ideas of inner sense; in logic, according to what intellectual consciousness suggests" (Kant 1907, AK. VII, p. 134; Kant 2006, p. 23). The error and the intrinsic insufficiency of psychology does indeed come from its failure to maintain a distinction between the apperception and the inner sense. In turn, pragmatic anthropology will not discredit that which is given through inner experience, but will approach it with a new attitude: while from the point of view of (rational) psychology, "the mind, which is represented as a mere faculty of feeling and thinking, is regarded as a special substance dwelling in the human being," (pragmatic) anthropology, in turn, "abstract[s] from the question of whether the human being has a soul or not (as a special incorporeal substance)" (Kant 1907, AK. VII, p. 161; Kant 2006, p. 53). The *Gemüt* that the *Anthropology* deals with, just like the *Gemüt* of transcendental philosophy, does not belong to the domain of psychology, whether rational or empirical. Following this description, it is once again tempting to consider Kant's anthropology as a discipline that accomplishes a peculiar form of phenomenological reduction, by refusing to objectify the data of internal experience and by remaining equally distant from the metaphysical, rational psychology and from empirical psychology. This point provides us with a further justification of Kant's intention, expressed within the *Critique of Pure Reason*, of transforming empirical psychology into a "complete anthropology" (Kant 1904 (A 849/B 877), AK. III, p. 548; Kant 1998, p. 700). From psychology to anthropology, it is indeed necessary to redefine the object of inquiry by joining the outer man to the inner man and by articulating the first-person and the third-person approach.

If Kant insists upon the necessity of separating pure apperception from the empirical one with such vehemence, he does so in order to delimit transcendental philosophy (and logic, in particular) from psychology, the error of the psychological approach – that Husserl will later denounce under the name of psychologism – being, once again, that of confusing the inner sense as "psychological (applied) consciousness" with "pure, logical consciousness" (Kant 1907, AK. VII, p. 142; Kant 2006, p. 33). Yet even this necessary demarcation will not suffice to dissipate the difficulties of self-knowledge: as an important passage of Kant's *Anthropology* (§ 7) puts it,

> [...] knowledge of the human being through inner experience, because to a large extent one also judges others according to it, is more important than correct judgment of others, but nevertheless at the same time perhaps more difficult. For he who investigates his interior easily *carries* many things into self-consciousness instead of merely observing. (Kant 1907, AK. VII, p. 143; Kant 2006, p. 34)

In other words, even when it is limited in its pretensions and carefully distinguished from pure apperception, the inner sense is unable to fulfill the promise of a perfect self-knowledge. This is the reason why the consideration of the "inner man" has to be complemented by that of the "outer man," in order to refrain from the propensity "to accept the play of ideas of inner sense as experiential cognition, although it is only a fiction" (Kant 1907, AK. VII, p. 161; Kant 2006,

p. 54) – a fiction which carries the name of *Schwärmerei*. In this respect, the *Anthropology* gets even more categorical at the end of § 24, which deals precisely with the inner sense, and where Kant stresses that the "tendency to retire into oneself, together with the resulting illusions of inner sense, can only be set right when the human being is led back into the external world and by means of this to the order of things present to the outer senses" (Kant 1907, AK. VII, p. 162; Kant 2006, p. 54).[12] The conviction expressed in this quote can easily be contrasted with Husserl's espousal of Saint Augustine at the very end of his *Cartesian Meditations*: "*Noli foras ire, in te redi, in interiore hominis habitat veritas*" (*De vera religione*, 39, 72).[13] Therefore, one should not hastily believe that the analytic of *Gemüt* deployed in the *Anthropology* leaves aside the human being regarded as a citizen of the world or that it forgets its initial intention to provide a knowledge of the world (*Weltkenntnis*) by means of anthropology: quite the contrary, its specific approach accomplishes and justifies the transition from the "inner man" to the "outer man," a transition in which, as Foucault puts it in a curiously serious manner, "the secret of [subjective] Power reveals itself in the dazzle of the Phenomenon" (Foucault 2008a, pp. 44–45; Foucault 2008b, pp. 71–72), or where the transition from *Vermögen* to *Erscheinung* takes the shape of an adventure that both manifests and challenges the "I" as a "being-in-the-world."

Thus, it has progressively emerged that far from being inessential or redundant, anthropology is a vital and necessary extension with respect to critical philosophy. Indeed, Kant's 1798 *Anthropology* addresses a postcritical necessity, and proves that instead of venturing an anthropological prohibition, the *Critique* launches a call for an anthropology.[14] But is this not a point in respect to which Kant's and Husserl's paths are irredeemably meant to part, just as they did when the fate of psychology from the standpoint of transcendental philosophy was at stake?

---

12 See also "Reflection 284" (Kant 1913, AK. XV, p. 106).
13 It is significant that this quote from Augustine should also appear in a 1930 text where Husserl presents and defends his proposal of a "true, philosophically authentic anthropology [*die wahre, die philosophisch echte Anthropologie*]" (Husserl 2002, Hua XXXIV, p. 246).
14 In this respect, I agree with Alix Cohen, who speaks of "A Pragmatic Counterpart to the Transcendental Project" in *Kant and the Human Sciences. Biology, Anthropology and History*, and considers that the "pragmatic counterpart" "entails a crucial re-interpretation of the transcendental project itself" (Cohen 2009, pp. 143–145). Moreover, she also pays special attention to the idea of a transcendental anthropology (Cohen 2009, p. 183, note 1).

5 Transcendental Phenomenology and Anthropology

If the aim of the famous 1931 conference on "Phenomenology and Anthropology" consists mainly in distinguishing and separating the two, Husserl's research manuscripts from the same period thoroughly explore and elaborate what the conference had already designated as their "intrinsic affinity [*innere Affinität*]" (Husserl 1989, Hua XXVII, p. 181; Husserl 1997, p. 500). This suggests that instead of always excluding each other, transcendental phenomenology and anthropology are not necessarily condemned to collide or take different paths – insofar as they are, on the one hand, the science of the transcendental and, on the other, the science of the empirical. Furthermore, the link that can be established between the two is not only that of the transcendental-apriorical foundation of the empirical-factual, but equally one of the rooting of the transcendental within the concrete facticity of human subjectivity. As previously seen, if Kant had considered that "[e]verything that obtains its rule not on objective, but on subjective grounds [...] pertains to anthropology" (Kant 1913, AK. XV, p. 384), in Husserl's research manuscripts one can similarly read the following: "Transcendental philosophy is necessarily related to me and thus to a humanity, to my humanity" (Husserl 1993, Hua XXIX, p. 332).[15] But the remaining question is one of knowing what the nature of this mutual presupposition might be, and under which condition it might result not merely in a parallelism but rather in a "reciprocal envelopment," as Merleau-Ponty put it in his famous article on "The Philosopher and the Sociologist" (Merleau-Ponty 2001 [1960], p. 166; Merleau-Ponty 1964, p. 102),[16] and as the exergue of this study also suggests.

Yet, far from immediately embracing such a conciliatory perspective, Husserl spoke, in his 1931 public lecture, of "a fundamental decision between anthropologism and transcendentalism" (Husserl 1989, Hua XXVII, p. 165; Husserl 1997, p. 486), and firmly rejected the former as being quite the opposite of the phenomenological attitude. To some extent, this rejection reflects the profound disappointment that Husserl experienced while reading Heidegger's *Being and Time*. Indeed, his annotations show that he had fully measured the abyss separating the existential analytic from transcendental phenomenology:

---

[15] "Die Transzendentalphilosophie [...] notwendig auf mich und von mir aus auf eine, meine Menschheit bezogen [ist]." This passage comes from the important 1936 work manuscript entitled "The Anthropological World," edited by Reinhold N. Smid in the XXIXth volume of the *Husserliana*, which contains complements to the *Crisis of European Sciences*.
[16] See also Merleau-Ponty 2001, p. 95.

> Heidegger transposes or changes [*transponiert oder transversiert*] the constitutive-phenomenological clarification of all regions of entities and universals, of the total region of the world, into the anthropological; the whole problematic is shifted over [*die ganze Problematik ist Übertragung*]: corresponding to the ego there is *Dasein*, etc. In that way everything becomes ponderously unclear, and philosophically loses its value. (Husserl 1994b, p. 13; Husserl 1997, p. 284)

As can be observed here, in Husserl's view, Heidegger's existential problematic is a mere "anthropological transposition" of his own transcendental analysis. The careful separation between phenomenology and such anthropological inquiries,[17] which he subsequently effectuates, must then be understood as a reaction against such an *Übertragung*. One might consider, however, that Husserl only rejects a certain kind of philosophical anthropology: namely, one that entirely dissolves the transcendental into the empirical and, in doing so, fully "naturalizes" human subjectivity. Yet, one has to keep in mind that the 1930 *Nachwort* to the *Ideas...I* dismissed just as firmly the "transcendental anthropologism" (Husserl 1952, Hua V, p. 139), designating the fact of attributing a transcendental value and significance to the forms of *human* knowledge, which appeared to be quite a harmful avatar of psychologism. For this reason, as seen previously, such a transcendental anthropologism, which Husserl reckoned himself to have found in Kant, was held to be an error even more serious than the concession to empirical anthropology insofar as it threatened the objective and universal grounding of knowledge in general (and of science in particular). For Husserl, this is what ultimately justifies the necessity of a "fundamental decision between anthropologism and transcendentalism." If anthropologism appears as an omnipresent drift, embracing the path of transcendentalism requires a particular methodological turn:

> The reduction is the means of access to this new realm, so when one gets the meaning of the reduction wrong then everything else also goes wrong. The temptation to misunderstandings here is simply overwhelming. For instance, it seems all too obvious to say to oneself: "I, this human being, am the one who is practicing the method of a transcendental alteration of attitude whereby one withdraws back into the pure Ego; so can this Ego be anything other than just a mere abstract stratum of this concrete human being, its purely mental [*geistiges*] being, abstracted from the body?" But clearly those who talk this way have fallen back into the naive natural attitude. Their thinking is grounded in the pregiven

---

[17] Similarly, while reading and annotating the 37th paragraph of Heidegger's *Kantbuch*, which deals with "The Idea of a Philosophical Anthropology," Husserl had immediately recognized in it "the prejudgment of Scheler, Heidegger, Dilthey, and of the whole anthropological line of thought [*das Vorurteil von Scheler, Heidegger, Dilthey und der ganzen anthropologischen Richtung*]" (Husserl 1994b, p. 56; Husserl 1997, p. 455).

world rather than moving within the sphere of the epoché. For, to take oneself as a human being already presupposes an acceptance of validity of the world. What the epoché shows us clearly, however, is that the Ego is the one in whose life-process the apperception "human being," standing within the universal apperception "world," acquires and maintains its sense of being. (Husserl 1989, Hua XXVII, pp. 172–173; Husserl 1997, p. 493)

As one can plainly see here, for Husserl, anthropological reflection remains prisoner to the pregivenness of the world without being able to question it. For this reason, the anthropological problematic is intrinsically a mundane one: here, we discover the Kantian equivalence between *Menschenkenntnis* and *Weltkenntnis* (Kant 1907, AK. VII, p. 120; Kant 2006, p. 4),[18] albeit cast in a new light and in a new relationship with the transcendental problematic. For Husserl, indeed, the transition to the transcendental attitude simultaneously leaves behind the anthropological and the mundane plan: "When, by virtue of the transcendental reduction, I become aware of myself as this kind of Ego, I assume a position above all worldly being [*weltliches Sein*], above my own human being and human living" (Husserl 1989, Hua XXVII, p. 174; Husserl 1997, pp. 494–495). Consequently, anthropology seems to pertain to a level that the phenomenological attitude will necessarily overcome by going beyond the pregivenness of the world by virtue of the (ultimately) transcendental reduction.

And yet, this does not suffice to demonstrate the impossibility of a genuinely phenomenological anthropology, insofar as the task remains to "understand, on ultimate transcendental grounds, why [...] anthropology [...] is in fact not just a positive science along with the natural sciences, but rather has an intrinsic affinity with philosophy, with transcendental philosophy" (Husserl 1989, Hua XXVII, p. 181; Husserl 1997, p. 500).[19] Thus, in contrast with transcendental anthropologism, which is the plain negation of the epistemological ambitions of phenomenology, a legitimate phenomenological anthropology can be envisioned, and it could deserve to be called "transcendental" neither because of its neglecting, or denaturing the empirical, nor because of its naturalizing the transcendental, but insofar as it would aim mutually to reshape the transcendental in the light of the anthropological and the anthropological in the light of the transcendental. Thus, instead of a merely mechanical and diminishing "transposition" of the transcendental problematic, such a "transcendental anthropology" would pro-

---

18 *Cf.* also "Reflection 1482," Kant 1913, AK. XV, p. 659.
19 In this quote, it is first and foremost the proximity between psychology and transcendental philosophy that Husserl intends to emphasize. Nevertheless, the contemporary research manuscripts display a specific interest in the idea of a phenomenological anthropology: see, for instance, Husserl 1973, Hua XV, texts n° 29 and 30.

vide us with an anthropological *realization, continuation* or *fulfillment* of transcendental phenomenology.[20] And if the 1931 conference only mentions the "intrinsic affinity" that allows a reconciliation of phenomenology and anthropology, several research manuscripts from the 30s indicate the means to unveil and elaborate this affinity more explicitly.

6 More than an Oxymoron?

But even if it is not unwarranted to attribute to Husserl the project of a phenomenological anthropology grounded in transcendental philosophy – does this nonetheless give us the right to speak of a "transcendental anthropology?" This expression, already a *hapax* in the Kantian context, designates, in Husserl, a group of research manuscripts (E III)[21] and is not easy to find as such in the texts themselves (whereas a 1929 text belonging to the C-Manuscripts, for instance, plainly speaks of a "transcendental sociology" and importantly defines it with reference to "the community of human beings and its world [*Menschengemeinschaft und ihrer Welt*];" Husserl 2006, Hua Mat. VIII, p. 165).[22]

In order to give a certain consistency to this apparently oxymoronic expression, I will begin by examining the characterization of anthropology that can be found in the 1932 research manuscript edited by Iso Kern in volume XV of the *Husserliana* (text n° 30): "*Universale Geisteswissenschaft als Anthropologie.*" This unfinished and yet relatively developed text makes a claim that could appear quite surprising, should one forget the intimate solidarity that exists, in Husserl's view, between the human and that which pertains to the world: "anthropological knowledge *encompasses all world knowledge in general*" (Husserl 1973, Hua XV, p. 480). More precisely, the universality of anthropology is grounded in the fact that any science is the result of human activity, is a human configuration (*Gebilde*) (*cf.* Husserl 1973, Hua XV, p. 481): therefore, the science of the human has the status of a "science of science." It is noticeable that this kind of intrinsic reflexivity specific to the anthropological approach is not very different from the one that the author of the *Critiques* had in mind while speaking of an "*anthropologia transcendentalis*;" and even in the less controversial context of

---

[20] Arion L. Kelkel has similarly spoken of an "anthropological vocation of phenomenology" (Kelkel 1991). See also Marosán 2016, p. 152.
[21] *Cf.* Husserl 2014, Hua XLII, p. 531.
[22] In two other texts from 1930, Husserl also speaks of a "transcendental person" (Husserl 2002, Hua XXXIV, p. 201) and even of a "transcendental humanity [*transzendentales Menschentum*]" (Husserl 2002, Hua XXXIV, p. 153).

the famous 1773 Letter to Marcus Herz, quoted above, where Kant depicts the intention of his "Anthropology" lecture and stresses the fact that his "plan is quite unique," the epistemic implications are far from being absent: "I intend to use it to disclose the sources of all sciences [*die Quellen aller Wissenschaften*]" (Kant 1969, AK. X, p. 145; Kant 1999, p. 141).[23] Even more radically, in the eyes of Husserl, the particular epistemic status of anthropology implies that no science can be exterior to it, and from this point of view, the separation between human and natural sciences and the presumptuous epistemic privilege of natural sciences both deserve to be challenged:

> Is there a science of nature apart from the universal anthropology? An exact, descriptive science of nature [...]? The science of the human seems to be a particular science. The human being is *within* the world and does not contain the world – and yet, the science of the human, without going beyond the human being as such, encompasses all the sciences. (Husserl 1973, Hua XV, p. 481)

Here, the claim of the universality of anthropology is rooted in a particular vision of scientific activity for which the consideration of the subject of science is far more important than that of its object. But in fact, Husserl goes even further: by asserting the universality of anthropology, his ultimate intention is to emphasize and prepare the transition from a "naturalistic" to an "anthropological attitude" – the latter being, in fact, strikingly close to the transcendental attitude, given that its aim is to highlight the subjective accomplishment that underlies all scientific production. It is in this sense that Husserl suggestively writes:

> It is only when, in an anthropological universal approach, the human person becomes thematic, that the cognizing thematization and the whole operative dimension of the I [*alles fungierende Ichliche*] become thematic. [...] The human person is indeed present in every individual act and within every particular theme, [...] but it depends upon the new task of accomplishing a universal reduction. (Husserl 1973, Hua XV, pp. 482–483)

Here, it appears that the universality of anthropology can only be properly grasped from the standpoint of transcendental phenomenology, or by accomplishing what it would be quite tempting to call, by transposing Foucault's diagnosis onto a phenomenological context, an *anthropologico-transcendental repetition*. This is undoubtedly paradoxical: "We, who are human beings within the world, egological subjects [*Ichsubjekte*], we are those who experience the world and eventually gain a scientific knowledge of the world. Does this not mean that

---

[23] Quite inexplicably, the English translation chooses to limit the range of this statement to practical sciences.

the world in which we find ourselves as subordinate events is our configuration [*Gebilde*] and so that we are ourselves our own configuration? What a nonsense, what a paradox! How can it be solved as an apparent absurdity that nonetheless harbors some truth?" (Husserl 1973, Hua XV, p. 483). Indeed, what appears as nonsense here is only such from the perspective of the natural attitude. The absurdity is resolved by embracing the anthropological attitude, which therefore appears to be intimately close to the transcendental attitude: the key to comprehending the universality of anthropology comes from understanding that both the world and the knowledge of the world are relative to the "operating subjectivity [*fungierende Subjektivität*]" (Husserl 1973, Hua XV, p. 483) and that this relativity is a transcendental one.

7 Coincidence Without Identity?

And yet, even if Husserl's argumentation brings them significantly closer, the anthropological and the transcendental dimension of subjectivity do not fully coincide. Furthermore, their complete coincidence seems strictly impossible, should one want to preserve both the rigor of the transcendental attitude and the concreteness of the anthropological fact. This is undoubtedly the greatest difficulty that the project of a "transcendental anthropology" would have to face. The paradox is newly expressed in a 1933 manuscript: the phenomenological "I" is "the same as an I and as a human person," and "yet I am not the same" insofar as "the egological human life within the world is [...] my transcendental configuration [*Gebilde*]" (Husserl 1973, Hua XV, pp. 540–541). However, this does not simply imply that my being human should be erased behind the transcendental dimension of my life; rather, their entanglement is the condition of a new way of apprehending them both: a transcendental view of the human, on the one hand, and a concrete reshaping of transcendental subjectivity itself, on the other. By adopting this two-sided perspective, which should lead to the eventual acceptance that "the human I and the transcendental I must coincide [*sich decken*]" (Husserl 1973, Hua XV, p. 542), a renewed, phenomenological gaze upon subjectivity and humanity can be reached.[24]

From this standpoint, it becomes difficult to follow unconditionally Blumenberg when he reads Husserl in the exclusive light of an "anthropological prohibi-

---

[24] This is also suggested by the eloquent testimony of a letter to Georg Misch on the 3rd of August 1929: "I [...] understood phenomenology as a radical and universal 'humanistic science,' in a far more radical way than Dilthey did, due to the phenomenological reduction" (Husserl 1994a, Hua Dok. III/6, p. 277, quoted in Kisiel and Sheehan 2010, p. 397).

tion" and defines the latter as "the apotropaic action through which the position of the transcendental spectator is fortified."[25] Indeed, the breakthroughs of Husserl's late research show that transcendental phenomenology can neither ignore nor exclude that which pertains to the anthropological concreteness of the "I." As another famous 1933 work manuscript summarizes it, while analyzing the functioning of subjective life: "It all eventually depends on my facticity [*Faktizität*] and on the facticity of my world" (Husserl 1973, Hua XV, pp. 518–519). As we can see, Husserl does not hesitate to admit the priority or even the primacy of the anthropological fact with respect to the transcendental ego.

This also means that Husserl could on no account approve of Fink's conception of the transcendental spectator as requiring an *Entmenschung*, a de-humanization of the "I" (Fink 1988, Hua Dok. II/1, pp. 130 and 132; Fink 1995, pp. 118 and 120). Importantly, he will temper the claim of his disciple by stating, in turn, that "the phenomenological activity belongs [...] to every human soul as a possibility" (Fink 1988, Hua Dok. II/1, p. 189). But what, then, is the specific relationship that Husserl acknowledges between the transcendental and the anthropological, which traces his median path between Fink's insistence upon the dehumanization of the transcendental "I" and Heidegger's emphasis on the worldly inscription of subjectivity?[26] Several texts from the 30s conceive of the relationship between transcendental subjectivity and the human person as a necessary "self-objectification" (*Selbstobjektivation* or *Selbstobjektivierung*). The 54th paragraph of the *Crisis of European Sciences* is eloquent in this respect: "each human being 'bears within himself a transcendental I' [...] insofar as he is the self-objectification, as exhibited through phenomenological self-reflection, of the corresponding transcendental 'I'" (Husserl 1954, Hua VI, p. 190; Husserl 1970, p. 186). A research manuscript from 1931 expresses the same idea in monadological terminology:

> The self-objectification of the total transcendental subjectivity [*Allsubjektivität*], as it exists in a transcendental intertwining [*Ineinander*], is realized in every transcendental monad [...]. In every monad, the individual self-objectification is a transcendental self-veiling [*Selbstverhüllung*]. (Husserl 1973, Hua XV, p. 388)

How is this dynamic of self-objectification and self-veiling to be understood, insofar as it appears to be a remarkable expression of the entanglement between

---

[25] "*Das Anthropologieverbot ist dann die apotropäische Handlung, mit der die Position des transzendentalen Zuschauers verteidigt wird*" (Blumenberg 2006, p. 91).
[26] See Husserl 1962, Hua IX, p. 274, footnote 1: "*Gehört nicht eine Welt überhaupt zum Wesen des reinen ego?*," and the comments provided by John D. Scanlon (Scanlon 1972).

the transcendental and the anthropological? Suggestively, Husserl presents it as the tension between the finite and the infinite. The finite life of the human being is that in which "its transcendental being as a transcendental subjectivity remains veiled," that in which "the transcendental subjectivity lives under the veil of its humanity [*in seiner Menschlichkeit die transzendentale Subjektivität als verhüllte lebt*]." From this standpoint, "the human being is a finite being which has a constant consciousness of infinity [*Das menschliche Sein ist Sein in der Endlichkeit derart, dass es beständiges Sein im Bewusstsein der Unendlichkeit ist*]," insofar as the unveiling of its transcendental dimension is necessarily possible for it (Husserl 1973, Hua XV, p. 389). The finite life that the "I" leads as a human being is consequently a life that is most of the time hidden from itself, a life which is unaware of the infinite potentialities which are harbored within it. This limitation is one specific to the natural attitude, and Husserl will also speak of it in terms of "transcendental blindness [*Verblendung*]" when writing that "[w]orldliness is a transcendental blindness which, prior to the transcendental reduction [...], makes the transcendental necessarily inaccessible" (Husserl 1973, Hua XV, p. 389). Reading this statement, it becomes easier to comprehend what was meant in the 1931 conference by the assertion that, should the meaning of the reduction be misconstrued, everything would be misunderstood: without accomplishing the phenomenological reduction, the human being remains hidden to him- or herself and ignores the infinity that he or she contains as a transcendental being. Only through reduction can one become conscious of the fact that "the life of every transcendental I is the life of the finite within an infinity, a life which, so to speak, reflects itself into the veiling of human finitude and manifests itself into this very veiling" (Husserl 1973, Hua XV, p. 390). In other words, the human life is not simply that in which the transcendental is masked or veiled: it also manifests the transcendental; however, only the attitude deployed through the phenomenological reduction can make it fully apparent and explicit.

As has become clear by now, Husserl's phenomenology has not only not submitted itself to the "anthropological prohibition," but can also hardly be accused of an "anthropological indifference [*anthropologische Indifferenz*]" (Blumenberg 2006, p. 814). Rather, Husserl's steadfast and patent intention is to reconquer the anthropological issue without abandoning the transcendental phenomenological perspective. This program corresponds precisely to the fine median path that is equally distinct from the rejection of the anthropological and from transcendental anthropologism. Even if such a path clearly does not meet Blumenberg's expectations regarding a phenomenological anthropology (given that, for him, such an anthropology should "make evident the presuppositions of phenomenology as anthropological," Blumenberg 2006, p. 167), it might not, after all, be lacking in interest.[27] The intention of my analysis has been precisely to show that the hazardous path of a transcendental anthropology, differently and yet jointly considered by Kant and Husserl, is neither fully aporetic nor disappointingly poor.

Bibliography

Blumenberg, Hans (2006): *Beschreibung des Menschen*. Frankfurt am Main: Suhrkamp Verlag.
Brandt, Reinhard (1996): "Aux origines de la philosophie kantienne de l'histoire: l'anthropologie pragmatique". In: *Revue germanique internationale*, vol. 6, pp. 19–34.
Brandt, Reinhard (1999): *Kritischer Kommentar zu Kants Anthropologie in pragmatischer Hinsicht*. Hamburg: Felix Meiner Verlag.
Cohen, Alix (2009): *Kant and the Human Sciences. Biology, Anthropology and History*. New York: Palgrave Macmillan.
Fink, Eugen (1988): *VI. Cartesianische Meditation. Teil I: Die Idee einer transzendentalen Methodenlehre*, Husserliana Dokumente II/1. Ed. Hans Ebeling, Jann Holl and Guy van Kerchoven. Dordrecht: Kluwer Academic Publishers.
Fink, Eugen (1995): *Sixth Cartesian Meditation: The Idea of a Transcendental Theory of Method*. Trans. Ronald Bruzina. Bloomington & Indianapolis: Indiana University Press.
Foucault, Michel (2008): "Introduction à l'*Anthropologie*". In I. Kant: *Anthropologie du point de vue pragmatique*. Paris: Vrin, pp. 11–79.
Foucault, Michel (2008): *Introduction to Kant's Anthropology*. Trans. Robert Nigro and Kate Briggs. Los Angeles: Semiotext(e).
Husserl, Edmund (1952): *Ideen zu einer reinen Phänomenologie und phänomenologischen Philosophie. Third Book: Die Phänomenologie und die Fundamente der Wissenschaften*. *Husserliana*, vol. V. Ed. Marly Biemel. The Hague: Martinus Nijhoff.
Husserl, Edmund (1954): *Die Krisis der europäischen Wissenschaften und die transzendentale Phänomenologie. Eine Einleitung in die phänomenologische Philosophie*. *Husserliana*, vol. VI. Ed. Walter Biemel. The Hague: Martinus Nijhoff.
Husserl, Edmund (1956): *Erste Philosophie (1923–1924)*, first part: *Kritische Ideengeschichte*. *Husserliana*, vol. VII. Ed. Rudolf Boehm. The Hague: Martinus Nijhoff.
Husserl, Edmund (1962): *Phänomenologische Psychologie. Vorlesungen Sommersemester 1925*. *Husserliana*, vol. IX. Ed. Walter Biemel. The Hague: Martinus Nijhoff.
Husserl, Edmund (1970): *The Crisis of European Sciences and Transcendental Phenomenology*. Trans. David Carr. Evanston: Northwestern University Press.
Husserl, Edmund (1973): *Zur Phänomenologie der Intersubjektivität. Texte aus dem Nachlass. Dritter Teil: 1929–1935*. *Husserliana*, vol. XV. Ed. Iso Kern. The Hague: Martinus Nijhoff.

---

[27] It is this path that Merleau-Ponty himself follows when, in his 1951–52 lecture on "Human Sciences and Phenomenology," he assigns to his research the task of "reflecting upon this *transcendental human being*" (Merleau-Ponty 2001, p. 47).

Husserl, Edmund (1976): *Ideen zu einer reinen Phänomenologie und phänomenologischen Philosophie*. First Book: *Allgemeine Einführung in die Phänomenologie*. Husserliana, vol. III/1. Ed. Karl Schuhmann. The Hague: Martinus Nijhoff.
Husserl, Edmund (1977): *Phenomenological Psychology. Lectures, Summer Semester, 1925*. Trans. John Scanlon. The Hague: Martinus Nijhoff.
Husserl, Edmund (1983): *Ideas Pertaining to a Pure Phenomenology and to a Phenomenological Philosophy*. First Book: *General Introduction to a Pure Phenomenology*. Trans. Fred Kersten. The Hague: Martinus Nijhoff.
Husserl, Edmund (1989): "Phänomenologie und Anthropologie". In: *Aufsätze und Vorträge (1922–1937)*. Husserliana, vol. XXVII. Ed. Thomas Nenon and Hans Rainer Sepp. Dordrecht/Boston/London: Kluwer Academic Publishers.
Husserl, Edmund (1993): *Die Krisis der europäischen Wissenschaften und die transzendentale Phänomenologie. Ergänzungsband: Texte aus dem Nachlass (1934–1937)*. Husserliana, vol. XXIX. Ed. Reinhold N. Smid. Dordrecht/Boston/London: Kluwer Academic Publishers.
Husserl, Edmund (1994a): *Briefwechsel: Philosophenbriefe*. Husserliana Dokumente, vol. III/6. Ed. Karl Schuhmann. Dordrecht/Boston/London: Kluwer Academic Publishers.
Husserl, Edmund (1994b): "Randbemerkungen Husserls zu Heideggers *Sein und Zeit* und *Kant und das Problem der Metaphysik*". Ed. Roland Breeur. In: *Husserl Studies* vol. 11 (1–2), pp. 3–63.
Husserl, Edmund (1997): *Psychological and Transcendental Phenomenology and Confrontation with Heidegger (1927–1931)*. Trans. Thomas Sheehan and Richard E. Palmer. Dordrecht/Boston/London: Kluwer Academic Publishers.
Husserl, Edmund (2002): *Zur phänomenologischen Reduktion. Texte aus dem Nachlass (1926–1935)*. Husserliana, vol. XXXIV. Ed. Sebastian Luft. Dordrecht/Boston/London: Kluwer Academic Publishers.
Husserl, Edmund (2006): *Späte Texte über Zeitkonstitution (1929–1934). Die C-Manuskripte*. Husserliana Materialien, vol. VIII. Ed. Dieter Lohmar. Dordrecht/Heidelberg/London: Springer.
Husserl, Edmund (2014): *Grenzprobleme der Phänomenologie: Analysen des Unbewusstseins und der Instinkte, Metaphysik, späte Ethik: Texte aus dem Nachlass (1908–1937)*. Husserliana, vol. XLII. Ed. Rochus Sowa and Thomas Vongehr. Dordrecht/Heidelberg/London: Springer.
Kant, Immanuel (1903): *Kritik der reinen Vernunft* (1. Auflage). *Prolegomena. Grundlegung zur Metaphysik der Sitten. Metaphysische Anfangsgründe der Naturwissenschaft*. Kants Gesammelte Schriften, vol. IV. Ed. the Royal Prussian Academy of Sciences. Berlin: G. Reimer.
Kant, Immanuel (1904): *Kritik der reinen Vernunft* (2e Auflage). Kants Gesammelte Schriften, vol. III. Ed. the Royal Prussian Academy of Sciences. Berlin: G. Reimer.
Kant, Immanuel (1907): *Der Streit der Fakultäten; Anthropologie in pragmatischer Hinsicht*. Kants Gesammelte Schriften, vol. VII. Ed. the Royal Prussian Academy of Sciences. Berlin: G. Reimer.
Kant, Immanuel (1913): *Anthropologie*. Kants Gesammelte Schriften, vol. XV. Ed. the Royal Prussian Academy of Sciences. Berlin: G. Reimer.
Kant, Immanuel (1969): *Briefwechsel*. Kants Gesammelte Schriften, vol. X. Ed. the Royal Prussian Academy of Sciences. Berlin/Leipzig: Walter de Gruyter.

Kant, Immanuel (1998): *Critique of Pure Reason*. Trans. Paul Guyer and Allen W. Wood. Cambridge: Cambridge University Press.
Kant, Immanuel (1999): *Correspondence*. Trans. Arnulf Zweig. Cambridge: Cambridge University Press.
Kant, Immanuel (2004): *Metaphysical Foundations of Natural Science*. Trans. Michael Friedman. Cambridge: Cambridge University Press.
Kant, Immanuel (2006): *Anthropology from a Pragmatic Point of View*. Trans. Robert Louden. Cambridge: Cambridge University Press.
Kelkel, Arion L. (1991): "Husserl and the Anthropological Vocation of Phenomenology". In: *Analecta Husserliana*, vol. 34–35, pp. 35–55.
Kisiel, Theodore/Sheehan, Thomas (Eds.) (2010): *Becoming Heidegger: On the Trail of His Early Occasional Writings, 1910–1927*. Seattle: Noesis Press.
Louden, Robert (2000): *Kant's Impure Ethics. From Rational Beings to Human Beings*. Oxford: Oxford University Press.
Marosán, Bence Péter (2016): "Transzendentale Anthropologie. Sinnbildung, Persönliches Ich und Selbstidentität bei Edmund Husserl und ihre Rezeption in László Tengelyis Phänomenologischer Metaphysik". In: *Horizon. Studies in Phenomenology*, vol. 5, n° 1, pp. 150–170.
Merleau-Ponty, Maurice (2001) [1960]: *Signes*. Paris: Gallimard.
Merleau-Ponty, Maurice (1964): *Signs*. Trans. Richard C. McCleary. Evanston: Northwestern University Press.
Merleau-Ponty, Maurice (2001): *Parcours deux: 1951–1961*. Lagrasse: Verdier.
Renaut, Alain (1993): "Présentation". In: I. Kant: *Anthropologie du point de vue pragmatique*. Paris: Garnier-Flammarion.
Renaut, Alain (1997): "La place de l'anthropologie dans la théorie kantienne du sujet". In: *L'année 1798. Kant sur l'anthropologie*. Ed. Jean Ferrari. Paris: Vrin, pp. 49–63.
Scanlon, John D. (1972): "The Epoché and Phenomenological Anthropology". In: *Research in Phenomenology*, vol. 2, n° 1, pp. 95–109.
Schmidt, Claudia M. (2007): "Kant's Transcendental, Empirical, Pragmatic, and Moral Anthropology". In: *Kant-Studien*, vol. 98, n° 2, pp. 156–182.
Vandewalle, Bernard (1997): "Actualité de l'anthropologie kantienne". In: *L'année 1798. Kant sur l'anthropologie*. Ed. Jean Ferrari. Paris: Vrin, pp. 184–185.
Wilson, Holly L. (2006): *Kant's Pragmatic Anthropology. Its Origin, Meaning, and Critical Significance*. Albany: State University of New York Press.

Section II: The Ego and the Sphere of Otherness

Inga Römer
Transcendental Apperception and Temporalization

Husserl on Kant

Abstract: The chapter analyzes Husserl's interpretation and appropriation of Kant's idea of transcendental apperception. The first part sketches three famous reinterpretations of the transcendental deduction and transcendental apperception by Hegel, Cohen, and Heidegger. The second part considers Husserl's reception of the transcendental deduction in general. And the third part is specifically dedicated to his interpretation of transcendental apperception. I will defend the thesis that the most fundamental layer of time-constitution can be understood as Husserl's final answer to the problem of a phenomenological transcendental apperception. On this interpretation, temporalization, characterized by anonymity and drive-intentionality, is the 'highest' or rather the 'lowest point' of transcendental phenomenology. Temporalization, however, has a sense very different from that proposed by Heidegger.

Husserl understands his phenomenology as an "attempt […] to realize the deepest sense of Kantian philosophizing" (Husserl 1956, Hua VII, p. 287 (1924)). The phenomenological transformation of the transcendental deduction has a central place in this project. The present study will focus on a specific aspect of this project and inquire into the role Husserl assigns to transcendental apperception or, more precisely, the phenomenological transformation of transcendental apperception. Transcendental apperception is a notion that Kant introduces in the first version of the transcendental deduction of the categories. In the second version of the transcendental deduction, this notion undergoes a reformulation and is termed the "original-synthetic unity of apperception" (Kant 1787, B 131) and referred to as the "highest point" (Kant 1787, B 134) of transcendental philosophy. The notion of transcendental apperception has been decisive for several reinterpretations, or rather transformations, of Kant's philosophy. And even though Husserl interprets the Kantian texts in much less detail than other thinkers, he seems to discover, over the course of his investigations, that transcendental apperception, properly understood, has a central role in a phenomenological version of a transcendental deduction.

The hypothesis of the present study is that the most fundamental layer of time-constitution can be understood as Husserl's final answer to the problem of a phenomenological transcendental apperception. Temporalization is thus the 'highest' or rather the 'lowest point' of transcendental phenomenology. Temporalization in the Husserlian context, however, has a sense very different from Heidegger's use of this term. The following interpretation is indebted to classic studies by Iso Kern (1964), Klaus Held (1966), and Eduard Marbach (1974), which remain indispensable for the questions discussed. Marbach examined Husserl's appropriation of Kant's transcendental apperception in detail with respect to the phenomenological problem of the I, but he did not focus on the problem of time-constitution in particular. Kern identified the importance of the C-manuscripts on time-consciousness for the deepest layer of a phenomenological transcendental apperception, but he did not himself develop a detailed interpretation of this point. Held analyzed the late manuscripts on time-consciousness using the I as his guideline, but he did not focus on the relation of this problematic to Kant's transcendental apperception in particular.

The first part of the present study presents an overview of three famous reinterpretations of the transcendental deduction and transcendental apperception, namely those found in the work of Hegel, Cohen, and Heidegger. The second part considers Husserl's reception of the transcendental deduction in general. The third part is specifically dedicated to Husserl's interpretation of transcendental apperception. This third part does not present an interpretation of Kant's own argument; the latter is, rather, discussed only insofar as it is relevant to Husserl's appropriation of it.[1]

1 Hegel, Cohen and Heidegger on Transcendental Deduction and Transcendental Apperception

Some of the most important receptions of Kant's transcendental deduction can be found in the works of Georg Wilhelm Friedrich Hegel, Hermann Cohen, and Martin Heidegger. All three can be situated within a movement that started when Kant was still alive. This movement began with Reinhold, continued with Fichte, Schelling, and Hegel, and was then renewed by Cohen and Heidegger. The common idea shared by these very different thinkers was this: even if Kant's thinking contained a major key to the future of philosophy, Kant himself had remained satisfied with a dualism between intuition and concept, between

---

[1] For a recent instance of such an interpretation of Kant's argumentation itself, see Allison 2015.

sensibility and understanding. He had thus failed to identify a first principle or root starting from which all the elements of his new transcendental philosophy could be developed. Nevertheless, they believed that Kant had given some important hints concerning such a principle, the most important of which are to be found in the two versions of the transcendental deduction and in the schematism of pure understanding.

In *Faith and Knowledge* from 1802, Hegel both critiques and praises Kant. On the one hand, he objects to the "shallowness of the deduction of the categories" (Hegel 1986, p. 304; Hegel 1977, p. 69). In Hegel's eyes, Kant's starting point for this deduction, namely, the table of judgments, is erroneous. But in spite of this "shallowness," Hegel detects an essential insight within the "original synthetic unity of apperception" insofar as Kant could have understood this transcendental unity as the "principle of intuition and of understanding" (Hegel 1986, pp. 304–305; Hegel 1977, pp. 69–70, translation modified). Over the course of his argument, however, it becomes clear that Hegel actually believes that the productive imagination is this original principle and that he thinks that "this productive imagination is only called understanding" (Hegel 1986, p. 308; Hegel 1977 p. 73, translation modified) insofar as the understanding determines certain forms of the imagination in concepts.

In the first edition of his *Kant's Theory of Experience* in 1871, Cohen already emphasizes the following phrase from the *Critique of Pure Reason:* "And thus the synthetic unity of apperception is the highest point to which one must affix all use of the understanding, even the whole of logic and, after it, transcendental philosophy; indeed this faculty is the understanding itself" (Kant 1787, B 134; see Cohen 1871, p. 140). Cohen understands this "highly important phrase" (Cohen 1871, p. 140) as an indication that Kant ultimately took the synthetic unity of apperception to be the single highest principle of transcendental philosophy as such. This principle is, for Cohen, the understanding. However, the understanding is ultimately the form of pure synthesis and not a human faculty (see Cohen 1871, p. 141).

In a lecture course from 1927–28 dedicated to a phenomenological interpretation of Kant's first *Critique*, Heidegger proposes a specific reading of the A-deduction. He deliberately transforms Kant's argument in such a way that the productive imagination is regarded as the root of all three Kantian syntheses and emerges as the common "root" of "pure intuition" and "pure thinking" (Heidegger 1995, GA 25, p. 417; Heidegger 1997, p. 283). These three syntheses are themselves interpreted with respect to the three ecstases of Heidegger's own conception of temporality: Apprehension is situated within the ecstasis of the present, reproduction is related to the ecstasis of the past, and recognition is reinterpreted as "precognition" (Heidegger 1995, GA 25, pp. 359–368; Heidegger

1997, pp. 243–249), i.e., as the ecstasis of the future. Kant's notion of transcendental apperception is problematic on Heidegger's reading because of "the lack of connection between time and the transcendental apperception" (Heidegger 1995, GA 25, p. 358; Heidegger 1997, p. 242).

While Cohen lauds transcendental apperception as the highest point of a transcendental philosophy that has the understanding as the form of synthesis, Heidegger rejects transcendental apperception because of its atemporality. Heidegger does so in favor of productive imagination, which is itself interpreted as temporality. In a sense, Hegel can be said to be situated between these two positions. He praises transcendental apperception because of its – as he sees it – secret status as a first principle, but he shifts its meaning into the domain of the productive imagination and considers the understanding to be only a derivative element.

2 Husserl on Kant's Transcendental Deduction

The first part of the lecture course on *First Philosophy* from 1923–24, as well as the manuscripts preceding this course from the years 1903 to 1924 (included as annexes in *Husserliana* VII), are an essential source for Husserl's understanding of Kant's transcendental deduction. A further important text for this issue is the lecture course *Nature and Spirit* from 1927. I will use these sources in order to point out some of the most essential aspects of Husserl's perspective on Kant's transcendental deduction in general.

Husserl tends to read Kant's whole argument in the spirit of Neo-Kantianism in that the Transcendental Aesthetic and Analytic up to the Principles (*Grundsätze*) of the pure understanding are seen as an argument by deduction. "Kant himself requires and carries out 'deductions', the deductions he calls metaphysical and transcendental, deductions of the forms of intuitions, of the categories; he also deduces the schematism, the necessary validity of the propositions of pure understanding etc." (Husserl 1956, Hua VII, p. 197). While Kant himself does not speak of a deduction of the schematism or of the principles, this reading takes the whole positive part of the *Critique of Pure Reason* to be one unified argument by deduction (see also Husserl 2001, Hua XXXII, p. 87).

In a move that is also in accord with Neo-Kantian interpretations, Husserl criticizes what he regards as Kant's tendency towards psychologism and anthropologism in the first *Critique*. Kant was on the right path when he analyzed objectivity in relation to subjectivity, but his analyses of pure subjectivity remain in an "enigmatic milieu" insofar as Kant makes use of "transcendental capacities that remain mythical" (Husserl 1956, Hua VII, p. 198). The subject is the human subject with its "psychical faculties" and the "*a priori* character of law, by which transcendental subjectivity [...] shapes objectivity, ultimately only has the signification of a universal anthropological fact" (Husserl 1956, Hua VII, p. 401 (1915), p. 199). This leads, in Husserl's eyes, to a situation where Kant's "turn to relativism and anthropologism" is "just as skeptical" as Hume's philosophy, or even "to an even greater extent" (Husserl 1956, Hua VII, p. 354 (1903)). Kant's deductions have, according to Husserl, an anthropological and thus ultimately a skeptical character that needs to be overcome in a rigorously scientific transcendental philosophy.

Furthermore, Husserl believes that Kant's transcendental philosophy also has a "natural-scientific prejudice" that needs to be "overcome" (Husserl 1956, Hua VII, p. 282 (1924)). Kant "does not see that transcendental philosophy cannot be narrowed down in the way he believed it could and he does not see that a radically clear, that is, a radically scientific implementation of such a philosophy is only possible when the concrete full life of consciousness and its constituting activity is studied in detail in all its correlative sides and in a completely differentiated manner – and that in the realm of a unified, concrete intuitive transcendental subjectivity" (Husserl 1956, Hua VII, p. 281 (1924)). An overcoming of Kant's 'natural scientific prejudice' would not only lead to an exploration of the correlation between subject and object beneath the higher-level realm of the natural sciences, but it would also be able to "include the humanities in the transcendental consideration" (Husserl 1956, Hua VII, p. 282 (1924)). Thus the realm of transcendental philosophy needs to be deepened and enlarged.

One central objection to Kant is that he "does not see the required method for a true transcendental science" (Husserl 1956, Hua VII, p. 197). The "solution" of "transcendental problems" requires "that all that is transcendent to consciousness is bracketed in radical resoluteness, that the study is set on the ground of pure consciousness" (Husserl 1956, Hua VII, pp. 400*sq*. (1915)). Kant's major fault was that he did not discover the necessity of the ἐποχή and the method of phenomenological reduction. Instead, he introduces "his fundamental problem with respect to the cognizing human being" (Husserl 1956, Hua VII, p. 401 (1915)). Kant's 'anthropology' needs to be overcome by phenomenological reduction.

However, Husserl praises Kant for the fact that he "saw eidetic structures" in the "subjectivity" he analyzed "with an unprecedented intuitive force" (Husserl 1956, Hua VII, p. 197). "Kant seeks in subjectivity or respectively the correlation between subjectivity and objectivity the ultimate determination of the sense of objectivity that is cognized by cognition [*die durch Erkenntnis erkannt wird*]. In this respect, we agree with Kant, but we determine and had to determine 'subjectivity' as phenomenological subjectivity" (Husserl 1956, Hua VII, p. 386

(1908)). Even if Husserl objects that Kant's deduction "is a constructive procedure of thinking, which is then followed by intuition, and not a bottom-up procedure" (Husserl 1956, Hua VII, p. 197) which starts with intuition, he believes that Kant has taken several important steps in the analysis of subjectivity. Husserl thus privileges the transcendental deduction of the first edition (see Husserl 1956, Hua VII, p. 387 (1908) and p. 288 (1924)), not only because it proceeds 'from bottom to top,' but also because it ascribes greater importance to the analysis of the acts of subjectivity. He praises the "first deep insights into the *a priori* of the sense-bestowing life of consciousness and the connections between the bestowing of sense and sense itself [*Zusammenhänge von Sinngebung und Sinn selbst*]" that Kant had undertaken "under the title 'subjective deduction' (in the first edition of the *Critique of Pure Reason*)" (Husserl 1956, Hua VII, p. 281 (1924)). While Kant states that the problem of a subjective deduction is less important than that of an objective deduction (see Kant 1781, A XVI*sq.*), Husserl emphasizes the importance of the subjective deduction, because its task is to study "the unified, concrete intuitive transcendental subjectivity" (Husserl 1956, Hua VII, p. 281 (1924)). Like Heidegger, Husserl privileges the A-deduction, even though they certainly cannot be said to reach the same conclusions.

In 1908, Husserl had already situated his own phenomenology in relation to a positive assessment of Kant's project of a deduction. By avoiding all the Kantian problems listed above and employing the proper method of the phenomenological reduction, Husserl aims at a phenomenological reformulation of a transcendental deduction in the broad sense discussed in our first point. The correlation between subjectivity and objectivity needs to be analyzed within the phenomenological reduction so as to show how subjectivity and its correlative objectivity develop in a process of constitution that truly proceeds from the bottom to the top: "The valuable thought that pervades in the demand of a deduction of the categories and specifically in their introduction seems to be" a concentration on "the pure correlation of objectivity and knowledge" (Husserl 1956, Hua VII, p. 387 (1908)). The idea of a transcendental deduction, properly understood, is thus a phenomenological study of the essence of the correlation between subjectivity and objectivity. However, for Husserl such a phenomenological transformation of the transcendental deduction goes hand in hand with an *overcoming of Kant's dualism* between sensibility and understanding. If Kant had seen the true – that is to say, the phenomenological – task of a transcendental deduction, he "would have had to teach that space and time are products of a synthesis of a lower level and that the synthesis of objectifying understanding is only a higher one" (Husserl 1956, Hua VII, p. 405 (1915)). A phenomenological deduction thus needs to study the "layers [*Stufen*] of synthesis" without reproducing the Kantian "theories," which "are undoubtedly wrong" (Husserl 1956, Hua VII, p. 405 (1915)).

In the lecture course *Nature and Spirit* (1927), Husserl provides an even more positive assessment of Kant's transcendental deduction. He now sees Kant himself as more of an ally than the Neo-Kantian Heinrich Rickert. Husserl claims that Rickert's version of a deduction contains "[f]ormal constructions" that are "very dangerous" (Husserl 2001, Hua XXXII, p. 90). In contrast to Rickert, Kant's own "transcendental deductions" are "truly epistemological" insofar as "they are situated in the realm of a concrete, even though universal, consideration of our experience and our world of experience as well as our sciences of this world of experience [...]. Here, Kant asks his questions and conceives his deductions while always remaining within the realm of a concrete intuition of the whole" (Husserl 2001, Hua XXXII, pp. 96*sq.*). In contrast to Rickert, Kant now appears as the philosopher who proceeded in a more 'bottom-up' fashion, as a philosopher who does not fall prey to a natural-scientific prejudice and its unjustified abstractions, and as someone who considered experience in a more encompassing sense than his Neo-Kantian successor: "Kant as a philosopher [...] oversaw the typically universal of this life, asks the proper questions with respect to a deeper, but still concrete, understanding of the sense and possibility of such activities [*Leistungen*] and the validity of goals and universal normative ideals to be set" (Husserl 2001, Hua XXXII, p. 99). It was "first Kant" who cleared the "ways" to "deduce" properly "the radical norms and forms of a possible science of the world and an existing world as its correlate." If Husserl still does not follow an entirely Kantian path, it is "because he [Kant] did not go far enough in exploring the world in a concrete-intuitive way, the world in correlation with the subjectivity who cognizes and lives in the world" (Husserl 2001, Hua XXXII, p. 102). Moreover, Husserl now believes that Kant, in contrast to his Neo-Kantian successors, had not only already gone a long way towards concreteness and intuitiveness, but he also thinks that Kant had already worked more or less within the realm of the phenomenological reduction, even if he had not yet developed this method explicitly: "Kant takes his starting point from a fact of universal experience and science of experience [...], [b]ut insofar as he asks for the possibility in principle and the sense of this fact [...], the fact loses the character of a standing presupposition and unquestioned validity; making comprehensible its possibility in principle leads to its 'bracketing'" (Husserl 2001, Hua XXXII, p. 98).[2]

---

[2] Already in 1924, Husserl writes: "Kant's thinking and researching moves *de facto* within the realm of the phenomenological attitude" (Husserl 1956, Hua VII, p. 236).

Husserl thinks that Kant's questioning concerning the conditions of possibility of experience is an implicit phenomenological reduction.

The essential idea in Husserl's interpretation of the task of transcendental deduction can be summarized as follows: Husserl sets himself the positive task of developing a phenomenological version of a transcendental deduction in the broad sense. This deduction will operate within the phenomenological reduction and analyze the correlation between transcendental subjectivity and transcendental objectivity from its most fundamental to its most complex layers. On the one hand, Husserl criticizes Kant's 'top to bottom' procedure, his natural scientific prejudice, his 'theories' of a fundamental separation between sensibility and understanding, and ultimately his anthropological interpretation of the mind's structures (which latter, Husserl claims, results in relativism and skepticism). On the other hand, Husserl holds the project of a transcendental deduction as such in high regard and he increasingly sees Kant as a predecessor of his own transcendental phenomenology. This is because, on his interpretation, Kant implicitly works within the phenomenological reduction, because he provides rich analyses of the experience underlying the scientific attitude, because Kant was largely guided by intuitiveness, and finally because Kant carried out essential analyses of subjectivity in the A-deduction.

3 Husserl on Kant's Transcendental Apperception

In 1924 Husserl is still formulating strong critical objections to Kant's transcendental apperception. He enumerates several "'metaphysical', in the bad sense of the word, components of the critique of reason," among which figures "the mythology of the transcendental apperception" (Husserl 1956, Hua VII, p. 235). However, Husserl finally aims to carry out a phenomenological reformulation, in an affirmative sense, of this central element of the Kantian transcendental deduction. What such a reformulation entails becomes particularly clear in passages from manuscript A VI 30, most likely written in 1926.[3] The present section will, on the basis of this manuscript, first elucidate what Husserl understood as a phenomenological transcendental apperception. In a second step, I will follow this

---

[3] The importance of this manuscript for the problem of a phenomenological transcendental apperception was discovered by Iso Kern. See Kern 1964, § 26. Since the manuscript is unpublished, I will not only give a translation, but will also cite the German original. I thank Dieter Lohmar from the Husserl Archive in Cologne for having given me access to this manuscript, Thomas Vongehr for having checked the quotes, and Julia Jansen from the Husserl Archive in Leuven for the permission to quote from it.

idea to its deepest phenomenological layers, i.e., into time-consciousness as it is discussed in the C-manuscripts.

In manuscript A VI 30, Husserl speaks of the "problem" of "the true sense of the transcendental apperception and a 'transcendental deduction' belonging to it."[4] He neither gives an interpretation of the letter of the Kantian text nor does he even explicitly summarize what he holds to be the central idea of Kant's transcendental apperception. But his central point of reference seems to be the reciprocity between the I and the object in Kant. The synthesizing activity of the 'I think' is, for Kant, the condition for the object; and it is only by this synthesizing activity, which provides the conditions for objectivity, that the identity of the I can itself be represented – without the I, no identical object; without the identical object, no identical I (see especially Kant 1787, B 133). Husserl's central question concerning "the true sense of the transcendental apperception" is how this mutual conditioning of identity can be understood in a phenomenological sense. This mutual conditioning cannot be understood in the way it is understood in Kant, where the formal 'I think' synthesizes and brings about objects on the basis of categories which are themselves established by way of the table of judgments. How can one account phenomenologically for the reciprocal constitution of the unity of the I and the unity of its objective correlate?

Husserl indirectly criticizes Kant by directly criticizing himself for excessive formalism in his having previously taken the I to be a mere pole: "I is not merely identical I-pole," "I-pole is not I."[5] The "source point of the 'I of the transcendental apperception'" is rather a concordance [Einstimmigkeit] with itself in its own judgments.[6] A "standing and persisting I" (a formulation directly taken from the A-deduction, even though not presented as a quote)[7] is constituted by "a constant rule [...], through which I am directed, under the title world of experience, towards an ideal unity of conviction, in which all single convictions would come to a unity of concordance [Zusammenstimmung]."[8] The unity of the I is constituted by a constant rule of world-constitution, and the world and its objects are constituted in their objectivity by this same constant rule. By experiencing

---

4 "[...] das eigentliche Problem [...] des echten Sinnes der transzendentalen Apperzeption und einer zugehörigen 'transzendentalen Deduktion'" (A VI 30, 37a).
5 "Aber das Ich ist nicht bloß identischer Ich-Pol" (A VI 30, 36b). "Ichpol ist nicht Ich" (A VI 30, 54b).
6 "Quellpunkt des 'Ich der transzendentalen Apperzeption'" (A VI 30, 44a). This idea of a unity of the I through concordance with itself in its judgments is actually already present in the summary of Kant's position Husserl gives in 1915. See Husserl 1954, Hua VII, p. 398.
7 "stehendes und bleibendes Ich" (A VI 30, 38b). See Kant 1781, A 123, translation modified.
8 "eine feste Regel" (A VI 30, 38b).

what is given, the I acquires a habitus which has the persisting object and world as its correlate. The acquisition of such a habitus, constantly nourished by the given, goes hand in hand with the acquisition of "new capacities [*Vermögen*]."[9] These capacities are not anthropological facts, as Husserl interprets them as being in Kant, but capacities constituted within the phenomenological reduction which imply a genuine flexibility and openness. The unity of the I has as its correlate the objects which have "persisting being, [...] the objects being posed [*Gesetztheiten*] as such have persisting validity for the subject."[10] The unity of the objective correlates depends on the persisting convictions of the I, and the unity of the I depends on the persisting convictions about these objective correlates.

But if the unity of the I depends on such a concordance of judgments and convictions, the question of the limits of such a concordance is essential. Husserl must thus deal with a phenomenological analogy to the chaos hypothesis Kant formulates in § 13 as an objection that the deduction needs to overcome. According to Kant, "appearances could after all be so constituted that the understanding would not find them in accord with the conditions of its unity, and everything would lie in such confusion that, e. g. in the succession of appearances nothing would offer itself that would furnish a rule of synthesis and thus correspond to the concept of cause and effect" (Kant 1781/1787, A 90/B 123). For Husserl, the threat lies in a 'thing' that would "change its determinations without any law" and a subject that would not have anything more than a "chaos of opinions."[11] Husserl considers the idea of chaos and wonders whether there could be an I that exists "without world [*weltlos*]" but with a "unity of my life [...] in the unity of immanent time."[12] But he tends towards the idea that, at the least, a "relative consistency"[13] is needed in order to speak of the unity of an I and of its objective world. A relative consistency is distinguished from a "pure consistency"[14] by the fact that relative consistency is given when the I corrects some of its judgments and convictions and integrates this history of revision into its

---

[9] See A VI 30, 40a: "*jede Habe ist zugleich Index für neue Vermögen des Subjekts und neue Wesensbestimmungen desselben als Subjekts.*"
[10] "*bleibendes Sein,* [...] *Gesetztheiten als solche haben für das Subjekt bleibende Geltung*" (A VI 30, 45b).
[11] "*Wechselte ein Ding gesetzlos seine Bestimmungen...*" A VI 30, 38a. "*Durcheinander von Meinungen,*" A VI 30, 54a.
[12] "*weltlos;*" "*Einheit meines Lebens* [...] *in der Einheit der immanenten Zeit.*" A VI 30, 52b.
[13] "*relative Konsequenz,*" A VI 30, 46a.
[14] "*Idee des Ich der puren Konsequenz,*" A VI 30, 45a.

system of concordance. Pure consistency, however, would mean that all its convictions are absolutely stable, which is "an idea lying in the infinite."[15]

These manuscript passages, likely from 1926, show quite clearly what Husserl understood by a phenomenological reformulation of transcendental apperception: the phenomenologist needs to show from within the phenomenological reduction how the I and its objective correlate are reciprocally constituted 'from bottom to top.' This is a process that aims for total stability in subjective conviction and its objective correlate. However, such a *telos* is an idea lying in the infinite which would constitute the highest or ideal point of a phenomenological apperception. But how can the deepest, and not the highest, point of this phenomenological transcendental apperception be understood? In order to answer this question, it is necessary to turn to the problem of time-constitution as it is discussed in the C-manuscripts.[16]

These manuscripts were written between 1929 and 1934 and are of particular importance for the problem of a phenomenological transcendental apperception because they ascribe to the I an essential role in what Husserl holds to be the deepest point of phenomenological constitution: time-consciousness. In an oft-quoted passage from the second edition of the *Logical Investigations*, Husserl 'discovers' the I (see Husserl 1984, Hua XIX/1, p. 374 (B 361)). In the *Bernau Manuscripts on Time-Consciousness*, considered to be the beginning of genetic phenomenology (see Bernet/Lohmar 2001, p. XLVI), Husserl analyses the relation of this I to time-consciousness. However, the I is only treated in texts Nr. 14 and 15. It is thematized there essentially as an I-pole and as an I objectified in reflection. In other words, it does not yet have the sense which it will be ascribed in the 1926 manuscript. It is only with the C-manuscripts that the I is intrinsically woven into the depths of time-constitution.

In the C-manuscripts published in *Husserliana Materialien*, volume VIII, Husserl only explicitly speaks of "transcendental apperception" in two passages (Husserl 2006, Hua Mat. VIII, p. 124 (1932), footnote, p. 126 (1932)). Moreover, there are no passages that discuss the general problem of a transcendental deduction. The sense in which the term "transcendental apperception" is used in a 1932 manuscript seems closely related to that of A VI 30. But it also goes a step further: Husserl now speaks of a "life in 'transcendental apperception' under constant systematic development of transcendental apperceptions" (Husserl 2006, Hua Mat. VIII, p. 126). The unifying subjective instance is now *life* and there is a *plurality* of transcendental apperceptions within it that contribute to

---

15 "*eine im Unendlichen liegende Idee*," A VI 30, 45a.
16 I am following a hint from Iso Kern. Kern 1964, p. 287, and also footnote 2 on this page.

the one transcendental apperception of life itself. How is this to be understood? In order to find a promising answer to this question, we need to go beyond the passages where Husserl explicitly situates his analyses within the realm of a phenomenological transcendental apperception. For the question is: How are the I and its correlates reciprocally related in the deepest levels of time-constitution?

In the C-manuscripts, Husserl sees the origin of time-constitution in the interdependence between the hyletic sphere and the original I. He speaks of a "pure hyletic sphere" of "pure association" (Husserl 2006, Hua Mat. VIII, p. 52), which is passively guided by an "original kinesthesis[,] a unified aimless 'activity [*Tun*]', together with an undifferentiated [*ungeschiedenen*] totality of *hylē*" (Husserl 2006, Hua Mat. VIII, p. 225). This hints at an anonymous and aimless unification of associations within the original hyletic sphere. The deepest layers of this sphere might be called "unconscious" insofar as they belong to the sphere of the "Being-for-me" but "not properly valid for me" (Husserl 2006, Hua Mat. VIII, p. 193). This process of association brings about unities, "outstanding figures [*Abgehobenheiten*]" (Husserl 2006, Hua Mat. VIII, p. 309) that might at some point attract the attention of the I. The "original I [*Ur-Ich*]" is an "anonymous" "originally functioning I" (Husserl 2006, Hua Mat. VIII, p. 2) that is "hidden, unthematic" (Husserl 2006, Hua Mat. VIII, p. 16). It is thus not adequately given, even though it is apodictic in its facticity. This I is a "unity of striving [*Einheit eines Strebens*], which is driving [*treibend*] in it, a total instinct, which affects all active life" (Husserl 2006, Hua Mat. VIII, p. 254). Neither the hyletic sphere nor the original I are in time, but their interplay originally constitutes time and beings. This has three main implications for the problem of a phenomenological transcendental apperception, respectively concerning temporality, drive, and anonymity.

For Kant, transcendental apperception is rooted in understanding and as such is not itself temporal but is applied to time. In Husserl's late analyses of time, we also find a relation between a non-temporal and a temporal sphere, but in a very different way: a pre-temporal, temporalizing sphere of association, unified by an aimless original kinesthesis, passively brings about outstanding figures which affect the equally pre-temporal I. If these outstanding figures attract the attention of the I, the I may react by constituting temporal beings and the persisting validity of these temporal beings will in turn constitute the habitus of the I. In the living present, a pre-temporal sphere of *hylē* and the unity of the original kinesthesis interacts with the pre-temporal unity of the original I. This constitutes time to the same degree as the reciprocal constitution of a concordant world and a concordant subject in time. Phenomenological transcendental apperception is thus ultimately grounded in the living present of an I that is fragmentarily affected by outstanding figures which catch its attention against the background of a "night of the unconscious" (Husserl 2006, Hua Mat. VIII, p. 184). This I would indeed be split into a plurality of 'transcendental apperceptions' which are only held together by the stream of 'life' in one 'transcendental apperception.' This claim, however, only touches the surface of the phenomena concerned because phenomenological analysis has to study the complex procedures of retention, protention, secondary memory, anticipation, phantasy, and association which structure the interplay between the I, on the one hand, and the *hylē*, together with the original kinesthesis, on the other. This interplay provides the concrete content for the reciprocal constitution of subjectivity and objectivity. But the phenomenological version of transcendental apperception is this interplay of the double pre-temporal sphere which constitutes the temporal reciprocity of the I and its objective world.

What for Kant is the synthesizing function of the 'I think' is for Husserl an original I driven by instinct. Instinct here is not to be understood in a naturalistic biological sense, but rather in the sense of an "instinctive drive-intentionality" (Husserl 2006, Hua Mat. VIII, p. 327). In other manuscripts, now published in *Husserliana XLII*, Husserl develops this idea in more depth. The original drive-intentionality does not have a determined object; it could be "founded in a representing intention, but not in one that means something determinate, something known beforehand (even if it is only determinate with respect to general characteristics), rather in one that is in this respect entirely undetermined, and in one that acquires determination for itself only by fulfillment" (Husserl 2014, Hua XLII, p. 84 (1916–1918)). The "what" of its directedness "is ambiguous, is not fully determined" (Husserl 2014, Hua XLII, p. 94 (1930)). This structure of drive-intentionality is transferred to all higher levels of constitution. Husserl writes: "Each creative achievement [*Leistung*] of an entirely new kind, which becomes determinate for future mankind, presupposes a dark drive directed at the new, a dark drive that shows its teleological sense only in fulfillment" (Husserl 2014, Hua XLII, p. 120 (1933)). While in Kant the formal 'I think' synthesizes intuitions by logical categories and brings about objects of experience, in Husserl the object of original drive-intentionality is still entirely undetermined and can only be determined retrospectively.

And finally, the original I of phenomenological transcendental apperception is anonymous. It is an anonymous, hidden, and inadequately given I that stands in an equally anonymous interplay between the realm of original *hylē*, original kinesthesis and its background, the phenomenological unconscious. Following Klaus Held, it can be asked whether this realm of original anonymity is the proper basis of intersubjectivity (see Held 1966, pp. 151–163). The anonymous, pretemporal interplay of the original *hylē*, the original kinesthesis, and the I with its drive-intentionality seems to be precisely the sphere where the striving of the original I not only intersects with an original *hylē*, but also with the striving of others. Beneath the determinate, identifiable personal habits that might form the character of a personal I, there would thus lie an anonymous intertwining of affection and striving.

These three elements show the deepest point of a phenomenological transcendental apperception as it was conceived by Husserl. In contrast to the Kantian 'I think,' which synthesizes via categories established beforehand through the table of judgments, Husserl speaks of a transcendental apperception that begins in the temporalizing interplay of the original I and the original *hylē* with its original kinesthesis. This interplay is characterized by anonymity and drive-intentionality.

Conclusion

Returning now to the first part of this paper where the interpretations of the transcendental deduction by Hegel, Cohen, and Heidegger were summarized, we arrive at the following paradox with respect to Husserl: Husserl's phenomenological appropriation seems close to Heidegger's interpretation of Kant insofar as, for both, temporalization is the central element. However, while Heidegger excludes transcendental apperception from his own appropriation of Kant's transcendental deduction, Husserl takes it to be its heart. And while Heidegger understands the three syntheses of the A-deduction as 'rooted' in the three ecstases of his own conception of temporality, Husserl sees the deepest point of a deduction as lying in a phenomenological apperception which is a temporalizing interplay of an anonymous I. This anonymous I is characterized by a teleologically open drive-intentionality and an original *hylē* with its original kinesthesis of aimless association. And even if Heidegger does relate his conception of temporality to a drive (*Drang*) in his interpretation of Leibniz, his notion of temporality remains very different from the temporality Husserl discusses. The projective drive is for Heidegger "primordially *unifying*" by projecting a horizontal unity; it is "anticipating-encompassing [*vorgreifend-umgreifend*]" (Heidegger 1978, GA 26, p. 116; Heidegger 1984, p. 94). Temporality, and the ecstasis of the future in the case of drives, has a holistic character to the extent that the whole horizon of understanding is projected. Husserl's temporalizing sphere is much more fragmented in its associative, affecting, and projecting elements. Pure association is aimless, only some of it affects the I, and the drive-intentionality of the original I does not have a determined *telos*. Furthermore, Husserl ascribes a much greater significance to the anonymity of this original sphere: It is neither the *Dasein* nor the human being as such (as Heidegger thinks at the end of the 1920s) that projects a unified horizon of understanding, but fragmentary and essentially open 'projections' (if Husserl's drive-intentionality can be so described) which occur in a realm of anonymity.

It is such a sphere, outlined by Husserl in the late C-manuscripts on time-consciousness, which would be the origin of a phenomenological version of transcendental apperception and thus ultimately the' ground for a phenomenological deduction as such. It would not be the highest, but rather the deepest, point of transcendental philosophy as phenomenology. The phenomenological transcendental apperception would then extend the reciprocity analyzed by Husserl in manuscript A VI 30 between transcendental subjectivity and its correlative transcendental objectivity. This reciprocity was understood as a process of continued confirmation and disappointment that results in the formation of a more or less concordant personal I with a more or less concordant objective world as its correlate. But does this conception of a phenomenological transcendental apperception not fundamentally disturb the project of an eidetic transcendental philosophy? It can simply be noted here that Husserl does not go beyond the discussion of more or less constant concordances (*Einstimmigkeiten*) in his late analyses of a phenomenological transcendental apperception. However, the question of a possible eidetic transcendental philosophy is, at least on the explicit level, not at the center of his argument.[17]

Bibliography

Allison, Henry E. (2015): *Kant's Transcendental Deduction. An Analytical-Historical Commentary*. Oxford: Oxford University Press.
Bernet, Rudolf/Lohmar, Dieter (2001): "Einleitung der Herausgeber". In: Husserl, Edmund: *Die Bernauer Manuskripte über das Zeitbewusstsein (1917/1918)*. Husserliana, vol. XXXIII. Ed. Rudolf Bernet and Dieter Lohmar. Dordrecht: Kluwer Academic Publishers, pp. XVII–LI.
Cohen, Hermann (1871): *Kants Theorie der Erfahrung*, 1st edition. Berlin: Ferd. Dümmler's Verlagsbuchhandlung. [(1885): *Kants Theorie der Erfahrung*, second revised edition. Berlin: Ferd. Dümmlers Verlagsbuchhandlung.]
Hegel, Georg Wilhelm Friedrich (1986): "Glsauben und Wissen oder Reflexionsphilosophie der Subjektivität in der Vollständigkeit ihrer Formen als Kantische, Jacobische und Fichtesche Philosophie". In: *Werke*, vol. 2: *Jenaer Schriften 1801–1807*. Frankfurt am Main: Suhrkamp.
Hegel, Georg Wilhelm Friedrich (1977): *Faith and Knowledge*. Trans. W. Cerf and H. S. Harris. New York: State University of New York Press.

---

[17] I am indebted to Aengus Daly and to Kourken Michaelian for their linguistic revision of this article.

Heidegger, Martin (1978): *Metaphysische Anfangsgründe der Logik im Ausgang von Leibniz. Gesamtausgabe*, vol. 26. Ed. Klaus Held. Frankfurt am Main: Vittorio Klostermann.
Heidegger, Martin (1984): *The Metaphysical Foundations of Logic.* Trans. M. Heim. Bloomington: Indiana University Press.
Heidegger, Martin (1995): *Phänomenologische Interpretation von Kants Kritik der reinen Vernunft. Gesamtausgabe*, vol. 25. Ed. Ingtraud Görland. Frankfurt am Main: Vittorio Klostermann.
Heidegger, Martin (1997): *Phenomenological Interpretation of Kant's Critique of Pure Reason.* Trans. P. Emad and K. Maly. Bloomington: Indiana University Press.
Held, Klaus (1966): *Lebendige Gegenwart. Die Frage nach der Seinsweise des transzendentalen Ich bei Edmund Husserl, entwickelt am Leitfaden der Zeitproblematik. Phaenomenologica*, vol. 23. The Hague: Martinus Nijhoff.
Husserl, Edmund (1956): *Erste Philosophie (1923/24). Erster Teil: Kritische Ideengeschichte. Husserliana*, vol. VII. Ed. Rudolf Boehm. The Hague: Martinus Nijhoff.
Husserl, Edmund (1959): *Erste Philosophie (1923/24). Zweiter Teil: Theorie der phänomenologischen Reduktion. Husserliana*, vol. VIII. Ed. Rudolf Boehm. The Hague: Martinus Nijhoff.
Husserl, Edmund (1984): *Logische Untersuchungen. Zweiter Band: Erster Teil: Untersuchungen zur Phänomenologie und Theorie der Erkenntnis. Husserliana*, vol. XIX/1. Ed. Ursula Panzer. The Hague: Martinus Nijhoff.
Husserl, Edmund (2001): *Natur und Geist. Vorlesungen Sommersemester 1927. Husserliana*, vol. XXXII. Ed. Michael Weiler. Dodrecht: Kluwer Academic Publishers.
Husserl, Edmund (2013): *Grenzprobleme der Phänomenologie. Analysen des Unbewusstseins und der Instinkte. Metaphysik. Späte Ethik. Texte aus dem Nachlass (1908–1937). Husserliana*, vol. XLII. Ed. Rochus Sowa and Thomas Vongehr. Dordrecht: Springer.
Husserl, Edmund (2006): *Späte Texte über Zeitkonstitution (1929–1934). Die C-Manuskripte. Husserliana Materialien*, vol. VIII. Ed. Dieter Lohmar. Dordrecht: Springer.
Husserl, Edmund (1909–1925): *Ms A VI 30.* Unpublished Manuscript, quoted with the permission of the Husserl Archives.
Kant, Immanuel (1998a): *Kritik der reinen Vernunft.* Ed. Jens Timmermann. Hamburg: Meiner.
Kant, Immanuel (1998b): *Critique of Pure Reason.* Trans. P. Guyer and A. Wood. Cambridge: Cambridge University Press.
Kern, Iso (1964): *Husserl und Kant. Eine Untersuchung über Husserls Verhältnis zu Kant und zum Neukantianismus. Phaenomenologica*, vol. 16. The Hague: Martinus Nijhoff.
Marbach, Eduard (1974): *Das Problem des Ich in der Phänomenologie Husserls. Phaenomenologica*, vol. 59. The Hague: Martinus Nijhoff.

Vincent Gérard
"The Ego beside Itself"

On Birth, Sleep, and Death from Kant's *Anthropology from a Pragmatic Point of View* to Husserl's *Late Manuscripts on Time-Constitution*[1]

Abstract: We know that Husserl had knowledge of the *Anthropology from a Pragmatic Point of View*, which he had at least partly read in Hartenstein's edition of Kant's *Sämtliche Werke*. In the section called "On the inhibition, weakening, and total loss of the sense faculties," Kant poses the problem of death in terms comparable to those of Husserl. Here, I argue that in his analysis of sleep, birth, and death in the so-called *C-Manuscripts*, Husserl makes a transcendental use of Kant's non-transcendental anthropology. If we can say, along with Saulius Geniusas, that the *C-manuscripts* "mark the emergence of the problematic of birth, death, and sleep into the critical scope of Husserl's phenomenology of time," then we need to add that the analysis of the sense faculties in the Anthropological Didactic marks its period of gestation.

Phenomenologically, birth, sleep, and death can be understood in two different ways. Firstly, they can be seen as "marginal problems" (*Randprobleme*), an unsatisfactory wording, as by these words Husserl does not mean that they are secondary or minor problems, but that they are "borderline cases" (*Limesfälle*) or "borderline phenomena" (*Limesphänomene*). In other words, they are phenomena that elude our experience, escape what is self-given because no one can experience their own birth, their own death, or their own sleep – we will see later in which sense this last word needs to be understood. However, they are also phenomena that can be foreshadowed through experiences that every person has – or can have. Not through "normal" experiences, which as such do not teach us anything about these phenomena, but through anomic experiences understood as intentional modifications of our "normal" experiences: sickness, childhood, or animality.

---

[1] This contribution is the edited English translation of a paper originally published in French in the special issue of *Meta: Research in Hermeneutics, Phenomenology, and Practical Philosophy*, vol. VIII, n° 2 / December 2016: *Husserl and Kant: The Transcendental-Phenomenological Project*, pp. 571–595.

https://doi.org/10.1515/9783110564280-008

From a slightly different perspective, birth, sleep and death can also be seen as "higher problems" (*Höhenprobleme*), as "supreme and ultimate problems," or in other words as metaphysical or ethical issues. While confronted with these "states," we are also confronted with questions about the meaning of life and the nothingness from which we come at birth and to which we will return when we die. Thus for example, in 1932, Husserl wrote to his friend Gustav Albrecht that

> The issues of the highest order are metaphysical issues: they concern birth and death, the ultimate being of the "I" and of the "We"–objectivized as "Humankind"–teleology which ultimately takes us back to transcendental subjectivity and to its transcendental historicity and naturally the supreme question: the being of God as the ultimate foundation of such a teleology. (Husserl 1994, Hua Dok. III/9, p. 83)

This paper will be centered upon an investigation of birth, sleep, and death as borderline cases of pathological anomy and of early childhood in the *Späte Texte über Zeitkonstitution* (1929–1934). In particular, it will analyze the text of the *C8 Manuscript* which Husserl considered "the best elucidation of the idea of the limit" (Husserl 2006, Hua Mat. VIII, p. 159), and which, for this reason, has already interested some of his editors and commentators.[2] Through this analysis, it will address the following questions: how can it be explained that, in these manuscripts, Husserl brings together the anomic or sick human being, the young child, and the animal? What is there in common between the phenomenological descriptions of deafness or blindness and those of childhood or animality? Why are birth, dreamless sleep, and death then brought together and seen – as a whole – as borderline cases of anomy? Why does Husserl add to these cases, to complete the picture, the "loss of consciousness" (Husserl 2014, Hua XLII, p. 8), and even the experience of religious "conversion" (Husserl 2008, Hua XXXIX, p. 478)?

The answer probably lies in part in the fact that Husserl was a mathematician who drew from his scientific and mathematical work the tools he then used to discuss such borderline phenomena. This is what Rochus Sowa and Thomas Vongehr have highlighted in their Introduction to the *Grenzprobleme der Phänomenologie*:

---

2 On this point, see Geniusas 2010, pp. 71–89; 2013, pp. 44–60, Sowa and Vongehr 2014, pp. XXXI–XLV. See also Natalie Depraz's analysis of birth and death as "borderline cases of non-donation" which imply a non-donation of life itself as "structure of the totality" (Depraz 1991, pp. 464–65).

For the mathematician Husserl, the way to make comprehensible the 'metaphysical', 'transcendental' or 'monadic' birth, as well as the analogous death, is to construct ideal limits. In other words, it is to construct, at the limits of our ability to have such experiences ourselves, the everyday life experiences, such as waking up and falling asleep or growing up and getting old, that foreshadow these limits. Just like an ideal geometric shape – which by definition cannot be perceived – is foreshadowed by the real but imperfect straight lines that look like it and that we experience when we perceive straight lines that are drawn or used in constructed artefacts (such as straight edges). (Sowa and Vongher 2009, p. XXXVIII)

However, Husserl is not only a mathematician. He is also part of a specific philosophical tradition: the tradition of empirical psychology and pragmatic anthropology. Furthermore, empirical psychology – even though Kant had expelled it from the field of metaphysics because it contradicts the very idea of metaphysics – is a domain that, since Leibniz, has developed a deep interest in phenomena such as "deep sleep without dreams" and "loss of consciousness" (Leibniz 1885, pp. 610–611).

We know that Husserl knew the *Anthropology from a Pragmatic Point of View*, which he had at least partly read in Hartenstein's eight-volume edition of *Kant's Sämtliche Werke* (Kant 1868, pp. 429–658).[3] In the section entitled "On the inhibition, weakening and total loss of the sense faculties," Kant approached the question of death in terms comparable to those of Husserl. On the one hand, he claimed that "no human being can experience his own death (for to constitute an experience requires life), he can only observe it in others" (Kant 1917, AK. VII, p. 167; Kant 2006, p. 59). On the other hand, he put together a series of concepts such as inebriation, sleep, ecstasy, loss of consciousness – in which he saw "a foretaste of death" (Kant 1917, AK. VII, p. 166; Kant 2006, p. 59). This paper will argue that in his exploration of egological sleep, birth, and death, Husserl uses Kant's non-transcendental anthropology both non-anthropologically and transcendentally. It can be said with Saulius Geniusas that the late manuscripts on the constitution of time "mark the emergence of the problematic of birth, death, and sleep in the critical scope of Husserl's phenomenology of time" (Geniusas 2010, p. 71), and it could be added that Kant's analysis of the sense faculties in the *Anthropology from a Pragmatic Point of View* constitutes its period of gestation. In order to establish this point, we shall review the *C8 Manuscript* and analyze how the meanings of birth, sleep, and death are constituted in it.

---

[3] We borrow this information from Iso Kern (1964, p. 430).

1 Birth

The *C8 Manuscript* dates from October 1929, written at the time when Husserl was reworking his *Cartesian Meditations*. A few months earlier, in February 1929, Husserl had delivered his Paris lectures. Back in Fribourg, he reworked the text of his lectures several times for the French translation that was to be published in 1931. However, the text sent to Jean Hering in May 1929 did not satisfy Husserl, who kept amending and enriching it for a further German edition. In the *C8 Manuscript*, the primordial reduction exposed in § 44 of the *Cartesian Meditations* is explicitly put in place; but unlike what happened in § 44 of the *Cartesian Meditations*, the primordial reduction is not put in place within the transcendental reduction.

Husserl is very clear on this point: the analysis of the birth of the ego is strictly a matter of natural attitude. It concerns internal psychology:

> This reductive consideration, Husserl writes, does not yet need to be transcendental. Within a natural attitude, it means that humankind has a psychological genesis, in which we gradually discover ourselves as human beings while we also discover the world, first as a close world and then as a distant world. (Husserl 2006, Hua Mat. VIII, p. 154)

Hence the non-radical start of the analysis; in order to reveal the way the ego is born to itself and to the world, we need to start with an ego that is already a human being and that already has a sophisticated sense of its own being-in-the-world:

> The problem of the constitution of the world as a real (*real*) spatio-temporal world – both in terms of psychological and transcendental constitution – is that it requires to start from the factual reality of such a world; and this factual reality needs to be unveiled in the static constitution of its meaning. This meaning of the being-in-the-world is offered as an extremely complex configuration (*Gebilde*): what then does the constitution of this meaning (*Sinnbildung*), this static constitution of its meaning, signify? (Husserl 2006, Hua Mat. VIII, p. 154)

Hence a series of consequences for the concept of the birth of the ego.

First, the birth of the ego does not refer to a physiological event that could be perceived from the outside and inscribed on a birth certificate; the birth of the ego is the beginning of life in a world to which it is the role of the ego itself to give a meaning; it is a birth "perceived from the inside" (Husserl 2006, Hua Mat. VIII, p. 155); and from this point of view it is not "a fact that can be experienced" (*Erfahrungsfaktum*). This expression that Husserl introduced in a 1916 text is, however, slightly ambiguous. Birth as a "fact that can be experienced" does not exactly refer to the beginning of independent life, characterized by the beginning of pulmonary breathing at the moment when the fetus is ejected from the mother's body, because for Husserl the fetus is already born and the human embryo is a soul that has to awaken to life. The birth is the moment when a complex aggregate of material elements becomes a lived body – i.e. at the time when the main organs are formed. Birth is an organogenesis:

> In nature, writes Husserl in a 1916 text, new complex physical elements, that initially were "no more" than matter are constantly constituted as lived bodies. Once this stage is reached, there is an embryo and consequently, from the perspective of every individual who has an external perception of all this but who is also able to experience empathy, a soul awakens to life (*ein erwachtes Seelenleben*), a subject is born. (Husserl 2014, Hua XLII, p. 17)

The birth of the ego is not the "generative birth" either. Husserl highlights this in his text: "Naturally, he says, a beginning – as the awakening of an ego that is emerging to life – does not mean the same thing as a birth in the generative sense" (Husserl 2006, Hua Mat. VIII, p. 155); because the ego should be able to be present at its own genesis, as an incarnated and human ego "before a human being has in front of itself other human beings, in other words before the plural makes any sense" (Husserl 2006, Hua Mat. VIII, p. 155). The primordial ego is born to itself without a father or a mother. It becomes human without needing to recognize itself as a human being amongst human beings or as a member of humankind. Its birth as a subject that has intersubjective relations, its birth to "the world of those who are awake," and its generative birth is something different again. This will be a topic of Husserl's 1931 *C17 Manuscript*:

> Birth is the awakening (*Wach-Werden*) of a Monad and its self-constitution while its remains awake. The reverse question, starting with the phenomenon of the world, leads to transcendental intersubjectivity as the *universum*, in the awake state or the universum of vigilance (*Wach-Universum*). (Husserl 2006, Hua Mat. VIII, p. 426)

In this perspective, which correlates with what Husserl calls transcendental anthropology, it is understandable that Husserl occasionally uses the point of view of pragmatic anthropology; what is more surprising is the way he uses it within the primordial sphere.

The birth of the ego is a borderline case that needs to be "methodologically – and somehow abstractly – constructed" (Husserl 2006, Hua Mat. VIII, p. 154) by the phenomenologist. It is a pure possibility which is the result of "a transformation of meaning *(Sinnabwandlung)* which itself has a meaning" (Husserl 2006, Hua Mat. VIII, p. 158). How is this transformation carried out? And for a start, what is the transformed meaning that acts as the starting point of such a construction?

The starting point of such a transformation is to be found in what Husserl calls "the structure of meaning (*Sinnesstruktur*) of the living present" (Husserl 2006, Hua Mat. VIII, p. 154), in other words the structure of meaning of the world of experience under the temporal form of the world of current experience. This is specifically the starting point of the *Empirical Psychology*'s theory of sensation, because "sensations" (*sensationes*) are "representations of the current state of the world" (Baumgarten 1779, p. 157; Baumgarten 2013, p. 205). But this structure of meaning of the living present is not exclusively limited, according to Husserl, to the field of perception. On the one side, the meaning of the world that exists for the ego extends constantly towards the future; this has to do with what Husserl calls "the progressive genesis of experience," which means that the present world is a world that is always present again. On the other hand, all our past present, which we can call back through memories, is a present that is poorer in terms of meaning – it throws us back to an "anterior genesis of experience." Such is the meaning structure of the living present, which acts as the starting point of this structured transformation.

The transformation of meaning thus implies that we adhere to the indications of the structure of meaning of the living present; it implies that the ego retreats through memory into its own past and becomes a witness to the gradual impoverishment of the meaning it goes through, in parallel with the impoverishment of the meaning which the world that surrounds it goes through too. Going back, so to speak, into its own past, the ego is first taken back to "the field of near experience" which comprises all the objects it can see. Visibility is an empirical concept. In *Empirical Psychology*, this field of visibility was called "the sphere of sensation" (*sphaera sensationis*). It was "the place in which bodies so disposed can still appropriately move a sense organ such that they are clearly sensed" (Baumgarten 1779, p. 189; Baumgarten 2013, p. 206). Transcendentally interpreted, the concept of "visibility" allows Husserl to conceive of our accessibility to "the near world" by contrast to the distant world: "Visibility, writes Husserl, has no other signification than being a reference for such an accessibility" (Husserl 2006, Hua Mat. VIII, p. 155).

As it continues this journey into its own past, the ego is brought back to its own body as the nucleus of the sphere of what is near; but the lived body is no longer the instrument of the ego's possibility of controlling the surrounding world, "the bare ego only reigns over its lived body" and the lived body is reduced to its own "self-reflexivity" (*Zurückbezogenheit auf sich selbst*). As it was stated in § 44 of the *Cartesian Meditations*, "I can perceive one hand by means of the other, an eye by means of a hand" (Husserl 1950, Hua I, p. 128; Husserl

1960, p. 97). Consequently, for the impoverished ego, the body organ becomes an object and the object becomes a body organ.

However, the lived body has necessarily itself been self-constituted in its perceptibility and its availability. It can be said that here we reach a limit. As far as its meaning is concerned, any present sends us back to an anterior genesis of experience, and any present that is past, whose meaning is poorer, also sends us back, in turn, to an anterior genesis. Birth is the idea of a past present that is so poor in terms of meaning that it does not send us back to any anterior genesis. In other words, any living present is followed by a successor whose meaning is richer than its own meaning was, while it also comes after a past present whose meaning was poorer. Birth is the degree zero of meaning, it is the present that is followed by all others and that comes after none of them.

However, this transformation of meaning should not remain a purely abstract construction. It should be possible "to establish constitutively in the life in the world" (Husserl 2006, Hua Mat. VIII, p. 158) the borderline cases that it helps build. These borderline cases require echoing figures in "concrete life." The concrete life situation that echoes this birth of the ego which cannot be experienced is the moment of waking up. Each time we wake up echoes the time we were born:

> Just as the ego is awake or in other words just as it has a perception field – even if it may not yet have a 'field of things' [*Dingfeld*] – there is also, as its borderline, the waking up ego, the ego as it wakes up to life, the ego that keeps on constituting itself and becomes – consciously for itself – a human ego. (Husserl 2006, Hua Mat. VIII, p. 155)

Husserl does not only resort to a structured transformation that leads him to the idea of a borderline beginning, he also resorts to a comparison. The transformation of meaning progresses and shifts from a proper meaning to a figurative one: it is a trope, as waking up in its proper meaning is the transition moment from being asleep to being awake.

What is it that justifies this metaphor? In empirical psychology, there is a great similarity between sleep and death, to such an extent that Baumgarten can conclude his analysis of the sense faculty: "Therefore sleep, a syncope, and death are quite similar to each other" (Baumgarten 1779, p. 197; Baumgarten 2013, p. 211). What they have in common is even so important that if, like Husserl, we accept the hypothesis of a dreamless sleep, there remains no difference at all between these two notions: such is precisely the reason why Kant, in his *Anthropology from a Pragmatic Point of View*, rejects this hypothesis – we will return to this point later. The comparison between sleep and death in empirical psychology has a very clear strategic dimension: it is an anti-Cartesian motion.

The polemical dimension of this comparison is obvious in Meier's parallel study in § 551 of the *Empirical Psychology:* "There are people who absolutely deny that the soul can be awake or asleep and who believe that these modifications only concern the body" (Meier 1757, p. 123). Yet, there is a solidarity between this comparison of sleep and death and a certain idea of the state of a soul that is awake. If sleep and death are so very much alike, it is because the state of being asleep and the state of being awake are two very different states of the soul, much more different than the Cartesians were ready to admit. When it is awake, the soul has clear sensations while in sleep or in death, it only has obscure sensations: "I am awake (*vigilio*) when I am sensing an external being clearly; thus, while I am starting to sense, I am awaking (*evigilio*)" (Baumgarten 1779, p. 195; Baumgarten 2013, p. 210). To wake up is to leave the world of darkness; it is as if we were "newborn in the world" (Kant 1917, AK. VII, p. 166; Kant 2006, p. 58).

Thus, the birth of the ego is neither "the birth as a fact that can be experienced" nor "the generative birth." It is a borderline case of the impoverishment of meaning of the living present, it is a past present without any possible anterior past; but this borderline case can be anticipated in the very concrete experience of waking up: birth is a case of waking up to life. What is, then, the death of the ego? Exactly like its birth, the death of the ego is a borderline case whose concept must be constructed through a law of a series; and this borderline case requires echoing figures in concrete life. The death of the ego appears as the borderline case of the dreamless sleep which results from an intentional modification of a pathological experience.

2 Disease

The term *Erkrankung* which Husserl uses in the *C8 Manuscript* does not mean to be sick so much as it means to become sick, to contract a disease, to be affected by it. It is a transitory and dynamic state, understood on the basis of the state it modifies: "the normal constitution" of the body in what Husserl calls "normal life." What is a "normal life"? What is a normally constituted lived body?

Health as a "normal constitution" is first of all characterized as a control (*Beherrschung*) over the lived body, which means a control over the body organs, a control over the lived body as an organ and a practical control over nature because the control of the lived body allows the ego to gain control over nature and because the practical control of nature allows in return the body as an organ to loosen up, and the lived body to become more agile. The hand of the carpenter framing a house, the hand of a locksmith constructing a lock, gain a certain amount of dexterity as they accomplish their correct movements:

> In my life in the world, I learn through it [the lived body] a practical control over nature and bringing into play the lived body in the different orientations of these aspirations and satisfactions, I somehow constitute it and I also constitute myself as a carpenter, a locksmith etc... I learn the correct movements. (Husserl 2006, Hua Mat. VIII, p. 156)

Health is further characterized by the gain of corporal strength, by the experience of the strengthening of the lived body which gradually increases the ego's power: "I continually become stronger physically, I constantly have more and more power" (Husserl 2006, Hua Mat. VIII, p. 156). Using a Kantian terminology, it could be said that the ego develops a certain degree of "mechanical capacity" ("I can if I want to"), or in other words it develops a "*facility* in doing something" (Kant 1917, p. 147; Kant 2006, p. 38).

Finally, health is also characterized by an increase in spiritual and psycho-corporal strength; it is indeed the ego which gives various directions to the development of its strengths, maps the *praxis*, and decides the tasks that have to be accomplished. Using a Kantian terminology again, the ego has at its disposal "a certain degree of will, acquired through the frequently repeated use of one's faculty" (Kant 1917, p. 147; Kant 2006, p. 38): it does not just have facility in doing something, but a "skill (*Fertigkeit*) in such actions," in other words a *habitus*, and § 32 of the *Cartesian Meditations* tells us that the ego is not only the empty identity pole of its *cogitations*, but the "substrate of its habitualities" (Husserl 1950, Hua I, p. 100; Husserl 1960, p. 66). When the ego makes a decision, the action wears off but the decision remains; however, it does not remain as a necessity, nor does it create within the ego a form of "habit." It rather matches that which, in his *Metaphysics of Morals*, Kant describes as a "free aptitude" (*habitus libertatis*) (Kant 1907, AK. VI, p. 407; Kant 1996, p. 535), partly as a way for the ego to remain faithful to its decisions, because it recognizes itself in them, and partly as a way for the ego to change itself if it does not recognize itself in them anymore.

In this context, a disease is to be seen as a case of temporary decline of corporal, as well as spiritual, strength. Such a decline may just mean a simple alteration of the habitus due to a lack of practice. The hand becomes clumsier, the movement less accurate, the body more awkward: "I lose my touch, writes Husserl, I need more practice to go back to my initial level of ability" (Husserl 2006, Hua Mat. VIII, p. 156). In the case of a disease, an injury, or a burn, the decline of forces is due to an alteration of the normal constitution of the lived body; but nothing is irreversible here either: diseases get cured, injuries heal, and those who are born blind may be operated upon.

Yet, the lived body can also permanently deteriorate. A constant decline of the strengths constitutes the first instance of a "limit" which is not yet the borderline case of death or of dreamless sleep. Using a mathematical metaphor, it could be said, with Husserl, the curve of the life of the ego reaches the turning point (*Wendepunkt*) where the sign of the derivative changes. The ego enters a "maturation period" (*Reife-Periode*) when the normal growth of physical and spiritual strength flips over and becomes its opposite: it has started to age. Everything happens then as if "the progressive genesis of experience" that keeps feeding the ego and presenting it with new presents is no longer enough to compensate for the loss of strength it now experiences. While it keeps expanding because of this genesis, the primordial ego and the world around it keep getting poorer from that second point of view; it is the moment when the future starts looking like the past, not in its content but in the structure of its meaning, that remains exclusively bound to the nucleus of the living present, to the flowing, original impression. The experience of the living body's deterioration in the ageing process is then characterized by a decline of physical strengths: the precision of eyesight is reduced, mobility is impaired, space and time themselves are reduced; and these determinations of the empirical ego have a transcendental meaning. For instance, the fact that "relative distances perpetually increase" signifies that, in the language of absolute facts, "the sphere of accessibility decreases" (Husserl 2006, Hua Mat. VIII, p. 156). Furthermore, the permanent deterioration of the living body translates into a decline of spiritual strengths: the ego is no longer in a position to project itself towards the future "the sphere of the tasks that remain to be conceived and achieved becomes smaller;" and finally, it is its own past that starts missing, with the deterioration of the faculty of recall and the various pathologies of memory.

How can we explain that normality is to be understood as a form of self-control and pathological anomaly as a form of self-dispossession? After all, it is by no means self-evident that a normal state should be defined in this way nor is it obvious that the concept of self-control (even more so if we use it in its Kantian sense) should be in any way helpful here, for self-control is a virtue which characterizes some human beings and which distinguishes them from others. It is not only the virtue of Augustus who, in the words of Corneille in his play *Cinna*, is in control of himself and of the whole world and is thus able to regulate and overcome his just anger, but more generally it is the virtue of the Stoic sage. This is so to such an extent that in Kant's *Groundwork of the Metaphysics of Morals*, self-control has a pragmatic value – in a context where pragmatics are opposed to ethics and are defined in relation to them: "moderation in affects and passions [*Mässigung in Affekten und Leidenschaften*]", "self-control [*Selbstbeherrschung*]," "calm reflection" cannot be seen as good without limitation (however unconditionally they were praised by the ancients), because there are also plenty of murders that are accomplished cold-bloodedly. How could the *Anthropology from a*

Pragmatic Point of View be useful to Husserl when he approaches the experience of the disease? How does it provide him with a proper anthropological concept of self-control?

Self-control or self-mastery, according to *The Metaphysics of Morals*, constitutes one of the two conditions of "inner freedom," which requires these two things: "self-control" (*animus sui compos – seiner selbst Meister sein*) and "self-governance" (*imperium in semetipsum – über sich selbst Herr sein*). What is the difference between "self-control" and "self-governance?" The latter is the ability to "govern one's passions [*seine Leidenschaften zu beherrschen*]," or in other words to regulate the pathological states of our faculty of desire (such as hatred); the former is the ability to "subdue one's affects [*seine Affecten zu zähmen*]," or in other words to discipline the pathological states of our sense of pleasure and pain (such as anger). Self-control and self-governance are at the foundation of noble characters, vile characters are those who lack these qualities: "In these two states one's character [*indoles*] is noble [*erecta*]; in the opposing case it is mean" (Kant 1907, AK. VI, p. 408; Kant 1996, p. 535). But self-control must govern pathological states that are different from the pathological states subdued by self-governance; as strictly speaking affects are not vices – they are at most "non-virtues."

This concept of self-control is used again in the *Anthropology from a Pragmatic Point of View* in the context of the analysis of the degrees of inhibition of sensations (§§ 26–27). It is indeed possible for the sense faculty to be weakened, inhibited, or even totally suppressed. This explains why pragmatic anthropology – as metaphysics before it – is so preoccupied with the states of drunkenness, sleep, loss of consciousness, and death. What is the place of the concept of self-control in such inquiries? Moreover, why does Kant mention the *Tramontano*? For Kant, all this is about being able to think the kind of inhibition of the sense faculty that can be encountered in the one who is affected in his own body by pathological emotional states: anger, joy, or horror (the last of which is the worst for Kant). It is then said that "he [or she] is disconcerted, beside himself [or herself] (with joy or fear), *perplexed, bewildered, astonished,* he [or she] has lost his *Tramontano*". In brief, he [or she] has no "control over himself [or herself] [*seiner selbst mächtig*]."

This state of inhibition of the sense faculty and the state of being asleep are thought analogically. The inhibition of the sense faculty is not exactly a "waking dream" (Kant 1917, AK. VII, p. 202; Kant 2006, p. 97, trans. modified), which constitutes according to Kant a true mental derangement in the fields of sense representations or of judgment, touching people who exempt themselves from having to confront their imaginings with the laws of experience, because it is very possible to ramble in our judgments and to lose any sense of the representations of our senses without being at all emotional. This loss of countenance is thus more accurately conceived as a waking *sleep* and a "momentary sleep" (Kant 1917, AK. VII, p. 166; Kant 2006, p. 59). As far as sleep is concerned, it is not the "visionary" or "melancholic" dimension (Kant 1917, AK. VII, p. 202; Kant 2006, p. 97) that interests Kant, it is the numbing of the organs of the body, which as our composure is being lost, "brings the play of the sense representations to a standstill." The experience of the temporary paralysis of the body when a person is beset by violent emotions is foreshadowed in the numbness of sleep.

This use of the concept of self-control, borrowed from Stoic philosophers, is not very original; Kant is here in line with the tradition of empirical psychology, as the analysis of § 26 of the *Anthropology from a Pragmatic Point of View* echoes back to those of § 552 of Baumgarten's *Empirical Psychology*, developed by Meier in § 552 of his *Metaphysics:* "If all sensations have a degree of clarity that is usual in a sound person, someone is then said to be in control of oneself (*sui compos*)" (Baumgarten 1779, p. 195; Baumgarten 2013, p. 210). The sound person must thus be awake, because when we are awake, we are in a state where our external sensations are clear. But even when I am awake my sensations may or may not have their normal degree of clarity: in the first case, I am not only awake but also healthy (in other words I have self-control), and in the second case, some sensations do not have their normal level of clarity.

Thus Husserl sees normality as a state of control over one's lived body, which imparts the ego with a potentially infinite power, a free habitus; in other words, he sees it in the light of Kant's concept of "self-control." It is not our goal here to decide if this concept is specifically anthropological or ethical, nor even to determine if this distinction remains meaningful in a thorough reading of Kant.[4] It is enough to understand that pathological anomality is seen by Husserl as a form of numbness, a temporary sleep that strips the ego of the use of its sensorial organs and deprives it simultaneously of its "fundamental ubiquity" (Desanti 1976, p. 97) – a "normal" ubiquity that allows it to be present at various points of time. The point is not, for Husserl, to produce a transcendental theory of emotions. At the infra-reflective level where the ego is affected, dispossessed, deprived of any practical future and of the opportunity to relate to its own past, the point for Husserl is to characterize the constitution of the spatio-temporal world of the primordial ego and its own constitution as a human ego. It remains, however, to see how, on this basis, the ego can also constitute the meaning of its own egological death.

---

[4] On this topic, see Harder 2009, pp. 161–184.

3 Sleep and Death

The concept of the death of the ego is constructed in the *C8 Manuscript* relatively abstractly, by applying a process of transformation of meaning to another borderline case: the case of the dreamless sleep, itself understood as an intentional modification of the situation of catching a disease or becoming sick. As it is the case in pragmatic anthropology and empirical psychology, the same transformation leads from the brutal inhibition of the sense faculty in the instance of sickness to its total annihilation in the instance of death via its temporary termination in the instance of sleep. But the comparison with the process put in place in the *Anthropology from a Pragmatic Point of View* is fraught with yet another difficulty, because Husserl and Kant do not always mean the same thing when they use the word "sleep." Sleep as a borderline phenomenon is a dreamless sleep, a pure sleep. Yet Kant rejects the possibility of a dreamless sleep.[5] In the *Anthropology from a Pragmatic Point of View*, he asserts that "one can take it as certain that there could be no sleep without dreaming, and whoever imagines that he has not dreamed has merely forgotten his dream" (Kant 1917, AK. VII, p. 190; Kant 2006, p. 83). If it were possible for the soul not to dream while it asleep, it would mean that sleep and death were the same, which is absurd. Hence, dream and sleep are inseparable. How, in these conditions, can a phenomenology of sleep use the conclusions of pragmatic anthropology?

First, it can be noticed that this has not always been Kant's position on this particular point. In his first lessons on Anthropology during the winter term of 1772–73, he argued that although people never dream during deep sleep phases, they do dream during lighter sleep phases and moments of slumber:

> The only difference between slumber [*Schlummer*] and sleep [*Schlaf*] is that in slumber we still have numb sensations, even if the representations we have of these sensations are usually completely flawed. *We only dream in slumber, never in deep sleep*, because strictly speaking we then have no sensations [*sinnliche Empfindungen*]. (Kant 1997, AK. VII, p. 72)

Hence, Kant goes back to the topic of the great similarity between deep sleep and death: "We are thus very much like the dead" (Kant 1997, AK. XXV/2, p. 72). From this point of view, dreams are a mixture of numb sensations and powerful imaginations that prevent sleep more than they reveal it:

---

5 On this point, see Hanne Jacobs's investigations on the continuity of consciousness during sleep (Jacobs 2010, p. 336).

> True dreams [by contrast with the waking dreams] happen when you are asleep, to dream is to be at the border between being asleep and being awake and it is a child of slumber [*Kind des Schlummers*]. A dream always starts with a specific sensation that we experience in slumber. But as these kinds of sensations are weak and numb, while the productions of our imagination are much more powerful, when the two get mixed together the fictive images get taken for real impressions. When all connections with our senses stop, the dream is suspended. We dream when we sleep lightly and usually in the morning. If we have had a heavy meal in the evening which disturbs our sleep, then we dream all through the night. (Kant 1997, AK. XXV/2, p. 101)

Furthermore, it could be said that in his analysis of the sense faculty in the *Anthropology from a Pragmatic Point of View*, Kant has to acknowledge that, to a certain extent, there is a dreamless sleep – a hypothesis that he rejects in his analysis of the imaginative faculty – precisely because he follows the structure of Baumgarten's *Empirical Psychology* in his analysis of the cognitive faculty. The kind of sleep that is the topic of § 26 of the *Anthropology from a Pragmatic Point of View* is a kind of sleep during which dreams produced by our oneiric imagination may arguably occur, but which will be considered here from the strict point of view of the soul and of its sensations. He thus temporarily disregards all kinds of phantasmagories of the imagination. In spite of Kant's evolution on this topic of the dreamless sleep, which gradually led him to get rid of a corpus of theories that he had inherited from Leibniz, we must acknowledge that in Kant, Husserl, and in the various texts we have considered, the same word refers to the same thing. Yet what are the main features that, according to Husserl, characterize the dreamless sleep?

In the *C-Manuscripts*, Husserl describes sleep as an interruption of the flow of the concurring experiences of the world that we experience when we are awake:

> To wake up is to wake up to the sphere of the memories that are at our disposal and which (with the exception of dreams that – for us – do not exist when we experience dreamless sleep) is synthetically put together with the new sphere that opens up as we wake up, in that way: a gap in our experience, an empty sphere of memories in the in-between, in which however things and events have lasted. (Husserl 2006, Hua Mat. VIII, pp. 156–157)

This extract requires explanation. When I wake up, I do not exclusively wake up to the present moment and to the moment that will follow it. I also wake up to my own past, to a "sphere of memories that are at my disposal." What is this sphere? It is the sphere that accommodates what happened before I fell asleep, the memories of the moments that preceded my falling asleep. But the synthesis of those two periods of consciousness can only be realized through a "gap in our experience" because of the disjointedness introduced by the dreamless sleep in our concurring experiences of the world. Do periods of paradoxical sleep reintroduce some form of continuity into this disjointed experience? Or does the dream add nothing to the figure of this synthesis? This is not an issue here for Husserl, who totally disregards dreams, his only concern being to highlight that they are fully absent from dreamless sleep.

In the *C4 Manuscript*, Husserl further describes sleep as an inhibition of the interest and activity of the ego:

> The sleep is thus the sleep of the ego, of the center of the affection and the action. The ego is asleep, it does not deal with any affection and remains passive. All the interests remain too but they are inactive, at rest. The ego, the ego of aspirations, the ego of volitions is totally at rest. (Husserl 2006, Hua Mat. VIII, p. 98)

In waking life, affects and excitations compete – so to speak – for the interest of the ego: "The ego that is affected by affective stimulations is active: battles of stimulations, battles, conflicts of interests; current, dominant, temporary interests, and on the other hand by interests that provisionally burst in" (Husserl 2006, Hua Mat. VIII, pp. 99–100). Then again, in sleep the ego becomes apathetic. It does not have the strength to react to the stimuli of the senses: "Here there is no conflict of affections. Although they concern the ego, although they – so to speak – touch it, although they are here for it, they have no strength; and this is how the mutual conflict of strengths destroys itself" (Husserl 2014, Hua XLII, pp. 34–35).

In these conditions, death is conceived as a "final sleep," or in other words as a dreamless sleep where waking up is impossible. To be more precise, based on the restraining experience of being sick or of getting older, the ego can envision the possibility of an ultimate ageing or of an incessant restraint by sickness that would lead to a pre-set ending: losing its sight, losing its hearing, eventually losing all its abilities and ultimately perhaps losing all its past and all its future.

What is it, then, that this analogy with a dreamless sleep and a loss of consciousness teaches us regarding our own death? It teaches us that there is nothing to fear about death. Meier, in § 554 of the *Empirical Psychology*, had already recognized the consoling dimension of this analogic vision of death:

> Just as it does not hurt anybody to fall asleep or to lose consciousness at the moment they do it, the moment of death itself, even if sensations of fear may have preceded it, causes admittedly no painful sensations either, because death makes the soul immediately oblivious to any sensations, because it makes it lose any awareness of its own body. (Meier 1757, p. 129)

Nature thus teaches us, through the experiences of sleep and lack of consciousness, that there is nothing to fear about the moment of death: however, is this really what we fear about death?

Kant goes Back to Meier's argument to dispel the fear of death. He argues that the conclusions we tend to draw from our external observation of other people's death should be revised in light of what our experience of sleep and loss of consciousness teaches us: "Whether it is painful cannot be judged from the death rattle or convulsions of the dying person; it seems much more to be a purely mechanical reaction of the vital force, and perhaps a gentle sensation of the gradual release from all pain" (Kant 1917, AK. VII, p. 167; Kant 2006, pp. 59–60); but if Kant does indeed go back to Meier's argument, he also immediately signals that it is an ineffective argument. The argument misses its target; indeed it aims at the wrong target, and Kant believes he has found in Montaigne the reason why this argument is powerless and does not have the effect its authors had hoped for: fear of death is not a fear of the experience of death, it is a fear of the idea of death:

> The fear of death [*Furcht vor dem Tod*] that is natural to all human beings, even the unhappiest or the wisest, is therefore not a horror of *dying* [*Grauen vor dem Sterben*] but, as Montaigne rightly says, horror at the thought of *having died* [*vor dem Gedanken gestorben zu sein*] (that is of being dead). (Kant 1917, AK. VII, p. 167; Kant 2013, p. 60)

Whether they are miserable and inclined to want to end their life to put an end to their sufferings, or wise and willing to be convinced by philosophical arguments, there is only one thing that the human being fears about death: the thought of having died, that is of being dead.

It is probable that Kant does not understand Montaigne well or that his reading of the text of the *Essays* is very free, because in Book II, chapter 13, Montaigne expresses precisely the opposite position to the one Kant will attribute to him: "I do not want to die, but I am quite indifferent to being dead" (Montaigne 1992, p. 608) – responding thus to Lucretius's argument who, to deliver us from the fear of death, stated: "Don't you know that death will not let live, after you have died, another you which, being alive, could stand over your body crying?" Kant does not repeat in the *Anthropology from a Pragmatic Point of View* the details of Lucretius's arguments against those who fear being deprived of a proper burial, or who dread the possibility that their remains may be devoured by vultures. We fear, according to Kant, the thought of death; in other words, we fear the apprehension of our own death which is to be, the state of our body buried in a grave or lying elsewhere, as if it were still us and as if we were able to say to ourselves: I am dead. Thus, if the arguments of the Epicureans are valid in theory, because they identify rightly the object of our fear of death, they are not more effective than those of Meier, for they do not abolish our fear of being dead. Essentially, it is the idea that the fear of death could be alleviated by any "appropriate" arguments that is an illusion: "This illusion cannot be pushed aside, for it lies in the nature of thought as a way of speaking to and of oneself" (Kant 1917, AK. VII, p. 167; Kant 2006, p. 60). Because we are language beings, it is in our very nature to tell ourselves the story of our own death, to create narratives about our death.

Conclusion

We have seen that there are two ways to understand birth, death, and sleep in Husserl's phenomenology. Either they are specifically metaphysical problems that deal with ultimate issues about the meaning of life – and this is the point of view that is chosen in some texts of the Freiburg period about monadology or about ethics (*cf.* sections 3 and 4 of the *Grenzprobleme der Phänomenologie*) – or they are borderline cases of anomaly within the general issue of the constitution of the world, the point of view that Husserl favors in his manuscripts of the 1930s. When he approaches questions of birth, sleep, and death this way, Husserl appears to be following Kant's program of freeing empirical psychology from metaphysics. As a matter of fact, this Kantian inspiration is here more an appearance than a reality. Husserl actually has no further reason to maintain this exclusion, because he uses the concepts of pragmatic anthropology in a metaphysical way; and, in order to think the birth and the death of the ego, he uses them outside of the field that he, Husserl, calls the field of transcendental anthropology. In that sense it can be said that Husserl uses Kant's non-transcendental anthropology both non-anthropologically and transcendentally.

From a methodological point of view, this transcendental use of non-transcendental anthropology is allowed by the fact that in these texts, the primordial reduction is relatively autonomous from the transcendental reduction. A more orthodox practice, one that would better conform to Husserl's theory, would have made this use very problematic; but theory is one thing, practice is another, and Husserl has indeed acknowledged that he occasionally took the liberty of making some accommodation with the theory of reduction:

> It seems initially (I have myself started to share some aspects of that perspective), he writes in 1933, that it [the reduction to primordiality] is possible on natural grounds as a 'pure' reduction and that it requires the pathway of the transcendental, universal reduction, which remained only unnoticed and not theoretical. (Husserl 1973, Hua XV, p. 530)

Everything happens as if the concepts of the Kantian non-transcendental anthropology could be used as an index and call upon themselves for their own transcendental interpretation.

This analysis may thus allow us to cast a new light on the concepts of the birth and death of the ego. The death of the transcendental ego is unthinkable, because even if it is possible for our experience of the world to deteriorate and even to lose its form of experience of the world, on the other hand it is "impossible for me that I disappear transcendentally" (Husserl 2006, Hua Mat. VIII, p. 97); nevertheless, this disappearance of future multiplicities can be understood on the basis of the issues of disease and deep sleep. The concepts of sleep and of the death of the ego are examined by Husserl based on the concept of 'self-control' that Kant introduced in his Anthropology lectures in 1772–1773 and to which he went back in his *Anthropology from a Pragmatic Point of View* in his analysis of the degrees of inhibition of the sense faculty; in other words, they are examined as borderline cases of "concrete life" situations where the ego is beside itself, where it has lost its presence to itself. In loss of consciousness or in religious conversion, which Husserl sees as other borderline cases, the structure of the ego is fundamentally ecstatic. When it faces a limit to its extraordinary power to be present to itself, the ego is beside itself; and it could be said of the *Dasein* that it is an ego suffering from vertigo.

This analogical conception of death could, however, be criticized for limiting itself to external analogies, and it is precisely for this that Fink will criticize it (although he never mentions Husserl directly). Interestingly, when during the 1966–67 Fribourg winter term Fink and Heidegger gave a lecture on Heraclites together, the topic of one of their sessions would be sleep and dream.

Fink will start by restating that some metaphorical expressions deserve, up to a certain point, to be taken seriously because they make one think: "We move into a metaphorical manner of speaking, when we speak of sleep as the brother of death. Someone who wakes up out of a deep sleep and reflects on sleep says: 'I have slept like a dead man'. This metaphorical expression is doubtful" (Heidegger 1986, GA 15, p. 222; Heidegger 1979, p. 137). If such expressions deserve to be taken seriously, it is mostly because they allow us to question the thesis that links intrinsically sleep and dreams ("no dreamless sleep") – a thesis that removes the existential difference between the one who dreams and the dreamed I of the dream world by asserting that all sleep implies dreaming. From this point of view, Fink and Heidegger follow in Husserl's footsteps. But these metaphors are in truth no more than the expression of an "everyday way of thinking," or even an "everyday philosophy," that sees life and death as terms which are mediated through the link of sleep: "In Leibniz, argued Fink, we find the philosophical tendency to attempt to understand the being of the lower monads through dreamless sleep, impotence, and death, which is no death for him in the strict sense" (Heidegger 1986, GA 15, p. 241; Heidegger 1979, p. 148). Death as a borderline case is not death – it is a borderline case of life.

Bibliography

Baumgarten, Alexander Gottlieb (1779): *Metaphysica*. 7th ed. Halle: Herman Hemmerde.
Baumgarten, Alexander Gottlieb (2013): *Metaphysics. A Critical Translation with Kant's Elucidations, Selected Notes, and Related Materials*. Trans. C. D. Fugate and J. Hymers. London: Bloomsbury.
Depraz, Natalie (1991): "La vie m'est-elle donnée ? Réflexions sur le statut de la vie dans la phénoménologie". In: *Les Études philosophiques*, n° 4, pp. 459–473.
Desanti, Jean-Toussaint (1976) : *Introduction à la phénoménologie*. Paris: Gallimard.
Geniusas, Saulius (2010): "On Birth, Death, and Sleep in Husserl's Late Manuscripts on Time". In: *On Time – New Contributions to the Husserlian Phenomenology of Time*. Eds. Dieter Lohmar and Ichiro Yamaguchi. Dordrecht: Springer, pp. 71–90.
Geniusas, Saulius (2013): "On Nietzsche's Genealogy and Husserl's Genetic Phenomenology. The Case of Suffering". In: *Nietzsche and Phenomenology: Power, Life, Subjectivity*. Eds. Elodie Boublil and Christine Daigle. Bloomington, Indianapolis: Indiana University Press, pp. 44–60.
Harder, Yves-Jean (2009): "Kant : les émotions d'un point de vue pragmatique". In: *Les émotions*. Ed. Sylvain Roux. Paris: Vrin, pp. 161–184.
Heidegger, Martin (1986): *Seminare. Gesamtausgabe*, vol. 15. Ed. Curd Ochwadt. Frankfurt am Main: Vittorio Klostermann.
Heidegger, Martin (1979): *Heraclitus Seminar 1966/67*. Trans. Charles H. Seibert. Tuscaloosa: The University of Alabama Press.
Husserl, Edmund (1950): *Cartesianische Meditationen und Pariser Vorträge*. Husserliana, vol. I. Ed. Stephan Strasser. The Hague: Martinus Nijhoff.
Husserl, Edmund (1960): *Cartesian Meditations. An Introduction to Phenomenology*. Trans. Dorion Cairns. The Hague: Martinus Nijhoff.
Husserl, Edmund (1973): *Zur Phänomenologie der Intersubjektivität. Texte aus dem Nachlass. Dritter Teil: 1925–1935*. Husserliana, vol. XV. Ed. Iso Kern. The Hague: Martinus Nijhoff.
Husserl, Edmund (1994): *Briefwechsel: Familienbriefe*. Husserliana Dokumente, vol. III/9. Ed. Karl Schuhmann. Dordrecht: Kluwer Academic Publishers.
Husserl, Edmund (2006): *Späte Texte über Zeitkonstitution (1929–1934). Die C-Manuskripte*. Husserliana Materialien, vol. VIII. Ed. Dieter Lohmar. Dordrecht: Springer.
Husserl, Edmund (2008): *Die Lebenswelt. Auslegungen der vorgegebenen Welt und ihrer Konstitution. Texte aus dem Nachlass (1916–1937)*. Husserliana, vol. XXXIX. Ed. Rochus Sowa. Dordrecht: Springer.
Husserl, Edmund (2014): *Grenzprobleme der Phänomenologie. Analysen des Unbewusstseins und der Instinkte. Metaphysik. Späte Ethik. Texte aus dem Nachlass (1908–1937)*. Husserliana, vol. XLII. Ed. Rochus Sowa and Thomas Vongehr. Dordrecht: Springer.

Jacobs, Hanne (2010): "Towards a Phenomenological Account of Personal Identity". In: *Philosophy, Phenomenology, Sciences: Essays in Commemoration of Edmund Husserl*. Eds. Carlo Ierna, Hanne Jacobs and Filip Mattens. Dordrecht: Springer, pp. 333–361.
Kant, Immanuel (1868): *Anthropologie in pragmatischer Hinsicht*. Leipzig: Leopold Voss. [Edition used by Husserl].
Kant, Immanuel (1907): *Die Religion innerhalb der Grenzen der blossen Vernunft. Die Metaphysik der Sitten*. In: *Kants gesammelte Schriften*. AK. VI. Berlin: Georg Reimer.
Kant, Immanuel (1917): *Der Streit der Fakultäten. Anthropologie in pragmatischer Hinsicht*. In: *Kants gesammelte Schriften*. AK. VII. Berlin: Georg Reimer.
Kant, Immanuel (1996): *Immanuel Kant Practical Philosophy*. Trans. Mary J. Gregor. Cambridge: Cambridge University Press.
Kant, Immanuel (1997): *Vorlesungen über Anthropologie. Zweiter Hälfte*. In: *Kants gesammelte Schriften*. AK. XXV/2. Berlin: Walter de Gruyter.
Kant, Immanuel (2006): *Anthropology from a Pragmatic Point of View*. Trans. Robert B. Louden. Cambridge: Cambridge University Press.
Kern, Iso (1964): *Husserl und Kant. Eine Untersuchung über Husserls Verhältnis zu Kant und zu Neukantianismus*. The Hague: Martinus Nijhoff.
Leibniz, Gottfried Wilhelm (1885): "Monadologie". In: *Die Philosophische Schriften*, vol. VI. Ed. Carl Immanuel Gerhardt. Hildesheim, New York: Georg Olms Verlag.
Meier, Georg Friedrich (1757): *Metaphysik*. Vol. III: *Die Psychologie*. Halle: Gebauer.
Montaigne, Michel de (1992): *Les Essais*. Ed. Pierre Villey in 3 volumes. Paris: Presses universitaires de France.
Sowa, Rochus and Vongehr, Thomas (2014): "Einleitung". In: Husserl 2014, pp. XIX–CXV.

Corijn van Mazijk
Kant and Husserl on Overcoming Skeptical Idealism through Transcendental Idealism

Abstract: Both Kant and Husserl claim to endorse a form of transcendental idealism which includes some sufficient form of realism in itself. This chapter offers a systematic comparison of this claim for both authors. The first half of this chapter discusses (i) Kant's criticism of Cartesian skepticism, (ii) his identification of transcendental realism as a fallacious source of that position, and (iii) his own solution based on the fusion of empirical realism with transcendental idealism. I subsequently discuss (iv) whether the negative concept of noumenon Kant accepts obscures this position, and I argue that it need not. Turning to Husserl, the second part discusses his criticism of Cartesian skepticism and the problem of the relation between the intentional and the real object. I argue that Husserl's position resembles Kant's on important points. I then turn to Husserl's concept of a "world beyond ours" in *Ideas I* and argue that Husserl's account of the material counter-sense, but also logical possibility of a world beyond consciousness, mirrors Kant's negative noumenon. I conclude that, disregarding details of their respective proof structures, both views on transcendental idealism are similar in important respects, also regarding the possibility of a noumenal world.

1 Overview

Difficulties interpreting Kant's position on the realism-idealism debate have recently steered new discussions which, as Allais puts it, show not "even a tendency toward convergence" (Allais 2015, p. 3). Allais herself takes an anti-realist stance at least insofar as Kant, on her view, bars us from access to aspects of reality: "things (objects) of which we have empirical cognition […] have natures or aspects that are entirely independent of us, which ground appearances" (Allais 2015, p. 59). In a similar vein, Guyer and Horstmann (2015) recently argued for Kant's "indeterminate ontological realism," with Guyer noting earlier that this indeterminate world is the one to which "we ultimately intend to refer" (Guyer 1987, p. 335). Other recent contributions within this camp include those of Westphal (2004) and Rockmore (2007), who both read Kant as being committed to a world beyond human cognition (Westphal 2004, p. 67; Rockmore 2007, p. 9), and Braver (2007), who holds Kant responsible for a whole new wave of anti-realism in continental philosophy.

But numerous scholars have also expressed disagreement with such readings. An early example of this is Bird (1962), who suggests that phenomenon and noumenon are two ways of looking at the same thing "because, on Kant's view, there is only one thing at which to look, namely appearances" (Bird 1962, p. 29). Prauss's (1974) early discussion on the concept of the thing in itself points in the same direction, arguing that Kant's preferred locution is not "thing in itself" (which suggests its actual existence) but "thing considered as it is in itself" (Prauss 1974). In more recent days, Allison (2004, pp. 50–57) and Luft (2007, p. 371) have provided like-minded readings, with Jansen (2014) boldly suggesting that anti-realist readings of Kant are plainly "symptomatic of a persisting confusion" (Jansen 2014, p. 83).

Is it a coincidence that things stand no differently with regard to Husserl, the other great self-proclaimed transcendental idealist? In recent years, scholars have ascribed virtually all possible positions to Husserl, including realism (Ameriks 1977), mentalism (Carman 2003, p. 62), internalism (Rowlands 2003), anti-realism (Wiltsche 2012), and solipsism (Blackburn 2016, pp. 229–230). Some have argued that the noema (the object as intended by consciousness) and the real object must be "completely distinct entities" (Smith and McIntyre 1989, p. 162), where the first "mediates" between act and object (Smith and McIntyre 1975, p. 115). Yet others claim that the noema does not "intervene between us and ordinary things" (Rouse 1987, p. 231), that the view of Smith and McIntyre is "mistaken" (Banchetti 1993, p. 81), and that it "distorts Husserl's theory of intentionality" (Drummond 2009, pp. 593–594).

However, recent studies of both Kant and Husserl also include attempts to demonstrate the compatibility of idealism and realism. H. Allison, for instance, claims that Kant employs a "metalanguage" (Allison 2004, p. 73) of things in themselves, the heuristic value of which derives from the paradigm of transcendental realism before him. Rightly understood, Kant's transcendental idealism is a realist position, his anti-realist tendencies stemming from a metalanguage employed to situate his view in a different philosophical landscape. Likewise, Zahavi (2017) and others interpret Husserl's transcendental idealism in a way that is not necessarily hostile to realism. Zahavi, for instance, remarks that for Husserl "the world of experience can have all the required reality and objectivity" (Zahavi 2017, p. 69).

This chapter interprets Kant's and Husserl's claims to transcendental idealism in a way sympathetic to such recent attempts. I argue that, for both, transcendental idealism is a form of non-problematic idealism which should include all the realism we need. This means, on the one hand, that both are realists: for Kant, physical objects are genuinely "outside us" (Kant 1781, A 376), and for Husserl, "a 'physical thing' as correlate [of consciousness] is not a physical thing"

(Husserl 1971, Hua V, p. 85; Husserl 1980, p. 72), because the latter alone exists independently of immediate intentional awareness. On the other hand, for both, this realism still derives from consciousness: for Kant, "external things [....] are [...] nothing but mere appearances" (Kant 1781, A 371–372), and for Husserl, no object signifies a "reaching out beyond the world which is for consciousness" (Husserl 1976, Hua III/1, p. 100; Husserl 1983, p. 121).

I further argue that the apparent incompatibility of these suggestions is overcome by both authors by challenging the tacit presupposition of transcendental or metaphysical realism: the implicit standard specifying that the real must be measured by the ideal of absolute mind-independence. Transcendental idealism then resets the norm for the real within the scope of possible experience; in other words: it is, for Kant as well as for Husserl, essentially a rejection of transcendental realism. While the concept of noumenon could be taken to problematize this position regarding Kant, I argue that Kant can plausibly be read as rendering the thing in itself a mere logical possibility without concrete sense or meaning. As I show, this matches to some extent Husserl's position on the logical possibility, but material counter-sense, of a world beyond consciousness in *Ideas I* – which should not be understood as compromising transcendental idealism either.

All of this warrants, I think, the claim that there is substantial overlap between Kant and Husserl on the point of transcendental idealism and its compatibility with some form of common sense or empirical realism. Moreover, it reveals that contemporary misunderstandings of Kant and Husserl on this point are largely symmetric. At the same time, it should be noted that manuscripts indicate Husserl's dissatisfaction with Kantian transcendental idealism, which Husserl believed to be anthropocentric, and which he actively sought to improve upon by insisting on the universal *a priori* correlation. This expands transcendental idealism beyond the human mind to the pure possibility of an object. Moreover, it should be noted that the core transcendental idealist commitment they share does not affect the fundamental differences between them regarding the method, scope, and nature of evidence of transcendental inquiry – points on which Husserl repeatedly sought to differentiate himself from Kant.[1]

---

[1] See van Mazijk 2016, 2019 and 2020, where I discuss aspects of Husserl's criticism of Kant in more detail.

2 Kant: The Cartesian Endeavor

Kant's most interesting discussions of the problem of idealism in the first *Critique* appear in the Refutation of Idealism (added in the B-edition), in Phenomena and Noumena, in crucial sections on the Paralogisms (in the A-edition), and in the Antinomies of pure reason.² In the Refutation of Idealism, among other places, Kant distinguishes between two sorts of idealism: skeptical and dogmatic (Kant 1787, B 274–275). A skeptical idealist – Descartes is Kant's favorite example – is defined as someone who denies that the existence of objects "is known through immediate perception" and who consequently holds that we "can never [...] be completely certain as to their reality" (Kant 1781, A 368–369). Skeptical idealism is thus defined specifically by an epistemic restriction. It specifies that although we may have experiences and knowledge of real objects, we can never be totally sure about this.

This contrasts with dogmatic idealism, which Kant ascribes to Berkeley. A dogmatic idealist is one who "regards the things in space as merely imaginary entities" (Kant 1787, B 274). Later on in the Paralogisms, Kant characterizes the dogmatic idealist as denying "the existence of external objects of the senses" (Kant 1781, A 368). Unlike the skeptical idealist, then, the dogmatic idealist makes an ontological claim. While the skeptical idealist puts a restriction on our claims to knowledge about the real world, the dogmatic idealist goes further in denying altogether the existence of external objects, claiming instead that they are nothing but imaginary entities. This dogmatic view thus naturally includes the weaker epistemic restriction of skeptical idealism in itself.

It does not matter for our purposes whether Kant is right in ascribing these positions to Descartes and Berkeley respectively, so I will not go into this. In fact, the distinction between both forms of idealism is not crucial to understanding Kant's position regarding them. For Kant, both positions are alike in that they share a certain hostility to realism. More importantly still, Kant believes that they both result from the same, single error of thought. If we can get rid of this error, the appeal of both views should vanish. As Kant puts it at one point, eliminating

---

2 My discussion in what follows strongly focuses on the fourth Paralogism and less on the Refutation of Idealism, which according to some scholars contradicts the fourth Paralogism (for instance Vaihinger 1988, Kemp Smith 1918, and Bader 2012). Guyer believes that "exactly *what* thesis the refutation is supposed to prove is unclear" (Guyer 1987, p. 280). I tend to think there is no contradiction between the refutation and the fourth Paralogism, and that the refutation does not bear directly on the thing in itself as some of these authors have assumed. I will here leave this issue aside, however. For recent discussions on the place of the Refutation of Idealism in Kant's second edition of the first *Critique*, see also Dicker 2008 and Bader 2012.

the error removes "*all controversy* in regard to the nature of the thinking being and its connection with the corporeal world" (Kant 1781, A 395, my italics).

Kant thus opposes idealism because it cannot accommodate realism. This indicates that the preferred transcendental idealism is not just any familiar form of idealism; it isn't one that can be framed in terms of the opposition between realism and idealism within early modern philosophy. Likewise, the realism Kant defends cannot be the "usual" realism – the one which conceptually opposes both Berkeley's ontological, and Descartes's epistemic, idealism. After all, the whole controversy of realism *and* idealism is claimed to be ill-founded. For that reason, Kant subsequently attempts to expose a tacit presupposition onto which the early modern debate is allegedly founded, in order to then draw out the right form of transcendental idealism.

Kant's discussion of this tacit presupposition appears most clearly in the fourth Paralogism section, which focuses on Descartes. Kant starts out by stating his sympathy for the Cartesian starting point, which seeks certainty in immanent consciousness. He agrees with Descartes that there "can be no question that I am conscious of my representations; these representations and I myself, who has the representations, therefore exist" (Kant 1781, A 370). Kant appears to favor less Descartes's subsequent procedure, however. He continues to criticize him specifically for the strategy of inference he then employs: "[For Descartes] I am not […] in a position to *perceive* external things, but can only infer their existence from my inner perception, taking the inner perception as the effect of which something external is the proximate cause" (Kant 1781, A 368). In this way, Kant thinks, Cartesian representationalism is born, and with it the problem of consciousness's relation to the world.

Kant believes this Cartesian fate can be avoided by reconceptualizing the relation between object and appearance in the original Cartesian model. Thus he presents his solution to the Cartesian inferentialist problem: "external objects […] are mere appearances, and are therefore nothing but a species of my representations […]. Thus external things exist as well as I myself, and both, indeed, upon the immediate witness of my self-consciousness" (Kant 1781, A 371). The solution, plainly put, consists of eliminating the idea that perceptions *indicate* the real world, as that strategy invokes the problem of our (inferential) access to the real based on appearance. Instead, we have to conceive of external objects as themselves species of representations. Real objects, Kant repeatedly notes, "are mere appearances;" "external things, namely matter, are in all their configurations and alterations nothing but mere appearances" (Kant 1781, A 371–372). Therefore, Kant concludes, the existence of external things is "immediately perceived," and the "need to resort to inference" has been dispensed (Kant 1781, A 371).

A superficial reading of Kant's suggestion may tempt one to conclude that the proposed solution simply downgrades the real object to mere appearance, hence falling prey to dogmatic idealism. Kant, however, aware of this threat, introduces a crucial distinction between empirical and transcendental idealism – a distinction which crosses with another one between empirical and transcendental realism.[3]

According to Kant, an empirical idealist is someone who considers objects to be mere empirically-produced ideas in the mind or brain, from which point the best one can do is infer the existence of external objects. Both Descartes and Berkeley, then, on Kant's reading of them, can be considered empirical idealists. Importantly, Kant now maintains that these forms of empirical idealism results from transcendental realism (Kant 1781, A 369); all empirical idealists that Kant claims to know are transcendental realists (Kant 1781, A 372). To identify the problems of skeptical and empirical idealism, then, we must turn to transcendental realism.

On Kant's view, a transcendental realist does not necessarily have to uphold transcendental realism as a theory. Instead, we can follow Allison in positing that transcendental realism is an "implicit norm in the light of which human cognition is analyzed" (Allison 2004, p. 28). The norm at stake is one which specifies the real by the ideal of radical mind-independence. As Stang puts it, transcendental realism concerns the (tacit) assumption that "reality 'is in itself' independently of how we cognize it" (Stang 2016).[4] Put differently, Kant believes that if one is prone to think of the world as a place out there beyond what can be given in appearance, and one subsequently reflects on one's sensibility to find only appearances, then the problem of the real world's immediate manifestation is unavoidable. Indeed, the threat of empirical idealism can always re-emerge – and indeed the entire problematic of our access to the real world with it – as long as transcendental realism sets the norm.

Now we can see how Kant believes erroneous forms of idealism follow from an implicit transcendental realism, the latter doctrine being the "common prejudice" (Kant 1781/1787, A 740/B 768) accepted by all philosophers before Kant. Interestingly, Kant offers something of an explanation as to why transcendental realism is so attractive, one which is somewhat akin to Husserl's descriptions of the so-called natural attitude. According to Kant, objects of experience have this "deceptive property that [...] they detach themselves as it were from the soul and

---

[3] The distinction between empirical and transcendental investigation is made earlier on already (Kant 1781/1787, A 97/B 118–120). The relevant distinction, however, occurs in Kant 1781, A 371–373.
[4] Note that Stang's definition pertains to Allison's account.

appear to hover outside it" (Kant 1781, A 385). It belongs, he notes, to ordinary experience to posit objects "as objects outside us, [thereby] completely separating them from the thinking subject" (Kant 1781, A 389). This results in "the ordinary concepts of our reason with regard to the communion in which our thinking subject stands with the things outside us" (Kant 1781, A 389); in other words: it leads to the ordinary (transcendental realist) conception of objects as enjoying radical independence from experience. However, as long as we do this, "we are dogmatic, looking upon them as real objects existing [radically] independently of us" (Kant 1781, A 389).

3 Kant: The Solution

The problems caused by transcendental realism bring us to the other combination of views: empirical realism with transcendental idealism. This new combination should provide the solution to all the skeptical problems that stem from transcendental realism. From the new viewpoint, Kant notes, objects are genuinely "outside us" (Kant 1781, A 376). This is Kant's empirical realism. At least in the usual (veridical) case, "outer perception [...] yields immediate proof of something real in space [...]. In this sense empirical realism is beyond question" (Kant 1781, A 375). On Kant's view, then, we have immediate, non-inferential access to real objects. But what does it mean for an object to be real here?

Clearly, for an object to be real does not mean, as with transcendental realism, that it exists *radically* independently from us. Instead, Kant's transcendental idealism specifies that they are to be considered *transcendentally* inseparable from us. That is to say, objects "need" us – as a transcendental condition of possibility – in order to be objects at all. Certainly, however, this does not mean that things not currently perceived by anyone do not exist. As Kant notes, "that there may be inhabitants in the moon, although no one has ever perceived them, must certainly be admitted" (Kant 1781/1787, A 493/B 251). In other words, we can legitimately treat the world as a place filled with real objects, as empirical realism specifies. Yet this thesis can be properly maintained only within the confines of transcendental idealism. The reality of objects can be granted exclusively from within the scope of possible experience, not outside of it, as transcendental realism has it.

This should help address Kant's otherwise confusing remarks that external objects are "mere appearances" (Kant 1781, A 371–372), and that transcendental idealism sees objects as "representations only" (Kant 1781, A 369). In saying so, Kant does not intend to contradict his commitment to empirical realism, which postulates that objects are truly "outside us," only to relapse into empirical idealism. Interpreting Kant this way "would be unjust" (Kant 1781/1787, A 491/B 519). That objects are mere appearances in us states that they are transcendentally "in" us, that is, transcendentally dependent on us. Yet they *appear as* being outside of us, and it is on that peculiar appearance structure that the natural sciences are legitimately erected. Transcendental idealism is thus merely the explication of the thesis that nothing more than this type of empirical realism is demanded, while transcendental realism, by contrast, is the tacit conviction that we need more.

Kant thus effectively seeks to deny that appearances are empirical ideas. They do not have a status akin to that of illusions, hallucinations, or dreams, and hence they are legitimately considered real (provided they accord with the categories). This point is also emphasized in the *Prolegomena*. Here, Kant writes that "the difference between truth and dream, however, is not decided through the quality of the representations that referred to objects, for they are the same in both, but through their connection according to the rules" (Kant 2004, AK. IV, p. 290). In other words, a non-veridical perception is not distinguished from a veridical one for failing to establish a causal connection to mind-independent external objects. Rather, what defines veridical perception is the way in which representations are connected by rules of understanding. Kant, then, is a conjunctivist regarding perception insofar as the external object is not regarded as a necessary constituent of veridical perception. In true perception there "is contained not the least illusion or temptation toward error," because here representations "can be connected together correctly in experience according to rules of truth" (Kant 2004, AK. IV, p. 291), and that settles the matter of reality to which perception makes claim.

This position in *Prolegomena* is perfectly in line with what Kant defends in the fourth Paralogism. Both texts support the idea that we should not measure the capacity of perception to give us real things by some norm conceptualizing the real as being outside of the scope of possible experience. The right mark of reality is a correct synthetic arrangement of representations through functions of understanding – not a (causal) relation to a radically mind-independent object.

And thus, Kant thinks, is the century-old problem of empirical idealism transcended. Proof of anything more than empirical realism of the sort Kant has argued for simply is not needed (Kant 1781, A 375–376). To the contrary, the only reasons for seeking for more stem from the false prejudice of transcendental realism. From now on, "the question is no longer of the communion of the soul with other known substances of a different kind outside us [transcendentally speaking], but only of the connection of the representations of inner sense with the modifications of our outer sensibility" (Kant 1781, A 386).

4 Kant: Phenomena *and* Noumena?

Ever since its first edition, Kant's first *Critique* has seen a steady branch of anti-realist or representationalist interpretation.[5] In Kant's own time this included Eberhard, Jacobi, Maimon, and Garve and Feder (to whom Kant responded in the *Prolegomena*). In twentieth-century philosophy, this tradition was furthered by Strawson (1966), who claimed that for Kant "reality is supersensible and [...] we can have no knowledge of it" (Strawson 1966, p. 16). More recent representationalist interpretations include Guyer (1987, p. 335), Westphal (2004, p. 67), Braver (2007), Rockmore (2007, p. 9), Allais (2015, p. 59), and Guyer and Horstmann (2015), among numerous others.

If these authors are right that Kant is ontologically committed to a reality beyond the one we can experience, then this obviously threatens Kant's empirical realism as I have just outlined it. This is because empirical realism depends on transcendental idealism, whereas these authors see Kant (in some important sense at least) as being committed to transcendental realism. Without discussing the detailed arguments of all these scholars, this section argues that Kant is not committed to a supersensible reality in a way that would threaten the proposed conjunction of empirical realism and transcendental idealism.

In a section in the chapter on Phenomena and Noumena (deleted in the B-edition), Kant first defines "*phaenomena*" as "objects according to the unity of the categories" (Kant 1781, A 248–249). Phenomena, in other words, are appearances; they are representations of which we can acquire knowledge. Second, Kant offers a (more striking) definition of *noumena*. There are, Kant contends, "things which are mere objects of understanding, and which, nevertheless, can be given as such to an intuition, although not to one that is sensible – [...] such things would be entitled *noumena*" (Kant 1781, A 249). A bit further on, Kant aligns this concept of noumenon with that of the thing in itself: "apart from the constitution of our sensibility (upon which the form of our intuition is grounded), [there] must be something in itself, that is, an object independent of sensibility. There thus results the concept of a *noumenon*" (Kant 1781, A 252).

---

[5] Note that I will not deal with Kant's practical philosophy in this section, which some scholars believe involves a stronger ontological commitment to the noumenon than is to be found in his theoretical work. At the moment I am most sympathetic to Adams (1997) on this point, who concludes, after discussing the import of Kant's practical philosophy, that "uncertain as it may be of the real possibility of noumenal causality, theoretical reason seems justified in affirming [only] the logical possibility of the concept" (Adams 1997, p. 821).

Not unimportantly, Kant also invokes a challenging distinction between *our form of intuition* – which, Kant maintains, is necessarily sensible – and intuition *as such*. Apparently, then, another kind of intuition is conceivable which is not sensible, as it is with us. There might be, although this is not necessarily so, "intelligible entities to which our sensible faculty of intuition has no relation whatsoever" (Kant 1787, B 309). Elsewhere, he writes that he has *not* proven "that another kind of intuition is possible," although neither has he proven "that sensible intuition is the only possible intuition" (Kant 1781, A 252).

Things are further complicated by a distinction between a positive and a negative noumenon (in the second edition, but the first edition discussion is, I think, not essentially different). Subscribing to a positive noumenon would amount roughly to acknowledging that we can comprehend the possibility (Kant 1787, B 307) or that we have the ability to comprehend (Kant 1781/1787, A 255/B 310) "an *object* of a *non-sensible intuition*" (Kant 1787, B 307). Crucially, this capacity for comprehension Kant *denies*. For Kant, the very "thing" the concept of a thing in itself denotes is not something we could possibly comprehend. This is why Kant repeatedly emphasizes that the concept is without "sense" (Kant 1781/1787, A 240/B 299), without "meaning" (Kant 1781/1787, A 241/B 300), and that it "signifies nothing at all" (Kant 1787, B 306).

The positive concept of a thing in itself, then, which is the cornerstone of noumenalist readings such as Strawson's (1966), is refuted by Kant.[6] Yet, while the concept is thus without "sense," it is not, Kant maintains, "in any way contradictory." This, he argues, is because "we cannot assert of sensibility that it is the sole possible kind of intuition" (Kant 1781/1787, A 254/B 310). Therefore, as he puts it later on in the *Critique*, "a place remains open for other and different objects; and consequently that these latter must not be absolutely denied, though [...] neither can they be asserted as objects for our understanding" (Kant 1781/1787, A 287–288/B 344). Kant, then, makes a distinction between the concept of noumenon as denoting a real intuitive possibility and as a merely

---

[6] There is also some debate about whether several of Kant's remarks stress that things in themselves are explicitly *not* spatiotemporal (Kant 1781/1787, A 26/B 42; A 32/B 49; A 492/B 520), which would of course contradict his other remarks that the thing in itself is merely a transcendental concept, and not a "thing" we can know determinatively. If things in themselves are explicitly non-spatiotemporal, this could lead to a position we may call dogmatic transcendental idealism (Guyer 1987, p. 335). I am sidestepping this issue here, but see particularly Allison 1976 – whose position on the issue I am most sympathetic to – and Guyer (1987, pp. 333–344) for more discussion.

formally-coherent concept[7] and makes it clear that he believes the concept is without sense or meaning but formally non-contradictory (thus he accepts the latter but not the former).[8]

Kant subsequently moves from the mere formal possibility of things in themselves to arguing for their *necessity* (Kant 1781/1787, A 254/B 310). It is crucial, however, to understand this necessity as the necessity *of* the concept of the mere logical possibility. This necessity is further qualified by Kant as being of a transcendental kind. That is to say, the negative concept of noumenon is a necessary *a priori* product of the transcendental structure of our experience. It is produced "to prevent sensible intuition from being extended to things in themselves" (Kant 1781/1787, A 254/B 310). It is "not only admissible, but as setting limits to sensibility [...] likewise indispensable" (Kant 1781/1787, A 256/B 311).

This yields the question of how human experience transcendentally generates the negative concept of noumenon. While the workings of sensible intuition may seem a plausible candidate here, this is not Kant's view. As Kant notes, "the understanding is not limited *through* sensibility; on the contrary, it itself limits sensibility by applying the term noumena to things in themselves [through which it at the same time] sets limits to itself" (Kant 1781/1787, A 256/B 312). In other words, it is the understanding which is "not satisfied with the substrate of sensibility, and [...] therefore add[s] to the phenomena noumena which only the pure understanding can think" (Kant 1781, A 251). Likewise, in the *Prolegomena*, Kant says that "the understanding, just by the fact that it accepts appearances, also admits of the existence of things in themselves, [this] is not merely permitted but also inevitable" (Kant 2004, AK. IV, p. 315).

Kant, then, by accepting the negative concept of noumenon, does not commit ontologically to things in themselves – the positive concept of noumenon he rejects. Instead, Kant deems things in themselves as (i) only logically possible – a possibility rooted in the fact that a non-sensible intuition of noumenal reality cannot be logically excluded, even though it isn't a real possibility – and (ii) transcendentally necessary, since it is transcendentally engrained in our understand-

---

[7] This reading of Kant as committed solely to the formal or logical possibility of the noumenal world but not to its real possibility is in broad agreement with the reading provided by Adams (1997).
[8] Note that the logical space of the thing in itself as here illustrated is not confined exclusively to an unknowable shadow side of appearances to which we have access, as some versions of the double aspect view have it. See also Ameriks 2003, who develops the point that "some things in themselves could lack appearances" – at least such a thing cannot be *logically* excluded either – which means a "one-on-one-mapping" of things in themselves (as thought entities) onto real things is impossible (Ameriks 2003, pp. 34–35).

ing's response to operations of sensibility. The necessity pertains, however, only to the negative concept of noumenon; in other words: we are of necessity capable of conceiving of the logical possibility of a reality beyond ours, and this, likewise with necessity, accrues our cognition with a sense of limitation. Nothing more is at stake in these discussions than this transcendental necessity of the negative concept of the noumenon. It is "a merely *limiting concept*" and "therefore only of negative employment" (Kant 1781/1787, A 255/B 310–311).

This should make it clear that the concept of noumenon which Kant defends in fact can have no ontological import. On Kant's terms, there is nothing "real" about the noumenon, as "reality" does not derive its sense from the parameters of transcendental realism but from qualifications concerning the synthetic orderings of representations instead. While an object beyond possible experience may *always* be logically conceived, it *cannot possibly* have "sense" (Kant 1781/1787, A 240/B 299) or "meaning" (Kant 1781/1787, A 241/B 300). The noumenon is not, then, that to which "we ultimately intend to refer" (Guyer 1987, p. 335). It is, to the contrary, better understood as having no significance when it comes to determining the conditions that must be satisfied for the ascription of a sense of reality to something.

5 Husserl: The Cartesian Endeavor

Like Kant, Husserl claims to endorse a form of transcendental idealism. At the same time, he suggests that there can be no stronger realism[9] and that no ordinary realist has ever been so realistic and concrete as he has been (Husserl 1994, p. 16).[10] In what follows, I first focus on Husserl's famous reading of Descartes in the first *Cartesian Meditations*, which should compare nicely to Kant's discussion of Descartes dealt with earlier. I then reconstruct Husserl's complicated views on the relation between the intentional object and the real object, for which I draw on a variety of later works and manuscripts.[11] Lastly, I discuss a section from

---

9 "A stronger realism therefore cannot be given, when this word says nothing more than: 'I am conscious of being a human being living in this world etc., and this I doubt not the slightest bit'" (Husserl 1976, p. 191, my translation).
10 "No ordinary 'realist' has been so realistic and concrete as I, the phenomenological 'idealist'" (Husserl 1994, p. 16, my translation).
11 I leave out *Logical Investigations* here, which was written prior to Husserl's transcendental turn, although I do not think Husserl's position there yields a very different picture of the relation between intentional and real object. See also Zahavi 2017, who offers a more elaborate case against representationalist readings of *Logical Investigations* in his recent book on Husserl.

Ideas I where Husserl discusses the logical possibility of a noumenal world. These discussions all illustrate that Husserl's thinking about the pitfalls of transcendental realism as well as the proposed solution of transcendental idealism are fundamentally akin to Kant's.

As is well-known, Husserl offered an(other) introduction to his philosophy for a French audience in 1929, in which he departs from Descartes's attempt to reform "philosophy into a science grounded on an absolute foundation" (Husserl 1950, Hua I, p. 43; Husserl 1960, p. 1). There has been an unfortunate tradition of scholarship which appears to have taken the fact of this starting point to indicate the neo-Cartesian nature of Husserl's own position,[12] suggesting that he upholds an inherently internalist, solipsist, and/or representationalist philosophy. A close reading of the first Meditation, however, should suffice to rebuff such a view.

Above all, the first Meditation reveals Husserl's deep admiration for the radicalism of Descartes's philosophical endeavor. Descartes is worthy of Husserl's appraisal as being one who "seriously intends to become a philosopher," an attempt which required Descartes to "withdraw into himself and attempt, within himself, to overthrow and build anew all the sciences that, up to then, he has been accepting:" Descartes, Husserl thinks, saw that philosophy is of its essence a "personal affair" (Husserl 1950, Hua I, p. 44; Husserl 1960, p. 2). He understood that radical philosophy demands beginning anew within oneself because of the recognition that absolute evidence can never take its departure from the naively accepted existing world or the opinions of others. It must, at least at first, withdraw from that world into the immediacy of immanent consciousness.

Husserl continues to grant Descartes's initial success in finding a correct starting point for philosophy – just as Kant did before him. Descartes's "famous and very remarkable method of doubt" successfully reveals that the world's existence is not given absolutely, and Descartes correctly follows up on that intuition by claiming that "the being of the world must remain unaccepted at this initial stage" (Husserl 1950, Hua I, p. 45; Husserl 1960, p. 3). Descartes thus "keeps only himself, qua pure ego of his *cogitationes*, as having an absolutely indubitable existence, as something that cannot be done away with" (Husserl 1950, Hua I, p. 45; Husserl 1960, p. 3).[13] This way, the Cartesian path of philoso-

---

[12] Husserl himself suggests that "one might almost call transcendental phenomenology a neo-Cartesianism, even though it is obliged – and precisely by its radical development of Cartesian motifs – to reject nearly all the well-known doctrinal content of the Cartesian philosophy" (Husserl 1950, Hua I, p. 43; Husserl 1960, p. 1).

[13] Already in his much earlier reading of Descartes in lectures from 1907, Husserl notes that he "can latch onto this point" (Husserl 1950, Hua II, p. 49; Husserl 1999, p. 38).

phy leads, correctly according to Husserl, "from naïve Objectivism to transcendental subjectivism" (Husserl 1950, Hua I, p. 46; Husserl 1960, p. 4).

It is only in appropriating the significance of this discovery of certainty that Descartes goes amiss. Descartes "stands on the threshold of the greatest of all discoveries [but] he does not grasp its proper sense" (Husserl 1950, Hua I, p. 64; Husserl 1960, pp. 24–25). In spite of the attempted radicalism, Husserl maintains that certain "prejudices were at work" (Husserl 1950, Hua I, p. 63; Husserl 1960, p. 24), by which he refers specifically to the "ideal of science" (Husserl 1950, Hua I, p. 48; Husserl 1960, p. 7) of the modern period, namely geometrical-axiomatic deduction. This assumed ideal led Descartes to conceive of the *ego cogito* as "the axiom of the ego's absolute certainty of himself" (Husserl 1950, Hua I, p. 49; Husserl 1960, p. 8), thus transforming the ego into "a little *tag-end of the world*," after which "the problem is to infer the rest of the world by rightly conducted arguments" (Husserl 1950, Hua I, p. 63; Husserl 1960, p. 24).

According to Husserl, then, Descartes erred in assuming that philosophy should be modeled on mathematics, an assumption which subsequently perverts the problem of the mind's relation to the world as one of inference. Descartes falls short of his own pursued radicalism by failing to see that, properly undertaken, even "logic is deprived of acceptance by the universal overthrow" (Husserl 1950, Hua I, p. 53; Husserl 1960, p. 13) of the world's certainty through methodical doubt. The *ego cogito*, in other words, simply isn't the inferential base Descartes thought it was, and he could – at least in principle – have seen this, had he freed himself more fully from bias.

It is worth mentioning that, from Husserl's viewpoint – although it is not elaborated in *Cartesian Meditations* –, Kant's transcendental philosophy is similarly unsuccessful in eliminating biases stemming from the Galilean paradigm.[14] In the end, both Descartes and Kant fail (i) to uncover transcendental subjectivity as one's "own pure conscious life, in and by which the entire objective world exists for me and is precisely as it is for me" (Husserl 1950, Hua I, p. 60; Husserl 1960, p. 21), and (ii) to erect subsequently an eidetic science on this which operates exclusively within the confines of pure subjectivity, and which accepts nothing but what can be gained on the basis of the immediate epistemic access which essentially characterizes it.

However, Husserl's deeper allegations regarding the supposed mythical and ungraspable nature of Kant's allegedly groundless metaphysics need not concern

---

[14] Kant's failures are not, however, exactly the same as Descartes's, but time does not permit me to discuss this here.

us here.¹⁵ What matters for our purposes is the similar extent of their respective appraisals of Descartes. As I discussed earlier, Kant, too, applauded Descartes's proof of the fact that "these representations and I myself [...] exist" (Kant 1781, A 370). Moreover, Kant's appraisal likewise terminated with Descartes questioning our "position to *perceive* external things" (Kant 1781, A 368) and the resort to inference that follows from it. What remains to be seen now is whether, abstracting from minute details, their solutions are also similar.

6 Husserl: The Solution

What has been said so far concerning Husserl's criticism of Cartesian representationalism leaves open how Husserl seeks to (dis)solve the problem to which Descartes reacted. In other words, we need a positive account of Husserl's construal of the relation between the world *as* experienced and the empirically real world outside of consciousness.

There is a long-standing debate (the so-called "noema-debate") between East Coast and West Coast interpreters of Husserl which deals with just this problem. On the one hand, there are those who, eager to avoid subscribing dogmatic idealism to Husserl, maintain a rigid distinction between the *experience* of an object and the *being* of an object. Here I gather West Coast readers Føllesdal (1969), Dreyfus and Hall (1982), Smith and McIntyre (1982, 1989), McIntyre (1986), Smith (2007, 2013), among others. These authors emphasize that the noema or the object *as* experienced is categorically distinct from the object *as* real. The aim of this conceptual distinction is to ensure that while Husserl's language of phenomenological constitution may apply to appearances of objects and our intentional directedness to them, it does not apply to their actual existence. Put differently, intentional consciousness can let a physical world appear to a subject, but it cannot for all that *create* the world.

While this strategy successfully eliminates the threat of dogmatic idealism, it risks doubling the intentional object, as others have keenly pointed out.¹⁶ In doing so, the West Coast interpreters could undesirably make Husserl susceptible to the kind of representationalism he consistently argued against. Moreover, interpreting the intentional and real object as "distinct entities" (Smith and McIntyre 1989, p. 162) fits uncomfortably with Husserl's frequent denial that the two senses of object can be held apart. For instance, Husserl argues that re-

---

15 See: Husserl 1976, Hua VI, pp. 116–118; Husserl 1956, Hua VII, p. 362.
16 This includes Drummond (1990, 2009) and Zahavi (2004, 2008, 2010), among many others.

ality does not somehow contain two types of being which "dwell peaceably side by side" (Husserl 1976, Hua III/1, p. 93; Husserl 1983, p. 111). Elsewhere, he notes that the "true being of nature is not a second one next to mere intentional being" (Husserl 2002a, Hua XXXV, p. 276, my translation). Also, the *Cartesian Meditations* stress that the real object isn't radically beyond consciousness: it "necessarily acquires all the sense determining it, *along with its existential status*, exclusively from my experiencing" (Husserl 1950, Hua I, p. 65; Husserl 1960, p. 26, my italics).

In spite of the noema-debate's central status in Husserl scholarship, I think it can be solved relatively easily. On the one hand, West Coast readers are right that (i) Husserl maintains that talk of real objects must be kept separate from talk of objects' appearances. Both *Logical Investigations* and *Ideas I* emphasize that whereas we can say about a real tree that it can burn down, we cannot do so about the tree's appearance (Husserl 1976, Hua III/1, pp. 182–184; Husserl 1983, pp. 214–216; Husserl 1984, XIX/1, pp. 359–390). Likewise, *Ideas III* stresses that "a 'physical thing' as correlate [of consciousness] is not a physical thing [...]. The theme is therefore a totally different one" (Husserl 1971, Hua V, p. 85; Husserl 1980, p. 72). In some sense, then, real objects are not mere appearances for Husserl.

Yet West coast readers tend to either downplay or overlook the fact that Husserl repeatedly states that (ii) the real, burnable tree also ultimately derives from consciousness. As Husserl puts it in his *Cartesian Meditations*, "that every sense that any existent whatever has or can have for me – in respect of its 'what' and its 'it exists and actually is' – is a sense in and *arising from* my intentional life" (Husserl 1950, Hua I, p. 123; Husserl 1960, p. 91). In his *Natur und Geist* lectures (1927), Husserl notes that every thinkable world in general is only thinkable as relative to the reality of consciousness (Husserl 2001, Hua XXXI/1, p. 78). Likewise, manuscripts on the phenomenological reduction emphasize that the world is only thinkable as idea from within the coherence of transcendental subjectivity (Husserl 2002b, Hua XXXVI, p. 26). In short, while a real object is certainly given *as* independent of consciousness and in that sense also distinct from a mere appearance, Husserl also seems to believe that the object ultimately derives its reality-sense from consciousness.

The solution to this ambiguity lies in the fact that Husserl, like Kant, seeks to blend realism within idealism. Simply put, (i) real objects and appearing objects are categorically distinct, yet (ii) both are also in a deeper sense rooted in consciousness. As with Kant, a superficial reading could lead one to conclude that point (ii) must contradict point (i) – yet Husserl, like Kant, denies this. On Husserl's view, it is consistent to say, for instance, that one believes that the physical world truly exists independently of one's personal experiences, while at the same time believing that that conviction ultimately derives all its sense (including that which the conviction is about) in some way from one's experiences. To make this more concrete: one can believe that the Big Bang created our universe 13.8 billion years ago (*a posteriori*, since it pertains to natural facts), while also believing that even the Big Bang and "all the sense determining it" comes, in the end, "from my experiencing" (*a priori*, since all sense-determination comes from experiencing consciousness) (Husserl 1950, Hua I, p. 65; Husserl 1960, p. 24).

Husserl's transcendental commitment to (ii), then, which is generally emphasized by East Coast readers, does not change the potency of the distinction defended by West Coast readers made in (i). This is also made pretty clear in lectures on phenomenological psychology, where Husserl notes that a "physical thing [is] *a priori*, like any object at all, referable to a subjectivity, as experienceable and knowable by it; but [...] in its sense as an object, a thing includes nothing of a subjectivity related to it" (Husserl 1962, Hua IX, p. 118; Husserl 1977, p. 89).[17] This illustrates that conceptually differentiating them does not necessitate their ontological differentiation.[18] This is also why Husserl insists that the phenomenologist doesn't study separate mental entities. To the contrary, phenomenology makes "the world *as such* our theme together with every natural consideration of the world" (Husserl 1962, Hua IX, p. 222; Husserl 1977, p. 170, my italics); it studies the "always known and knowable world, precisely as it is known and knowable" (Husserl 1956, Hua VII, p. 272; Husserl 1974, p. 43).

For Husserl, then, as for Kant, the Cartesian conviction that an account of the communion of consciousness with radically mind-independent entities must be given has to be rejected. Reality does not derive its sense from a relation to mind-independent objects. To the contrary, transcendental idealism relocates the norm for reality ascription to within the scope of possible experience: the "space of possible absolute consciousness encompasses *all meaningful questions and answers, all meaningful truth and existence*" (Husserl 2002a, Hua XXXV, pp. 270 –

---

17 The same point is emphasized in *Ideas III*: The issue we need to understand is "how '*the same thing*' functions as to concepts and propositions in ontological [scientific] and phenomenological [transcendental] research [respectively]" (Husserl 1971, Hua V, p. 80; Husserl 1980, p. 68, my italics).

18 This reading brings not only the noema-debate to its only viable solution, but also, I think, Ameriks's (1977) early dispute with Solomon (1972), Ingarden (1973), and others about the term 'constitution' in Husserl's work and about the meaning of consciousness as productive source of the world. One can agree with Ameriks's realist reading that the world for Husserl is not "a part of consciousness" and that constitution does not signify "creation" or "invention." One can accept all that while still agreeing with Ingarden (1973) that Husserl regarded external objects rooted in the productivity of transcendental consciousness.

271, my translation). This means that, again in line with Kant, the mark of veridical perception cannot be the presence of a relation to radically mind-independent objects. As Husserl puts it: "everything depends upon the interconnections [in consciousness] that present intelligible unity. They themselves constitute objectivity [...] It is only in these connections that the objectivity of the objective sciences [...] constitutes itself" (Husserl 1950, Hua II, p. 75; Husserl 1999, p. 55).

7 Husserl: Phenomena *and* Noumena?

Husserl scholars may have this advantage over Kant scholars: that the former's work is not pervaded with puzzling remarks on the existence of noumena. Yet Husserl does, precisely in what is arguably the most idealist section in *Ideas I*, address the issue of the noumenon in a paragraph entitled "The Logical Possibility and the Material Countersense of a World Outside Ours" (Husserl 1976, Hua III/1, pp. 90–91; Husserl 1983, pp. 108–109). Focusing on this paragraph should help draw out more clearly that, in spite of the widespread acceptance of the contrary view, Husserl's position on the noumenon and on the faults of transcendental realism are, in its broad outlines, very similar to Kant's.

Starting from the paragraph's title, the first question that arises is what Husserl means by *logical* possibility/countersense and *material* possibility/countersense.[19] This demands a clarification of the concepts of material and formal in Husserl's work. In brief, for Husserl, so-called formal ontology includes only formal entities (or concepts), which constitute the study province of formal logic. The formal character of such entities at the same time suggests that they do not belong to any particular material-ontological region. Instead, material regions all abide by and in some sense at least make use of formal principles. Material ontology can in turn be divided into different regions to which various sciences correspond, such as biology, geometry, or phenomenology ("organism," "space," and "consciousness" would be their respective material-ontological regions). Any region of inquiry which is not strictly formal is thus to be considered material (so the term has nothing to do with "physical matter").

The second question which now rises is what constitutes a countersense on both levels. First, a material countersense is, for Husserl, any expression whose concrete content matter is inherently contradictory. For instance, the proposition

---

[19] Unimportant in the present context, Husserl also differentiates the countersense from the nonsense, which "results when the formation-rules for complex terms and sentences are violated" (Centrone 2010, p. 117). One example of this would be meaningless gibberish (a sentence without meaning whatsoever).

that "if something is clearly red all over then it is clearly green all over" is a material countersense.[20] Also, "a round square" – often used by Husserl – is a material countersense.

Second, a formal countersense is an expression whose content involves an inherent formal contradiction, as for instance in the proposition that "for any properties x and y, if something has both x and y then it does not have x and y."

From here a third and more urgent question can finally be raised, namely why the existence of a world beyond possible experience is in fact a material countersense. That this idea is not logically contradictory is deemed evident by Husserl: "something real outside this world is, of course, 'logically' possible; obviously it involves no formal contradiction" (Husserl 1976, Hua III/1, p. 90; Husserl 1983, p. 108). Husserl, then, like Kant, accepts at least the formal coherence of this idea. So where, according to Husserl, does its material contradiction lie?

The answer is: in the material region of transcendental consciousness. What does that mean? Husserl believes that while we may be capable of conceiving the merely empty possibility (its formal coherence) of a world beyond ours, as soon as "we ask about the essential conditions on which its validity would depend," we "recognize that something transcendent *necessarily must be experienceable* not merely by an ego conceived as an empty logical possibility but by *any actual ego*" (Husserl 1976, Hua III/1, p. 90; Husserl 1983, p. 108, my italics).[21] In other words, any object whatsoever presupposes the possibility of being intended by a consciousness. This universal *a priori* correlation between object and consciousness, insofar as it states a universal law for the being of any object, is a material – not a formal – law. Obviously, this correlation claim does not pertain to any physical law governing things; but that is not required to make it a material law. For Husserl, it is material in the sense of being a "philosophical" or "transcendental" law at the fundamental level of transcendentally constituting consciousness.[22]

---

[20] Example taken from Centrone 2010, p. 118. See also Leichtle 2002 for a more elaborate discussion of this.
[21] The word "any" [meaning "every"] may surprise here. Husserl elaborates on this further on, noting that "what is cognizable by one ego must, of essential necessity, be cognizable by *any* ego" and that there exist "eidetically regarded, *essential possibilities of effecting a mutual understanding*" such that "worlds of experience separated in fact become joined by concatenations of actual experience to make up the one intersubjective world" (Husserl 1976, Hua III/1, p. 90; Husserl 1983, p. 108). In what follows, I speak simply of a (not just any) ego.
[22] One could ask here why the logical possibility of a radically mind-independent world is not in fact more important than its material countersense. Does formal logic not stand in the highest possible regard, above that of any conceivable material inquiry? But the answer, for Husserl at

And so Husserl concludes, in a manner reminiscent of Kant, that the "formal-logical possibility of realities outside the world [...] materially proves to be a countersense" (Husserl 1976, Hua III/1, p. 91; Husserl 1983, p. 109).[23] It may be worth highlighting an apparent difference though, namely that whereas Husserl here focuses on the formal possibility of a world beyond ours, Kant seemed instead to focus on the limits of intuition. As discussed earlier, Kant emphasized in particular that he had proven neither "that another kind of intuition is possible" nor "that sensible intuition is the only possible intuition" (Kant 1781, A 252).[24] Still, I do not think this makes for a substantial difference between both accounts. Kant's point was that we have no intuition of a noumenal world and cannot even truly imagine the reality of such an intuition. Since for Kant all justification of propositions with content must come from intuition – since "thoughts without content are empty" (Kant 1781/1787, A 51/B 75) – the concept of such a world as well as of a corresponding non-sensible intuition lacks real justification and becomes a mere formal postulation. Kant explicitly acknowledges this, saying that we "are in no way justified" in positively accepting another kind of intuition that is non-sensible (even though the idea is formally non-contradictory) (Kant 1781/1787, A 259/B 309).

Thus, for Kant, the possibility of a non-sensible intuition of a noumenal world proved to be, in spite of its formal coherence, not a real possibility. So while Kant, indeed, unlike Husserl, focused on intuition to discuss the possibility of a world beyond ours, the conclusion he reaches still turns out pretty much the same – namely that although we cannot imagine what such an intuition would be like (since it has no intuitive or "material," justificatory ground, in Husserl's idiom) it is still formally coherent (we have an empty concept for it).

---

least, is negative. That the *a priori* correlation is universal means that it holds for all formal expressions as well. Put differently, even logic derives its sense and validity from transcendental consciousness – since *no object* [including ideal ones] signifies a "reaching out beyond the world which is for consciousness" (Husserl 1976, Hua III/1, p. 100; Husserl 1983, p. 121).

23 Leichtle (2002) comes to a similar conclusion based on Husserl's much earlier *The Idea of Phenomenology* (from 1907), writing that Husserl "will attempt to demonstrate the countersense of construing the problem of transcendence as that of understanding how 'real immanence' correlates with 'absolute transcendence'" (Leichtle 2002, p. 386).

24 Thanks in particular to Stefano Vincini for pointing this out to me.

Conclusion

This chapter has offered a general systematic-historical comparison of Kant and Husserl regarding their defenses of transcendental idealism. I argued that for both, transcendental idealism is genuinely a form of idealism, albeit one which is motivated precisely by the attempt to overcome skeptical idealism by incorporating realism. Both defenses further share a point of departure in Descartes's philosophy, which both Kant and Husserl take to be rooted in a transcendental realism that has to be overcome by relocating the norm for reality ascription within the scope of possible experience. I suggested that Kant is plausibly read as being consistent on this matter, and that the negative concept of noumenon remaining in his philosophy entails nothing but the necessary concept of the empty logical possibility of a world beyond ours – something that can also be found in Husserl.

At the same time, I wish not to downplay the fact that Husserl's exploration of transcendental idealism through the universal *a priori* correlation as a synthetic (material) *a priori* truth is quite different from Kant's. Further differences would, I think, become apparent through a more detailed exposition of Husserl's intricate proof structure, which would involve a discussion of Husserl's concept of *a priori*[25] and of his theory of *a priori* intuition.[26] Most notably, perhaps, this would draw out (i) the different theories of *a priori* evidence that underlie their respective proofs, and how this subsequently (ii) leads Husserl to distance him-

---

[25] I cannot dwell on the details of Husserl's concept of *a priori* here, although a further elaboration would be required for a complete exposition of the universal *a priori* correlation. In brief, Husserl maintains that *a priori* refers to pure possibility, i.e. to pure imaginative possibility in detachment from actuality. Any *a priori* proposition is one which holds valid in pure possibility, and therefore "prescribes rules" to the actual (as an instance of the possible). Euclidean geometrical propositions are instances of regionally valid *a priori* propositions (valid within a Euclidean manifold). Husserl, however, maintains that "there is not the slightest reason to consider the methodological structure of *a priori* thinking [...] as an exclusive property of the mathematical sphere" (Husserl 1997, p. 353). This is while the capacity for the free variation of possibilities in pure imagination involved in *a priori* cognition is "everywhere the same" (Husserl 1997, p. 354). As a result, "from *every* concrete actuality, and every individual trait actually experienced in it or capable of being experienced, a path stands open to the realm of ideal or pure possibility and consequently to that of *a priori* thinking" (Husserl 1997, pp. 353–354). Phenomenology itself is an example of a non-mathematical *a priori* discipline. In the same manner, the necessity of the correlation of object to consciousness can be known to hold *a priori* in pure possibility. See also van Mazijk 2018 where I discuss this extensively.

[26] On Husserl's view, in contradistinction to Kant's, *a priori* truths can be directly intuited by us. See Tieszen 1984 and Uehlein 1992 for discussions on Husserl's concept of *a priori* intuition.

self from Kant's philosophy, which Husserl read as pertaining exclusively to humans, rather than to the pure possibility of an object in general.[27] Lastly, this would also, I think, reveal that Husserl does not just attempt to "save" empirical realism as Kant does (the reality of spatiotemporal things), but the reality of any intended object – reality understood each time within the essential limitations of the respective region. These deeper divergences, however, lie outside the scope of the present chapter, which was concerned with fleshing out more generally the similarities between Kant's and Husserl's attempts to overcome skeptical idealism through transcendental idealism.[28]

Bibliography

Adams, Robert M. (1997): "Things in Themselves". In: *Philosophy and Phenomenological Research*, vol. 57, n° 4, pp. 801–825.
Allais, Lucy (2015): *Manifest Reality: Kant's Idealism and his Realism*. Oxford: Oxford University Press.
Allison, Henry E. (1976): "The Non-Spatiality of Things in Themselves for Kant". In: *Journal of the History of Philosophy*, vol. 14, n° 3, pp. 313–321.
Allison, Henry E. (2004): *Kant's Transcendental Idealism: An Interpretation and Defense*. New Haven, London: Yale University Press.
Ameriks, Karl (1977): "Husserl's Realism". In: *The Philosophical Quarterly*, vol. 86, n° 4, pp. 498–519.
Ameriks, Karl (2003): *Interpreting Kant's Critiques*. Oxford: Oxford University Press.
Bader, Ralf M. (2012): "The Role of Kant's Refutation of Idealism". In: *Archiv für Geschichte der Philosophie*, vol. 94, n° 1, pp. 53–73.
Banchetti, Marina P. (1993): "Føllesdal on the notion of the noema: A critique". In: *Husserl Studies*, vol. 10, n° 2, pp. 81–95.
Bird, Graham (1962): *Kant's Theory of Knowledge: An Outline of One Central Argument in the Critique of Pure Reason*. London: Routledge & Kegan Paul.
Braver, Lee (2007): *A Thing of this World: A History of Continental Anti-Realism*. Evanston, Illinois: Northwestern University Press.
Carman, Taylor (2003): *Heidegger's Analytic*. Cambridge, UK: Cambridge University Press.
Centrone, Stefania (2010): *Logic and Philosophy of Mathematics in the Early Husserl*. Dordrecht: Springer.
Dicker, Georges (2008): "Kant's Refutation of Idealism". In: *Noûs*, vol. 42, n° 1, pp. 80–108.

---

27 See Husserl 1956, Hua VII, pp. 357–364, 377–381.
28 I am grateful to the participants of the 2018 Husserl Circle at UNAM in Mexico City for providing useful feedback, and in particular to Stefano Vincini, as well as to the participants of the Via Moderna meeting at University of Groningen, Faculty of Philosophy, for their comments on an earlier version.

Dreyfus, Hubert. L., Hall, Harrison (1982): *Husserl, Intentionality, and Cognitive Science.* Cambridge, Massachusetts: MIT Press.
Drummond, John (1990): *Husserlian Intentionality and Non-Foundational Realism: Noema and Object.* Dordrecht, Boston, London: Springer.
Drummond, John (2009): "Phénoménologie et ontologie". Trans. G. Fréchette. In: *Philosophiques*, vol. 36, pp. 593 – 607.
Føllesdal, Dagfinn (1969): "Husserl's Notion of Noema". In: *Journal of Philosophy*, vol. 66, n° 20, pp. 680 – 687.
Guyer, Paul (1987): *Kant and the Claims of Knowledge.* Cambridge: Cambridge University Press.
Guyer, Paul, Horstmann, Rolf-Peter (2015): "Idealism". In: *The Stanford Encyclopedia of Philosophy* (Fall 2015 Edition), Ed. E. N. Zalta. URL = https://plato.stanford.edu/entries/idealism/.
Husserl, Edmund (1950): *Cartesianische Meditationen und Pariser Vorträge. Husserliana,* vol. I. Ed. S. Strasser. The Hague: Martinus Nijhoff.
Husserl, Edmund (1950): *Die Idee der Phänomenologie: Fünf Vorlesungen. Husserliana,* vol. II. Ed. W. Biemel. The Hague: Martinus Nijhoff.
Husserl, Edmund (1956): *Erste Philosophie (1923/4). Erster Teil: Kritische Ideengeschichte. Husserliana,* vol. VII. Ed. R. Boehm. The Hague: Martinus Nijhoff.
Husserl, Edmund. (1960): *Cartesian Meditations: An Introduction to Phenomenology.* Trans. D. Cairns. The Hague, Boston, London: Martinus Nijhoff.
Hussserl, Edmund (1962). *Phänomenologische Pyschologie: Vorlesungen Sommersemester 1925. Husserliana,* vol. IX. Ed. W. Biemel. The Hague: Martinus Nijhoff.
Husserl, Edmund (1971): *Ideen zu einer reinen Phänomenologie und Phänomenologischen Philosophie: die Phänomenologie und die Fundamente der Wissenschaft. Husserliana V.* Ed. M Biemel. The Hague: Martinus Nijhoff.
Husserl, Edmund (1974): "Kant and the Idea of Transcendental Philosophy". In: *Southwestern Journal of Philosophy*, vol. 5, n° 3, pp. 9 – 56.
Husserl, Edmund (1976): *Krisis der europäischen Wissenschaften und die Transzendentale Phänomenologie: Eine Einleitung in die Phänomenologische Philosophie. Husserliana,* vol. VI. Ed. W. Biemel. The Hague: Martinus Nijhoff.
Husserl, Edmund (1976): *Ideen zu einer reinen Phänomenologie und Phänomenologischen Philosophie: allgemeine Einführung in die reine Phänomenologie. Husserliana,* vol. III/1. Ed. K. Schuhmann, The Hague: Martinus Nijhoff.
Husserl, Edmund (1977): *Phenomenological Psychology: Lectures, Summer Semester, 1925.* Transl. J. Scanlon. The Hague: Martinus Nijhoff.
Husserl, Edmund (1980): *Ideas Pertaining to a Pure Phenomenology and to a Phenomenological Philosophy: Third Book: Phenomenology and the Foundation of the Sciences.* Trans. T. E. Klein & W. E. Pohl. The Hague, Boston, London: Martinus Nijhoff.
Husserl, Edmund (1983): *Ideas Pertaining to a Pure Phenomenology and to a Phenomenological Philosophy: First Book: General Introduction to a Pure Phenomenology.* Transl. F. Kersten. The Hague, Boston, Lancaster: Martinus Nijhoff.
Husserl, Edmund (1984): *Logische Untersuchungen, Band I – II. Husserliana,* vol. XIX/1 – XIX/2. Ed. U. Panzer. The Hague: Martinus Nijhoff.
Husserl, Edmund (1994): *Briefwechsel: Wissenschaftler Korrespondenz. Husserliana Dokumente,* vol. III/7. Ed. K. Schuhmann. Dordrecht: Springer.

Husserl, Edmund (1997): *Experience and Judgment: Investigations in a Genealogy of Logic.* Evanston, Illinois: Northwestern University Press.
Husserl, Edmund (1999): *The Idea of Phenomenology.* Trans. L. Hardee. Dordrecht, Boston, London: Kluwer Academic Publishers.
Husserl, Edmund (2001): *Natur und Geist: Vorlesungen Sommersemester 1927. Husserliana,* vol. XXXII. Ed. M. Weiler. Dordrecht: Kluwer Academic Publishers.
Husserl, Edmund (2002a): *Einleitung in die Philosophie: Vorlesungen 1922/23. Husserliana,* vol. XXXV. Ed. R. Bernet, U. Melle. Dordrecht: Springer.
Husserl, Edmund (2002b): *Zur Phänomenologischen Reduktion: Texte aus dem Nachlass. Husserliana,* vol. XXXVI. Ed. S. Luft. Dordrecht: Springer.
Jansen, Julia (2014): "Taking a Transcendental Stance: Anti-Representationalism and Direct Realism in Kant and Husserl". In: *Husserl und die klassische deutsche Philosophie.* Ed. Fabbianelli, F. & Luft. Dordrecht: Springer.
Kant, Immanuel (2004): *Prolegomena to Any Future Metaphysics That Will be Able to Come Forward as Science.* Ed. G. Hatfield. Cambridge: Cambridge University Press.
Kant, Immanuel (2007): *Critique of Pure Reason.* Trans. N. K. Smith. New York: Palgrave MacMillan.
Kemp Smith, Norman (1918): *A Commentary to Kant's Critique of Pure Reason.* London: Macmillan and Co.
Leichtle, Sean (2002): "*The Idea of Phenomenology:* Husserl's Program". In: *The New Yearbook for Phenomenology and Phenomenological Philosophy.* Eds. B. Hopkins & S. Crowell. London, New York: Routledge.
Luft, Sebastian (2007): "From Being to Givenness and Back: Some Remarks on the Meaning of Transcendental Idealism in Kant and Husserl". In: *International Journal of Philosophical Studies,* vol. 15, n° 3, pp. 367–394.
McIntyre, Ronald (1986): "Husserl and the Representational Theory of Mind". In: *Topoi,* vol. 5, n° 2, pp. 101–113.
Melle, Ullrich (2010): "Husserls Beweis für den transzendentalen Idealismus". In: *Philosophy, Phenomenology, Sciences: Essays in Commemoration of Edmund Husserl.* Eds. C. Ierna, H. Jacobs & F. Mattens. Dordrecht, Heidelberg, London: Springer.
Prauss, Gerold (1974): *Kant und das Problem der Dinge an sich.* Bonn: Bouvier Verlag Herbert Grundmann.
Rockmore, Tom (2007): *Kant and Idealism.* New Haven, Connecticut: Yale University Press.
Rouse, Joseph T. (1987): "Husserlian Phenomenology and Scientific Realism". In: *Philosophy of Science,* vol. 54, pp. 222–232.
Rowlands, Mark (2003): *Externalism: Putting Mind and World Back Together Again.* Montreal & Kingston: McGill-Queen's University Press.
Smith, David Woodruff (2007): *Husserl.* New York: Routledge.
Smith, David Woodruff (2013): "Phenomenology". In: *The Stanford Encyclopedia of Philosophy* (Winter 2013 Edition). Ed. Edward N. Zalta. URL = http://plato.stanford.edu/archives/win2013/entries/phenomenology/.
Smith, David Woodruff, McIntyre, Ronald (1975): "Husserl's Identification of Meaning and Noema". In: *The Monist,* vol. 59, n° 1, pp. 115–132.
Smith, David Woodruff, McIntyre, Ronald (1982): *Husserl and Intentionality: A Study of Mind, Meaning, and Language.* Dordrecht, Boston: D. Reidel Publishing Co.

Smith, David Woodruff, McIntyre, Ronald (1989): "Theory of Intentionality". In: *Husserl's Phenomenology: a Textbook*. Eds. J. N. Mohanty and W. McKenna. Washington, DC: University Press of America, pp. 147–179.

Stang, Nicholas F. (2016): "Allison on Transcendental Realism and Transcendental Idealism". *Stanford Encyclopedia of Philosophy*. Ed. E. N. Zalta. URL = https://plato.stanford.edu/entries/kant-transcendental-idealism/supplement2.html.

Strawson, Peter F. (1966): *The Bounds of Sense: An Essay on Kant's Critique of Pure Reason*. London: Methuen.

Tieszen, Richard (1984): "Mathematical Intuition and Husserl's Phenomenology". In: *Noûs*, vol. 18, n° 3, pp. 395–421.

Uehlein, Friedrich A. (1992): "*Eidos* and Eidetic Variation in Husserl's Phenomenology". In: *Phenomenology, Language & Schizophrenia*. Eds. Spitzer, M, Uehlein, F. A., Schwartz, M. A. & Mundt, C. New York, Berlin, Heidelberg: Springer Verlag.

Vaihinger, Hans (1884): "Zu Kants Widerlegung des Idealismus". In: *Straßburger Abhandlungen zur Philosophie*. Akad. Verlagsbuchhandlung. Heidelberg: Mohr, pp. 85–164.

Van Mazijk, Corijn (2016): "Kant and Husserl on the Contents of Perception". In: *The Southern Journal of Philosophy*, vol. 54, n° 2, pp. 267–287.

Van Mazijk, Corijn (2019): "Husserl's Covert Critique of Kant in the Sixth Book of *Logical Investigations*". In: *Continental Philosophy Review*, vol. 52, pp. 15–33.

Van Mazijk, Corijn (2020): *Perception and Reality in Kant, Husserl, and McDowell*. New York, London: Routledge.

Westphal, Kenneth. R. (2004): *Kant's Transcendental Proof of Realism*. Cambridge, New York, Melbourne: Cambridge University Press.

Wiltsche, Harald A. (2012): "What is Wrong with Husserl's Scientific Anti-Realism?". In: *Inquiry*, vol. 55, n° 2, pp. 105–130.

Zahavi, Dan (2004): "Husserl's Noema and the Internalism-Externalism Debate". In: *Inquiry: An Interdisciplinary Journal of Philosophy*, vol. 47, n° 1, pp. 42–66.

Zahavi, Dan (2008): "Internalism, Externalism, and Transcendental Idealism". In: *Synthese*, vol. 160, n° 3, pp. 355–374.

Zahavi, Dan (2010): "Husserl and the 'Absolute'". In: *Philosophy, Phenomenology, Sciences: Essays in Commemoration of Edmund Husserl*. Eds. C. Ierna, H. Jacobs & F. Mattens. Dordrecht, Heidelberg, London: Springer.

Zahavi, Dan (2017): *Husserl's Legacy: Phenomenology, Metaphysics, and Transcendental Philosophy*. Oxford: Oxford University Press.

Antoine Grandjean
"Pure Ego and Nothing More"[1]

> "As what is absolutely given, or what can be brought to givenness in the *a priori* possible view of fixating reflection, [the pure ego] is by no means whatsoever something mysterious or mystical."
> (Husserl 1952, Hua IV, p. 97; Husserl 1989, p. 103)

Abstract: According to the *Ideas*, conscious life is the life of an ego which is a *"pure I and nothing more."* This expression is decisive: here is largely at stake what makes Husserlian transcendental phenomenology different from a number of other philosophical trends, whether phenomenological or not (Neokantianism, Sartrian or Heideggerian phenomenology); it describes a specific moment in Husserl's working out of his own point of view by distinguishing a central stage of his philosophy from previous and subsequent ones. We start with an analysis of the polarization of conscious life by an irreducible *I*, whose non-substantial signification and transcendence within immanence have to be explained. We maintain here that it is only when it became idealist that phenomenology could become egological. Secondly, we study the *purity* of this I: differing from any *psychological ego*, it implies a proper transcendental meaning of egoity. Then we consider Husserl's refusal of any additional property of this *I*, which is only the title of an identity stating itself in each of its acts, *and nothing more*. We finally ask if maintaining such an egological polarization is not *too much*, and if it could reveal a lack of phenomenological radicality.

According to *Ideas I*, the phenomenologist who is attentive to the general structures of pure consciousness cannot help but acknowledge that besides its acts within this consciousness, there is an ego inseparable from (but also dependent upon) these very acts:[2] "pure ego and nothing more [*reines Ich und nichts weit-*

---

[1] This chapter is the English translation of an article published in the volume *Husserl. La science des phénomènes*, edited by A. Grandjean and L. Perreau (Paris: Editions du CNRS, 2012, pp. 161–186), under the title "Je pur et rien de plus."
[2] *Cf.* Husserl 1952, Hua IV, p. 99; Husserl 1989, p. 105: "On the one hand, we must definitely here distinguish the pure ego from the acts themselves, as that which functions in them and which, through them, relates to objects; on the other hand, this distinction can only be an abstract one. It is abstract to the extent that the ego cannot be thought of as something separated from these

er]" (Husserl 1976, Hua III/1, p. 179; Husserl 1983, p. 191). Our objective in this chapter is to clarify this phrase. Indeed, firstly, the phrase accurately summarizes what the analysis reveals, i.e. Husserl's thesis concerning the egoical nature of consciousness. Moreover, it is central, both from an internal and an external point of view: internal, because it makes it possible to locate the *Ideas I* within Husserl's very own philosophical journey and distinguishes the book published in 1913 from what preceded it as well as from subsequent publications; external, because giving the ego such a transcendental dignity makes Husserl's phenomenology stand out from his rivals. This contribution will revolve around the following question: What does it mean for the transcendental to be egoical?[3]

1 Ego

1.1 A Natural Life from a First-Person Perspective

The suspension of the "natural attitude" of consciousness, a suspension which also opens up the thematic field of its pure lived-experiences, i.e. of transcendental subjectivity, concerns a consciousness which first and foremost exists in a first-person perspective. The natural life of consciousness is the life of "someone" who perceives him- or herself as an "I" (Husserl 1976, Hua III/1, p. 59; Husserl 1983, p. 54), whose experiences are constantly given in a first-person perspective[4] in a course of life that he or she perceives as belonging to him- or herself.[5] The various acts of this consciousness come under the *cogito* (Husserl 1976, Hua III/1, p. 59; Husserl 1983, p. 54), according to Descartes' broad definition in the second Meditation,[6] about which Husserl writes that it denotes "con-

---

lived experiences, from its 'life,' just as, conversely, the lived experiences are not thinkable except as the medium of the life of the ego." We have sometimes tacitly modified the English translations of Husserl's works.

3 This question undoubtedly echoes the one raised by Jocelyn Benoist (Benoist 1994, pp. 41–61): "What does it mean for the subject to be 'transcendental'?"

4 See Husserl 1976, Hua III/1, p. 56; Husserl 1983, p. 51: "I am conscious of a world", "intuitively I find it immediately, [...] I experience it", "corporeal physical things [...] are *simply there for me*", "animate beings too – human beings, let us say – are immediately there for me: I look up; I see them; I hear their approach; I grasp their hands; talking with them I understand immediately what they objectivate and think, what feelings stir within them, what they wish or will."

5 See Husserl 1976, Hua III/1, p. 59; Husserl 1983, p. 54: "Living along naturally, I live [...]." And also Husserl 1973a, Hua XIII, pp. 112*sq.*

6 Descartes 1982, p. 22; Descartes 1993, p. 54: "What is a thing which thinks? It is a thing which doubts, understands, [conceives], affirms, denies, wills, refuses, which also imagines and feels."

sciousness in the pregnant sense of the term, in the sense which first comes to mind" (Husserl 1976, Hua III/1, p. 70; Husserl 1983, p. 68): "'I perceive, I remember, I phantasy, I judge, I feel, I desire, I will', and thus all egoical lived-experiences which are at all similar to them, in their countless flowing particular formations."[7] The very object of the first phenomenological act is thus the *cogito*. Consciousness, in so far as it is a stream of lived-experiences (Husserl 1976, Hua III/1, p. 67 and 104; Husserl 1983, p. 64 and 110), is also the consciousness of these lived-experiences as so many forms of "I live."

1.2 An Ego that Remains Irreducible

While the meaning of ego is profoundly altered, the egoical nature of conscious life remains unscathed when the natural attitude is excluded. Indeed, while it is important to distinguish the 'pure' ego from the psychic ego in which we live our natural lives, the ego appears as an irreducible element of conscious life: the "phenomenological ego" cannot be reduced to a "transcendental nothing" (Husserl 1976, Hua III/1, p. 123; Husserl 1983, p. 132).

In its essence, conscious life entails a dual polarity. If consciousness is always a consciousness of something, it is also naturally consciousness *of* the ego, in the subjective sense of the genitive.[8] Each perception is perception from a first-person perspective, each recollection is an "I remember," each imagination is an "I imagine," each judgment is an "I judge," each joy is an "I rejoice:" "in all such acts I am present [*bin ich dabei*], *actionally* present" (Husserl 1976, Hua III/1, p. 179; Husserl 1983, p. 190). The connection between the lived-experience and the ego goes beyond the sphere of actionality. Admittedly, a large part of conscious life occurs without any vigilant ego. Given its conscious nature, however, every unawakened consciousness may be attached to a wakeful conscious life, which is the place where it is consistently possible for the ego to 'enter the scene'. This is, according to Husserl, the true meaning of the Kantian thesis, which he reformulates as follows: "The pure ego must be able to accompany all my representations" (Husserl 1952, Hua IV, p. 108; Husserl 1989, p. 115): every *cogitatio* comes under a *cogito* (Husserl 1976, Hua III/1, p. 123; Husserl 1983, p. 133), although not always in an actional way. The lived experiences that do not have the character of the *cogito*, and which "form the universal milieu for the

---

[7] This "pregnant sense" is distinct from "a broad sense" which denotes all lived experiences (Husserl 1976, Hua III/1, p. 67; Husserl 1983, p. 64).
[8] As Husserl will write in 1929, "All consciousness is consciousness of my Ego" (Husserl 1962, Hua IX, p. 315, quoted in Benoist 1994, p. 19).

egoical actionality," "also have their share in the pure ego and the pure ego has its share in them:" "they 'belong' to it as 'its own', they are *its* consciousness-background, *its* field of freedom." (Husserl 1976, Hua III/1, p. 179; Husserl 1983, p. 191).[9]

Indeed, the characteristic orientation of any act of consciousness requires two references: the thematic "of" reference (intentionality) and the "from" reference. However, the need for the "from reference" alone is not sufficient to guarantee that what is referred to is something with any form of consistency. The centrifugal nature of consciousness can be understood as proving its true centered being only if the diversity of its acts emerges as the declension of an identity, where this very identity ascertains that there is a unique source of this multiplicity. This is what the reflection shows: "Each '*cogito*', each act in a distinctive sense, is characterized as an act of the Ego, it 'proceeds from out of the Ego', it 'lives' 'actionally' in the act" (Husserl 1976, Hua III/1, p. 178; Husserl 1983, p. 190).[10] The intentionality of consciousness, the fact that it is directed toward objects, is also a "proceeding from" which is inconceivable without a source-center, "the Ego-point [*Ich-Punkt*]" which is the *terminus a quo* of all acts (Husserl 1952, Hua IV, p. 105; Husserl 1989, p. 112). We will also see that the ego denotes nothing more than the identity of the focal point *from which* all that is directed *toward* the object is taken to be emanating and *to which* it is, in the same way, possible to *return*. The egoity of consciousness is thus the other side of its intentionality, as an intentionality in which the identity of intention is given to itself. The same eidetic status must then be acknowledged to this egoity:

> No excluding can annul the form of the *cogito* and cancel out the "pure" subject of the act: the "being directed to," the "being busied with," "the taking a position toward", the "undergoing," the "suffering from" *necessarily* includes in its essence this: that it is "emanating from the ego" or in the reverse direction of the ray, "toward the ego" – and this ego is the *pure* ego, no reduction can do anything to it. (Husserl 1976, Hua III/1, p. 179; Husserl 1983, p. 191)

As all lived-experience is likely to appear as an "I live" and thus as what the "ego lives" in, "the relationship of each lived-experience to the 'pure' Ego" can be raised to the first rank among the "universal essential peculiarities per-

---

9 See also Husserl 1976, Hua III/1, p. 123; Husserl 1983, p. 132: "In every actional *cogito*, the ego lives out its life in a special sense. But all background lived-experiences belong to it; and it belongs to them."
10 See also Husserl 1976, Hua III/1, p. 75; Husserl 1983, pp. 75*sq.*: "To the *cogito* itself there belongs, as immanent in it, a 'regard-to' the object which, on the other side, wells forth from the 'ego' which therefore can never be lacking."

taining to the transcendentally purified realm of lived-experiences" (Husserl 1976, Hua III/1, p. 178; Husserl 1983, p. 190).

1.3 To Whom Does Ego Refer?

What does the term 'ego' really mean? Any attempt to respond to this question must begin by establishing where the ego resides. This ego, however, resides nowhere. Indeed, it is not a lived-experience, precisely because it is a pole of identity of all flowing lived-experiences (Husserl 1976, Hua III/1, p. 123; Husserl 1983, p. 132; Husserl 1962, Hua IX, p. 208; Husserl 1977, p. 159). Nor is it a "fragment" of the lived-experience, i.e. a real (*reel*) component of lived-experiences (Husserl 1952, Hua IV, pp. 102*sq.*; Husserl 1989, p. 109). Indeed, the flow in question is not a framework within which lived-experiences occur, but it rather characterizes the very fabric of these entirely fluid experiences. However – and we will have to come back to this point – one cannot assume that what is not a lived-experience is simply nothing. If the ego is neither a lived-experience nor a part of this experience, it is precisely because the ego is present in each lived-experience: if the pure ego "cannot *in any sense* be considered as a *real element or moment* of lived-experiences themselves," it is because it is "something absolutely identical throughout every actual and potential change in lived-experiences" (Husserl 1976, Hua III/1, p. 123; Husserl 1983, p. 132).[11] The non-local nature of the ego is the nature of what is, at least potentially, omnipresent, and this omnipresence is the correlate of its necessity: if, in principle, every *cogitatio* is "something transitory," "the pure ego seems to be *something essentially necessary*." If the ego cannot be found when one examines lived-experiences, if it does not reside *within* these experiences, it is precisely because it is, wherever lived-experiences are to be found, always inclined to appear as an "I live." The reason why it cannot be temporally situated is because it is something permanent where everything flows. However, it is not a permanent *within* the flow, whose universality cannot be restricted. The essence of the ego is not that of a rock in a river. The ego is not stubborn, and no positive metaphor drawn from the order of things can adequately present it: "this continualness is obviously not that of a stupidly persistent lived-experience, a 'fixed idea;' instead, the ego belongs to each coming and going experience." A distinct sense of belonging is here at stake, and it implies a

---

[11] See also Husserl, Ms K II 4, p. 43b, quoted in Marbach 1974, p. 304: "In consciousness, the ego is everywhere."

corollary: the ego belongs to each lived-experience, and is thus given as an event within the life which is its own.

The word "ego" thus refers to the irreducible identity of consciousness: "the ray of regard changes with every *cogito*, shooting forth afresh with each new one as it comes and vanishing with it. The ego, however, is something identical." This identity is not so much a property of the ego as its entire content, if we consider its form as the form of a center from which all the rays of conscious life originate:

> [...] in the accomplishment of each act, there lays a ray of directedness I cannot describe otherwise than by saying it takes its point of departure in the ego, which evidently thereby remains undivided and numerically identical while it lives in these manifold acts. (Husserl 1952, Hua IV, p. 98; Husserl 1989, p. 104)

Conscious life, as the life of an ego directed toward objects, is thus essentially bipolar in nature, but in no way is this bipolarization homogeneous.[12] Indeed, the egoical pole is a radically non-substantial one, a pole so absolutely devoid of properties that, separated from the rays that emanate from it, it means nothing in and for itself: "This pure ego, as a pole, is nothing without its acts, without its flow of lived-experience, without the living life so to speak flowing from itself" (Husserl, Ms E III 2, 1920–1921, p. 5a, quoted in Marbach 1974, p. 303); "The ego is nothing isolated. *The ego gives itself only with the cogito*" (Husserl, Ms K II 4, 1913–1916, p. 43b, *idem*). This is why, despite prevalent vision-oriented metaphors,[13] the analogy between the ego and an eye is in no way totally satisfying; not only because this analogy presents the ego as a spectator, ignoring that it is inherently involved in and by its lived-experiences (driven by what repels or attracts it, captured by what it likes, potentially engulfed in sorrow, etc.; *cf.* Husserl 1952, Hua IV, p. 98; Husserl 1989, p. 104); but also, and especially, because it may lead to assigning to the ego the real identity of a *thing*, like the eye is identical to itself, without considering its actional looking. Indeed, given its radical non-substantiality, the ego is nothing more than the identity

---

12 *Cf.* Husserl 1973b, Hua XIV, p. 30: the ego is "to a certain extent similar to the object-pole (affective pole, thematic pole, etc.), which is what it is as a support, substratum of accidents and changing attributes. Yet it is something entirely different: the ego-pole [*Ichpol*] is what it is, not as a support, as a substratum for action and affection, and so forth, but precisely as ego, a point from which rays flow, a functional center for affections, a radiation center, a center of activities and acts. It resides 'within' its states [...] and 'within' its acts..." (1920–1921).
13 See for example Husserl 1976, Hua III/1, p. 123; Husserl 1983, p. 132: "Its 'regard' is directed 'through' each actual cogito to the objective something."

of this very vision. It can only reside within the living of each lived-experience, and is nothing besides it:

> In these particular combinations of 'its' lived-experiences, the living ego is not something taken *for itself* and which can be made into an object *proper* of an investigation. Aside from its "modes of relation" or "modes of comportment," the ego is completely empty of essence-components, has no explicatable content, is undescribable in and for itself: pure ego and nothing more. (Husserl 1976, Hua III/1, p. 179; Husserl 1983, p. 191)

Ego without qualities thus represents the unique without properties.[14] While the ego is an object, that is, it is something and not nothing,[15] it is empty of all objective content, i.e. it lacks properties which may constitute the subject of predication. We must state, however, that the inconsistency of the ego as an object is what makes its description an *infinite* one. Its qualitative emptiness is the other side of a never-ending description, what cannot be described in and for itself being in fact described in every description. What is nothing in and for itself, but simply what lives each lived-experience, is inexhaustible. Insofar as there is a flowing life, the ego lives: "for this reason there is still the occasion for a multiplicity of important descriptions, precisely with respect to the particular ways in which it is an ego living in the kinds or modes of lived-experiences in question" (Husserl 1976, Hua III/1, p. 180; Husserl 1983, p. 191). From this stems the irreducible relevance of the egoic theme in the strict sense, understood as "the pure ego pertaining to the living [*das reine Ich des Erlebens*]" distinguished from the "lived-experience itself," a distinction that is phenomenologically legitimate and necessary, despite their irreducible entanglement. In a broader sense, phenomenology as a whole is an eidetic description of the ego, but one which knows what this ego is, i.e., that which lives every lived-experience, and nothing more: "the phenomenologically pure ego-center remains a great phenomenological theme which is ultimately interwoven with everything else" (Husserl 1962, Hua IX, p. 315; Husserl 1997b, p. 224).

---

14 See Husserl 1973b, Hua XIV, Supplement II, 1921, p. 43: "*The ego is nothing else than a pole, deprived of any quality, for acts* and draws all its determinations form this polarization;" Husserl 1973b, Hua XIV, Nr. 2, p. 29: "*The ego is a functional center* which, at any given time, *can* be the functional center of a given function [...]. So we have an identical ego which is nothing in and for itself, and which, perceived abstractly, is completely empty of content, which considered in and for itself has only this one specific universal figure, that it is a functional center in general and here, *within this* flow, to be its general functional center."

15 On the definition of the object as a something, see for instance Husserl 1976, Hua III/1, p. 27, 31, 47.

1.4 A Delayed Necessity

Neither a lived-experience nor a real component of lived-experiences, the ego cannot be said to be immanent, as in § 41 of *Ideen I*. Nevertheless, as "belonging" to the flow of lived-experiences, in no way can it be assigned a real transcendence, i.e. the mode of being characteristic of things. The ego cannot really find its place in the life of which it is the center, but it is unable to reside elsewhere. Living in all lived-experiences, but – or rather *precisely for this reason* – without being something one could meet *within* them, the ego upsets and destabilizes the very principle of binary partition and imposes that a "quite peculiar transcendence" should be acknowledged to it: "a transcendence within immanence" (Husserl 1976, Hua III/1, p. 124; Husserl 1983, p. 133).[16]

We know that due to conceptual constraints, Husserl began by excluding the ego from the pure life of consciousness. In the first edition of *Logical Investigations* (1901 for the section we are concerned with), Husserl, who reconsidered this point in § 57 of *Ideen I*, professed "skepticism" where the ego was concerned (Husserl 1976, Hua III/1, p. 124; Husserl 1983, p. 133), for a twofold reason, stating that the ego, in addition to its fundamental defect which makes it untraceable, is also superfluous.

It is *superfluous*, first, contrary to what (Neo-)Kantianism suggests, because no synthetic instance is required to ensure the unity of the flow of lived-experiences, such a unity being immanent within this flow, and ultimately rooted in temporality itself. In the fifth *Investigation*, Husserl rejects the idea that the unity of this flow of lived-experiences requires something like an ego. He argues that this unity depends on their immanent relationship alone, and that contents go hand in hand with the laws that consistently govern their interconnections. From here proceeds, in a strictly immanent way,[17] the unity of lived-experiences

---

[16] See also Husserl, Ms F III 1, p. 3a; quoted in Marbach 1974, p. 127. Concerning this egoical transcendence, there is an apparent hesitation. Indeed, initially stating that this was a "non-constituted transcendence" (*ibidem*), Husserl later announced the constitution of the ego itself, leaving this constitution aside and simply noting that it was linked to temporality (Husserl 1976, Hua III/1, p. 182; Husserl 1983, p. 193). As noted by Marbach, in one of his personal copies, Husserl replaced "non-constituted" by "to some extent non-constituted" (Husserl 1976, Hua III/2, p. 502; Marbach 1974, p. 212). What is excluded, therefore, is not so much the constitution of the ego but its *constitution from a multiplicity* (Husserl, Ms F III 1, p. 6a), i.e. the constitutively derived character of its sense of identity.

[17] The anti-Kantian nature of these notes is general, since the immanent nature of essential laws – and therefore of unity – of the manifold excludes "here as elsewhere," i.e. *both for the unity of the ego and for the unity of the object*, the need for a synthetic operator which

that we *refer to* as an ego, and which is ultimately rooted in temporality (Husserl 1984, Hua XIX/1, p. 369; Husserl 2001, p. 88). Hence an egoical nominalism which strictly identifies "the phenomenological ego" and the "stream of consciousness" (Husserl 1984, Hua XIX/1, p. 363; Husserl 2001, p. 85) or "the complex of reflectively graspable lived-experiences" (Husserl 1984, Hua XIX/1, p. 374; Husserl 2001, p. 92). The ego is simply the title of the unity of lived-experiences which results from their immanent legal unification, and does not require an "egoical principle [*Ichprinzip*]" to confer unity onto something which already possesses unity by itself.

It is *untraceable*, secondly and especially, lying neither outside the lived-experience nor within the flow which possesses no identical term, precisely because of its nature as a flow. What is neither an object nor a lived-experience in Husserl's *Investigations* cannot have real consistency. *Descriptively egoical*, without doubt, the life of consciousness cannot be *ontologically* grasped as *the life of an ego*,[18] and it must be said that it is "the thinking of no one" (Husserl 1973c, Hua XVI, p. 41; Husserl 1997a, p. 34). "The phenomenologically reduced ego is therefore nothing peculiar [*Eigenartiges*] floating above the many lived-experiences: it is simply identical with their own interconnected unity" (Husserl 1984, Hua XIX/1, pp. 363sq.; Husserl 2001, p. 86), i.e. it is nothing besides the "corresponding 'bundle' of lived-experiences" (Husserl 1984, Hua XIX/1, p. 390; Husserl 2001, p. 101).[19] The ego is either empirical content or the title of the unity of the immanent relation of lived-experiences: *The pure ego is nothing from which "something more" can be excluded because it is not even something*.

The second edition of the *Investigations*, written at the same time as the *Ideen I*, repeatedly features Husserl's retraction on this point (Husserl 1984, Hua XIX/1, pp. 364, 368, 374, 376, 391). The question that arises, however, is to know exactly on what retraction the addition of an ego to the life of consciousness is based. It is tempting to think that Husserl was reconsidering the *superfluity* of the pure ego, especially in view of the dialogical context which showed, for instance, that he had appropriated Kant's well-known quote that it must be possible for the "I think" to accompany all representations (Husserl 1976, Hua III/1,

---

would be external to the unified manifold (Husserl 1984a, Hua XIX/1, p. 364; Husserl 2001, p. 86).

18 "In the *description* relation to a living ego is inescapable; but the lived-experience described is not itself a complex which contains the ego-representation as a partial lived-experience" (Husserl 1984a, Hua XIX/1, p. 391; Husserl 2001, p. 101).
19 As is well known, Husserl shares here Hume's views in the *Treatise on Human Nature* (I, IV, 6).

p. 123; Husserl 1983, p. 133[20]),[21] while his egoical skepticism was at the center of a controversy against Natorp's Neo-Kantianism,[22] from whom Husserl later said he had learned a lot.[23] However, we must not be misled by this context: it is clear that it is neither as a synthetic operator nor as the basis for the unity of the flow that pure egoity is now admitted. In no way does the abandonment of the egoical skepticism mean that Husserl retracted on the need for unity, nor does the ego come into consciousness as a synthetic principle. Nowhere does Husserl argue that there must be a pure ego to ensure a unity of the flow of consciousness. What he now says is that every actual *cogito* makes the egoical polarization *of* this flow explicit, whose unity is unceasingly guaranteed phenomenologically in and for itself. In short, neither in 1913 nor earlier is the unity of the flow based on the pure ego, which is foremost *one* flow; and time, which is the original form of synthesis,[24] has no need for an external principle to synthesize it. The temporality of consciousness does not allow discontinuity,[25] as is typical of the atomistic position of representation which, shared by both Kantianism and classical empiricism, grounds the synthetic requisite. The unity of conscious life, the identical polarization of which is simply marked by the ego, cannot be regarded as a performance of the latter, because it is sufficiently supported by its own temporality: "this phenomenological time, the unitary form of all lived-experiences within *one* flow of lived-experiences (the one pure ego)" (Husserl 1976, Hua III/1, p. 181; Husserl 1983, p. 192).[26] The unity of conscious life is not based

---

20 It should be noted that in no way does this text concern the need for a synthetic ego, but rather something very different, which is the belonging of the sphere of non-actuality to the ego.
21 Among more ancient texts, in which, to the contrary, Husserl sharply opposed Kant's "I think," we can mention in particular the *Letter to Hocking* written on September 7, 1903 (Husserl 1994, Hua Dokumente, III/3, pp. 147*sq.*; see also the 1908 text in Husserl 1956, Hua VII, p. 387). The exclusively empirical assignment of the ego is thus in line with Husserl's anthropological interpretation of the Kantian theory of subjectivity.
22 Husserl quotes and discusses his *Introduction to Psychology According to Critical Method* (Natorp 1888) (Husserl 1984a, Hua XIX/1, pp. 372 *sq.*).
23 In 1912, in his *General Psychology According to Critical Method*, Natorp responded to the criticism raised by Husserl in 1900 (see Natorp 1912, Chapter 2, § 6).
24 *Cf.* Husserl 1973d, Hua I, p. 79; Husserl 1960, p. 41.
25 See Husserl 1976, Hua III/1, p. 182; Husserl 1983, p. 194: "Each actual lived-experience […] is necessarily an enduring one; and with this duration it finds its place within an infinite continuum of duration – in a fulfilled continuum. It has necessarily an all-around, infinitely fulfilled temporal horizon. Which also means: it belongs to *one* endless 'flow of lived-experiences'."
26 See also Husserl 1976, Hua III/1, p. 184 and Husserl 1973a, Hua XIII, pp. 184*sqq*. Marbach interprets all these texts (and other similar ones) as if they were assuming, rather than a strict reciprocation, a foundation of the temporal unity on the ego, whose entry into phenomenology

on the ego. The ego simply marks the identity in each of the acts of which this life, itself unitary, is the fundamental element. If there is a foundational relation between the unity of consciousness and the ego, it is thus quite the opposite one.[27]

The ego's superfluity where synthesis is concerned is not attenuated, and it is not on this point that Husserl's position changed. This change was actually driven by an ontological discovery which reversed the initial findings concerning the untraceable nature of the ego. Indeed, the egoical turn of phenomenology required that the identity of the subjective and of the lived-experience be broken down, while the *Investigations*, using a metonymy whose erroneous nature Husserl later perceived, held that real immanence exhausted the sense of immanence.[28] Where all that is phenomenological is restricted to lived-experiences (Husserl 1984, Hua XIX/1, pp. 359*sq.*; Husserl 2001, p. 83), no room remains for the pure ego. To argue that more may be found within subjectivity than within lived-experiences, "within" must have a broader sense than real immanence. If

---

would be marked by *The Basic Problems of Phenomenology* (1910 – 1911). This interpretation can be contested on two accounts. *First*, in this text, the phenomenological ego is not, any more than elsewhere, the principle of the unity of conscious life; it shares a strictly mutual relationship with this unitary life, of which it simply marks the *proper* character, by differentiating it from the other lives it may be conscious of, indirectly, in empathy. The "ego" thus refers to the appropriation of unitary conscious life whose unity is not accountable to that ego. The "ego" does not help us to understand the unity of multiplicity (of lived-experiences), but rather refers to a differential unity within a multiplicity (of lives) – moreover, this designation does not provide a foundation of this differential unity, which simply depends on the data mode (all original lived-experiences which are directly accessible belong *ipso facto* to this life which is mine, and no one else's, as the texts written after the admission of the pure ego will attest). See, for example, Husserl 1973b, Hua XIV, Nr. 24, 1927, p. 429. *Second*, the *Basic Problems of Phenomenology* remains fundamentally undecided about the issue of the pure ego, understood as the centre or pole of consciousness, rather than as the simple title of the unitary life of oneself. See, for example, Husserl 1973a, Hua XIII, p. 155. While lived-experiences cannot be perceived anymore as the lived-experiences "of nobody," because they present themselves as my own lived-experiences, nothing is certain about the consistency of a pure ego that couldn't be reduced to the acts from which it is inseparable. In the *Basic Problems of Phenomenology*, Husserl therefore argues that there exists a quality of *mineness* phenomenologically speaking, but he does not affirm the phenomenological consistency of the *pure ego*.

27 This is why Husserl was able to note, as in § 57 and certainly long before any regard for intersubjectivity, that the pure ego is a pure ego "in principle different for each flow" (Husserl 1976, Hua III/1, p. 124; Husserl 1983, p. 133). See also Husserl 1962, Hua IX, p. 416: "Separation of the flows of consciousness, leaving aside the issue of the ego."

28 Husserl 1976, Hua III/1, p. 296; Husserl 1983, p. 307. That explains, for instance, the rejection of Brentano's theory of intentional immanence (Husserl 1984a, Hua XIX/1, pp. 385*sq.*; Husserl 2001, p. 98).

the pure ego ceases to be untraceable, it is not because Husserl eventually focused on it by dutifully analyzing the same field, but because he opened up a new dimension of subjectivity in which the ego was able to reside. In other words, the intentional sense of immanence had to be discovered to enable the descriptive irreducibility of the egoical dimension of consciousness to pave the way to the acknowledgement of the existence of a pure ego. Thus, it is this discovery which led phenomenology to both idealism and egology. Moreover, given that the idealistic turn of phenomenology occurred in 1906–1907,[29] it is hardly surprising that this egoical conception of the unity of consciousness emerged only thereafter[30] and was only later taken up, despite Husserl's persistent reluctance.[31]

Thus, the pure ego is never an issue of the *unity* of conscious life, but rather of the *identity* at work in each of its *acts*. It is an issue *imposed* by things themselves and whose egoical *solution* required an idealistic position. By extending "immanence" to "intentional immanence," Husserl includes every object within the subject. Certainly, the transcendence-in-immanence of the ego is not the intentional transcendence of the noema, because it is not the transcendence of what is lived but rather the transcendence of who is living. However, by assuming that *all* transcendence means intentional immanence, Husserl discovers a non-real transcendence sphere which may host this transcendence-in-immanence which characterizes the *ego*, and nothing else. While much remained to be done, Husserl was encouraged by the opening up of a space where the ego could reside, as well as by the descriptive irreducibility of the egoical form of conscious life. In no way does the decline of Husserlian skepticism regarding the ego mean that he had scruples about his anti-Neo-Kantianism. Rather, it reflects the adoption of a new ontological position: the discovery of the intentional

---

29 See *Einleitung in die Logik und Erkenntnistheorie* (Husserl 1984b, Hua XXIV) and *Die Idee der Phänomenologie* (Husserl 1950, Hua II).

30 On Husserl's "difficulties" concerning the ego, which are evidenced in the manuscripts of 1907–1908, see Marbach 1974, pp. *59sq*. Marbach, however, does not associate Husserl's overcoming of these difficulties with the conquest of an idealistic ontological position. In any case, it is striking to see that it is precisely in the texts published at the end of 1907 that Husserl largely reflects on whether, in addition to the ego-phenomenon and the immanent temporal unity of lived-experiences, there may be an ego that, the one and only, lives in each and every act of consciousness. See, for example, Ms B II 1 (September 1907), p. 22b and 23a (quoted in Marbach 1974, p. 76).

31 See, in 1912 once more, Husserl's hesitations in the MS F III 1, p. 3a and 3b (quoted in Marbach 1974, p. 128). Husserl repeatedly indicates the (anti-)metaphysical nature of his hesitations (Husserl 1984a, Hua XIX/1, p. 374; Husserl 2001, p. 92; Husserl 1971, Hua V, p. 24; Husserl 1980, p. 22).

immanence of the objective transcendence which paved the way for the invention of a transcendence within the subjective dimension of immanence itself. Without making it a theorem, even if testing this view from other perspectives would be worthwhile, it thus seems legitimate to say that idealism (immanence of the transcendent) and the egoical style of Husserl's phenomenology (transcendence in immanence) are two sides, albeit not identifiable, of the same invention, which is none other than the invention of an immanence that exceeds the realm of lived-experiences, or the invention of a non-real immanent sphere.

2 "Pure"

The *purity* of the pure ego means that it is the *reduced* ego[32] which is referred to, distinguished from the impurity synonymous with worldliness, i.e from the "human ego" (Husserl 1976, Hua III/1, p. 105; Husserl 1983, p. 112) or psychic ego. Indeed, "empirical subjectivity" (Husserl 1976, Hua III/1, p. 124; Husserl 1983, p. 133) is a moment of the world itself and "I, the human being" (Husserl 1976, Hua III/1, p. 179; Husserl 1983, p. 190) suffer the exclusion. The ego which appears under the reduction does not refer to the natural ego, meaning both that the *ego* makes sense from a transcendental perspective, and that the ego has a transcendental sense. The first point has already been explained; let us now explain the second.

In order to fully understand the issue, we must begin with a characterization that occurred later. In *Cartesian Meditations*, Husserl writes that in the realm of "the transcendental-phenomenological self-experience" (Husserl 1973d, Hua I, p. 65; Husserl 1960, p. 26), I am "no longer" who I was.[33] This means three things: 1) in the natural attitude, I experienced myself to be part of the world; 2) in the transcendental attitude, the 'I' now emerges as what

---

[32] § 57 of *Ideas I* is, by anticipation, sufficiently clear about the fact that it is the fate of the reduced ego which is at stake here. See also this explicit equation about the lived-experience: "'in' the reduced perception (in the phenomenologically pure lived-experience)" (Husserl 1976, Hua III/1, p. 105; Husserl 1983, p. 216).

[33] Husserl 1973d, Hua I, pp. 64 *sq.*; Husserl 1960, pp. 25*sq.*: "'I exist, *ego cogito*', that no longer signifies: 'I, this man, exist'. No longer am I the man who, in natural self-experience, finds himself as as a man"; "By phenomenological epoché, I reduce my natural human ego and my psychic life – the realm of my psychological self-experience – to my transcendental-phenomenological ego, the realm of transcendental-phenomenological self-experience." The permanence of the possessive ("my ego") in the transition from the psychological to the transcendental clearly highlights the difficulty which involves thinking the transcendental and the psychic as two modes of being of the same subject.

makes the world appear; 3) there is nevertheless sufficient continuity between the two to state that *I was* what *I no longer am!* There is a connection between the psychic ego and the pure ego because one may relate to the other as its own past. We face here a non-synonymy which is not a pure or simple homonymy; the issue is thus to think about it positively. It confronts us with "a difficult and even paradoxical relation" (Husserl 1954, Hua VI, p. 207; Husserl 1970, p. 203): the relationship between the transcendental and the worldly, but appearing to occur in one and the same place which, moreover, is the one which clearly defines identity itself – namely, the *ego*. From this arises the "paradox" (Husserl 1954, Hua VI, p. 182; Husserl 1970, p. 180) of this apparent phenomenological chiasm of an ego which, as the transcendental ego, constitutes the world in which it resides as a psychic ego: "Do I not say I in both cases?" (Husserl 1974, Hua XVII, p. 245; Husserl 1969, p. 238).

This ambiguity which is no homonymy may be explained by the radical nature of the incarnation in which the pure ego emerges under the worldly nature of psychism. The incarnation is actually the reification (*Realisierung*) (Husserl 1976, Hua III/1, p. 117; Husserl 1983, p. 125) of consciousness as a soul or mind. Indeed, while egoity is an eidetic trait of consciousness, the pure ego is not a consciousness that is a mere spectator. It is always the ego *of* a body, first in the sense that it is *from* a body. However, the radical phenomenological nature of incarnation implies that *localization* (from) means in fact a *belonging* (of). The body *from* which the ego lives, which is irreducibly *its* place, is actually its *own* body, and the ego objectivates itself as the ego of this body, the pole of the psychic phenomena, as worldly as the body (*Leib*), outside of which the psyche would be untraceable (Husserl 1952, Hua IV, p. 139; Husserl 1989, p. 146). This is the psychic ego, an identical subject in which whatever is transcendentally grasped as a pure lived-experience occurs as a property or as a state of mind, "a *sequence* of conscious *states* of an identical *real* ego-subject" (Husserl 1976, Hua III/1, p. 117; Husserl 1983, p. 126),[34] who is intended to "in its unity with the appearing body." While we commonly speak about "states of mind," we might as well say that the mind is the consciousness described as the realm of the states of a bodily subject. In some ways, the transcendental is nothing other than what it constitutes, and the psychic ego is no more than the manner in which, being incarnated, the pure ego appears to itself.

Against all transcendental psychologism, or the type of transcendental realism taking the reality which is the mind for the transcendental subject, one

---

[34] Husserl takes the example of joy, which can appear in turn as pure lived-experience or as a mental state of the joyful subject. See also Husserl 1976, Hua III/1, p. 195; Husserl 1983, p. 206.

should not, however, settle for repeatedly stressing that pure consciousness is not the mind. It must be mentioned, because while the mind may return to itself[35] and thus *isolate itself from the rest of the world*, it is not what would remain after the exclusion of the natural world; the mind is part of the world[36] and it is *body and mind* (the mind because of the body) that the human being is put in parentheses. However, one must go further, because while there is a difference between the transcendental dimension and the psychic one, the transcendental sense of egoity is also in principle non-identical to its psychic sense, the psychic ego being not simply a bodily ego but also a bodily ego *among others*. The transcendental is neither bodily nor intersubjective, because it is the principle of intersubjectivity itself. The *egoical sense of the transcendental* must thus be understood as a *transcendental sense of ego*. The pure ego is not what *remains* of the natural attitude after reduction. It is not a limit to the reduction. It emerges, in its purity, only under the condition of reduction (Husserl 1954, Hua VI, pp. 409*sq*.).

Indeed, the pure ego is not *straightforwardly* the first person. It is first *the* person if this term means the being to whom his [her] self-identity appears; or it is strictly impersonal, if personality is perceived as an identity whose meaning can only be differential.[37] The ego of the empirical and contingent individual is itself constituted by the pure ego which, precisely because it is unique, is not specific, at least not initially. As Husserl will write in *The Crisis of European Sciences and Transcendental Phenomenology*, the "original ego [*Ur-Ich*]" (Husserl 1954, Hua VI, p. 188; Husserl 1970, p. 185) is not "the I of the personal pronouns" (Husserl 1954, Hua VI, p. 270; Husserl 1970, p. 336), which makes no sense without a "you." It is not *an* ego, but *the* ego (Husserl 1954, Hua VI, p. 84; Husserl 1970, p. 82), and it is only in the constitution of the *alter ego* that it also constitutes itself as the *first* person. Egoity thus precedes personality: the personal sense of egoity is a secondary sense that the pure ego assigns itself according to the self-personalization which is strictly contemporary to its constitution of otherness.

---

[35] Indeed, every ego, whether worldly or transcendental, must be able to relate to itself. See Husserl 1973d, Hua I, p. 102; Husserl 1960, p. 68.

[36] Even though, *within that which appears*, the mind does not appear externally, it is no less, *as something which appears*, external (from a non-spatial perspective) to the ontological realm of that which makes that something appears: *psychological immanence is phenomenological transcendence*. See for example Husserl 1974, Hua XVII, p. 238; Husserl 1969, p. 230.

[37] Transcendental consciousness is thus "a non-personal consciousness" (Husserl 1976, Hua III/1, p. 119; Husserl 1983, p. 127).

3 "And Nothing More": The Transparency of the Ego

Bear in mind the methodical restrictions associated with the requirements of phenomenology: the transcendental ego must belong to the realm of evident reduced data (Husserl 1976, Hua III/1, p. 124; Husserl 1983, p. 133). Accepting only the pure ego's egoity "and nothing more" is denying that nothing pertains to it apart from this obvious egoity, in order to underscore the nature, indescribable in itself, of what is nothing besides its commitment in each actual lived-experience, with its double horizon of non-actionality. The *Ideas* explore a radically transparent ego whose absolute necessity is paid for in radical poverty. The characteristic adequacy of its evidence, which excludes that there is anything "more" than the actual given, goes beyond what lies in general in the sphere of lived-experience. The latter means that from lived-experience, everything is immediately given, unlike real transcendence, which is necessarily presented in adumbrations and is thus always incomplete. However, if, in what concerns the ego, everything is there from the outset, it is because it has nothing to give. To the inadequate givenness of the thing and the completeness of the lived-experience, one must thus add the ego's characteristic adequacy resulting of its emptiness.

The ego, which cannot be isolated from its own life, thus lacks even the consistency of a style, because nothing it experiences can configure it. The unyielding interlacing between the "lived-experiences" and the ego does not incorporate the ego itself. This explains why its static vacuity cannot be reconsidered from a dynamic perspective. While the inadequacy of reality may increase if its historicity is added to its perpetual forth-shadowing, no history can enlarge the ego presented in the *Ideas*. At the time, Husserl excluded all historicity from the pure ego and transferred properties, dispositions and various characters to the realm of the real: while the human being has a character, a history, and capacities, the pure ego does not; it basically *has* nothing, because it *is* simply the performance of acts: "As pure ego it does not harbor any hidden inner richness; it is absolutely simple and it lies there absolutely clear. All richness lies in the *cogito* and in the mode of the function which can be adequately grasped therein" (Husserl 1952, Hua IV, p. 105; Husserl 1989, p. 105). The reflexive dimension of the phenomenological method can thus not be confused with an introspective enterprise. "And nothing more" does not mean that nothing remains to be found, but that there is nothing to look for, in terms of properties of the ego. The expression is not a conclusion of the analysis; it excludes the analysis. One act of reflection, and of the ego nothing remains to be seen: "in order to know that the pure ego is and what it is, no ever so great accumulation of self-experiences can profit me more than a single experience of one sole and simple *cogito*" (Husserl 1952, Hua IV, p. 104; Husserl 1989, p. 105).

However, the inaugural and definitive nature of this "and nothing more" was challenged by the genetic and monadological developments of phenomenology.[38] When Husserl writes, in the *Cartesian Meditations*, that "this centering ego is not an empty pole of identity" (Husserl 1973d, Hua I, p. 100; Husserl 1960, p. 66),[39] he is going against what he affirmed in *Ideas I*, § 80. Indeed, the pure ego is not an ego devoid of history. The issue of the ego's self-constitution cannot be sufficiently resolved by a reference to the phenomenological temporality, understood as the simple emergence of the flow. This is possible only starting from a historical configuration of temporality, understood as the element of a proper genesis. Indeed, if each lived-experience and each act is located in a flow of time, each single "now" does not simply and purely disappear for the benefit of the next one. Each "performance," i.e. each constitutive act, situated at a point of the flow, remains in the following points, as an act that has happened, and, at the same time, it paves the way to a future that is not fully indeterminate. All its "performances," which are always motivated (by which they consistently attest a manner of motivation specific to the ego, i.e. a style that belongs to the Ego[40]) and are immediately motivating, *particularize* the constituent consciousness, which thus constitutes itself within its particularity, *within its productions:* its specific performances then constitute the consciousness as a specific one.[41] The specificity of the modes of constitution in consciousness is the constitution of its own specificity as a consciousness. The ego, inseparable from its lived-experiences, is thus their pole of identity, but a pole which is not itself empty. Indeed, each new constitution of sense is *ipso facto* the constitution of a property of the constituent ego as an ego *which has (already) constituted that sense*. Each constitution gives rise to a sedimentation, to a habitus (Husserl 1952, Hua IV, p. 214; Husserl 1989, p. 226), i.e. to a sustainable achievement which may become actual again at any time: the habitus of an ego, which is then the specific ego of this habitus. The pure ego as a "substrate of habitualities" (Husserl 1973d, Hua I, p. 100; Husserl 1960, p. 66) thus *grows* each time it constitutes a sense, the *history of its constitutions* being, at the same time, the *history of its self-constitution*. The identity of the ego is not one of emptiness.

---

38 Marbach notes that in one of Husserl's copies, several question marks and exclamation points can be found in the margins of the "nothing more" (Husserl 1976, Hua III/1, p. 505; Marbach 1974, p. 205).
39 See also Husserl 1962, Hua IX, p. 211; Husserl 1977, p. 161.
40 See Husserl 1962, Hua IX, p. 215; Husserl 1977, p. 164; and also Husserl 1973b, Hua XIV, p. 18.
41 See the 1921 text in Husserl 1973b, Hua XIV, p. 44.

It must be understood as the *identity of consequence* (and inconsistency is simply one of its modes);[42] not self-consequence but rather consequence as the very form of the constitution of the self, which cannot be found outside and before it. In brief, all its constitutions constitute the constituent as an irreplaceable individuality, meaning that consciousness is always monadic[43] and, as Leibniz initially said about substance, includes all its predicates: consciousness is constituted by its past constitutions which, to some extent, outline its future acts.

Consciousness is not pure act and the pure ego is not an empty functional center: it is *what it did*; hence its specific identity, which is not an empirical one. In short, in the temporal flow occurs "a unity of universal genesis of the ego" and "the ego constitutes himself for himself in, so to speak, the unity of a 'history'" (Husserl 1973d, Hua I, p. 109; Husserl 1960, p. 75).[44] This historicity of the transcendental thus makes it possible to go beyond the alternative of the empty pure ego and of the concrete psychic ego: the transcendental is an individuation process,[45] and the concrete identity of the ego occurs in the history of its constitution of the world.

4 Nothing Excessive?

Natural existence is, foremost, life in a first-person perspective. At the same time, however, the transcendental receives its egoical nature from outside the realm of reduction. Husserl does not proceed from the transcendental to the egoical, but from an egoical natural life to the transcendental. Asking whether, for the phenomenological sphere, the pure ego is or is not *something excessive* thus means questioning a certain egoical continuity between natural attitude and phenomenological attitude. Questions have been raised about knowing whether this continuity is or not the sign of a possible flaw of radicalism.

The first issue is that of a relative *thematic* continuity. This does not mean that the phenomenological reception of the egoical nature of conscious life is pure passivity. As we saw earlier, Husserl reflected deeply on the possible reduc-

---

42 See Husserl 1952, Hua IV, p. 112; Husserl 1989, p. 119. Ms F III 1 (1912), p. 248b.
43 See Husserl 1973d, Hua I, p. 102; Husserl 1960, p. 68. The monadic concept of the ego, which paves the way for conceiving a genetic individuation process, dates from the end of the 1910s. It differs from a first use of the term "Monad", which, at the beginning of the same decade, simply defined the static closure of the flow of consciousness. On the Husserlian concept of monad, see Pradelle 2006.
44 See also Husserl 1962, Hua IX, pp. 211*sq.*; Husserl 1977, pp. 161*sq.*
45 *Cf.* Housset 2000, p. 177.

ibility, consistency, and identity of this ego, which must be distinguished from the psychic ego, even in terms of egoity. Nonetheless, the phenomenological attitude accepts the identity of conscious life *as* the life of the ego. As such, we can say that the analysis of the ego after the reduction means the reaffirmation of its relevance from a transcendental perspective,[46] or the explanation of the proper transcendental status of what is given *before* reduction.

Second, we find here a *formal* continuity, which increases the risk of natural bias in the consideration of the transcendental subject. Indeed, while the life of pure consciousness derives its egoical sense from the natural life of consciousness, the phenomenologizing act which makes it possible to identify it is itself simply the extension of the natural act through which the ego appears. In other words, the phenomenologizing act which allows one to grasp the life of pure consciousness in an intuitive presence only prolongs that through which the natural life of consciousness grasps itself as the life of an ego. The risk, then, lies in attributing to the transcendental what is simply the effect of a natural projection.

This act, which is made possible by the nature of all lived-experiences, and which reveals the relationship of the lived-experience to this ego which is not itself a lived-experience, is none other than *reflection*. Indeed, each conscious experience may become the object of a new lived-experience, i.e. the object of an experience of reflection, designating the conversion of consciousness back to itself. The nature of the lived-experience allows it to be reflected upon (see Husserl 1976, Hua III/1, pp. 77, 95, 162, 166 and Husserl 1952, Hua IV, p. 101) in an intuitive reflection to which it is "given-in-person," in its originary presence. Husserl was able to write at the very beginning of his book, as if it were self-evident: "we have originary experience of ourselves and of our states of consciousness in internal perception or self-perception" (Husserl 1976, Hua III/1, p. 11; Husserl 1983, p. 6).[47] Unlike Brentano, Husserl describes this perception as "immanent" and as something which, while it may be less clear and more fleeting than transcendent perception (Husserl 1976, Hua III/1, p. 146; Husserl 1983, p. 158), is just as perceptive and the only one likely to be adequate.

It is in this *natural* reflection that the empirical ego appears. Indeed, it is only when being reflected upon that a lived-experience can appear as an "I live," i.e. as the ego's lived-experience. Reflection alone may reveal the entirely egoical nature of conscious life. Seeing an apple tree in bloom is not seeing it as an object of my sight. This means that seeing this apple tree is neither seeing this

---

46 See Benoist 1994, p. 71.
47 See also Husserl 1952, Hua IV, p. 101; Husserl 1989, p. 107.

sight of the apple tree, nor seeing me see it. Husserl makes a similar argument concerning the pure ego: reflection, made possible by the essence of the lived-experience, is thus required to reveal the relationship to the ego included in all lived-experiences.[48] Reflection is the act that reveals the egoical nature of all lived-experiences in general, including those in which the ego is somewhat self-forgetful.[49] Better still: reflection does not simply show the egoical nature of transcendental consciousness. It fully *gives* the ego that polarizes the life of consciousness. The *reflecting* lived-experience is the *lived-experience of the ego*, in the objective sense of the genitive.[50] According to Husserl, the act of reflection is characterized by its immediacy.[51] This implies a sound *identity* between the reflective ego and the reflected ego, an intuitive identity between the subject of the act and its object, which places this reflective intuition alongside intellectual intuition as it was conceptualized by German idealism: "The pure ego can be posited as an object by the pure ego which is identically one with it" (Husserl 1952, Hua IV, p. 101; Husserl 1989, p. 107). Reflection, where "the appearing" and what "makes it appear" coincide, is the actual refutation of the scruples expressed by Natorp: the center of all objectification clearly occurs as an object for itself, providing that we do not allow, through an undue metonymy, the "thing-like" object to exhaust the sense of objectivity.

In these conditions, the question of a possible natural bias in the consideration of the transcendental arises because, although the phenomenologizing act leans on the thematically radical break that constitutes the epoché, it remains the extension of this natural reflection, itself made possible by the potential re-

---

[48] *Cf.* Husserl 1976, Hua III/1, p. 168; Husserl 1983, p. 180: "It is only through acts of *experience* in a reflective mode [*reflektiv* erfahrende] that we know something of the flow of lived-experiences and of its necessary relatedness to the pure ego; we thus know that it is a field of free accomplishing of *cogitationes* belonging to one and the same pure ego; that all lived-experiences of the flow are the egos' precisely insofar as it regards them or can direct its regard 'through' them to something other than the ego." See also Husserl 1973a, Hua XIII, p. 246.

[49] The Ms A I 18 (March-April 1914) refers to them as "*Selbstvergessenheit*" (pp. 18a*sq.*, quoted in Marbach 1974, pp. 178*sq.*).

[50] "It pertains in general to the essence of every *cogito* that a new *cogito* of the kind called by us 'ego-reflection [*Ich-Reflexion*]' is in principle possible, one that grasps, on the basis of the earlier *cogito* (which itself is thereby phenomenologically altered) the pure subject of that earlier *cogito*. It consequently pertains [...] to the essence of the pure ego that it be able to grasp itself as what it is and in the way it functions, and thus make itself into an object" (Husserl 1952, Hua IV, p. 101; Husserl 1989, p. 107).

[51] "In the case of an immanently directed or, more briefly expressed, of an *immanent* (the so-called 'internal') perception, *perception and perceived* form *essentially an unmediated unity*, that of a single concrete *cogitatio*" (Husserl 1976, Hua III/1, p. 78; Husserl 1983, p. 79).

flexivity necessarily included in the nature of each lived-experience: "The phenomenological method operates exclusively in acts of reflection" (Husserl 1976, Hua III/1, p. 162; Husserl 1983, p. 174),[52] the "transcendental" or "pure" (via the epoché) species of which is identical to its "natural" one (Husserl 1956, Hua VII, p. 268).

This permanence in the revolution can be a source of suspicion. Indeed, while the appearing of the ego is necessarily reflexive, and while reflection is an act which is not exclusively phenomenological but also natural, the indisputable relevance of the former depends on the phenomenological validation of the latter. This validation lies in the recognition of the immediate nature of reflection, itself attached to the temporality of lived-experiences. The latter guarantees the absence of any solution of continuity between the pre-reflective lived-experience and the reflected experience. Indeed, "to the lively flowing present itself belongs a realm of immediately conscious past" (Husserl 1959, Hua VIII, pp. 149*sq*.), and "it belongs to the essence of the intuition of time that in each point of its duration [...], it is consciousness *of what has just been* and not mere consciousness of the now-point of the object that appears as enduring" (Husserl 1966, Hua X, p. 32; Husserl 1991, pp. 33*sq*.). Retention, as a "still-being-conscious" (Husserl 1966, Hua X, p. 80; Husserl 1991, p. 85), makes it possible to look back on the lived-experience without having to "let it go," and thus ensures continuity between the pre-reflected and reflection, in the absence of any break between the present (of the reflection) and that which has just been and is now reflected upon.[53] Husserl could thus write that "all of the objections that have been raised against the method of reflection are explained on the basis of ignorance of the essential constitution of consciousness" (Husserl 1966, Hua X, p. 120; Husserl 1991, p. 124), i.e. of its temporality. Retention guarantees that reflection and presence are not mutually exclusive, or that reflection, which is obviously a modification, does not imply, nonetheless, any mediation. Husserl thus argues that reflexive objectification cannot stand for the alteration of what is reflected upon, from which derives "the absolute legitimacy of the immanent perceiving reflection, i.e. immanent perception *simpliciter*" (Husserl 1976, Hua III/1, p. 168; Husserl 1983, p. 180).

---

[52] See also Husserl 1976, Hua III/1, p. 165; Husserl 1983, p. 177.
[53] See Husserl 1966, Hua X, pp. 118*sq*.; Husserl 1991, pp. 122*sq.:* "When a primal datum, a new phase, emerges, the preceding phase does not vanish but is 'kept in grip' (that is to say, precisely 'retained'); and thanks to this retention, a looking-back at what has elapsed is possible; [...] But since I keep the elapsed phase in my grip, I can direct my regard to it in a new act that we call reflection (immanent perception) or recollection [...]. We therefore owe it to retention that consciousness can be made into an object."

We can simply note here that the retentional guarantee of the absolute validity of reflection, and of the egoical nature of the phenomenological, may ultimately not appear to be absolutely final. While it explains that reflection doesn't *need* any distance to be established, it fails to exclude all alteration *due to* the fact of reflection. In other words, it is not because reflection requires no alteration (i.e., alteration is not a precondition for reflection) that it does not produce one (i.e., alteration is not an effect of reflection). Retention preserves reflection from all vacuity, but it does not ensure that what is reflected upon is unaltered.

The general anti-skeptical argument, which consists in ascribing some sort of performative contradiction to skepticism, and which Husserl mobilizes in this particular case (Husserl 1976, Hua III/1, p. 174; Husserl 1983, p. 185), seems to be somewhat of a fallacy: in order to question the immediately revealing nature of reflection, there is no need to compare – within a new reflection – the reflected and the non-reflected. Such a suspicion does not necessarily include an assumption of alteration. To know that there is reflection, that there is the reflected and the non-reflected, and to know it through reflection, hardly means that one knows and *has evidence* concerning what these three terms mean. Rather, it is up to the one who assumes the legitimacy and the immediate nature of reflection to establish it! To this end, he or she must show that retention and reflection are homogeneous, and this is not at all self-evident. Indeed, in contrast to reflection, retention is a non-objectifying act, so that while retention provides reflection with its material ground, the acts of both retention and reflection are completely heterogeneous: "The retention itself is not a looking-back that makes the elapsed phase into an object" (Husserl 1966, Hua X, p. 118; Husserl 1991, p. 122); there is thus "a new act," and this is reflection. We thus believe that the point is not sufficiently clear-cut. Indeed, while retention offers reflection upon something which is not altered, it offers no guarantees about the non-disruptive nature of the reflective form. What if its form provides, *in addition*, the evidence of the ego? What if the "wonder of all wonders"[54] was, in part at least, a spell cast by reflection? Many of Husserl's successors believed so, in different ways.

---

54 Husserl 1971, Hua V, p. 75; Husserl 1980, p. 64: "the wonder of all wonders is pure ego and pure consciousness." See also Husserl 1999, p. 207; and Husserl 1973d, Hua I, p. 102; Husserl 1960, p. 43.

Bibliography

Benoist, Jocelyn (1994): *Autour de Husserl. L'ego et la raison*. Paris: Vrin.
Descartes, René (1982): *Oeuvres*, vol. IX-1: *Méditations et Principes: traduction française*. Ed. Charles Adam & Paul Tannery. Paris: Vrin.
Descartes, René (1993): *Meditations on First Philosophy in Focus*. Trans. Elizabeth Sanderson Haldane. Ed. Stanley Tweyman. London: Routledge.
Husserl, Edmund (1950): *Die Idee der Phänomenologie. Fünf Vorlesungen*. Husserliana, vol. II. Ed. Walter Biemel. The Hague: Martinus Nijhoff.
Husserl, Edmund (1952): *Ideen zu einer reinen Phänomenologie und phänomenologischen Philosophie*. Zweites Buch: *Phänomenologische Untersuchungen über die Konstitution*. Husserliana, vol. IV. Ed. Marly Biemel. The Hague: Martinus Nijhoff.
Husserl, Edmund (1954): *Die Krisis der europäischen Wissenschaften und die transzendentale Phänomenologie. Eine Einleitung in die phänomenologische Philosophie*. Husserliana, vol. VI. Ed. Walter Biemel. The Hague: Martinus Nijhoff.
Husserl, Edmund (1956): *Erste Philosophie (1923–1924)*, Erster Teil: *Kritische Ideengeschichte*. Husserliana, vol. VII Ed. Rudolf Boehm. The Hague: Martinus Nijhoff.
Husserl, Edmund (1959): *Erste Philosophie (1923–1924)*, Zweiter Teil: *Theorie der phänomenologischen Reduktion*. Husserliana, vol. VIII. Ed. Rudolf Boehm. The Hague: Martinus Nijhoff.
Husserl, Edmund (1960): *Cartesian Meditations. An Introduction to Phenomenology*. Trans. D. Cairns. The Hague: Martinus Nijhoff.
Husserl, Edmund (1962): *Phänomenologische Psychologie. Vorlesungen Sommersemester 1925*. Husserliana, vol. IX. Ed. Walter Biemel. The Hague: Martinus Nijhoff.
Husserl, Edmund (1966): *Vorlesungen zur Phänomenologie des inneren Zeitbewusstseins*. Husserliana, vol. X. Ed. Rudolph Boehm. The Hague: Martinus Nijhoff.
Husserl, Edmund (1969): *Formal and Transcendental Logic*. Trans. Dorion Cairns. The Hague: Martinus Nijhoff.
Husserl, Edmund (1970): *The Crisis of European Sciences and Transcendental Phenomenology. An Introduction to Phenomenological Philosophy*. Trans. David Carr. Evanston: Northwestern University Press.
Husserl, Edmund (1971): *Ideen zu einer reinen Phänomenologie und phänomenologischen Philosophie*. Drittes Buch: *Die Phänomenologie und die Fundamente der Wissenschaften*. Husserliana, vol. V. Ed. Marly Biemel. The Hague: Martinus Nijhoff.
Husserl, Edmund (1973a): *Zur Phänomenologie der Intersubjektivität. Texte aus dem Nachlass. Erster Teil: 1905–1920*. Husserliana, vol. XIII. Ed. Iso Kern. The Hague: Martinus Nijhoff.
Husserl, Edmund (1973b): *Zur Phänomenologie der Intersubjektivität. Texte aus dem Nachlass. Zweiter Teil: 1921–1928*. Husserliana, vol. XIV. Ed. Iso Kern. The Hague: Martinus Nijhoff.
Husserl, Edmund (1973c): *Ding und Raum: Vorlesungen 1907*. Husserliana, vol. XVI. Ed. Ulrich Claesges. The Hague: Martinus Nijhoff.
Husserl, Edmund (1973d): *Cartesianische Meditationen und Pariser Vorträge*. Husserliana, vol. I. Ed. S. Strasser. The Hague: Martinus Nijhoff.

Husserl, Edmund (1974): *Formale und Transzendentale Logik. Versuch einer Kritik der logischen Vernunft. Husserliana*, vol. XVII. Ed. Paul Janssen. The Hague: Martinus Nijhoff.
Husserl, Edmund (1976): *Ideen zu einer reinen Phänomenologie und phänomenologischen Philosophie. Erstes Buch: Allgemeine Einführung in die Phänomenologie. Husserliana*, vol. III/1 Ed. Karl Schuhmann. The Hague: Martinus Nijhoff.
Husserl, Edmund (1977): *Phenomenological Psychology. Lectures, Summer Semester, 1925*. Trans. John Scanlon. The Hague: Martinus Nijhoff.
Husserl, Edmund (1980): *Ideas Pertaining to a Pure Phenomenology and to a Phenomenological Philosophy. Third Book: Phenomenology and the Foundations of the Sciences*. Trans. F. Kersten. The Hague: Martinus Nijhoff.
Husserl, Edmund (1983): *Ideas Pertaining to a Pure Phenomenology and to a Phenomenological Philosophy. First Book: General Introduction to a Pure Phenomenology*. Trans. T. E. Klein and W. E. Pohl. The Hague: Martinus Nijhoff.
Husserl, Edmund (1984a): *Logische Untersuchungen. Zweiter Band: Untersuchungen zur Phänomenologie und Theorie der Erkenntnis. Husserliana*, vol. XIX/1. Ed. Ursula Panzer. The Hague: Martinus Nijhoff.
Husserl, Edmund (1984b): *Einleitung in die Logik und Erkenntnistheorie. Vorlesungen 1906–1907. Husserliana*, vol. XXIV. Ed. Ullrich Melle. The Hague: Martinus Nijhoff.
Husserl, Edmund (1989): *Ideas Pertaining to a Pure Phenomenology and to a Phenomenological Philosophy. Second Book: Studies in the Phenomenology of Constitution*. Trans. R. Rojcewicz and A. Schuwer. Dordrecht: Kluwer Academic Publishers.
Husserl, Edmund (1991): *On the Phenomenology of the Consciousness of Internal Time (1893–1917)*. Trans. J. B. Brough. Dordrecht: Kluwer Academic Publishers.
Husserl, Edmund (1994): *Briefwechsel: Die Göttinger Schule. Husserliana Dokumente*, vol. III/3. Ed. Karl Schuhmann. Dordrecht: Springer.
Husserl, Edmund (1997a): *Thing and Space. Lectures of 1907*. Trans. R. Rojcewicz. Dordrecht: Springer.
Husserl, Edmund (1997b): *Psychological and Transcendental Phenomenology and the Confrontation with Heidegger (1927–1931)*. Trans. Thomas Sheehan and Richard E. Palmer. Dordrecht/Boston/London: Kluwer Academic Publishers.
Husserl, Edmund (1999): *Phänomenologische Methode und phänomenologische Philosophie (Londoner Vorträge)*. In: *Husserl Studies*, vol. 16, n° 3, pp. 183–254.
Husserl, Edmund (2001): *Logical Investigations*. Volume II. Trans J. N. Findlay. London and New York: Routledge.
Housset, Emmanuel (2000): *Husserl et l'énigme du monde*. Paris: Seuil.
Marbach, Eduard (1974): *Das Problem des Ich in der Phänomenologie Husserls*. The Hague: Martinus Nijhoff.
Natorp, Paul (1888): *Einführung in die Psychologie nach kritischer Methode*. Tübingen: Mohr/Siebeck.
Natorp, Paul (1912): *Allgemeine Psychologie nach kritischer Methode*. Tübingen: Mohr Siebeck.
Pradelle, Dominique (2006): "Monadologie et phénoménologie". In: *Philosophie*, vol. 92, pp. 56–85.

Irene Breuer
Towards a Phenomenological Metaphysics
The Contingent Core of the ego and of all Eidetic Forms

Abstract: Husserl defines eidetically-based transcendental phenomenology as "First Philosophy." Accordingly, in *Ideas I* he conceives of the I as an "eidetic particularization" grounded on apodictic eidetic universalities. Insofar as the positing of the ego's facticity is necessary to enable any self-reflection leading to the task of the eidetic variation, it seems to be necessary only on methodological grounds. Later on, however, at the end of his *Cartesian Meditations* and in a supplementary sheet to his *First Philosophy*, he establishes contingency and the "irrationality of the transcendental fact" as the contents of a "metaphysics in a new sense:" Phenomenological metaphysics encompasses originary primal facts (I, world, bodily existence, intersubjectivity, historicity) that are absolutely self-given and thus the condition for the possibility of the existence of every other fact. An embodied ego becomes thus ontologically necessary. The novelty lies in the insight that contingency not only characterizes the "core" of primal facts but even the very ego's essence due to its qualitative "openness," as stated in *Ideas II*. Hence, the order of foundation is revised: a phenomenological metaphysics comprising these primal facts underlies transcendental phenomenology. This paper will focus on these transformations and distinguish among different senses of a concomitant 'phenomenological openness.'

Introduction

Husserl conceives of eidetically-based transcendental phenomenology as "First Philosophy." On the basis of the eidetic method, transcendental phenomenology must determine the possibilities from which realities or actualities (*Wirklichkeiten*) should be derived and understood. Phenomenology is based on the method of eidetic variation, which yields the universal, i.e., the *eidos*, as the invariant structure inherent to all possible factual realities. Later on, however, at the end of his *Cartesian Meditations*, Husserl briefly develops the idea of a phenomenological metaphysics that is to deal with "the problem of the 'accidental factualness'" and which characterizes the limit issues of factual life (destiny, death…), thereby disclosing the apodictic facticity of the world and of the ego. Contingency not only characterizes the "core [*Kern*]" of the primal facts but even the ego's very essence due to its qualitative "openness." While in the *Ideas I* the ego was

https://doi.org/10.1515/9783110564280-011

only hypothetically and methodically necessary in order to enable the eidetic variation, now, as a primal fact, it becomes ontologically necessary. Hence, the order of foundation is revised: transcendental phenomenology is grounded upon a phenomenological metaphysics. In what follows, I will show how and why Husserl moves from a transcendental philosophy understood as an eidetic science to a phenomenological metaphysics based on originally given primal facts, focusing on the transformation of the concept of the ego. The inquiry into the realm of the primal facts as the objects of a phenomenological metaphysics will reveal an essential 'phenomenological openness' that in the first instance concerns the essence and consciousness of the ego and which also accounts for the contingency and irrationality of its surrounding world.

1 Eidetic Transcendental Phenomenology as First Philosophy

In *Ideas I*, Husserl defines eidetically-based transcendental phenomenology as the "incessant precondition for every metaphysics [...] that will be able to make its appearance as science" (Husserl 1976, Hua III/1, p. 8; Husserl 1982, p. XXII); as such, it is "First Philosophy" (Husserl 1950, Hua I, p. 106; Husserl 1960, p. 72; Husserl 1956, Hua VII, p. 14; Husserl 2019, p. 14). Actually, as early as 1910–11 Husserl defines phenomenology as a rigorous science of the pure essences of psychic phenomena in *Philosophie als strenge Wissenschaft* (Husserl 1987, Hua XXV, pp. 3–62). But it is only in *Ideas I* that Husserl exposes and executes this program. In this work, Husserl argues that the only philosophy that can provide a rigorous clarification of consciousness as such is transcendental phenomenology by means of descriptive eidetic analyses. Phenomenology's rigor is based on the fact that its results are eidetic, i.e. universally true for any consciousness, be it animal or human, whether it exists or not. Non-empirical, i.e. eidetic analysis provides the universality and necessity that characterize scientific results. In the first section Husserl argues that an individual object possesses qualitative determinations that make up its essence. In an Aristotelian way, Husserl defines the essence as the "what" of an individual being. Just as the "empirical intuition" grasps the individual in its bodily singularity, the "eidetic intuition" is presentive of a "pure essence [...] in its 'personal' selfhood" (Husserl 1976, Hua III/1, p. 15; Husserl 1982, p. 10). The two sorts of intuition are "essentially different" insofar as one grasps matters of fact, i.e. individual factual existences, while the other intuits an *eidos* or idea, "the *pure essence*." Essences can be seized both from experiential data and from data of mere phantasy. They encompass many different sorts of objects: spatial forms, melodies, social practices, acts of liking or disliking, etc., taken either as particular exemplified types or as examples of whatever, i.e. taken as a generalities (Husserl 1976, Hua III/1, p. 16; Husserl 1982, p. 11).

While for Aristotle, only existing things have an essence, for Husserl essences are independent of existence, i.e. they do not imply *"the positing of any individual factual existence, pure eidetic truths contain not the slightest assertion about matters of fact,"* insofar as they can be the product of a free phantasy or memory (Husserl 1976, Hua III/1, p. 17; Husserl 1982, p. 11). Even though intuition of an essence implies no positing of existence, the intuition of something individual or the consciousness thereof – be it existent or not – is required to intuit an essence (Husserl 1976, Hua III/1, p. 15; Husserl 1982, p. 10). Husserl clearly distinguishes between cognition of matters of fact and eidetic cognition about essences: while any predication concerning individual facts grounds on experience, thinking about pure essences grounds on the seizing of essences. Concerning thinking about essences, Husserl claims that essences can be seized as the objects of an eidetic judgment in two ways: either as a judgment about essences and relationships about essences or in a vague, universal manner, i.e. "in the mode *Any [überhaupt] about the individual, though purely as a single particular subsumed under essences [Einzelheit der Wesen]*," and any of them can be converted into the other (Husserl 1976, Hua III/1, p. 17; Husserl 1982, p. 12). As G. Heffernan remarks, Husserl's eidetic phenomenology is "double-sided in so far as it both describes phenomena in eidetic terms and thematizes essences as objects in their own right" (Heffernan 2018, p. 78). Essences are thus the objects of formal logic, i.e. of a judgment, be it universal or about single particulars, and have no ontological reality.

The distinction between matters of fact and essences is further developed in texts dating from around 1920. In the first part of *Erste Philosophie*, Husserl distinguishes between phenomenology as first philosophy and metaphysics. Metaphysics as "'second' philosophy" presupposes the "First Philosophy," i.e. the eidetical phenomenology, as "a science of the totality of the pure (*a priori*) principles of all possible knowledge and of the totality of *a priori* truths contained systematically within (i.e. purely deducible from) these principles." Second philosophy, i.e. metaphysics, concerns "the totality of 'genuine' factual sciences, i.e., of 'explanatory' sciences employing a rational method." These sciences attain the unity of a relational system through the "systematic unity of the highest *a priori* principles themselves" (Husserl 1956, Hua VII, p. 14; Husserl 2019, p. 14). The realm of metaphysics concerns the correlation between the sciences of matters of fact, and "the unity of the factual reality." (Husserl 1956, Hua VII, p. 14; Husserl 2019, pp. 13*sq.*) Metaphysics has thus lost its priority insofar as, for transcendental phenomenology, the world is not just "a fact *simpliciter*, it is not reality existing *simpliciter*," but

> is posited in cognizing subjectivity as 'meant and intuited fact' in its immanent experiencing and theoretical accomplishing, more precisely in activities creating ever new meaning, in [subjectivity's] exhibiting 'evident' confirmations and reasonings. (Husserl 1956, Hua VII, p. 369; Husserl 2019, p. 434)

According to these statements, metaphysics as a rational investigation of the factual actuality presupposes eidetic phenomenology as a science of possibilities.

2 Transcendental Phenomenology: Eidetic Variation and Actuality

In *Ideas I*, Husserl claims that

> [t]he old ontological doctrine that the cognition of 'possibilities' must precede the cognition of actualities is, in my opinion, insofar as it is correctly understood and made useful in the right ways, a great truth. (Husserl 1976, Hua III/1, p. 178; Husserl 1982, *Ideas I*, p. 190)

On the basis of the eidetic method, transcendental phenomenology must determine the possibilities from which actualities should be derived and understood. Even at the time of the *Cartesian Meditations*, Husserl grounds this conception on the apriority of eidetic laws, out of which the *Ego cogito* should constitute and understand the *de facto* world in its reality:

> [A]ll the rationality of the fact lies, after all, in the Apriori. Apriori science is the science of radical universalities and necessities, to which the science of matters of fact must have recourse, precisely in order that it may ultimately become grounded on such radical principles. But apriori science must not be naive; on the contrary, it must have originated from ultimate transcendental-phenomenological sources. (Husserl 1950, Hua I, p. 181; Husserl 1960, p. 155)

Phenomenology, like mathematics, does not deal with realities as stated above, but with ideal possibilities and laws showing a universal and invariant structure: the *eidos*, obtained by eidetic variation or intuition. This method of eidetic variation yields the universal, i.e., the *eidos*, as the invariant structure inherent to all the possible factual realities (Husserl 1959b, Hua IX, § 9; Husserl 1977, § 9). It is the work of phantasy to intuit the pure *eidos*, disengaged from every positing of existence (Husserl 1939, EU, pp. 426*sq.*; Husserl 1972, pp. 352*sq.*). When an *eidos* is obtained through free eidetic variation, it does not depend on its factual actualization or non-actualization. Reality is thus conceived "as a possibility among other possibilities, and even as an optional possibility for phantasy" (Husserl 1959b, Hua IX, p. 74; Husserl 1977, p. 55). Hence, "the essence of purely eidetic science thus consists of proceeding in an exclusively eidetic way" (Husserl 1976, Hua III/1, p. 21; Husserl 1982, p. 16), so that the "factual actuality" is "completely irrelevant" (Husserl 1959b, Hua IX, p. 74; Husserl 1977, p. 55), and experience is only a starting point for eidetic variation. The insight into this universal *eidos* allows us to discern *a priori* every conceivable singularization as a particularization of this *eidos*, i.e. as an example of a chain of singular pure possibilities.

Contrary to the sciences of matters of fact, the grounding of eidetic sciences "is not experience but rather the seeing of essences" (Husserl 1976, Hua III/1, p. 21; Husserl 1982, p. 16), while experience is only an exemplary starting-point for the phantasy variation that does not imply any positing of factual existence. This is why Husserl conceives individual existence as "*contingent*. It is thus; in respect of its essence it could be otherwise" (Husserl 1976, Hua III/1, p. 12; Husserl 1982, p. 7). This is why all essential predicables of an object necessarily belong to it while any singularization of this object, i.e. any material thing whatsoever, may have any determinations whatsoever and is as such contingent. Any real object is at the same time a possible one and can be regarded as an example or case of a pure possibility transformed into a variant. On the contrary, every description of essence "expresses an unconditionally valid norm for possible empirical existence" (Husserl 1976, Hua III/1, p. 177; Husserl 1982, p. 189). This is why any eidetic particularization of an eidetic necessity holds for any matter of fact. The consciousness of the necessity is called an "*apodictic* consciousness" (Husserl 1976, Hua III/1, p. 19; Husserl 1982, p. 14.) because it involves the consciousness of a particularization of an eidetic universality.

Husserl claims that factual egos are uncovered by "irrevocable [*undurchstreichbar*]," (Husserl 1973a, Hua XIV, p. 154*sq.*), i.e. "apodictic principles" pertaining to this "*eidos* ego: the essential universalities and necessities by means of which the fact is to be related to its rational grounds (those of its pure possibility)" (Husserl 1950, Hua I, p. 106; Husserl 1960, p. 72). The eidetic concepts are therefore universal and absolutely valid for every contingent individual case. As I. Kern remarks, this foundational order leads to the establishment of philosophy as a universal and pure eidetic science, which retrospectively grounds its own reality on absolute terms by reverting to its own rationality (Kern 1975, p. 336). In the line of this interpretation, Husserl states that

> [t]he ideal possibility of a reflection having the essential characteristic of an evidently indefeasible positing of factual existence is grounded in the essence of *any Ego whatever and of any mental process whatever*. (Husserl 1976, Hua III/1, p. 98; Husserl 1982, p. 103)

This is the true sense of phenomenological idealism: It is the task of the factual existing ego to "retroactively [*rückwärts*]" constitute the sense of every other factual existence (Husserl 2002b, Hua XXXV, p. 141).

3 Transcendental Phenomenology: Facticity and Necessity of the Ego – *Eidos* as Invariant Structure

We can now take up our reflections on the role of essences: particular essences are the objects of an "apodictic" judgment as derived from a universal judgment that concerns universal essences. The fact that something real or actual corresponds to "purely eidetic propositions" is not a "mere fact," i.e. something accidental, but an "eidetic necessity" as a particularization of eidetic laws. Thus, only the actual thing is conceived as a fact (Husserl 1976, Hua III/1, pp. 19*sq.*; Husserl 1982, pp. 14*sq.*). This distinction runs parallel to the delimitation between the "apodicticity of the fact" – that of the egos for themselves – and apodicticity in the "special sense" of eidetic laws (Husserl 2002b, Hua XXXV, p. 287). The ego unifies in itself both modes of apodicticity insofar as it recognizes and perceives its individual cogito. This is why the *Ego cogito* is "an essential eidetic principle and at the same time, is a universal eidetical-apodictical necessity" (Husserl 2002b, Hua XXXV, p. 287). Hence, the *Ego cogito* is endowed with apodictical certainty, an "absolutely indubitable positing" which Husserl compares to the "'contingent' positing" of the world (Husserl 1976, Hua III/1, p. 98; Husserl 1982, p. 102).[1] In this context, Husserl states that the "pure I" has an eidetic necessity, inasmuch as each "eidetic predicatively formed affair-complex," thereunder the I is a "matter of fact, insofar as it is an individual predicatively formed actuality-complex" (Husserl 1976, Hua III/1, p. 19; Husserl 1982, p. 15). In correlation with this, each predicatively formed affair complex is an "eidetic necessity in so far as it is a singularization of an eidetic universality:" "Eidetic universality and eidetic necessity are therefore correlates" (Husserl 1976, Hua III/1, p. 19; Husserl 1982, p. 14).

---

[1] *Cf.* Landgrebe 1982, p. 120.

Hence, at the time of *Ideas I* Husserl still conceives of the I as an "eidetic particularization" grounded on apodictic eidetic universalities (Husserl 1976, Hua III/1, p. 19; Husserl 1982, p. 14) and factual existence in general in terms of any example whatsoever (Bernet, Kern, Marbach 1996, pp. 74–80). When the eidetic variation yields the *eidos*, it is independent from any possible factual actualization, so that any singularization of this *eidos* can be conceived as an example of a chain of pure possibilities. This is why individual existence is conceived as contingent (Husserl 1976, Hua III/1, p. 12; Husserl 1982, p. 7).

But the relationship between the factual I and the *eidos* of any I whatever having been obtained through eidetic variation is an exception to the law according to which a universal essence belongs by necessity to any possible single case of this essence, as K. Held and L. Landgrebe both point out (Held 1966, p. 147; Landgrebe 1982, p. 176).[2] As Husserl remarks in 1931, while the being of an *eidos*, i.e. the being of eidetic possibilities, is free from any actualization, the "*eidos* of the transcendental I is inconceivable without any transcendental I as factual" (Husserl 1973b, Hua XV, p. 385). This is indeed the case, because the last acting I is not simply the accidental actualization of one of the infinite number of eidetic possibilities. On the contrary, this last acting I as the origin of all constitutional work precedes any positing of a difference between fact and *eidos* (Held 1966, p. 147). Consequently, the actuality of the I is methodologically and hypothetically necessary in order to allow for the eidetical variation – a type of necessity which Husserl later revises.

Hence, Husserl stresses the impossibility of going beyond the actual I insofar as the I is a "primal fact" in the process of eidetic variation, through which it retrospectively discovers the "primal structures of [its] facticity." In Husserl's words:

> I am the primal fact in this process, I recognize, that in addition to my factual ability for eidetic variation, these and those own primal stock of components yield to me as primal structures of my facticity in response to my factual retrospective inquiries. [...] I cannot go beyond my factual I. (Husserl 1973b, Hua XV, p. 386)

This insight leads Husserl to posit the apodictic facticity of the world as well as of the I. Indeed, the phenomenologizing Ego is now conceived of as the "absolute irrevocable fact" (Husserl 1973a, Hua XIV, p. 154) of the self-reflective process that is involved in any eidetic inquiry insofar as it is given with an "apodictic evidence as the primal evidence of the 'I-am'" (Husserl 1973a, Hua XIV, p. 154). Thus, the Ego can vary its qualitative determinations, its being-thus; but both its

---

[2] While Held views this turning point as an "exception [*Ausnahme*]" to the general law, Landgrebe regards it as "relinquishment [*Preisgabe*]" of the earlier conception.

and the world's existence, i.e. its "ground of existence," are apodictically necessary to allow for the eidetic variation. This means that the monad – here the Ego – is an "absolute actuality" (Husserl 1973b, Hua XV, p. 386) whose non-being is in conflict with the other monads. In conclusion, the positing of the facticity of the Ego is necessary to enable any self-reflection leading to the task of the eidetic variation. As such, it seems to be necessary only on methodological grounds.

4 Phenomenological Metaphysics – Ontology of Primal Facticity

In the context of his later writings, however, Husserl carries out a deeper investigation of the kind of evidence that characterizes the ego and the world.[3] His inquiry into a primal facticity leads him to revise his claim about the priority of the cognition of possibilities over the cognition of realities and consequently to revise the order of foundation by conceiving a "phenomenological metaphysics" as underlying phenomenology. Indeed, we may recall that in the *Cartesian Meditations*, Husserl still adheres to his conception of phenomenology as an eidetic science grounded on *a priori* insights:

> The universal *de facto* structure of the given Objective world – as mere nature, as psychophysical being, as humanness, sociality of various levels, and culture – is, to a very great extent [...] an essential necessity [...]. Such an ontological *A priori* [...] does confer on the ontic fact, on the *de facto* world in respect of its "accidental" features, a relative intelligibility, that of an evident necessity of being thus and so by virtue of eidetic laws. (Husserl 1950, Hua I, p. 164; Husserl 1960, p. 137)

But he had already realized in 1922 that "if I have no real ground of existence, no experiential basis, I have no possibilities" (Husserl 1973a, Hua XIV, p. 153). These inquiries overcome the distinctions posed in *Ideas I* and in the *Lectures on First Philosophy*. As the brief outline of a metaphysics of primal givenness at the end of his *Cartesian Meditations* shows, a phenomenological metaphysics, which is grounded upon the experience of apodictically given primal facts (which are themselves absolutely given), is the condition for possibility of the eidetic variation and thus cannot be subject to it. Indeed, the later Husserl seems to rework his early insights, insofar as the reflection is no longer restricted to the reality of an "eidetic-phenomenological interpretation of the science of matters-of-fact" (Bernet, Kern, Marbach 1989, p. 211). Already in a supplementary sheet to his

---

3 *Cf.* Breuer 2018.

First Philosophy of 1923–24, Husserl extends the scope of this problematic to the realm of the "irrationality of the transcendental fact" as the content of a "metaphysics in a new sense" (Husserl 1956, Hua VII, 188 fn.; Husserl 2019, p. 194 fn.), a phenomenological metaphysics, on which the transcendental-eidetic phenomenology is grounded and which no longer allows any distinctions between 'static' and 'genetic.' The problem of the "irrationality of the transcendental fact, which expresses itself in the constitution of the factual world and of factual spiritual life" concerning the "metaphysical" interpretation of the "universe" (Husserl 1956, Hua VII, 188 fn.; Husserl 2019, p. 194 fn.) is closely related to those of "accidental factualness" because contingency characterizes the problems of death, destiny, illness, and misery (Husserl 2014, Hua XLII, p. 398), the "'meaning' of history," and even "ethico-religious problems" (Husserl 1950, Hua I, p. 182; Husserl 1960, p. 156). In Husserl's words: "The being of absolute human beings and absolute communities" is a mere "contingency, contingency of their surroundings, upbringing, education, health and illness" (Husserl 2014, Hua XLII, p. 409 and p. 300). The world is "unpredictable; would it itself be predicable, it would be of no avail to the I, which has bumped into it by hazard and fate and which is dragged around by and in it" (Husserl 2014, Hua XLII, p. 286). Hence, phenomenology's realm is enlarged to encompass the problems concerning irrationality, indeterminacy, and contingency, the causes of which are indeterminate.

Metaphysics is thus enlarged to "limit issues" of factual life, i.e. "primal facts [...] last necessities, the primal necessities" (Kern 1975, p. 340), upon which all eidetic relations are dependent. These specific issues open the way to the disclosure of the apodictic facticity of the world and of the I. Husserl realizes that for a bodily Ego, the possession of the world (*Welthabe*) is a primal fact insofar as the experience of the world – in contrast to any experience generally – cannot be modalized. Hence, the certainty of the world is apodictically given. In Husserl's words:

> [d]oubt and not-being possible for a real particular are possible only on the grounds of continual certainty of the world. [...] No matter how I modalize myself as a personal, human I, I remain as having the world and living in this structure. (Husserl 2008, Hua XXXIX, p. 246)

The apodictic structure of transcendental reality thus belongs to these primal necessities insofar as "the certainty of the being of the world as world is apodictical" (Husserl 2008, Hua XXXIX, p. 256). In research manuscripts published in *Husserliana XV* (Husserl 1973b), he states that these primal structures encompass the apodictic evidence of the world (p. 386), the intersubjectivity (p. 366), the bodily existence (p. 385), and the historical teleology (p. 381) that are inherent to "the absolute actuality" (p. 386). These primal facts, to which space and time as apodictic pregivenness should be added, are the "primal structures of my facticity" insofar as "I am the primal fact" (p. 386) underlying them. Hence, Husserl clearly states that the "actuality" (p. 381) of a transcendental Ego is only within the framework constituted by a spatio-temporal world (p. 362), an "intentional intertwining" (p. 372), an "universal will [...] referred to the ideal telos" (p. 380), and finally a bodily "concrete individuality" (p. 381).

Husserl's metaphysics differs from traditional metaphysics insofar as these primal facts are conceived as "originary givenness," as L. Tengelyi accurately remarks (Tengelyi 2011, p. 129). It grounds itself, contrary to the Kantian metaphysics, on a transcendental sphere of facts, which has an a-posteriori and apodictic character. These originary primal facts (I, world, bodily existence, intersubjectivity, historicity, space, time) are absolutely self-given and thus the condition for the possibility of the existence of every other fact. Although every experience of common facts can be put into question or modalized, the originary experience of these primal facts is not modalizable. This 'impossibility of modalization' (*Unmodalisierbarkeit*) resulting from their absoluteness and apodicticity is to be regarded as the criterion that distinguishes these primal facts from facts in the common sense. The eidetical variation within the transcendental-eidetical metaphysics presupposes these primal, originary given facts. Hence, phenomenology comes to be grounded on these primal structures which account for the ontology of the living world.

But in my view, Husserl's 'archeological' dismantling reveals an ultimate originary sphere on which these primal structures are in turn grounded. In a 1931 text published in *Husserliana XV*, Husserl claims that "the condition for the possibility" of actuality's being and essence lies in "its being-referred-to the primal fact of the *hylē*" comprising "primal kinaesthesias, primal feelings and primal drives" (Husserl 1973b, Hua XV, p. 385). In his *Bernauer Manuskripte* Husserl calls this primal *hylē* the "originary sensibility [*ursprüngliche Sinnlichkeit*]" (Husserl 2001, Hua XXXIII, p. 275), which origin he locates in the time-consciousness. The fundamental affectivity of the *hylē*, i.e. this "sensuousness devoid of Ego [*ichlose Sensualität*]," is further characterized as an "originary vitality [*ursprüngliche Lebendigkeit*]" or a "universal drive intentionality [*universale Triebintentionalität*]" and can therefore be understood as an originary drive. This originary sensibility owes its force to the intentionality of drives: When understood – as I'd like to suggest – as an intensive affective vitality, it 'enlivens' the aforementioned primal facts and endows them with an affective power that can only be bodily sensed. As affective primal material and insofar it is caught up in all the other primal facts, it cannot appear in itself, but only through those primal facts. Hence the *hylē*, or affective sensibility, should be regarded as a 'special primal fact,' i.e. as a 'grounding primal fact of appearance.'

These reflections lead us to the conclusion that in this context 'facticity' does not mean a contingent fact whose not-being is possible (as stated in *Ideas I*), but a "primal fact" (Husserl 1973b, Hua XV, p. 385) which precedes any contingent fact and apodictically makes every positing of reality possible. In Husserl's words:

> A full ontology is teleology but it presupposes the factum. I am apodictically and apodictically in the belief in the world. The worldliness lies in the factum for me, the teleology is disclosable, transcendental. (Husserl 1973b, Hua XV, p. 385)

L. Tengelyi remarks that this inquiry outlines a metaphysics that replaces the threefold structure of the I, the world, and God by a fourfold structure of the I-subject, the *Welthabe*, intentional intertwining, and historicity. Phenomenological metaphysics is thus conceived as a "doctrine of the primal facts," "which do not permit being led back to first causes and hence cannot be speculatively fathomed" (Tengelyi 2014, p. 186). This new meaning of the concept of 'fact' is accompanied by a revision of the order of foundation: now, the eidetic variation within the transcendental-eidetic metaphysics presupposes these originary given primal facts, which thus make up an 'ontology of the primal facticity.' These primal facts are the originary apodictic ground of the experience of every other contingent experiential fact, which latter, according to *Ideas I*, belongs to the realm of a metaphysics as a science of facts. Phenomenology as an eidetic science is thus grounded upon a phenomenological metaphysics. Metaphysics, which had lost its priority in favor of phenomenology as an eidetic science, now regains this priority through a change in its grounding structures. The order of foundation is renewed: a metaphysics of the primal facts, i.e. an ontology of primal facticity, underlies a phenomenological eidetic science and a formal ontology, which furnishes the metaphysics of a science of facts with *a priori* determinations.[4]

---

4 *Cf.* Breuer 2019.

5 Phenomenological Metaphysics – Primal Contingency of Eidetic Forms

When it comes to the role of the Ego within this renewed metaphysics, Husserl states that "my being as that which experiences itself is apodictically included in each experience of the world" (Husserl 2002a, Hua XXXIV, p. 432). The transcendental consciousness is to be regarded as the most universal realm of existential positedness. Its evidence is apodictic, "because without its evidence, all other evidences (those of the world and the objectivities) basing on it would be annulled" (Taguchi 2006, p. 199). For Husserl it is clear that

> [t]he being of this world is purely self-included in the content of this life and that this being is inseparable from me as subject of this life [...]. My life is in itself the first, it is the primal ground, to which all other groundings must refer back to. (Husserl 1959a, Hua VIII, p. 396)

It thereby turns out that the "I am, I live" is to be considered as the final primal evidence. Husserl claims that

> I am presumptively certain, that the world is – certainly, as long as I live the way I do. The first certainty: I am, I live, absolutely uncancellable [...]. The pure subjectivity is for itself absolute, and all originally capable to be experienced or even presumed belongs to it, in so far as it has the character of that which must be fulfilled by experience. (Husserl 1973a, Hua XIV, p. 442)

This irrevocability characterizes the fact of my own life, i.e. my actual being as embodied subject, because I am the one who remembers, expects something, phantasizes, judges, desires, feels, etc. (Husserl 2002b, Hua XXXV, p. 402). What is at issue here is the apodicticity of the Ego's existence: "As matters of fact, they are absolute" (Husserl 2002b, Hua XXXV, p. 321). Egos have a *"double being:* an *absolute being* and a *appearing-for-themselves-and-for-another"* (Husserl 1959a, Hua VIII, p. 506; Husserl 2019, p. 632); they are *"the absolute* <they are the subjectivity> without whose cogitative life [...], all *real* substances *would not exist"* (Husserl 1959a, Hua VIII, p. 505; Husserl 2019, p. 632). This means they are apodictically necessary.

At this point we should distinguish between contingency, i.e. the empirical necessity of the modalizable facts pertaining to eidetic phenomenology, and the apodictic necessity of the unmodalizable primal facts belonging to this "metaphysics in a new sense" or phenomenological metaphysics. While individual existence is conceived as "contingent" (Husserl 1976, Hua III/1, p. 12; 1982, p. 7), the necessity of a "lived experience [...] given 'in person'" is called the "necessity of a fact" (Husserl 1976, Hua III/1, p. 98; 1982, pp. 102*sq.*, modified translation). This necessity of a fact, as a special case of the empirical necessity applying to any existence whatsoever (Husserl 1976, Hua III/1, p. 98 fn.; 1982, p. 103, fn.), implies that the fact of the Ego's existence is contingent, i.e. dependent on its having experiences. As such, its existence is merely hypothetically necessary – as long as I have *Erlebnisse*, my existence is necessary. In later writings, however, Husserl revises this conception: the Ego's existence is no longer hypothetically, but absolutely, i.e. apodictically, necessary. As stated above, the Ego becomes an absolute irrevocable fact given with apodictic evidence (Husserl 1973a, Hua XIV, p. 154). Husserl realizes that the Ego's "possession of the world" (Husserl, 2008, Hua XXXIX, pp. 246 and 256), and the primal facts as the Ego's primal structures are absolutely and irrevocably given (Husserl 2002b, Hua XXXV, p. 321); as such, they are apodictically necessary and not modalizable.[5]

Hence, in the transcendental consideration there lies the absolute, that which "cannot even be called 'necessary'" because it "lies at the basis of all possibilities, all relativities, endowing them with sense and being" (Husserl 1973b, Hua XV, p. 669). In this context, R. Boehm points out that "the absolutely given is at first the absolutely doubtless being" (Boehm 1959, p. 221). The "absolute I" is the Ego in the "immediate present life-evidence" (Taguchi 2006, p. 115). We may therefore conclude that the I as primal fact is now no longer necessary for methodological reasons, but is *ontologically necessary* to ground all eidetic investigations.

These statements, far from grounding a renewed subject-metaphysics, point to something new (Tengelyi 2014, p. 184): All eidetic forms obtained through eidetical variation host a "core of 'primal contingency'" (Husserl 1973b, Hua XV, p. 386). By this "primal contingency" Husserl means the open possibilities of the "irrational/senseless [*Unsinnigkeiten*]" – destiny, death, illness, and misery (Husserl 2014, Hua XLII, p. 398) and of "senseless fortuitousness [*unsinnige Zufällen*]" insofar as the being of human beings is a mere contingency (Husserl 2014, Hua XLII, p. 409). Human beings are therefore inevitably subject to the strokes of destiny and fate. Furthermore, these primal facts are primal structures of the Ego's facticity, i.e. they ground on the life of the phenomenologizing Ego. In Husserl's terms, they are "primal components [...] as primal structures of my facticity" (Husserl 1973b, Hua XV, p. 386) The I bumps into an already existing world – as Husserl claims: "I haven't chosen my life" (Husserl 2014, Hua XLII, p. 409) – and is born amid a family and a certain community, in a particular surroundings under particular historical circumstances, in a cultural tradition, in a

---

5 *Cf.* Breuer 2018, pp. 281–290.

determinate place in time and space and so forth which were already constituted by others and which it has to endow retroactively with sense. Therefore, self-givenness is not to be confused with self-grounding: This sense-endowing praxis can be called an 'ontological praxis' insofar as the Ego has to constitute these originally given facts in their sense 'for it' which, as originally given, "cannot be the object of any further reflective questioning" (Landgrebe 1982, p. 106). It is only through self-reflection that the phenomenologizing Ego uncovers these originally given primal facts and comes to realize that these primal facts determine its own essential core. These reflections have a far-reaching impact on eidetic phenomenology, insofar as it is now grounded upon this new metaphysics that comprises not only the given factual structures that belong to the Ego's very essence but also irrational or senseless and fortuitous events that may overcome the Ego in the actualization of its factual life. This means that the Ego is subject not only to pre-existing structures imposed upon it, but to future contingencies within the course of its life. Transcendental consciousness, formerly conceived of as a strong, self-grounded subjectivity on which everything else grounds in its sense, turns out to be pre-structured by and even grounded upon primal factual structures. These not only condition its present, but also its future life as embodied subject. The Ego is thus subject to both pre-existent structures and unpredictable blows of fate; it has thus – at least partially – not only lost control over its own life but also to a certain extent its self-determining power. This doesn't mean that Husserl relinquishes the egoical embedding of his phenomenology, but the Ego's realm is extended. In view of this intentional intertwining, Husserl concludes: "Not only am I no *solus ipse*, but no conceivable absolute is *solus ipse*, this is completely senseless" (Husserl 1973b, Hua XV, p. 371). Hence, these primal facts become ontologically necessary insofar they are the 'primal material' for eidetic variation, which latter is applied to a particular singularization of this material in order to establish its invariant *eidos*. Husserl later puts this invariance into question in the context of his consideration of the contingencies and indeterminacies of life.

6 Phenomenological Metaphysics – Contingent Core of the Ego, Essential Openness

As for the I as primal fact, its "core of 'primal contingency'" concerns "essential forms, forms of facultative functioning, upon which the essential necessities are grounded" (Husserl 1973b, Hua XV, p. 386). Husserl's assertion of this contingent core suggests a modification of his conception of the relationship between essence and existence. Indeed, in *Ideas I*, Husserl conceived of individual existence as contingent. The sense of this contingency, which Husserl called "factualness," is correlative to a necessity that has the character of "eidetic necessity and with this a relation to eidetic universality" (Husserl 1976, Hua III/1, p. 12; Husserl 1982, p. 7). Thus, all essential predicates of an object necessarily belong to it, while any singularization of this object is contingent. In Husserl's view, the Ego is the carrier of the world, the others, and the horizons whose singular actualization is rather possible but not necessary. This is why the openness within the field of eidetic possibilities entails the sense of 'not-necessary actualization,' as we have already seen.

But later on, in the above cited 1931 text published in *Husserliana XV*, by affirming that the Ego has a contingent "core," Husserl acknowledges the influence of these primal facts on the very essence of the *cogito*. The Ego's essence is thus subject to change according to the temporal/spatial/historical/social/cultural determinations imposed on it by these primal facts. Here, Husserl seems to question the Aristotelian principle of the invariable *eidos*, a step that he definitely takes in *Ideas II*. In the context of his inquiries about the ontology of the person in *Ideas II*, Husserl develops the notion of the "personal Ego." He ascribes to it a spiritual individuality and, by considering the experiences it has and/or is subject to in cultural and social life, he is finally led to revise his conception of the invariable essence. The process, which can be sketched in two steps, starts by the recognition of the qualitative individuality of the personal I and culminates in the positing of the essential openness of the Ego resulting from its being exposed to varying circumstances. Hence, this openness characterizes not only the eidetic variation, but even the essence of the Ego.

The first step is Husserl's conception of the personal I as a person in a specific, strong sense, as "the subject of acts which are to be judged from the standpoint of reason, the subject that is '*self-responsible*,' the subject that is free" (Husserl 1952, Hua IV, p. 257; Husserl 1989, p. 269). It is a matter of a demand not only of self-responsibility, but also of an active positioning and active thinking of the I, an Ego that makes decisions and takes positions for itself and does so "in the mode of reason" (Husserl 1952, Hua IV, p. 269; Husserl 1989, p. 282), i.e. it "makes decisions based on 'grounds'" (Husserl 1973a, Hua XIV, pp. 20*sq.*). The personal I is therefore a "*person as the subject of acts of reason*, whose motivations and motivating powers come to givenness in our own original lived experience as well as in the lived experience, available to us in empathy, of others" (Husserl 1952, Hua IV, p. 269; Husserl 1989, p. 282). What is here displayed is its individuality, i.e. its "individual idiosyncrasy" (Husserl 1973a, Hua XIV, p. 23). By "personal individuality" (Husserl 1973a, Hua XIV, p. 21) Husserl means the qualitative unity concerning the freedom of the I to take decisions. There is an *a priori* manifold of possible acts or positions, but each act is "necessary out of pure possibility," i.e. it is "'*a priori*' (necessary) in a new special sense" (Husserl 1973a, Hua XIV, p. 22). Husserl defines this *a priori* necessity in a new sense as an "individual necessity" (Husserl 1973a, Hua XIV, p. 24). It concerns the essence of the individual being: If the I is "an identical I," i.e. if the essence of a person is unchangeable – in Husserl's words: If "I hold to myself as the I, that I am" – then "only one thing is possible as the case may be for each I and this is for it thus necessary," such that the real decision is the sole reasonably possible one (Husserl 1973a, Hua XIV, pp. 22*sq.*). The I can think of manifold possibilities, but it is able to realize "intuitively" whether the possibility under consideration is compatible or incompatible with its own essence. An incompatible possibility for the I implies that the I is fantasized as "another I" (Husserl 1973a, Hua XIV, p. 24). Husserl still conceives of essence in an Aristotelian sense: there are certain possibilities potentially available for the unchanging essence, possibilities which are *a priori* necessary but which vary according to each individual.

In a second step, Husserl enlarges his conception of openness as qualitative individuality of character paired with an unchanging essence and defines a new sense of openness as modifiable *eidos*. Husserl asks himself whether a thing is "an identical subject of identical properties" and whether its behavior is "predelineated by its own essence." The groundbreaking question, which breaks with the Aristotelian tradition, reads:

> But does each thing [...] have such an essence of its own in the first place? Or is the thing, as it were, always underway, [...] in principle only a relatively identical something, which does not have its essence in advance or graspable once and for all, but instead has an open essence, one that can always take on new properties according to the circumstances of givenness? (Husserl 1952, Hua IV, p. 299; Husserl 1989, p. 313)

Even the Ego's core, its essence, is open to modifications whose actualization is possible but not necessary. The Ego can not only think of itself as being-other by means of eidetic variation but can even become other than it actually is thanks to its "essential openness," as we may call it. What remains a pure potentiality in the first case becomes an entelechy – a process of actualization – in the second. In this sense, not only the world and physical things, but also the Ego's *eidos* is subsumed into a *kinesis*, a process of becoming which may entail the unpredictable assumption of new qualities according to varying circumstances. Events that overcome us may force our essential qualities to change. This means that even though the being of our Ego – its essence – is as such absolutely necessary, the qualities invested in it are but contingent – exposed to unpredictable strokes of fate.

This leads Husserl to acknowledge that the Ego is not an empty pole but is the "bearer of its habitualities," i.e. it has "its individual history." Although a personal Ego has an absolute individuation, as stated above, it "allows itself to be determined by its 'over and against' in the surrounding world" and by its own "history" (Husserl 1952, Hua IV, pp. 300*sq.*; Husserl 1982, pp. 314*sq.*), so that it acquires new properties. This means that the I as ensouled nature acquires new habits in response to its cultural environment, habits which were not part of its original essence. This insight, as E. Marbach has shown, leads Husserl to a revision of the pure I as an empty I-pole contained in *Ideas I* and to the concretion of his conception of the monad (Marbach 1974, p. 305). In a supplementary note to *Ideas II*, Husserl comes to the realization that "the doctrine of the pure Ego – before all else as pole – must be [revised?]." He now claims that the pure I is not isolated from his context, but is given as a pole of "affects and actions" (Husserl 1952, Hua IV, p. 310; Husserl 1989, p. 324). The I as "pure I" is self-conscious and unchanging in itself, while as "personal I" it is changing in its practices, in its activities and passivities (Marbach 1974, pp. 313–316). Moreover, it is "a 'steadfast and persistent' Ego" (Husserl 1952, Hua IV, p. 113; Husserl 1989, p. 120) which is a "center of an identity" (Husserl 1952, Hua IV, p. 310; Husserl 1989, p. 324); it remains unchanged as long as it remains of the same "lasting conviction" (Husserl, Hua IV, p. 113; Husserl 1982, p. 120), i.e. although the Ego remains self-identical as a pole, it changes along with its varying convictions. Consequently, the pure I possesses a core of selfhood insofar as it is able to grasp its comportment and its motivations. This core of selfhood is itself unreflected insofar as it is the intentional object of the pure I. By way of self-reflection the I "know(s) about (its) unreflected Ego-life" (Husserl 1952, Hua IV, p. 248; Husserl 1989, p. 260). Thus, the reflective I presupposes a pre-reflective I self-individualised by its actions and passions. The unreflected selfhood unfolds thus in factual life as factual existence and is retroactively experienced as an I endowed with personality by way of the pure I's reflection: the pure I comes across itself as an already existent and singular I. This means that the pre-reflective self as pre-existent is retroactively uncovered as such by the pure, transcendental I. Hence, to be a person means not only to be the subject of the Ego-acts, i.e. of active intentionality, but also to be subject of affections and habitualities, i.e. of passive intentionality.

This world concerns the person insofar as it engages itself not only in "experiencing" "universal life" (Husserl 1973a, Hua XIV, p. 46) but also with the activities of other "social communities," such as social and religious institutions, and more generally law, morals, the state, etc. (Husserl 1952, Hua IV, p. 133; Husserl 1989, p. 141). The participation of individual persons pertaining to this "transcendent surrounding world" in these institutions and in their dependence on them is defined as "monadic life," i.e. "the unity of the universal life within the lived experience" (Husserl 1973a, Hua XIV, pp. 46*sq.*). In everyday life, the I-human being in its commerce with things and others is "*as a being who maintains* [...] *his individuality throughout*" (Husserl 1952, Hua IV, p. 141; Husserl 1989, p. 148). This implies that the I qua person is self-same, i.e. an individual being, although becoming other in response to the influence of its environment. There is a "dependence on 'circumstances'" with respect to which Husserl distinguishes "the totality of sensations" and "their concomitant reproductions," the present and earlier "stock of lived experience," and "the intersubjective dependence of psychic reality." Husserl concludes that "the *whole life of consciousness is already affected by this dependency*" (Husserl 1952, Hua IV, pp. 134*sq.*; Husserl 1989, pp. 142*sq.*). The condition for the possibility of this capacity for transformation is the 'flexible' nature of our consciousness: "Consciousness has its own essence, one in flux and not determinable exactly" (Husserl 1952, Hua IV, p. 301; Husserl 1989, p. 315). It is important to note that Husserl attributes a certain flexibility or essential indeterminacy to consciousness so that not only essence but consciousness, being both subject to a process of development and change, can adapt to varying contexts. As such, Husserl terms it a "concrete essence," a bearer of qualities and "substantial contents" (Husserl 1952, Hua IV, p. 300; Husserl 1989, p. 314). The concepts of "human being" and of the "I" are thus conceived according to two different modes of apprehension and experience: the "psychological" one and the "personal" one, which respectively concern the "spiritual Ego" and the I as "personal Ego" (Husserl 1952, Hua IV, p. 143; Husserl 1989, p. 150).

In order to restore the unity of the psychological and the personal approaches we need to relate this essential openness of consciousness to the I as person, pertaining to the first and the second modes respectively. Husserl does precisely this when he claims that "[a]bsolute individuation enters into the *personal* Ego. [...] What is uniquely and originally individual is consciousness taken concretely with its Ego" (Husserl 1952, Hua IV, p. 301; Husserl 1989, p. 315). This means that the person – not the human being as such – is the only reality which has a personal, individual I, is bearer of habitualities, and therefore has a personality with an individual history. This is why Husserl distinguishes between the "*originary* individuation," i.e. the absolute individuation acquired by way of the Ego's constitutive or sense-endowing activities, and the "*secondary* individuation," i.e. the individuation it acquires by allowing itself to be determined "over and against" its surrounding world or by actively determining the latter (Husserl 1952, Hua IV, p. 301; Husserl 1989, p. 315). Hence, the essence of the personal I can therefore change and assume new properties, according to its own history, while being related to nature through its cultural and scientific achievements.

7 Final Remarks – Towards a 'Phenomenological Openness'

Following the above analyses, we can distinguish different senses of 'openness:' first, the *openness of eidetic variation*, where the field of eidetic possibilities entails the sense of 'not-necessary actualization;' second, the *openness of the core of all eidetic forms* obtained through eidetic variation, which hosts a core of 'primal contingency' that allows for the open possibilities of the 'irrational' and thus has an arbitrary character; third, *openness as 'qualitative individuality of character'* concerning the freedom of the I to make decisions; fourth, an *'essential openness'* which denotes the possibility of the Ego to undergo qualitative changes in response to the primal contingencies of its factual life; finally, the *'openness of a consciousness* endowed with a certain 'flexibility' or 'essential indeterminacy' implying that not only essence but also consciousness is subject to a process of development and change in response to varying cultural, historical, social, or scientific surroundings to which the Ego not only is subject to but to which it also endows sense. Hence, with the exception of the first meaning of 'openness,' which corresponds to phenomenology as eidetic science, *openness accounts for the unforeseen or unpredictable events of factual life,* i.e. it accounts for everything that might overwhelm or befall the Ego in the course of its life. In conclusion, the inquiry into the realm of primal facts as the objects of a phenomenological metaphysics has revealed an essential *'phenomenological openness'* that, while concerning in the first instance the essence and the consciousness of the Ego, accounts for the contingency and irrationality of its surrounding world.

Bibliography

Bernet, Rudolf; Kern, Iso; Marbach, Eduard [1989] (1996): *Edmund Husserl. Darstellung seines Denkens*. Hamburg: Meiner.

Boehm, Rudolf (1959): "Zum Begriff des 'Absoluten' bei Husserl". In: *Zeitschrift für philosophische Forschung*, vol. XIII, n° 2, pp. 214–242.

Breuer, Irene (2018): "Aristotle and Husserl on the Relationship between the Necessity of a Fact and Contingency". In: D. De Santis, E. Trizio (Eds.): *The New Yearbook for*

Phenomenology and Phenomenological Philosophy XV – 2017. Edmund Husserl between Platonism and Aristotelianism. London/New York: Routledge, pp. 269–296.

Breuer, Irene (2019): "Husserl und die kritische Rehabilitierung der aristotelischen Ontologie". In: *Husserl Studies*, vol. 35, pp. 203–224.

Held, Klaus (1966): *Lebendige Gegenwart*. The Hague: Martinus Nijhoff.

Heffernan, George (2018): "Husserl's Aesthetic of Essences. Critical Remarks on Phenomenology as an Eidetic and 'Exact' Science". In: D. De Santis, E. Trizio (Eds.): *The New Yearbook for Phenomenology and Phenomenological Philosophy XV – 2017. Edmund Husserl between Platonism and Aristotelianism*. London/New York: Routledge, pp. 70–83.

Husserl, Edmund (1939): *Erfahrung und Urteil. Untersuchungen zur Genealogie der Logik*. Ed. L. Landgrebe, Prag: Academia. Cited as EU.

Husserl, Edmund (1950): *Cartesianische Meditationen und Pariser Vorträge*. Ed. S. Strasser. *Husserliana*, vol. I. The Hague: Martinus Nijhoff.

Husserl, Edmund (1952): *Ideen zu einer reinen Phänomenologie und phänomenologischen Philosophie. Zweites Buch. Phänomenologische Untersuchungen zur Konstitution (Ideen II)*. Ed. M. Biemel, *Husserliana*, vol. IV. The Hague: Martinus Nijhoff.

Husserl, Edmund (1956): *Erste Philosophie (1923/1924). Erster Teil. Kritische Ideengeschichte*. Ed. R. Boehm. *Husserliana*, vol. VII. The Hague: Martinus Nijhoff.

Husserl, Edmund (1959a): *Erste Philosophie (1923/1924). Zweiter Teil. Kritische Ideengeschichte*. Ed. R. Boehm. *Husserliana*, vol. VIII. The Hague: Martinus Nijhoff.

Husserl, Edmund (1959b): *Phänomenologische Psychologie. Vorlesungen Sommersemester 1925*. Ed. R. Boehm. *Husserliana*, vol. IX. The Hague: Martinus Nijhoff.

Husserl, Edmund (1960): *Cartesian Meditations: Introduction to Phenomenology*. Trans. D. Cairns. The Hague: Martinus Nijhoff.

Husserl, Edmund (1973): *Experience and Judgment. Investigations in a Genealogy of Logic*. Ed. Ludwig Landgrebe. Trans. J. S. Churchill, K. Ameriks. Evanston: Northwestern University Press.

Husserl, Edmund (1973a): *Zur Phänomenologie der Intersubjektivität, Zweiter Teil: 1921–1928*. Ed. I. Kern. *Husserliana*, vol. XIV. The Hague: Martinus Nijhoff.

Husserl, Edmund (1973b): *Zur Phänomenologie der Intersubjektivität. Texte aus dem Nachlass. Dritter Teil: 1929–1935*. Ed. I. Kern. *Husserliana*, vol. XV. The Hague: Martinus Nijhoff.

Husserl, Edmund (1976): *Ideen zu einer reinen Phänomenologie und phänomenologischen Philosophie. Erstes Buch. Allgemeine Einführung in die reine Phänomenologie. 1. Halbband. Text der 1.–3. Auflage*. Ed. K. Schuhmann. *Husserliana*, vol. III/1. The Hague: Martinus Nijhoff.

Husserl, Edmund (1977): *Phenomenological Psychology. Lectures, Summer Semester, 1925*. Transl. J. Scanlon. The Hague: Martinus Nijhoff.

Husserl, Edmund (1982): *Ideas Pertaining to a Pure Phenomenology and to a Phenomenological Philosophy. First Book*. Trans. F. Kersten. The Hague: Martinus Nijhoff.

Husserl, Edmund (1987): *Aufsätze und Vorträge (1911–1921). Mit ergänzenden Texten*. Ed. Th. Nenon, H.-R. Sepp. *Husserliana*, vol. XXV. Dordrecht/Boston/Lancaster: Martinus Nijhoff.

Husserl, Edmund (1989): *Ideas Pertaining to a Pure Phenomenology and to a Phenomenological Philosophy. Second Book. Studies in the Phenomenology of Constitution*. Trans. R. Rojcewicz, A. Schuwer. Dordrecht: Kluwer Academic Publishers.

Husserl, Edmund (2001): *Die Bernauer Manuskripte über das Zeitbewußtsein (1917–1918)*. Ed. R. Bernet und D. Lohmar. *Husserliana*, vol. XXXIII. Dordrecht: Kluwer Academic Publishers.

Husserl, Edmund (2002a): *Zur Phänomenologischen Reduktion. Texte aus dem Nachlass (1926–1935)*. Ed. S. Luft. *Husserliana*, vol. XXXIV. Dordrecht: Kluwer Academic Publishers.

Husserl Edmund (2002b): *Einleitung in die Philosophie. Vorlesungen 1922/23*. Ed. B. Goossens. *Husserliana*, vol. XXXV. Dordrecht: Kluwer Academic Publishers.

Husserl, Edmund (2008): *Die Lebenswelt: Auslegungen der vorgegebenen Welt und ihrer Konstitution. Texte aus dem Nachlass (1916–1937)*. Ed. R. Sowa. *Husserliana*, vol. XXXIX. Dordrecht: Springer.

Husserl, Edmund (2014): *Grenzprobleme der Phänomenologie. Analysen des Unbeswusstseins und der Instinkte. Metaphysik. Späte Ethik. Texte aus dem Nachlass (1908–1937)*. Ed. R. Sowa, Th. Vongehr. *Husserliana*, vol. XLII. Dordrecht: Springer.

Husserl, Edmund (2019): *First Philosophy. Lectures 1923/24 and Related Texts from the Manuscripts (1920–1925)*. Trans. S. Luft, Th. M. Naberhaus. Dordrecht: Springer.

Kern, Iso (1975): *Idee und Methode der Philosophie*. Berlin: Walter de Gruyter.

Landgrebe, Ludwig (1982): *Faktizität und Individuation*. Hamburg: Meiner.

Marbach, Eduard (1974): *Das Problem des Ich bei Husserl*. The Hague: Martinus Nijhoff.

Taguchi, Shigeru (2006): *Das Problem des 'Ur-Ich' bei Edmund Husserl. Die Frage nach der selbstverständlichen 'Nähe' des Selbst*. Dordrecht: Springer.

Tengelyi, László (2011): "Necessity of a Fact in Aristotle and Phenomenology". In: *Philosophy Today* 55, [SPEP Supplement], pp. 124–132.

Tengelyi, László (2014): *Welt und Unendlichkeit. Zum Problem phänomenologischer Metaphysik*. Freiburg/München: Karl Alber.

Raymond Kassis
The Transcendental Grounding of the Experience of the Other (*Fremderfahrung*) in Husserl's Phenomenology

Abstract: This chapter argues that, from within the attitude of supposed Solipsism, the solipsistic ego is not, and cannot be, alone unless its own solitary existence is determined by otherness. This demonstration is based on a different understanding of the worn-out and overused concept of Empathy. Indeed, the traditional use of the concept of empathy already presupposes what it sets out to prove and is therefore a logical sophism. However, empathy can be used effectively if its own possibility is grounded from inside this supposed solipsism. This article shows that the solitude of the ego is paradoxically due to a general Ego which transcends every possible individual one and which, as an intersubjective subjectivity, will ensure the unity of the scientific and the life-world. The ultimate consequence is that the concept of Ego is close to traditional German Idealism, especially to the one which does, and at the same time does not, differentiate between the Ego as mind (*Geist*) and the ego as Self (*Selbst*). Reference is made to the author's previous research on intersubjectivity and to texts published in *Husserliana* volumes XIII, XIV, XV and in the *Cartesian Meditations*.

1 A Reminder of the Justification of the Idea of Reduction

In order not to go so far back as the earliest *Outlines of Pyrrhonism* of Sextus Empiricus or even the more recent *Enquiries of Human Nature* of David Hume concerning *the phenomena*, and therefore to proceed directly to the justification of the transcendental attitude in the Husserlian sense, it is necessary to recall the main idea which is at the base of this phenomenological attitude; namely, the absurdity of a world considered as an independent and really transcendental unity beyond that which is given in the intentionality of consciousness.[1] In addition to the fact that this absolutely transcendental unity can appear as a transcendental illusion or as an idea produced instead by the very reason which

---

[1] Among the numerous texts which express this idea, the most explicit one is probably Text Nr. 17 of *Husserliana XIV*: "Der Widersinn des transzendentalen Realismus..." (Husserl 1973b).

thinks it, this justification can be founded on the fact that it is extremely difficult to imagine a consciousness which will be able to retreat from itself in order to affirm that there could be a reality which is one in itself and different from the one which is given to the consciousness of multiple subjects! If it is difficult to imagine a consciousness capable of going out of itself in order to bear witness to a reality (or a non-reality) other than that which is given in different ways, the transcendental reduction can therefore appear as non-arbitrary, and this is beyond all other traditional motives that are founded on intentional analysis. The same result could be obtained if the hypothesis were to be pushed to the extreme, by imagining *a pure experience* (*reine Erfahrung*) somewhat similar to that of R. Avenarius, stripped of the constitutive elements of its identity, coinciding totally with a universal world supposedly non presentable to a consciousness armed with its subjective constitution. For, in this hyperbolic hypothesis, it is always possible to wonder if the unity of such a projected universal world is not correlative of the unity of such an experience purified in this way of that which makes an experience an experience!

2 The Outcome of the Reduction

As this transcendental reduction is purified of every suspicion of a transcendental realism resulting from one or other of the schools working on the exegesis of Kant's philosophy,[2] the set of problems of the conceptual duality of the transcendental ego to which Husserl's reduction leads becomes apparent.

The result of the reductive step invoked can be summed up in the formula *ego cogito cogitatum*. But the boundary between the problems of Husserl's transcendental reduction and Kant's transcendental deduction is clearly fixed, and Husserl's reduction, the *ego cogito*, is carefully separated from the previous idealistic interpretations of Kant's transcendental ego (particularly those of Fichte[3] and the early Schelling[4]). It is clear that this formula, in the way it announces the ego as the unquestionable being in opposition to the essential possibility of the

---

[2] As expressed explicitly by Dermot Moran in his book *Edmund Husserl Founder of Phenomenology:* "Adopting the Kantian critical position, Husserl understood transcendental idealism to mean that there is no such thing as 'being-in-itself' or 'objectivity as such': every form of objectivity, the constitution of everything, from the natural world to the world of spirit, culture and history is constituted [...]" (Moran 2005, p. 56).

[3] Especially in his 1797 *Erste und Zweite Einleitung in die Wissenschaftslehre* (Fichte 1920).

[4] Especially in his *Vom Ich als Princip der Philosophie* (Schelling 1856).

reduction (of *destruction: Vernichtung*)⁵ of the world, will be the source for Husserl of many more difficult questions than it was for Descartes. It will be enough to ignore for a moment the bitter criticisms which were directed (especially those of Kant) at the arguments which Descartes used to escape his hyperbolic doubt and the subjective limits of his ego, in order to see that what Descartes could allow himself to say, Husserl could not. The radicalization of the transcendental reduction to the sphere of the ego could not permit Husserl to retain the idea of an absolute supreme perfect being whose total perfection includes or attributes to him an unquestionable intrinsic transcendent existence. This was not because of the criticisms which were directed at the fallacious foundation of the Cartesian proof, but mainly because of the idea of a transcendence beyond the intentionality of consciousness. But, abandoning with difficulty the attitude which was his in the *Logical Investigations* and proceeding cautiously towards a phenomenology described as transcendental, Husserl was induced, for justifiable reasons, to complete the epoché by what is called transcendental reduction. But the radicalization of this reduction which reaches a certain level in the period of the *Ideen I* could not allow him to go beyond the transcendental ego which he had just discovered. And although the sphere of phenomenological immanence revealed by the reduction is clearly distinguished from the sphere of psychological immanence, the pure ego where the reduction suddenly stops is an ego as a principle, with an ambiguous character, which cannot be compared with the ego of the main streams of idealist transcendental philosophy which preceded it; rather, it is closer to the center of Descartes's egology or Leibniz's monadology.

3 The Unity of the World

The questions which therefore arise from within the sphere of the real and intentional immanence of the ego of the *cogito* are numerous and more difficult. Only some of them will be dealt with here. Let us admit for an instant that the world of life⁶ in which science emerges, as well as the scientific world, is such as it is rediscovered as a result of the transcendental reduction, rather a *cogitatum* or a

---

5 Idea and terminology which started to emerge in the last paragraph of *Thing and Space* (Husserl 1973d, Hua XVI; Husserl 1997) and was fully developed in the *Ideas I* (Husserl 1976, Hua III/1; Husserl 1982b).
6 Life-world (*Lebenswelt*) as the originally intuitive world with all its complexity and misunderstandings and before its practicality, in the language used by Pierre Kerszberg in *La science dans le monde de la vie* (Kerszberg 2012), chapter 10 in particular: "Le monde de la vie comme monde premier en soi."

correlate *noumenon* referring to noetic structures belonging to the ego. If so, how would it be possible to show that the unity of this *cogitatum* dependent on the intentional structures of the constituting ego is a single unity, that is to say, an objective unity by its universality in relation to every other possible subject? The answer to this question which must come to the aid of this irreducible ego and bring the guarantee of the universality and objectivity of the unity of the world which it retains as a *phainomenon*, cannot be guaranteed by any other superior being. The only phenomenological support which is acceptable can come from a transcendental intersubjectivity. Otherwise, the objection of solipsism would be inevitable in so far as this ego, declared (*Ideas I*) as a phenomenological ego endowed with a specific transcendence, still remains confined to its egological sphere, and as the world retrieved is only a *cogitatum* intentionally transcendent for an ego which is not personal in a psychological sense but which without a doubt pertains to an individual.[7]

4 The Shadow of Solipsism

This problem, which remains of course theoretical, is not as simple as may have been imagined but, on the other hand, not so unimportant that one can just ignore it; it is not, in Rickert's terms, "a fortress [*Grenzfestung*] on which one can, even while knowing it is invincible, turn one's back."[8] Neither is this problem so minor that it only deserves a single chapter among others, which is the false impression given by the fifth *Cartesian Meditation*, as it must occupy the first "stratum" above aesthetics, as has already been stated here. On comparing the fifth *Meditation* to the numerous manuscripts Husserl devoted to this problem, it becomes clear that this *Meditation* is only one tree which hides a forest[9] which was unknown to several prestigious authors. We can also say that without a radical

---

[7] Several of Husserl's texts express it in this way. The most explicit is that of the *Ideas I*, where Husserl underlines the passage in which he states the opposition of the thesis of the contingency of the world to the thesis of the unquestionable necessity of one's own ego, saying: "Over against the positing of the world, which is a 'contingent' positing, there stands then the positing of my pure ego and ego-life which is 'necessary,' absolutely indubitable positing." (Husserl 1976, Hua III/1, § 46, p. 108; Husserl 1982b, p. 102) But other texts of the 1920s (published in Husserl 1973b, Hua XIV) openly use for the "one's own ego" sphere the expression "*the solipsistic subjectivity*" (*Die solipsistische Subjektivität*). See for example Text n° 5.
[8] See Rickert 1928, p. 6.
[9] We mean the three volumes of *Husserliana* (Hua XIII, XIV and XV: Husserl 1973a, b, c) that contain the posthumous work on the question of intersubjectivity, which show that this problem had been a major concern since 1905.

solution to this question, the validity of the phenomenological discourse on subsequent ontologies of all sorts, material, scientific, existential of the lived world, or formal, remains very much in dispute. For the reduction of the world necessarily includes that of the other (*fremdes Ich*). The other is just as involved in so far as it is, although in a different way, an object of perception presented in the same reduced external world. Therefore, if on the one hand in order to get out of the solipsist sphere, and on the other, in order to provide an irrefutable proof of the objective universality of the unity of the phenomenal *cogitatum*, it is absolutely necessary to have the support of another element, i.e. another ego; it is imperative to be able to prove that there can be another independent ego beyond its noematic character resulting from the universal reduction.

In other words, in order to show that the unity of the *cogitatum* is dependent on an intersubjective rather than a solipsistic constitution of the unique "one's own ego" sphere (*Eigenheitssphäre*), or, to express this in more recent terminology, the ownness of "experiential selfhood,"[10] it is necessary to constitute this other ego which in its turn would have this eminent role of co-constituting the same world and of making the multiple worlds coincide in the same unity, which would consequently be legitimately qualified as an intersubjectively objective unity. In other words, so that this unity is not apprehended as a private unity, a unity which is always mine, a solipsist one like the ego which carries it in its intentionality, the participation of the other ego is absolutely indispensable. It must be intersubjectively constituted, instituted, baptized, and transhistorically sedimented and inherited. But for that to happen, the individual ego must first of all constitute the other ego as such. It is only in this way that the other can play this delicate role after having been swallowed up in the expanding current of the transcendental reduction. If this reduction is not arbitrary, would it be possible to avoid a vicious Husserlian circle culminating in an irremediable solipsism? Is the critique of solipsism not justifiable and does it not represent one of the reasons for the emergence of other types of phenomenology? But before examining Husserl's reactions to the different disciplines which, in his time, had to deal with questions of the perception of the Other, we should note in advance that not only for numerous recent researchers and phenomenologists in various countries, but primarily for Husserl himself, the enigma of solipsism is an *illusion*, as he qualifies it in *Formal and Transcendental Logic*[11] and in *Cartesian Meditations*. But we must point out that each time Husserl states

---

10 As for example in Zahavi's *Self and Other: Exploring Subjectivity, Empathy, and Shame* (Zahavi 2014). See Part I in particular.
11 See for example § 96 from *Formal and Transcendental Logic* (Husserl 1974, Hua XVII; Husserl 1969).

that it is an *illusion*, he immediately adds a sentence which shows that the question itself has not really been clarified. We choose here only one example. The last paragraph of the *Cartesian Meditations* says: "The *illusion* of a solipsism is dissolved," adding: "*even though* the proposition that everything for me must derive its existential sense exclusively from myself, from my sphere of consciousness retains its validity and fundamental importance" (Husserl 1950, Hua I, p. 150, emphasized in italics in the text by Husserl).

Obviously Husserl was not unaware of this problem, as several posthumous texts, the majority of which were published in the three volumes of *Husserliana*, show, long before the fifth *Cartesian Meditation*.[12]

5 Husserl's Debate with the Main Psychological Currents about the Question of the Other Ego

At this point it is necessary briefly to examine Husserl's initial treatment of the question of the experience of the other. This is in order to know if the path followed by Husserl, that of a typically static phenomenology, was in itself sufficient to dispel the critique of solipsism, or if, on the contrary, it necessitated resorting to other complementary paths. Constituting the other means, as it did for other schools at the time, showing and describing the ways in which the other, as an object, makes itself representable (*vorstellig werden*), 'appresented' (*appräsentiert*), and apperceived (*apperzipiert*) for the consciousness of the 'own ego.'

---

12 See for example, in Husserl 1973a, Hua XIII, § 18, p. 154, the text from 1910 (modified in 1924) about the critique of solipsism where Husserl first specifies the meaning of solipsism: "*Solus ipse* – that means I am alone...*,*" and then defends himself concerning the confusion between the spheres of psychological immanence and that of phenomenology. Two important points should be noted: 1) that the doctrine of epistemological solipsism was present in German philosophy towards the end of the 19th and at the beginning of the 20th century, notably in the many currents of the philosophy and psychology of immanence and especially in the works of some authors of the empirico-criticist tradition. Husserl knew them very well, here I will quote only one. See for example Schubert-Soldern in his *Der Kampf um die Transcendenz*, in *Vierteljahrschrift für Wissenschaftliche Philosophie* of 1886, where he writes: "This is why I am *a theorist of the solipsist theory of knowledge, all knowledge has in me its beginning and its end*" (author's translation). The text is underlined by the author himself. Husserl knew these schools of thought well, and according to K. Schuhmann (Schuhmann 1977, p. 73), he read the main work of Schubert-Soldern, *Grundlagen einer Erkenntnisstheorie* (1884) in September 1902. 2) The second point is that the transition to the transcendental reduction, the concept of the transcendental ego in Husserl, although claimed as a phenomenological ego, was not and could not yet be firm and clear. See on this topic Kassis 2001, chapter III, § 2.

This object-subject is then, in Husserlian language, a particular noema which refers to specific noetic structures of apprehension and different from those in which physical things present themselves. These specific noetic structures to which the special *cogitatum* which is the other refers, are no other than those of the phenomenon of empathy or of the experience of the other, in which the modes of apperception of the other are revealed, the ways in which the other is given to the sphere of '*ownness*.' How is this fundamental experience produced? The psychological schools which dealt with this theme at that time, and which Husserl felt obliged to oppose, were many and varied. The way in which he reacted to some of the latter is very revealing of his innermost thoughts on the subject.

The main theses of the schools contemporary to Husserl which are of particular interest to us here were, on the one hand, those which based the experience of the other on reasoning by analogy (*Analogieschluss*), of which Husserl considered B. Erdmann to be the most important representative. On the other hand there were those who based it on direct intuition, or on empathy as sympathy (*Mitleid*), or on empathy as identifying with one's object (*Einsfühlung*), or on empathy as imitation (*Nachahmung*), one of the main representatives of which Husserl considered to be his friend, Th. Lipps. Let us examine the first case. Here it is a question of a proportional analogy with four pillars: the body (*Körper*) of the other which behaves in a certain way (anger, joy, etc..) and one's own body, both of which are already constituted in the space and time of the objective world. Next, there is the physical resemblance (*Ähnlichkeit*) between the two bodies, on the basis of which a reasoning or a comparison is produced which, through the power of *phantasia*, associates and transposes the internal intellectual processes to the physical processes perceptible on the body of the other.[13] Kant talked rather of the transfer through which the body of the other will be represented as the *Körper* of another thinking being.[14] Husserl calls this operation of comparative reasoning *sophisma*, and bases his refusal on the theory

---

[13] See Lipps 1907, p. 46, which Husserl quotes in Annex IX of *Husserliana* XIII (Husserl 1973a, p. 36).

[14] Kant, of whose first *Kritik* B. Erdmann published a new edition, already had all the philosophical tools which enabled him to maintain that only by this transfer ('*Übertragung*') is it possible for the other to be represented as a thinking being: "Now I cannot have the least representation of a thinking being through an external experience, but only through self-consciousness. Thus such objects are nothing further than the transference of this consciousness of mine to other things, which can be represented as thinking beings only in this way" (Kant 1976/Kant 1998, A 347).

of Th. Lipps.¹⁵ This favored the idea of an empathy as direct perception without mediation.¹⁶ It is important to specify that this theory was not the only one which places empathy in this way under the sign of the immediacy of the perception of the other ego.¹⁷

6 Husserl's Opposition

The question to be asked at this point is: if in order to counter the theory of reasoning by analogy, Husserl relies on the arguments of Th. Lipps, to what extent was his own phenomenology capable of sharing the same starting points which permitted Th. Lipps to refute such a theory? Obviously, behind the thesis of reasoning by analogy lies another thesis, namely that of the reference in relation to which the assimilation of the other ego is constructed and transposed towards the physical processes of the perceived body (*Körper*) of the other ego. This ultimate reference can only be the ego of the individual who perceives, compares, assimilates, and projects through appresentation of *phantasia*. This ego of central reference cannot therefore escape the objection of solipsism. Even if the main statements of Th. Lipps insist on the immediacy and the precedence of the perception of the other in relation to one's own ego, it is possible to observe in his psychology the residual traces of the use of analogy. Therefore, this objection of solipsism cannot be addressed to him. The reason lies in his concept of the ego, which prevents this.¹⁸ Furthermore, if we focus on Husserl's own posi-

---

15 Husserl says clearly: "What has still to be formulated as a reasoning by analogy? Therefore this is a sophism," and the footnote adds, "As already recognized by T. Lipps!" (Husserl 1973a, p. 38). Husserl means in his allusion the *Leitfaden der Psychologie* of Th. Lipps. It is remarkable that Husserl's phenomenology, especially that of the *Logical Investigations* (1901), already showed astonishing similarities to Th. Lipps's psychology of *Das Selbstbewusstsein. Empfindung und Gefühl* (Lipps 1901).
16 In his *Leitfaden der Psychologie* (Lipps 1909, p. 48), Th. Lipps says for example that the proposition: "I 'judge' the other ego's life manifestations by analogy with those which belong to me, is a totally wrong reply".
17 In addition to the psychology of Th. Lipps, which was welcomed by Husserl, this thesis was common in many psychologies similar to those for example of H. Münsterberg (Münsterberg 1908, p. 106), and of M. Scheler in *The Nature of Sympathy*, particularly part III, *Other Minds* (Scheler 1973/2017, chapter C: "Vom fremden Ich"), etc.

In the subsequent pages, all quotations for which there are no published English translations will be translated by the author.
18 It is very important to note that when for Th. Lipps it is a question of the belonging of the consciousness or of the ego, this consciousness "is not in itself an individual consciousness but simply a consciousness; or, this ego (*Ich*) is not in itself my ego or 'this' ego, but it is simply

tion and on the manner in which he interpreted Th. Lipps and the other schools of that period, we can see that, in spite of his confidence in the reaction and argument of Lipps against reasoning by analogy, he does not appropriate either the thesis of the precedence of the perception of the other or that of immediate empathetic perception. However, it appears on the other hand that he does not really reject the apperception by analogy and by the action of *phantasia*, or, at least if he rejects a certain aspect of it, he does not reject it in the same way. Th. Lipps destroys the theory of reasoning by analogy by following a threefold movement: first by showing the evidence that it is impossible to perceive one's own exterior expressions of one's own psychical processes while they are being produced.[19] Next, he bases the relation of the exterior expressions to the inner processes of which they are a manifestation on the "impulse of exteriorization [*Äusserung*]"[20] and then on the instinct of belief (in Hume's sense). Finally, he completes this impulse by another which he calls the impulse of imitation (*Nachahmung*), which will be considered as a constitutive element of another instinct, namely that of empathy: "The name is: instinct of empathy. The same name contains in itself (...) two aspects, or it is the product of two factors. One of the two is the instinct or the instinctive impulse of the manifestation of life. The other is the instinct of imitation." (Lipps 1907, p. 713) However, it is necessary to stress the point that, for this typical instinct, it is not a question of contagion, but a transmission by thought (*sich hineindenken*), of a self-projection into the other's lived experience which the naked eye cannot see. It is a question of living the same experience as the other, in one word, of sympathy.[21]

7 Results of Husserl's Opposition

This brief reminder shows us that Husserl's reference to Th. Lipps in his criticism of reasoning by analogy does not reveal a real agreement with the fundamental concepts on which the latter built his enormous works. But it will also allow us to have an in-depth understanding of Husserl's thought, not only thanks to his

---

[*schlechthin*] an ego." For the confrontation of the theory of Husserl and of Th. Lipps, see Kassis 2001, chapter II.
[19] See Lipps 1907, p. 699.
[20] "*Der Trieb der Äusserung*," in Lipps 1907, pp. 713 and 715. *Leitfaden der Psychologie* describes this activity as an "inexpressible singularity" (Lipps 1909, p. 230).
[21] Th. Lipps says: "The representation of the affect in the gesture of the other ego or this act of thinking it in projecting it on the gesture of the other becomes then an act of living the same affect, a co-feeling, a sympathy" (Lipps 1907, p. 719).

interpretation of Th. Lipps but also due to the way in which he will later criticize him. Indeed, this agreement does not mean they share the same point of view, especially as far as the phenomenon of empathy is concerned.[22] From a phenomenological point of view, Husserl will react several times against the theories of Th. Lipps on two main topics. Firstly, against the explanation of the phenomenon of empathy by an irrational element such as impulse or instinct.[23] Secondly, Husserl completely rejects this theory which was useful for him at the start[24], as he interprets in his own way the act of co-living or co-feeling as a consciousness of image or of an analogon of oneself, lived (*erlebt*) within oneself and projected by thought (*hineingedacht*) in the other.

If it is not a question of sympathy or of co-living, it is even less a real transposition of the own experience in the other: "I cannot therefore transpose myself really in the other, but I could only represent to myself how I would feel if I were like the other." (Husserl 1973a, Hua XIII, Text n° 13, p. 338) It is therefore a question of representation of *phantasia* (*Phantasievorstellung*). The term 'representation' is fundamental here, for it introduces the in-depth thought of Husserl in all its complexity and finesse and presents the pivotal point of the relationship between the 'ownness,' the *oneself of the selfhood*, and the possibility of the other. The possibility of the other is necessarily linked to the possibility of the experience of the other, and this is in its turn linked to the experience of oneself. The experience of the other (empathy) is then neither a real transposition nor co-living nor completely an immediate apperception, because it necessitates a certain representation which includes a certain analogy with the experience of oneself as shown in the text quoted above. But nor is it an analogy based on mental deduction which will be finally transferred to the perceptible physical body of the other. It is not as imagined by Erdmann and the school he represents, which had just been criticized by Husserl, neither is it as imagined by Th. Lipps and his school, whose ideas were approved by Husserl. Husserl will show how his posi-

---

22 For a systematic comparison, see Kassis 2001, chapter II, and Kassis 2003.
23 Husserl 1973a, Hua XIII, Beilage XXXI, p. 242 says: "I cannot adopt Lipps's conception of empathy. I cannot proceed with inexplicable instincts."
24 See Husserl 1973a, Hua XIII, § 38, pp. 187–188: "Must one say that it is a question of consciousness of image, a consciousness which makes the other analogous by the intermediary of a simultaneous similar own consciousness? I mean by this that Th. Lipps was making such good progress that he was strongly opposed to the traditional, and in fact lamentable, psychology of empathy although I cannot accept everything he says about empathy. [...] Thus one's own experience or act, that of anger for example, should fulfill the function of analogon (changed later into image, '*Bild*') for the other. But it is a nonsense [*ein Unsinn*]. For, when in the relation of I-you, I feel the anger in you, I am not angry myself; I am even less so when imagining this state than when remembering it."

tion has changed when he says: "Reasoning by analogy is false but the critique of Th. Lipps and my initial critique are equally wrong."[25] The consequences of this are numerous and of great importance. Here we will only mention those which will help us, on the one hand, to understand the question of the experience of the other, and on the other, to pursue the thesis of the condition of the unity of an intersubjective world.

8 The Paradoxes and the Subtlety of Husserl's Thought

What will be retained from what was approved at one time and criticized at another in the different, previously examined positions, is the following: if the apperception of the Other must be considered in a phenomenological way as immediate, without reasoning, without mental deduction, this does not mean that the role of analogy, of the representation which the *phantasia* obtains in modifying the ego of oneself in an analogon, *de facto* disappears. This role will be considered in the fifth *Meditation* as that of varying and associating (*paarend*) the *Modifikat* to that which will be considered as the apperceived other ego in an immediate apperception. Consequently, what Husserl does not approve is that the consciousness that the ego has of this representation which is obtained thanks to the modification or variation of itself and in which the other is phenomenologically given as itself originally present (*Selbstgegeben*), is interpreted as a consciousness of portrait-image (*Abbildung*). This very fine line of Husserl's thought, namely that the consciousness of the representation in which the other is given vividly should not be confused with a consciousness of an image, needs to be very delicately handled; otherwise it will lead to serious misunderstandings, and indeed already has. This is the case despite the fact that the other could in no way and for an essential reason be originally, and in an immanent manner, given in the same way as the ego of oneself could be given to itself. It is a very puzzling paradox. In the process of apperception of the other, what Husserl criticizes in Erdmann's '*Analogieschluss*' is rather the deduction '*Schluss*;'[26] what he retains from it is the analogy which will be detected by the reference to the 'ownness' of oneself (*dem eigenen Ich*). What he retains from Th. Lipps's immediacy is that of an immediate apperception which is neither the equivalent of a sympathy

---

[25] See Husserl 1973a, Hua XIII, Appendix n° X, p. 38 (author's translation).
[26] The § 50 of *Cartesian Meditations* says: "Apperception is not inference, not a thinking act" (Husserl 1950, Hua I, p. 141; Husserl 1982a, p. 111).

or a real co-living (*miterlebend*), nor of a consciousness of an image (*Bildbewusstsein*) of oneself. This apperception can, however, reach such a degree of immediacy that one's own ego sees itself merged with (*Verschmelzung*)[27] the *Modifikat* which is associated with it, or that one's own ego disappears in it.[28] But considering that in this merging and in this disappearing (*Auslöschen*) the referring back to one's own ego as a source is indispensable, this merging cannot be a union (*Einsfühlung*): "It is not a matter of a *union*, as if I were transposed in the other or I were living in the other or I lived myself in the other [...], nevertheless the other ego is nothing but variation of myself, and when I have the experience of him, I have the experience of myself in variation."[29]

As a firm consequence, however original the apperceptive donation of the other may be, the other can in no way really be given as my own lived experience is given to myself, lest the other ego lose its transcendence and become "a mere moment of my own being."[30] This is imposed by the intentional essence which characterizes the givenness and the apperception of the other, whose fulfillment can never be realized other than by the means of other appresentations which, in their turn, could likewise not be fulfilled other than by other appresentations, etc. A text published in *Husserliana* XIII will express this more clearly than the § 52 of the fifth *Meditation:*

> In empathy it is a part of the essence of this appresentation that it cannot in principle be fulfilled by the means of an original presentation of a psychical element. On the other hand, the fulfillment is accomplished again in psychical appresentations which accompany parallel physical presentations (manifesting themselves in the expression of the body), which essentially exclude here the presentative fulfillment. (Husserl 1973a, Hua XIII, appendix XXVII, p. 225)

---

[27] It is the terminology of the fifth *Cartesian Meditations*, § 54: "Every overlapping-at-a-distance, which occurs virtue of associative pairing, is at the same time a fusion and therein, sofar as incompatibilities do not interfere..." (Husserl 1950, Hua I, p. 147; Husserl 1982a, p. 118).
[28] A text published in *Husserliana* XIII will say: "so in a certain way I live in the other. My life is extinguished, in a certain way transformed into the other" (Husserl 1973a, Hua XIII, p. 337).
[29] Husserl 1973b, Hua XIV, p. 527. Other texts will state explicitly that the other ego is an Analogon analogized or in an appresentative way constituted as an intentional modification of my objectified (*objektiviert*) ego as a modification of myself. In § 52 of *Cartesian Meditations* Husserl says: "It is therefore conceivable only as an analogue of something included in my peculiar ownness. Because of its sense-constitution it occurs necessarily as an 'intentional modification' of that Ego of mine which is the first to be objectivated [...] a 'modification' of myself" (Husserl 1950, Hua I, p. 144; Husserl 1982a, p.115).
[30] According to the *Cartesian Meditations*, § 50 (Husserl 1950, Hua I, p. 139; Husserl 1982a, p. 109).

So, from both these perspectives, the other can neither be given originally at the risk of disappearing as a real part of one's own ego, nor given intentionally as such, as in the apperception or the immediate appresentation that I have of it, what I apperceive is nothing but myself in variation, a variation of myself, as expressed strikingly in the text quoted above. In this line of analysis, it is impossible to affirm with an apodictic evidence similar to that of one's own ego that the other ego is possible as such, independently and beyond the noetic status to which it refers as an analyzed noema in the phenomenon of empathy.

9 The Necessity of Taking a Subjective Turn: The Meaning of the Own Ego

Let us now turn to the initial theme in the light of these consequences. In order to constitute the unity of the world as a noematic phenomenon of the ego which is in need of nothing in order to exist after the reduction (*nulla 're' indiget ad existendum*, *Ideen I*, § 49), it was inevitable that Husserl guarantee the objectivity of this unity by another ego, by intersubjectivity. Without this guarantee, the objection of solipsism of this unity which is equal to the solipsism of the ego which carries it, would be unavoidable. That is why it was indispensable for Husserl to analyze the noetic structures to which the other, as a noema, relates. This direction, which starts with the noema-object-index and goes towards the appropriate noetic structures, can be described as an objective one with a static structural character.

The analyses which followed this path can lead only to problematic results which are neither firm nor definitive. Thanks to this type of analysis, the own ego (*die Thesis meines reinen Ich und Ichlebens*, *Ideen I*, § 46) of the *cogito* cannot go beyond its limits traced by the reduction, and consequently neither can it guarantee, with apodictic evidence, another ego, beyond the status of a constituted noema. Nor can it raise the subjective unity of its world to the level of a unity which is intersubjectively one and objective: it is each time its own unity. The dilemma reaches its paroxysm if on the one hand we cannot go beyond the inseparable noematic structures from their constitutive noeses, and on the other hand if the movement of the universal reduction is stopped at this ego to which those structures belong, and which affirms itself ontologically as an undoubted *factum* in its *being*. This leads inevitably to the following: if the other is constituted as a variation of myself, a variation appresented and projected through a *Phantasievorstellung* in the already objectified (in many ways) *Körper* of the other, would it not be necessary to have another Other, a third, another ego other than the one which is in such a way constituted, in order to co-constitute the unity of this constituted ego, and to affirm that the unity of this constituted ego is an objective one and equivalent to an independent one, and so on *ad infinitum?* What would happen to the unity of the world which, in order to have the value of a universal one, should be constituted by this same other ego? Are there not here some difficulties which bear the signature of their own reasons, whether in the analysis of the noetic structures or in the primordial factum, in the Archimedean point where the transcendental reduction abruptly stopped? It will be enough here to underline that at a certain time, precisely in certain texts of the 1930s written for the preparation of the 'systematic work,' Husserl tries indirectly to remove this type of problem in such a way that gives the impression that he is in an utter contradiction with the inescapable following step of his initial epoché, i. e. the universal transcendental reduction. He goes so far as to ask himself: "When I apply an authentic epoché, that of the apperception of the world as a ground of any particular theme, then does it not mean also putting out of action the other in general?" The answer: "that means this epoché does not suppress the appearing modes of the others, or the others themselves." (Husserl 1973c, Hua XV, Text nr. 8, p. 113) And he even asserts that "the other is not a mere sense of being which I formed and accepted in my constitutive operation." (Husserl 1973c, Hua XV, Text nr. 7, p. 108) No doubt, but the question which we are entitled to ask is: suppose the other ego himself is not submitted to the logical consequence of the epoché (the transcendental reduction), or even that it remains presupposed as a being which really transcends the noematic status (which will be a full contradiction) – where will it be possible to find this other ego after having, by this authentic epoché, withdrawn and neutralized the world in which it was given as an animate body? To say that the constitution of the other ego is different from that of its *Körper* as a physical phantom (*Sehding*) extended in a spatio-temporal schema, is phenomenologically undeniable. Will it be possible to find again this other ego, in its sense as well as in its possibility of being, elsewhere than in the own transcendental ego which resisted the epoché and the reduction of the world and all corporal bodies (mine and his) included in it?

Is it not this own ego itself which modifies or varies itself and then transposes itself through a representation of *phantasia* in the *Körper* of the other in order to simulate what it would have been able to feel or to think if it had been the "null point" of orientation which transforms that other *Körper* in front of me into a *Körper* of will and of another ego? To what extent can the ego vary itself?

10 Conversion to the Own Ego: The Pre-Ontological Meaning of My and Your Ego

It follows that if the other ego cannot be withdrawn from the reduction, and if the analysis of the phenomenon of empathy can only give it as a noema – index – variation – *Modifikat* or analogon of a model referring to myself, the remaining possibility of going beyond the solipsistic egological circle can only be provided by a conversion, by a return from the noematic object and from the noetic structure towards the ego itself to which the latter belong. In this return, it is principally no longer a question of knowing how the other ego is given and what are the noetic structures of the operations in which it is given, but of knowing what is the basis upon which the subject of reference, i.e. the own ego (*das eigene Ich*) (*the selfhood*) as a transcendental undoubted factum, can function as a model, can be varied, can undergo a variation and have an analogon. It is more a question of proceeding from a phenomenology of a transcendental ego which affirms its apodictic factual existence in thinking its own objects to a pre-ontological, properly transcendental phenomenology which seeks to understand to what extent this undoubted factum can be this factum, and in which sense this ego can be an own ego, and how this own ego just in so far as it is own (*eigen*) can essentially not be alone and cannot be different. This extreme level is that of the transcendental eidetic phenomenology.

It is only by unveiling the *a priori* eidetic basis of one's own ego, whereby the initial transcendental reduction stopped, with the help of what Husserl will call the *a priori* eidetic, that the meaning and the pre-ontological possibility (*im Vorsein*) of one's own ego, and those of the other ego, can be explained. Both, namely meaning and the pre-ontological possibility of one's own ego, are contained within the universe of a pre-ontological ego-eidos which covers *a priori* the possibilities of all conceivable egos. This eidetic starts from the fact that what is appresented in the varying or modifying representation is one's own ego itself, but in another (under the modus of other). In the merging (*Verschmeltzung* and *Auslöschen*) mentioned above, what is apperceived in the pairing appresentation is one's own ego presentiated (*vergegenwärtigt*) as another. The possibility *a priori* of being-otherwise (*Anderssein*), in the modus of a fictitious appresentation, belongs to one's own ego, to the primordial factum (*Urfaktum*) as being factually so (*Sosein*) and not as being otherwise, which is obtained by self-transformation.

This possibility of being otherwise (*Anderssein*) through *phantasia*, while being really at the same time being-so (*Sosein*) and the same, is an *a priori* possibility: this being otherwise is not an image of the self, because the ego cannot internally have an image of itself, and the consciousness it has of this being otherwise is not a consciousness of an image as we saw a moment ago with the confrontation with Th. Lipps. The splitting of one's own ego into being-so, as it is in fact, and into being-otherwise, as it is not in fact, is a possibility which must be clearly specified and indicated as a status of essence of the one's own ego, as one of its pure potentialities. In this splitting, the other ego which I apperceive as so and so embodied in a phantom-*Körper*-there, like myself in the mode of a modified self (*als ob ich so wäre*), whether it exists in itself or not, corresponds to one possibility (*Möglichkeit*) in the system of my possibilities or modalities being-otherwise: "In the comprehensive perception of the other ego [...], and through the known analogization [*Analogisierung*] I have a presentiating [*vergegenwärtigende*] and motivated position of another ego which is, according to its pure possibility, contained [*enthalten*] in the system of my ego's being-otherwise." (Husserl 1973b, Hua XIV, p. 161)

The countless possibilities of being-otherwise belong to the closed system of one realized, embodied possibility in one monad or one factual, undoubtedly existing ego. To each possibility of "another ego separated from me corresponds generally a possibility of my being-otherwise." (Husserl 1973b, Hua XIV, p. 155) If the variation or modification begins freely from my own factual apodictic ego, then "each such a possibility of variation gives as a result a possible subject, and also the evidently existing ego (*das evident seiende ich*) becomes therefore one of these possibilities." (Husserl 1973b, Hua XIV, p. 94) My ego implodes, one can say, inside its own possibilities. And "my non-being is only representable under the form of my being-otherwise." (Husserl 1973b, Hua XIV, p. 159) Those possibilities which are *a priori* contained in each other (*Ineinandersein*) form the cosmos of an ego in general:

> I have the evidence of being able to be otherwise, and the field of the possible being-otherwise lies *a priori* in me; I could intuitively go through all the possible variations of my ego. And this universe of my being-otherwise possibilities has simultaneously the same extension (coincides with: *deckt sich mit*) as the possibilities of the universe of an ego in general [*Ich überhaupt*]... (Husserl 1973b, Hua XIV, appendix XX, p. 154)

This universe of an ego-eidos to which belong each of the in-each-other-included possibilities, pre-exists eidetically to each factual or possible existing ego, therefore to my in-its-undoubted-being ego, from which the process of transformation took its departure. My ego, which is irreducible in its being as a fact, is included inside as one of those potentialities, whether realized or not yet, and therefore is in its essence never alone. Through this variation of *phantasia*, which reveals here its own internal justification, it is possible to assert that each ego as an original factum (*Urfaktum*) contains intentionally its *alter ego* and at the same time it is itself intentionally contained, so that the system of the wholes, or the universe of the wholes which belongs to each factual or possible ego forms, in a sort of teleological harmony, pure multiples of one-all-one (*All-Einheit*):

> Then I come back to this point that my primal ego contains an infinity of primal egos, each of which, departing from itself contains also this infinity: my ego is included within this infinity in which all this is included, just as my ego is included again in each. All being, in any imaginable sense, is in me [*liegt in mir*] – with the teleological harmony which makes possible the totality as an all-unity. But all the others in their totality of infinity are [*liegen*] in me and they are in me as including each other in every sense... (Husserl 1973c, Hua XV, pp. 587–588)

This internal intentional inclusion of one in the other, described thus intuitively, is a metaphysical original fact of primordial importance: "This interiority of being one for each other as an interiority of the intentional one being in the other is the original metaphysical fact, it is the being-in-each-other of an Absolute." (Husserl 1973c, Hua XV, p. 366) Accordingly, if some scholars refute the metaphysical aspect of Husserl's transcendental phenomenology while others accept it, it is possible to state that this metaphysical aspect is indispensable but is neither hypothetical, nor mystical, but intuitive and descriptive. Considered from a different perspective,[31] if we take into full consideration this Absolute, which is discovered inside the *solipsisity* (*Solipsizität*) of each embodied possibility, it will also be possible to say that the apodictic individual transcendental ego, precisely when it thinks that it is alone, cannot be alone, seeing that it is already essentially linked to an infinitely undetermined encompassing Ego in general (*Ich überhaupt*).

11 Final Conclusions: The Universal Ego and the Intersubjective Unity of the World

The consequences of all this are numerous. Here we can only consider some of them:

(A) If the ego of the initial own original fact (*Urfaktum*) was accused of solipsism regarding the fact that the noematic analyses of empathy could not go beyond the noematic status of one's own ego, the eidetic analysis shows that this own ego is not only swallowed up as one of the infinite possibilities of es-

---

[31] Like that of Georg Römpp, for example in his *Husserls Phänomenologie. Eine Einführung* (Römpp 2005). See chapter III in particular: "Das Problem der Solipsizität des absoluten Ego."

sence intentionally contained one in the other in the unity of a universal ego, but that it implodes within its own possibilities and its solipsist sphere (*Eigenheitssphäre*).[32] The objection of solipsism, this invincible *fortress*, is consequently removed and irrelevant.

(B) The irreducible own ego, whose existence is not in doubt, has a pre-ontological status which is descriptively undeniable. It is in its *a priori* status as a pre-existing and persisting essential potentiality, before it has a temporal genesis, or, to express it in specifically Husserlian terms, before being *awakened*,[33] a possibility, a variant, an analogon, a *Modifikat* of an infinity of other variants which are unified in one universal ego. Therefore, the individual transcendental *factum* is, *a priori*, in its egoic essence nothing other than a variant of an infinity of variants of a transcendental universal *ego-eidos*. And the variation operated on the own ego is not arbitrary and does not transgress it because it is based on the infinite possibilities contained in and unified by this universal. Therefore the act of variation, which is operated by the powerful transposing *phantasia*, and which gives birth to the phenomenon of empathy, has retrospectively its *a priori* necessary conditions in this unified intentional being one in another (*Ineinandersein*).

(C) The eidetic status of the individual own ego finds its complement in another wider fundamental status. The eidetic which phenomenology takes to its highest level reveals the essence of the original *factum* in a variety of potentiality intentionally contained in the infinity of possible variants, therefore of one universal ego which unifies and penetrates all its varieties. Otherwise the varieties would phenomenologically no longer be varieties: "Eidetic phenomenology thus studies the universal *a priori*, without which, I and a transcendental ego is not at all or not in general 'imaginable'."[34] This universal *a priori* does not, therefore, belong exclusively to one or another of its variants. It belongs to each one of them, within the perimeter of its individual essence. So if the transcendental ego of the *ego cogito* is revealed to be like an ego with a status of pre-ontological individual potentiality, this status turns out to be dual: an individual status intrinsically founded in a universal transcendental ego belonging relatively to each

---

[32] One's own ego can transpose itself, as Husserl describes (in most of the texts devoted to the *Fictum*, particularly in the appendix XIX of Hua XIV, Husserl 1973b), into one of the possibilities which lie in its sphere of being-otherwise (*Anderssein*), and can imagine through *phantasia* its initial real being as a fictitious possibility of its being otherwise.

[33] A sentence which Husserl often repeats. See in particular Husserl 1973c, Hua XV, p. 604: "The I of this pole can neither come into being nor cease to be, it can only be awakened."

[34] According to the *Cartesian Meditations* (Husserl 1950, Hua I, p. 106; Husserl 1982a, pp. 71–72).

of its potentialities or varieties. The individual is only individual because it is the variation of a universal. Consequently, if the transcendental ego unveiled by the reduction in the formula *ego cogito cogitatum* has given rise to a series of objections, of which I have only taken here that of solipsism, it results, at the end of a long life of uncompleted phenomenological reflections, that the formula *ego cogito* contains an ambiguity and entails a misunderstanding which are difficult for the beginner to avoid:

> When, in phenomenology, it is a question principally of the *ego cogito* as an expression of the ego to which the reduction leads, this is an ambiguity, a beginning, with an absolutely necessary equivocation (*Äquivokation*). Then, it is only later that it can be clear that the primitive Ego of the flux is the absolute Ego which carries in itself one's own Ego as an own Ego, and carries all other egos as an intentional modification of this Ego. (Husserl 1973c, Hua XV, Text nr. 33, p. 586)

Other texts will also say: "by the transcendental method, I discover my 'transcendental subjectivity.' But this does not mean in the first place: my own primordial being, which is how it would be designated as an inevitable confusion of the beginner." (Husserl 1973c, Hua XV, Text nr. 21, p. 368)

(D) If we now return to the theme of the unity of the world, which was threatened by the objection of solipsism, we can draw the following conclusion in so far as the ego is in its essential individual status intrinsically intersubjective. Such a status belongs already to a universal *a priori* ego unifying all its possible variations: therefore, it is evident that the world constituted by the intentions of each of its variations is one intersubjective unity for each real and possible ego.

Bibliography

Avenarius, Richard (1908): *Kritik der reinen Erfahrung*. Zweite Auflage: Leipzig: O.R. Reisland.
Erdmann, Bruno (1907): *Wissenschaftliche Hypothesen über Leib und Seele*. Köln: Verlag der M. D-S. Buchhandlung.
Fichte, Johann Gottlieb (1920): *Erste und Zweite Einleitung in die Wissenschaftslehre*. Leipzig: Felix Meiner.
Hume, David (1992): *Enquiries Concerning Human Understanding*. Oxford: Oxford University Press.
Husserl, Edmund (1950): *Cartesianische Meditationen und Pariser Vorträge*. Husserliana, vol. I. Ed. Stephan Strasser. The Hague: Martinus Nijhoff.
Husserl, Edmund (1982a): *Cartesian Meditations*. Trans. Dorion Cairns. The Hague: Martinus Nijhoff.
Husserl, Edmund (1974): *Formale und transzendentale Logik*. Husserliana, vol. XVII. Ed. Paul Janssen. The Hague: Martinus Nijhoff.

Husserl, Edmund (1969): *Formal and Transcendental Logic*. Trans. D. Cairns. The Hague: Martinus Nijhoff.
Husserl, Edmund (1973a): *Zur Phänomenologie der Intersubjektivität. Texte aus dem Nachlass*, Erster Teil (1905–1920). *Husserliana*, vol. XIII. Ed. Iso Kern. The Hague: Martinus Nijhoff.
Husserl, Edmund (1973b): *Zur Phänomenologie der Intersubjektivität*, Zweiter Teil (1921–1928). *Husserliana*, vol. XIV. Ed. Iso Kern. The Hague: Martinus Nijhoff.
Husserl, Edmund (1973c): *Zur Phänomenologie der Intersubjektivität*, Dritter Teil (1929–1935). *Husserliana*, vol. XV. Ed. Iso Kern. The Hague: Martinus Nijhoff.
Husserl, Edmund (1973d): *Ding und Raum, 1907*. *Husserliana*, vol. XVI. Ed. Ulrich Claesges. The Hague: Martinus Nijhoff.
Husserl, Edmund (1997): *Thing and Space: Lectures of 1907*. Trans. Richard Rojcewicz. Dordrecht: Springer.
Husserl, Edmund (1976): *Ideen zu einer reinen Phänomenologie und phänomenologischen Philosophie. Erstes Buch: Allgemeine Einführung in die Phänomenologie. Husserliana*, vol. III/1. Ed. Karl Schuhmann. The Hague: Martinus Nijhoff.
Husserl, Edmund (1982b): *Ideas Pertaining to a Pure Phenomenology and to a Phenomenological Philosophy*. First Book. Trans. Fred Kersten. The Hague: Martinus Nijhoff.
Husserl, Edmund (1997): *Psychological and Transcendental Phenomenology and the confrontation with Heidegger (1927–1931)*. Ed. and trans. Thomas Sheehan & Richard E. Palmer. Dordrecht: Kluwer Academic Publishers.
Kant, Immanuel (1976): *Kritik der reinen Vernunft*. Hamburg: Felix Meiner Verlag.
Kant, Immanuel (1998): *Critique of Pure Reason*. Ed. and trans. Paul Guyer & Allen W. Wood. Cambridge: Cambridge University Press.
Kassis, Raymond (2001): *De la phénoménologie à la métaphysique*. Preface by Paul Ricœur and presented by Bernard Besnier. Grenoble: Jérôme Millon.
Kassis, Raymond (2003): "Les sources historiques de la phénoménologie husserlienne de l'intropathie (*Einfühlung*): T. Lipps and Avenarius". In: *Annales de phénoménologie*, n° 2, pp. 49–97.
Kerszberg, Pierre (2012): *La science dans le monde de la vie*. Grenoble: Jérôme Millon.
Lipps, Theodor (1901): *Das Selbstbewusstsein. Empfindung und Gefühl*. Wiesbaden: Verl. v. J. F. Bergmann.
Lipps, Theodor (1907): *Das Wissen von fremden Ichen*, in *Psychlogische Untersuchungen*, vol. I. Leipzig: Verl. v. W. Engelmann.
Lipps, Theodor (1909): *Leitfaden der Psychologie*. 3rd edition. Leipzig: Verl. v. W. Engelmann.
Lipps, Theodor (1912): "Zur Einfühlung". In: *Psychologische Untersuchungen*, vol. II. Leipzig: Verl. v. W. Engelmann.
Moran, Dermot (2005): *Edmund Husserl Founder of Phenomenology*. Cambridge: Polity.
Münsterberg, Hugo (1900): *Grundzüge der Psychologie I*. Leipzig: J. A. Barth.
Münsterberg, Hugo (1908): *Philosophie der Werte*. Leipzig: J. A. Barth.
Rickert, Heinrich (1928): *Der Gegenstand der Erkenntnis*, 6th edition. Tübingen: J. C. B. Mohr.
Römpp, Georg (2005): *Husserls Phänomenologie. Eine Einführung*. Wiesbaden: Marixverlag.
Scheler, Max (1973): *Wesen und Formen der Sympathie*. Bern/München: Francke Verlag.
Schelling, Friedrich Wihelm (1856): *Vom Ich als Princip der Philosophie. Sämmtliche Werke, erster Band (1792–1797)*. Stuttgart and Augsburg: J. G. Cotta.

Schubert-Soldern, Richard von (1882): *Über Transcendenz des Objekts und Subjects*. Leipzig: Fues.
Schubert-Soldern, Richard von (1884): *Grundlagen einer Erkenntnisstheorie*. Leipzig: Fues.
Schubert-Soldern, Richard von (1886): *Der Kampf um die Transcendenz*. In: *Vierteljahrschrift für Wissenschaftliche Philosophie*.
Schuhmann, Karl (1977): *Husserl-Chronik*. Band 1. The Hague: Martinus Nijhoff.
Sextus Empiricus (1933): *Outlines of Pyrrhonism*. Trans. R. G. Bury, Litt. D. Vol. 1. London: William Heinemann LTD.
Zahavi, Dan (2014): *Self and Other: Exploring Subjectivity, Empathy, and Shame*. Oxford: Oxford University Press.

Section III: Aesthetic, Logic, Science, Ethics

Julien Farges
Aesthetic, Intuition, Experience
Husserl's Redefinition of the Transcendental Aesthetic[1]

Abstract: This chapter approaches the relationship between Kant's and Husserl's transcendental philosophies from the point of view of the transcendental aesthetic. The phenomenological conception of the transcendental aesthetic is rebuilt by studying its relationship with transcendental analytic, then with transcendental logic. The first perspective shows not only that Husserl's concept of a transcendental aesthetic aims at a double-leveled task, but that the second level implies a non-Kantian integration of causality along with time and space in the aesthetic frame. On this basis, it is possible to see Husserl as an heir of Schopenhauer's critique of Kant's philosophy. The second perspective shows that Husserl has always seen the transcendental aesthetic as the first step of a new type of logic: first, a "real logic," then a "world-logic," namely the transcendental logic itself in a genetic point of view, describing the world's "history" within the subject's intentional life.

In a letter to Ernst Cassirer dated April 3, 1925, Husserl points out Kant's role in his own philosophical itinerary and admits that his "original hostility" has faded as he became aware that "the science which was growing in [him] encompassed – by means of a very specific method – the whole of Kant's problematic." Thus, he could "confirm, in a rigorously scientific foundation and delimitation, Kant's main results" despite the explicit recognition of the flaws of his method and the deficiency of his analysis (Husserl 1994, Hua Dok. III/5, p. 4). Until his manuscripts from the *Krisis* period, Husserl maintains this rather ambivalent appreciation of Kant's philosophy, where praise and criticism intermingle in a way that can easily cause many "misunderstandings [...] about phenomenological transcendentalism" (Husserl 1956, Hua VII, p. 238). Beyond retrospective considerations, explicit claims of a "Kantian legacy" (Husserl 1956, Hua VII, p. 286), or public statements in academic context, these possible misunderstandings are fa-

---

[1] This chapter is a translated, corrected, and slightly extended version of a previous article ("L'esthétique, l'intuitif et l'empirique. La refonte husserlienne de l'esthétique transcendantale" published in: *Meta. Research in Hermeneutics, Phenomenology and Practical Philosophy*, vol. VIII, n° 2 / December 2016, Guest Editor: Iulian Apostolescu, pp. 546–570). I thank Iulian Apostolescu and Claudia Serban for welcoming it in this volume.

vored by the fact that Husserl takes up a large number of Kantian concepts to name not only some fundamental aspects of his phenomenology's theoretical program but also the main moments of its unfolding. This obviously applies to the term "transcendental" itself, but also and above all to some of the major divisions of the *Critique of Pure Reason*, especially Transcendental Aesthetic, Logic, and Analytic.

In this chapter, I would like to focus on the transcendental aesthetic because, as numerous studies have pointed out, it is one of the places where the issues related to Husserl's reception of Kant's philosophy are particularly striking, either from an internal and architectonic perspective (related to the very definition of transcendental philosophy) or from an external and more historical one (related to the opposition between phenomenological and Neo-Kantian reception of Kant). However, these studies all tend to neglect or minimize the fact that Husserl determines the transcendental aesthetic according to *two very distinct approaches*[2] – a duality highly indicative of his critical relationship with critical philosophy: sometimes, according to the structure of the "Transcendental Doctrine of Elements" of the *Critique of Pure Reason*, the field of transcendental aesthetic is phenomenologically redefined as opposed to that of transcendental *logic*; sometimes, ignoring this Kantian division, it is redefined as opposed to the field of the *analytic*. Now, as a matter of fact, these two approaches don't lead to exactly the same definition of the transcendental aesthetic. To be more precise: taking as a guide this twofold approach, I would like to show that it allows not only, on a structural point of view, a better understanding of the phenomenological conception of transcendental logic and of the role of causality in this framework, but also, on a historical point of view, the assumption of a probable – yet generally unrecognized – presence of Schopenhauer in the background of Husserl's criticism of Kant. In both cases, we will see how intuition, understood in relationship to empirical evidence, becomes in Husserl the criterion of what must be called "sensible" while implying a strong distinction between aesthetic and mere sensibility.

---

[2] The exception is represented here by Michela Summa, who pays explicit attention to this double distinction (Summa 2014, pp. 46–47). But she relates it only to Husserl's criticism of Kant's anthropologism and in the next steps of her work, only the first distinction (that between transcendental aesthetic and analytic) plays a structuring role (see Summa 2014, pp. 49–52).

1 Duplication of the Aesthetic and Aesthetization of Causality

In order to sketch out the phenomenological conception of transcendental aesthetic first in its relation to the transcendental analytic, I shall start with a statement dated 1919 which shows how balanced Husserl's reception of Kant's distinction is:

> We must [...] point out *another fundamental stratification*, expressed in Kant's brilliant distinction between *transcendental aesthetic and transcendental analytic*, a distinction worthy of admiration despite the fact that all the distinctions mentioned here as well as the essence of what is in his view "aesthetic" in the transcendental sense have remained obscure to him, which is not unrelated to the fact that his theories are far from possessing the scientific power to which he aspired with so much ardor. (Husserl 2002, Hua Mat. IV, p. 171)

These lines don't suggest a phenomenological elimination of the distinction between aesthetic and analytic, but rather its modification, its revision, and at the same time its critical justification, by bringing it back to its true meaning, compatible with the requirement of a return "to the things themselves." Let us recall the general principles of such a revision.

As Dominique Pradelle recently argued (Pradelle 2012, 2014), Husserl's redefinition of the distinction between transcendental aesthetic and analytic implies a twofold criticism. First, Husserl criticizes Kant's anthropologism, that is the presupposition of a transcendental subject, provided with distinct and pre-determined faculties (sensibility as a receptive faculty and the understanding as a spontaneous faculty) whose functioning is supposed to be valid only for us, human subjects. Suspending such a presupposition implies for Husserl something like a "de-subjectivation" of the distinction between the sensible and the intellectual, insofar as it is no longer referred to human subjective faculties but to possible types of objects in correlation with distinct types of intuitive givenness. Accordingly, not only is the distinction between sensibility and understanding redefined as a distinction between what is sensible and what is categorial, but moreover, space and time are no longer determined as *a priori* forms of sensibility but as *a priori* "forms of the 'sensible object of a possible experience'" (Pradelle 2014, p. 296), of the "appearing object" itself, that is to say as "immanent structures within the sense contents" (Pradelle 2012, pp. 265–266).

Husserl's second criticism does not concern Kant's presupposition of subjective faculties, but rather the operating mode of those faculties. More precisely, Husserl casts away Kant's definition of the understanding by synthetic activity as well as the consecutive reduplication of the distinction between aesthetic and analytic by the distinction between what is pre-synthetic and what is synthetic in consciousness. On the contrary, because synthesis is for Husserl "the primal form belonging to consciousness" (Husserl 1950, Hua I, p. 77; Husserl 1960, p. 39), it is "coextensive with all the intentional life of pure consciousness" (Pradelle 2012, p. 277) and therefore already operates at the aesthetic level in the constitution of space and time themselves as pure intuitions, so that phenomenology can describe their genesis instead of presupposing them as already constituted structures. And since Kant himself seems to acknowledge a synthetic operation at the aesthetic level of sensible intuitions even if he mentions it only in the context of transcendental analytic, Husserl spots a contradiction between Kant's aesthetic and analytic (Husserl 1956, Hua VII, p. 405), a contradiction which he sums up in the following anti-Kantian alternative:

> Without the study of the "synthesis" in which the spatio-temporality of an experiential world is constituted, the ontological necessities such as Kant elaborates them are empty from a transcendental point of view. But if synthesis determines the distinction between aesthetic and analytic, then space and time would remain precisely excluded from aesthetic, and we would then remain only with the sensitivity of sensations as a residue. (Husserl 2002, Hua Mat. IV, p. 180)

What conception of transcendental aesthetic and of its relations with analytic results from this twofold criticism? Two main aspects can be underlined.

First of all, the texts in which, from 1919, Husserl expressly confronts this set of problems show a *splitting* (or a *duplication*) *of the phenomenological transcendental aesthetic*. But such a splitting is far from being the effect of an equivocation in the definition of the task of transcendental aesthetic. On the contrary, Husserl clearly emphasizes the thematic unity of the aesthetic as opposed to the analytic. While the latter is dedicated to the description of the modes of idealization according to which an exact and objective, physico-mathematical nature is constituted, the task of the transcendental aesthetic is to elucidate the necessary structures and modalities of constitution of empirical and intuitive objectity, or, as Husserl puts it, of "nature as it is precisely given in experience" (Husserl 1920–1926, p. 13b), i.e. in a simply perceptive way before any idealizing synthetic activity. But this one task is in fact divided into two layers, corresponding to two constitutive levels of the "thing" which is intuitively given in experience: first its mere *sensory* determination, and second the fundamental properties in which its *reality* unfolds.

The first of these two layers corresponds to what Husserl calls a "systematic ontology of the phantom," this last term referring to the "pure sense-thing" (Husserl 2002, Hua Mat. IV, pp. 174, 172), that is to say the pre-empirical and purely sensory unity that each sense allows to grasp from the thing, whether this unity has a spatial extension or not. For example, this sheet of paper in front of me can be described by its visual phantom (the pure visual thing) or its tactile phantom (the pure tactile thing), both implying an extension whose congruence or covering (*Deckung*) constitutes space in its originarity. It is also possible to describe the sound (the pure tonal or acoustic thing) detached from the material reality related to its conditions of production (for example a violin in the side room). It then remains "a tonal spatial phantom, appearing with a determinate orientation" (Husserl 1952, Hua IV, p. 22; Husserl 1989, p. 24). Because phantoms are thus "concrete units of experience" which constitute "an *a priori* necessary lower layer" (Husserl 2002, Hua Mat. IV, p. 174) in any experience of a thing, the highlighting of their own structures is a crucial moment in the elucidation of the constitution of the intuitive experienced thing and, jointly, in that of the constitution of space and time as *a priori* forms of its intuitive givenness (see Summa 2014, pp. 136–142). It is well-known that Husserl develops such analysis as early as the 1907 lectures on *Thing and Space* (Chapter IV, §§ 19–25) or in the first part of *Ideas II* (§§ 10 and 15b). However, the deepening of his constitutive problematic leads him gradually to integrate them into the systematics of a transcendental aesthetic, but only as a first layer. Indeed, the phantom is not the intuitive thing itself, as it is given in experience, but just one of its components, gained by a certain abstractive procedure. Interrupting or suspending this abstraction is precisely what is required to reach the upper layer of the transcendental aesthetic.

What exactly was set aside by this abstraction in the first level of aesthetic? The answer is *causality*, understood in a non-physico-mathematical way but according to its intuitive determination as a simple relation of regulated mutual dependence between the data of experience. Conversely, with the re-introduction of causality, the phenomenological description of the intuitive datum changes level by opening itself to *reality* as such, with its essential character of substantiality:

> A deformation of a physical body followed by a movement is of course a process within the phantom, for example in the visual thing as a pure visual thing. But this does not yet give the elasticity, which is a truly real property, a property of the physical thing. The pure phantom is not yet a physical thing. What does the term "elastic" mean? Well, the continuous property of a thing according to which, under certain circumstances and if it is hit in a certain way, it undergoes certain typical deformations followed by oscillating movements. Seeing a deformation followed by a movement for example in a cinematographic phantom, is different from seeing the elasticity. But if we see an elastic plate oscillate, then we [...] *experience* that because the plate was hit, it oscillates, and so on. (Husserl 2002, Hua Mat. IV, pp. 180–181; see also Husserl 1930, p. 56a)

This rather long quotation shows very clearly that the intuitive content of concrete experience goes far beyond the mere sensory (or aesthetic in the narrow sense of the word) content of the things given in it. And it shows at the same time that if causality allows this enrichment, it is because it implies together substantiality, materiality – and thus reality (Husserl 1956, Hua VII, p. 41). This is confirmed by the following synthetic notation:

> If we stick to reality, then causal properties belong to things and these are, as substrates, substances for such properties. (Husserl 1920–1926, p. 20b; see Husserl 2002, Hua Mat. IV, p. 182)

As a result, it appears that first, the specific task of the transcendental aesthetic's second layer is a description of the constitution of the properly intuitive (and no longer simply sensory) unity of the real thing given in experience (and, by extension, the constitution of a possible world of experience); second, that within such an ontology of reality (or of materiality), causality represents a necessary structural form (Husserl 1930, p. 57a).

Given this last result, it is easy to see what characterizes the second fundamental aspect of transcendental aesthetic in its phenomenological re-definition: the *aesthetization of causality* and, with it, of a significant part of what is categorial in Kant's sense. As a synthetic result of the highlighting of an intuitive causality within experience and of the conception of aesthetic ruled by intuition rather than mere sensibility, this aspect reveals a proper phenomenological subversion of Kant's distinction between aesthetic and analytic, insofar as it implies that at its second level, the transcendental phenomenological aesthetic coincides with some of the tasks that Kant ascribed to the analytic:

> Having sketched out the clear and well-defined horizon of the problems and the researches which refer to an ontology and a phenomenology of phantoms, we would have to come to a transcendental aesthetic of the immediately superior layer, which, in Kant, doesn't stand under the title of a "transcendental aesthetic," but is rather integrated with the transcendental analytic. (Husserl 2002, Hua Mat. IV, p. 179)
>
> In Kant's transcendental analytic is to be found much of what must be called in the authentic sense a transcendental aesthetic, that is, in our view, a transcendental aesthetic of materiality. (Husserl 2002, Hua Mat. IV, p. 198)

For a better understanding of this "part" of Kant's analytic which the phenomenological topology ascribes to aesthetic, we can refer to what Husserl calls in the *Krisis* Kant's "great discovery" (while stressing at the same time that it has remained for Kant himself only a "preliminary discovery"), namely, the two-fold functioning of the understanding (Husserl 1954, Hua VI, p. 106; Husserl 1970, pp. 103–104). On the first hand, the understanding is the faculty which produces the idealizations, the concepts, and the norms of intersubjective scientific objectivity. On the other hand (and, so to speak, "in concealment"), the understanding simultaneously works to "rationaliz[e] sense-data," i.e. to constitute the "sensibly intuited world of objects" (Husserl 1954, Hua VI, p. 97; Husserl 1970, p. 94); in short: the world of the perceptual experience upon which the scientific idealization operates (Kern 1964, pp. 261–269; Pradelle 2012, pp. 289–294). In other words, against Hume's sensualism, Kant discovers that "mere sensibility, related to mere data of sense, cannot account for objects of experience," but that "these objects of experience point to a hidden mental accomplishment" which "enables [...] pre-scientific experience, through logic, mathematics, mathematical natural science, to be knowable with objective validity" (Husserl 1954, Hua VI, pp. 96–97; Husserl 1970, pp. 93–94). If the proper task of the analytic is to give an account of the constitution of the scientific world by highlighting the acts of idealization upon which it is grounded, highlighting the acts of identification which rule over the pre-scientific constitution of an intuitive world is the proper task of a transcendental aesthetic which, in its broadest sense, coincides with the idea of a "transcendental theory of experience" (Pradelle 2012, p. 294).[3] Furthermore, because the "concealed" functioning of understanding is related to the aesthetic constitution of an intuitive world of experience, whereas its "manifest" functioning is related to the constitution of an objective nature, it seems possible to claim that Husserl's redefinition of Kant's topology ultimately consists in *reducing the tri-partition between sensibility, understanding, and reason to the duality of the intuitive and the discursive, the given and the constructed, or between experience and thought.*

2 Schopenhauer's Shadow?

On this basis, I would now like to emphasize something generally ignored in secondary literature, namely the fact that this criticism and reorganization of Kant's topology is very similar to the criticism that Schopenhauer, one century earlier, raised against Kant. It is true that Schopenhauer's name is sometimes mentioned as far as Husserl's concept of the living-body as *Willensorgan* is concerned, but never – at least to the best of my knowledge – in relation to Husserl's

---

[3] In his analysis, D. Pradelle opposes the tasks of transcendental aesthetic and transcendental logic, clearly identifying the latter with the transcendental analytic. On the contrary, my claim is that the opposition between aesthetic and logic represents a different level of analysis, which I shall address in the third part of this paper.

redefinition of the transcendental aesthetic or analytic.[4] And yet, as I would like to show now, the two philosophers stand in such proximity to each other on this matter that it is may be possible to support *the assumption of Schopenhauer's influence on Husserl*. After all, we know for sure that Husserl acquired Schopenhauer's *Sämmtliche Werke* in 1880 (Sommer 2012, pp. 293–294)[5] and dedicated two seminars in 1892–93 and 1897 respectively to some aspects of his philosophy (Schuhmann 1977, pp. 9, 34, 51). If we also take into consideration two convergent statements of Husserl to Dorion Cairns in 1931, revealing that Schopenhauer was among the first philosophers he read (Cairns 1976, pp. 47, 60), it is not unreasonable to assume that Schopenhauer's criticism of Kant could have played a role in Husserl's thought.

I shall begin with an external observation. As a result of his integration of causality into the field of transcendental aesthetic, Husserl frequently mentions time, space, and causality *in conjunction with each other* as the three basic dimensions of reality, or the three aspects of a unique aesthetic *a priori* of the world. In other words, as the "necessary structural forms" of a possible world of experience, determining its "global style" and allowing a "science of the world's universal structure" (Husserl 1962, Hua IX, pp. 89, 68 and 64). Now, such a conjunction of time, space, and causality is one of the key features of Schopenhauer's theory of representation. In an explicitly critical relation to Kant's distinction between aesthetic and analytic, Schopenhauer conceives of them not only as the "conditions" of "our faculty of apprehension," but also and consequently as "the essential [...] and therefore universal forms of any object," or as the "laws according to which all phenomena are connected to one another" (Schopenhauer 1977a, pp. 513–514, 31 and 516; Schopenhauer 1969, pp. 418, 5 and 420). While it could be a mere terminological coincidence, we must go back to the principle of such a conjunction of time, space, and causality in Schopenhauer's philosophy to check whether the phenomenological redefinition of transcendental aesthetic can be seen as its distant inheritor.

The texts in which Schopenhauer outlines his criticism of Kant's philosophy clearly show that this principle is closely related to *the requirement of a rigorous definition of the sphere of intuitiveness as such*, which, for Schopenhauer, is co-

---

[4] It is instructive to note that even Michela Summa, in her detailed and thorough study of Husserl's transcendental aesthetic, mentions Schopenhauer only when it comes to the role played by the living-body (Summa 2014, pp. 287–290), but not once as far as the integration of causality in the spatio-temporal constitution of the aesthetic thing is concerned.

[5] This paper also shows that the highlighting of Schopenhauerian aspects in Husserl's phenomenology plays a significant role in Michel Henry's work, but also in the program of a "phenomenologically inspired" philosophical anthropology (notably in Hans Blumenberg).

extensive with experience and its conditions (Schopenhauer 1977a, pp. 32 and 39; Schopenhauer 1969, pp. 6–7 and 13). This requirement is indeed the root of one of Schopenhauer's main critical arguments against Kant: that of having confused intuitive knowledge with abstract knowledge, or what is intuitive with what is abstract in knowledge (Schopenhauer 1977a, pp. 532, 535, 579 and 580; Schopenhauer 1969, pp. 434, 437, 473 and 474). Now, in Schopenhauer's view, the iconic place of this confusion is the theory of categories, of the pure concepts of the understanding which, according to Kant, are constitutive of a possible experience in general.

Schopenhauer's critical argument has two sides: first, he claims that only intuition provides a relation to an object, so that any conceptual element is dismissed as an abstraction:

> Generally, according to Kant, there are only concepts of objects, no intuitions. On the other hand, I say that objects exist primarily only for intuition, and that concepts are always abstractions from this intuition. (Schopenhauer 1977a, p. 549; Schopenhauer 1969, p. 448)

In other words, Kant's mistake is to give to conceptual abstractions a constitutive function for experience that should only be granted to intuition. But far from globally rejecting Kant's categories, Schopenhauer highlights in a second step the particular status of causality:

> Kant ascribes the objects themselves to *thinking*, in order to make thus experience and the objective world dependent to the *understanding*, yet without letting the understanding be a faculty of *intuition*. [...] But actually [...] our empirical intuition is at once *objective*, just because it comes from the causal nexus. (Schopenhauer 1977a, p. 543; Schopenhauer 1969, p. 443)

In pointing out that causality gives our intuition an objectifying power, Schopenhauer clearly draws a boundary between this category, related to intuitive knowledge, and the eleven others, "only" conceptual and abstract. But where does causality get this privilege of intuitiveness from?

The answer can be found in Schopenhauer's claim that the sensitive impression, "mere sensation in the sense-organ" (Schopenhauer 1977a, p. 538; Schopenhauer 1969, p. 438), is, strictly speaking, not a representation because sensation does not imply any relation to an object as such (see Schopenhauer 1977b, p. 66). In other words, sensibility is reduced to mere sensoriality, so that, in Schopenhauer's view, it couldn't constitute any experience of an empirical object without the intervention of an additional element bestowing an objective significance on our intuition. It is precisely this element that is causality, i.e. the law according to which an object is real only as the effect of another one or as cause for another one. To be sure, causality is intellectual and, as such, takes root in the understanding. However, it is important to emphasize that for Schopenhauer, causality is simply the link that unites time and space (Schopenhauer 1977a, p. 35; Schopenhauer 1969, p. 10; see also Schopenhauer 1977b, pp. 43–44). As such, causality remains, so to speak, at the same level of intuitiveness as time and space, so that the sphere of intuitiveness goes beyond that of sensibility taken in the narrow sense of sensoriality. Thus, experiencing an object is possible, in Schopenhauer's view, only if the understanding applies the law of causality to the impressional sense-data: in doing so, it "converts the mere sensation into objective empirical intuition," which means "into a *representation*," which now "exists as *object* in space and time" (Schopenhauer 1977a, pp. 552 and 538; Schopenhauer 1969, pp. 451 and 439).

While this statement could simply be regarded as a new form of the classical distinction between sensation and perception, its full significance is actually related to causality in a way that directly affects transcendental topology. On the one hand, causality becomes the only necessary *and* sufficient constitutive condition for any empirical object and, more broadly, of a real "world of experience" (Schopenhauer 1977b, pp. 44 and 58). That is why Schopenhauer feels justified in retaining only this category as a subjective condition of experience and in "throw[ing] away" the eleven others (Schopenhauer 1977a, p. 549; Schopenhauer 1969, p. 448). On the other hand, and in return, causality is sufficient to define the essence of the understanding, reduced to the only function of causal objectification, a function that is intellectual to be sure, and yet not conceptual, but intuitive (Schopenhauer 1977a, pp. 37–38, 538 and 547; Schopenhauer 1969, pp. 11, 439 and 446; see also Schopenhauer 1977b, pp. 92–93). In contrast, the eleven other categories are indeed concepts, products of reason, and reason is conceived in a deflationary way as a mere faculty of abstract representations (Schopenhauer 1977a, pp. 580–581; Schopenhauer 1969, p. 475; see also Schopenhauer 1977b, pp. 84 and 112–113).

On this basis, I would like to suggest that *Husserl's critical diagnosis of a "twofold functioning of the understanding" in Kant is prefigured by Schopenhauer's claim that, in his theory of categories and with his concept of the understanding, Kant confuses two different things: first, the process through which a possible world of experience is intuitively constituted for us, and, second, an abstract conceptuality stemming from a rational activity of the mind which in fact presupposes the intuitive world of experience.* Therefore, it is already possible to find in Schopenhauer the critical gesture that we have previously identified in Husserl; namely, the reduction of the tri-partition between sensibility, understanding, and reason to the duality of the intuitive and discursive. *In both philosophers, intuition is released from its narrow and merely sensory meaning, and extended to the categorial sphere* (Schopenhauer, 1977a, pp. 580–581; Schopenhauer 1969, p. 475). Thus, Husserl could have seamlessly taken up Schopenhauer's diagnosis, according to which Kant was right in distinguishing between intuition and thought, "although here, the nature of this distinction is a fundamentally false one" (Schopenhauer 1977a, p. 580; Schopenhauer 1969, p. 474).

Against such a convergence, one might argue that the aesthetization of causality, as one of the fundamental aspects of Husserl's criticism of Kant, has nothing to do with Schopenhauer in so far as Schopenhauer specifically relates causality to the understanding and defines causality as the one and only object of the understanding (Schopenhauer 1977a, p. 38; Schopenhauer 1969, p. 11). However, I believe that this is less a real divergence between the two than a difference between two possible and symmetrical readings of the same revision, so to speak, of Kant's distinction between aesthetic and analytic; a revision guided by the requirement of intuitiveness and leading to the discovery of the analytic's internal duality. Hence, I suggest that *what appears in Husserl as an aesthetization of causality corresponds exactly to what appears in Schopenhauer as an intellectualization of intuition*, and that the difference is related to what is at stake for each of them in criticizing Kant. Whereas the claim of an intuitive causality allows Husserl, despite the extension of the synthesis to the sensibility, to oppose the Neo-Kantian who, like Cohen, argues for an absorption of the aesthetic within the analytic (see Pradelle 2012, pp. 135, 160, 274; Pradelle 2014, p. 304), Schopenhauer's demonstration of the role of understanding for the possibility of empirical intuition allows him to bring out the idea of an intellectual intuition while firmly opposing the speculative conception of such an intuition in Fichte or Schelling (Schopenhauer 1977a, pp. 38–39 and 549; Schopenhauer 1969, pp. 11–12 and 448–449; see also Schopenhauer 1977b, p. 65).

Whatever the case may be, the close relationship between the two philosophers in their common criticism of Kant's distinction between transcendental aesthetic and transcendental analytic is confirmed by the fact that *once put into intuitive continuity with space and time, it is causality which allows Schopenhauer's philosophy, as well as Husserl's phenomenology, to address the question of the conditions not only of experience but of empirical reality*. In a way that strikingly anticipates Husserl's approach, Schopenhauer shows that causality immediately implies materiality, and the latter substantiality (Schopenhauer 1977a, p. 36; Schopenhauer 1969, pp. 10–11). These three concepts are finally identified with each other[6] and represent together what might be called the *a priori* coordinates of reality.

---

[6] Schopenhauer explicitly identifies causality and materiality (Schopenhauer 1977a, p. 37 and

For all these reasons, it is possible to suggest that what Husserl sees as the task of the transcendental aesthetic (once its relation to the analytic is phenomenologically clarified) corresponds to and inherits from what Schopenhauer saw as the task of highlighting the principle of sufficient reason of an intuitive representation of the world.

3 Aesthetic and Logic: From "Real Logic" to "World-Logic"

Let us now turn to Husserl's last determination of the transcendental aesthetic, specifically from the point of view of its relation to the whole of the transcendental logic, not just the analytic. In this perspective, a new anti-Kantian feature can be stressed in Husserl's thought: *the incorporation of the transcendental aesthetic within the transcendental logic*. Such an integration, which obviously presupposes a redefinition of the transcendental logic and its tasks, does not happen all at once in Husserl but results from an evolution which I shall briefly reconstruct.

First, it is important to emphasize that in his oldest texts dedicated to the idea of a phenomenological transcendental aesthetic (especially the 1906–1907 lectures *Introduction to Logic and Theory of Knowledge*), Husserl conceives of such an aesthetic as a part of a logic which he calls "real logic" (*reale Logik*). He defines real logic in opposition not only to formal logic but also – and perhaps more surprisingly – to Kant's transcendental logic. In fact, this idea of a real logic is related to the way Husserl sought at that time to carry out the program of a material ontology as it emerged in the third of the *Logical Investigations*. The discovery of a material and synthetic *a priori*, irreducible to the formal *a priori* and related to the object's real content, required the development of a science which could provide a logical analysis of this material ontological sphere in its specificity and which could refer the heterogeneous variety of empirical sciences to its internal structure. This material and concrete logic is exactly what Husserl calls "real logic" in 1906–1907. By taking into consideration not only

---

546; Schopenhauer 1969, pp. 11 and 445; see also Schopenhauer 1977b, p. 98), but also materiality and substantiality (Schopenhauer 1977b, pp. 44, 58 and 98), and hence, by inference, causality and substantiality, as Husserl does. The only difference is that Husserl often describes their mutual involvement before introducing materiality, which is rather mentioned as a complement (see for example Husserl 1920–1926, p. 21a: "Causality and constitution of things, then of a world of things as permanent substances of changing properties.").

the factual reality as it is dealt with in the empirical sciences, but also the reality as an idea (i.e. in the most general sense of all the necessary conditions of a factual reality), this logic aims at "the ascertainment of the truths grounded in the universal essence of real Being as such" (Husserl 1984, Hua XXIV, p. 100; Husserl 2008, p. 98). Its particular task is then to bring out material categories, concepts "in which what is real as such is to be understood in terms of its essence," "concepts like thing, real property, real relation, state, process, coming into being and passing away, cause and effect, space and time, that seem to belong necessarily to the idea of a reality" (Husserl 1984, Hua XXIV, p. 101; Husserl 2008, p. 98). Even if Husserl doesn't explicitly speak of transcendental aesthetic in this context, this indicative list of concepts obviously shows that its thematic field is exactly congruent with the definition of a real ontology and logic. A clear confirmation is to be found a few pages later:

> However, despite their kinship, really partial overlapping, with Kant's transcendental logic, one will not be able to identify the idea of such an ontology in the sense we have in mind without further ado. [...] Attention would [...] have to be turned to the Kantian distinction between transcendental esthetic and transcendental logic, which I cannot go into here. (Husserl 1984, Hua XXIV, p. 113; Husserl 2008, p. 109)

It is not difficult to understand why Kant's distinction between logic and aesthetic is mentioned by Husserl in order to reject any identification between his real logic and Kant's transcendental logic. In the earlier list of material categories provided by Husserl, some concepts belonging to the logical sphere or, in Kantian terms, categories (such as cause and effect) are brought together with concepts belonging to the aesthetic sphere, or pure intuitions (space and time). This simple observation indicates that Husserl's real logic implies a new definition of the relations between transcendental aesthetic and logic, in critical tension with Kant's conception. As a *logic*, it implies a categorial dimension which Kant could only locate in the analytic moment of his transcendental logic; but as a *real* logic, it can't be limited to the merely formal conditions of an object in general. In this context, the controversial dimension of Husserl's discovery of a material, synthetic *a priori* becomes clear: in Husserl's view, in fact, Kant's distinction between transcendental logic and esthetic implies that the true sense of such an *a priori* is completely ignored or – which is all the same – that apriority is tacitly reduced to formality. Such an exclusively formal conception of the *a priori* makes it impossible to develop the idea of a real logic as a science of the material *a priori* in the terms of Kant's architectonic. Thus, because it is necessarily tied to Kant's transcendental esthetic *and* logic, Husserl's real logic, as the "general basis of all individual sciences of reality" (Husserl 1984, Hua XXIV, p. 114; Husserl 2008, p. 110), can't be identified with the entire transcendental logic as opposed to formal logic, nor can it be, as a science of the synthetic a *priori*, with Kant's transcendental aesthetic as opposed to the analytic moment of his transcendental logic (Husserl 1984, Hua XXIV, p. 113; Husserl 2008, pp. 109–110).

Still, this idea of a real logic is strongly affected by the "genetic turn" according to which Husserl's constitutive phenomenology no longer limits itself to the particular task of exhibiting the subjective modes of constitution corresponding to each single type of object. Rather, it seeks to describe the temporal and motivational connections between the acts which constitute these objects from the level of associative passivity, in order to bring out the "history" of these objects within consciousness and, correlatively, the "history" of the living subjectivity itself. Indeed, this new orientation allows Husserl to provide a genetic interpretation of the presupposition according to which the world's predicative and scientific determination refers to its intuitive and pre-predicative determination in the passive syntheses of the pre-scientific and perceptive life. As a result, the program of a transcendental logic as a science that accounts for the possibility and the modalities of a rational determination of the world in the positive sciences turns into that of a "world-logic [*Welt-Logik*]" (Husserl 1974, Hua XVII, p. 296; Husserl 1969, p. 291). Namely, the science that elucidates the various world-constituent performances (*Leistungen*) in their genetic sequence, from pre-theoretical passivity to active scientific conceptualization, thus tracing the world's "history" within consciousness. According to this definition, the transcendental logic absorbs and relativizes that which was the task of the real logic (the foundation of the positive sciences of reality): it is now a mere local task, which corresponds to a particular stratum of the world's "history" in the subject's intentional life.

In this new perspective, Husserl still considers the transcendental aesthetic as taking part in a logic. However, at a further distance from Kant's topology, this logic is henceforth the transcendental logic itself, conceived as a genetic logic. If it is to be distinguished from all dogmatic sciences (including logic in the usual formal sense) to the extent that "it wants to be the ultimate science that goes back to ultimate givennesses, namely, to those givennesses that are already presupposed in all other givennesses, in all naive givennesses" (Husserl 1966, Hua XI, p. 255; Husserl 2001, p. 389), the aesthetic then represents its first moment, which brings out precisely the structures of the passive pregivenness of the experiential world, before the ego's categorial spontaneity adds various layers of idealities to it:

> "*Transcendental aesthetics*" – in a new sense of the phrase (which we use because of an easily apprehensible relationship to Kant's narrowly restricted transcendental aesthetics) – functions as the ground level <in a world-logic>. It deals with the eidetic problem of any possible world *as a world given in "pure experience"* and thus precedes all science in

the "higher" sense; accordingly it undertakes the eidetic description of the allembracing *Apriori*, without which no Objects could appear unitarily in mere experience, prior to categorial actions (in our sense, which must not be confounded with the categorial in the *Kantian* sense), and therefore without which the unity of a Nature, the unity of a world, as a passively synthetized unity, could not become constituted at all. (Husserl 1974, Hua XVII, p. 297; Husserl 1969, pp. 291–292)

Hence, the genetic perspective allows us to come back to the meaning of the phenomenological distinction between transcendental aesthetic and analytic as we have highlighted it at the end of the first part of this study, and to complete it. From the noetic point of view, the transcendental aesthetic is the "the science of consciousness that pre-gives meant reality" (Husserl 1966, Hua XI, p. 256; Husserl 2001, p. 389), and its task is to elucidate the primal forms of objectification as they take place in passive, essentially perceptive syntheses in the sphere of pre-theoretical sensible receptivity, as opposed to that of categorial spontaneity, studied by transcendental analytic (Husserl 1966, Hua XI, p. 361; Husserl 2001, pp. 444–445). From the correlative noematic point of view, the transcendental aesthetic is the science of the world constituted in this passive and pre-theoretical givenness within the framework of the perceptive, pre-predicative experience. It must therefore provide the *a priori* of the aesthetic world. In other words, the *eidos* of an experiential world in general, now defined as a perceptual world since perception is *par excellence* the intuitive mode of givenness (Husserl 1966, p. 295; Husserl 2001, pp. 581–582).

Finally, I want to emphasize that in the context of a transcendental logic conceived as a world-logic, the distinction between transcendental aesthetic and analytic paradoxically goes hand in hand with a fundamental genetic continuity from one to the other. They correspond to two successive degrees of a single process of constitution and allow the phenomenologist to bring out *the genesis of predicative ideality from that of empirical evidence*. In this perspective, the proper task of the transcendental aesthetic is to account for the process through which the true world of science proceeds from the world of experience as it is always already passively given. This process, which the famous § 9 of the *Krisis* describes as "Galileo's mathematization of nature" or as an idealization of the life-world (Husserl 1954, Hua VI, pp. 20 *sq.*; Husserl 1970, pp. 23 *sq.*), without any reference to the transcendental aesthetic, belongs to it *de jure* nevertheless, as many of Husserl's lectures and manuscripts since the mid-20's undoubtedly confirm it. I won't develop further this well-known theme, but will simply highlight a very important feature of Husserl's later thought: if this theory of idealization as a process that leads from relative and situated life-world evidences to irrelatively exact evidence of science brings to light a genetic continuity from experience to science in the form of an *archaeological rooting* of the former in the latter, Husserl doesn't neglect the reverse movement, which brings back the higher formations of science to experience in the form of a *teleological sedimentation* of science in experience. One of the first descriptions of this process can be found in the 1927 lectures on *Nature and Spirit*:

> The products of thought are not something that could be found next to the experiential world, but they belong to this world, they bear its print although they are not themselves new intuitive and sensitive features in this world. Any other act, any way of being active while being affected by the ambient world of each moment creates thereby at the same time aspects which fit into this ambient world and become experienced in their own way by an isolated subject or in an intersubjective way. (Husserl 2001, Hua XXXII, pp. 228–229)[7]

Taking into account this downward movement responding to the upward movement of idealization allows us to introduce the important precision according to which the aesthetic world is at the same time – and in a non-contradictory way – the intuitive basis of scientific activity while made of the conceptual sedimentations of such an activity. In other words, it is undoubtedly pre-predicative, but not really pre-theoretical.

* * *

In conclusion, I would like to emphasize that the multiple aspects of Husserl's phenomenological re-definition of Kant's transcendental aesthetic can be referred to *the unfolding of a unique intuitionist requirement that frees intuition from its dependency on a narrow empiricist or sensualist conception of sensibility and thus implies a disjunction between what is aesthetic and the mere sensory content of sensibility*. But if this means that we enter the sphere of transcendental aesthetic as soon as we are "in the sphere of intuition which is the sphere of experience" (Husserl 2002, Hua Mat. IV, p. 193), then it is possible to claim that the transcendental aesthetic, phenomenologically understood, is no longer primarily determined by an *object* which would be its specific theme (like, in Kant, the pure forms of sensible intuition). Rather, it is determined by a *mode of givenness* which is irreducible to the mere sensory *datum* and which has nevertheless to serve as a standard for what "sensible" means, namely "the original self-exhibi-

---

[7] What is here articulated *sich einfügen* will become, in the 1930's and in the context of the *Krisis*, a theme of analysis and fundamental descriptions under the title of the *Einströmen*, the "inflow" of theoretical idealities within the life-worldly experience (see Husserl 1954, Hua VI, pp. 115, 141 (note) and 212–213; Hua 1970, pp. 113, 138 (note) and 208–209).

tion" (Husserl 1954, Hua VI, p. 118; Husserl 1970, p. 116).[8] This intuitionistic feature lies at the root of the aesthetization of causality, now conceived along with time and space as an *a priori* structure of empirical reality and, more broadly, of a possible world of experience. Together with "the reintegration, within the transcendental aesthetic, of the synthesis as *Urform* of consciousness" (Pradelle 2012, p. 304), this aesthetization ensures, on the one hand, the subversion of Kant's distinction between transcendental aesthetic and *analytic*, and on the other hand it simply cancels Kant's distinction between transcendental aesthetic and *logic*. Indeed, insofar as the transcendental aesthetic now coincides with the science of the prescientific constitution of an intuitive world of experience (i.e. of this life-world on which the scientific production of idealities is grounded), it presents itself as the first moment of a transcendental logic meant to provide a genetic elucidation of the empirical and then theoretical constitution of the world within the subject's intentional life. Finally, this same intuitionist feature seems the deepest vindication of the convergence I brought out between Husserl's redefinition of the aesthetic-analytic distinction and a central aspect of the criticism raised against Kant by Schopenhauer a century before. The way both philosophers define space, time, and causality in conjunction with each other as the conditions, which are themselves intuitive, of any empirical intuition seems significant enough in my view to support the assumption that Husserl's "original hostility" (Husserl 1994, Hua Dok. III/5, p. 4) towards Kant is not due solely to Brentano's influence but also to the more diffuse but no less real influence of Schopenhauer, whose philosophy might have facilitated one of young Husserl's first encounters with Emmanuel Kant's thought.

Bibliography

Cairns, Dorion (1976): *Conversations with Husserl and Fink.* The Hague: Martinus Nijhoff.
Husserl, Edmund (1920–1926): *Ms A VII 14: Transzendentale Ästhetik.* Unpublished manuscript.
Husserl, Edmund (1930): *Ms A VII 20: Möglichkeit der Ontologie.* Unpublished manuscript.
Husserl, Edmund (1950): *Cartesianische Meditationen und Pariser Vorträge. Husserliana*, vol. I. The Hague: Martinus Nijhoff.
Husserl, Edmund (1960): *Cartesian Meditations. An Introduction to Phenomenology.* Trans. Dorion Cairns. The Hague: Martinus Nijhoff.

---

8 Hence Husserl's important notation a few pages before: "Here we can now clarify the very limited justification for speaking of a sense-world, a world of sense-intuition, a sensible world of appearances" (Husserl 1954, p. 108; Husserl 1970, p. 106).

Husserl, Edmund (1952): *Ideen zu einer reinen Phänomenologie und phänomenologischen Philosophie, Zweites Buch: Phänomenologische Untersuchungen zur Konstitution. Husserliana*, vol. IV. Ed. Marly Biemel. The Hague: Martinus Nijhoff.

Husserl, Edmund (1989): *Ideas Pertaining to a Pure Phenomenology and to a Phenomenological Philosophy. Second Book: Studies in the Phenomenology of Constitution.* Trans. Richard Rojcewicz and André Schuwer. Dordrecht: Kluwer Academic Publishers.

Husserl, Edmund (1954): *Die Krisis der europäischen Wissenschaften und die transzendentale Phänomenologie. Eine Einleitung in die phänomenologische Philosophie. Husserliana*, vol. VI. Ed. Walter Biemel. The Hague: Martinus Nijhoff.

Husserl, Edmund (1970): *The Crisis of European Sciences and Transcendental Phenomenology. An Introduction to Phenomenological Philosophy.* Trans. David Carr Evanston: Northwestern University Press.

Husserl, Edmund (1956): *Erste Philosophie (1923–1924). Erster Teil: Kritische Ideengeschichte. Husserliana*, vol. VII. Ed. Rudolf Boehm. Ed. Rudolf Boehm. The Hague: Martinus Nijhoff.

Husserl, Edmund (1962): *Phänomenologische Psychologie. Vorlesungen Sommersemester 1925. Husserliana*, vol. IX. Ed. Walter Biemel. The Hague: Martinus Nijhoff.

Husserl, Edmund (1966): *Analysen zur passiven Synthesis. Aus Vorlesungs- und Forschungsmanuskripten 1918–1926. Husserliana*, vol. XI. Ed. Margot Fleischer. The Hague: Martinus Nijhoff.

Husserl, Edmund (2001): *Analyses Concerning Passive and Active Syntheses. Lectures on Transcendental Logic.* Trans. Anthony J. Steinbock. Dordrecht: Kluwer Academic Publishers.

Husserl, Edmund (1974): *Formale und transzendentale Logik. Versuch einer Kritik der logischen Vernunft. Husserliana*, vol. XVII. Ed. Paul Janssen. The Hague: Martinus Nijhoff.

Husserl, Edmund (1969): *Formal and Transcendental Logic.* Trans. Dorion Cairns. The Hague: Martinus Nijhoff.

Husserl, Edmund (1984): *Einleitung in die Logik und Erkenntnistheorie. Vorlesungen 1906/07. Husserliana*, vol. XXIV. Ed. Ullrich Melle. The Hague: Martinus Nijhoff.

Husserl, Edmund (2008): *Introduction to Logic and Theory of Knowledge. Lectures 1906/07.* Trans. Claire Ortiz Hill. Dordrecht: Springer.

Husserl, Edmund (1994): *Briefwechsel: Die Neukantianer. Husserliana Dokumente*, vol. III/5. Dordrecht: Kluwer Academic Publishers.

Husserl, Edmund (2001): *Natur und Geist. Vorlesungen Sommersemester 1927. Husserliana*, vol. XXXII. Ed. Michael Weiler. Dordrecht: Kluwer Academic Publishers.

Husserl, Edmund (2002): *Natur und Geist. Vorlesungen Sommersemester 1919. Husserliana Materialien*, vol. IV. Ed. Michael Weiler. Dordrecht: Kluwer Academic Publishers.

Kern, Iso (1964): *Husserl und Kant. Eine Untersuchung über Husserls Verhältnis zu Kant und zum Neukantianismus.* The Hague: Martinus Nijhoff.

Pradelle, Dominique (2012): *Par-delà la révolution copernicienne. Sujet transcendantal et facultés chez Kant et Husserl.* Paris: Presses universitaires de France.

Pradelle, Dominique (2014): "Sur le sens de l'idéalisme transcendantal: Husserl critique de Kant". In: François Calori/Michaël Fœssel/Dominique Pradelle (Eds.): *De la sensibilité. Les esthétiques de Kant.* Rennes: Presses Universitaires, pp. 285–305.

Schopenhauer, Arthur (1977a): *Die Welt als Wille und Vorstellung*. Zürcher Ausgabe: *Werke in zehn Bänden*. Band 1. Zürich: Diogenes Verlag.

Schopenhauer, Arthur (1969): *The World as Will and Representation*, 2 Volumes. Trans. E. F. J. Payne. New York: Dover.

Schopenhauer, Arthur (1977b): *Über die vierfache Wurzel des Satzes vom zureichenden Grunde*. Zürcher Ausgabe: *Werke in zehn Bänden*. Band 5. Zürich: Diogenes Verlag.

Schuhmann, Karl (1977): *Husserl-Chronik. Denk- und Lebensweg Edmund Husserls. Husserliana Dokumente*, vol. I. The Hague: Martinus Nijhoff.

Sommer, Christian (2012): "Présentation". In: *Les Études philosophiques*, vol. 102, pp. 291–296.

Summa, Michela (2014): *Spatio-Temporal Intertwining: Husserl's Transcendantal Aesthetic*. Dordrecht: Springer.

Daniele De Santis
Synthesis and Identity

Husserl on Kant's Contribution to the History of Philosophy[1]

> "Si può dire che chi non accetta la sintesi *a priori* è fuori della strada della filosofia moderna, anzi della filosofia senz'altro."
> (Benedetto Croce, *Logica come Scienza del Concetto Puro*)

Abstract: The present chapter explores a very specific theme concerning Husserl's relation to Kant, namely, the connection between the idea of (transcendental) synthesis and the notion of "identity" construed as its correlate. According to Husserl, the introduction of a transcendental conception of "synthesis" represents Kant's crucial contribution to the history of (modern) philosophy. Now, in order to fully appreciate the significance of such claim, we will first have to explain in what sense Husserl takes "the determination of the identity of being" as the problem lying at the very heart of philosophy, notably, of its "Greek" origin. Accordingly, the present chapter will be divided into two parts: after discussing the way in which Plato tackles and addresses the question of the determination of the identity of being, we will switch to Kant and his "contribution" to the history of modern philosophy as Husserl understands it. In this way, we will be able to ascribe to Kant a clear and specific position in the history of philosophy, which, as we firmly believe, can represent the starting point for any future attempt at discussing and shedding light on the relation between Kant and the father of phenomenology.

Introduction

Despite the quite narrow and specific topic suggested by its title, *Realitätswissenschaft und Idealisierung. Die Mathematisierung der Natur* (Husserl 1962, Hua VI, pp. 279–293; Husserl 1970, pp. 301–314) has the great merit of providing a succinct overview of the history of Western philosophy, notably of its Greek "origin,"

---

[1] This work was supported by the European Regional Development Fund-Project "Creativity and Adaptability as Conditions of the Success of Europe in an Interrelated World" (No. CZ.02.1.01/0.0/0.0/16_019/0000734).

understood as an incessant and rational effort at addressing a single, yet crucial, problem: *the determination of the "identity" of being as a "real being."*

That at the origin of Greek philosophy (prior to any distinction between philosophy and science as we, modern humanity, have come to understand it (Husserl 2012, Hua Mat. IX, pp. 7–27)) there lies the problem of "the determination of the identity of being" is a thesis that Husserl argued for, though in different forms, since nearly the very beginning of his carrier, that is, at least since the 1902–1903 lectures *Allgemeine Erkenntnistheorie* (see Husserl 2001a, p. 82).[2] Here, too, more than twenty years later, Husserl opens his analyses by stressing that *vor ihr* – pointing at something for *philosophy* to be faced with and thereby successfully to address – "is the question about the flux of being in becoming and about the conditions of the possibility of the identity of being in becoming" (Husserl 1962, Hua VI, p. 280; Husserl 1970, p. 301). Now, according to the manner in which Husserl accounts for how philosophy came originally to tackle such a question, Plato is the one who plays the decisive role: it is in Plato that – as we will show – the problem is originally addressed and a first and preliminary articulation of *synthesis* and *identity* can be found. Nevertheless, this being the major "thesis" that this paper is going to propose and defend, if *der Göttliche* does not really succeed in securing *the identity of being in becoming* (hereafter: DIB), it is because he lacks a *transcendental notion of synthesis*; such, in Husserl's view, is Kant's contribution to the history of philosophy, namely, the introduction of a transcendental understanding of the notion of synthesis, only one upon whose basis DIB can be addressed. As a consequence, this study will be divided into two main sections: after a preliminary assessment of Husserl's account of the "inaugural" role of Plato (which will provide us with the necessary backdrop) (1.1, 1.2, and 1.3), we will move on to Kant to see how Husserl understands his position in this history (2.1, 2.2, 2.3). In order to do so, we will mostly rely upon Husserl's manuscripts from the 20s and 30s – these being the crucial years in which the most systematic and unitary interpretations of the history of philosophy are developed.

As we firmly believe, approaching Kant based on the problem of "the determination of the identity of being" will result in two major advantages: one, it will

---

[2] "According to what the Eleatics affirm, all becoming, all coming into being and disappearing, all self-alteration is mere illusion; only the absolutely identical being is real or actual, and such identical being that excludes all change, hence all multiplicity, is not to be perceived, yet grasped by means of philosophical thought. On the other hand, Heraclitus teaches us that the essence of things lies precisely in change and becoming. What is rigid, namely, all fixed identity is just appearance, for in reality there is only a becoming determined by the supreme ἀνάγκη, i.e., by an eternal, necessary lawfulness."

help us ascribe to Kant a specific position within a quite determined and unitary history (whose origin dates back to Plato); two, it will explain why Husserl was always particularly fond of the first edition of the transcendental deduction of the *Critique of Pure Reason*. As the title of our paper suggests, all our effort will be directed entirely toward elucidating Kant's contribution to the history of philosophy; the way in which Husserl intends to correct Kant's "doctrine of synthesis," and thereby develop it further, will be only hinted at in the conclusion, for it opens up a completely new topic (3.).

1.1. Let us start from the very beginning. In its original meaning, "philosophy" means nothing other than "universal science," science of the universe and of "the all-encompassing unity of all that is" (Husserl 1962, Hua VI, p. 321; Husserl 1970, p. 276). Husserl describes such "All" (*Weltall*) by means of the non-technical expression "all things" (*alle Dinge*),³ and quite explicitly includes in his account Thales and Anaximenes, Anaximander and Parmenides, Heraclitus, Anaxagoras and Democritus (Husserl 1956, Hua VII, p. 311).⁴ In Husserl's view, what all these philosophers have in common is their attempt to identify a "principle" capable of explaining all things in terms of such and such a particular form of all-encompassing becoming.⁵ As Husserl goes on to say: "Soon the interest in the All, and hence the question of the all-encompassing becoming and being in becoming begins to particularize itself according to the general forms and regions of being" (Husserl 1962, Hua VI, p. 321; Husserl 1970, p. 276). If, then, the "birth" of philosophy coincides with the emergence of the question of the totality of things understood as the all-encompassing becoming and being in becoming (which will slowly particularize itself according to the different forms of being

---

3 In this sense, philosophy was "originally" a "universal factual science of the All given in a natural way [*universale Tatsachenwissenschaft von dem natürlich gegebenen Weltall*]" (Husserl 2012, Hua Mat. IX, p. 283).
4 "All things, humans, animals and heavenly bodies stem out of water, ἄπειρον or of air. All things are the mere appearance of the unalterable One; all things are appearance, for in reality [they are] mere forms of an eternal and lawful becoming, which is to be traced back to the primordial process of becoming of the primordial fire (out of which everything stems and into which everything sinks back once again). All things spring out of the elements by means of a supreme νοῦς. All things consist of unalterable atoms, and the ordinary sensible things are appearances of the senses and stem out of the atoms' lawful process of becoming."
5 "Universal knowledge on which the entire word, including all its realities, rests: how everything has become what it is; whence it derives and what it thereby carries within itself; what it is in-itself; how all becoming comes into being, and what is it that shows itself and must show itself in what becomes; how all stable entities stem out of the harmony of opposites, and how a necessary rule dominates everything" (Husserl 1956, p. 288).

(Husserl 2008, Hua XXXIX, pp. 281–293)), it is exclusively in Plato, and his "doctrine of ideas," that the problem of *the determination of the identity of being as that being which becomes* is directly set out as the central task of philosophy.[6] Let us consider what Husserl asserts at the very beginning of *Realitätswissenschaft und Idealisierung. Die Mathematisierung der Natur*:

> Science has its origin in Greek philosophy with the discovery of the idea and of the exact science that determines by means of ideas. It leads to the development of pure mathematics as pure science of ideas, science of possible objects in general as objects determined by ideas. Science is confronted with the problem of that which is, as the real which exists in itself, existing in itself over against the multiplicity of subjective manners of givenness belonging to the particular knowing subject; [it is confronted with] the question about the flux of being in becoming and about the conditions of the possibility of the identity of being in becoming, of the identical determinability of an existing real. (Husserl 1962, Hua VI, p. 279; Husserl 1970, p. 301)

This passage contains a series of intertwined claims that need to be carefully disentangled and unpacked.

(α) In the first place, the turn of phrase *the discovery of the idea* explicitly refers to Plato: it is only on the basis of the doctrine of ideas, in fact, that the question as to "the determination of the identity of being" can be raised and addressed.

(β) "The discovery of the idea" makes possible "exact science," notably "pure mathematics" (and, though Husserl does not mention it here, "pure geometry" (Husserl 1987, pp. 132–133)). This point should not be underestimated: for Husserl is clearly maintaining that these sciences determine by means of ideas (*durch Ideen bestimmenden*). In other words: it is only because the *ideas themselves determine*, that these sciences, too, can determine "by means" of them: *the determining function of the ideas is therefore prior to their being employed by exact sciences.*

(γ) As it seems to us, Husserl distinguishes between two "variations" on the theme "determination of the identity of being": indeed, there is (i) the determination of the identity of being *in becoming*, as well as (ii) the determination of the identity of being "over against the multiplicity of subjective manners of givenness belonging to the particular knowing subject." If the first can be considered more "ontological" and the notion of *identity* is opposed to that of *becom-*

---

6 For a detailed presentation of Husserl's account of the twofold origin of ancient philosophy, and of the role played by the sophists' objections against the naiveté of the pre-Socratics, see Majolino 2017. By focusing on DIB, our account of the "Husserlian" history of philosophy in general (modern philosophy in particular), therefore of Kant's "role" therein, substantially diverges from Kern 1964, pp. 304–320.

ing, the second has a much more "gnoseological" nature and the opposition is that between *identity* and *subjective manner of givenness:* now, if Husserl seems to go without any solution of continuity from the one to the other, his line of thought is directly based upon the Platonic text.

In a nutshell, "the discovery of the idea" (α) marks a decisive turning point in the history of the ancient Greek origin of philosophy: in place of the interest in the "All" and the general problem of "being and becoming," DIB imposes itself as the central task of philosophy (β) according to the two varieties presented above, the ontological one and the gnoseological one (γ).[7] Perhaps it would be better to assert that with the discovery of the idea, and its determining function, the determination of the identity of being becomes possible for the first time.

---

[7] In between the original interest in *Werden und Sein im Werden* and the Platonic attempt at DIB stands Socrates and his return to self-evidence. As Husserl describes it, Socrates' problem is "the identity of the 'object'" as "intended" (*das Vermeinte*): "The Socratic return to self-evidence represents a reaction; and specifically this is making clear to oneself, by means of example, the fields of pure possibilities, the free variation which upholds the identity of meaning, identity of the object as substrate of determination, and makes it possible to discern this identity. Over against these alterations are others which break the identity" (Husserl 1962, Hua VI, p. 280; Husserl 1970, p. 302; Husserl 2012, Hua Mat. IX, pp. 22–27). Socrates, in Husserl's view, raises the problem of the object as an identical correlate of multiple determinations of thought; yet, his appeal to self-evidence will be realized by Plato, for "it [the Socratic questioning] forces a radical consideration of the conditions of possible truth and possible being; and it forces the recognition that not vague thinking and talking but only radical thinking, aimed at the ultimate showing of possible being [...] can help in assuring ourselves of truth and being" (Husserl 1962, Hua VI, p. 261; Husserl 1970, p. 303). Plato will be the one who recognizes the correlation between *genuine knowledge, genuine truth* and *being* in the strict sense of the term (Husserl 1956, Hua VII, p. 13). Were we to represent the sequence in question, we would distinguish the pre-Socratic determination of "being" in terms of "becoming," the Socratic need for a determination of the object as an identical "correlate" of multiple "meaning-intentions," and Plato's own attempt at DIB according to the *gnoseological* ("*knowledge-truth*-being") and the *ontological* ("knowledge-*truth-being*") variety.

        (I) The <u>Pre-Socratic</u> determination of *alle Dinge*
                      in terms of "becoming"

        (II) The <u>Socratic</u> problem of determining
       the identity of the object as an "intended" one

(III) The <u>Platonic</u> determination of the identity of being as a real being
                (III') Gnoseological Variety
                (III'') Ontological Variety

1.2. Among the many texts dedicated to Plato, the 1919–1920 Freiburg lectures *Einleitung in die Philosophie* (Husserl 2012, Hua Mat. IX) are those that, by far, present one of the most articulated and systematic assessments of Plato's thought and the greatest number of implicit and explicit citations from his texts: *Meno* (p. 299), *Symposium* (pp. 44, 197), *Republic* (60), *Philebus* (p. 123), *Phaedrus* (p. 197), *Phaedo* (pp. 65, 196–197), *Theaetetus* (pp. 30, 54, 67), and *Timaeus* (pp. 191, 196, 198) are often referred to.

Most importantly, these are the lectures where Husserl directly tackles Plato's account of DIB in light of the *Entdeckung der Idee:* the dialogue on which his interpretation builds being, as we will see, *Phaedo* (even though the text is never explicitly named in these pages).[8] Why *Phaedo* exactly? Because it is the dialogue where DIB emerges – as a problem – in terms of the relation between the well-known "two kinds of beings [δύο εἴδη τῶν ὄντων]" (*Phaedo*, 79a-b), one "visible" and another "invisible," and the "invisible" is always "the same as itself," while the visible "is never in the same state [καὶ τὸ μὲν ἀειδὲς ἀεὶ κατὰ ταὐτὰ ἔχον, τὸ δὲ ὁρατὸν μηδέποτεκατὰ ταὐτά]." Now, as Husserl remarks, "in contrast to the fixed being-in-itself of the world of ideas, the fundamental characteristic of the empirical world is motion, alteration, in general: becoming [*Werden*]" (Husserl 2012, Hua Mat. IX, p. 196). In perfect compliance with the two "varieties" distinguished above (γ), Plato does not only describe the δύο εἴδη τῶν ὄντων in terms of opposition between what always becomes, and is also subject to alter-ation (as both μεταβολή and ἀλλοίωσις) (78d), and what exists "by itself," but also as what can be grasped by sensibility and intellect respectively: "You can see these and touch them and perceive them by the other senses [αἰσθήσεσιν], whereas the things that are always the same can be grasped only by means of the intellect [διανοίας], and are invisible and not to be seen."

As Husserl describes the "empirical world": "Everything is contingent here, therefore it could be otherwise and could have been otherwise. It can assume infinitely many other shapes different from the ones, which it has factually come to display [*Alles ist hier zufällig, denn es kann auch anders sein, es konnte anders geworden sein, und in unendlich vielen anderen Gestalten kann es werden, als in welchen es faktisch werden wird*]." (Husserl 2012, Hua Mat. IX, pp. 196–197) This being observed, Husserl goes on to raise the decisive questions, those directly bearing on DIB: "Why, in general, is this world of becoming? Why does it become in this way rather than otherwise [*Warum ist überhaupt diese Werdenswelt*

---

[8] It is worth remarking that the pages we are going to comment on come immediately after a series of observations on Anaxagoras, Empedocles, and Heraclitus's famous motto *Alles Sein ist Werden:* "Becoming characterizes the essence of life. The world is then an infinite living process, a process of becoming" (Husserl 2012, Hua Mat. IX, p. 191).

und warum wird sie so und nicht anders]?" (Husserl 2012, Hua Mat. IX, p. 197) The answer, as could be easily guessed, consists in the doctrine of "participation" – which is recalled by Husserl according to the bottom up ("all empirical things partake in the idea and its truth") and the top down "direction" ("the ideas – no matter how in-itself they are – descend toward the empirical and inhabit it, though imperfectly"). Plato himself – to show how accurate Husserl's references are – speaks of things that, though imperfectly (ἐνδεῖ), aim at being like what "properly is" (τῶν ὄντων) (74d); of participation (μετέχει), as well as – *in umgekehrter Betrachtung* – of "presence" of the ideas (εἴτε παρουσια εἴτε κοινωνία) in the realm of unstable and ever-changing bodies (100d).

So far, so good. Here comes, then, the problem of synthesis and the Platonic configuration of the plexus *synthesis-identity*. In what, exactly, does the participation consist? Or, to speak in the manner of *Realitätswissenschaft und Idealisierung*, what is the ideas' own determining function all about? In what does it consist? Let us read Husserl's answer by paying careful attention to his language:

> Now, everything [*jedes Ding*] is constantly becoming. For the thing [*für das Ding*], to become means not to hold its predicates, to change them, to abandon predicates and assume new ones. Always new ideas descend toward the empirical and inhabit it. The world of ideas does not stay still or rigid, but puts itself in action and sets itself in motion. The ideas connect themselves [*Ideen verbinden sich*]: they correspond to the plurality of predicates with which a thing [*ein Ding*] comes into existence and which is newly generated as the thing becomes. They [= the ideas] separate [*sie trennen sich*] again in the process of decay. (Husserl 2012, Hua Mat. IX, p. 197)

In order to appreciate fully this excerpt, three observations are necessary.
– First of all, Husserl is clearly stepping beyond the boundaries of *Phaedo:* in fact, by speaking of "action" (*Aktion*) and "motion" (*Bewegung*) of the ideas, Husserl seems to have in mind the *Sophist*, where Plato's main concern is not the distinction/relation between the world of heavenly ideas and the world of earthly bodies, but the exclusive domain of the ideas and its "internal" dynamism (the *Sophist* being the dialogue where τὰ ὄντα in general are ascribed the power to act, δύναμις τοῦ [...] ποιεῖν (*Sophist*, 248c), and some sort of motion (κίνησις) characterizes also the ideas (248e-249e)).
– If we set aside this implicit reference to the *Sophist*, the excerpt is a clear description, not only of the "mechanism" of participation (according to its top down movement: "always new ideas descend toward the empirical"), but first and foremost of what it means for a thing (*ein Ding*) to "become." Preliminarily stated: for a thing "to become" (as a losing and acquiring "predicates") means that the ideas either *join up together* (*sich verbinden*) or *separate themselves* (*sich trennen*) in it; or, better, that a synthesis (*Verbindung*) and a sep-

aration (*Trennung*) of the ideas *in* a thing take place. Now, although it is not easy to tell what – in the Platonic dialogue – would correspond to such synthesis (unless we take it as referring to the *Sophist* again, and to the term συμπλοκή (240c)), Husserl here is addressing the heart of Plato's argument: the distinction between the δύο εἴδη τῶν ὄντων. Indeed, if the idea exists by itself, always remains the same as itself, and "never" in any way admits of any change, it is because of its being "uniform" (μονοειδές) (*Phaedo*, 78d) and uncompounded or, better yet, *a-synthetic* (ἀσύνθετα, as Plato also characterizes them (78c)); by contrast, if the domain of "bodies" is in constant "becoming," thereby subject to change, it is by virtue of its being multiform (πολυειδές) (80b) and compounded or, better yet, "synthetic" (Plato speaks of συντεθέντι, συνθέτῳ, σύνθετα (78c, 86a)). As Socrates himself puts it: "Now is not that which is synthetic and synthetically structured naturally liable to be divided (διαιρεθῆναι), in the same way in which it was synthetically composed (συνετέθη)? And if anything is a-synthetic (ἀσύνθετον) is not that, if anything, naturally unlikely to be divided?" (my trans.). Such is the Platonic configuration of the plexus *synthesis-identity* (hereafter S&I): that is, of what is *synthetic*, subject to alteration and "becoming" – and thereby never *identical* to itself; and what is *a-synthetic*, admits of no change whatsoever and never becomes – being thereby always *identical* to itself. If the *identity* excludes the *synthetic*, the *synthetic* holds no *identity* whatsoever.

– That this is exactly what Husserl has in mind is also proved by the presence of the term *Ding* and *Dinge*, which translate the Greek πρᾶγμα and πράγματα as they are used by Socrates toward the end of the dialogue in one of his replies to Cebes: "We said before that the opposite thing is generated from the opposite thing [ἐκ τοῦ ἐναντίου πράγματος τὸ ἐναντίον πρᾶγμα γίγνεσθαι], while now we assert that the opposite itself can never become its opposite [αὐτὸ τό ἐναντίον ἐατω ἐναντίον οὐκ ἄν ποτε γένοιτο]" (*Phaedo*, 103b). The distinction is between το πρᾶγμα, *das Ding* that is nothing else but a constant and never-ending becoming of opposites from opposites, and το αὐτὸ, the "identical" that never becomes – which is "the opposite itself" as an "idea."

Were we to represent these distinctions, the following diagram could be proposed:

Το Αὐτὸ	Τα Πράγματα
A-Synthetic	Synthetic
Uniform	Multiform
Always the Same as Itself	Never in the Same State
Indissoluble	Dissoluble

If the doctrine of ideas, with their determining function, was supposed to secure the determination of *the identity of being in becoming*, what the ideas end up securing is, by contrast, the *identity* of what *lies outside the flow of becoming:*[9] the ideas – always "identical" to themselves (το αὐτὸ) – "connect" (*sich verbinden*) "in" a thing (ἐν τῇ φύσει) (*Phaedo*, 103b) and thereby determine it as something that, being "synthetically" structured (συνετέθη), becomes and thus displays no identity whatsoever. Husserl acknowledges this expressly: "Only the ideal has a rigorous identity" (Husserl 1962, Hua VI, p. 292; Husserl 1970; p. 313; Husserl 2012, p. 53); the "real" (τὰ σώματα) turns out to be nothing but aggregates deprived of any identity of their own (Prauss 1966; Mann 2000).[10] In a nutshell, in order for DIB to be successfully addressed, S&I undergoes a disjunction: whatever is S has no identity whatsoever; and whatever, on the contrary, displays I is not synthetic.

1.3. Both the "necessity" and the "advantage" of this Platonic *detour* should be evident by now: as a systematic background, it will help us elucidate Kant's own position – not only with reference to the history of modern philosophy (as is usually done) – but primarily against the backdrop of an all-embracing problem (DIB) that harks back to the ancient Greek origin of philosophy. If, historically speaking, it has already been recognized that Kant's great merit is to have worked out the notion of "synthesis" from a transcendental perspective (Kaulbach 1967; Bärthlein 1976), our aim here is to assess Husserl's own understanding of the Kantian position vis-à-vis DIB. As already announced at the outset, although what follows will not be dealing with how Husserl intends to critically "take up" Kant's doctrine, we will nevertheless try to clarify to what extent the latter contributed to the development and, so to say, self-understanding of some phenomenological "themes."

2.1. Kant, Husserl asserts with conviction, is not simply a great philosopher: Kant is one of those that Husserl labels *Urheber*, "initiators" – these occupying, in the "history of philosophy," "a quite distinguished place": "They are the representatives of developments which have a unified meaning because of their work, be-

---

9 As Husserl remarks: "such essentialities are peculiar objectivities, for they constitute a domain of specific, and absolutely stable being to be grasped in absolute indubitability. It is a being that stands, in fixed identity, over against the entire flux of temporal existence;" "All ideas are fixed identities" (Husserl 2012, Hua Mat. IX, pp. 43 and 62).
10 An analysis of how these problems are developed by Aristotle is provided by Calogero 1927, notably Chapter I. To what extent these problems still affect a certain phenomenological tradition is what De Santis 2016 tries to argue for.

cause of the new universal objectives outlined in their developed theories" (Husserl 1962, Hua VI, p. 194; Husserl 1970, p. 191). Great philosophers continue to have their effects in all subsequent historical periods, whereas an "initiator" delivers a "motif" (*Motiv*) able to give unity to a historical sequence, that is to say, "a motif that works as a driving force and sets a task that must be fulfilled, such that its fulfillment brings to an end the historical period of development." As an *initiator*, Kant opens up a "new" line of development, which – this being Husserl's major claim – only phenomenology will eventually be able to bring to its final expression (*Endform*).[11]

Before we embark on the examination of the "new line" inaugurated by Kant, we should clarify in what the line of development "concluded" right before Kant consists! Now, in the history of modern philosophy outlined by Husserl, Kant appears immediately at the end of the "cycle" that runs from Descartes (through Locke and Berkeley) to Hume, and which is mainly characterized by a twofold "dialectics": the one between subjectivism and objectivism, and, within the former, between transcendentalism and naturalism (Husserl 1962, Hua VI, § 14). Even without going over the entire account and the position occupied by the individual protagonists in detail, and in order to understand in what sense this line is "concluded" before Kant, who opens up a new one, we could confine ourselves to raising the question of Hume's contribution – Hume who stands at the end of this "pre-Kantian" phase of modern philosophy. In light of the Cartesian return to the *ego cogito*, which inaugurates the history of modern philosophy, the main difference between the French thinker and Berkeley/Hume consists in this: while in the first the *ego cogito* stands in a "representative" relation to the "world" (Husserl speaks of *Weltbild*), in Berkeley and Hume it stands in such a relation to a "production" (*Erzeugung*) (Husserl 1962, Hua VI, p. 92; Husserl 1970, pp. 89–90).[12] With Berkeley, Husserl contends, only the "cor-

---

[11] Husserl's account of the history of modern philosophy from Descartes to Kant, as well as his notion of "conclusion" (*Abschluß*), should be compared with those provided by two important "heirs" of Giovanni Gentile's "formal idealism": Calogero 1938 and Bontadini 1966. The analogies and differences between the former's conception of *Abschluß* and *Endform* and the latter two's ideas of *conclusione* would be of great help in better understanding Husserl's own position vis-à-vis the history of modern philosophy, notably Kant's transcendental critique of reason.
[12] "No offense was taken if, in Descartes, immanent sensibility engendered pictures of the world; but in Berkeley this sensibility engendered the world of bodies itself; and in Hume the entire soul, with its 'impressions' and 'ideas', the forces belonging to it, conceived of by analogy to physical forces, its laws of association (as parallels to the law of gravity!), engendered the whole world, the world itself, not merely something like a picture – though, to be sure, this product was merely a fiction, a representation put together inwardly which was actually quite vague. And this is true of the world of the rational sciences as well as that of *experientia vaga*."

poreal things" are reduced "to aggregates of sense-data" (Husserl 1962, Hua VI, p. 89; Husserl 1970, pp. 86–87). With Hume, the reduction reaches its peak and, so to say, "conclusion" (*In diesen Richtungen geht Hume bis ans Ende*), so that *the problem of the determination of the identity of being* becomes apparent by showing all its dramatic force – indeed, not only "the *identity* of persisting bodies supposedly found in immediate, experiencing intuition," but also "the supposedly experienced *identity* of the person" (Husserl 1962, Hua VI, p. 89; Husserl 1970, p. 87) are "reduced" to being nothing but complexes of sense-data, and are thereby mere "fictions."

Three quick remarks are immediately necessary.

– In contrast to those interpretations asserting that Husserl tends to understand Kant as primarily concerned with saving the "objectivity" of the science of the natural world from Hume's "skeptical" attack (Ferrarin 2011, p. 406), our approach shows how Kant is reacting to Hume's dissolution of the *identity*, the problem of the "objectivity" of science being exclusively a "consequence" of DIB (Husserl 1962, Hua VI, p. 90; Husserl 1970, pp. 87–88), yet not at all Kant's major preoccupation.[13] Accordingly, Husserl takes what Kant refers to as *das Humesche Problem* as consisting of a two-sided problem: "the *identity* of the material world" and "the *identity* of the ego" (Husserl 1956, Hua VII, p. 174).[14]

---

[13] "All categories of objectivity – the scientific ones through which an objective, extra-psychic world is thought in scientific life, and the prescientific ones through which it is thought in everyday life – are fiction" (Husserl 1962, Hua VI, p. 89; Husserl 1970, p. 87).

[14] Now, to whomever argued that this does not correspond to Kant's account of *das Humesche Problem* at the beginning of the *Prolegomena*, the following could be objected. Though Kant focuses on one single problem, or better, "concept," i.e., "causality," as a "metaphysical" one (*Hume ging hauptsächlich von einem einzigen, aber wichtigen Begriffe der Metaphysik, nämlich dem der Verknüpfung der Ursache und Wirkung* (Kant 2011, vol. III, p. 115)), his main reproach goes directly against Hume's *general inability to think the notion of "synthesis"* (*Verknüpfung*), due to his not understanding the necessity of the "deduction" of such pure concepts, only upon whose basis our understanding can think *a priori* the synthesis of things: "So I first tried whether Hume's objection could not be put into a general form, and soon found that the concept of a synthesis of cause and effect was by no means the only concept by which the understanding thinks the synthesis of things [*Verknüpfung der Dinge*] *a priori*" (Kant 2011, vol. III, p. 119). In general, Husserl takes Hume's critique of "causality" to be just *one single case of his more general attempt at reducing "identity" to "fiction."* As Husserl writes: "Hume had shown that we naively read causality into this world and think that we grasp necessary succession in intuition. The same is true of everything that makes the body of the everyday surrounding world into an identical thing with identical properties, relations, etc." (Husserl 1962, Hua VI, p. 96; Husserl 1970, p. 93).

- The sense of such *being*, whose *identity* is progressively dissolved, needs to be traced back to the very *origin of the modern spirit* (Husserl 1962, Hua VI, p. 58; Husserl 1970, p. 57) and the "scientific" model which brings about a radical "transformation of the idea of the world" (Husserl 1962, Hua VI, p. 61; Husserl 1970, p. 60): "here the exemplary role of physics' conception of nature, and of the scientific method, has the understandable effect [...] that a mode of being is ascribed to the soul which is similar in principle to that of nature." The first and most immediate consequence of it – the one that triggers, so to speak, the process of dissolution that Hume will bring to a conclusion – is Descartes's substance dualism (Husserl 1962, Hua VI, pp. 81, 217–222; Husserl 1970, p. 213). In a nutshell: the *being* whose *identity* is "consumed" within the development of the early phase of modern philosophy is the one construed based on the Cartesian dualism of *res cogitans* and *res extensa* (Husserl 1956, Hua VII, p. 158): "The soul is something self-contained and real by itself, as is a body; in naive naturalism the soul is now taken to be like an isolated space, like a writing tablet, in his famous simile, on which psychic data come and go" (Husserl 1962, Hua VI, p. 87; Husserl 1970, p. 84).[15]
- The analogy between Plato's position, as outlined in the first part of this text, and Kant's should be apparent by now: as Plato "responds" to the pre-Socratic comprehension of the totality of being in terms of "all-encompassing becoming," Kant "reacts" to the modern dissolution of the identity of being to mere aggregates of "sense-data." If Plato, with the determination

---

15 A second "consequence" of the scientific paradigm must be briefly mentioned: the so-called *Sensualismus*, i.e., the conviction according to which "the sole indubitable ground of all knowledge" is the immanent domain of sense-data (Husserl 1962, Hua VI, p. 89; Husserl 1970, p. 86). Now, were we to present the full development of the pre-Kantian history of modern philosophy, we would distinguish "three" steps. According to Husserl: (i) the Cartesian *res* is first declared unknowable by Locke based upon his *Sensualismus* (it is his famous *Je ne sais quoi* (Husserl 1962, Hua VI, § 22)); (ii) then, and in perfect compliance with the *Sensualismus*-thesis, the entire "material" world will be reduced to a complex of sense-data by Berkeley; (iii) finally, Hume will radicalize the process through his dissolution of the identity of the "ego."

Descartes's substance dualism – Naturalistic paradigm

(i) Locke's *Datensensualismus:* "Je ne sais quoi"
↓
(ii) Berkeley's *Sensualismus:* reduction of the identity of the corporeal world to sense-data
↓
(iii) Hume's *fictionalism:* reduction of all "identity" to mere fiction

of the identity of being and his own configuration of S&I, opens up a new "line of development" in the history of ancient philosophy, so does Kant after the Humean *conclusion* of the early phase of the history of modern philosophy. Plato and Kant are two *initiators*, not just "great philosophers."

We are now in a position to answer the question of what the "line of development" "concluded" before Kant actually consists in. It consists in the progressive consummation or self-dissolution of the identity of being – first of the domain of the corporeal world, then of the ego as well. If in Plato the reduction of τὰ σώματα to only synthetic aggregates with no identity of their own was the consequence of his approach to S&I, in Kant it is the starting point (*das Hume'sche Problem*) for re-thinking DIB through a new configuration of S&I.

2.2. With no hesitation, Husserl characterizes the Kantian doctrine of "synthesis" as a "profound" one (*tiefsinnige Lehre von der Synthesis*) which "basically already discovered the specificity of the intentional connections [*die Eigenart intentionaler Zusammenhänge*]" (Husserl 1956, Hua VII, p. 237). Now, no matter how vague such a bald assertion on the part of Husserl might sound, its implications are of such a nature that, as we will see, some basic assumptions about the notion of intentionality have to be re-thought. However, on a closer look it is apparent that Husserl is not maintaining that Kant already discovered the notion of intentionality itself: rather, he is suggesting that, with his *profound doctrine of synthesis*, Kant discovered the *specificity*, i.e., what is peculiar to the idea of "intentional connections." If such a "claim" does not necessarily imply the quite different thesis that Kant was aware of what he had *de facto* discovered (it does not rule it out either), it implies (as something involved in the very idea of a "discovery") that before Kant the *specificity* in question had not yet been discovered. If we understand Husserl correctly, he is maintaining that the pre-Kantian phase of modern philosophy had no clue about the *specificity* of the "intentional connections."

Accordingly, this preliminary Husserlian remark gives us the chance to distinguish three possible scenarios (actually there is also a fourth option, which will be mentioned later on):

(A) <u>First Scenario</u>: The specificity of the "intentional connections" has been discovered, but not the intentionality itself;

(B) <u>Second Scenario</u>: Neither the specificity nor the intentionality have been discovered;

(C) <u>Third Scenario</u>: The intentionality has been discovered, but not the specificity of the intentional connections.

As for (A), Kant falls under it: as we have started to see, the great merit of Kant's doctrine of synthesis consists in its discovery of the *specificity of the intentional connections*; yet, Husserl never maintains that Kant also discovered the idea of "intentionality" as a universal feature of consciousness. When it comes to (B), the perfect example is Descartes: "To be sure, there is no question of a true presentation and treatment of the theme of 'intentionality' [in Descartes]" (also Husserl 1974, Hua XVII, § 97) – and yet, as he goes on to say, Descartes inaugurates the modern "theory of knowledge" (*Erkenntnistheorie*), understood as an effort to "metaphysically" transcend the ego (*das ego metaphysisch transzendierende Erkenntnis*) (Husserl 1962, Hua VI, p. 85; Husserl 1970, p. 83). This should not come as a surprise: since Descartes did not discover the specificity of the intentional connections, nor does he know the notion of *intentionality*, the issue of knowledge necessarily arises as that of bridging the gap between two separate substances.[16] As for (C), the example is without a doubt Brentano; now, when it comes to his master, Husserl's language switches from the terminology of "discovery" (Husserl 1973, Hua I, p. 79; Husserl 1993, p. 41; Husserl 1974, Hua XVII, p. 268; Husserl 1969, p. 261) to that of a less emphatic *Geltendmachung* (the latter meaning the "claim" or "assertion" of a certain right) (Husserl 1974, Hua XVII, p. 218; Husserl 1969, p. 210). This might be due to two different – yet tightly connected – reasons. On the one hand, it might derive from Brentano *de facto* never using the noun *Intentionalität* itself, but merely a series of variations on the adjective *intentional*, i.e., intentional object, intentional content, relation, and existence (see De Santis 2012). In this sense, if Brentano, as Husserl would say, never "discovered" the *Intentionalität*, he nevertheless laid claim to the right (*Geltendmachung*) of the "intentional object" and its "ontological" status (Husserl 1962a, Hua IX, p. 354). On the other hand – as suggested by a manuscript on *Die Bedeutung der Synthese für die Intentionalität* (Husserl 1962a, Hua IX, pp. 420–427) – by not recognizing the *synthesis* (this being Husserl's main argument against his former master), Brentano is unable to make sense of the *identity* of an *intentional object*, i.e., of an object as *intended* by "consciousness" as always *identical* to itself.[17]

---

16 In Husserl 1974, Hua XVII, § 86, the *Blindheit für Intentionalität* affects the entire *Sensualismus* of modern philosophy.
17 "I see the syntheses between consciousness and consciousness, syntheses of identification, etc. I see the object in its mode of appearance and the modes of appearance as modes of consciousness in a specific sense, i.e., in such a way that each one of them includes its reference to the object [*ihr 'von' hat*] thanks to the essential possibility of the syntheses themselves. Are we not always amid syntheses between consciousness and consciousness, the latter understood as identification-syntheses or as syntheses of the continuous unity of consciousness? Otherwise,

This brings us back to Kant: for, although Kant did not actually "discover" the *Intentionalität*, by discovering the synthesis he has *de facto* also discovered what makes "intentionality" possible. As Husserl explicitly points out in the *Cartesian Meditations:* "Only the elucidation of the peculiarity [*Eigenheit*] of the synthesis makes fruitful the exhibition of the *cogito*, of the intentional experience, as a consciousness of" (Husserl 1973, Hua I, p. 79; Husserl 1993, p. 41). Differently stated: without Kant's "profound doctrine," the Brentanian notion of "intentional object" or "relation" remains completely useless. That without *synthesis* there is no *intentionality* is a thesis that Husserl has always upheld, in both the "static" and the "genetic" framework. If in the lectures on *Passive Syntheses*, Husserl remarks that it is only by virtue of "passively emerging syntheses" that a *Vorstellung* acquires a new character, "the character of the specific 'intention'" (Husserl 1966, Hua XI, p. 76; Husserl 2001b, p. 118), the *Ideen I* (§ 86) already explain that what we call "consciousness of..." emerges (*Bewußtsein von etwas so zustande bringen*) only at the level of the so-called "functional problems," where *das Stoffliche* is animated and combined into a series of syntheses (*das Stoffliche beseelend und sich zu mannigfaltig-einheitlichen Kontinuen und Synthesen verflechtend*) (Husserl 1976, Hua III/1, p. 196; Husserl 2014, p. 169). If this is the case, then it is no surprise that as early as the 1902–1903 lectures, Husserl dedicates a great deal of energy toward working out a first system of syntheses of consciousness and in re-interpreting Brentano's famous principle ("Every psychical act is either a representation or is based on a representation") in terms of "syntheses," namely, different levels of "identification-synthesis" (Husserl 2001a, Hua Mat. VIII, p. 124). We have just touched upon the crucial point, the one whose importance and significance will bring us, once again, back to Kant's profound doctrine and to our main problem: S&I. For Husserl is clear: the basic form of synthesis (*die Grundform der Synthesis*) – the one without which there would be no intentionality – is that of *identification* (Husserl 1973, Hua I, p. 79; Husserl 1993, p. 41; see Pradelle 2012, pp. 277–285; Rizo-Patrón de Lerner 2012, p. 227).

Before we move on, let us sum up what has been argued thus far.

- Kant's profound doctrine of synthesis expresses the specificity of the intentional connections, i.e., that without which (as Husserl urges repeatedly in his texts and lectures)) "intentionality" cannot even emerge as such: "If one intends to understand what consciousness does […], it is not enough, here or anywhere else, to speak of the 'directness' of consciousness. […]

---

how can the talk of intentional object be justified? What is it that drives Brentano?" See also De Santis 2018.

One has to trace [the multiplicities of consciousness] back to their *synthetic transitions*" (Husserl 1974, Hua XVII, p. 172; Husserl 1969, pp. 163–164).
- Brentano, unlike Kant, has discovered the notion of "intentional object" but has no clue about the specificity of the intentional connections – this, Husserl continues, is the reason why, in a certain sense, he has not really discovered the *Intentionalität*.[18]
- And this is the case – as Husserl would go on to add – because the most "fundamental form" of synthesis (which Brentano altogether lacks) is the so-called "identification-synthesis."

This being said, we should try to understand what Kant's *profound doctrine of synthesis*, and therefore his discovery of the specificity of the intentional connections, consists in as a "response" to the dissolution of the identity of being brought to a radical conclusion by Hume.

Husserl's description, if not definition, of Kant's "synthesis" is, we would maintain, quite straightforward: Kant introduces (*führt... ein*) the term "synthesis" to mean the operation (*Leistung*), accomplished in the subject, consisting in the "unification" of a multiplicity of representations into a unitary and interconnected experience of an identical external object.[19] Now, it is not clear why, as argued by Kern, the synthesis that Husserl has here in mind is, or should be, only the *synthesis speciosa* or *figürliche Synthesis* (Kern 1964, p. 247).

Two arguments seem to speak against such thesis. First, Husserl's account not only complies with Kant's general presentation of the synthesis in the B-deduction (*Verbindung ist die Vorstellung der synthetischen Einheit des Mannigfaltigen* (Kant 1996, p. 176, B 130–131)), but it seems to be almost an "indirect" citation from what Kant says at the very beginning of the section *Von den reinen Verstandesbegriffen oder Kategorien:* "By *synthesis*, in the most general sense of the term, I mean the act of putting together various representations and apprehending their manifold in one cognition [*Ich verstehe aber unter Synthesis in der allgemeinesten Bedeutung die Handlung, verschiedene Vostellungen zu einander hinzuzutun, und ihre Mannigfaltigkeit in einer Erkenntnis zu begreifen*]" (Kant 1996, p. 130, A 77/B 103). In addition to this, it must be emphasized that

---

18 See, for example, the way in which Husserl presents Brentano's problem in Husserl 1956, Hua VII, p. 106; Husserl 1966, Hua XI, pp. 236–237; Husserl 2001b, pp. 368–370.

19 "Kant introduces the term 'synthesis' that is so peculiar to him. In so doing, he refers to the operation (*Leistung*) of apperceptive unification that accomplishes itself in the subject, and by means of which the conscious manifold of representations acquires the meaning of a unitary and co-belonging experience of precisely one and the same external object" (Husserl 1956, Hua VII, p. 397).

Husserl speaks of "experience" – which in Kant is the "result" of the activity of the understanding upon our perceptions (Barale 1988, pp. 62–66).[20] This excludes, *contra* Kern's opinion, the limitation to the synthesis of imagination: Husserl's account is broad enough, we believe, to be held as a general description of the meaning of the "synthesis" as such – hence, as embracing the totality of its *Leistungen*.

What is striking, though, about Husserl's account in relation to Kant's own words is the way in which he presents the "outcome" of the synthesis: *the identity of the object* ("*zur Einheit eines identischen äußeren Objekts*"). We stand at the threshold of Kant's assessment of DIB. If in Plato the *synthetic* had no *identity* of its own and determined itself in opposition to it, and in the pre-Kantian phase of modern philosophy *identity* ended up being dissolved in the immanence of the *Sensualismus*, in Kant we are confronted with a new configuration of the plexus S&I: *identity* as a result of *synthesis*.

As we will immediately strive to show, this can "contribute" to explaining – if not completely explain – why Husserl was particularly fond of the A-edition of the Transcendental Deduction.

2.3. To put it as bluntly as possible: the general problem which Kant presents at the outset of what in the B-edition is § 13 ("Of the Principles of a Transcendental Deduction As Such"), and which consists in the question as to the concepts' reference to objects *a priori* (*wie sich Begriffe a priori auf Gegenstände beziehen können*) (Kant 1996, pp. 142–143, A 86/B 118), is tackled in two different ways, depending on which edition we consider. In the second edition, Kant's major preoccupation is to present a more objective deduction and the stage is dominated by the emphasis on what gives *sense and meaning* (*objektive Gültigkeit*) to the categories (Kant 1996, pp. 189–190, B 149); the A-edition (with its distinction between "synthesis of apprehension," "synthesis of reproduction," and "synthesis of recognition") places emphasis upon the *identity of the object* being the "result" of the interplay of our faculties. The terminology of both the *Selbst* and the *identisch* is crucial here and characterizes all the main steps of the argument (we are referring to the section before the *Schematism*, which remains unaltered): Kant's chief burden amounts here to bringing to the fore the way in which the different faculties, and their synthesis, contribute to its determination. This, we

---

[20] "Experience is comprehended perception. We understand it [*Wir verstehen sie aber*], however, as we represent it under the guide of the understanding [*des Verstandes*]. Experience is the specification of the concepts of the understanding *via* given appearances."

believe, is what makes the text, in this context and in this specific respect, particularly interesting to Husserl.

Without getting into a detailed commentary on the entire text of the deduction (which is a task that would take us far beyond the limited scope of this text), let us confine ourselves to recalling a series of passages exemplifying what was just argued: the first text worthy of a brief analysis is the one on the "synthesis of reproduction." After pointing out that all our "representations" cannot but arise as "modifications" of our *Gemüt*, in such a way that the "manifold" of our representations becomes a "unity" by means of the synthesis of apprehension (Kant 1996, p. 153, A 99), Kant moves on to the contribution of the faculty of "imagination," and the "transcendental affinity" it brings about (for a general introduction to the theme, see Ferrarin 2009). Kant's examples here are crucial and quite telling; as he explains, the empirical law of reproduction presupposes that the appearances themselves are actually subject to such a rule (*einer solchen Regel unterwerfen sind*) – otherwise our imagination, understood as an "empirical" faculty, would never get to do anything conforming to its own ability.

> Suppose that cinnabar were now red, then black, now light, then heavy; or that a human being were changed now into this and then into that animal shape; or that on the longest day of the year the land were covered now with fruit, then with ice and snow. In the case my empirical imagination could not even get the opportunity, when presenting red color, to come to think of a heavy cinnabar. Nor could an empirical synthesis of reproduction take place if a certain word were assigned now to this and then to that thing; or if the same thing (*dasselbe Ding*) were called now by this and then by another name, without any of this being governed by a certain rule to which appearances by themselves are already subject. (Kant 1996, pp. 153–154, A 100–101)

The examples are meant to illustrate what would happen if the empirical law of reproduction were not grounded in the *Leistung* of the synthesis of imagination. Yet, upon a closer investigation, the state of affairs is not that easy; for, by speaking of "a certain rule" Kant is *de facto* already hinting at the contribution of the "synthesis of recognition,"[21] which recognizes "the identity or affinity between

---

[21] Here is a crucial excerpt: "the unity that the object makes necessary can be nothing other than the formal unity of consciousness in the synthesis of the manifold of the representations. When we have brought about synthetic unity in the manifold of intuition – this is when we say that we recognize the object. This unity is impossible, however, unless the intuition can be produced according to a rule through a function of synthesis, namely, a function of synthesis that makes the reproduction of the manifold necessary *a priori* and makes possible a concept in which this manifold is united. […] Now this *unity of the rule* determines all that is manifold, and limits it to conditions that make possible the unity of apperception" (Kant 1996, p. 157, A 105).

present and past intuitions in the unity of a concept" (Ferrarin 1995, p. 68). As far as we understand Kant's line of thought, here quite dense as usual, the point he is making can be so presented: if there were no concept capable, as a "rule," of recognizing and thus unifying a series of present and past intuitions, such a series (in terms of affinity brought about by the synthesis of imagination) would present itself solely as a combination without any identity of its own.²² Kant is elaborating on the contribution of the synthesis of imagination by already having in view its relation to the synthesis of recognition. To reverse the order of Kant's argument: were things to hold no stable identity of their own (as recognized in the unity of a concept), and hence randomly change, the empirical faculty of imagination would be unable to think of a "heavy cinnabar," which is also "red," as one and the same thing with the same properties. As Kant writes again at the outset of Section III while describing the outcome of the deduction: "*Sense* presents the appearances empirically in *perception*; *imagination* does so in association (and in reproduction); *apperception* does so in the *empirical consciousness* of the identity of these reproductive representations through which they were given, and hence in recognition" (Kant 1996, p. 164, A 115). The text sheds a retrospective light on each of the three layers individually: the *Identität* (better: the "consciousness of identity"), eventually determined by the apperception, rests on the appearances being given to perception and associated by imagination. In terms of the three syntheses: "all of perception is based *a priori* on pure intuition [...]; association is consciousness based *a priori* on the pure synthesis of imagination; and empirical consciousness is based *a priori* upon pure

---

22 See the beautiful and very insightful analyses developed by Summa 2015, who, if we understand her correctly, relates this Kantian excerpt to the expression *regelloser Haufen von Vorstellungen* (Kant 1996, p. 168, A 121) – the latter standing for the possible "chaos" that would arise in case the synthesis of imagination did not take place. If this is the case, then a question will arise as to the "cogency" of Kant's examples: for, the case of the "cinnabar," which is now "red" and then "black," or that of a "human being," which is now changed into this and then into that animal shape, do not suggest a *Haufen von Vorstellungen* understood as a form of "chaos." Quite the contrary: in order for us to speak of something – be it *a* piece of cinnabar or *a* human being that would randomly change – a minimal and recognizable "identity" must already be present. Otherwise, it would be impossible to even "speak" of *a* human being or of *some* cinnabar unlawfully changing. One of two things: either Kant's examples are unfitting, or the term "chaos" should be replaced by a different notion because it is not what Kant intends to suggest. As far as we understand Kant, the *regelloser Haufen von Vorstellungen* is to be understood as Kant's way of presenting *the Humean dissolution of the identity of being*, and its reduction of a series of immanent "sense-data." In fact, if Hume were right and the identity of being were only a "combination" of subjective impressions, then it would be impossible to speak of an object "regularly" changing while maintaining its identity: every "new" identity simply boiling down to a new combination of subjective impressions.

apperception, i.e., on the thoroughgoing identity of oneself in all possible representations" (Kant 1996, pp. 164–165, A 115–116).

This last excerpt introduces a new and crucial element; as one could easily frame it: the ultimate goal of the transcendental deduction is to secure or to explain, through its transcendental conditions, the *identity* of the object as the correlate of "self-consciousness" as *das stehende und bleibende Ich* (Kant 1996, pp. 169–170, A 123): "For in this constant and enduring I [...] consists the correlate [*das Correlatum*] of all our representations insofar as becoming conscious of them is so much as possible." As Kant does not fail to recognize explicitly, "nothing can enter cognition without doing so by means of this original apperception. This identity must, then, necessarily enter into the synthesis of everything manifold in appearances" (Kant 1996, pp. 162–163, A 113). The "identity" of the object as the correlate of *das stehende und bleibende Ich* (consciousness of identity) is the final outcome of the transcendental deduction (that is to say, of the application of the categories of understanding to the givennesses of sensibility), to which each of the three syntheses contributes in its own way (see the extensive analyses by Hoppe 1983, pp. 176–194). If it is the case, then, that the major achievement of the A-edition of the transcendental deduction can be described as the "determination" of the "identity" of being, now construed as an objectual correlate of the "identity" of self-consciousness (*das stehende und bleibende Ich*),²³ then a conclusion must be drawn that we were right in contending that Husserl's understanding of Kant's *Humesches Problem* consists in the first place in the "dissolution" of the "identity" of being brought to a radical conclusion by Hume himself (see above, section **2.1**).

That this is the way Husserl has almost always approached Kant's problem, notably the A-edition of the deduction, is shown by two very different texts that are at least ten years apart. In a 1908 manuscript on Kant (*Zur Auseinanderset-*

---

23 In *Erste Philosophie*, Husserl himself refers to such Kantian expression in his account of the synthetic constitution of the identity of the object: "Moreover, in relation with this one must see that the conscious identity of an object, which precisely justifies talk of *one object*, refers back to a synthesis in which several [states of] consciousness—for example, distinct and multifarious perceptions—are connected into a consciousness of one and the same object, where this 'one and the same' is itself consciously co-present, is itself intentional. And in turn one has to see that, parallel with the type of continuously governing synthesis that makes conscious, as objects for the ego, the unity and identity of this or that, and thus *of objects in general*, conversely, the ego itself is the index of a *universal* synthesis, by means of which all of this infinitely diverse consciousness, the consciousness that is mine, has a universal unity—not the objectual, but the *egological* unity. Alternatively, it must be seen that through this type of synthesis, the 'fixed and abiding ego' of this conscious life is constantly constituted and made conscious (our italics)" (Husserl 1956, Hua VII, p. 109).

zung meiner transzendentalen Phänomenologie mit Kants Tranzendentalphilosophie, Husserl 1956, Hua VII, pp. 381–395) as well as in the famous lectures on *Passive Synthesis*, Husserl discusses the A-edition of the transcendental deduction and tackles the problem of *identification* (Husserl 1956, Hua VII, p. 389) and that of the constitution of immanent and transcendent *identity-unities* (Husserl 1966, Hua XI, pp. 125–127; Husserl 2001b, pp. 170–172): the critical point being that Kant "has sketched out an initial system of transcendental syntheses in the transcendental deduction of the first edition of the *Critique*" (Husserl 1966, Hua XI, p. 125; Husserl 2001b, p. 170) in relation to the higher level of constitution, yet he never comes to address the constitution of the so-called immanent identities (Husserl 1966, Hua XI, p. 127; Husserl 2001b, p. 172). We should not forget, in fact, that in the passage on Kant's synthesis quoted above, Husserl describes its result as the "*Einheit eines identischen* äußeren *Objekts*" – the unity of an identical *external* object.

3. We have finally reached the end of our analysis; it is time to sum up its main upshots. In a few words, our goal can be so described: to explain the way in which Husserl understands Kant and his "position" in the history of philosophy, notably the history of modern philosophy. In order to do so, what we preliminarily needed was a specific "problem," which – as a sort of "filter" – could help us better and more directly comprehend Husserl's assessment: such a "problem" being what we have dubbed *the determination of the identity of being* (DIB) that dates back to one of the very origins of Greek philosophy, namely Plato. This gave us the chance of looking at Kant from the perspective of an all-embracing theme, thus of understanding his specific position vis-à-vis DIB in opposition to Plato's. As we believe, any attempt at comparing Kant and Husserl – the former's transcendental critique of reason and the latter's transcendental phenomenology – is bound to one-sidedness[24] until we clearly identify the *historical problem* (i.e., in terms of the history of philosophy) that, according to Husserl, Kant is dealing with. As we have tried to show, such a problem is – *in the more general terms of the history of philosophy* – the problem of the "determination of the identity of being" (as inaugurated by Plato) and – *in terms of the history of modern philosophy* – that of the dissolution of the identity of being brought to a "conclusion" by Hume (Kant's famous *Humesches Problem*).

---

24 "Quoi qu'il en soit de ces divergences d'interprétation, entre les deux pôles extrêmes, entre l'opposition radicale et l'identification pure et simple des intentions respectives de la phénoménologie husserlienne et de la critique kantienne, il y a place pour autant de conceptions nuancées différentes, mais toutes en définitive impliquent une certaine préconception soit de la philosophie de Kant, soit de la pensée de Husserl" (Kelkel 1966, p. 155).

It is a double "framework," so to speak, which turns out to be decisive when it comes to answering the very thorny question of Kant's contribution to the history of philosophy. As we have tried to argue, this contribution is "two-sided," depending on whether we look at it *from the standpoint of Kant's problem* or *from Husserl's retrospective standpoint*. In the former case, Kant's contribution is the introduction of the transcendental idea of synthesis, thereby the approach to the determination of the identity of being as a "result" of such a system of synthesis; from the latter standpoint, Kant's contribution amounts to the discovery of the *specificity of the intentional connections*, that is, the synthesis as what makes intentionality (in its most basic form: the "synthesis of identification") possible. As a consequence, and no matter how unusual this might sound, Husserl can claim that by not recognizing the "synthesis" as expressing the specific *specificity of the intentional connections*, Brentano cannot really be said to have "discovered" the "intentionality," though he has laid claim to the idea of "intentional object" and the issue of its ontological status.[25]

Accordingly, a fourth scenario in addition to the three already presented (**2.2**) can be described as the scenario in which – the *specificity of the intentional connections* having been discovered, and thus combined with the Brentanian "ontological" concern of the "intentional object" – the notion of "intentional synthesis" (*echte intentionale Synthesis*) becomes the dominant one and thus opens up a brand new field of investigation. It is the date of birth of phenomenology:

> What is new in the *Logical Investigations* is found not at all in the merely ontological investigations that had a one-sided influence contrary to the innermost sense of the work, but rather in the subjectively directed investigations [...]. The genuine intentional synthesis is discovered in the synthesis of several acts into one act, such that, in a unique manner of binding one meaning to another, there emerges not merely a whole, an amalgam whose parts are meanings, but rather a single meaning in which these meanings themselves are contained, but in a meaningful way. With this the problems of correlation, too, already announce themselves; and thus, in fact, this work contains the first, though of course very imperfect, beginnings of "phenomenology". (Husserl 1962, Hua VI, p. 237; Husserl 1970, p. 234)

What remains to be decided (this being the topic of future investigations, for which this paper is intended only to pave the way) is whether the "proliferation"

---

25 Husserl 1962, Hua VI, p. 237; Husserl 1970, p. 234, asserts that Brentano and *seine ganze Schule* can be said to have developed a "psychology of intentionality" only "formally" (*formell*). For a comprehensive and insightful study of the current state of the debate on "intentionality," see Majolino 2016.

of the notion of "synthesis" in Husserl's phenomenology merely represents the "final form" of the one inaugurated by Kant, or whether it also opens up a new line of development.

Bibliography

Barale, Massimo (1988): *Kant e il metodo della filosofia*. Pisa: ETS.
Bärthlein, Karl (1976): "Von der 'Transzendentalphilosophie der Alten' zu der Kants". In: *Archiv für Geschichte der Philosophie*, Volume 58, pp. 353–392.
Bontadini, Gustavo (1966): *Studi di filosofia moderna*. Brescia: La Scuola.
Calogero, Guido (1927): *I fondamenti della logica aristotelica*. Firenze: Le Monnier.
Calogero, Guido (1938): *La conclusione della filosofia del conoscere*. Firenze: Le Monnier.
De Santis, Daniele (2012): "Appunti sul problema dell'"intenzionalità' in Roman Ingarden ed Edmund Husserl". In: *Syzethesis. Rivista di filosofia on-line*.
De Santis, Daniele (2016): "Jean Hering on *Eidos, Gegenstand* and *Methexis*. Phenomenological Adventures and Misadventures of 'Participation'". In: *Discipline filosofiche*, Volume XXV-1, pp. 145–170.
De Santis, Daniele (2018): "'Metaphysische Ergebnisse': Phenomenology and Metaphysics in Edmund Husserl' *Cartesianische Meditationen*. Attempt at Commentary". In: *Husserl Studies*, Volume 34, Issue 1, pp. 63–83.
Ferrarin, Alfredo (1995): "Kant's Productive Imagination and its Alleged Antecedents". In: *Graduate Faculty Philosophy Journal*, Volume 18, pp. 65–92.
Ferrarin, Alfredo (2009): "Kant and Imagination". In: *Fenomenologia e società*, Volume XXXII, pp. 7–18.
Ferrarin, Alfredo (2011): "Come è possibile comprendere i giudizi sintetici *a priori*". In: L. Amoroso, C. La Rocca, A. Ferrarin (Eds.): *Critica della ragione e fenomenologia dell'esperienza*. Pisa: ETS, pp. 395–414.
Hoppe, Hansgeorg (1983): *Synthesis bei Kant. Das Problem der Verbindung von Vorstellungen und ihrer Gegenstandsbeziehung in der "Kritik der reinen Vernunft"*. Berlin: Walter de Gruyter.
Husserl, Edmund (1956): *Erste Philosophie (1923–1924). Erster Teil. Kritische Ideengeschichte*. Husserliana, vol. VII. Ed. Rudolf Boehm. The Hague: Martinus Nijhoff.
Husserl, Edmund (1962): *Die Krisis der europäischen Wissenschaften und die transzendentale Phänomenologie*. Husserliana, vol. VI. Ed. Walter Biemel. The Hague: Martinus Nijhoff.
Husserl, Edmund (1962a): *Phänomenologische Psychologie*. Husserliana, vol. IX. Ed. Walter Biemel. The Hague: Martinus Nijhoff.
Husserl, Edmund (1966): *Analysen zur passiven Synthesis*. Husserliana, vol. XI. Ed. Margot Fleischer. The Hague: Martinus Nijhoff.
Husserl, Edmund (1969): *Formal and Transcendental Logic*. Trans. Dorion Cairns. The Hague: Martinus Nijhoff.
Husserl, Edmund (1970): *The Crisis of European Sciences and Transcendental Phenomenology*. Trans. David Carr. Evanston: Northwestern University Press.
Husserl, Edmund (1973): *Cartesianische Meditationen*. Husserliana, vol. I. Ed. Stephan Strasser. The Hague: Martinus Nijhoff.

Husserl, Edmund (1974): *Formale und transzendentale Logik. Husserliana*, vol. XVII. Ed. Paul Janssen. The Hague: Martinus Nijhoff.
Husserl, Edmund (1976): *Ideen zu einer reinen Phänomenologie und phänomenologichen Philosophie. Erstes Buch. Husserliana*, vol. III/1. Ed. Karl Schuhmann. The Hague: Martinus Nijhoff.
Husserl, Edmund (1987): "Phänomenologie und Erkenntnistheorie (1917)". In: *Husserliana*, vol. XXV. Ed. Thomas Nenon and Hans Rainer Sepp. Dordrecht, Boston, Lancaster: Kluwer Academic Publishers, pp. 125–206.
Husserl, Edmund (1993): *Cartesian Meditations*. The Hague: Kluwer Academic Publishers.
Husserl, Edmund (2001a): *Allgemeine Erkenntnistheorie. Vorlesung (1902–1903). Husserliana Materialien*, vol. III. Ed. Elisabeth Schuhmann. Dordrect, Boston, London: Springer.
Husserl, Edmund (2001b): *Analyses Concerning Active and Passive Syntheses*. Trans. Anthony J. Steinbock. Dordrecht, Boston, London: Kluwer Academic Publishers.
Husserl, Edmund (2008): *Die Lebenswelt. Auslegung der vorgegebenen Welt und ihre Konstitution. Texte aus dem Nachlass (1916–1937). Husserliana*, vol. XXXIX. Ed. Rochus Sowa. Dordrecht, Boston, London: Springer.
Husserl, Edmund (2012): *Einleitung in die Philosophie. Vorlesungen (1916–20). Husserliana Materialien*, vol. IX. Ed. Hanne Jacobs. Dordrecht, Boston, London: Springer.
Husserl, Edmund (2014): *Ideas I*. Trans. Daniel O. Dahlstrom. Indianapolis: Hackett.
Kant, Immanuel (1996): *Critique of Pure Reason*. Trans Werner S. Pluhar. Indianapolis: Hackett.
Kant, Immanuel (2011): *Werke in sechs Bänden*. Darmstadt: WBG.
Kaulbach, Friedrich (1967): "Die Entwicklung des Synthesis-Gedankens bei Kant". In: *Studien zu Kants Philosophischer Entwicklung*. Hildesheim: Georg Olms, pp. 56–92.
Kelkel, Arion (1966): "Husserl et Kant: Réflexions à propos d'une thèse récente". In: *Revue de métaphysique et de morale*, pp. 154–198.
Kern, Iso (1964): *Husserl und Kant. Eine Untersuchung über Husserls Verhältnis zu Kant und zum Neukantianismus*. The Hague: Martinus Nijhoff.
Majolino, Claudio (2016): "Intentionnalités, ontologies: quel Aristote en héritage ? Esquisse d'une cartographie militaire". In: *Revue philosophique de Louvain*, vol. 114, pp. 485–546.
Majolino, Claudio (2017): "The Infinite Academy: Husserl on how to be a Platonist with some (Aristotelian?) Help". In: D. De Santis, E. Trizio (Eds.): *Edmund Husserl between Platonism and Aristotelianism. The New Yearbook for Phenomenology and Phenomenological Research*, XV, pp. 164–221.
Mann, Wolfgang-Rainer (2000): *The Discovery of Things. Aristotle's Categories and their Context*. Princeton: Princeton University Press.
Pradelle, Dominique (2012): *Par-delà la révolution copernicienne. Sujet transcendantal et facultés chez Kant et Husserl*. Paris: Presses universitaires de France.
Prauss, Gerold (1966): *Platon und der logische Eleatismus*. Berlin: Walter de Gruyter.
Rizo-Patrón de Lerner, Rosemary (2012): *Husserl en diálogo. Lecturas y debates*. Bogotá D. C.: Siglo del Hombre Editores.
Summa, Michela (2015): "Ein sinnloses Gewühl? Die Hypothese des Chaos und ihre Implikationen bei Kant und Husserl". In: C. Asmuth, P. Remmers (Eds.): *Ästhetisches Wissen*. Berlin: Walter de Gruyter, pp. 189–210.

Bernardo Ainbinder
Questions of Genesis as Questions of Validity
Husserl's New Approach to an Old Kantian Problem[1]

Abstract: Can Husserl's phenomenology be understood as a variety of transcendental philosophy in Kant's sense? To compare their uses of this term would require examining the various places where Husserl's and Kant's paths seem to diverge.

Husserl's insistence on including within the field of phenomenological inquiry allegedly causal, pre-personal, cognitive mechanisms seems to be one such divergence. In particular, it conflicts with Kant's clear-cut distinction between questions of genesis and questions of validity. In this chapter, I claim that Husserl's genetic analysis – at least in part – can be understood as a way of defending a transcendental perspective in the strong sense and of overcoming some of the flaws that he found in Kant's critical philosophy. I will claim that Husserl's appeal to mechanisms is transcendentally motivated: if transcendental philosophy is the inquiry into the conditions of possibility of cognition in terms of the justification of the validity of our claims to knowledge, analyzing the mechanisms involved and their transcendental role contributes to understanding what rational grounding is and how rational norms can inform our cognitive processes.

1 Husserl on Kant's 'Mythology'

It is a well-acknowledged fact that Husserl's phenomenology can be adequately characterized as transcendental philosophy. At least since *Ideas I* and all the way up to and past his last major work, the *Krisis*, Husserl himself took up the label "transcendental" for his own inquiries. Nevertheless, whether Husserl's phenomenology and notion of the transcendental can be conceived as continuous with

---

[1] This paper was written during a Research Stay at the University of Wollongong, Australia, thanks to a generous grant by the Chilean National Council for Scientific Research (REDI170493). I am indebted to Pablo Guiñez, with whom I discussed the main ideas of this paper at its early stage, and to Zachary Hugo, who provided me with valuable references and discussed my ideas throughout the process.

https://doi.org/10.1515/9783110564280-015

Kant's critical philosophy and with his own transcendental program is a far more complicated issue.

Since Iso Kern's monumental work (Kern 1964), many have attempted to explain to what extent Husserl follows Kant and where exactly he has found the limits of critical philosophy (see Seebohm 1962, Mohanty 1996, Luft 2007, Nenon 2008; for a more general look at the relation between phenomenology and the transcendental, see the papers in Heinämaa *et al.* 2014). I don't think that the problem can be solved in any straightforward way. This is not only due to the fact that there is no single unambiguous notion of transcendentality in both Kant's and Husserl's work, but also to the fact that Husserl's own transcendentalism is haunted by tensions that are not so easy to resolve (see Ainbinder 2018). Given this state of affairs, the question of whether Husserl was and remained a Kantian still affords a legitimate source of puzzlement.

In order to cut through some of the brambles in this monumental discussion, one might adopt a more modest and focused strategy by attempting to show that we cannot *prima facie* exclude the possibility of understanding the phenomenological use of 'transcendental' in its legitimate Kantian sense. To compare their uses of this term would require examining the various places where Husserl's and Kant's paths seem to diverge.

In this paper, I will look at one such divergence, namely, Husserl's later insistence (proper to his genetic phenomenological writings from at least 1917 onwards) on including within the field of phenomenological inquiry allegedly causal, pre-personal, cognitive mechanisms: e.g. instincts, drives, stimuli (*Reize*), passive associations, and the like.[2] The inquiry into such themes seems to indicate a decided abandonment of Kantian transcendentalism and an endorsement of some hybrid form of *a priori* analysis and naturalistic inquiry.

This evaluation of Husserl's genetic phenomenology seems *prima facie* valid. However, my main contention in this paper will be that Husserl's genetic analysis – at least in part – can be understood as a way of defending a transcendental perspective in the strong sense and overcoming some of the flaws Husserl found in Kant's critical philosophy. I will claim that Husserl's appeal to mechanisms is transcendentally motivated: if transcendental philosophy is the inquiry into the

---

[2] As a matter of fact, as is apparent from the manuscripts on the *Studien zur Struktur des Bewusstseins*, to be published in the forthcoming *Husserliana* volume, Husserl's engagement with such topics is to be found much earlier, at least since 1908. I am grateful to Zachary Hugo for pointing this out to me. This speaks for a close and internal connection between genetic analyses and transcendental inquiry, like the one I am defending here, and discredits the idea of a "turn" in Husserl's later thought. Having said that, I will only refer here to works and manuscripts from his later period.

conditions of possibility of cognition in terms of the justification of the validity of our claims to knowledge, analyzing the mechanisms involved and their transcendental role contributes to understanding what rational grounding is and how rational norms can inform our cognitive processes. This is a question that troubled Husserl ever since the *Prolegomena to Pure Logic* and which led him to contend one of Kant's central methodological distinctions, that between questions of genesis and questions of validity.

1.1 Kant on Transcendental Philosophy: Questions of Validity vs. Questions of Genesis

At the very beginning of the Transcendental Deduction, Kant introduces, by recourse to his time's legal parlance, the famous distinction between questions of validity (or legitimacy) and questions of (factual) genesis: "Jurists, when they speak of entitlements and claims, distinguish in a legal matter between the questions about what is lawful (*quid juris*) and that which concerns the fact (*quid facti*)" (Kant 1781/1787, A 84/B 116). To the latter corresponds an explanation of the possession of a pure cognition, such as Locke's "tracing of the first endeavors of our power of cognition to ascend from individual perceptions to general concepts," a "physiological derivation" (*ibid.*). But this would not suffice to grant legitimacy or validity to a claim, which Kant calls 'deduction.' That is, in order to ground validity, "which should be entirely independent of experience, an entirely different birth certificate than that of an ancestry from experiences must be produced" (Kant 1781/1787, A 86–87/B 119).

The distinction between cognitive mechanisms qua causal (or cum-causal) processes and their explanatory role and normative justification is surely a complex matter. For the purposes of this chapter, I will refer to cognitive mechanisms as the biological mechanisms that underpin the abilities of a given organism, including but not limited to neurophysiological and psychological processes. As such, they can be described in third-person terms and may not be immediately accessible to the first-person point of view. If normative assessment and justification involve being able to present the justificatory credentials for a given belief, it seems to be *prima facie* apparent that such mechanisms cannot fulfill such a function. And if they were completely third-person and inaccessible to the subject they could not. But, as I will show, there are good reasons to contest that there exists such a clear-cut distinction between the realm of the pre-personal and the realm of what is first-personally accessible, the realm of causality and the realm of normativity, the realm of the concrete and the realm of the *a priori* conditions for rationality. Questioning such a distinction and showing an alternative model of how those realms are articulated, as well as of the import of cognitive mechanisms for rational justification, is, I will claim, at the core of Husserl's engagement with genetic analyses.

In the context of the Deduction, Kant seems to think that causal-genetic questions and transcendental questions are to be kept apart. If we reflect on the juridical parlance in which he presents the point, the distinction is perfectly natural. If we consider a question such as "Why are you the owner of that car?," a response of the sort "because I found it over there with the keys in it" has no application at all: the question concerns one's right to the ownership of the vehicle, which is not the same as a story of how one came to get one's hands on it. Kant's point is that the same goes for the transcendental question concerning the validity of the application of the category of, e.g., causality to the objects of experience (i.e. as a synthetic principle to unify them).

It is in this regard that Hume's associationist account of our cognition of objects falls short. Just as the *fact* that I found a car somewhere is perfectly consistent with Joanne's *claim* that it is her car, the psychological (or physiological, as Kant would put it) tendency to synthesize experiences in relations of cause and effect would make the use of the notion of causality a purely contingent matter. Reimagining a famous Kantian scenario, for example, I could die right before one billiard ball hits a second one and hence no association would necessarily obtain. As Tom Nenon puts it, "'transcendental knowledge' should concern necessities; it should be non-empirical, non-contingent, and therefore cannot be based on anything we learn from the senses. Put in Kantian terms: it must be '*a priori*'" (Nenon 2008, p. 430).

The philosophical upshot is that the subjective structures upon which Kant will ground the validity of the application of the categories to objects cannot depend on contingent factual features of the actual subjects performing the synthesis or of their cognitive ("physiological") processes.[3]

Does that mean that Husserl abandons *bona fide* transcendentalism – despite his insistence on the use of the term – and relapses into a sort of Humeanism? In the next section I will examine this question.

---

[3] This is exactly the conclusion that Nenon draws when underscoring the contrast between Kant's view of transcendental subjectivity and Husserl's inquiries into concrete subjectivity and its cognitive processes. See Nenon 2008, p. 432.

1.2 Husserl on Kant: Transcendental Philosophy as a Mythology and the Problem of Fulfillment

One of Husserl's most systematic examinations of Kant's understanding of transcendental philosophy takes place in the *Krisis*, more specifically in the first section of the third part.[4] At the very end of the second part, in § 26, Husserl presents his own position as transcendental philosophy in open contrast to Kant: "[T]he expression 'transcendental philosophy' has been much used since Kant, even as a general title for universal philosophies whose concepts are oriented toward those of the Kantian type." In contrast to Kant, he claims to use the word to refer to "the motif of inquiring back into the ultimate source of all the formations of knowledge, the motif of the knower's reflecting upon himself and his knowing life in which all the scientific structures that are valid for him occur purposefully, are stored up as acquisitions, and have become and continue to become freely available" (Husserl 1954, Hua VI, pp. 100*sq.*; Husserl 1970, pp. 97*sq.*).[5] Shortly thereafter he adds: "This source [of universal, i.e. transcendental, philosophy] bears the title *I-myself*, with all of my actual and possible knowing life and, ultimately, my concrete life in general" (Husserl 1954, Hua VI, p. 101; Husserl 1970, p. 98).

The reference to a Cartesian motif is surely perplexing in this context, where an appeal to concrete subjectivity, including its bodily, affective, and other cognitive "physiological" (in Kant's sense) processes is transformed into the very source of transcendental philosophy, i.e. of rational grounding.[6] I will deal with this in the final section of the paper. But at this stage I would like to focus on the reasons why Husserl turns his gaze to complex, concrete, actual cognitive life. The confrontation with Kant in the following sections of the *Krisis* illuminates this problem.

Husserl's main contention is that Kant's notion of subjectivity is no more than a "mythical construction;" it is "his own sort of mythical talk, whose literal

---

[4] See also his 1924 treatise entitled *"Kant und die Idee der Transzendentalphilosophie"* (Husserl 1956, Hua VII, pp. 230–287). For Husserl's more general and rough overview of Kant, see his 1916–1920 lecture course on the history of philosophy (Husserl 2012, Hua Mat IX, pp. 468–477).
[5] References to Husserl are to the English translation, when available. Otherwise, I quote the *Husserliana* edition, and translations are my own.
[6] Husserl expresses a similar idea already in *Ideas I*, where he refers to the conscious life of the transcendental subject "in the entire fullness of its concreteness" (Husserl 1983, p. 70) as the proper field of transcendental inquiry. This allows one to identify an underlying problematic thread that leads from static to genetic phenomenology, even if, of course, genetic phenomenology attempts a more elaborate analysis of what that concreteness means.

meaning points to something subjective, but a mode of the subjective which we are in principle unable to make intuitive to ourselves, whether through factual examples or through genuine analogy" (Husserl 1970, p. 116). Kant's failure – according to Husserl's diagnosis – was not due to an improper understanding of the transcendental but to an inadequate notion of psychological inquiry that he shared with Locke and Hume. Kant, by understanding the mundane I as "the soul conceived in naturalistic terms and as a component of the psychophysical man in the time of nature," cuts loose the connection between the mundane I and the transcendental I (Husserl 1970, p. 120). As a consequence, he was incapable of seeing the connection between the mundane I and transcendental grounding, between psychological considerations and the problem of validity. In sum, Kant failed to see how questions of genesis and questions of validity are connected in relevant ways when one adopts a different notion of subjectivity. In a way, reintroducing the *quaestio facti* into the picture offers, according to Husserl, a way of avoiding Kant's mythical way of speaking and of grounding the transcendental perspective. But while Husserl's appeal to concrete subjectivity as a ground of this transcendental perspective avoids Kant's mythical constructions, one may wonder if this upshot comes at a price. Namely, wouldn't Husserl then be reducing validity to mere psychological or physiological conditioning, as in Hume?

1.3 Husserl on Concrete Subjectivity

Before considering that objection – which I will only be able to fully respond to in the final section – let us take a brief look at what Husserl calls 'concrete subjectivity.'

As is well known, from *Ideas II* onwards, Husserl asserts that the specific form and matter of the experience of a subject depend on its bodily makeup (Husserl 1989, p. 56). Such aspects are not essential, i.e. they cannot be ascribed to an essential form of subjectivity, "whose highly multifarious constituents we obtain with progressive evidence when we uncover to intuition our own concrete subjectivity and then, with the aid of a free changing of its actuality into 'other' possibilities of any concrete subjectivity as such, direct our regard to the invariable that can be seen throughout" (Husserl 1969, 30). For instance, it is not *a priori* necessary that we are capable of perceiving colors or sounds (*ibid.*) and we can perfectly well conceive of a blind or deaf subject that is nevertheless rational (see also Husserl 1999, p. 63). Husserl acknowledges that, if we restrain ourselves to the realm of pure reason, we are dealing with the essence of subjectivity in this formal sense.

Nevertheless, that would not suffice to understand the way in which the world is constituted. What Husserl calls "concrete subjectivity" (Husserl 1969, p. 30) involves factual features such as "the use of objects, the role of cultures and specific make-up of bodily motility" (Nenon 2008, p. 437) as well as the particular sense through which the *hylē* is apprehended, the peculiar temporal form of experience and the like that constitute the realm of the *contingent a priori* (Husserl 1969, p. 29) and which have an explanatory role in transcendental constitution. As Mohanty puts it, "a transcendental subjectivity that is to serve as the domain within which all meanings have their genesis needs to be, in the first place, a concrete field of experience (and not an essence of it)" (Mohanty 1985, p. 211).

This opens up an important difference with the Kantian notion of necessity. As Kenneth Gallagher clearly described it: "the insight into necessity, far from being a formal condition for the experience of objects, is rendered possible through the experience of certain objects. He [Husserl] is therefore simply rejecting the Kantian view that universality and necessity cannot be founded upon experience" (Gallagher 1972, p. 343). Gallagher is talking about judgments, such as 'Everything colored is extended' or 'Nothing that is red is green,' which cannot be reduced to mere logical necessity. There is a twofold dimension to such judgments: on the one hand, they express essences that are to be attained through free variation in phantasy; that is the way in which Husserl gives an account of the necessity of material *a priori*. But they are also grounded on the factual concrete constitution of subjectivity and the correlative experience of objects. For example, the judgment "Nothing that is red is green" requires us to be capable of seeing both red and green and to be able to sort out the difference in most cases.

This will provide us with a first hint as to why Husserl thought that an account of the "physiological" mechanisms involved in cognition must be included in a well-grounded development of transcendental philosophy. This goes hand in hand with his criticism of Kant's methodological insight which preserves the universality of the subjectivity-based norms that constitute rationality by sacrificing their experienceability.

1.4 Crowell on Husserl and the Seductions of Naturalism

Let me now consider a powerful objection to such a connection, based on a novel and, in my opinion, correct understanding of what is at stake in transcendental philosophy. It is due to Steven Crowell, one of the more consistent defenders of a strong transcendental reading of Husserl and of phenomenology in general. In his "Transcendental Phenomenology and the Seductions of Naturalism," Crowell distinguishes two intellectual strands within transcendental phenomenology: "a *Geltungs*-theoretical (or normative) strand and an experience-theoretical (or psychological) strand. It is this combination that distinguishes it from other forms of transcendental philosophy, including Kant's [...]" (Crowell 2012, p. 27).

According to Crowell, the transcendental approach concerns the question of validity, i.e. the question regarding our (rational) responsiveness to the norms that govern experience qua rationally grounded. Only in this way can subjects refer objectively to the world and bind themselves by the norm of truth. In this sense, the psychological strand must submit itself to the constraints posed by such an account of norms: "if transcendental phenomenology concerns the constitution of all transcendence, it can no longer be understood as psychology – 'descriptive' or otherwise – since the very consciousness to which such psychology appeals, the psyche, is itself a transcendent entity, constituted by certain norms of validity" (Crowell 2012, p. 28). Doing otherwise would mean illegitimately importing into the realm of rational grounding – which is essentially first-personal, since it involves acting in light of norms and being responsible for such acting (see Crowell 2007) – a merely third-personal description of human existence as if it were any other transcendent object. This obviously echoes the Kantian concern about turning the I into a mere object of the inner sense, both in the Transcendental Deduction and in the Paralogisms.[7] Crucially, according to Crowell's reading, Husserl himself has fallen prey to such an illegitimate move:

> When Husserl claims that the subject of the personalistic attitude is a 'human being' [*Mensch*], he believes that he is entitled to the idea that the sense, 'human being', carries with it reference to natural kinds – not merely in some culturally relative sense in which the pregiven world contains various familiar 'types' of organism, but in the strict sense of scientific naturalism. [...] But the importation of this sort of third-person assumption into transcendental phenomenology is pernicious, because it makes it seem as though the *pre-personal processes characteristic of consciousness conceived as a natural function could somehow be 'reconstructed', in the absence of first-person evidence, as constitutive abilities of transcendental subjectivity.* (Crowell 2012, p. 41, my emphasis)

---

[7] Husserl himself deemed this Kantian identification of psychology with an objectification of subjectivity as a result of Kant's own misunderstanding of the nature of a proper philosophical psychology. See Husserl 1970, pp. 116–117. The same misunderstanding seems to underlie Crowell's criticism of Husserl.

I think Crowell is right that in order for pre-personal, factual mechanisms to acquire constitutive status something else is needed; but that does not mean that the description of the contingent and factual mechanisms involved becomes irrelevant. Rather, given the contingency of the starting point, the question concerning rational grounding becomes all the more pressing. Such a question would take the following form: how can the norms that govern rationality, the very norms that can be endorsed in first-person once we perform the reduction, actually inform the behavior of contingent, factual, and concrete subjects? How can they inform their bodily movements, their passive associations, their attentional shifts?

This is a problem that Husserl raised as early as 1900, in his *Prolegomena to Pure Logic*. If the main argument of the book is addressed against psychologism in logic, he nevertheless assumes, at the same time, what we may call the "truth of psychologism." Husserl states it immediately after discussing the insufficiency of Kant's distinction, in *Logik Jäsche*, between how one in fact thinks and how one ought to think as a ground for differentiating psychology and logic. He says that such a distinction could be easily overridden by the advocates of psychologism. After all, "the necessary use of the understanding is, all the same, a use of the understanding and belongs, with the understanding itself, to psychology" (Husserl 2001, p. 66). Much of Husserl's discussion in the subsequent logical investigations can be seen as an attempt to make sense of this thesis. But suffice it to say, for now, that the 'truth of psychologism' is that any account of how the norms of rationality inform our behavior must be such that it could specify the way in which such norms can have a grasp on the very behavior they inform. To put it bluntly, the correctness of thinking (call it rightness, aiming at truth, or objective purport) must be the correctness of the thinking of the thinkers we are, instantiated in specific cognitive processes with factual concrete characteristics.

This is the path that will lead to a more articulated criticism of Kant and will lead Husserl to focus, especially in his genetic inquiries, on the various mechanisms at play in consciousness. A robust and well-grounded account of rationality requires explaining how a norm can inform actual and factual behavior. And doing this, in turn, requires understanding the kind of behavior that is at stake.

1.5 Two Questions about Mechanisms and Rational Grounding

In light of the foregoing, we can mark out two separate but related questions that Husserl needs to address.

(1) What are the mechanisms characteristic of cognitive subjects that allow them to be capable of intentional behavior or, in Crowell's wording, that allow them to refer objectively to the world and bind themselves to the norm of truth?

The *Geltungs*-theoretical strand to which Crowell refers is concerned with the fact, already underlined by Kant, that when it comes to cognition, it is not sufficient to explain the way in which we come into contact with the world; it is also necessary to understand intentional states as involving a normative claim to truth, i.e. a claim to present the object as it is and to submit itself to being assessed in light of how and what the object really is.[8]

Characterizing cognition as involving such normative claims does not exempt us, though, from tackling the equally important question about what specific form concrete subjectivity must have in order to be capable of this sort of normative assessment. See for instance the following passage from *Husserliana XIV:* "it is also a transcendental question to what extent a psycho-physical 'parallelism' of this factual kind is a condition of the possibility of human scientific knowledge (and of an objective and unlimited science of the psyche [*Seelenwissenschaft*]" (Husserl 1973a, Hua XIV, p. 72, my translation). Without this reference to the factual constitution of concrete subjectivity, we would easily relapse into the kind of *a priori* mythology that Husserl denounces in Kant.

Husserl's answer is that a teleological tendency to self-coherence and self-preservation is what is required in order for biological organisms to be capable of intentional behavior. Cognitive mechanisms must be understood in light of that tendency. Such a tendency is definitive of life itself, which progressively becomes his word of choice to speak of concrete subjectivity considered as a whole.

That is why – to the surprise of interpreters with a rather strong notion of transcendentality, such as Crowell – Husserl can claim that animals are transcendental subjects,[9] at least insofar as they exhibit the kind of mechanisms

---

[8] This distinction underlies the Kantian one between judgments of perception (such as "This rock looks big") and judgments of experience (such as "The rock is big"). The orthodox Kantian explanation states that only the latter involve subsuming the sensible manifold under the categories, that is, that only judgments of experience involve objective rules that go beyond the mere psychological association involved in pure sensibility. See Longuenesse 1998, pp. 170–180.
[9] See for instance Husserl 1973a, Hua XIV: Beilage XI, Nr. 6; Beilage XIII; Beilage XXX, Nr. 13, pp. 5–8; and Husserl 1973b, Hua XV: Beilage X; Beilage XLVII.

that are required for normative claims to be in place. Since such mechanisms are, I will claim, necessary but not sufficient conditions of rationality, this statement obviously stands in need of qualification and justification. And in light of the fact that cognitive mechanisms do not entail *eo ipso* rationality, a second question arises:

(2) How does rational grounding emerge from such mechanisms and how does it transform them?

This is the question that brings the first-person perspective with which Crowell is concerned back into the picture, and which allows one to distinguish human rationality from other forms of cognitive mechanisms that can be in place in other animals. I will tackle the first of these questions in the next section and the second question in the final one.

2 Husserl on Cognitive Mechanisms and Validity

2.1 Husserl on the Contingent A Priori and Psychophysical Parallelism

Before turning to the question regarding what mechanisms need to be in place for an organism to be capable of normative behavior and, by that same token, able to engage in the specific kind of activity that is rational grounding, let me first explore what specific contribution mechanisms would amount to what Crowell calls "constitutive abilities of transcendental subjectivity" (Crowell 2012, p. 41).

For starters, this way of posing the problem leads immediately to a puzzlement, the very puzzlement Crowell puts forward in a rather Kantian vein: namely, how could we legitimately include in the realm of transcendental necessity determinations that are factual and contingent? To put it more simply: how can there be a contingent *a priori*?

It is well known that, at least since *Ideas II* and the *Analyses to Passive Synthesis*, Husserl assumes that the only way of making sense of how transcendental norms refer to psychological operations and govern them is by identifying the transcendental subject with the empirical one. As Mohanty puts it, "transcendental consciousness is said to be parallel to empirical consciousness. It is the same consciousness which as belonging to the world is empirical, and as constituting the world is transcendental" (Mohanty 1996, p. 25).

This strategy raises two important concerns: one, which I will only tackle in the final section, is whether the transcendental – i.e. the system of norms governing rationality – is finally identified with some kind of causal determination inscribed in our biological constitution, our cultural affiliation, our personal preferences. The second one concerns whether, inasmuch as transcendental subjectivity is permeated by empirical contingent facts, we can still speak of the transcendental as *a priori* conditions of possibility of the constitution of the world. The two questions are related but still distinct. The first question concerns the status of the constraints that norms impose on us: are they causal or properly normative-rational? The second question involves the problem of how our factual cognitive setup can be constitutive of objectivity, i.e. how it can be an *a priori* of the correlation, to put it in more classical Husserlian terms?

In what follows I will deal with this second problem concerning the status of *a priori* conditions once we identify (at least in terms of numerical identity) empirical and transcendental subjectivity.

Husserl struggles over the next two decades to provide a satisfactory answer to the question of an *a priori* that involves material determinations grounded on contingent facts about human and animal nature. In a text from 1921, for instance, Husserl presents the problem of organic development and its consequences for the perspectival and intersubjective character of cognition as follows:

> *Is it shown to be a transcendental necessity* that a world in general can only be constituted in conjunction with [*in eins mit*] a system of the development of animals and animal monads, with a certain parallelism of psychic [*seelischer*] and organic [*leiblicher*] development (here pursuing aspects of knowledge)? (Husserl 1973a, Hua XIV, p. 128 – my translation, my emphasis)

Despite the metaphysical overtones that permeate much of the *Beilage*, the central phenomenological upshot is that the constitution of the world – i.e. the existence of stable objects that can be the correlates of intentional acts characteristic of what we understand by cognition – requires the existence of certain kinds of biological organisms that relate to their environment and interact with each other.

In light of what Husserl understands by objectivity and knowledge thereof, the existence of such biological organisms (and, as we will see, the fact that they exhibit a certain set of typical abilities instantiated in biological mechanisms) is an *a priori* condition for objectivity and knowledge. It is of course not a pure *a priori*, since it involves material elements and concrete contingent determinations. The notion of objectivity *per se* does not modally require, for instance, organic corporeality; but the notion of objectivity as applied to the experience of concrete epistemic subjects does. Understanding this latter notion of objectivity such that it can be applied to the objects of experience to which we are intentionally related requires understanding which of the contingent features of one's experience are relevant for *a priori* determining the possibility of referring to objects. This is what Husserl calls the *material a priori* or, in *Formal and Transcendental Logic*, the *contingent a priori*.[10]

In light of this, it is necessary to examine what kind of mechanisms in our contingent concrete experience allow for the constitution of a world and of our possibility of knowledge, i.e. what mechanisms *need to be in place* for the constitution of objectivity as a correlate of human (or animal) knowledge. Husserl presents this relation in terms of necessity: the necessity so exhibited is not of course a metaphysical necessity; that is why the *a priori* in question is contingent. But it is a form of necessity in its own right, a "transcendental necessity," i.e. the necessity of what is thus exhibited in the correlation. As a factum, the correlation between the existence of certain biological organisms with certain sets of mechanisms and the very existence of the world as a possible correlate for cognitive activities gains transcendental necessity.

In order for such a correlation to be more than a mere postulate, Husserl must be capable of showing exactly what aspects of biological life, both animal and human, contribute to the constitution of objectivity as such. This is precisely where genetic phenomenological analyses come into the picture.

2.2 Cognitive Mechanisms and the Constitution of Objectivity: A Look at Genetic Analyses

While recent publications from Husserl's *Nachlaß* have shown that Husserl's interest in genetic questions began quite early, his work from the 1920s and onward exhibits a notable surge in writings on topics that seem to push the very limits of phenomenological inquiry: passivity, affectivity, drives and instincts, questions of generativity, and even birth, sleep, and death.[11] While this list of topics is not meant to exhaust the scope of genetic phenomenology, it is worth noting that such genetic themes have to do with non-rational and, at

---

10 Not surprisingly, Husserl can also speak (as in Husserl 1960, pp. 28, 38 *et passim*) of "*a innate A priori*." Once again, while this may sound to a Kantian like a monstrous hybrid of empirical and transcendental determinations, this is perfectly consistent with Husserl's own efforts to account for an *a priori* that can be exhibited in experiencing subjectivity.

11 In many of the same texts and especially in the C-manuscripts (Husserl 2006, Hua Mat. VIII), Husserl also engages with a rather different line of inquiry, what we may call an archaeological rather than a genetic inquiry into the proto-forms of subjectivity (such as proto-temporalization, the *Ur-Ich* and the like). I think this line of inquiry follows a different yet methodologically important problem in Husserlian phenomenology. I have argued for this distinction and explored the significance of this archeological quest in another paper (Ainbinder 2016).

least *prima facie*, non-normative cognitive mechanisms definitive of concrete, factual (*faktisch*) subjectivity.

If my hypothesis is right, then the analyses of such phenomena must be oriented towards explaining their contribution to the constitution of the world and to the emergence of the full-fledged normative practice that aims at truth, i.e. knowledge. I will analyze two of those phenomena which in my opinion paradigmatically show the motivation of the Husserlian approach: repetition (*Wiederholung*) and normality and abnormality. I will then draw out some general conclusions regarding the role played by Husserl's notions of teleology and self-preservation, which will lay the basis for my argument in the final section of this paper.

a) Repetition

In a manuscript from 1932, Husserl refers to an "instinctive drive to repetition" (*instinktiver Wiederholungstrieb*) in the context of discussing the basic form of the will that is to be found in the dialectics of inclination (*Neigung*) and satisfaction (Husserl 2014, Hua XLII, pp. 109–111, my translation). Husserl adopts here what is a typical strategy when undertaking genetic analysis: he identifies a problem that arises at higher levels of constitution (in this case the problem of free will as based on practical possibilities) and looks for a precursor at a more basic level of constitution in which the I is not actively participating. Importantly, this inquiry is not merely motivated by an ungrounded tendency to go beyond what is first-personally given; rather, it is necessitated by transcendental analysis itself. As I have shown, the only way of accounting for the transcendental capacity of free will (the "*I can*" which Husserl identified in *Ideas II* as a key element in the description of intentional acts: Hua IV, Husserl 1989, § 60) as permeating the very acts of the concrete subject is to explain what is to be found in such acts that warrants the possibility of such a capacity without presupposing it:

> The problem regarding how a repetition is possible, e.g. repetition of kinesthesia, the datum [of the] kinesthesis diminishing, [and] returning. [...] Cancellation and ever new repetitions, until the same comes. To develop a conviction through successful repetitions. One single successful repetition is not enough, because after each deviation the tendency must be revived, that is, the tendency to a new repetition. (Husserl 2014, Hua XLII, p. 110, my translation)

The instinctual inclination to repetition grounds the possibility of a synthesis of identification of similar but never identical data, corresponding to correlative bodily movements. Certain kinesthesia express expectations that the world will appear in more or less typical ways, that is, they belong to a typical horizon for our experience. Without this instinctual drive, the rational capacity involved in the assessment of truth would not get off the ground. Indeed, Husserl immediately characterizes such an instinctual drive as the very "experience of the 'I can', of practical potentiality [*Vermöglichkeit*]" (*ibid.*).

If, as is well known, "for Husserl all constitution involves an infinity, the possibility of reiteration and the idea of '*immer weiter*'" (Mohanty 1985, p. 116), the identification of an instinctual drive to repetition is an answer to the question about the mechanisms involved in the constitution of objectivity:

> If I can say that the world repeats itself, that is, that it runs its course in a typical and normal fashion [*in einer typischen Normalität*], then to this belongs the normal typology [*die normale Typik*] of its ever new becoming in the establishment of human formations, and correlatively, that human situations repeat themselves typically [...]. (Husserl 2014, Hua XLII, pp. 110*sq.*, my translation)

It is easy to see how the contingent factual condition of organisms capable of cognition – i.e., their bodily nature, the fact that they experience the world in partial spatial adumbrations through time, but also the fact that they are capable of performing typified movements and recognize them as such in an instinctual and pre-reflective way – gains transcendental necessity and determines the norm for knowledge. For instance, it determines the fact that pursuing the truth amounts to the rehearsal of repetitions in order to confirm or disconfirm the coherence of the whole experience as given in the corresponding modes of appearance of the world. In this sense, such features are part of the contingent *a priori* conditions for the possibility of knowledge.

In another text from 1927, we find another example of the transcendental necessity that links factual determinations and transcendental constitution. There, Husserl explains that the possibility of bodily movements grounds the unity of the perceptual field in a complex process that involves distinct fields for different senses and at the same time a unified field for all of them:

> Every organ of perception in [its] perceptual function, which runs its course with the "I move," has a certain unity with the perceptual field; namely in accordance with the separation between the visual organ, tactual organ, auditory organ, etc. we have particular relations to the fields of sensation [...]. (Husserl 1973a, Hua XIV, p. 448, my translation)

Both the plurality of senses and the capacity of bodily movement are facts about the organism's bodily makeup. Yet, they determine the problems that a theory of constitution must deal with (the problem of the unification of the different data provided by different senses) and, at the same time, they pre-delineate the solution (the unity of movement, i.e. of the body as the ground for the unity of the perceptual field).

b) Typicality, Normality, and Abnormality

If factual aspects of concrete subjectivity and its bodily makeup inform the *a priori* of constitution, it should come as no surprise that this *a priori* is not a homogeneous and univocal realm but rather a realm of typicalities that admit of deviations. As Husserl puts it, "every subject has – not qua subject of acts, but rather in regard to its passivity – possible normality and abnormality (*Anomalität*). And the index of this distinction is the organic body" (Husserl 1973a, Hua XIV, p. 67, my translation). This has some important consequences for Husserl's notion of rationality.

First, unlike the nomological structure of physical laws, the biological nature of the body involves a dimension of individuality[12] where the conditions under which something can be said to be the kind of organism it is depend not on its falling under a given law but rather on its being normatively assessed against the background of a spectrum of normality and abnormalities.

Second, since abnormalities are frequent, the characterization of the *a priori* capacities involved in cognition – and the correlative characterization of the world that is thereby known – are not of a piece, but rather admit degrees and must be thought against a background of optimality. We might be tempted to think of them as empirical-inductive or statistical generalizations which constitute what counts as normal. But if that were so, there would be no way of grounding objectivity. How would we be able to specify what is normal in the first place? Would what is the case change if what is to be considered normal changes? Thus, Husserl needs to account, on the one hand, for the possibility of distinguishing normality from abnormalities and of identifying abnormal experiences as such. This is required to avoid the risk of a normative solipsism where the way in which I perceive the world through my potentially abnormal body immediately becomes (for me) the way the world really is. On the other hand, if normality is to be more than a mere statistical prevalence, he would need to explain how the "normal" *a priori* can be properly normative, i.e. provide the norm for truth and objective knowledge.

---

12 See Husserl 1973a, Hua XIV, p. 67.

As to the first question, Husserl provides an account of how we experience normality in terms of intra-subjective and inter-subjective comparisons.[13]

As to the second one, which is much more relevant for Husserl's conception of rationality, Husserl identifies normality not with a statistical prevalence of certain features but rather with an unattainable optimum in the apprehension of objects: "To normal corporeality belongs a system of better and worse possibilities of exhibition, and to this there belongs in turn the idea of an optimal mode of givenness or of a possible optimal system of modes of givenness, which, at a certain level, is representative of the truth" (Husserl 1973a, Hua XIV, pp. 120*sq.*, my translation).

Once again, it is apparent how certain features of the contingent factual constitution of organic beings – in particular the variability and individuality of organisms – pervade the transcendental account of the conditions of possibility of objective knowledge and truth. In particular, it determines the peculiar kind of normative relation that holds between the subject's cognitive performances and the ideal givenness of the world as truthful. The normative strand in transcendental thinking already brought to the fore by Kant finds a further grounding in the factual concrete aspects of subjects as biological organisms.

2.3 The Body, Self-Preservation, and Teleology

In reviewing these few but central Husserlian remarks regarding cognitive mechanisms from a genetic perspective, it has come to the fore that a certain kind of being, namely, biological organisms, can neither be characterized in terms of general laws, as in physics, nor in terms of features that are necessary and sufficient for them to count as such, given the frequency and centrality of abnormalities. Such organisms, on the contrary, reveal a peculiar kind of normativity which is exhibited in the drive to repetition and the adjustments of perception and other cognitive processes towards relevant optima.[14] This opens up a new realm with its own peculiar legality:

> Physical nature is already a universal heading for legalities of constitutive passivity, legalities which concern all subjects alike. And corporeality is yet another particular heading, insofar as there belongs to nature in general an empirical lawful necessity of organization (*and perhaps also an a priori belonging to it, insofar as physicalistic legality is transcenden-*

---

13 See Husserl 1973a, Hua XIV, p. 69*sq.*
14 On Husserl's notion of perceptual optima, see Doyon 2018.

tally insufficient) and an empirical necessity of a development of organisms up to the human organic body. (Husserl 1973a, Hua XIV, p. 74, my translation, my emphasis)

As is well known, in his "Analytic of Teleological Judgment," Kant had already noted this peculiarity of organisms and the insufficiency of physical laws to account for them. But while Kant paid no attention to the fact that the knowing subject, the mundane I, is such an organism, Husserl brought that fact to the center of the philosophical and methodological challenges of adopting a transcendental point of view. Such a move was required to overcome the mythical character of Kant's I and bridge the gap between the transcendental and the mundane I.

This has important consequences for the role of teleology in both accounts. Whereas Kant focused on the peculiarly limited reach of teleological judgments when it comes to providing knowledge, Husserl made of teleology a central feature of his transcendental approach. This required gaining an internal perspective on the organism to account for its own identity in teleological terms. From an external perspective, the teleologically informed drives are mere physical processes.[15] But by adopting a view from within, which is the genuine transcendental point of view – as Crowell rightly notes – the proper teleological dimension comes to the fore:

> In internal observation – which is not that of the investigator of physical nature [...] but rather the [manner of] observation whereby one places oneself in the perspective of psychic subjectivity and, qua transcendental, whereby one places oneself in this perspective [psychic subjectivity] in a transcendental turn – there we have the animal subject as the subject of its pregiven environment and we have it as subject of its drives, of its drive-habitualities, of its acquired directions-toward and its correlative acquisitions, in which the identical objects lie. (Husserl 2014, Hua XLII, p. 97, my translation)

Now, the possibility of a transposition of phenomenological insights concerning one's own psychic subjectivity into an animal subjectivity remains, of course, problematic; despite Husserl's insistence upon empathic procedures, the description of animal instinctive drives and the like from within seems to be deemed merely analogic. But this difficulty notwithstanding, there is a sense in which the perspective from within becomes less problematic.

This is where the all-important notion of self-preservation (*Selbsterhaltung*) comes into view. Immediately after the above passage, Husserl asks: "Yet, from the internal-perspective, what sense does it make to speak of 'self-preserva-

---

15 See Husserl 2014, Hua XLII, p. 96.

tion' and 'preservation of the species [*Gattungserhaltung*]'? That is, at this primitive stage?" (Husserl 2014, Hua XLII, p. 97, my translation). It is precisely at this stage, I would like to suggest, that the question gains its significance. From an external point of view, the tendency to cohere and the tendency to assume stable forms can be explained away as in the case of any other physical system. It is only from the point of view of the individual organism that the structure of instinctive drives, movements, and self-adjustments according to a norm of optimality can be seen as responding to a teleological orientation that is none other than the preservation of the organism itself.[16]

Self-preservation is the way in which the norms which are exhibited in the factual constitution of human and animal subjectivity – but which, as Husserl claims, have transcendental necessity and inform the contingent *a priori* that governs their own lives – gain a normative foothold in the organism itself.[17] This was the problem first posed in Husserl's *Prolegomena* with regard to the laws of logic, but now it is generalized to apply to transcendental norms in general. To be more precise, *Selbsterhaltung* names the fact that organisms are governed by those norms. The I itself is "a unity through a tendency toward self-preservation; that is, by striving to be and by striving to be itself" (Husserl 2014, Hua XLII, p. 338, my translation).

Up to this point, I have tried to show in which way cognitive mechanisms – i.e. Kant's question regarding genesis – are not only relevant for transcendental inquiries into validity but also shape the very way in which we account for the transcendental. But this may lead to the conclusion that Husserl's account of the transcendental is no more than the formalization of certain factual mechanisms, a sort of Humean associationism in a biological disguise. In his efforts to avoid Kantian formalism, Husserl might then be guilty of throwing the baby out with the bathwater. In the following section, I will try to assuage this concern by arguing that these teleologically-oriented biological mechanisms are a necessary but not a sufficient condition for rationality.

---

16 See Okrent 2007, ch. 2.
17 In his doctoral dissertation, Zachary Hugo develops the thesis that self-preservation plays the fundamental role in grounding the normative force of reason in Husserl's account by providing a *sui-generis* form of self-governing norm-responsiveness. See esp. Hugo 2017b, pp. 342sq.

3 The Baby and the Bathwater: Rationality as a Claim to Justification

3.1 From Cognitive Mechanisms to Normativity

Up till now I have reviewed Husserl's take on cognitive mechanisms and have underlined how his genetic analyses transform the conception of the *a priori*. Nevertheless, I have not yet shown how Husserl accounts for the role such mechanisms play in rational grounding nor how they are thereby transformed. In order to avoid a conclusion such as Crowell's – namely, that Husserl's genetic analyses are motivated by a naturalistic assumption that is independent of the transcendental question concerning validity – I will now turn to my second question in § 5 above, namely, how does rational grounding emerge from such mechanisms and how does it transform them?

Let me start with a very significant passage concerning this problem, where Husserl discusses blind instincts and how they can gain normative import for rational grounding:

> Each original and each acquired instinct is blind. Yet if one introduces the consideration of value through reason and follows up the immediate and mediate connections of values, in this way the instinctive drive, which has a blind absoluteness of the "I must," gains the character of an insightful "I ought," that is necessarily directed, in the evidence precisely of this "I ought," toward values [...]. It is thus said that blind drives – the original and acquired ones, are not entirely without a sense [*sinnlos*], but rather they harbor in themselves so to speak hidden or already familiar valuations [*Wertmeinungen*], as such [they] stand under critique and by means of this critique they lead into an evident absolute ought with *a personal sense of value* [*Wertsinn*]. (Husserl 2014, Hua XLII, p. 385 note 1, my translation, my emphasis)

This passage clearly describes what we may call the rational transformation of the instinctive drives. In Husserl's terms, what was previously a blind (i.e. cum-causal and pre-personal) determination – an "I must" – is transformed into a normative endorsement – an "I ought." This is precisely the way in which Husserl describes rationality, as the capacity to assess and endorse our beliefs in terms of a norm (the norm of coherence, of truth, of objectivity) through a process of self-criticism.[18] But in order for that to be so, and this is the important point here, such instincts must already have a certain value-as-

---

[18] On the role of normativity in Husserl's phenomenology of reason, see Walton 2017 and Hugo 2017b.

sessment in them. There must then be continuity between pre-personal mechanisms and the person-level activity of rational grounding.

The Kantian clear-cut distinction between rational grounding and cognitive processes is then blurred. It is not just the case that cognitive mechanisms have an influence on the way in which the kind of organisms we are come to be rational – though they certainly do play a role. It is rather that the distinction between the realm of natural processes and the realm of rationality is not there. Bruzina, who locates such a theoretical move in the *Natur und Geist* lectures, explains it as follows: "Husserl proposes an approach in which nature and spirit need to be, and can be, rethought so as to allow recognition of the intrinsic play of each within the other" (Bruzina 2010, p. 92).

This calls for a different take altogether on the notion of cognitive mechanisms. Strictly speaking, it would not be precise to speak of mechanisms if we understand thereby merely mechanical causal processes. Rather, such mechanisms are to be understood as part of a dynamical system of possibilities for acting:

> Primordial drives, primordial instincts are not mechanical powers. They are the sources of all potentiality, all systems of potentialities [*die Quellen alles Könnens, aller Könnenssysteme*]. In the developed I, the world has its correlate in a system of abilities [*Vermögenssystem*], which is a systematic unity of abilities: Each possible experience is a series of mastery [*Linie der Gekonntheit*]. Each empirical thought of mind is an empirical thought of my abilities; and my abilities are in constant development and have their source in primordial abilities. (Husserl 2014, Hua XLII, p. 102, my translation)

Instincts and drives are not, Husserl claims, mechanical forces. But that does not mean they are not mechanisms in my sense. Rather, what Husserl is underlining is the insufficiency of a purely physical consideration of mechanisms to account for the role these play in organic life: "The full and true concrete zoological investigation concerns nevertheless the animal in its concrete real existence and not the merely physical-organic thing in the context of physical nature" (Husserl 2014, Hua XLII, p. 98, my translation). I take this to be the way in which Husserl understands the tendency, already present in Kant, of understanding biological life in terms of a teleologically oriented whole, or, as he puts it here, a system of abilities. This is why Husserl's description of mechanisms can be legitimately extended to animal life, which results in the perplexing statement that animals can also – to a certain extent at least – count as transcendental subjects. This would allow for the capacity for rational grounding – in the form of self-criticism or, more precisely, as I will show, of justification (*Rechtfertigung*) – to gain a grasp on such cognitive mechanisms. But before telling that story, let me now clarify the problems involved in the description of cognitive mechanisms, problems that have given rise to criticisms of genetic phenomenology such as Crowell's.

3.2 The Problem of Description and the Problem of Rational Grounding

If we take a closer look at Husserl's description of cognitive mechanisms, there are two different problems that need to be kept apart. One is what we may label the methodological problem concerning the contrast between the view from within (*Innenbetrachtung*) and a view from without (*Außenbetrachtung*) and the limits that the impossibility of properly placing oneself into animal life, what Husserl calls "placement" or *Hineinsetzen*, entails for zoological investigation.

This is a very important question. Husserl's engagement with animal life – which goes to as far as to attribute transcendental capacities to animals – has been one of the preferred targets of those who have seen in Husserl a relapse into some form of naturalism incompatible with transcendental inquiry.[19]

Husserl underlines such methodological problem in passages like the following:

> The zoologist in his or her experience of discovering animals as realities in the world, observing, scientifically investigating: the animal being [*das tierische Dasein*] in its subjective environment, of which it is aware, the life of instinct of the animal in its inner development, its concrete spiritual (psychical, egoic-intentional) life and its egoic development in correlation with the development of its subjective environment. (Husserl 2014, Hua XLII, p. 98, my translation)

This turns out to be, Husserl goes on to say, "problematic: animality in the view-from-within or inner apprehension and in parallel to the view-from-without, of the biophysical perspective" (*ibid.*). Now, it is true that from the point of view of the phenomenological evidence for such a description, no direct intuition can be offered. This rather calls for a reconstructive method that goes beyond what can be phenomenologically given. Crowell (2012) gets this right. According to Husserl: "only from a psyche, from that of the knower, to whom alone this is *a priori* primarily given [*der ihm a priori allein urgegebenen*], can each other and thus each possible content of empathy be investigated [...]" (Husserl

---

[19] For an analysis along these lines, see Crowell's and Jacobs' contributions to Heinämaa *et al.*, 2014.

1973a, Hua XIV, p. 125, my translation), so that "my lived-body in the 'inner apprehension' is the proto-apperceived and provides the necessary norm. All the rest are modifications of this norm" (Husserl 1973a, Hua XIV, p. 126, my translation).

The motivation for such a reconstruction must nonetheless lie in the persistence of instincts in us, i.e. in the mature and developed subject, and in the role that such mechanisms play in our existence. If Kant (and Crowell) thought that understanding animal life as teleologically oriented and norm-governed could only be derivatively grounded on the ascription of human features to other animals, Husserl draws the opposite conclusion: only to the extent that we ourselves exhibit mechanisms that are part of our animal and biological constitution, and to the extent that such mechanisms can be accessible to us even as rational constituting subjects, can we understand animals as akin to us.

The second problem is the problem of how such mechanisms (understood now as systems of potentialities or abilities, *Könnenssysteme*) can be at the basis of rational grounding. As I have said, they are necessary enabling conditions (in the sense in which our factual contingent concrete biological constitution underlies the possibility of rational grounding as an activity of the concrete contingent kind of subjectivity that we are), but not sufficient ones.

Husserl briefly distinguishes the way in which we are to be distinguished from animals in the following way: "The lower animal has an 'implicit,' but not an explicit, that is real [*wirkliches*] consciousness of a world which exists for it, of [the] I and not-I, etc." (Husserl 2014, Hua XLII, p. 99, my translation). How are we to understand such a distinction? What does it mean to gain an explicit, real consciousness of the world and of oneself as distinct from it?

Husserl warns us that this is not to be understood as an annulment of instinct. In discussing basic instincts such as breathing and eating in humans, Husserl makes this clear: "it is still the same instinctive happening, striving performance [*Tun*], but 'understood' as eating" (Husserl 2014, Hua XLII, p. 106, my translation). Such "understanding" is none other than the acknowledgment of the instinct as *my* potentiality. Thus, referring to breathing, he claims that "despite each lack of a specific action on the part of the I [*Ichaktion*], [this letting-it-run-its-course (*Verlaufenlassen*) is] nonetheless something egoically subjective, belonging to the realm of the I, which at the same time is a realm of the possible 'I can'" (Husserl 1973a, Hua XIV, p. 447, my translation). If this is implicit in animals – who are also *Könnenssysteme* –, it underpins the properly human capacity for rational assessment, i.e. the possibility of acknowledging the subjective character of such instincts and of cognitive mechanisms in general. For only in this way can mechanisms be normatively assessed in light of value: "Were the subject of instincts able to progressively disclose the instinct, then she would have to come to chains of value [*Wertverkettungen*] and she would have to will at each stage not merely the next disclosed goal, but rather the goal for the sake of its value and these values again for the sake of higher values, etc." (Husserl 2014, Hua XLII, p. 385, my translation).

3.4 Rational Endorsement: Mechanisms, Potentialities, and Norms

We are now able to answer the question that I posed in 2.1: namely, how does rational grounding emerge from these cognitive mechanisms and how does it transform them?

Rational grounding arises, I can now claim, when the teleologically-oriented processes that underpin our capacity to disclose the world are explicitly assumed as governed by a value. Such value – truth, science, objectivity, even ethical life – is posed as the norm against which the processes will now be assessed.

Let's consider the case of repetition again. Repetition characterizes, as we have seen, cognitive processes as they extend through time. It allows one to establish a correlation between, for instance, bodily movements and adumbrations of the world. They bear in themselves an "if… then" structure. In that sense, they reflect accurately the way in which biological organisms are organized in terms of a system of potentialities. They involve expectations and may well involve adjustments and corrections when what is expected does not occur. In that sense, we could speak of a certain natural normative tendency in drives. Nevertheless, that does not suffice for rationality to be in place. For that, something else is required, namely, that the whole process takes place in the light of a value that is taken to be the norm that governs mechanisms as such. So, if we for example think of perceptual mechanisms (involving kinesthesia, multisensory coordination, lighting variations and the like), such mechanisms would only count as being part of perception in the full-fledged rational sense (say, of being a perceptual experience) if they are governed by the norm of correctness (*Rechtigkeit*). Such a norm as a value incorporates the teleological orientation already exhibited in cognitive mechanisms – the tendency to fulfillment, striving after coherence –, but does so by instituting a value as the criterion to assess the cognitive performance of the subject.

This is even more clear in the case of the role played by normality. As I have said, normality cannot count as a mere statistical generalization. In a sense, that was an overstatement. From a certain point of view, what counts as a normal case of, say, perception, depends on the contingent constitution of our perceptual apparatus, of the temporal and contingent character of our experience, etc.

But taking the normal to be a norm against which to assess our cognitive performance, an optimum, involves more than that. In particular, it involves endorsing a certain value as governing the cognitive process.

Sophie Loidolt makes the point quite clearly, referring to the way in which truth becomes a value, when she states: "Thus, truth or rather evidence as the lived-experience of self-givenness must not only be conceived naively as the measure of the correctness of the content, but also transcendentally as the ground of all validity" (Loidolt 2009, p. 93; my translation).

This is what Husserl calls justificatory responsibility (*Rechtfertigung*).[20] Justificatory responsibility is a key topic in Husserl's reflections on ethical life. This does not mean that Husserl lets the question concerning epistemic justification dissolve into the realm of practical philosophy in general and ethics in particular, but rather that the disclosure of truth is to be seen as part of an overall conception of rationality as an ideal for human life.

The series of papers Husserl wrote for the Japanese journal *Kaizo* are especially illuminating in this respect.[21] There, Husserl defines *Rechtfertigung* as the process of rational striving which not only tends toward truth and justification but also and at the same time toward giving "one's personal life the form of insight to [...] its position-takings or rather to bring them into an appropriate relationship with what gives them correctness [*Rechtmässigkeit*] or rationality" (Husserl 1988, Hua XXVII, p. 26, my translation).

This rational demand is expressed on the subjective side as a requirement for renewal (*Erneuerung*). This ideal of renewal draws together many significant Husserlian methodological topics – such as the always-again (*immer-wieder*), or the iterability of experience, the presumptive character of evidence, among others – in the form of an ethical maxim and a call to answer for oneself as a rational being. The idea of renewal involves a call to be willing on each occasion to provide new evidence, to seek out further experience, to revise our prior beliefs, to change ourselves, in the quest for rightness (*Rechtheit*). This makes the exercise of reason an exercise of freedom, of autonomy. Being rational does not only amount to believing what we are completely justified to believe on perfect evi-

---

20 The notion of *Rechtfertigung*, as will become apparent, has the advantage of combining both the notion of justification as providing evidence, which is the standard in theoretical contexts, and the broader notion of proving oneself right, in the sense of exhibiting one's rational credentials as the ground for one's own values (see Husserl 1988, Hua XXVII, p. 33). For further elaboration on this see my paper: Ainbinder 2018.
21 This has been underlined in Nenon 2003, pp. 66*sq*.

dential grounds, but also to willingness to question our evidence and our justification at any given time.[22]

As Kant correctly argued against Hume, no causal fact could function as a criterion for assessing what is right and what is wrong. That I cannot but experience objects perspectivally depends at least in part on what perception is for the kind of organisms that we are; but if I happened to experience the sides of the object I perceive as coming together incoherently, I would need to revise my experience, my position-takings and my positings, and that requires assessing my actual experience in light of norms that determine what experience *ought* to be like. This is the way in which the "must" becomes an "ought," and such a transformation is the very definition of rational life in Husserl's terms.

I have developed in detail the crucial role of what I translated as justificatory responsibility (*Rechtfertigung*) elsewhere (Ainbinder 2018) and cannot get into the details here. There, I assumed the perspective of rational grounding against a Humean reading of transcendental conditions. What I intended to do in this chapter was to take seriously what I now understand to be an essential trait of Husserl's understanding of transcendental philosophy, namely, the way in which rational norms are instantiated in our lived, concrete biological existence and the way in which our rationality cannot be properly understood without taking into account the mechanisms upon which rational assessment (partially) supervenes.[23] What I mean by partial supervenience here is that the mechanisms at stake are such that, were they not in place, the rational assessment involved in objective thinking would not be possible even if their mere proper functioning does not guarantee the rationality of the associated thought. This is where abnormalities are especially illuminating. To perceive truthfully (believing myself to be doing so) a ball in front of me involves my being disposed to offer rational justification for my (perceptual) claim, which at least partly involves my being willing to withdraw it if I touch the ball and my hand goes through it. It was, after all, a hallucination, I would think. But if my capacity for rational assessment rides on my capacity to track the ball through space and time, to compare the data provided by my different senses, to voluntarily repeat my movements to get a better look at the ball, etc., failures in such mechanisms will have a potentially destructive impact on my capacities for rational assessment. So, for instance, a deficit in my short term memory mechanisms may make me incapable of tracking the object if the perceptual process is not continuous and hence

---

22 See Melle 2007, p. 7.
23 In talking of partial supervenience, I am loosely following Yoshimi 2010, § 2.

makes me *eo ipso* incapable of accounting for my belief that there is in fact a ball there.

What is more, the fact that human rationality involves a normative dimension, an appeal to values and an ethical demand, all depends on the contingent fact that, on the one hand, we are biological organisms that have identities based on teleologically oriented capacities, a system of potentialities, and, on the other hand, that we are capable of assuming such potentialities as something to which we need to respond, as an "ought" rather than a "must." If we neglect the roots of reason in these contingent concrete mechanisms, we risk losing a grip on how rational norms can govern our thinking at all, which is precisely what, in the eyes of Husserl, happened to Kant.

Bibliography

Ainbinder, Bernardo (2016): "'Trascendental a posteriori'. La autofundamentación de la fenomenología trascendental y los límites de la donación". In: *Studia Heideggeriana*, vol. V, pp. 147–186.

Ainbinder, Bernardo (2018): "Transcendental Experience". In: Cimino, A. & Leijenhorst, C. (Eds.): *Phenomenology and Experience: New Perspectives*. Leiden: Brill, pp. 28–45.

Bruzina, Ronald (2010): "Husserl's "Naturalism" and Genetic Phenomenology". In: *New Yearbook for Phenomenology and Phenomenological Philosophy*, vol. 10, n° 1, pp. 91–125.

Crowell, Steven (2007): "Phenomenology and the First-Person Character of Philosophical Knowledge". In: *Modern Schoolman*, vol. 84, n° 2–3, pp. 131–148.

Crowell, Steven (2012): "Transcendental Phenomenology and the Seductions of Naturalism: Subjectivity, Consciousness, and Meaning". In: Dan Zahavi (Ed.): *The Oxford Handbook of Contemporary Phenomenology*. Oxford: Oxford University Press.

Doyon, Maxime (2018): "Husserl on Perceptual Optimality." In: *Husserl Studies*, vol. 34, n° 2, pp. 171–189.

Gallagher, Kenneth (1972): "Kant and Husserl on the Synthetic A Priori". In: *Kant-Studien*, vol. 63, n° 1–4, pp. 341–352.

Heinämaa, Sara; Hartimo, Mirja & Miettinen, Timo (Eds.) (2014): *Phenomenology and the Transcendental*. London: Routledge.

Hugo, Zachary (2017a): "Horizon, Modality, and Reason: Another Look at Husserl and the Normativity of Perception." In: *Études Phénoménologiques – Phenomenological Studies*, vol. 1, pp. 65–93.

Hugo, Zachary (2017b): *The Normativity of Perceptual Experience in Husserl's Phenomenology*. Unpublished Dissertation, Alberto Hurtado University, Santiago, Chile.

Husserl, Edmund (1956): *Erste Philosophie (1923/24)*. Erster Teil: *Kritische Ideengeschichte*. *Husserliana*, vol. VII. Ed. Rudolf Boehm. The Hague: Martinus Nijhoff.

Husserl, Edmund (1960): *Cartesian Meditations*. Trans. Dorion Cairns. The Hague: Martinus Nijhoff. German Edition: Husserl, E. (1973): *Cartesianische Meditationen und Pariser Vorträge*. *Husserliana*, vol. I. Ed. Stephan Strasser. The Hague: Martinus Nijhoff.

Husserl, Edmund (1969): *Formal and Transcendental Logic*. Trans. Dorion Cairns. The Hague: Martinus Nijhoff. German Edition: Husserl, E. (1974): *Formale und transzendentale Logik. Versuch einer Kritik der logischen Vernunft. Husserliana*, vol. XVII. Ed. Paul Janssen. The Hague: Martinus Nijhoff.

Husserl, Edmund (1970): *The Crisis of European Sciences and Transcendental Phenomenology. An Introduction to Phenomenological Philosophy*. Trans. David Carr. Evanston: Northwestern University Press. German Edition: Husserl, E. (1976): *Die Krisis der europäischen Wissenschaften und die transzendentale Phänomenologie. Eine Einleitung in die phänomenologische Philosophie. Husserliana*, vol. VI. Ed. Walter Biemel. The Hague: Martinus Nijhoff.

Husserl, Edmund (1973a): *Zur Phänomenologie der Intersubjektivität. Texte aus dem Nachlass. Zweiter Teil. 1921–28. Husserliana*, vol. XIV. Ed. Iso Kern. The Hague: Martinus Nijhoff.

Husserl, Edmund (1973b): *Zur Phänomenologie der Intersubjektivität. Texte aus dem Nachlass. Dritter Teil. 1929–35. Husserliana*, vol. XV. Ed. Iso Kern. The Hague: Martinus Nijhoff.

Husserl, Edmund (1983): *Ideas Pertaining to a Pure Phenomenology and to a Phenomenological Philosophy. First Book. General Introduction to a Pure Phenomenology*. Trans. Fred Kersten. Dordrecht/Boston/London: Kluwer Academic Publishers. German Edition: Husserl, E. (1952): *Ideen zur einer reinen Phänomenologie und phänomenologischen Philosophie. Zweites Buch: Phänomenologische Untersuchungen zur Konstitution. Husserliana*, vol. IV. Ed. Marly Biemel. The Hague: Martinus Nijhoff.

Husserl, Edmund (1988): *Aufsätze und Vorträge. 1922–1937. Husserliana*, vol. XXVII. Ed. T. Nenon and H.R. Sepp. The Hague: Kluwer Academic Publishers.

Husserl, Edmund (1989): *Ideas Pertaining to a Pure Phenomenology and to a Phenomenological Philosophy. Second Book. Studies in the Phenomenology of Constitution*. Trans. Richard Rojcewicz and André Schuwer. Dordrecht/Boston/ London: Kluwer Academic Publishers. German Edition: Husserl, E. (1977): *Ideen zu einer reinen Phänomenologie und phänomenologischen Philosophie. Erstes Buch: Allgemeine Einführung in die reine Phänomenologie*, 1. Halbband: Text der 1.–3. Auflage – Nachdruck. *Husserliana*, vol. III/1. Ed. Karl Schuhmann. The Hague: Martinus Nijhoff.

Husserl, Edmund (1999): *The Idea of Phenomenology. A Translation of "Die Idee der Phänomenologie", Husserliana II*. Translation and Introduction Lee Hardy. German Edition: Husserl, E. (1973): *Die Idee der Phänomenologie. Fünf Vorlesungen. Husserliana*, vol. II. Ed. Walter Biemel. The Hague: Martinus Nijhoff.

Husserl, Edmund (2001): *Logical Investigations. In Two Volumes*. Trans. John Niemeyer Findlay. London: Routledge. German Edition: Husserl, E. (1975): *Logische Untersuchungen. Erster Teil. Prolegomena zur reinen Logik. Text der 1. und der 2. Auflage. Husserliana*, vol. XVIII. Ed. Elmar Holenstein. The Hague: Martinus Nijhoff.

Husserl, Edmund (2006): *Späte Texte über Zeitkonstitution (1929–1934). Die C-Manuskripte. Husserliana Materialien*, vol. VIII. Ed. Dieter Lohmar. New York: Springer.

Husserl, Edmund (2012): *Einleitung in die Philosophie. Vorlesungen 1916–1920. Husserliana Materialien*, vol. IX. Ed. Hanne Jacobs. Dordrecht: Springer.

Husserl, Edmund (2014): *Grenzprobleme der Phänomenologie. Analysen des Unbewusstseins und der Instinkte. Metaphysik. Späte Ethik (Texte aus dem Nachlass 1908–1937). Husserliana*, vol. XLII. Ed. Rochus Sowa & Thomas Vongehr. Dordrecht: Springer.
Kern, Iso (1964): *Husserl und Kant. Eine Untersuchung über Husserls Verhältnis zu Kant und zum Neukantianismus.* The Hague: Martinus Nijhoff.
Loidolt, Sophie (2009): *Anspruch und Rechtfertigung.* Dordrecht: Springer.
Luft, Sebastian (2007): "From being to givenness and back: Some remarks on the meaning of transcendental idealism in Kant and Husserl". In: *International Journal of Philosophical Studies*, vol. 15, n° 3, pp. 367–394.
Melle, Ullrich (2007): "Husserl's personalist ethics". In: *Husserl Studies*, vol. 23, n° 1, pp. 1–15.
Mohanty, Jitendranath (1996): "Kant and Husserl". In: *Husserl Studies*, vol. 13, n° 1, pp. 19–30.
Mohanty, Jitendranath (1985): *The Possibility of Transcendental Philosophy.* Dordrecht: Kluwer Academic Publishers.
Nenon, Thomas (2003): "Husserl's Conception of Reason as Authenticity". In: *Philosophy Today*, vol. 47, pp. 63–70.
Nenon, Thomas (2008): "Some differences between Kant's and Husserl's conceptions of transcendental philosophy". In: *Continental Philosophy Review*, vol. 41, n° 4, pp. 427–439.
Okrent, Mark (2017): *Nature and Normativity: Biology, Teleology, and Meaning.* London: Routledge.
Seebohm, Thomas (1962): *Die Bedingungen der Möglichkeit der Transzendentalphilosophie.* Bonn: Bouvier.
Walton, Roberto (2017): "Horizonality and Legitimation in Perception, Affectivity, and Volition". In: Walton, Roberto; Shigeru Taguchi & Roberto Rubio (Eds.): *Perception, Affectivity, and Volition in Husserl's Phenomenology.* Dordrecht: Springer.
Yoshimi, Jeff (2010): "Husserl on Psycho-Physical Laws". In: *New Yearbook for Phenomenology and Phenomenological Philosophy*, vol. 10, pp. 25–42.

Dale Allen Hobbs, Jr.
Philosophical Scientists and Scientific Philosophers

Kant and Husserl on the Philosophical Foundations of the Natural Sciences

Abstract: This chapter explores the varying conceptions of science as such put forth by Kant and Husserl, particularly with respect to the essential connections that each posit between the natural sciences and the field of transcendental philosophy. Although both philosophers follow a similar path in spelling out a strict set of conditions for scientificity, this chapter largely sets out to investigate the ways in which their views on the subject differ. In particular, I discuss certain limitations on Kant's view of science that do not recur on Husserl's model; one major purpose of the chapter is thus to defend Husserl's views as a more developed account of the relationship between science and transcendental philosophy than are those of his philosophical forebear.

What is a scientist? Taken in a sufficiently broad sense, the term calls all sorts of images to mind: the chemist in a white lab coat, the physicist or mathematician puzzling over symbols on a chalkboard, perhaps even the theorist in an armchair, struggling to carry out Edmund Husserl's famous "philosophy as rigorous science" as he stares at the copper ashtray before him. In light of the extremely wide variety of contexts in which the term "science" might be employed, it is no simple task to give it a precise definition. Nonetheless, if fields as diverse as philosophy and physics are to be characterized as sciences without equivocation, some essential relationships among the methods employed in those disciplines must be found.

This issue is especially relevant to transcendental idealism, broadly construed. After all, it is perhaps this field that most explicitly endeavors to establish certain basic links between philosophy as a rigorous science of cognition and the very possibility of attaining genuinely scientific knowledge of the world. In particular, this chapter will set out to investigate the conceptions of science as such that are operative within the work of Immanuel Kant and that of the aforementioned Edmund Husserl. Both philosophers share a commitment to the claim that there exist essential connections between transcendental philosophy and the natural sciences, with the former playing a foundational role. However,

https://doi.org/10.1515/9783110564280-016

they disagree about the precise nature of this role, and thereby espouse differing views about the scope of science as a whole. The purpose of this project is to explore both these similarities and these differences, with the ultimate aim of determining which view of the natural sciences offers the more fruitful account of the relationship between philosophy and other modes of investigating the world of experience.

1 Kant's Conception of the Natural Sciences

Let us begin with Kant, the leading light of transcendental idealism and the forefather of anything like a critical philosophy of scientific cognition. For Kant, the problem of scientific knowledge in general is a major focus of any genuine philosophy, and the fundamental approach he takes to this problem – the transcendental turn carried out in the first *Critique* – is already well-known in philosophical circles. Nonetheless, in order to illuminate more clearly the ramifications of Kant's views in their specific connections to the *natural* sciences, it will be useful to examine the basic requirements that he posits for science as such. In particular, I want to examine three of Kant's central claims about the necessary preconditions for scientificity. Namely, on his model, any genuinely scientific discipline can be identified by its overarching systematicity, its focus on relations of grounding and consequence, and its ultimate appeal to apodictic evidence; all three of these criteria must be met for any field of investigation to be considered a science at all.

For Kant, perhaps the foremost *conditio sine qua non* of all authentic knowledge of the world (as opposed to the broader notion of *doctrine*, of which scientific knowledge is only the most venerated part) is its systematic character. That is to say, truly scientific knowledge must, by definition, be rooted in an architectonics, and not merely pursued haphazardly. As he notes in his work on *Physical Geography*, to give just one example, "we need to become acquainted with the objects of our experience *as a whole*. Thereby our knowledge is not an *aggregation* but a *system*; for in a system the *whole* is prior to the parts, while in an aggregation the *parts* have priority" (Kant 2012, § 2, p. 446). Kant's discussion of this point at the very beginnings of his inquiry is no accident; his claim is the bold one that any body of knowledge, insofar as it is to partake in the status of science at all, must be carried out in this systematic manner, such that it can never accurately be represented as merely a *collection of facts*. The key difference here lies in the programmatic structure of scientific investigation vis-à-vis other ways of understanding the world; while it is certainly acceptable, in some circumstances, merely to account for the "facts on the ground" in a more or less rhapsodic way, genuine science must move beyond this lack of rigor. Science and systematicity go hand-in-hand. This requirement is clearly met in several cases, from the rigor of transcendental philosophy (e.g., the careful layout of Kant's own *Critiques*) to the experimental precision of theoretical physics and beyond.

Nonetheless, systematicity by itself is insufficient to establish a given discipline as a genuine science, on Kant's model. *In addition to* discussing its subject matter in architectonic fashion, a truly scientific field of study must go beyond the level of mere (empirical) description to focus also on the fundamental structures of the field of experience that it studies. That is, science is distinguished by the fact that it focuses not merely on a set of (systematically understood) facts, but rather, as Kant puts it, on the various relations of grounding and consequence among those facts. In the preface to his treatise on the *Metaphysical Foundations of Natural Science*, Kant thus distinguishes between a mere "*historical doctrine of nature*, which contains nothing but systematically ordered facts about natural things," and "natural science" in the full sense (Kant 1963, AK. IV, p. 468; Kant 2004, p. 4). Although certain methods for laying out the facts on the ground (e.g., a physical geography that proceeds in an orderly fashion through discussion of mountains, valleys, rivers, etc.) might well be fully systematic in character, that is simply not enough to permit them to seize upon the title of science. Rather, something else is required: an appeal to the *underlying principles* of the subject matter in question – not merely detailing what is empirically the case, but rather explaining *why* it is the case (and must be so).

Indeed, Kant carries out his own investigations in the natural sciences in just such a manner. His *Physical Geography*, for instance, begins not with an account of certain facts about rivers, valleys, or any other feature of the natural world, but with a consideration of what he calls purely "mathematical geography," the general principles of physics governing the "shape, size, and motion of the earth, as well as its relationship to the rest of the universe" – and he claims that this beginning is an absolutely necessary foundation for everything that follows (Kant 2012, § 6, p. 453). He dedicates much of the geography lectures to exploring these "preliminary mathematical concepts," and for good reason: without strict attention to these underlying mathematical concerns, the discipline of geography could not, for Kant, properly aspire to the status of science at all. Here, again, we see the connection between science as it concerns the natural world and the scientific philosophy that was Kant's hallmark; just as a genuine science of cognition can only establish its own credibility through rigorous examination of the basic structures of consciousness itself, the natural sciences must be rooted in similar investigations into their own fundamental principles if they are to be valid as science in the first place. It is only because of its (systematic, architectonic, but also more than merely empirical) investigations into fundamental principles, Kant maintains, that any so-called science can justify a claim to that title.

Finally, there remains one basic requirement of scientificity on Kant's model that must be discussed. Namely, in addition to carrying out a systematic investigation into the fundamental principles of its subject matter, any genuine science must ultimately, for Kant, be capable of grounding itself on evidence that is known with *apodictic certainty*. Returning to the *Metaphysical Foundations*, Kant writes the following: "What can be called proper science is only that for which certainty is apodictic; cognition that can contain mere empirical certainty is only knowledge improperly so-called" (Kant 1963, AK. IV, p. 468; Kant 2004, p. 4). That is to say, it lies in the very definition of scientific knowledge that no purely empirical enterprise can ever be a science in the full sense, on Kant's interpretation; all genuine sciences, in order to qualify themselves as fully fledged modes of knowledge, must ultimately have some claim to complete and utter indubitability. This claim is evidenced both in philosophical sciences and in natural ones; for Kant, the appearance of any object via the categories is no more capable of being doubted than is the mathematical delimitation of space dealt with in physics, and it is on the basis of that fact that both disciplines can lay claim to the title of science.

Of course, we must be careful not to over-interpret Kant here. Particularly, it is critical to note that this requirement for apodicticity need not extend to *every* claim that might be subsumed under a given field of scientific investigation. As Peter Plaass rightly notes in his seminal investigation into Kant's view of the natural sciences, "it is to be observed that the certainty of a science spoken of here does not *eo ipso* mean that each proposition of this science, each bit of knowledge contained in it, is apodictically certain (as, e.g., in geometry)," and such a mischaracterization of Kant's true position on the subject is fastidiously to be avoided (Plaass 1994, p. 233). Rather, all that is required for a discipline to be scientific is that the method which the discipline follows be *in principle* based on such apodictic evidence (as, e.g., physics is rooted in the immutable truths of mathematics in their application to the spatial world, as well as in the insights produced by the philosophical consideration of spatiality in Kant's transcendental aesthetic), rather than merely employing such evidence in a peripheral way or – worse yet – ignoring it entirely. Kant thus demands only that any genuinely scientific field of investigation be possessed of a purely apodictic *core*, a fundamental basis derived from wholly *a priori* cognition, and not that it mandate that all possible derivations from that core be themselves purely apodictic. As Kant writes, all "*proper* natural science therefore requires a *pure* part, on which the apodictic certainty that reason seeks therein can be based," and it is only this pure element of the science that must meet this strict criterion (Kant 1963,

AK. IV, p. 469; Kant 2004, p. 5). The requirement of apodicticity is thus not as excessive as it might appear at first glance; natural science must be rooted in the apodicticity that, as I will discuss, is possible only through critical philosophy, but it is not simply *reducible* to that foundation. Physics, e. g., can certainly include empirical observations in the scope of its genuinely scientific investigations – the calculation of the speed of light, for instance – while nevertheless remaining grounded in principle on legitimately apodictic insights. Nonetheless, the connection between science and apodicticity remains vital.

To return to the topic of the relationship between the natural sciences and transcendental philosophy, it should be noted that these claims about the essential connections among science, systematicity, and an apodictic investigation into fundamental principles are by no means a passing fancy on the part of Kant. Rather, they are deeply rooted in his conception of the conditions for the possibility of knowledge as such. Given the fact that any real science must, for Kant, result in the acquisition of genuine knowledge (and not mere belief), as well as the fact that the knowledge pursued by the *natural* sciences is precisely supposed to be knowledge *of the world* (and thus not merely analytic), it is plain to see that these disciplines must contain, at least as an essential part, the sort of cognitions that Kant refers to as both synthetic and *a priori*. Even from the very beginnings of his critical investigations, Kant admits as much. Speaking of his paradigmatic example of a true natural science, physics, Kant writes in the first *Critique* that it "*contains* a priori *synthetic judgments as principles,*" mentioning specifically the judgments that "in all changes of the material world the quantity of matter remains unchanged; and that in all communication of motion, actions and reaction must be equal" (Kant 1787, B 17; Kant 2003, p. 54). But all such conclusions – that is to say, apodictic conclusions drawn from reason totally *a priori*, but which necessarily remain applicable to the world of experience – are possible, Kant claims, only on the basis of the particular conception of knowledge as such put forth by transcendental idealism. It is only possible for any investigation of the world to attain knowledge that is both necessary and generally applicable if it remains essentially connected to a transcendental view of cognition as a whole. Thus, the fact that any genuine science must, by virtue of its necessary appeal to apodictic principles, reach back to the transcendental investigations that Kant began in the first *Critique* is, at least on this model of scientificity in general, indisputable.[1]

---

[1] Of course, this essential link between Kant's views on the requirements of science and his conception of knowledge as such is by no means a novel development in Kant studies. Peter Plaass' 1965 treatise (published only in 1994) makes more or less the same observation, and in more detail. He notes that Kant's criteria for science are "not by any means an observation

As such, any investigation into the natural world, if it is to come forth as a science, must ultimately be rooted in transcendental philosophy. Although the first two conditions of science could potentially be satisfied without such reference, Kant holds that only transcendental idealism is able to attain the synthetic, *a priori* truths that are necessary for apodictic knowledge to be applied to the natural world. It is certainly possible for there to exist modes of investigating the world of experience that are fully systematic without making any intrinsic reference to transcendental philosophy: descriptive geography, for one, could be carried out in a completely architectonic fashion, without venturing one step beyond a mere catalog of facts. It is even reasonable, on Kant's account, for there to exist certain systematic investigations into fundamental principles that nevertheless have no (direct) connection to philosophy, as I will discuss in what follows. Nevertheless, any genuine attainment of *knowledge* that can apply to all experience, knowledge that appeals back to the apodictically certain, *a priori* conditions for the possibility of experience as such, is only possible on the basis of the transcendental turn that is the hallmark of Kant's idealism. For Kant, transcendental philosophy is thus the foundation of all genuine science, with each other possible science having its roots in the insights which only the transcendental philosopher can unlock.

Of course, Kant by no means claims that *only* the philosopher is capable of being a genuine scientist. As we have already seen, Kant certainly holds that at least some of what are ordinarily considered to be the natural sciences also have a legitimate claim to that term – his paradigmatic example is always that of rigorous physics, which is both a true science in its own right and irreducible to even the most advanced philosophical investigations. But how can this possibly be the case, if the hallmark of the natural sciences is that they venture beyond the more austere conclusions of critical philosophy, even to the point of deriving many of their most noteworthy conclusions from merely empirical data (e. g., in physics, the calculation of the speed of light through empirical experiments involving mirrors)?

Kant's answer, hearkening back to his nuanced portrayal of the apodictic character of science in general, is that any genuine science must be founded

---

incidentally put forth here, but [are] well grounded in the [*Critique of Pure Reason*]," and that "only this necessity would be able to make something like *a priori* knowledge in this field legitimate" (Plaass 1994, pp. 237–238). My interpretation of Kant on this point owes much to Plaass as one of the first to examine these critical links. But it is important to make these general observations once again, at least briefly, if the ramifications of Kant's view of the natural sciences are to be understood completely in light of their relevance to transcendental philosophy in general.

on certain *a priori* judgments that are themselves grounded on the results of transcendental philosophical investigations, but which perhaps remain distinct from specifically philosophical conclusions. Physics, for instance, rests on certain basic conclusions – the laws of physics, say – that, while seeming to be merely empirical on the surface, are truly derived *at core* from *a priori* judgments (e. g., about the nature of spatiality as such). As Michael Friedman artfully demonstrates in his analysis of Kant on matter and motion, we can "know *a priori* that there are two general types of objects of our senses: objects of inner sense and objects of outer sense. The concept of matter" – i.e., its fundamental determinations, though not, of course, the empirical properties of any specific instance of matter – "is simply that of an arbitrary object of outer sense – the concept of an object in space. And, in this sense, its content then appears to be entirely *a priori*" (Friedman 2013, p. 54). But, of course, the basic determinations of an "object of outer sense in general" are themselves only intelligible through philosophical investigation – namely, the very one that Kant himself carries out as the transcendental aesthetic. The "laws of physics," then, can be seen to be rooted in specifically philosophical inquiry, even while they range beyond the limitations of philosophy *per se* – the physicist takes as the founding principle of his discipline certain conclusions about spatiality that are unlocked by the philosopher, but he or she employs those principles in rigorous, systematic investigations of a very different sort.[2] Only thus can physics be valid *as* science. Kant himself confirms this interpretation, noting that that the entire sphere of natural science "presupposes, in the first place, metaphysics of nature" as a necessary precondition for its scientific character (Kant 1963, AK. IV, p. 469; Kant 2004, p. 5).

Accordingly, Kant's view of science as a whole as rooted in transcendental philosophy has little trouble accounting for some of our ordinary uses of the term; physics can be just as much a genuine science as the most rigorous philosophy, precisely because of its reliance on that philosophy. And yet, Kant does run into problems when he attempts to extend his definition of science beyond this

---

[2] Specifically, these investigations in *natural* science are carried out by unifying the pure *a priori* laws grasped by transcendental philosophy with the empirical content studied by the natural science in question, e. g., the particular determinations of actual instances of matter and energy in physics. This shift in focus allows the natural sciences to range beyond the more limited sphere of transcendental philosophy as such. As Paul Guyer notes, the pure *a priori* content of philosophy, taken by itself, can never "logically imply any empirical laws of nature because empirical intuitions are always needed to give them empirical content, just as empirical intuitions must be added to the pure forms of intuition to represent any objects located at any determinate region of space or time" (Guyer 2005, p. 40).

level. Recall that the basic preconditions for scientificity demand the employment of apodictic insights as the foundational principles of any supposedly scientific field of investigation, just as physics employs Kant's insights about space in the transcendental aesthetic. Certainly, such a foundation is possible for at least some disciplines that we would ordinarily count among the natural sciences – but do *all* such disciplines appeal to such a basis so overtly? In fact, this is not the case. Only relatively few of the fields that we ordinarily think of as natural sciences make (direct) use of transcendental, apodictic insights in the way that Kant demands from a genuine science. Since he claims that science as such requires such a foundation, Kant is thus forced into the unenviable position of denying the status of science proper to many apparently scientific disciplines – his philosophical rigor demands no less.

Let us take as our chief example of this distinction the field that Kant himself discusses as the paradigmatic case of an "improper" science, a discipline only mistakenly numbered among the real sciences: chemistry. Certainly, chemistry seems on the surface to be quite scientific, and chemists to be real scientists; after all, the stereotypical depiction of a scientist dressed in a white lab coat and holding a Bunsen burner is closely associated with the field. And yet, chemistry is also a field of study far more concerned with empirical details than even its close relative, physics; whereas physics studies the laws of motion, etc., *in general*, chemistry has a much more specific aim (i.e., the study of the interactions among particular – determinate – sorts of elements or molecules). It is thus difficult to see a parallel in chemistry to physics' appeal to the transcendental conditions of objects of outer sense as such, an explicit connection to the genuinely apodictic conclusions of transcendental philosophy. As a result, Kant is forced by his own criteria for scientificity to reject chemistry as a proper science at all. As he writes: "If, however, the grounds or principles themselves are still in the end merely empirical, as in chemistry, for example, and the laws from which the given facts are explained through reason are mere laws of experience, then they carry with them no consciousness of their necessity (they are not apodictically certain), and thus the whole of cognition does not deserve the name of a science in the strict sense," ultimately concluding that "chemistry should therefore be called a systematic art rather than a science" (Kant 1963, AK. IV, p. 468; Kant 2004, p. 4). While chemistry might be a truly systematic avenue of investigation, and while Kant certainly admits its usefulness, it is eternally barred from the status of a genuine science on the Kantian model, precisely because of its essentially empirical character. The same would hold true for most other examples of supposed natural sciences, from geology to (especially, on Kant's view) biology, none of which have the same overt connection to the truly apodictic truths of transcendental philosophy that lie at the foundation of physics. While useful, they have a merely subordinate role to play in the grand scheme of human knowledge.

Let us examine the subject in more detail. What really distinguishes physics from these so-called "improper" sciences? Kant justifies this distinction by appealing to his restriction of genuinely scientific investigation of the natural world (i.e., the world given in genuine experience) to the purely mathematical elements *contained within* certain supposed natural sciences as their principled core. That is to say, only fields of inquiry that are, at root, based on theoretical, mathematical reason, *and which derive their principles purely therefrom*, may be genuine sciences. In the *Metaphysical Foundations*, Kant asserts

> that in any special doctrine of nature there can be only as much proper science as there is mathematics therein. For, according to the preceding, proper science, and above all proper natural science, requires a pure part lying at the basis of the empirical part, and resting on *a priori* cognition of natural things. Now to cognize something *a priori* means to cognize it from its mere possibility. But the possibility of determinate natural things cannot be cognized from their mere concepts; for from these the possibility of the thought (that it does not contradict itself) can certainly be cognized, but not the possibility of the object, as a natural thing that can be given outside the thought (as existing). Hence, in order to cognize the possibility of determinate natural things, and thus to cognize them *a priori*, it is still required that the intuition corresponding to the concept be given *a priori*, that is, that the concept be constructed. Now rational cognition through construction of concepts is mathematical. (Kant 1963, AK. IV, p. 470; Kant 2004, p. 6)

I quote this account at length because it strikes to the heart of Kant's views about science's limitations. Only those aspects of a field of study that are truly capable of derivation from *a priori* principles in a *purely mathematical* way (e.g., the most rigorous branches of theoretical physics) are genuine sciences, for Kant. Chemistry – as rigorous and systematic as it may be – does not deal with the notion of, e.g., "objects in space" in a purely mathematical way, but rather ranges well beyond that level, to the point where its primary focus is on the interactions of specific sorts of objects *in terms of their determinate content*.[3] Kant thus writes that

---

3 Of course, it is possible that more recent developments in *molecular* chemistry as a very mathematical discipline could permit the establishment of a more thoroughgoing connection between the field and the genuinely apodictic conclusions of, e.g., a transcendental philosophy of matter as such than would have been possible in Kant's time. I make no definitive claim on this subject here. Nevertheless, even if such a rehabilitation of the scientific status of chemistry on Kant's model would be possible in light of such developments, the problem would recur in countless other ostensibly scientific fields: the aforementioned fields of geology and biology, certainly, are essentially dependent on merely empirical investigations in a way that does not seem likely to

"its principles are merely empirical, and allow of no *a priori* presentation in intuition" (Kant 1963, AK. IV, p. 471; Kant 2004, p. 7).

Even though physics too is rooted not only in the pure *a priori* laws of transcendental philosophy, but also in empirical intuitions about the motion of matter, these latter intuitions are relevant to that science only insofar as they are *particular determinations* of the former laws, particular ways in which those laws manifest themselves in actual experience.[4] In chemistry, by way of contrast, the principles studied are *merely* empirical, and thus require a more explicitly empirical mode of study than the rigorously mathematical methods of theoretical physics. Whereas one can figure out a great deal about theoretical physics by considering, e.g., the application of "the concept of nature in general to the empirical concept of the electron [...] without taking anything more from experience," this accomplishment is, for Kant, not repeatable when we move beyond this limited sphere to the concrete determinations of particular sorts of molecules, etc. (Plaass 1994, p. 243). The same is, of course, true for most other supposed natural sciences – few fields have anything like the rigorously mathematical purity or abstraction of physics, especially once we venture into the rather messy realms of biology, sociology, etc.

Accordingly, Kant's conception of the natural sciences is a rather restrictive one, for all its nuance. It precludes, most especially, the possibility of making *genuinely scientific* advances in many fields of inquiry; even if the work carried out by the chemist or the biologist is useful (or even necessary for a full understanding of the world), it can never be fully *scientific* on Kant's model. That is not to say, of course, that Kant devalues these disciplines in any thoroughgoing way. Science, even taken as a whole, does not account for the sum total of human cognition, any more than the discipline of transcendental philosophy carried out in Kant's critical work encompasses all of science; there is plenty of room left over for chemistry, or even wider-ranging disciplines like anthropology or sociology, to make genuinely *pragmatic* advances in their respective fields.[5] Nevertheless, as demonstrated previously, genuine science is, for Kant, the elevated core of all true knowledge of the world of experience, and is more worthy of esteem than all unscientific disciplines. As such, the modern thinker inquiring into the subject of the scientific status of such disciplines might well find Kant's portrayal of science to be lacking in certain respects – it would be a grievous blow indeed if we were required to strip the title of scientist from all chemists or biol-

---

permit this sort of mathematization, and the same applies to many such disciplines, from meteorology to astronomy and beyond.
4 *Cf.* Guyer 2005, p. 40.
5 See Makkreel 2001 for further discussion of these alternatives to science, properly so-called.

ogists, and that move would necessitate a radical shift in our ordinary way of thinking about the validity of such fields. Thus, although Kant is well able to account for the solid, foundational link between science and philosophical inquiry that is sought after by any aspiring transcendental philosopher, the question can still reasonably be asked as to whether or not some alternative means of explaining this link can be found that would rid us of the need for such reappraisal. Without some feasible alternative, the disestablishment of certain ostensibly scientific disciplines from that status that is made necessary by Kant's model cannot be avoided while remaining within the realm of transcendental philosophy as such.

2 Husserl's Phenomenological Account of Science

It is fortunate, then, that transcendental philosophy by no means came to a halt after the death of Kant. Even beyond the various schools of Neo-Kantianism, the transcendental turn carried out in the first *Critique* remains a strong influence in many regions of philosophy, perhaps most notably that of transcendental phenomenology. First formalized by Edmund Husserl, this school carries out the project of transcendental philosophy in a way that – at least, in its own estimation – goes beyond the limitations of Kant's attempts. Nonetheless, when it comes to the question of defining science as such, phenomenology gives similar answers to those of Kant discussed above. Ultimately, I hope to demonstrate how Husserl provides answers to the problem of scientificity that account for many of the same facts as does Kant's solution, while also going beyond Kant's formulation in important ways – particularly with respect to the relationship between scientific philosophy and the "messier" natural sciences that Kant considers to be only improperly so termed.

To begin, it is noteworthy that Husserl too claims that any genuine science must be rooted in transcendental philosophy, and that he does so for many of the same reasons as Kant. For Husserl, as for his philosophical forebear, science is inextricably related to the task of producing, as he puts it, an "archaeology" of knowledge; the task of any scientific discipline is to "investigate systematically" the foundational principles of whatever region of reality it purports to study, ultimately in such a way that "it can be originally secured with an absolutely clear conscience as *finished*, as not only valid but *'finally valid'*" (Husserl 1959, Hua VIII, p. 28). In broad terms, Husserl too thus endorses Kant's three criteria for scientificity. Any science worthy of the name must be fully systematic in character in order to serve as a genuine archeology of its subject matter, it must delve deeply into the fundamental structures of that subject matter if it is to be able to bring its investigations to completion, and it must – ultimately – be grounded on apodictic evidence in order to have the "final validity" mentioned above. The continuing influence of the transcendental philosophy established by Kant remains quite apparent in Husserl's take on the subject, and much of what was said previously about the nature of science on Kant's model continues to be accurate in a phenomenological context as well – Husserl is, after all, a transcendental philosopher in his own right, and thus committed to walking the path that the founder of transcendental philosophy laid out ahead of him.

Nevertheless, let us examine more carefully the peculiarities of Husserl's own views on the subject of science as such. While both Husserl and Kant are deeply concerned with the task of establishing an ineradicable link between the validity of the natural sciences and the transcendental science that is carried out by the philosopher, their motivations for this project are somewhat distinct. For Kant, as demonstrated, the point of this task is to uncover those aspects of the natural sciences that are truly worthy of the title, i.e., by disentangling the purely mathematical elements of the genuine sciences from the (merely empirical) conclusions of sciences only improperly so-called. Husserl, on the other hand, puts more of an emphasis on the role of transcendental philosophy in assisting the other sciences in coming to a full self-understanding of themselves than in weeding out certain disciplines from the scope of science as a whole. He carries out this task, in large part, in his examination of the systematic roots of knowledge as such collected as his lectures on *First Philosophy*. Since the basically Kantian connections between science and in-depth systematic investigation of the relevant subject matter are quite obvious throughout Husserl's work and require little further discussion – see, e.g., his famous thoughts on "Philosophy as Rigorous Science" –, let us focus our attention primarily on his views about the connections between science and the transcendental, particularly in light of the access that transcendental philosophy grants to genuine apodicticity.

Like his predecessor, Husserl too insists on the need for any genuine science to be grounded on evidence that is known apodictically if it is to be worthy of the name, and it is here (as in Kant) that the dependence of science on a genuinely transcendental philosophy is most apparent. He writes that all sciences whatsoever must be, at core, dependent on a transcendental philosophy of cognition as "a systematic advance of a completely novel, all-encompassing, thoroughgoingly transcendental science, a science that no longer contains any skeptical abysses, but in which, rather, everything is completely bright and clear and secure" (Husserl 1959, Hua VIII, p. 20).⁶ But why should this be the case? We have already seen Kant's insistence on the intrinsic interconnection between genuine knowledge and irrefutability, the insulation from doubt that is required by the transition to knowledge from the realm of mere opinion, but Husserl follows a slightly different path in reaching this conclusion. To understand why, on Husserl's model, any science whatsoever must be founded on the conclusions of transcendental philosophy, it is first necessary to look at one of the most central concepts of Husserl's phenomenology in general: that of *evidence*.

The notion of evidence, of course, is critical to scientificity. The natural sciences, even on the common view, count as legitimate pursuits of knowledge only because they seek to answer the questions of their various fields only on the basis of solid, publically available evidence.⁷ For Husserl, however, this notion of evidence is by no means as readily understandable as it might appear to be at first glance. What really counts as evidence, we might ask, and how are we to understand what sort of validity evidence has for us? It is only by answering these questions – and by doing so in a particularly phenomenological way – that Husserl believes that the validity of scientific inquiry in general can be understood at all.

For Husserl, the term "evidence" is to be interpreted literally, as that which *makes itself evident* to the cognizing subject. This view is essential to his philosophical methods; after all, what is phenomenology but the study of the world as a collection of interrelated *phenomena?* And what are these phenomena other than meaningful contents making themselves evident to an experiencing subject? Husserl thus identifies *evidence* as the objective counterpart to the experiential *insight* that is required to attain it (see, e.g., Husserl 1956, Hua VII, p. 9). All of this is nothing more than the basis of phenomenology, and it follows directly from Husserl's choice to follow Kant through the transcendental turn. But

---

6 All translations from this text in this chapter are drawn from a manuscript prepared by Sebastian Luft and Thane Naberhaus.

7 Note that this requirement of public availability is also a central component of Husserl's conception of science as such, as seen in his frequent characterization of the scientist as being essentially a member of an intersubjective community of fellow seekers of knowledge (a point of view especially prevalent in his later work, as well as in the texts of his followers, perhaps most prominently his assistant and collaborator Eugen Fink). I will not focus on this aspect of science in quite as direct a way as the others I mention, however, not because it is less relevant to our understanding of science than they are, but rather because it is in the links between science and transcendental philosophy established in science's requirement of apodicticity that it will be easiest to relate Husserl's views on science to those of Kant, as well as to explore the practical ramifications of the conceptual moves that Husserl makes to distinguish himself from his illustrious predecessor.

Husserl, given his own philosophical commitments, expands this view of experience in ways that go beyond Kant's focus on carrying out a critical analysis of reason. Instead, Husserl puts the focus of his investigations squarely on the *objects* to be investigated, namely, on the real phenomena that are supposed to make themselves evident and on the objective characteristics that enable them to do so (rather than solely on the transcendental conditions of consciousness that are necessary for such objects to *appear*).

It is here that his notion of evidence comes to the fore: an evidence, for Husserl, is a direct encounter with some phenomenon or set of phenomena that is to be understood, an encounter that is governed by its own special laws, which it is the task of the phenomenologist to investigate. An encounter with a visually perceived ball lying on the floor, for example, serves as evidence of the shape of the ball, its color, etc., while an encounter with a beautiful song or painting might provide evidence about the aesthetic quality of the piece. All of phenomenology, then, can be thought of as an extended investigation into the unique structures governing these various sorts of evidence: the evidence that is given in visual perception, for instance, versus that which goes along with our experiences of values. Phenomenology studies the necessary conditions for all these modes of evidence to be genuine components of our experiential world at all (e. g., Husserl's famous thoughts on the adumbrations of visual perception).

However, not all evidence is of equal stature. Just because something appears at first glance to be so does not, of course, mean that it is so. Indeed, a great deal of the evidence we encounter throughout our daily lives fails to justify the conclusions we are wont to draw from it in any really satisfying way. Imagine, to use Husserl's example, an encounter with a dimly-lit figure in a store window. This experience provides us with certain forms of evidence, perhaps that of a stranger gawking at us from within. Nevertheless, upon closer inspection, this evidence can turn out to be misleading: the figure in the window is not a human being at all, but a mannequin that merely appeared to be one in the bad lighting. This deception by no means obviates the fact that the initial experience was an evidence for us; it merely gives rise to the newer (and more complete) evidence that the figure is, in fact, not a living creature at all. This insight permits us to make useful distinctions between different *sorts* of evidence. Some evidence is more solid than others, while other evidences are opaque or misleading, ever remaining susceptible to revisions on the basis of new experiences. This is not to say that all such evidences (e. g., all sense data) are to be tossed out entirely; some such evidences are clearly more useful than others, just as a clearly seen figure in good lighting serves as better evidence than a dim figure at night. Husserl calls this sort of evidence *adequate* to its task, emphasizing that – while it remains, in some sense, dubitable and subject to revision – it is rare to encounter the opposing evidences that could put it into question. Even when such revision does become necessary, furthermore, adequate evidence never completely loses its force; it merely develops into newer and even more adequate forms of evidence, as when the figure in the window resolves itself into the mannequin. Nevertheless, Husserl does distinguish between adequate evidence and the "gold standard" of evidence, which he terms the apodictic. Recognition of this fact returns us to the overarching project at hand; if science is to be worthy of the name, for Husserl, then it must be rooted essentially in the latter form of evidence, a requirement which separates genuine science from all other modes of understanding the world around us.

Here, Husserl once again explicitly mirrors Kant. Any science worthy of the name must (in addition to its systematicity, etc.) be rooted in genuine *knowledge* about the world and grasped with a final validity, not merely in speculation or opinion based on insufficient evidence. But such conclusions are possible only on the ultimate basis of the absolutely certain knowledge unlocked by transcendental philosophy. In the *First Philosophy* lectures, Husserl declares that this insight has lain at the heart of genuine philosophy from its very beginnings, even before it became explicit in Kant's transcendental turn. He writes approvingly of the Platonic theory of the Ideas as establishing an encounter with "the original source of all legitimacy" as the basis of all real knowledge, claiming that the phenomenological insistence on a direct, intuitive encounter with genuine, apodictic evidence is nothing more than an updated (and more precise) version of the same approach: "[e]xpressed in our terms, [this encounter] occurs by recourse to perfect clarity, 'insight,' evidence,'" i.e., as "genuine knowing, producing itself through perfect evidence" (Husserl 1956, Hua VII, p. 9). For Husserl, it is this pursuit of apodictic truth that, taken alongside its thoroughgoing systematicity and unrestricted focus, distinguishes philosophy as the foundational science that is capable of unlocking knowledge *per se*. Philosophy's role is to sponsor a rigorous return to that which can be known absolutely – ultimately, phenomenology's famous return to "the things themselves," in light of the transcendental structures that govern their constitution by consciousness –, and it is the only discipline able to accomplish such a task in full.

Accordingly, while the natural sciences may be useful disciplines for the pursuit of knowledge in their own right by following the merely adequate evidence on which they are based (e.g., the physicist's experimental observations), they cannot *by themselves* attain the gold standard of knowledge without appeal to their philosophical roots. The physicist, for example, must rely on all sorts of conclusions taken from philosophy if his or her own investigations are to have any meaning: the adumbrations of visual perception, e.g., might have bearing on his or her experimental observations, while the mathematical calculations he or she employs might rely on the connection between mathematical consciousness and the real world established by Husserl's explorations into intellectual consciousness, and so forth. As in Kant, transcendental philosophy is thus the ur-science from which all other sciences derive their validity.

Moreover, without recourse to the truly apodictic conclusions unlocked by the transcendental turn, Husserl maintains that any supposed knowledge we could attain would remain mired in a transcendental naiveté. It is only once the cognizing subject understands the irrevocable link between consciousness and its object, between the real nature of any phenomenon that is to be known and the structures according to which that phenomenon gives itself to consciousness, that he or she can truly understand the object at all. This insight, known in technical terms as the correlational *a priori*, is perhaps the central claim of phenomenology as a distinct philosophical discipline, and is accessible only from the standpoint of the (transcendental) philosopher. Only once this grasp of the essential connections between reality and consciousness has been attained is it possible to produce knowledge in the fullest sense of the term, according to Husserl, since that knowledge (gained by an experiencing subject, but nevertheless applying to the experienced world) necessarily appeals to those connections for its ultimate validity – just as the world that these other sciences claim to study only becomes amenable to genuine knowledge when we understand how it is essentially constituted through consciousness. Husserl thus concludes that "transcendental philosophy in the phenomenological style" is "the *unum necessarium* for the attainment of ultimately sufficient cognition and ultimately scientific science," which has ventured beyond transcendental naiveté into as complete an understanding as possible of its own scientific validity (Husserl 1956, Hua VII, p. 186). He concludes that "none of our existing sciences, whether exact mathematics, natural science, or any human science, [are] however worthy of recognition on methodological grounds, as science in this ultimate sense" – i.e., without an irrevocable link to the transcendental philosophy that sheds light on their own sources of validity (Husserl 1956, Hua VII, p. 186).

Of course, as in Kant, the natural sciences continue to have a crucial and distinct role to play, even bearing in mind their essential connections to transcendental philosophy as the foundational science.[8] Husserl certainly does not dis-

---

[8] There are, of course, other forms of science than the transcendental science of philosophy and the natural sciences entirely – e.g., a science of aesthetics or of culture. Husserl distinguishes the natural sciences in particular by the fact that they, as he puts it, focus only on "pure cognition" of the experienced world, that the natural scientist "exclude[s], voluntarily and abstractively, all predicates the source of whose sense lies in the heart and will [...] In these sciences – that

parage the natural sciences in terms of their ability to produce helpful conclusions about (certain aspects of) the world in which we live. He writes approvingly of the "experimental method" employed by these sciences that it has been "brilliantly guaranteed [...] by countless successes" (Husserl 1911, p. 310; Husserl 1965, p. 103). Philosophy as such is by no means the only scientific mode of understanding the world around us. While the phenomenologist might be able to say some interesting things about the manner in which, say, the revolution of the moon around the earth is perceived, it takes a physicist to grasp the laws of motion that guide its path, and the latter is no less a scientist than the former. Insofar as they too are systematic in character, penetrating in scope, and (at least in principle) ultimately valid via their dependence on the apodictic conclusions first unlocked by transcendental philosophy, many of what are ordinarily considered to be natural sciences can remain genuinely scientific disciplines on the phenomenological model, even when the claims they make venture beyond the level of apodicticity to the realm of mere adequacy. Even though a physicist might be wrong about some particular question within his or her domain of inquiry, his or her research remains scientifically justified through its scientific methodology, i.e., through its systematic rigor, its propensity to uncover the underlying principles of its subject matter, and its (at least implicit) awareness of its own scientific validity via its rootedness in transcendental philosophy. Although phenomenology maintains that all of these sciences remain naive with respect to this ultimate source of validity without an explicit appeal to the transcendental science carried out by the philosopher, they remain quite capable of making genuinely scientific advances in a way that goes beyond the capabilities of philosophy, once that foundation has been established.[9]

Thus, it is apparent that the essential reliance of any science whatsoever on the conclusions of the foundational science of philosophy is a thread running through the field of transcendental idealism. Nonetheless, as noted, there are fundamental differences between the ways in which Kant and Husserl conceive of that relationship, not only in terms of how it is to be ascertained, but also in

---

is, in the natural sciences – the heart and will do contribute an influence, but only in the form of the will to cognition or, alternatively, of valuing-truth-as-cognitive-aim" (Husserl 1959, Hua VIII, pp. 24–25). But I will return to this point later, focusing for now primarily on the natural sciences that have thus far been our main topic of discussion.

9 This, of course, is a great part of the reason for Husserl's famous rejection of psychologism; psychology might well be a useful discipline for understanding human cognition on the empirical level – or even a genuine (empirical) science of cognition in its own right – but is it not capable of being the *foundational* science upon which all knowledge as such can be justified, precisely due to its failure to appreciate the sort of evidence unlocked by the transcendental turn.

the consequences that our understanding of it has for the scope of scientific inquiry as such. Most importantly, for our purposes, Husserl's focus on evidence as something inextricably linked with the world of lived experience – i.e., the fact that phenomenology focuses its investigations primarily on what Husserl calls the *lifeworld*, the world of our everyday concerns, interests, and involvements – necessitates, on the phenomenological model, a closer connection between scientificity and the full scope of our daily lives than was possible for Kant. Accordingly, Husserl does not limit the scope of science to the purely mathematical elements of what are ordinarily considered to be the natural sciences, but rather extends that category quite broadly in order to account for the possibility of scientific investigation into any number of regions of our ordinary experience – not only those, such as chemistry or psychology, which were essentially barred from the status of science on the Kantian view, but countless others as well.

Consider the Husserlian claim that the proper object of phenomenology is, in a more or less abstracted way depending on the particular sort of investigation to be carried out, the lifeworld. This standpoint is evident throughout Husserl's philosophy, predominantly in his later work, perhaps especially the *Crisis*. The lifeworld is the chief focus of phenomenological investigation as such because it is *that which is first and most fundamentally given* to us as experiencing subjects; that is to say, it is an absolutely immediate self-evidence for us. As Husserl describes it, the lifeworld "is always already there, existing in advance for us, the 'ground' of all praxis whether theoretical or extratheoretical. The world is pregiven to us, the waking, always somehow practically interested subjects, not occasionally but always and necessarily as the universal field of all actual and possible praxis, as horizon" (Husserl 1976, Hua VI, p. 145; Husserl 1970, p. 142). This world, which we both live in and investigate scientifically, is an ever-present pole of our experience, even prior to philosophical speculation of any kind; after all, before we philosophize, we must first wake up in the morning and eat breakfast, immersing ourselves in the quotidian embrace of the lifeworld. Whenever we seek to encounter or know the world in any way whatsoever, we are always ultimately directed towards the lifeworld (or its constituent elements, i.e., the objects and situations we encounter as part of that world) as the object of our intentions – even if we often focus on certain particular pieces of that world in a more or less abstract way, depending on our goals at the time.[10]

---

10 For instance, phenomenological investigation, taking place within Husserl's famous epoché, represents a fairly radical departure from the (transcendentally naive) ways in which we ordinarily encounter the lifeworld; it is a quite "unnatural attitude," in contrast to the natural attitude we ordinarily inhabit. And yet, the ultimate goal of such phenomenologizing is nothing more than to gain a fuller and more complete understanding of the experiential structures underlying

Accordingly, a science, if it is to have any real validity, must have its roots firmly planted in the soil of the lifeworld. In the context of the natural sciences, all such inquiries must be conducted in such a way as to shed light on the everyday world in which the scientist lives – and this applicability is a *conditio sine qua non* of the scientific validity of those disciplines. Husserl is clear that all natural sciences, from physics to chemistry and beyond, are ultimately aimed at addressing problems within the lifeworld. As he writes, "[w]hen science poses and answers questions, these are from the start, and hence from then on, questions resting upon the ground of, and addressed to, the elements of this pregiven world in which science and every other life-praxis is engaged" (Husserl 1976, Hua VI, p. 124; Husserl 1970, p. 121). His classification of science as a "life-praxis" is illuminating; the validity of, e. g., physics does not stem from an abstract set of facts floating in the aether, as it were, but is rather rooted in the here and now. Physics, like any other natural science, is an important, even necessary, undertaking, but only because it has meaning for the world that we always already experience, prior to any engagement in science at all. What this characterization indicates is that science, for Husserl, is by no means to be thought of as a "pure" enterprise in the strictly theoretical sense – notwithstanding the intense rigor that is required by all genuine sciences – but rather an activity that remains grounded *in terms of its goals* in the everyday world. Science has validity not because of the abstractions it is wont to make (even though such abstractions may, in a limited way, be an essential component of its methodology), but because it is a specialized mode of grasping the ordinary world in which we all (scientists included) live.

Accordingly, Husserl rejects all attempts to limit the scope of scientific knowledge as such to any mere abstractions. Especially in his later work (and nowhere is this fact more obvious than in the highly polemical *Crisis*), Husserl is deeply perturbed by the modern tendency to conflate all knowledge with purely *mathematized*, or at least mathematizable, knowledge – and it is here that his disagreements with the Kantian conception of science come to the fore. When the content of any body of knowledge is reduced to its merely abstract elements, such as the "pure part" of mathematical physics for which Kant wants to reserve the title of science, that body of knowledge loses its genuine significance. Husserl thus writes, for instance, that the "arithmetization of geometry" carried out under such a model "leads almost automatically, in a certain way, to the empty-

---

the lifeworld that we can never completely abstract away. But this point is somewhat tangential to the present discussion, and has been addressed in detail elsewhere, both by Husserl and others.

ing of its meaning. The actually spatiotemporal idealities, as they are presented firsthand in geometrical thinking under the common rubric of 'pure intuitions,' are transformed, so to speak, into pure numerical configurations, into algebraic structures" (Husserl 1976, Hua VI, p. 44; Husserl 1970, p. 44). If physics, as a genuine science, is *nothing more* than the purely mathematical conclusions that can be drawn from the notion of "an object in space" in general (or derived therefrom), then it has no true meaning *in the context of the lifeworld*. It has lost the necessary meaning-references that tie it to the world of pre-given experience, and has thereby ceased to be genuine knowledge *of the world* at all. For Husserl, this is an unjustifiable reductionism – though a quite popular one, considering the "crisis of the European sciences" from which the text takes its title.[11]

The point is that, for Husserl, any attempt to reduce the scope of the sciences to pure mathematics is, in principle, doomed to failure, precisely as a result of the fact that genuinely scientific knowledge must, by definition, remain applicable to the *real world*, of which the merely mathematized world is nothing more than an abstraction. While such abstractions may be quite useful to the scientist as a tactic to further his investigations (as a physicist might reduce the movements of particular bodies in space to equations on his or her chalkboard in order to consider them more carefully), the scope of science as such is not at all reducible to such terms in its entirety. For this reason, Kant's refusal to call subjects like chemistry or biology, which are less susceptible to such mathematization, genuine sciences is completely untenable on Husserl's model; the only possible justification for such a restriction would be the same mistaken substitution of an abstraction for the full scope of science that Husserl rejects in the *Crisis*.

Furthermore, Husserl does not endorse this extension of the scope of the sciences to encompass all sufficiently rigorous studies of the everyday world on a whim. As with Kant, Husserl has strong philosophical reasons for his delineation of the scope of science as a whole, reasons that link his views here with the philosophical commitments that inform his views on knowledge as such. On the Husserlian model, knowledge is only meaningful – indeed, it is only valid *as* knowledge – insofar as it can be traced back to the original evidences that are themselves found only in the lifeworld. It is thus implicit in the very conception

---

11 Certainly, Kant's rather restrictive view of the natural sciences may well have played a role in bringing about this crisis through the abstractization and mathematization of science that he mandates. However, he was hardly the only contributor to that process. Indeed, much of the *Crisis* is dedicated to Husserl's reconstruction of the way in which this mathematization gradually came to dominate the natural sciences as a whole, beginning with Galileo and continuing into the present day – but it is hardly necessary to recapitulate this historical tale here.

of science itself (i.e., the rigorous pursuit of genuine knowledge, which does not remain naive concerning its own sources of validity) that it should have these essential references to every region of the lifeworld that makes such knowledge meaningful. Consider that perhaps the chief distinguishing characteristic of any genuine science is, on the phenomenological model, the fact that it is essentially rooted in the original evidences that justify its claims. Transcendental philosophy is the ur-science because it is the discipline that deals with the most basic claims about the interrelations between the world we seek to know and our conscious experience thereof, physics counts as a genuine science because it is rooted in the evidences provided by experimental observation of that world (which are, in turn, founded on certain apodictic evidences uncovered by the philosopher), and so on. But what is the original source of all such evidences? The answer to that question can be nothing other than: the lifeworld. It is the everyday world in which we all live that gives rise to the genuine insights that are carried out in phenomenologizing, just as it is our ordinary experiences of motion that, in a highly rigorous and specialized manner, are employed by the physicist as evidence for his or her own claims. Husserl says as much quite openly: "The lifeworld is a realm of original self-evidences. That which is self-evidently given is, in perception, experienced as 'the thing itself,' in immediate presence, or, in memory, remembered as the thing itself […]. All conceivable verification leads back to these modes of self-evidence because the 'thing itself' (in the particular mode) lies in these intuitions themselves as that which is actually, intersubjectively experienceable and verifiable" (Husserl 1976, Hua VI, p. 130; Husserl 1970, pp. 127–128).

Husserl thus opens up more room for the expansion of the term "science" than was possible on the Kantian model. And, indeed, Husserl envisions this expansion to be vital to a fully scientific understanding of the world of experience. It is a fundamental component of that world, he notes, that our possibilities for understanding it always project themselves forward into new regions, which never come to an end (i.e., scientific understanding is possessed of ever-expanding "horizons," in phenomenological terms). Accordingly, the bare outlines of a "science" that is strictly limited to the *a priori* cognitions uncovered by transcendental philosophy or by purely mathematical inquiry proceeding therefrom are, for Husserl, quite incapable of encompassing everything that the term "science" must include: "every science, however exact, offers only a partially developed system of doctrine surrounded by a limitless horizon of what has not yet become science" (Husserl 1911, p. 335; Husserl 1965, p. 138). It is only when the notion of science expands beyond this limited level, incorporating all of the merely adequate data studied by philosophers, physicists, and chemists alike, Husserl maintains, that it becomes worthy of the name; science must not be understood as a potentially completable enterprise, but as a perennial drive towards a more-and-more expansive understanding of reality as such (as well as the consciousness that apprehends that reality). As such, it would be a completely illegitimate move to attempt to restrict the title of science to that which is purely subject to mathematization, precisely because such a restriction would foreclose on many of these necessary horizons for the expansion of science as such. Thus, science can no more be limited to the "pure part" of physics, as Kant would have it, than it can be reduced to the conclusions of philosophy as the transcendental science. Science as such is a far broader topic, not only including many of what are ordinarily considered to be the natural sciences, but investigations of many other regions of the lifeworld as well: sufficiently rigorous psychology as the science of subjective cognition (though not the foundational science of cognition as such carried out by phenomenology), physical geography as a science of the planet on which we live, aesthetics as a science of certain sorts of values, etc.

In summation, Husserl's model of science as an inextricable component of the lifeworld goes beyond the account put forth by Kant, insofar as the former is better able to account for the real interrelationships between our lived experiences and the knowledge unlocked by scientific inquiry than the latter – binding together consciousness and reality in a way that better satisfies the very goal of transcendental philosophy as such. That is not to say that Kant's views on the subject are without value. Quite the contrary; Husserl himself admits, in the *Crisis* and elsewhere, that Kant's transcendental philosophy serves as a necessary building block of anything like a phenomenological account of the lifeworld, or of phenomenology's genuinely scientific status. As he writes, Kant's philosophy is "in accord with the formal, general sense of a transcendental philosophy in our definition," even describing it as "the first attempt, and one carried out with impressive scientific seriousness, at a truly universal transcendental philosophy meant to be a *rigorous science* in a sense of scientific rigor which has only now been discovered and which is the only genuine sense" (Husserl 1976, Hua VI, p. 102; Husserl 1970, p. 99). Husserl merely claims that Kant failed to see the necessary extension of the status of science to encompass all these different (though still thoroughgoingly systematic, etc.) modes of investigating the world of experience because he had *taken for granted* the basic interconnections between knowledge as such and the lifeworld to which it is ultimately supposed to apply. Kant limited his definition of science to only the most purely philosophical or mathematical sorts of investigation because he simply overlooked the fact that all regions of the lifeworld contain similar structures amenable to rigorous investigations hearkening back to the conclusions of transcendental philosophy, though perhaps in a way made obvious only by Husserl's phenomenological methods. As Husserl notes in the *Crisis*, "Kant's inquiries in the critique of reason have an unquestioned ground of presuppositions which codetermine the meaning of his questions [...] from the very start in the Kantian manner of posing questions, the everyday surrounding world of life is presupposed as existing" (Husserl 1976, Hua VI, p. 106; Husserl 1970, p. 104).[12] Kant's understanding of science as such was certainly, on the Husserlian model, on the right track, but it remained naive with respect to its own source of validity in the lifeworld – precisely the mistake that prevents any line of inquiry whatsoever from genuinely attaining the level of science in its own right.

Conclusion

Overall, both Kant and Husserl tread largely on the same path when it comes to describing the nature of science as such. Both envision science as a necessarily rigorous and systematic enterprise, which directs itself towards uncovering the fundamental principles of the subject matter that it investigates, doing so with – at least in principle – apodictic certainty. Too, both posit transcendental philosophy as a sort of ur-science, from which all other scientific disciplines attain their own validity, and for the same reasons: no science is worthy of the name unless it produces knowledge, and true knowledge requires us to move beyond the transcendental naiveté that is unavoidable without philosophy. Nonetheless, there are significant differences in the ways in which they follow this path, especially when it comes to the limitations that each prescribes for the scope of scientific inquiry. While Kant restricts the title of science to a small portion of the disciplines ordinarily covered by the term, Husserl broadens the notion of science quite far as a result of his emphasis on the necessary application of any form of knowledge whatsoever to the lifeworld. For Kant, scientific knowledge is to be limited to what can be known with absolute (transcendental) clarity, or at least derived in a narrowly mathematical way from that body of knowledge; for Husserl, in contrast, scientific knowledge is always to be explicated in terms of the wide (and endlessly developing) variety of roles that it plays in our ordinary lives, in many different spheres.

Thus, assuming the truth of Husserl's views on the absolute priority of the everyday, of the lifeworld, to any encounter with knowledge whatsoever –

---

[12] Indeed, Husserl raises quite a few criticisms of what he sees as Kant's unexamined presuppositions throughout the *Crisis*. It is not, however, my intention here to carry out a full examination of Husserl's treatment of Kant, but rather merely to point out the ways in which Husserl's somewhat more nuanced model of science as such goes beyond the limitations of his predecessor.

a point which I am quite prepared to concede, given the lucidity of his conception of evidence as *that which is made evident* within that lifeworld –, it can be concluded that Husserl's views of science are more developed than those of Kant. This superiority pertains both to Husserl's progression down the path of transcendental philosophy in general – insofar as Husserl gives us a more direct way to tie the notion of scientific knowledge in with the experiential world to which it is supposed to apply – as well as to the everyday utility of Husserl's conception of science. It is, after all, an important point to be able to identify disciplines like chemistry, biology, or even the social sciences as genuine *sciences* in their own right (as long as that application can be justified philosophically) if they are to have their proper validity, and Husserl gives us a way to defend such a categorization. Thus, although Kant's views on science certainly informed Husserl's phenomenological take on the subject, and while those views have much to recommend them in their own right, the phenomenological model of science ultimately takes precedence over its forebear (in the context of transcendental philosophy). If nothing else, it can at least be said that Husserl's model of science gives us a formidable way of understanding the role that scientific inquiry and scientific knowledge have to play throughout our ordinary lives, as disciplines that assist us in comprehending the world in which we all live. In that task, at least, the phenomenological model of science is without parallel.

Bibliography

Friedman, Michael (2013): *Kant's Construction of Nature: A Reading of the Metaphysical Foundations of Natural Science*. Cambridge: Cambridge University Press.

Guyer, Paul (2005): *Kant's System of Nature and Freedom: Selected Essays*. New York: Oxford University Press.

Husserl, Edmund (1970): *The Crisis of European Sciences and Transcendental Phenomenology: An Introduction to Phenomenological Philosophy*. Trans. David Carr. Evanston, Illinois: Northwestern University Press.

Husserl, Edmund (1956): *Erste Philosophie (1923/4). Erster Teil: Kritische Ideengeschichte. Husserliana*, vol. VII. Ed. Rudolf Boehm. The Hague: Martinus Nijhoff.

Husserl, Edmund (1959): *Erste Philosophie (1923/4). Zweiter Teil: Theorie der phänomenologische Reduktion. Husserliana*, vol. VIII. Ed. Rudolf Boehm. The Hague: Martinus Nijhoff.

Husserl, Edmund (1976): *Die Krisis der Europäischen Wissenschaften und die Transzendentale Phänomenologie. Husserliana*, vol. VI. 2nd ed. Ed. Walter Biemel. The Hague: Martinus Nijhoff.

Husserl, Edmund (1911): "Philosophie als Strenge Wissenschaft". In: *Logos*, vol. 1, pp. 289–341.

Husserl, Edmund (1965): *Philosophy as Rigorous Science*. In: *Phenomenology and the Crisis of Philosophy*. Trans. Quentin Lauer. New York: Harper & Row.
Kant, Immanuel (1963): *Kritik der reinen Vernunft. Prolegomena. Grundlegung zur Metaphysik der Sitten. Metaphysische Anfangsgründe der Naturwissenschaft. Akademieausgabe*, vol. IV. Berlin: Walter de Gruyter.
Kant, Immanuel (2003): *Critique of Pure Reason*. Trans. Norman Kemp Smith. New York: Palgrave Macmillan.
Kant, Immanuel (2004): *Metaphysical Foundations of Natural Science*. Trans. Michael Friedman. Cambridge: Cambridge University Press.
Kant, Immanuel (2012): *Physical Geography*. In: *Natural Science*. Ed. Eric Watkins. Cambridge: Cambridge University Press.
Makkreel, Rudolf (2001): "Kant on the Scientific Status of Psychology, Anthropology, and History". In: Eric Watkins (Ed.): *Kant and the Sciences*. New York: Oxford University Press, pp. 185–204.
Plaass, Peter (1994): *Kant's Theory of Natural Science*. Trans. Alfred Miller and Maria Miller. Dordrecht, NL: Kluwer Academic Publishers.

Dominique Pradelle
A Phenomenological Critique of Kantian Ethics[1]

Abstract: We want to focus on Husserl's critique of Kantian ethics and to develop the following questions. As opposed to the empiricist orientation of Hume's ethics, the Kantian foundation of ethics has an *a priori* character; does this character have to be identified with the origin of ethical principles in pure subjectivity? If not, what is its phenomenological signification? The meaning of the Copernican revolution is that structures of objects accord with the universal structures of the finite subject; Husserl refuses this principle and assumes that every sort of object determines a regulative structure in the subject; is it possible to apply this anti-Copernican principle to the ethical sphere? As opposed to the Kantian principle of the supremacy of practical reason, we find in Husserl's thought a *supremacy of theoretical reason*; what is the meaning of this inversion? The concept of *foundation* has great importance in Husserlian phenomenology: every sort of truth of a higher degree is founded on the lower level of sensible truth; is it possible to apply this principle to the ethical sphere? Finally, the Kantian concept of liberty is not an empirical one, but a cosmological and practical idea; what is the phenomenological meaning of liberty?

1 A Few Guiding Themes for our Reading

We shall adopt a few guiding themes here, which can be summarized as a series of questions.

1. First, against the purely empirical and anthropological orientation characteristic of the "moral sentimentalists" (*Gefühlsmoralisten*), Kantian ethics possess an *a priori* foundation (see Husserl 2004, Hua XXXVII, pp. 125–171). Quite simply, *how is one to conceive of the* a priori *nature of duty, and of ethical norms in general?* Is this *a priori* character to be located from the outset in pure subjectivity (here, in the pure will), or not? If the answer is negative, then what is the properly phenom-

---

[1] This chapter is the English translation made by John Rogove of an article originally published in French in the special issue of *Meta: Research in Hermeneutics, Phenomenology, and Practical Philosophy*, vol. VIII, n° 2 / December 2016: *Husserl and Kant: The Transcendental-Phenomenological Project*, Guest Editor: Iulian Apostolescu, pp. 442–481.

https://doi.org/10.1515/9783110564280-017

enological (as opposed to Kantian) meaning of the *a priori* character of ethical norms?

2. And then, the second sense of Kant's Copernican revolution in theoretical philosophy is that the structures of the object as it appears are measured according to the faculties (sensibility, imagination, understanding) and to the supposedly invariant structures of any finite subject; and that the validity of any relation to an object has its origin and its grounding in pure subjectivity, and not outside of it. On the contrary, Husserl's fundamental theses overturn this Copernican revolution, in a specific sense that in no way implies a return to realism: "Any object in general [...] designates a regulative structure for the transcendental subject" (Husserl 1963/1976, Hua I, p. 90; Husserl 1982, p. 53; translations are here often modified tacitly); rather than the *a priori* structures of the object being measured according to the universal structures of the finite subject, it is instead the constitutive structures of any subjectivity in general that have their grounding in the essence of possible intentional objects. The essence of the object determines its mode of givenness as well as its mode of being meant as an intentional structure of a pure subject, whatever it may be; phenomenology thus frees itself of any presupposition regarding the pre-constitution of the finite subject, the essence of which, on the contrary, allows itself to be elucidated by envisaging every type of possible intentional object.

Is this anti-Copernican principle applicable to the ethical realm? To what extent? And what then is its exact meaning? Does this mean that the foundation of ethics and of ethical norms should never be sought in reason or in the pure will, insofar as they are faculties of the finite subject?

3. One essential principle guides the Kantian doctrine: that of the primacy of practical reason over theoretical (epistemological) reason, of *praxis* over *theoria*; the ultimate ends that determine man's essential destination reside in the realm of ethics and religion (see Kant 1781/1787, *Kanon der reinen Vernunft*, A 798/B 826).

And again what we find in Husserl is the inverse primacy of *theoria* or of theoretical reason, as opposed (implicitly but radically) to the Kantian primacy of practical reason: "But all the decisive battles, so to speak, are fought in the realm of theoretical reason" (see Husserl 1956, *Beilage* XXI, Hua VII, p. 406). *What consequences does this Husserlian primacy of theoretical reason have?* Is it a reactivation of Platonic, or even Aristotelian philosophy, directed against Kantian moral philosophy? *I.e.* of the primacy of the *Einsicht*, of rational self-evidence as the intellectual and spiritual guide of the acting will? And thus of the primacy of the intuition in ethics?

4. Husserlian phenomenology is guided by a fundamental principle that is determined by the relation of *foundation* or *grounding* (*Fundierung*): at the noe-

matic level, every object and every truth of the understanding is a higher-level objectity founded on concepts and truths of a sensory type and, ultimately, on the final level of perceptual objects; in the same way, at the noetic level, every intentional act taking such higher level objectities as correlates have their ultimate basis in the perception of sensory objects. The principle states, consequently, that no higher level objectity or truth floats anchorless in the air, but rather that they must be founded, immediately or mediately, on the realm of sensory arch-objects.

Is it possible to transpose or to apply this principle to the realm of moral or axiological philosophy? What, in such a realm, would its meaning then be? Would it mean that any ethical or axiological consciousness should have its foundation in the realm of sentiment – with all ethics referring in this case to sensibility, affectivity, and the faculty of having feelings (*Gefühlsvermögen*)? Is this a reactivation of a Humean morality against the rationalism of Kantian ethics, or, at least, an *attempt to reconcile the moralists of the understanding (Verstandesmoralisten) and of the sentiments (Gefühls-), of ethical rationality and of the empirical underpinning of ethics?*

5. Finally, for Kant the concept of freedom is absolutely not an empirical concept, but instead and primarily a cosmological Idea, and secondly a practical Idea that has both meaning as a principle and a foundational function without having any empirical content – there is, rigorously speaking, no experience of freedom.

What, then, is the phenomenological concept of freedom, as opposed to Kant's? Can it have the same principial and fundamental function as in the Kantian doctrine? If phenomenology requires that no concept float anchorless in the air, but that it always be grounded and brought back to a form of experience in which the objective correlate of its meaning is fulfilled such that the object or the meaning that corresponds to it can truly be given, does this not imply that there must necessarily be an experience of freedom to which its concept can be brought back?

2 The Common Point between the Moral Philosophies of Kant and Husserl: The Key Problem of the Overcoming of Skepticism and Realism

First of all, independently of Husserl's criticisms of Kantian ethics, both thinkers nevertheless share a common goal: *to combat and refute ethical skepticism in its various forms*. Later critiques should not allow us to forget that they share this common basis.

What are the forms that ethical skepticism takes? Husserl explicitly describes three. First of all, *historical and ethnological skepticism*, according to which there are such "enormous gulfs between the ethical institutions of diverse peoples and diverse epochs" (see Husserl 1988, *Ergänz. Text* Nr. 1, Hua XXVIII, p. 382) that no ethical law has any omni-temporal and omni-subjective validity; then there is *ethnico-cosmological skepticism*, according to which "ethicists presuppose free will" (Husserl 1988, Hua XXVIII, p. 382), whereas there is no reason why the human will should be thought to constitute an exception to the universal cosmological law of causality; and finally, *Humean-type ethical anthropologism*, according to which morality cannot be anything more than an emotivity-based morality with nothing other than universal ways of feeling as a foundation, which are in turn anchored in human nature and beyond which it has no validity, rather than being valid for all beings endowed with reason (see Husserl 1988, *Ergänz. Text* Nr. 2, Hua XXVIII, p. 385).

The fundamental characteristics of Kantian ethics emerge in opposition to these forms of skepticism.

First of all, against cosmological skepticism, the concept of freedom possesses, according to Kant, an unconditional validity as a practical Idea of freedom, and as such is the "stumbling block for all empiricists," as well as the keystone and necessary foundation for all supreme practical propositions (Kant 1788, *Vorrede*, p. 13; Kant 1908/1913, AK. V, p. 7; Kant 2015, p. 6). Secondly, against historical and ethnological relativism, it is not enough simply to affirm the "subjective necessity" (*subjektive Gültigkeit*) of ethical feelings, namely the fact that they have a universality that transcends the differences among epochs and cultures; one must rather find a grounding in "objective validity" (*objektive Gültigkeit*) for the principles of ethics, with the status of a rational necessity or of an *"intuited necessity"* (eingesehene *Notwendigkeit*) (Kant 1788, *Vorrede*, pp. 24–25 and 27; Kant 1908/1913, AK. V, pp. 12–13; Kant 2015, pp. 9–10). Thirdly, against Humean anthropologism, it is a matter of elaborating a critique of practical reason *in gen-*

eral, "which has only to give a complete account of the principles of its possibility, of its extent, and of its limits, without any special reference to human nature [*die nur die Prinzipien ihrer Möglichkeit, ihres Umfangs und Grenzen vollständig ohne besondere Beziehung auf die menschliche Natur angeben soll*]" (Kant 1788, Vorrede, pp. 14–15, Kant 1908/1913, AK. V, p. 8; Kant 2015, p. 7) while possessing an omni-subjective validity, for any being endowed with reason in general.

But, from this point of view, Husserl's position turns out to be close to Kant's: *ethical matters for Husserl cannot be matters of fact, but only matters of principle*.

In a general way, it is possible to speak of philosophy only where "it is not merely a matter of establishing what the facts are" (Husserl 1988, *Ergänz. Text Nr. 1*, Hua XXVIII, p. 383), but where matters of principle are involved: i.e., questions concerning the absolute or relative validity of ethical laws, the validity of idealism or materialism in ethics, the determination of "the ultimate source of all ethical regulation," the analysis of the normative ethical concepts "good" and "evil," and the "determination of the sovereign Good" (Husserl 1988, Hua XXVIII, p. 383). Here there is a sovereign principle of parallelism between logic and ethics: in both realms, we are not dealing with factualities (*Tatsächlichkeiten*), but with ideal norms or horizon concepts (Husserl 1988, *Ergänz. Text Nr. 2c*, Hua XXVIII, p. 397). In this way, the true is not that which is effectively judged or asserted, but that which is *behauptenswert*, i.e., that which possesses an assertoric value or which proves to be worthy of being asserted; by analogy, that which is morally good is not that which is approved of *de facto* (*tatsächlich gebilligt*), but that which is *billigenswert* or *billigenswürding*, i.e., worthy of approval. As a result, just as the true is the "content of an act of correct recognition [*Inhalt eines richtigen Anerkennens*]," in the same way, the good seems to be the "content of an act of correct approval [*Inhalt einer richtigen Billigung*]" (see Husserl 1988, Hua XXVIII, p. 397): ethical approval is subject to the requirement of rightness or rectitude (*Richtigkeit = rectitudo*), and is therefore regulated by norms and laws bearing ideal meaning and validity for anyone whomsoever and absolutely, whatever their nature may be (man, angel, or God). In moral philosophy, the sovereign principle is thereby one of *omni-subjective validity of the norms of ethical approval, which are themselves correlated to ideal laws of ethical rightness* – in the same way that in logic the sovereign principle is that of omni-subjective validity of the ideal norms of judgment and of reasoning, which are themselves correlated to ideal laws governing sequences of propositional forms.

The consequence of this is that a *strict distinction between the* de facto *and the* de jure *is required* – a distinction between the factuality of a people's positive law, and the ideality of the moral law. The requirements proper to the positive law and to the ethical rules of a people belong to the realm of empirical factuality; on the other hand, by the fact that they state ideal and supra-empirical requirements that are independent of the relativity of peoples, of eras and of species, morality is supposed to enjoy absolute and supreme authority:

> One must separate mores [*Sitte*] and law [*Recht*] on the one hand, and morality in the proper sense on the other hand. An *action* [...] is moral only if, even when it goes against mores and law, it is in conformity with the ideal and absolute prescriptions of the ethical norm. Ethical norms claim to be a supreme court for practical questions; they claim to judge mores and law themselves, and to determine their absolute value or lack of value, [...] and thus to set an absolute criterion for value, which is such because it is ultimate and supra-empirical. (Husserl 1988, *Ergänz. Text* Nr. 2a, Hua XXVIII, p. 386)

In conclusion, we find, following the parallelism between pure logic and pure ethics, the same *a priori* separation between morality and mores, between justice and positive law, as we find between logic and psychology: just as logical laws are not reducible to psychological truths stating how we think *de facto*, but that ideal laws determine norms for the ought-to-think *de jure* (see Kant 1923, AK. IX, pp. 13–14; Kant 1992, p. 529), so also moral laws cannot be reduced to any type of factual legality (be it psychological, sociological, ethnological, historical...) explaining why, *de facto*, we make such or such a judgment or subject our acts to such or such a rule, since they belong rather to a supra-empirical *regnum*. There exists an unbridgeable abyss between the generality of a fact (*Allgemeinheit einer Tatsache*) and the universality that characterizes justified validity (*Allgemeinheit einer berechtigten Geltung*): if the law of gravitation possesses universal validity, this is merely a matter of factual universality stating that "it is thus universally and necessarily," without any exception, but in no way is it a matter of a normative universality that states that "it must be thus" (Husserl 1988, *Ergänz. Text* Nr. 2a, Hua XXVIII, p. 388). We must therefore distinguish three degrees within the concept of *Allgemeinheit:* on the one hand, the *empirical generality* of a matter of fact within a finite plurality ("all the roses in this garden are red"); on the other hand, the *nomological universality* of a law that applies to an infinite totality of objects ("all equiangular triangles are equilateral"); and finally the *normative universality* of an ought-to-be for possible situations ("one ought always keep one's promises"), which is surely not reducible to any form of factual generality founded on empirical observations, but nor is it founded on any form of nomological generality within being. In Kantian terms, the division of philosophy into a metaphysics of nature (connected to the realm of beings) and a metaphysics of morals (which refers to the realm of what ought-to-be) (see Kant 1781/1787, *Transz. Methodenlehre, Architektonik*, A 840–841/B 868–869; Kant 1998, pp. 695–696) is the object of a phenomenological justification.

3 Husserl's Platonic Orientation: The Primacy of Theoretical Reason

In Kant's thought, there is a *double primacy of practical reason*.

On the one hand, the *ultimate ends* (*Endzwecke*) *of pure reason* in which the destination of man consists do not fall under the domain of speculative or theoretical reason, but rather under that of practical reason: if the essential ends of man are defined by the three questions of what I can know, what I must do and what I am allowed to hope for, these essential ends are nevertheless not supreme, but remain on the contrary subordinate to the uniquely supreme end determining the "total destination of man" – namely, the *moral* destination, which is governed by the questions of the Good and of salvation (see Kant 1781/1787, *Transz. Methodenlehre*, *Kanon*, A 804–805/B 832–833; *Architektonik*, A 840/B 868, Kant 2015, pp. 676–677 and 695; and Kant 1788, *Von dem Primat der reinen praktischen Vernunft*, pp. 215–219; Kant 1908/1913, AK. V, pp. 119–121; Kant 2015, pp. 96–98).

On the other hand and above all, the *conscience* is, for Kant, *independent of all theoretical knowledge*, insofar as it is capable, by itself and completely autonomously with respect to the theoretical order of knowledge of objects, of being an awareness of absolute duty:

> The most common understanding can distinguish without instruction what form in a maxim makes it fit for a giving a universal law [*Welche Form in der Maxime sich zur allgemeinen Gesetzgebung schicke, das kann der gemeinste Verstand ohne Unterweisung unterscheiden*]. (Kant 1788, *Von den Grundsätzen d. r. prakt. Vern.*, § 4, Lehrsatz III, Anmerkung, p. 49; Kant 1908/1913, AK. V, p. 27; Kant 2015, p. 25)
>
> What is to be done in accordance with the principle of the autonomy of choice is seen quite easily and without hesitation by the most common understanding [...] [*Was nach dem Prinzip der Autonomie der Willkür zu tun sei, ist für den gemeinsten Verstand ganz leicht und ohne Bedenken einzusehen [...]; d. i.: was Pflicht sei, bietet sich jedermann von selbst dar*]. (Kant 1788, *Grundsätze*, § 8, Lehrsatz IV, Anm. II, p. 64; Kant 1908/1913, AK. V, p. 36; Kant 2015, p. 33)
>
> [...] that there is, accordingly, no need of science and philosophy to know what one has to do in order to be honest and good, and even wise and virtuous [...] [*daß es also keiner Wissenschaft und Philosophie bedürfe, um zu wissen, was man zu thun habe, um ehrlich und gut, ja sogar um weise und tugendhaft zu sein*]. (Kant 1968, AK. IV, p. 404; Kant 1997, p. 16)

For Kant, the conscience belongs to any ordinary understanding, such that in order to become conscious of one's duty, there is no need for instruction of any sort, of any prerequisite knowledge, or of any particular perceptiveness or insightfulness, the exercise of which would belong to the understanding or to theoretical reason: on the one hand, awareness of the fundamental law of practical reason (that of the universalizability of the maxim presiding over the action) is a "fact of reason," that is, neither an empirical fact nor an awareness that is mediately derived from what is given according to pure reason, but an originary modality of consciousness in which reason recognizes itself as legislator (see Kant 1788, *Grundsätze*, § 7, *Grundgesetz*, pp. 55–56; Kant 1908/1913, AK. V, p. 31; Kant 2015, p. 28); on the other hand, far from being known through a complex reasoning process against the backdrop of multiple givens, the subsumption of the maxim in the form of universal legislation is known immediately, as an "identical proposition, which is therefore clear in itself" (Kant 1788, *Grundsätze*, § 4, *Lehrsatz* III, *Anmerkung*, p. 49; Kant 1908/1913, AK. V, p. 27; Kant 2015, p. 25). *As a matter of principle, there can be no such thing as ethical blindness or of obliteration of the conscience* out of a lack of theoretical evidence.

In contrast to this, Husserl frequently has recourse to reason in the practical sphere; and he does not understand this as an immediate consciousness of duty according to a specifically practical modality, but as a faculty of intuition or of insight (*Intuition, Einsicht, Einsehen*) into practical norms:

> If discernment [*Einsicht*] grasps what is good and bad, better or worse, if ethical evaluation and preference are not a blind but an intuitive act [*sehender Akt*] that can represent the intuited value as a unit of validity –, then it can be said from the outset that reason is the origin of ethical principles [*Ursprungsstätte der ethischen Prinzipien*]: because where else can one speak of "discernment" other than in the realm of reason? (Husserl 1988, *Ergänz. Text* Nr. 2a, Hua XXVIII, p. 385)[2]

In other words, *the conscience is a matter of perceptiveness, of clear-sightedness or of discernment*; and it must be enlightened by evidence or insight, i.e. an act of knowing the ethical norms relative to a given situation, which falls under the purview of theoretical reason. What indeed is designated here by the term *reason*? A passage from the *Lessons on Ethics* provides perfect clarity on this matter. Here, Husserl writes that reason does not designate a psychic faculty of the finite subject – namely the faculty of grasping supersensible Ideas and principles –, but that it is to be understood in a phenomenological or transcendental sense, namely as a fundamental structure of all intentional consciousness: "like a title designating the eidetic configurations of acts in which objectities [...] come to the givenness that attests to them" (Husserl 1988, § 7, Hua XXVIII, p. 274). Reason consequently designates the teleological orientation of any inten-

---

[2] We are following the usage established by M. de Gandillac in his translation, by translating "*Einsicht*" – "insight" – as "discernment."

tional meaning of an object towards the givenness 'in person' (*Selbstgegebenheit*) of that object, i.e., the tendency that orients any partially empty intentional consciousness toward the fulfillment or the intuitive attestation that truly and fully portrays the meant object (Husserl 1963/1976, § 24, Hua I, p. 93; Husserl 1982, p. 57).³

This teleological structure enjoys a universal applicability, which embraces the totality of areas or types of object: the problem of the attestation of being-valid can be extended to every object in general, be they theoretical (concepts, propositions, states of affairs), axiological (values), aesthetic (specifically aesthetic values), or practical (goods). Hence the possibility of applying it to the ethical sphere: values and goods are *also* objects, of which there has to be a giving intuition capable of attesting to its validity. Thus there exists, for example, an intuition of values, which is certainly not a *Wahrnehmung* (perception as grasping of the true), but a *Wertnehmung* (specific grasping of value) or a *Wertgegebenheit* (axiological givenness) (see Husserl 1988, § 7b, Hua XXVIII, p. 279); it is the same, in principle, for goods and ethical norms: there must be a form of giving intuition of ethical norms and of that which is good.

The result, in the practical realm, is an *eidetic distinction between blindness and clear-sightedness* (or perceptiveness): i.e., between, on the one hand, will and action that belong to blind instinct (*blind-instinktiv*) and, on the other hand, clear-sighted or insightful (*einsichtig*) will and action (see Husserl 1988, *Ergänz. Text* Nr. 2c, Hua XXVIII, p. 400). This fundamental distinction, moreover, provides Husserl with his essential objection to the Humean argument according to which, seeing that the same relations between actions and feelings are found in both animals and humans and that we do not attribute a conscience to the former, we have no more reason to attribute one to the latter (Hume 1854, vol. III, I, I, pp. 229–230). Against this, Husserl presents a parallel between the theoretical and practical domains: since the animal does not judge in an insightful way but against the backdrop of blind instinct, in the same way, while it is capable of evaluating (*bewerten*), it remains nevertheless incapable of differentiating between blind and insightful evaluation, and also of having an awareness of the rightness or wrongness of the evaluation; it is consequently incapable of knowing an ethical norm (Husserl 1988, *Ergänz. Text* Nr. 2c, Hua XXVIII, p. 400). Thus, there is a parallelism between the different forms of reason: in the same way as a judgment can be right or wrong (*richtig vs. unrichtig*), and as judicative reason fulfills its function against the backdrop of the self-evidence of the rightness

---

3 We analyzed this phenomenological definition of reason in *Par-delà la révolution copernicienne* (Pradelle 2012, pp. 199 *sqq.*).

or wrongness of the judgment passed, so in the same way can will and action be good or bad, morally right or wrong, ethical or not, and practical reason fulfills its function against the backdrop of the ethical rightness or wrongness of our acting and willing; again, just as evaluation can be true or false, axiological reason plays its role against the backdrop of the self-evidence of its truth or falsity (Husserl 1988, § 7b, Hua XXVIII, p. 280).

The Husserlian position in the ethical field turns out to be Platonist and anti-Kantian. Whereas Kant devotes his efforts to freeing the practical realm from the paradigm of the knowledge of objects and to rendering the conscience independent of any knowledge whatsoever, Husserl restores its paradigmatic function to object-oriented knowledge by setting up an equation between the good (*das Gute*) and that which is "true on a practical level [*das praktisch Wahre*]" (Husserl 1988, *Ergänz. Text* Nr. 2c, Hua XXVIII, p. 401, note): the good is that which can be attested to, in an intuition that is originarily given, as being worthy of approbation – to such an extent that it is possible to speak of an "interest for truth in feeling and will [*Wahrheitsinteresse im Gemüt und Willen*]" (Husserl 1988, Hua XXVIII, p. 401). *Ethics is a matter of discernment or of perceptiveness:* the important thing is to see clearly, to exercise ethical insight, to know what is good and just in each situation and in general – such that the self-evident consciousness of rightness has a rectifying function for it. In this sense, Husserlian phenomenology remains faithful to Brentano's teachings, which are summarized by the title of the 1889 lectures, *On the Origin of Ethical Knowledge* (Brentano 1969): within the ethical sphere, the central question remains how we recognize that something is better; and, in opposition to all forms of ethical blindness, only self-evident knowledge of what is better grounds the rightness or accuracy of the will and of action (Brentano 1969, §§ 29, 30 and 34) – such that we have grounds to draw a strict parallel between the true and the good, insofar as they are both anchored in the consciousness of *Richtigkeit* (Brentano 1969, § 23).

4 The Material *A priori* and the Formal *A priori*: The Demand for an Ethics that Proceeds "from the Bottom up"

While Husserl agrees with Kant concerning the fundamental distinction between facts and norms, the latter must (as for Kant) belong to the *a priori*, since in no case is it supposed to be derived from facts. However, should the *practical* a priori *be understood in the same way in phenomenology as it is in Kant?*

First of all, what does the *a priori* or objective character of the practical law mean for Kant? This implies, first, that the latter "can be recognized as being endowed with validity for the will of any being endowed with reason [*für den Willen jedes vernünftigen gültig erkannt*]" (Kant 1788, *Von den Grundsätzen d. r. prakt. Vernunft*, § 1, *Erkl.*, p. 35; Kant 1908/1913, AK. V, p. 19; Kant 2015, p. 17): the first criterion of apriority resides in objectivity, understood as designating a validity that is universally knowable and omni-subjective (*Allgemeingültigkeit*) (see Kant 1903, AK. IV, p. 298; Kant 2004, p. 50); and, second, that practical law has its exclusive origin "in pure reason, thought of as being its own faculty, separate from sensibility and from all the other faculties" (Husserl 1988, *Ergänz. Text* Nr. 3a, "*Kritik der Kantischen Ethik,*" Hua XXVIII, p. 404). Husserl establishes a connection between these two Kantian theses which renders the two inseparable: the objectivity of validity (*Objectivität der Geltung*) understood as a "bindingness for every being endowed with reason in general [*Verbindlichkeit für jedes Vernunftwesen überhaupt*]" implies that "the origin of the norm [is to be found] in pure reason [*Ursprung der Norm in der reinen Vernunft*]" (Husserl 1988, Hua XXVIII, p. 404). And it is precisely in opposition to this (supposedly Kantian) connection between the two characteristics of the *a priori* – universal validity and a purely rational, non-sensible origin – that Husserl asserts, as a matter of principle, that these theses must absolutely be separated. Why is this?

In order to understand why, it is necessary to allow oneself to be guided by Husserl's critique of the Kantian notion of the *a priori* in general, which is to be found in the texts presented in the appendix to volume I of *Erste Philosophie*. For Kant, necessity and universality are the distinctive characteristics (*Kennzeichen*) of the *a priori*, understood as "criteria of origin in pure subjectivity [*Kennzeichen des Ursprungs in der reinen Subjektivität*]": indeed, the *a priori* is what is not *a posteriori*, and therefore what is not derivable from the sensory experience the subject has of objects; thus the *a priori* resides in pure subjectivity itself, *i.e.*, in subjectivity insofar as it is unaffected from the outside by objects (*sofern sie nicht [...] von aussen affiziert ist*) (Husserl 1956, Beil. XXI, Hua VII, p. 402). But this, for Husserl, is nothing more than a "transcendental-psychological construct:" this thesis is indeed the product of an unfounded conceptual construct, and not of an eidetic state of affairs drawn from an originally presentative intuition; it is, moreover, a construct that mixes up transcendental considerations – concerning the problems of transcendental constitution and constituting consciousness understood in its non-worldly purity – and psychological considerations – concerning the human psyche in its supposedly invariant pre-constitution. Why is this? For the simple reason that the Kantian thesis has a tendency to assimilate *a priori* structures to subjective forms, which have their seat in subjectivity and which belong to its supposedly invariant constitution.[4] However, the true concept of the *a priori* has nothing to do with the question of whether or not the subject is affected from the outside, no more than it does with the question of whether the subject possesses certain invariant faculties and structures; in other words, it is in no way connected to the question of *exclusive origin in pure subjectivity*, but rather only to that of *validity for anyone in general*.

A Neo-Kantian would certainly respond that the veritable Kantian problem, far from being one of the determination of the native psychological structures of the subject, is precisely that of the conditions of possibility of the validity of the relation to an object, or of objective knowledge! (see Cohen 1918, pp. 141, 174, 178–179, 185, 199, 207, 237, and above all the entire 5th chapter, devoted to the distinction between the concepts of the *a priori* and the innate, pp. 255*sqq.*). But this notwithstanding, the Husserlian concept of the *a priori* can be distinguished from the Kantian one by three essential characteristics.

First of all, far from radically avoiding any anthropologistic presupposition of the facticity of *a priori* structures, Kant explicitly recognizes their existence in § 21 of the second Deduction: far from being able to account for the necessity that the subject be characterized by such forms as sensibility and understanding, this is simply a fact that cannot be completely justified (Kant 1781/1787, *Transz. Deduktion*, § 21, B 145–146); as subjective forms, *a priori* structures are contingent. *A priori* connections are, for Husserl, on the contrary, supposed to possess an unconditioned necessity.

Second, while it is possible to show in the Deduction the necessity of the categories as the condition of possibility of *scientific* knowledge, it is much more difficult, not to say impossible, to do so for certain categories of *pre-scientific or perceptual* experience: thus, that the laws of causality and conservation are necessary forms of the determination of objects for physics in no way implies that these laws have any necessary validity for the pre-scientific perception of objects. And it is precisely the task of eidetic variation to show what can be undone: the contingent forms of legality can be unimagined (Husserl 1956, *Beil.* XXI, Hua VII, p. 396).

Finally and above all, if the true *a priori* possesses absolutely universal validity, this is not because it is constitutive of any finite subject, but because it is given in eidetic intuition (*Wesenschau, Wesensintuition*): it is the "eidetic neces-

---

[4] This reading of the Kantian *a priori*, which attaches it to the idea of subjective formality, is radically opposed to the attempt by the Neo-Kantians to avoid all assimilation of the *a priori* to the innate, or of the *a priori* structures of the object to the native forms of the subject. Far from being isolated, this subjectivist reading was defended by C. Stumpf (see Stumpf 1873, p. 14) and then by Reinach in "*Über Phänomenologie*" (1913) (see Reinach 1989, p. 546).

sity or generality [*Wesensnotwendigkeit bzw. Wesensallgemeinheit*] that is absolutely given in eidetic intuition [*in der Wesensintuition absolut gegeben*]" (Husserl 1956, *Beil.* XXI, Hua VII, p. 404). *A priori* structures are not the subjective structures of intuition or of thought, but rather the *objective structures intuited in the form of self-evidence that is the intuition of essence:* they are absolutely necessary connections of essence endowed with validity for any subject in general.

But, does it follow from the fact that the apriority of a law can be identified with the possibility of its being given in an intuition of essence that any eidetic truth has its source in *pure* reason?

Absolutely not! On the contrary, large areas of *a priori* truths rest on *sensible*, and therefore *a posteriori*, representations. For example, that purple is qualitatively situated between red and blue, as grey is between black and white and not between red and green, or that three sounds are situated on a fixed scale of pitches, or that color is inseparable from extension, are all *a priori* truths (endowed with a necessity that is grounded in the essence of the representations in question), but they are also *material truths*, since they refer to (sensible) contents of knowledge (*sie beziehen sich auf eine Erkenntnismaterie*); they are in no way purely formal truths like those of logic or arithmetic, which are on the contrary independent of any material knowledge and have their foundation in the pure laws of thought (see Husserl 1988, *Ergänz. Text* Nr. 3a, Hua XXVIII, p. 403). The case of material *a priori* truths forces us to radically dissociate the two questions of validity and of origin. It in no way follows from the universally obligatory character of these truths for any being endowed with reason (*für jedes Vernunftwesen verbindlich*), i.e., capable of eidetic intuition, that they originate in pure reason "conceived as its own faculty, separate from sensibility and from all the other faculties" (Husserl 1988, Hua XXVIII, p. 404). In the cases just mentioned, the *a priori* character of the relations is compatible with the sensible origin of the representations: these relations are valid for anyone in possession of both sense representations and a capacity for *Wesenschauen*; but they are grounded in sensible matter, which is given *a posteriori*. In sum, the *a priori* can in no way be reduced to the formal *a priori* alone.

How does it stand, then, with the *application of this notion of material* a priori *to the ethical realm?*

The latter is governed by a double principle: an *a priori* relation is given in an eidetic intuition; and it has its foundation in the essence of representations, which can be *a posteriori*. Indeed, reason's relation to feelings has, in the practical domain, a function analogous to that of the relation to the senses in the epistemological domain: that "reason is the place of origin of ethical principles [*Ursprungsstätte der ethischen Prinzipien*]" (Husserl 1988, *Ergänz. Text* Nr. 2a, Hua XXVIII, p. 385), does not mean that they have their exclusive origin in pure reason thought of as an isolated faculty separate from the feelings; on the contrary, just as *a priori* truths can be grounded in the essence of sensory contents, so also can *a priori* truths "be grounded in the conceptual essence of emotive acts [*im begriffichen Wesen der Gemütsakte*]" (Husserl 1988, *Ergänz. Text* Nr. 2b, Hua XXVIII, p. 393)[5]. In this way, just as theoretical reason can come from some sensible matter and relate back to such a matter, in the same way, by analogy, can axiological and practical reason refer to a matter "that comes from the faculty of feeling and desire" (Husserl 1988, *Ergänz. Text* Nr. 3a, Hua XXVIII, p. 404); it can thus have the eidetic intuition (*Einsicht*) of an ethical norm, *i.e.* the self-evidence of an eidetic necessity that is grounded in the essence of feelings and desires. *Feeling and desire are, as a result, presupposed by the consciousness of the practical law: it is only on the basis of feelings and desires that we can acquire a clear intuition of the hierarchy of values and goods.*

A basic conclusion follows from this, which pertains to the concept of grounding (*Fundierung*): *ethics must be built as an "ethics from the ground up"* (*Ethik von unten*) (Husserl 1988, *Ergänz. Text* Nr. 3d, Hua XXVIII, p. 414) – from the bottom up: *i.e.* on the basis of affective *hylē*, upon which the higher objects that are ethical norms must be built.

A few consequences from this follow that are no less essential.

5 Reactivation of the Hegelian Critique of Kantian Formalism and Intellectualism

First of all, *Husserl appropriates the Hegelian critique of Kantian ethical formalism.*

Let us begin by recalling that "the fundamental law of pure practical reason," such as it is formulated by Kant at §7 of the *Grundsätze* of the *Critique of Practical Reason:* "Act such that your will's maxim is at the same time valid as a principle of universal legislation [*als Prinzip einer universalen Gesetzgebung*]" (Kant 1788, *Grundsätze*, §7, p. 54; Kant 1908/1913, AK. V, p. 30; Kant 2015, p. 28) – is discussed by Husserl in the lessons on ethics (Husserl 1988, *Ergänz. Text* Nr. 3e, Hua XXVIII, p. 414). This practical rule is unconditioned, since it makes demands of us as an *a priori* practical proposition that is not grounded in an intuition, because of the fact that here the pure will is "conceived as being determined *by the form of the law alone* [*durch die blosse Form des Gesetzes*]"

---

[5] And a bit further: "Cannot an *a priori* legality be grounded in the nature of feeling, or in the nature of the concepts that are grounded in the feelings?" (Husserl 1988, Hua XXVIII, p. 396).

(Kant 1788, *Grundsätze*, § 7, *Anm.*, p. 55; Kant 1908/1913, AK. V, p. 31; Kant 2015, p. 27), and not by any determinate representation of happiness or any material value. It is precisely for this reason that Husserl sees in this formula of the universalizability of one's maxim an "abstruse formalism [*abstruser Formalismus*]" (Husserl 1988, Hua XXVIII, p. 415). It contains, to be sure, a thesis that Husserl judges correct: namely that to be universal, the validity of an ethical demand must be "in accordance with a law" (*gesetzmässige Geltung*), without ever being dependent on particularities belonging to the actor or to circumstances; it must indeed express a binding "you must" for every subject in general. And yet, such nomological validity – that grounds the objective character of duty – cannot be reduced to or identified with the ability to universalize taken in a purely formal sense (*Verallgemeinerungsfähigkeit, rein formal genommen*), which remains totally empty (Husserl 1988, Hua XXVIII, p. 417). Why is this?

Let us distinguish and analyze Husserl's different arguments.

1/ The first argument is directed at the *absence of a heuristic or unveiling function of the abstract formula of the universalizability of one's maxim:* this formula "can never help us to find the law itself" (Husserl 1988, Hua XXVIII, p. 418), because it cannot, *on its own*, determine the concrete practical law that states what we must do in such and such a determinate situation. Here, it is a matter of the gap separating formal universalization and the particular content of the law, of passing from one to the other, and of the interpretation and the application of the law; indeed, "the character of being law is bound to what is specific about certain moments; there are circumstances that are meaningful [*relevante Umstände*], and others that are not" (Husserl 1988, Hua XXVIII, p. 417). In order to be able to determine the law in its particular content, we must carry out a preliminary separation of what is important (meaningful) from what is not, that is, determine the level of generality at which the law is to be applied; and this level is always defined with reference to circumstances that are more or less general: "Seeing as that in each case we can grasp the maxim in the most various ways, that we can accept sometimes one thing, sometimes another in it, and circumstances that are sometimes more, sometimes less general, the result of this is various and opposite possibilities of universalization" (Husserl 1988, Hua XXVIII, p. 415).

Let us take the Kantian example of savings left behind by a deceased person who has not left any will concerning it: if my maxim is to increase my wealth by any means, I will appropriate the savings for myself; but if I universalize this maxim, everyone then acquires the right to appropriate for themselves a savings that has been left *post mortem* in their hands without any will – which would have the effect of eliminating the value of any savings, and therefore to annihilate its possibility (Kant 1788, *Grundsätze*, § 4, *Lehrsatz* III, p. 49; Kant 1908/1913,

AK. V, p. 27; Kant 2015, p. 25). Nevertheless, the maxim can be understood at other levels of generality. One might formulate it in the following manner: "no one is bound to keep her promise," from which it would follow that no one would keep her promises any longer and the law would cancel itself out. If, on the other hand, one formulates it like so: "no one is bound to keep her promise if no written indication stipulates on what condition that promise can be considered fulfilled," this will simply make everyone more circumspect and attentive to the existence of written documents (Husserl 1988, Hua XXVIII, p. 415)!

2/ The second argument deals with the form taken by the test of universalizability of the subjective maxim governing the action, namely the *possibility of unveiling, on the basis of the universalization of the maxim, a contradiction that might invalidate it: to what type of logic does this contradiction belong* (Husserl 1988, Hua XXVIII, p. 418: "A contradiction with what?, must we also ask")?

Is it a purely formal-analytic contradiction? Most certainly not! It is on the contrary a *material contradiction*, namely an incompatibility with some content, in which case it is necessary to specify the nature of this content: a "contradiction with the nature of man, or with the nature of the specific particularities of the acts having to do with feeling or will" (Husserl 1988, Hua XXVIII, p. 418). Thus, in the case of the savings, the contradiction is not of a purely logical order: the maxim of enrichment by any means is not a formal contradiction, but contradicts the possibility of the promise as the ultimate foundation of the social bond, not to say of man's humanity. Thus is it always a matter of knowing *which material values the generalized maxim must be in agreement with*. There is therefore a parallel here among the logical, ethical, and aesthetic realms regarding the concept of *Richtigkeit* – as rightness in these domains can never be achieved through pure formal generalization (through the sole application of the universal quantifier), but in referring to the specific nature of the ideas in question, as well as to the self-evidence by which they are given:

> The law – whether aesthetic, ethical or logical – must necessarily be given self-evidently to us through the specific nature of ideas in which they are grounded [...]. The pure possibility of universalization does not ground any logical or aesthetic rightness, just as no pure possibility of universalization can ground ethical rightness. (Husserl 1988, Hua XXVIII, p. 418)

3/ The third argument consists in *re-appropriating Hume's skeptical doubt about the very idea of the efficacy of reason*, that is, about its ability to influence the practical determination to act.

For Hume, indeed, "reason alone can never be a motive to any action of the will" (Hume 1854, vol. II, III, III, p. 164 and vol. III, I, I, p. 215): only the expectation of the pleasure or pain caused by an object can make of it an object of propensity or aversion, thus causing a "sentiment of aversion or propensity," whereas reason possesses only the rectifying function consisting in determining the means satisfying a positive or negative impulse, without ever being able to create this impulse (Hume 1854, vol. II, III, III, pp. 165–167). Now, for Husserl, the same is true for pure practical reason's law of universalization: the thought of the formal universalization alone, insofar as it "is for me something totally indifferent [*etwas völlig Gleichgültiges*]" and "leaves the sentiment totally intact [*das Gefühl völlig unberüht lässt*]" (Husserl 1988, *Ergänz. Text* Nr. 3e, Hua XXVIII, p. 416), turns out to be incapable of constituting a determinative foundation for the will on its own. If practical rationality is confused with the possibility of universalizing the maxim that is the principle of the action, the discrepancy that separates the latter from the realm of feelings makes it unable to stimulate any feeling, and thereby to provoke an affective dynamic liable to put the will into motion. Here is something that corroborates Hume's thesis according to which "the understanding alone cannot create any morals" and "feeling holds an essential place in the emergence of ethical distinctions" (Husserl 1988, *Ergänz. Text* Nr. 2b, Hua XXVIII, p. 391): to speak of good and evil can only have meaning for a being in possession of the ability to feel and to desire.

Of course, from a Kantian point of view, one might object that Kant himself, in the doctrine of the motives (*Triebfeder*) of practical reason, notes that if feeling is not set in motion by the representation of the law, "neither can any practical effect come about from the latter" (Husserl 1988, *Ergänz. Text* Nr. 3e, Hua XXVIII, p. 416); in other words, the representation of the law must be able on its own to stimulate feeling or sentiment. It is with this in mind that Kant allows that the feeling of respect for the law is capable of setting the ability to desire into motion, without nevertheless presupposing a properly sensible feeling of pleasure (*Lust*): far from being produced by a preexisting feeling that is given *a posteriori*, respect is a positive feeling that is of purely intellectual origin, which has the effect of putting egotistical tendencies aside, of weakening or even defeating presumptuousness, and whose necessity can be the object of *a priori* self-evidence (*Einsicht*) (Kant 1788, *Von den Triebfedern d. r. pr. Vern.*, pp. 128–130; Kant 1908/1913, AK. V, pp. 72–73; Kant 2015, p. 61).

Husserl is aware of this, but thinks it is an incoherence (*Inkonsequenz*) of Kant's thought: indeed, on the one hand, Kant posits that ethical decision is not empirically derived from any pleasurable affect (*Lustaffektion*) and can find no foundation in it, but only in the formality of practical law (Kant 1788, p. 133; Kant 1908/1913, AK. V, p. 75; Kant 2015, p. 63); on the other hand, however, respect has to set the faculty of desiring into motion, and therefore to interest it, even though "the faculty of desiring is exclusively oriented towards pleasure" (Husserl 1988, *Ergänz. Text* Nr. 3e, Hua XXVIII, p. 417). The core of the incoherence is therefore the following: even though Kant explicitly denies that respect can be identified with pleasure (Husserl 1988, Hua XXVIII, p. 417),[6] he is ultimately forced to admit, in his *Metaphysics of Morals*, that "ethical decision rests upon an affection of pleasure;" for, in order to be motivated to want that which reason prescribes, it is necessary to have "a feeling of pleasure, of satisfaction at having fulfilled one's duty" (Husserl 1988, Hua XXVIII, p. 417). This is a return of the repressed: all of the egotistical tendencies that had been put aside by Kant to make room for the formality of the law here come back in the form of the interest taken in the moral act and of a moral satisfaction which, while it is not reducible to sensible pleasure, is pleasure nonetheless.

4/ The fourth argument is the most decisive one.

What is the foundation for Kant's conversion to what Husserl names his "extreme intellectualism" (Husserl 1988, *Ergänz. Text* Nr. 3d, Hua XXVIII, p. 412)? It resides in the fact that "if pure reason does not provide the foundations for the determination of willing, and the latter reside rather in feelings, in hedonism, egoistic utilitarianism is then the only coherent doctrine" (Husserl 1988, Hua XXVIII, p. 412). Why should this be the case? For the essential reason that Kant "only recognizes one type of difference between pleasure and displeasure, namely quantitative differences" (Husserl 1988, Hua XXVIII, p. 412):[7] if the determination of the will has its foundation in the feeling of pleasantness or of unpleasantness, the only relevant thing is to know the intensity and the duration of the pleasure, and the means by which it can be attained and renewed with ease (Kant 1788, *Grundsätze d. r. pr. Vern.*, § 3, *Lehrs.* II, *Anm.* I, p. 43; Kant 1908/1913, AK. V, p. 23; Kant 2015, p. 21); in the absence of a determining principle that is purely rational and refers to the moral law, the only possible position is Epicureanism, which only seems to recognize a quantitative difference between pleasure and displeasure (Kant 1788, *Grundsätze d. r. pr. Vern.*, § 3, *Lehrs.* II, *Anm.* I, pp. 43–44; Kant 1908/1913, AK. V, p. 24; Kant 2015, p. 22).[8]

Against this, Husserl evokes the Humean principle of the "admission of qualitative differences within feeling [*Annahme qualitativer Unterschiede im Gefühl*]," in virtue of which we "derive the difference between higher and lower feelings from moments that are internal to feeling [*innere Gefühlsmo-*

---

[6] See Kant 1788, *Triebfeder*, p. 137; Kant 1908/1913, AK. V, p. 77; Kant 2015, p. 64: "respect is so *little* a feeling of pleasure […]."

[7] See Kant 1788, *Grundsätze d. r. pr. Vern.*, § 3, *Lehrs.* II, *Anm.* I, p. 42; Kant 1908/1913, AK. V, p. 23; Kant 2015, p. 21: "the feeling of pleasure […] is of one type alone […], and it cannot differ from itself save by degree."

[8] See Husserl 1988, *Ergänz. Text* Nr. 3d, Hua XXVIII, p. 412). This is a crass misinterpretation of Epicureanism, both on Kant's part and on Husserl's.

mente], and not to purely and simply quantitative distinctions such as intensity and duration" (Husserl 1988, Hua XXVIII, p. 413). Far from a crass hedonism founded on an undifferentiated pleasure principle, we are brought back to the Greek principle of the hierarchy of the pleasures. Indeed, to refute the thesis of the univocity of the pleasures, it suffices that we compare the pleasure we take respectively in eating a good meal and in listening to Beethoven's *Eroïca* Symphony: we find that there is not simply a difference in quantity or in degree, but in the quality of the pleasure; "the artwork elevates, it makes us happy, and what it brings us cannot be reduces to a simple contentment" (Husserl 1988, Hua XXVIII, p. 413). As a result, if art in the supreme sense has primacy in the hierarchy of pleasures, this is by virtue of the "particularity of the feelings it stimulates," such that the difference between that which is vile and that which is elevated is a "distinction that is grounded in qualities [*ein in den Qualitäten gründender Unterschied*]," even though it is not immediately reducible to a difference in quality (Husserl 1988, Hua XXVIII, p. 413). To emphasize this, it suffices to underline the limits of the analogy with color: "elevated" and "vile" characteristics are not distinct qualities (like red and yellow), any more than they are types of quality (like color among types of visual quality); it is here a matter of "second degree difference, linked to qualities or to combinations of qualities," which have however nothing to do with a quantitative scale of degrees or of intensive quantities (like the difference between hot and cold, light and dark colors, etc.) (see Husserl 1988, Hua XXVIII, p. 413).

This refusal of the pure quantification of pleasure is moreover corroborated by a second argument. Within quantities, there is a difference between positive and negative quantities; if pleasure were merely a matter of quantity, the opposition between pleasure and displeasure would be reduced to a distinction between positive and negative quantities. However, qualitative differences are found right down to the realm we call "displeasure:" there is such a thing as noble sadness, just as there is noble indignation, etc. (Husserl 1988, Hua XXVIII, pp. 413–414).

The *main problem*, then, remains the *material hierarchy of values and goods, of pleasures and feelings:* what lies at the foundation of ethics is a universal doctrine of values, a material axiology that must be grounded in an axiological hierarchy of feelings and pleasures (Husserl 1988, Hua XXVIII, p. 414). Once again we see manifesting themselves the primacy of a relation of grounding or foundation (*Fundierung*) and the correlative demand for an ethics built from the bottom up (*Ethik von unten*): to ground ethics is to bring it back to its undergirding, which resides in the practical and axiological determinations of things, along with the hierarchical stratification of feelings and pleasures. This does not mean, of course, that such an undergirding suffices on its own to characterize what is ethical and to distinguish it from what is not: noble and beautiful feelings do not necessarily entail ethicity – but, on the other hand, the latter is grounded on the undergirding of the former: "Of course, this distinction is not appropriate without going any further for characterizing univocally ethicalness from non-ethicalness. All positively ethical feeling is noble and beautiful, but not all noble feeling is ethical" (Husserl 1988, Hua XXVIII, p. 414).

6 Critique of the Copernican Revolution

We begin by recalling Kant's two fundamental theses regarding anthropologism and finitude in the practical realm.

First, the theoretical realm always carries the inherent danger of anthropologism, i.e. the admission that the *a priori* structures of sensibility and understanding refer to the generic constitution of the human being. On the one hand, while Kant grants to space and to time the status of *a priori* forms of sensibility, he does so while simultaneously recognizing that they only have validity "for us humans" (*für uns Menschen*); on the other hand, while the categories of the understanding are not reducible to intellectually innate structures, but rather designate the necessary forms of the determination of empirical objects, Kant nevertheless recognizes, in the second edition of the Transcendental Deduction of the Categories, that we cannot account for the fact that the finite subject possesses these two forms of sensibility and this determinate number of categories (Kant 1787, *Transz. Deduktion*, § 21, B 145–146; Kant 1998, p. 254).[9] And if we move to the practical realm, Humean morality presupposes ways of feeling that turn out to be "profoundly rooted in human nature and constitution" (Husserl 1988, *Ergänz. Text* Nr. 2a, Hua XXVIII, p. 385). But this is precisely not the case with the *Kantian grounding of ethics*, which *on the contrary escapes any danger of sliding towards anthropologism:* as an *a priori* grounding, it turns out to be totally independent of any presupposition about a human nature. Indeed, the task of the *Critique of Practical Reason* consists in determining the principles of its possibility, its extent and its limits "absolutely without particular reference to human nature" (Kant 1788, *Vorrede*, p. 15; Kant 1908/1913, AK. V, p. 8; Kant 2015, p. 7); and practical principles are not supposed to have validity for the *human* will alone, but "for the will of any being endowed with reason" (Kant

---

9 See Husserl 1956, *Beil.* XV and XXI, Hua VII, pp. 354, 397 and 401: "the human subject [is] constantly understood in advance as the subject of psychic faculties." We adopted this formula, in *Par-delà la révolution copernicienne* (Pradelle 2012), as the red thread running throughout our interpretation of the opposition between Kantianism and Husserlian phenomenology.

1788, *Grundsätze*, § 1, *Erkl.*, p. 35; Kant 1908/1913, AK. V, p. 19; Kant 2015, p. 17). The authority of morality turns out then to be independent of any anthropological thesis.

Secondly, while the *fundamental distinction between finite and infinite (divine) beings* has an essential function in the theoretical sphere – where it is possible to posit, for the finite being, intuition and understanding as heterogeneous sources of knowledge –, this distinction *keeps its eminent role in the practical sphere for Kant*. Of course, far from being limited to humans, the principle of ethicity has the value of law for "all finite beings that have reason and will," and so also for the divine being (Kant 1788, *Grundsätze*, § 7, *Anm.*, p. 57; Kant 1908/1913, AK. V, p. 32; Kant 2015, p. 29); and, in contrast to the principle of self-love, which has only a contingent and subjective necessity, which refers to what finite beings accept as objects of pleasure, it has an objective necessity, without any reference to human predilections (Kant 1788, *Grundsätze*, § 3, *Lehrsatz* II, *Anm.* II, p. 47; Kant 1908/1913, AK. V, p. 26; Kant 2015, p. 24). And yet, it is only for *finite* subjects – which are at once affected and in possession of a will that is *pure* but not *holy* –, that the law offers a form of imperative or binding moral obligation: the grounding of the imperative form taken on by the moral law thus resides in the finitude of the will (Kant 1788, *Grundsätze*, § 7, *Anm.*, p. 57; Kant 1908/1913, AK. V, p. 32; Kant 2015, p. 29), such that *the Copernican revolution carried out in the theoretical realm is also valid in the practical realm*; just, indeed, as the *a priori* structures of the object were supposed to follow the formal structures of the finite subject, so here the form of the categorical imperativeness proper to the moral law follows the finite character of the will. This principle of the Copernican reversal is just as valid for the analysis of respect: to the extent to which it has an effect on sensibility, the respect for the moral law presupposes, as a moral feeling, that the being endowed with reason is also endowed with sensibility, therefore with the "finitude of such a being;" for non-sensible beings, there can hardly be such a thing as respect for the law (Kant 1788, *Triebfeder*, pp. 134–135; Kant 1908/1913, AK. V, p. 76; Kant 2015, p. 63: "... that respect for the *law* cannot be attributed to a supreme being or even to one free from all sensibility").

On the contrary, even though the phenomenological reduction is indeed a method that is Copernican in inspiration, since it consists in suspending the being of the world in order to return to the subjective realm of pure *cogitations* and to the subjective modes of appearing of beings (see Husserl 1994, letter to Pannwitz, April 14th 1937, p. 227; Husserl 1956, Hua VII, p. 240), *Husserl's fundamental position is of an anti-Copernican character*.

This can first be stated in the form of a general principle and grasped in the realm of perceptual experience, before being transposed into the practical realm:

in the realm of experience, "any object [...] designates in general a regulative structure of the transcendental ego" (Husserl 1963/1976, § 22, Hua I, p. 90; Husserl 1982, p. 53), whatever, moreover, the nature of this ego might be (man, angel, or God). For example, a spatial object cannot become perceptible except by presenting itself in a structurally inadequate way, through unilateral adumbrations: "no God can change this fact, no more than the fact that $1 + 2 = 3$ or the constancy of any essential truth" (Husserl 1976, § 44, Hua III/1, p. 92; Husserl 1983, p. 95); in the same way, any lived experience of mine cannot present itself other than by reflection, which entails a temporal gap between the reflected and the reflecting, such that "by this necessity that is absolute and given in an intuition of essence, God is therefore equally bound" (Husserl 1976, § 79, Hua III/1, p. 175; Husserl 1983, p. 189). In other words, the mode of givenness of an object has the status of eidetic necessity: it is prescribed by the type of object, and does not depend in any way on the type of subject that is having the experience; it turns out then to be independent of the difference between human finitude and divine infinity. From this point of view, nothing remains of Kant's Copernican principle according to which the object of knowledge is measured according to the *a priori* structures of the knowing subject; thus, even if phenomenology is characterized by a subjective orientation centered around the field of pure consciousness, the latter nevertheless does not possess a pre-constituted essence that is supposed to belong to any finite subject or to "us humans"; on the contrary, it is characterized by a set of constitutive structures that determine the types of object that can be given in experience.

Can this reversal of the Copernican principle be transposed to morals?

Indeed, it does seem that there is an analogous reversal in the practical realm:

> It is the essence of a practical law to express a duty [...]. It is a biased thesis of Kant's that such a law should only take the imperative form for a finite being [*nur für ein endliches Wesen die Imperativform annehme*]. (Husserl 1988, Ergänz. Text Nr. 3a, Hua XXVIII, pp. 404–405)

In other words, the imperative form that the moral law takes is the mode of givenness that belongs to it, and this mode of givenness depends only on the essence of the moral law, and not on the type of being that experiences it. What is the argument by which Husserl justifies this anti-Copernican principle?

He mobilizes the Leibnizian concept of God, as opposed to the Cartesian or Spinozist concept: of course God cannot but act in a good way, because His will is holy (Kant 1788, *Grundsätze*, § 7, Anm., p. 57; Kant 1908/1913, AK. V, p. 32; Kant 2015, p. 29), but He finds himself nevertheless in the same situation as any subject in general with respect to action: to be up to acting in a good way, He must have a preliminary discernment of what is good; if this were not the case, He would of course act in a good way, but He would do so in a blind and non-foresightful way – like the well-intentioned beautiful soul, who is characterized both by his moral blindness and by his sleep-walking infallibility. Essentially, God himself is subject to the demand of moral foresight:

> The determination of His will consists in the fact that He necessarily wants the good because He knows it as good, and this means that He knows it as something that he must do, which means that the rule governing His action is not an arbitrary law of nature, but a law of duty [*Sollengesetz*]. (Husserl 1988, Ergänz. Text Nr. 3a, Hua XXVIII, p. 405)

If God's holy will could not take leave of its duty, but accomplished it with an infallible necessity without having an intuition of it, such a fulfillment would then be of the order of blind necessity, analogous to that of the laws of nature; if the action of God must be able to be called moral in the supreme sense, then God Himself must have the clear intuition of practical duty, of what is absolutely valid from a moral point of view, and adjust His action to this preliminary intuition; God's not-being-able-to-do-otherwise is not a mechanical or analytic necessity (as if perfect actions followed analytically from His essence), but a necessity enlightened by the consciousness of duty and of the good. However, that God himself perceives the difference between what is and what ought to be entails that *the imperative form of the law rests only on the essence of the good*, and that *the imperative is the way in which the essence of the moral law gives itself to a subject, whatever its nature might be:* the presentation of the moral law in the form of an imperative is therefore not restricted to finite and fallible subjects alone, but turns out to be indifferent to the distinction between finitude and infinity, pure and holy will.

This anti-Copernican thesis leads, however, to a strange paradox.

Indeed, on the one hand, moral laws must not be valid only for beings endowed with reason, but for any sensing being in general, "be it man or angel" or God (Husserl 1988, Hua XXVIII, p. 406). As a result, God Himself must be characterized by the ability to have feelings, and be subject to all the necessities inherent in sensibility!

This was already true in the perceptual and theoretical order: far from being able to know directly the primary qualities of external things, God Himself was obliged not to be able to perceive them save through the mediation of secondary qualities, qualities which are of course proper to Him and different from ours, but are nonetheless essentially distinct from the primary qualities, the distinction between primary and secondary qualities is valid for God himself, such that He is subject to the constraints inherent in sensibility, as well as to the distinction between the thing such as it appears and such as it is in itself (Husserl 1952, § 18 g, Hua IV, p. 85; Husserl 1989, p. 90).

And it is the same in the practical realm. To show this, Husserl has recourse to the method of eidetic variation, which he applies to the concept of the subject of practical experience. Let us form the fiction of a subject that is perceiving and thinking, but is deprived of all ability to experience feelings (*Fähigkeit des Fühlens*), to have desires and to want (*des Begehrens, Wollens*); and indeed, without this faculty, such a subject would not have any notion of the distinction between good and evil, nor any principle of determination – since any act of the will has its ground in the act of evaluation, and the latter is in its turn grounded in feeling (see Husserl 1988, *Ergänz. Text* Nr. 2b, Hua XXVIII, p. 391). The moral sense is grounded in the realm of practical sensibility.

In sum, *the relation of foundation (Fundierung) has universal validity in Husserlian phenomenology*, and this permits the drawing of a parallel between the theoretical and practical realms. All essence and all eidetic truth being grounded in the realm of sensibility and of sensible objects, any being capable of knowing essences and truths such as these must necessarily possess a sensibility that allows it to know the objects situated at their ground: the foundation of the understanding on sensibility corresponds, in the subjective order of acts, to that of superior objectities on the sensible arch-objects in the objectal order. It is the same, by analogy, in the practical realm: since all discernment of the moral law or of ethical distinctions is grounded in evaluation, and the latter in turn in feeling, any being capable of such ethical insight – "be it man or angel" – must necessarily have the ability to experience feelings. Of course, the laws of duty must be characterized by an *a priori* intuitiveness, and are valid, as a result, for any being endowed with reason in general; but, insofar as many moral imperatives are *a priori* material laws, they can only be intuited by a sensing being in general (*für jedes fühlendes Wesen überhaupt*).

Thus, in order to be capable of theoretical and practical discernment, God must have both sensibility and the faculty of feelings. There is therefore, in Husserlian phenomenology, an *essential neutralization of the distinction between God and the finite subject, infinity and finitude*. No more on the theoretical level than on the practical level do we find in Husserl any analytic of finitude, but rather an absolutization of structures and properties which traditionally are only attributed to the finite subject: just as the essence of the temporal or spatial object imposes its mode of givenness and prescribes a corresponding constitutive structure to all subjects, so in the same way does the essence of ethical distinctions and laws prescribe to all subjects a mode of givenness in the imperative form and a grounding or foundation in the realm of feeling.

7 The Phenomenological Concept of Freedom

We return, in conclusion, to the concept of freedom: *is there, in Husserlian phenomenology, a doctrine of freedom?* Does it have anything in common with the Kantian concepts of transcendental freedom and practical freedom?

We recall that the concept of freedom is described by Kant as constituting the keystone of the entire edifice of the system of pure reason (see Kant 1788, *Vorrede*, p. 4; Kant 1908/1913, AK. V, p. 3; Kant 2015, p. 3). Indeed, on the one hand transcendental freedom constitutes the *ratio essendi* of the moral law insofar as the concept of absolute duty presupposes that acts can be imputed to the subject and, therefore, to the practical spontaneity of the latter; inversely, the moral law constitutes the *ratio cognoscendi* of freedom, since the conscience remains the condition of possibility of all revelation of our freedom (see Kant 1788, *Vorrede*, p. 5 and *Grundsätze*, § 6, *Anmerk.*, pp. 52–53; Kant 1908/1913, AK. V, 4 and pp. 29–30; Kant 2015, pp. 4 and 27). On the other hand, there is a compatibility between two forms of causality – causality as freedom grounded in ethical law, and causality as natural mechanism grounded in the laws of nature –, on account of the duality of the ontological status of the human: the first has to do with human being as it is in itself, the second with the human as an empirical phenomenon (see Kant 1788, *Vorrede*, p. 10; Kant 1908/1913, AK. V, p. 6; Kant 2015, p. 5). As a result, *there is in principle no experience for humans of their own freedom*; the latter remains a cosmological Idea and then a practical Idea, whose objective meaning is proved by the consciousness of the moral law. A particular experience seems, however, to offer itself as an equivalent (albeit a negative one) to the experience of freedom: in any ethical action, we are constantly aware of the resistibility of our sensible tendencies (see Kant 1788, *Grundsätze*, § 6, *Anm.*, p. 54; Kant 1908/1913, AK. V, p. 30; Kant 2015, p. 27); no sensible impulse imposes itself on us as endowed with an irresistible force, such that, for every finite being endowed with reason, the principle of the autonomy of the will is valid (see Kant 1788, *Grundsätze*, § 8, p. 58; Kant 1908/1913, AK. V, p. 33). Freedom thus appears as *a matter of pure principle*, even though we have a negative prescience of it by experiencing the resistibility of the inclinations.

What concept of freedom do we now find in transcendental phenomenology? Can the latter also grant it the status of transcendental Idea (i.e. of a concept to which no object that can be given in intuition corresponds; see Kant 1781/1787, *Transz. Dial.*, A 327/B 383) if, following phenomenology's intuitionist principle, any valid concept must be able to be confirmed in an originary giving intuition (see Husserl 1976, § 24, Hua III/1, p. 51; Husserl 1983, p. 44), so here in a form of *ethical experience?* And if we follow these intuitionist requirements, can we trace these Kantian concepts of freedom back to a giving intuition that can confirm them?

As far as the *transcendental* (cosmological) concept of freedom is concerned – freedom as the ability to start a chain of empirical processes (Kant 1781/1787, *Transz. Dial.*, A 445/B 473) –, Husserl grants it an intuitive validity by exemplifying it through the consciousness of my own fleshly acts: the ego reigns in a specific way, through its "somatic power" (*leibliches Können, Vermögen*), over its fleshly body and its various organs – a power that has the "characteristic of a subjective moving, an 'I move' [*Charakter des subjektiven Bewegens, des 'ich bewege'*]," of a moving that is by essence distinct from any mechanical movement (Husserl 1952, § 60a, Hua IV, p. 259; Husserl 1989, p. 271). The primitive experience of transcendental freedom thus resides in the automotive abilities of the subject, in which both its status as a voluntary agent and as a body of flesh and immediate organ of will reveal themselves at once. What we have here is indeed a pure and simple intuitive application of the cosmological idea of transcendental freedom; and what is at stake in this application is a form of psychophysical causality that is no more mysterious than other forms of causality: indeed, all causality is constituted by the law of motivation, *i.e.*, against the background of the perception of the relation "if...,then...," and the latter can assume many distinct forms – including, in particular, that of conditional consequence between voluntary intention and bodily movement.

Nevertheless, the practical concept of freedom cannot be exhausted by this immediate consciousness of fleshly freedom – far from it! Thus, remaining in the field of fleshly movements, one finds the exemplary case of "impulsive doing, for example the involuntary 'I move' [*das Tun als triebmässiges Tun, z. B. das unwillkürliche 'ich bewege mich'*]": for example, I involuntarily move my hand toward my cigar, without being aware of wanting it. This example reveals, *before* any voluntary willing, an undergirding endowed with a blind efficiency (*'blinde' Wirksamkeit*) and constituted by obscure associations, impulses, feelings, and tendencies that determine the course of consciousness by means of blind laws. We must, then, distinguish a double stratum in the essence of subjectivity: on the one hand a lower level of pure animality, and on the other hand a higher (and specifically mental or spiritual) level of the *intellectus agens*, "of the free ego as ego of free acts, including specifically rational acts" – *animale rationale* (Husserl 1952, § 61, Hua IV, p. 276; Husserl 1989, p. 289).

More generally, the double stratum of which the human is constituted is a *duality between reason and sensibility*, which are split apart by a chasm and are in constant struggle with each other. However, far from being limited to animal subjectivity, which is characterized by essentially impulsive blind needs, here sensibility designates *pre-constituted subjectivity* (*vorkonstituierte Subjektivität*), determined by a dark and obscure undergirding that embraces idiosyncrasies and hidden in-born dispositions; truly free and spiritual subjectivity (*echte freie une geistige Subjektivität*) is indeed influenced by this undergirding of passive impulses and pre-constituted dispositions. The result of this is an essential transformation of the Kantian concept of freedom: for, as opposed to the thesis of the principle of freedom understood as the autonomy of reason, there exists a *phenomenological experience of freedom, which is concretely realized in accordance with the differing concrete degrees of resistance and submission*; for example, I can resist my inclinations and impulses, tear myself free from the influence of sensibility or of my character, not allow myself to be sucked in (*ziehen*) or oppressed (*herabziehen*) by them; but I can feel myself incapable of this, my will proving itself to be too weak (*zu schwach*), without, however, this weakness of will ever being an invariable and definitive property of the ego – as mental or spiritual ego, I can always, throughout the course of my development, "become stronger [*stärker werden*]," "the weak will can make itself strong [*das schwache Willen kann sich stärken*]"; in the power struggle that opposes passive undergirding and active will of the subject, the latter can strengthen itself and become predominant (Husserl 1952, § 60b, Hua IV, p. 267; Husserl 1989, p. 279).

What then is the status of practical freedom? While it is still that of a Kantian Idea, it has nevertheless changed both its meaning and its function: it is no longer a foundational or principial Idea situated at the ground of the possibility of the moral act, but rather a *regulative and programmatic Idea, situated on the horizon of subjective potentialities*. Freedom is no longer a principial Idea inherent in our noumenal being, but is defined as the *ideal pole of a progressive liberation:* there is no pregiven and absolute noumenal freedom, but only the regulative Idea of freedom taken as a horizon concept, as a goal situated at the infinite end of an approximation or a personal progress, of a progressive liberation from any pre-constituted, blind, or obscure passivity. Thus, in the place of the principle of absolute rational freedom, we find the concrete experience of diverse forms of passive conditioning, joined together with the apperception of the possibility of overcoming them – of a path leading towards a freedom that must always be won and strengthened – towards liberation.

Bibliography

Brentano, Franz (1969): *Vom Ursprung sittlicher Erkenntnis*. Hamburg: Felix Meiner.
Cohen, Hermann (1918): *Kants Theorie der Erfahrung*, 3rd edition. Berlin: B. Cassirer.

Heidegger, Martin (1982/1994): *Vom Wesen der menschlichen Freiheit. Gesamtausgabe*, vol. 31. Ed. Hartmut Tietjen. Frankfurt/Main: Vittorio Klostermann.
Hume, David (1854): *A Treatise of Human Nature*, Vol. II: "Of the Passions". Vol. III: "Of Morals", in *The Philosophical Works of David Hume*, Vol.1. Boston/Edinburgh: A. and Ch. Black.
Husserl, Edmund (1952): *Ideen zu einer reinen Phänomenologie und phänomenologischen Philosophie*, Zweites Buch: *Phänomenologische Untersuchungen zur Konstitution. Husserliana*, vol. IV. Ed. Marly Biemel. The Hague: Martinus Nijhoff.
Husserl, Edmund (1956): *Erste Philosophie*, Band I. *Husserliana*, vol. VII. Ed. Rudolf Boehm. The Hague: Martinus Nijhoff.
Husserl, Edmund (1963/1976): *Cartesianische Meditationen. Husserliana*, vol. I. Ed. Stephan Strasser. The Hague: Martinus Nijhoff.
Husserl, Edmund (1976): *Ideen zu einer reinen Phänomenologie und phänomenologischen Philosophie*, I. Buch. *Husserliana*, vol. III/1. Ed. Karl Schuhmann. The Hague: Martinus Nijhoff.
Husserl, Edmund (1982): *Cartesian Meditations*. Trans. Dorion Cairns. The Hague: Martinus Nijhoff.
Husserl, Edmund (1983): *Ideas Pertaining to a Pure Phenomenology and to a Phenomenological Philosophy*. First Book: *General Introduction to a Pure Phenomenology*. Trans. Fred Kersten. The Hague: Martinus Nijhoff.
Husserl, Edmund (1988): *Vorlesungen über Ethik und Wertlehre (1908–1914). Husserliana*, vol. XXX. Ed. Ulrich Melle. Dordrecht/ Boston/London: Kluwer Academic Publishers.
Husserl, Edmund (1989): *Ideas Pertaining to a Pure Phenomenology and to a Phenomenological Philosophy*. Second Book: *Studies in the Phenomenology of Constitution*. Trans. R. Rojcewicz and A. Schuwer. Dordrecht: Kluwer Academic Publishers.
Husserl, Edmund (1994): *Briefwechsel: Wissenschaftler Korrespondenz. Husserliana Dokumente*, vol. III/7. Ed. Karl Schuhmann. Dordrecht/Boston/London: Kluwer Academic Publishers.
Husserl, Edmund (2004): *Einleitung in die Ethik. Vorlesungen Sommersemester 1920 und 1924. Husserliana*, vol. XXXVII. Ed. Henning Peucker. Dordrecht/Boston/London: Kluwer Academic Publishers.
Kant, Immanuel (1781/1787): *Kritik der reinen Vernunft*. Riga: Hartknoch [A = first original edition (1781); B = second original edition (1787)].
Kant, Immanuel (1788): *Kritik der praktischen Vernunft*, Originalausgabe. Riga: Hartknoch.
Kant, Immanuel (1903): *Prolegomena zu jeder künftigen Metaphysik. Kants Gesammelte Schriften*, Königlich Preußischen Akademie der Wissenschaften (AK.), vol. IV. Berlin: Georg Reimer.
Kant, Immanuel (1908/1913): *Kritik der praktischen Vernunft. Kants Gesammelte Schriften*, Königlich Preußischen Akademie der Wissenschaften (AK.), vol. V. Berlin: Georg Reimer.
Kant, Immanuel (1923): *Logik* (Jäsche). *Kants Gesammelte Schriften*, Königlich Preußischen Akademie der Wissenschaften (AK.), vol. IX. Berlin/Leipzig: Walter de Gruyter.
Kant, Immanuel (1968): *Grundlegung zur Metaphysik der Sitten. Kants Gesammelte Schriften*, Königlich Preußischen Akademie der Wissenschaften (AK.), vol. IV. Berlin/Leipzig: Walter de Gruyter.

Kant, Immanuel (1992): *Lectures on Logic.* Trans. J. Michael Young. Cambridge: Cambridge University Press.
Kant, Immanuel (1997): *Groundwork of the Metaphysics of Morals.* Trans. Mary Gregor. Cambridge: Cambridge University Press.
Kant, Immanuel (1998): *Critique of Pure Reason.* Trans. Paul Guyer and Allen W. Wood. Cambridge: Cambridge University Press.
Kant, Immanuel (2004): *Prolegomena to Any Future Metaphysics That Will be Able to Come Forward as Science.* Trans. Gary Hatfield. Cambridge: Cambridge University Press.
Kant, Immanuel (2015): *Critique of Practical Reason.* Trans. Mary Gregor. Cambridge: Cambridge University Press.
Reinach, Adolf (1989): *Sämtliche Werke*, vol. I. München/Hamden/Wien: Philosophia Verlag.
Scheler, Max (1916): *Der Formalismus in der Ethik und die materiale Wertethik.* Halle: Max Niemeyer.
Stumpf, Carl (1873): *Über den psychologischen Ursprung der Raumvorstellung.* Leipzig: S. Hirzel.

Section IV: Transcendental Philosophy in Debate

Alexander Schnell
Is There a "Copernican" or an "Anti-Copernican" Revolution in Phenomenology?[1]

Abstract: This chapter raises the question – based on the works of Marc Richir and Dominique Pradelle (in particular) – of if and how phenomenology deals with an "anti-Copernican" revolution, considering that the motif (which is initially Kantian) of a "Copernican" revolution seems to have gone through some modifications that reflect a certain deposition of the constitutive role of the subject. Its fundamental thesis is that a certain dimension "beyond" the Copernican revolution does not reestablish a "Ptolemaic" realism but rather opens a dimension "beneath:" beneath the subject and the object where a mutual relationship between an a-subjective constitutive power and a pre-empirical foundational being can take place. This dimension "beneath" means that the alternative does not concern a "pre-Copernican" realism, on the one hand, and an "idealism" – which leaves in the shadows the relationship between the transcendental method and an ontological perspective – on the other, but rather puts forward a constructive circularity between the transcendental constitution and an ontological foundation. It follows that "normativity" is not achieved on the basis of pre-given objectivity – because it would imply a *petitio principia* – but draws upon the "pre-immanent generativity."

Shortly before his death, Hegel, testifying to the heritage of classical German philosophy, asserted that "The effect of Fichtean idealism [...] on philosophizing should forevermore be to make it unavoidable to show the self-evidence [*Aufzeigen*] of *necessity*" (Hegel 1986, pp. 485 *et sq.*, italics ours). The reflection on necessity and its relation to a precise understanding of the "*a priori*"[2] continues in the debate between Kant's transcendental idealism and Husserl's phenomenological idealism. This questioning in particular is at the heart of an examination

---
[1] This chapter is the edited English version made by John Rogove of an article originally published in French in the special issue of *Meta: Research in Hermeneutics, Phenomenology, and Practical Philosophy*, vol. VIII, n° 2 / December 2016: *Husserl and Kant: The Transcendental-Phenomenological Project*, Guest Editor: Iulian Apostolescu, pp. 257–279.
[2] An explicit reference to this relation is to be found for example in the important *Beilage* XVI to *Erste Philosophie* (Husserl 1956, Hua VII, pp. 357*sq.*).

of the status of the "Copernican Revolution." As is well-known, the latter seeks to account for *a priori* knowledge by reversing the relation of constitutive priority between the objects which are to be known and the knowing subject. In the following, we would like to raise the question – stimulated by earlier work (Richir 1976) and by contemporary work[3] – as to whether and to what extent we can speak of an "*anti*-Copernican" revolution in phenomenology, given the fact that this motif, which is Kantian in origin, seems to have undergone modifications which imply the overthrow of the constitutive role of the subject (and, in particular, its role in instituting necessary "norms"). We shall begin by recalling the meaning that the latter has for Kant.

1 The "Copernican Revolution" in Kant's Criticism and "Transcendental Idealism" in Husserl's Phenomenology

The "Copernican revolution," such as it is presented in the *Critique of Pure Reason*, consists in the idea that the – eminently *epistemological* – project of grounding *a priori* knowledge demands, on the *ontological* level, that this "knowledge" be born not by the "things" such as they are in themselves, but on "objects" understood as phenomena, *i.e.*, insofar as they appear as a result of the pure forms of sensibility and insofar as they are synthesized (unified) by the categories of the understanding. These "objects" are dependent on the "transcendental subject" which Kant analyzes with respect to its faculties, among which sensibility, understanding, and imagination play a leading role in accounting for the conditions of the possibility of any and all knowledge.

However, while Husserl occasionally asserts that he is remaining faithful to the author of the *Critique of Pure Reason* concerning essential points,[4] he nevertheless criticizes the Kantian project. To what extent does this criticism affect the project of a "Copernican revolution?" Is Husserlian phenomenology a continuation of the latter or opposed to it?

Classically, Husserl (and Heidegger following him) insists on the idea that phenomenology is characterized by a specific *method*. At the heart of this

---

[3] On this topic, see the last chapter, "Une révolution anticopernicienne: le monde de la vie," in *Au cœur de la raison, la phénoménologie* (Romano 2010). See above all Pradelle 2012.

[4] For example, Husserl writes in 1924: "[...] we see ourselves in agreement with Kant in the essential results of our work growing systematically out of the absolutely ultimate sources of all knowledge ("*Kant und die Idee der Transzendentalphilosophie*," Husserl 1956, Hua VII, p. 235).

method are the epoché and the phenomenological reduction. In the context of a reflection on the relation between the "I" and the world, Husserl explains that, as regards these methodological tools, the "I" is not simply "opposite" the world, "facing" it – which, moreover, begs the (Cartesian) question of the status of the world –, but is the *intentional relation*, designated as "*cogitatio*," which puts the "I" and its objective correlate in an originary relation. The object, and by extension the world, cannot be considered "outside," or even "prior to" this dimension which endows it with "meaning" and validity."

But what exactly is to be understood by "subjective pole" (opposite to its objective correlate)? The *cogito* is not the empirical "I" but the pole around which the constitution of the meaning of appearing is centered in the regime of the epoché and the phenomenological reduction. The description of this pole requires a change of attitude with respect to pregiven and pre-established reality. By holding steadfastly to the epoché and the reduction, the field of phenomenological investigation that Husserl calls "subjectivity" is opened, which is precisely constitutive of meaning and of the meaning of the being of appearing. What is the sense of *transcendental idealism* that this method implies?

> If I give myself the task of making comprehensible how, in my subjectivity, I come therein constantly to have "the" world pregiven and given, this does not then signify thereby any "consciousness idealism." I am not saying here that the world has all its being in a being-for-me. I am only going on the idea that what is given for me under the heading "the world" gains in me all its meaning and its validity as a being. I am not saying that the world is somehow inside me, or even that it is in some way a product of materials from my own transcendental being and, as a result, a subjective formation, like a product from stone is a formation in nature, belonging to it as a part. I am not saying anything of the sort, but am only trying to make clear how, in me, that which emerges under that heading "nature and world" as a being, as something experienced, judged, etc., but also as verified effectivity or as appearance, as certainty or possibly as uncertainty, as questioning, as supposition, etc. – how, from which sources of consciousness it gets all of its meaning, and [comes] to its being possibly posited in self-evidence [...]. (Husserl 2002, Hua XXXIV, p. 114)

Phenomenological transcendental idealism thus proposes to account for the way in which Being and beings derive their meaning and their validity from the sources of transcendental consciousness. Husserl says so without ambiguity:

> But having-in-validity essentially means having-an-interest-field, a field of a universal life-theme, horizon of possibilities of the "I", living in it, being able to work [*hineinwirken*] in it, being able to preserve itself in it. The epoché is the phenomenological reduction to the "I"[5]

---

5 Concerning reduction to the "I," Husserl writes in chapter 3 (entitled "The activity of the I's natural life consciousness and the reduction to pure subjectivity") in the third section of the sec-

in the absolute sense, *i.e.*, in the type of being that encompasses all the possibilities of being, and thus all possible interest-fields accessible to me, insofar as they are free to be constituted from it and for it. (Husserl 2002, Husserliana XXXIV, p. 224)

What exactly does this *free constitution from me* and *for me* mean? What is the status of subjectivity and *what can transcendental life do?*

Let us first note that the two fundamental concepts of the preceding quote – the *meaning* of being (*Seinssinn*) and the *validity* of being (*Seinsgeltung*) – do not overlap purely and simply, even though Husserl often mentions them in the same context; thus, it is appropriate here to make distinctions that will allow for a clarification of the status of the Copernican (or anti-Copernican?) revolution in phenomenology. This work has been very usefully carried out by Dominique Pradelle in *Beyond the Copernican Revolution* (2012).

2 The Copernican (or Anti-Copernican?) Revolution in Phenomenology

According to Dominque Pradelle, there are reasons that plead in favor of the idea that there is an "anti-Copernican revolution" in phenomenology. What justifies this thesis? To answer this question, it is necessary to recall the extent to which phenomenology places itself, first of all, in *continuity* with the Kantian Copernican revolution.

---

ond part of *Erste Philosophie:* "In natural life [i.e., the natural attitude] [...] everyone knows about the life of his [her] I, about the relations of his [her] I with manifold real and ideal objectities. He [she] knows about it thanks to natural reflection. But this can never give knowledge of pure subjectivity, it does not even allow such a thing to be imagined. For, it is its nature always to have objectivities – through a pre-established and continuous objective knowledge – and therefrom to relate the I, as subject of acts, to these objectities [...]. In this natural reflection it is impossible to see (as long as it completely dominates) that each 'having' of objects and each determination of experience and of thought with which they are there for the 'I' are already an effectuation [*Leistung*] of the 'I' and of its conscious life, and the 'I' always establishes [*zustande bringt*] own-most and essential life and doing [...], the appearing and the validity of its objects. Therefore consciousness itself, intentional life – such as it lives in itself, such as in it are born [*erwachsen*] such and such subjective apperceptions with the corresponding characteristics of subjective validity out of pure motivations that are essential and proper to them – remains necessarily hidden; all of this life through which for me my respective world – things, humans, values, works, human affairs, societies, etc. – are there in one fell swoop" (Husserl 1954, Hua VII, pp. 120–121).

It is apparent in the *Krisis* (Husserl 1954, Hua VI, p. 202; Husserl 1970, p. 199), in its later revisions (Husserliana 1994, Hua Dok. III/7, p. 227; Pradelle 2012, p. 351), and elsewhere that an association of the Husserlian perspective with Kant's Copernican revolution is justified. In fact, it is here a question of a *radicalization* of this "Copernican revolution." According to this radicalization, the "transcendental subject" is not limited, as is still the case according to Husserl in the first *Critique*, to an *epistemological* apparatus (which orients itself with respect to the faculties of knowledge, and is characterized, in particular, by never delivering anything but the *conditions of possibility* of knowledge); rather, it unveils its *ontological* status, by virtue of a "transcendental experience" that opens up onto a "new world of pure subjectivity" (Husserl 1954, Hua VI, p. 260; Husserl 1970, p. 257). What, more precisely, is the ontological position expressed here by Husserl?

> Every imaginable sense, every imaginable being, whether the latter is called immanent or transcendent, falls within the domain of transcendental subjectivity, as the subjectivity that constitutes sense and being. (Husserl 1950, Hua I, p. 117; Husserl 1982, p. 84)

The ontological import of the Copernican revolution in phenomenology has to do with the fact that this realm is a "new region of being [*Seinsregion*][6] that has up till now never been delimited in its specificity" (Husserl 1976, Hua III/1, p. 67; Husserl 1983, p. 63). It becomes, therefore, a matter of clarifying how the relation between this new "dimension" and the constituting power of transcendental subjectivity is to be conceived.

Dominique Pradelle determines the notion of an "anti-Copernican revolution" in three stages: first, he characterizes it negatively; then, he proposes several positive determinations; and finally, he responds to a fundamental difficulty that allows, in particular, for a presentation of the nature of the "field of consciousness" at the center of this response to Kant (and Husserl). The negative determination of the anti-Copernican revolution takes place at two levels – with respect to method and relative to the presuppositions that must be removed.

On the methodological level, first of all, Pradelle insists on the necessity of substituting *description* and *reflection* for *construction*. By "construction" he actually means the *re*construction of an ideal subject of knowledge inasmuch as it

---

[6] In the *Krisis*, he speaks, concerning this, of a "new realm of being [*neue Seinssphäre*]" (Husserl 1954, Hua VI, p. 118).

possesses objective validity (or is capable of satisfying it).⁷ The phenomenological method, on the contrary, carries out a descriptive elucidation that relies on "transcendental reflection." He then turns to countering a double-presupposition of Kant's: the *substantialization* and *anthropologization* of the subject. Concerning substantialization, Dominique Pradelle asserts that Husserl denounces the Kantian identification of the unity of the "I" or of the ego with a worldly thing, *i.e.*, with a bearer or a substrate to which qualities or properties can be attributed. The psychologistic or anthropologistic presupposition refers to the idea that the *a priori* structures of the object are grounded in the *a priori* forms of the subject's faculties of cognition, which Dominque Pradelle characterizes as "anthropological invariants of any finite subject (space, time, categories)" (Pradelle 2012, p. 359). It is here a matter of an irreducible and "originary facticity" that causes Kant to slide towards anthropologism (as Husserl emphasizes in *Erste Philosophie*) (Husserl 1956, Hua VII, pp. 401*sq.*).

The strategy that allows these presuppositions to be eliminated then consists, for Pradelle, in pointing out that this I or this *ego* is rather a *pure ego*, one that is "indescribable" and without any explainable traits – "without qualities" (like Robert Musil's "man without qualities"); or, according to Husserl's famous formula: "a pure 'I' and nothing more [*reines Ich und nichts weiter*]" (Husserl 1976, Hua III/1, p. 179; Husserl 1983, p. 191).⁸ This 'I' must not be attained through an internal consciousness in the psychological or empirical sense of the term (it is on this point that Husserl's critique of Kant bears), but on an internal perception in the sense of transcendental experience,⁹ which would alone be capable of providing a "universal ground" in apodictic self-evidence. Dominique Pradelle reads Husserl here – convincingly, since it gives a concrete character to the Husserlian position – through the lens of the Heideggerian exegesis of transcendental apperception: the synthetic action of the latter is interpreted in terms of "effectivity of a discovering behavior" or of an "ability-to-make-self-evident" that covers the whole of the immanent flux of consciousness (Pradelle 2012, pp. 357*sq.*).

For Dominique Pradelle, the determination of transcendental apperception as "ability-to-make-self-evident" or as the "effectivity of a discovering behavior"

---

7 One must not therefore confuse this understanding of "construction," which relies on a hypothetical-deductive method, with that which Fink and Husserl put forth under the name of a "phenomenological construction" (*cf. infra*).
8 We note, however, that Dominique Pradelle himself recognizes that this idea can be reconciled with certain arguments of the transcendental dialectic in the first *Critique* (Pradelle 2012, p. 360 *et sq.*).
9 In the *Krisis*, Husserl calls it an "apodictic internal perception" (Husserl 1954, Hua VI, p. 119).

proper to the whole of the flux of consciousness nevertheless brings a risk. He seems, following J.-T. Desanti, to fear a slide into idealism: "Does not the accessibility of all lived experience of a single flux to the ego's power to make self-evident indicate a constructive ideal-type, an idealist presupposition or a methodological fiction, rather than an effective possibility? And if so, is the intuitive character of the subject that is obtained in this way not an illusion of transparency that runs up against the opacity of unrememberable lived experiences?" (Pradelle 2012, p. 358). The solution, which aims to avoid a retreat to the "subject," consists in no longer characterizing "transcendental apperception" as "ego" but, borrowing an expression from A. Gurwitsch and above all from Sartre, as "field of consciousness." What is its meaning and its status?

First of all, to respond to what was asserted on the first, methodical level, one must, according to Dominique Pradelle, undertake a "methodological inversion of the move in which the Copernican reversal consists": "let us put all faculties between brackets!"[10] This can be translated exactly as follows: "the clarification of the noetic acts, of the structures of receptivity and of subjective activity must happen according to the *types of objects* that are accessible to the subject. *Each category of object* (temporal object, spatial object, material thing, animate being, person, society, ideality…) *prescribes the legality of its modes of appearing to the subject*, as well as the style of the subjective acts necessary for the effectivity of its appearing" (Pradelle 2012, p. 363; emphasis ours). In other words: "since consciousness is intentional by essence, the structures of this concrete subject do not pre-exist as a nature of the immanent realm in itself (conceived on the model of all transcendent objects), but rather *only* allow themselves to be reflexively clarified *precisely when* intentionality is oriented towards an *object* of a determinate category" (Pradelle 2012, p. 364; our emphasis). If ever there is an "anti-Copernican revolution" in Husserl's phenomenology, it can only be identified on the level of this "inversion" that makes objects, types of object, categories of object, etc., into that according to which all subjective constitution structures itself.

Two essential consequences follow from this methodological specification. Dominique Pradelle sees in this anti-Copernican move, which seeks to avoid the risk of an anthropologization of the subject, the possibility of a "systematic refoundation of the doctrine of the faculties." This entails no longer considering them as invariant powers of a finite subject, but as "eidetic structures of the subject that are prescribed according to an essential legality by different categories of object" (Pradelle 2012, p. 365). The ontological implication of this refounda-

---

10 "*Schalten wir alle Vermögen* […] *aus*" (Husserl 1956, Hua VII, 387).

tion is sizeable: the constitutive structures of transcendental subjectivity now have their "*ratio essendi*" "in the categories of object, and in the order of stratification [*Schichtung*] or of foundation [*Fundierung*]" insofar as we can discern the hierarchy concerning the noematic correlates of the intentional structure, a hierarchy among 'founded' and 'founding' [or 'grounded' and 'grounding'] objects, 'mono-stratified' and 'pluri-stratified' objects." For Dominique Pradelle, the status of the subject is limited, then, to the quasi-oxymoronic (or at least highly paradoxical)[11] one of being a "transcendental mirror of its transcendent correlates" (Pradelle 2012, p. 365).

The second[12] consequence has to do with a redefinition of the *a priori* that amounts to its radical de-subjectivation, as Heidegger insightfully remarked (Heidegger 1979, GA 20, p. 101; quoted in Pradelle 2012, p. 367). Apriority is not linked to subjectivity, and still less to its so-called origin in it, but rather corresponds to *that which can be given in an intuition of essence*.[13] Dominique Pradelle can thus make a distinction between the "constitution" and the "establishment" of the laws of essence by the subject: "The fact that the laws of essence are constituted by the subject in no way means that they are *established* by the subject; constitutive analysis consists precisely in actualizing this process of making-self-evident, in order to elucidate its specific modalities" (Pradelle 2012, p. 368).

The (provisional) conclusion of this argument aiming to lock down the anti-Copernican move resides then in the identification of the "true phenomenological absolute": Dominique Pradelle abandons the idea of a self-grounding and constitutive transcendental subject – "constitutive" in the sense of "establishing [*instaurateur*]" – of all meaning of beings and replaces it with "the entirety of the anonymous and eidetic structures of appearing and of givenness, which decline the diversity of types of objects of possible experience and impose themselves on all subjects" (Pradelle 2012, p. 387). However, the whole problem is whether one should see in this the quintessence of an *anti*-Copernican revolution or whether the access to this "absolute" does not amount to the opening up of a field that is prior to the distinction between subject and object (we shall return to this).

Whatever the case may be, for Dominique Pradelle this absolutization of the *a priori* of correlation leads to a central difficulty within phenomenological tran-

---

[11] Indeed – isn't making the subject into a simple (transcendental) mirror tantamount to depriving the subject of its constitutive power?
[12] D. Pradelle enumerates two more still: one with respect to the opposition between passivity and activity in our cognitive faculties (Pradelle 2012, p. 366) and the other concerning the Husserlian elaboration of a purely transcendental theory of reason (Pradelle 2012, pp. 366–367).
[13] Without realizing it, Husserl was thereby rediscovering an idea first developed by Hegel.

scendental idealism. This difficulty resides in the opposition between two theses – the ontological thesis according to which the transcendental subject is the origin of the *Seinssinn* and of the *Seinsgeltung* – and the thesis (proper to the anti-Copernican move) which is both ontological and epistemological, expressing a reciprocal mediation (or "circularity") between subject and object, or more exactly the idea that the subject is the *ratio essendi* of the object and the object is the *ratio cognoscendi* and *essendi* of the subject. This opposition, in the eyes of Dominique Pradelle, is aporetic and essentially reproduces the fallacious alternative between an unsatisfying version of idealism and a no less unsatisfying version of realism (both already criticized by Fichte from the very first versions of the *Wissenschaftslehre*).

Three solutions seem to present themselves to avoid this aporia. The first, anti-Levinasian one as it were (we shall immediately see what justifies this qualification), consists in distributing in a strictly determined way the *rationes essendi* and *cognoscendi* between the transcendental subject, on the one hand, and the meaning and being of the world as well as of all worldly beings, on the other. And yet this solution is not Husserlian (and does not allow us to exit the circle): Husserl would not subscribe to a division between the phenomenological method and its idealist ontological implications; and, more generally, his phenomenology opens onto a realm of investigation that situates itself precisely on a level that is before or deeper than the division between epistemology and ontology.

The second solution is properly Levinasian: it assigns an ontological primacy to beings and relegates the constitutive power of the subject (this is therefore the opposite solution to the previous one – hence its characterization as "anti-Levinasian"). Even though Levinas refers to § 20 of the *Cartesian Meditations*, which is what legitimates in his eyes his allowing himself to do so, this solution is hardly Husserlian either: indeed, one must not confuse the excess of the intention with respect to what is intuited (a properly Husserlian thesis), with that of being with respect to consciousness (a Levinasian or Marionian thesis).[14] However, while Dominique Pradelle rightly criticizes the subjectivist after-taste of the Husserlian position, it must be conceded that such criticism does not apply to Levinas (who expresses this critique himself). Does not this refutation of the second thesis then miss its target?

Thus one might also wonder whether the "third way" taken by Dominique Pradelle, which consists in taking advantage of the opposition between *Seinssinn* ("meaning of being," but he translates this expression by "ontic meaning [*sens*

---

14 See for example Marion 1989, pp. 294 *et sq.*; Marion 1997, pp. 366 *et sq.*

ontique]") and *Seinsgeltung* ("validity of being", his translation being "ontological validity [*validité ontologique*]"), does not amount to a fundamental aspect that already appeared in the second solution.¹⁵ This aspect is nothing less than what Dominique Pradelle had already identified previously as the "anti-Copernican move:"

> [...] the giving of meaning that opens up the possibility of appearing [i.e., *Seinssinn*] is *subjective*, whereas the intuitive validation of this meaning [that is, the *Seinsgeltung*] – which confers it with the status of something that really is –, even though it is subjective insofar as it is a succession of noetic acts, possesses an *anonymous and universal structure*, imposed upon the subject and not established by it [...].¹⁶ (Pradelle 2012, p. 374)

What then can be said about the thesis (to say nothing of the "solution") defended by Dominique Pradelle? Concerning this, one must return to and specify the meaning of the "circularity" contained in this solution. Dominique Pradelle envisions two possible interpretations. Either one sees in it a *petitio principii*, or one recognizes in it the "essential situation of thought" that we must maintain and "seek to [...] think – *par excellence* a Heideggerian gesture" (Pradelle 2012, pp. 374 *et sq.*). He chooses the second option, while specifying the nature of the "region" or the "field" of consciousness at the heart of this situation: it must be identified with an "a-subjective field of appearance" and understood as a "*normed* realm of meaning-giving and of appearing of objects" (Pradelle 2012, pp. 375 *et sq.*). However, must we not, on account of the circularity inherent in this a-subjective field, see in this solution a *slippage* of the thesis of an "anti-Copernican" revolution toward the idea of displacement of the Copernican revolution (in which a fundamental role is given precisely to the field of consciousness), relativizing the "anti" in favor, precisely, of a "beyond?" Dominique Pradelle seems to admit as much at the end of his essay:

> Beyond the Copernican inversion [and not: by carrying out an "*anti*-Copernican inversion"]: this expression does not then consist in carrying out a Ptolemaic revolution in order to restore the pre-Copernican realism proper to the natural attitude, but in admitting that a *structural* eidos *of the field of consciousness – i.e., of the transcendental infra-egoical dimension – precedes any subject and any object*. Older than the subject, imposing its norms on it, so the structural essence of an anonymous field of consciousness is found to be. (Pradelle 2012, p. 385)

---

15 And even more, for D. Pradelle here returns to the Levinasian solution as much as he does to the ontological thesis (i.e. to the first term of the tension exposed above).

16 "Imposed on the subject" of course meaning "by a grounding [*fundierend*] being."

3 Reflections on the Transcendental Deduction of the Categories (1787)

It will now be a matter of accounting for this "absoluteness of the *a priori* of correlation within an anonymous transcendental field," which allows the simultaneous maintenance of, on the one hand, a *legitimation of knowledge*, and, on the other, an *ontological* foundation of that which is known as well as the methodological tools at the basis of the latter. In order to do this, we shall proceed in two stages: first, returning to Kant, we would like to show the extent to which the second edition of the transcendental deduction of the categories already responds effectively to the charges of "anthropologization" or "psychologization;" and then, we shall give a brief sketch of how the three "types" of phenomenological construction, in the framework of a "generative" phenomenology, reconcile the Kantian and the Husserlian perspectives without this entailing any confusion between the (constitutive and self-constituting) transcendental ego and the totality of the anonymous regulative and universal structures prescribed to the transcendental subject by constitutable objects (Pradelle 2012, p. 378).

We know that Kant judged it necessary to rewrite the core of the chapter on the transcendental deduction of the categories in the *Critique of Pure Reason* in order to counteract the charges of "psychologism" and "anthropologism" which were directed toward him immediately after the publication of the first edition of the work (notably relative to the role played by the "three syntheses" in the so-called "subjective" deduction). Kant was himself convinced that he had answered these criticisms satisfactorily. In what exactly does this response consist?

In the transcendental deduction of the categories from the second edition of the *Critique of Pure Reason*, Kant lays out three principle stages. But before we present them in detail, it is necessary, in our opinion, to modify the order he gave to these three stages, namely the *unity* of the consciousness of the object, the "*figurative synthesis*" and the *laws* of the connections of objects, making it possible for the objects of experience to be subject in turn to legality.

Of course, this order is architectonically justified because it follows that of the first deduction in which, on an empirical level, Kant had first distinguished between the synthesis of apprehension in intuition, the synthesis of reproduction in the imagination, and the synthesis of recognition in the concept. Next, he made clear, for these three empirical syntheses, a corresponding transcendental synthesis, whose triple operativity ensures this "subjective" deduction. However, to avoid any charge of empiricism, Kant is now careful not to emphasize the idea of the three "syntheses," but, in the end, the configuration remains the same. The fact that he preserves the same order in the second edition does not allow him to escape the charge of empiricism once again: Kant orients himself with respect to the three cognitive faculties (sensibility, understanding, imagination), and it is the order of empirical syntheses that commands the order of the corresponding transcendental syntheses.

On a *systematic* level, on the other hand, this order is no longer justified.[17] If one takes into account the transcendental operations that are actually carried out, one is obliged to note that the establishment of the unity of intuitive consciousness *follows* the figuration of the spatial and above all temporal framework opened by pure intuitions. Nothing can be unified in an object that has not first been deployed in the formal matrix that makes the appearance of an object possible.[18] In order better to distinguish the specific operations or effectuations of the transcendental syntheses, Kant would indeed have been better off following this systematic order. The establishment of the "objective validity of the categories" or, transposed onto phenomenological territory, that of the constitutive power of the dimension of pure phenomenality, therefore requires proceeding in the following order: first, with respect to the "*figurative synthesis*"; second, the institution of the *unity* of the consciousness of the object; and third, the establishment of the *legality* of the objects of experience.

The fundamental object of a transcendental deduction of the categories resides in the necessity – which comes before an understanding of how experience can be unified and harmonious *for us* and before showing what attaches these categories to their "ultimate point" – of demonstrating how these categories can be legitimately applied to intuitions. In other words, it is necessary to make self-evident the ultimate condition of the fact that the categories can have a constitutive value for the content of knowledge. This is the primary

---

17 This modification in the order has above all to do with the second synthesis (of the imagination). Whereas the *empirical* synthesis of the imagination must necessarily *succeed* the empirical synthesis of intuitive apprehension, given that nothing can be *re*produced that has not first been apprehended, the *transcendental* synthesis of the imagination, which is not *re*productive but *productive*, *precedes* the other syntheses – in this way, at least, it is possible to endow the transcendental imagination and the synthesis that corresponds to it with the architectonic place that it deserves.

18 This is the specificity of the relation between time as the pure form of sensibility and the categories as pure forms of the understanding: whereas, for that which concerns the connection characterizing the *understanding alone* (§ 15), synthesis precedes analysis, here, where it is a matter of understanding how the syntheses are articulated among one another on the levels of sensibility, imagination, and understanding, the "intellectual" synthesis can only take place on the basis of an act of synthesis of an entirely different nature (namely on the basis of a "figured" synthesis), which then reverses the relation between unity and multiplicity.

goal, the primordial *desideratum*, of an investigation aiming to establish the objective validity of the categories.

It is with this in mind that Kant proceeds, in § 24, to a *veritable genetization*, which is at the heart of his transcendental deduction. The argument proceeds as follows. The problem is one of knowing, we insist, how the categories (insofar as they are *unitary* functions of the understanding) can be applied to intuitions (characterized by a *multiple* manifold). The answer is given in two stages. First, it is a matter of understanding how there can be a "conformity [*Gemäßheit*]" thanks to which the "manifold of given representations" can be determined "*in conformity with*" the synthetic unity of apperception. This is possible thanks to the fact that there is a concordant harmony between internal sense (= time as *a priori* form of sensibility) and the spontaneity (*a priori* in turn) of the understanding. And what constitutes this harmony and this concordance? It is the case, secondly, by virtue of a very specific synthesis that allows the *a priori* "synthetic unity of the apperception of the manifold of sensible intuition" to be thought. What is this synthesis that, apparently, is of absolutely crucial importance in the transcendental deduction of the categories? It is the "*synthesis speciosa*" (which Kant also characterizes as "an *a priori and* necessary possibility"), an *originarily figured* synthesis that belongs to the *productive imagination*. Generalization consists in the circular (but by no means vicious!) back and forth between the *a priori* harmony between time and intellectual spontaneity, on the one hand, and the synthetic unity of the apperception of the manifold, on the other. The figured synthesis "floats" in between the two (just like, later, the imagination shall "float [*schweben*]," in Fichte, between sensibility and understanding).

However, the productive imagination does not on its own guarantee the relation to the object, and it does not thereby institute an "objective reality." Indeed, in order for this circular relationship not to float in a void, a unity is necessary to ensure that this "production" is not simply imaginary or fictional. In §§ 16 and 17 of the 1787 deduction of the categories, Kant thus seeks to show that the permanent (*durchgängig*) and concordant (*einstimmig*) character of experience demands the *consciousness of the synthesis of my representations* concerning this selfsame experience. Now, this synthetic unification presupposes the unity of this consciousness. "As a result," he concludes, "the unity of consciousness is *the only thing that constitutes the relationship between representations and object*, and therefore, the fact that they constitute knowledge [...]" (Kant 1787, B 137; emphasis ours). This synthesis only concerns the multiple manifold in intuition. While "[t]he synthetic unity of consciousness is therefore an objective condition for all knowledge," to which all intuition must be subject "in order to become an object for me, since in another way and without this synthesis the manifold could not become united to a consciousness" (Kant 1787, B 138; Kant 1998, p. 249), this is precisely the condition ensuring the unity of the consciousness of the object (which relies, as we can see, on the unity of consciousness itself).

Here we arrive finally at the third step. The transcendental deduction must not only explain how the content of experience can be determined by the categories and that which ensures the relation to the object, but it also has to account for the way in which objects can be known *a priori* according to the constitutive laws of their connections. This is what explains the legality of our knowledge of objects. The solution (delivered in § 26) is unsurprising; it reproduces the same principle as for the imaginative synthesis: "It is one and the same spontaneity that, there under the name of imagination and here under the name of understanding, introduces the connection into the manifold of intuition" (Kant 1787, B 162; Kant 1998, p. 262).

4 The Legitimation of Knowledge – A Perspective Belonging to "Generative Phenomenology"

How can this conceptual triad "figurativity – unity – legality" now be made fruitful for the problem of the legitimation of knowledge in a phenomenological perspective? In his excellent book on the concept of truth in Husserl and Heidegger, Ernst Tugendhat, when he reflects on the meaning and the limits of the idea of an ultimate legitimation such as it is understood in the framework of constitutive phenomenology, expresses a doubt whose full expression we see fit to reproduce here:

> One is permitted here to doubt whether, in the reflexive intuition [*Schau*], the manifold constituting acts that belong to a determinate objectity are actually given in their determinacy as clearly as Husserl claims (*cf.* for example *Ideen* II, pp. 90*sq.*). Even if all objective truth only has meaning relative to the possibilities of subjective demonstration, it is nevertheless a consequence of Husserl's dogmatism, *i.e.* of his conviction that everything that is immanent is *eo ipso* adequately given, that these possibilities of demonstration are in turn supposed to be transparent and ultimately knowable in an immanent analysis. One can especially wonder whether what is given in the depths of constitution is generally accessible to a simple reflection, and whether Husserl is not in reality *constructing* rather than describing the phenomenological facts [*Befunde*] [...]. But Husserl himself trusted so much in immanent intuition that this problem did not at all exist for him. (Tugendhat 1970, pp. 216 – 217, emphasis ours)

Tugendhat is asking here whether, on any constitution's ultimately constitutive level, the "given" allows itself really to be exposed in intuitive self-evidence, and whether it is therefore accessible to reflection (be it "transcendental"). He is certainly right to express such reservations; but instead of condemning an unjustified structure, it is better rather to make virtue of necessity and to perceive the soundness and phenomenological legitimacy of a constructive procedure – *i.e.*, of a construction that is neither hypothetico-deductive nor speculative, but properly *phenomenological*.

The perspective of "constructive" or "generative" phenomenology can be clarified by proceeding to place the fundamental result of the second deduction of the categories (Kant), the descent into the "pre-immanent" sphere of consciousness (Husserl), and the discovery of "reflexibility" (Fichte) into relation with one another. For Kant, as we have seen, we find the conceptual triad "figuration – unity – legality" insofar as any establishment of knowledge requires a phenomenalizing figuration, a unifying binding and the putting into place of legislation. This triad is combined with the necessity not to remain at the simple level of things as they appear, and thereby within the *immanent* field of consciousness, but to expose the operativity of the transcendental field in a "transcendental experience" (or in a "transcendental reflection") beneath that which is describable or given intuitively. And the final question, which is of absolute importance, is how to confer a "normative" power on these effectuations if it is the case that this power cannot be drawn from the immanent sphere itself. The answer in turn is composed of three moments: first, a phenomenalization-schematization that constitutes the concrete accomplishment of transcendental meaning-constituting consciousness; secondly, the installation (brilliantly anticipated by Levinas) of a reciprocal mediation between ontological grounding and transcendental constitution, a mediation which endows the constitutive power with an ontological aspect;[19] and, thirdly, the exploitation of the fundamental character of the transcendental that consists in doubling as a possibilizing power (in other words, in grounding reflection in that which makes it possible itself (= reflexibility)). We shall go no further here than a simple sketch of the methodological tools of such a procedure. It will be a question of the different "kinds" of phenomenological construction.

Phenomenological construction – as we have developed at length elsewhere (see Schnell 2015) – is the methodological tool allowing an orientation in the pre-immanent sphere that is not normed *a priori* by objective determinations

---

[19] We have developed this point in our study "La 'nouvelle ontologie' de la phénoménologie: Approches phénoménologiques et transcendantales du 'réel'" (Schnell 2016).

constituting themselves in the immanent sphere. Phenomenological construction is helpful when the limits of intuition (and of "transcendental reflection") are reached; and it prevents the operations and effectuations of the (productive) transcendental imagination from sliding into the purely imaginary. We distinguish three "kinds" of phenomenological construction.

Generally, the phenomenological constructions of the first kind correspond to an *originary phenomenalization-schematization of meaning*. While this term's orientation comes from the Fichtean idea of a "genetic construction," it is the idea of "genesis" (or rather of "generativity," because the term "genesis" means something else in Husserl) that takes priority over the idea of "construction" (which has the disadvantage of recalling the hypothetico-deductive or speculative constructions from which we firmly distance ourselves). More particularly, these phenomenological constructions of the first kind are required when, within the immanent sphere of consciousness, different *facta* are opposed to one another and make a construction necessary – which is carried out in the *pre-immanent* sphere of consciousness –, allowing the resolution of a *precise* problem, relative to a *determinate* field of objects. We have attempted to show, in a prior attempt (Schnell 2007), how these phenomenological constructions are concretely carried out in view of a phenomenology of *time*, of *intersubjectivity*, and of *impulse*. Other constructions are conceivable, for example in the phenomenology of logic and mathematics; but whatever the area under consideration, they will always and each time be dependent on a particular phenomenon and will not deliver a method that is identical in every case and which one could apply purely and simply to the object in question.

Phenomenological constructions of the second kind are to be placed on the horizon of what Catherine Malabou calls "plasticity" (see Malabou 2011, pp. 44 *et sq.*) and which expresses both an *annihilation* and a *generation*. Phenomenological constructions of the second kind "condense" the question of the emergence of meaning towards a "dimension" or a^{20} "horizon" of phenomenalization characterized by "virtuality" (in Richir's sense), which entails here a double movement between, on the one hand, this "dimension" or this "horizon" which is impossible to fix or to grasp and, on the other hand, the phenomenon presenting itself in the immanent sphere of consciousness. The point is that what we have here is a *unique* principle of phenomenalization in massive opposition to the plurality of *constructa* characterizing the phenomenological construction of the first kind. The phenomenological construction of the second kind reinterprets "plasticity" in terms of the "moment" of the genesis' formation

---

20 Hence the reference to the moment of *unity* (*cf. supra*).

and constitutes thereby a "bridge" between the geneticization of the "*facta*" and the "possibilizing" construction.

Phenomenological constructions of the third kind are the very ones that carry out *possibilizations* ("*Ermöglichungen*") and aim to account for them.[21] A possibilization designates not the simple fact of making possible... (experience, knowledge, *etc.*), but that which makes possible the very making of possibilities – therefore the law of a possibilizing *doubling*. Such a possibilizing does not consist in a simple return to... (and is therefore not equivalent in some way to a doubling of the phenomenological construction of the second kind), but *it unveils the legality of the doubling that belongs essentially to all transcendental conditioning*. It is this very possibilization that answers the question of the source and the origin of the transcendental attitude. But, while this phenomenological construction of the third kind also relates to a *single* phenomenon, it nevertheless takes place in three moments: a moment of "phenomenalization," a moment of "plasticity," and a moment of "possibilization" properly speaking. Thus does this phenomenological construction of the third kind integrate the principles of the three kinds of construction, just as each kind of construction is an echo of one of the three terms of the conceptual triad presented in the second transcendental deduction of the categories.

Conclusion

Is the "revolution" carried out by phenomenology "Copernican" or "anti-Copernican?" That which is "beyond" [*par-delà*] the Copernican revolution does not restore a "Ptolemaic" realism, but instead opens onto a "below," a "before" or a "beneath" [*en deçà*]: before the distinction between subject and object, where the reciprocal relation between an a-subjective constitutive power and a foundational pre-empirical being can be carried out. This "before" means that the alternative is not between a "pre-Copernican" realism and an "idealism" that leaves the relation between transcendental method and ontological method in the shadows, but rather puts forward a constructive circularity (first anticipated by Levinas) between transcendental constitution and ontological grounding. What follows from this in particular is that "normativity" is not gotten through borrowing from pregiven objectivity – since that would amount to a *petitio prin-*

---

21 Heidegger attempted different sketches of this, notably the one concerning anxiety as a *Grundstimmung* opening up access to the world (in *Sein und Zeit*), the self-projection of originary *temporality* (in the *Fundamental Problems of Phenomenology*), or the self-projection of the *world* (in *Fundamental Concepts of Metaphysics*) (*cf.* Schnell 2013).

cipii and would destroy all constitution – but has its source in pre-immanent generativity.

Bibliography

Hegel, Georg Wilhelm Friedrich (1986) [1831]: "Ohlert-Rezension". In: *Werke in zwanzig Bänden*, vol. 11: *Berliner Schriften 1818–1831*. Ed. Michel Moldenhauer. Frankfurt: Suhrkamp Verlag.
Heidegger, Martin (1979): *Prolegomena zur Geschichte des Zeitbegriffs. Gesamtausgabe*, vol. 20. Ed. Petra Jaeger. Frankfurt: Vittorio Klostermann.
Husserl, Edmund (1950): *Cartesianische Meditationen und Pariser Vorträge*. Husserliana, vol. I. Ed. Stephan Strasser. The Hague: Martinus Nijhoff.
Husserl, Edmund (1954): *Die Krisis der europäischen Wissenschaften und die transzendentale Phänomenologie. Eine Einleitung in die phänomenologische Philosophie*. Husserliana, vol. VI. Ed. Walter Biemel. The Hague: Martinus Nijhoff.
Husserl, Edmund (1956): *Erste Philosophie (1923/24). Erster Teil: Kritische Ideengeschichte*. Husserliana, vol. VII. Ed. Rudolf Boehm. The Hague: Martinus Nijhoff.
Husserl, Edmund (1959): *Erste Philosophie (1923/24). Zweiter Teil: Theorie der phänomenologischen Reduktion*. Husserliana, vol. VIII. Ed. Rudolf Boehm. The Hague: Martinus Nijhoff.
Husserl, Edmund (1970): *The Crisis of European Sciences and Transcendental Phenomenology*. Trans. David Carr. Evanston: Northwestern University Press.
Husserl, Edmund (1976): *Ideen zu einer reinen Phänomenologie und phänomenologischen Philosophie. Erstes Buch: Allgemeine Einführung in die reine Phänomenologie*. Husserliana, vol. III/1. Ed. Karl Schuhmann. The Hague: Martinus Nijhoff.
Husserl, Edmund (1982): *Cartesian Meditations*. Trans. Dorion Cairns. The Hague: Martinus Nijhoff.
Husserl, Edmund (1983): *Ideas Pertaining to a Pure Phenomenology and to a Phenomenological Philosophy. First Book: General Introduction to a Pure Phenomenology*. Trans. Fred Kersten. The Hague: Martinus Nijhoff.
Husserl, Edmund (1994): *Briefwechsel: Wissenschaftler Korrespondenz*. Husserliana Dokumente, vol. III/7. Ed. Karl Schuhmann. Dordrecht/Boston/London: Kluwer Academic Publishers.
Husserl, Edmund (2002): *Zur phänomenologischen Reduktion. Texte aus dem Nachlass (1926–1935)*. Husserliana, vol. XXXIV. Ed. Sebastian Luft. Dordrecht/Boston/London: Kluwer Academic Publishers.
Kant, Immanuel (1787): *Kritik der reinen Vernunft*. Riga: Hartknoch [A = first original edition (1781); B = second original edition (1787)].
Kant, Immanuel (1998): *Critique of Pure Reason*. Trans. Paul Guyer and Allen W. Wood. Cambridge: Cambridge University Press.
Malabou, Catherine (2011): *Que faire de notre cerveau ?* Paris: Bayard.
Marion, Jean-Luc (1989): *Réduction et donation. Recherches sur Husserl, Heidegger et la phénoménologie*. Paris: Presses universitaires de France.
Marion, Jean-Luc (1997): *Etant donné*. Paris: Presses universitaires de France.

Richir, Marc (1976): *Au-delà du renversement copernicien. La question de la phénoménologie et de son fondement. Phaenomenologica*, vol. 73. The Hague: Martinus Nijhoff.
Romano, Claude (2010): *Au cœur de la raison, la phénoménologie*. Paris: Gallimard.
Pradelle, Dominique (2012): *Par-delà la révolution copernicienne. Sujet transcendantal et facultés chez Kant et Husserl*. Paris: Presses universitaires de France.
Schnell, Alexander (2007): *Husserl et les fondements de la phénoménologie constructive*. Grenoble: Jérôme Millon.
Schnell, Alexander (2013): *En voie du réel*. Paris: Hermann.
Schnell, Alexander (2015): *La déhiscence du sens*. Paris: Hermann.
Schnell, Alexander (2016): "La 'nouvelle ontologie' de la phénoménologie. Approches phénoménologiques et transcendantales du 'réel'". In: *Annales de Phénoménologie*, vol. 15, pp. 119–132.
Tugendhat, Ernst (1970): *Der Wahrheitsbegriff bei Husserl und Heidegger*. Berlin: Walter de Gruyter.

Garrett Zantow Bredeson
Back to Fichte?
Natorp's Doubts about Husserl's Transcendental Phenomenology

Abstract: It is well known that Husserl's turn to a form of "transcendental" phenomenology troubled many of his followers in Munich and Göttingen. It was just as perplexing, though, for his contemporaries in the tradition of post-Kantian transcendental philosophy. Cohen had identified the living core of Kant's philosophy as the "transcendental method," and Natorp, in particular, had worked extensively to distinguish the principles of the Marburg recovery of Kant from his wayward appropriation by Fichte and others. In this chapter, I consider what the stakes of Husserl's transcendental turn looked like from the Marburg perspective. Natorp warmly welcomed Husserl's attempt to steer the nascent phenomenological movement in a "transcendental" direction, but he continued to wonder whether Husserl's turn towards this tradition was aligned with the true spirit of Kant, or whether, on the contrary, phenomenology would settle into a broadly Fichtean appropriation of Kant's legacy. Though Natorp's public position is markedly conciliatory, he barely conceals his suspicion that it was the Kant of Fichte's Jena, not the Kant of Cohen's Marburg, to whom Husserl was (perhaps unwittingly) turning. This, I argue, is the background against which the Natorp-Husserl encounter on the eve of World War I must be understood.

1 The Marburg Recovery of Kant

The Kantian renaissance of the late nineteenth century was, perhaps predictably, followed by a renaissance of interest in Fichte and Hegel. A few years before his death in 1906, Eduard von Hartmann was said to have referred to contemporary Germany thought as a *Repetitionskursus* – a repetition of the conceptual trajectory from Kant to Hegel.[1] Although it would be unfair to paint the Marburgers as uniformly hostile to the tendencies of this trajectory, in either its original or its repeated form,[2] it should go without saying that this is hardly a development

---

[1] See Ewald 1907, pp. 238*sq*. Note, however, that neither Oscar Ewald nor Heinrich Rickert (whom he quotes extensively in this connection at Ewald 1908, p. 400) sees this as a *threat* to the "sober inquiry" of the prevailing Kantian spirit of the age. *Cf.* Ewald 1910, p. 481.
[2] See, e.g., the appreciation for Hegel apparent in Natorp 1912b, pp. 210*sq*.

they could have welcomed with open arms.[3] By no means did they want to freeze Kant's philosophy in its eighteenth-century place;[4] everything depended, however, on Kant's achievement being developed *in the right way*,[5] and that, of course, had been the polemical point of going "back to Kant" in the first place. To make Kant a positive resource for modern science required putting the subjectivism and absolutism of the later developments of post-Kantian philosophy definitively to rest.

On Cohen's view, Fichte[6] had fallen into the trap of trying to demonstrate the conditions of the possibility of objective cognition by going back to the mental activities of the thinking subject.[7] Kantian-inspired motivations for this were not lacking, whether they lay in a crude understanding of Kant's "Copernican turn" or in a mistaken emphasis on the "subjective" version of Kant's Transcendental Deduction. But the consequence of this way of proceeding is that

> all objectivity, and indeed not only that consisting in things, but that consisting in laws, too, succumbs to the semblance of subjectivism. *Self-consciousness* is passed off as the source and guarantor of *natural laws*. And in this way Fichte would be the legitimate heir of Kant. (Cohen 1918, p. 397; also quoted in Edel 2013, p. 19)

Kant's demand on philosophy, as Fichte internalized it, would require an initial turn towards the structures and activities of the cognizing subject as a way to provide a proper justificatory grounding for the objective claims of putatively scientific cognition. For Cohen, to execute such a strategy would only be to relativize objective, scientific claims to the standpoint of the cognizing subject. To be sure, this is exactly how many in the nineteenth century understood the significance of Kant's Copernican turn anyhow. But Cohen was convinced that Kant's true achievement could not be understood at all if "transcendental" idealism

---

3 The 1905 polemical exchange between a young Ernst Cassirer and the neo-Friesian Leonard Nelson was still fresh in the mind not only of the Marburgers, but of Husserl, as well. See Husserl to Natorp (23 Dec 1908), Husserl 1994, Hua Dok. III/5, pp. 99*sq*. Again, the underlying question at the center of the exchange concerns the identity of the genuinely *Kantian* tradition. For background, see Kubalica 2016.
4 As announced emphatically at the outset of Natorp 1912b. *Cf.* Natorp 1904, p. 243.
5 See esp. the discussion at Natorp 1888, § 14.3, pp. 109*sq*.
6 Let me be unequivocally clear that I am by no means endorsing the Marburg interpretation of Fichte (or Kant, for that matter). Indeed, Natorp himself was far from harboring a completely negative attitude towards Fichte, as is made clear by his (early) reception of Fichte's pedagogical philosophy and his (later) attraction to Fichte's theoretical project.
7 See Edel 2013, pp. 17–21. I am basically following Edel's excellent presentation in this paragraph.

were divorced from actual science – indeed, science in its purest form, mathematical natural science.[8] Instead of following Fichte in offering a subjective ground for objective cognition, we must first look to what has actually been achieved in the realm of objective cognition itself. Only by adverting to the "fact of science," as the methodological primacy of the reference to on-hand objective cognition[9] came to be called, can the motives of a relativizing subjectivism be permanently rooted out. Philosophy need not relinquish its project of seeking out the conditions of the possibility of objectively valid cognition, but it must not turn its back on the foothold these very sciences provide for its project: the conditions of possibility of scientific cognition must be developed immanently from out of the accomplishments of the sciences themselves. To refuse this foothold by seeking out an *independent* subjective grounding of cognition would be to dive head-first back into a rudderless metaphysics – and to make Fichte into Kant's true heir.

Natorp gives a perceptive account of Cohen's basic move in his 1912 Halle lecture. Following Cohen, Natorp contrasts "transcendental" and "metaphysical" philosophy. Transcendental philosophy is constituted by its *method*, which has two parts:

> The first is the secure reference back to existing, historically verifiable facts of science, morals, art, and religion. For philosophy would be unable to breathe in the "airless space" of pure thought. [...] [The second part is] to demonstrate the ground of the "possibility" and hence the "legal ground" [*"Rechtsgrund"*] of the fact, i.e., to show the ground of the law and to show the unity of *logos* and the *ratio* in every creative cultural deed and work it out in its purity. (Natorp 1912b, p. 197; translation modified)

Beginning with the fact of science, now emphatically conceived as the collected facts of culture as a whole,[10] philosophy seeks out the rational law that forms its basis. This search "transcends" the scientific-cultural accomplishments themselves insofar as it seeks their *law*, yet "an immanent method cannot locate the law of objective formation anywhere else but in that objective formation itself, in the creation of human cultural life that is always at work and never concluded."[11] Natorp lays special emphasis on dissolving fixed "being" into the "movement" characterizing genuine thought.[12] Philosophy cannot arrive at an

---

[8] See esp. Cohen 1914, p. 66.
[9] See Luft 2015b, pp. 48–58.
[10] We already find the intention of making culture as a whole the object of critique (however imperfectly executed) in Cohen. See Luft 2015b, pp. 58–70.
[11] Natorp 1912b, p. 198.
[12] See Natorp's formulations at Natorp 1912b, p. 199.

overarching, rational principle that would render the manifestations of culture as a whole uniformly intelligible, but it can and must dive into the facts themselves and work through them towards an *ideal* of their unity, a unity which can itself never be "given." Reliance on any sort of "given" sells short the character of cognition as a *fieri*, an *activity*, a *doing*.[13] Kant's directive to search out the *a priori* conditions of the possibility of experience is not fulfilled by identifying given – and hence "metaphysical" – structures or activities of the cognizing subject, but by working towards identifying the law unifying scientifically purified experience.

Natorp's own project, however, should not be understood merely as a defense of Cohen. For Natorp, Cohen had been dismissive of Fichte to a fault, and a deeper appreciation of Fichte's motives was necessary to secure Cohen's accomplishment. Natorp shared with Cohen a deep revulsion for contemporary psychologism,[14] and while Fichte himself had not fallen into crude psychologism, he had given credence to the basic thought from which it later drew its plausibility: that of the absolute primacy of a subjective grounding of cognition. By failing to do justice to the inner, subjective side of cognition, upon which Fichte had so forcefully insisted, Cohen had inadvertently left his flank open to psychologistic attacks. Natorp thus set himself the task of redeeming Fichte's original motives in a manner compatible with Cohen's insistence on the primacy of the objective grounding of cognition.

Natorp concedes that Kant himself had been conflicted on this issue; both the motivations underlying Fichte's mistake and the decisive insight that should have prevented it can be found in Kant's text.[15] Natorp first systematically announced his own position in 1887 and developed it over the next two and a half decades, culminating with the 1912 publication of *Allgemeine Psychologie*. While his emphasis on the possibility, and even the necessity, of a subjective grounding of cognition may appear to contradict the Marburg line, Natorp is always careful to present his view as a complement to Cohen's approach. Near the beginning of his 1887 essay, Natorp remarks that cognition

> exhibits itself from the start in a two-sided manner: as "content" (as what is cognized or to be cognized) and as "activity" or experience [*Erlebnis*] of the subject (as cognizing). To be sure, in every cognition both relations are present together and closely connected. [...] We

---

13 See esp. Natorp 1912b, p. 200.
14 See Natorp 1887, § 3, pp. 264–267, and Edgar 2008.
15 For a particularly nice discussion of Kant's insight, see Natorp 1888, § 9.6, pp. 59–61.

must ask which of the two should be regarded as first, underlying, and determining in the grounding of cognition. (Natorp 1887, § 2, p. 260; translation modified)[16]

Any cognition claiming objective validity, e. g., a law discovered in natural-scientific research, is related on the one hand to its cognizer or cognizers (i. e., to the scientist or the community of scientists) and on the other hand to the natural processes constituting the object of the cognition. When it comes to providing a justificatory ground for this cognition, then, it appears we must first decide whether the cognition of the law is to be justified by reference to the activity of *cognizing* the natural law or else by reference to, say, what constitutes a natural law *itself* (lawfulness). In this light,

> the "deed" [*That*] of cognizing seems as if it must be the first thing, while cognition, taken as content, seems to be the dependent result or product [*Erzeugnis*]. The product [*Product*] may be called objective; the factors [*Faktoren*] are subjective. True, on this view logic inevitably becomes dependent on psychology, a conclusion which at least the more consistent advocates of the subjective view have not shied away from. (Natorp 1887, § 2, p. 262; translation modified)[17]

Natorp is referring here to any view that accepts the premise that acts of cognition are *prior* to the content cognized through them – prior at least in the sense that the justification of the content thus cognized is demonstrated by making an essential reference to the nature of the cognizing act. On such a view, psychology grounds logic in the sense that the justification of a cognition requires an antecedent analysis of the mental acts of a cognizing subject.

In the next year's *Einleitung*, Natorp makes the historical provenance of such a mistake explicit and follows Cohen in singling out Fichte:

> Determining the manifold to a unity, the objectification itself, can easily appear to be a subjective act [*Act*], the "deed" [*"That"*] of the determining I, the "subject" or consciousness. The turn to subjectivism is actually rooted in this notion. Kant, by his manner of expression, has at the very least not sufficiently forestalled this, by depicting precisely this determination of the manifold to a unity, to which all objectification refers, as an "action of the mind" [*"Handlung des Gemüths"*] and attributing it to a "spontaneity" (self-activity) of the understanding. Fichte's titanic subjectivism latched onto these expressions (action, spontaneity); to refer the entirety of objectivity to an "action," to a "positing" on the side of the "I," was very much to his liking. (Natorp 1888, § 14.6, p. 114)

---

[16] "Nowadays," he adds in the *Einleitung*, "there is hardly any other question on which 'standpoints' differ as sharply as this one" (Natorp 1888, § 14.1, p. 104).
[17] *Cf.* Natorp 1888, § 7.1, pp. 33sq.

Interestingly, Natorp goes on to connect the legacy of Fichte's mistake with J. F. Herbart's psychology. This brings Natorp's implicit history of the nineteenth century full circle, for Cohen himself had started out in the orbit of the Herbartians,[18] and the decisive rejection of this heritage launched the Marburg School as such. Herbart and Fichte, despite their differences,[19] share one important (and plausibly even Kantian) presupposition, namely, that it is through mental *acts* that subjective consciousness is to be approached scientifically.[20] It thus turns out that both the idealist metaphysicians and their apparently sober, empirically-minded opponents had appropriated Kant's reference to the spontaneity of the understanding in the same, mistaken way.

Cohen's turn away from Herbart breaks through the psychologistic impasse. Cognitions that claim objective validity can only be justified by reference to further objectively valid cognitions. The relation of, say, a natural law to its justification can never be that of an objective law to a subjective act; rather, "the explaining ground can never be in any other relationship to that which is explained by it than that of universal to particular, of law and recognized instance of the law" (Natorp 1887, § 2, p. 263). To this point we are entirely on Cohen's well-trodden turf. But even the practice of the positive sciences indicates that this explaining ground can be turned on its head – and even *must* be, as, e.g., Newton understands when he emphatically requires that the law unifying the phenomena be able to be traced back to the unified phenomena. However far it proceeds towards objective unification through the discovery of increasingly universal laws, scientific practice would be unintelligible and ungrounded without such a demand. Now, to be sure, what Newton has in mind by "phenomena" are not *absolutely* subjective facts standing over against the fully objective laws at whose articulation the sciences aim (Natorp 1887, § 5, pp. 274*sq*.). But if we take seriously the demand implicit in the scientific procedure to provide the phenomena for the law, we can hardly justify stopping short of what *is* absolutely subjective, and indeed positivist psychologism, however misguided, is a symptom of the widespread recognition of this fact in the nineteenth century.[21]

---

18 See Beiser 2014, pp. 468–471.
19 For the story of Herbart's own gradual break from Fichte, see Beiser 2014, pp. 94–109.
20 See esp. Natorp 1888, § 5.1, pp. 15–17. Note, though, that Natorp always treats Herbart sympathetically, as someone drawn unwittingly into metaphysical-naturalist excesses by a train of basically sound inferences based on a fundamental error. See esp. Natorp 1888, § 7.5, pp. 40–43.
21 "Today the question of the particular and the universal no longer concerns merely the relationship of the particular thing, particular occurrence, or particular instance of a relation to the universal of this thing, this occurrence, or this relation. It concerns at bottom the relation of the

The mistake often made here is that of supposing that such subjective grounds can be found in ultimate psychological "facts" already on hand, which need only be scientifically observed and analytically isolated. It is supposed that, prior to their unification by means of the law, appearing phenomena are given as simple elements (sense data, perhaps, for the empiricists, or intuitions, as opposed to concepts, to speak with the Kantians), reference to which (in tandem, now, with acts of the subject) will provide the sought-after subjective grounding for objective cognition. But the subjective aspect of cognition turns out to be conditioned by objectivity no less (and, as we will see, in a specific sense *more*) than its objective side is conditioned by subjectivity. While the *demand* that we get down to what is ultimately subjective is justified enough, any attempt to fulfill it itself involves some degree of objectification:

> [Subjectivity] can only be grasped, in as far as this is possible at all, in concepts, because there is absolutely no other organon of cognition. Yet when it is grasped in concepts it is no longer absolutely immediate and subjective, but has always already been objectified. (Natorp 1887, § 7, p. 283; translation modified)

To be sure, taken to its logical conclusion, the (scientifically respectable) demand to trace objective cognition back to its subjective "foundations" *presupposes* the "absolutely immediate and subjective," but this must be understood as a *methodological* presupposition, not a substantive, *metaphysical* guarantee that such elements are actually on hand. However justified the presupposition may be, it by no means indicates a possible or necessary *starting point* for philosophy. As Natorp puts it much later, "To lend *logos* to *psyche*, language to the soul, is not the first, but rather exactly the last task of philosophy" (Natorp 1912b, p. 198).

It is the *last* task of philosophy because, despite Cohen's tendency to overlook the rights of the subjective, he was perfectly correct to recognize the epistemological priority of the objective. The common facts from which all grounding of cognition must begin are the facts established by modern science; they provide the only secure foothold for gaining access, however indirect, to the conscious activities through which they are established.

> We actually only first infer back from the unity given in the content to the act of consciousness [*Bewusstseinsact*] constituting it, and in doing so, we do not, in addition, cognize a

---

final, absolutely particular subjective representation or appearance to that which has somehow already been raised to universal and so objective significance" (Natorp 1887, § 6, p. 277).

> new fact [*Thatsache*] preceding and underlying the actual consciousness of the unity. (Natorp 1888, § 14.0, p. 103)[22]

And for this reason,

> the primary thing *for cognition* is precisely the unity in the objective contents of consciousness, and the unity of consciousness is first *reconstructed* from it and is, properly speaking, only the subjective expression for it. *For cognition*, the subjective relation is more conditioned by the objective one than the latter is by the former. (Natorp 1888, § 14.7, p. 116)

Cognition is always given to us as a *fait accompli*, as it were – even if the discovery of increasingly comprehensive objective laws is always possible. *Psychology* is distinctive in that, whereas the direction of progress in other sciences is measured in terms of the increasing objectification of (what are revealed to be merely) subjective phenomena, progress in psychology is measured in terms of the increasing subjectification of the phenomena thus objectified, with the reconstitution of the immediately "given" (but in fact only presupposed) facts of consciousness serving as its infinitely distant goal. For Natorp, therefore, psychology is uniquely *re*constructive – and hence dependent on original, constructed objective unities. On the one hand, this gives a definitive answer to the basic question posed by the 1887 essay: the original grounding of cognition is thoroughly objective (Natorp 1887, § 7, p. 285). On the other hand, Natorp has (as Cohen had not) carved out a genuine role for modern psychology to play: *beginning* with the already-objective results of modern science, its task lies in the stepwise reconstruction of the subjective experience expressed in those results. Instead of delimiting a specific region of properly "psychological" phenomena to which some further method could then be applied, Natorp's psychology inquires into the *same* contents afforded by the objective sciences from a different direction.

A few corollaries of Natorp's general orientation to psychology deserve our attention in light of the later encounter with Husserl.

For Natorp, consciousness (*Bewusstsein*) can be considered according to three aspects: first, the *content* of which we are conscious; second, the *I* for which the content is conscious; and, finally, the *relation* between the two, which Natorp typically calls *Bewusstheit*.[23] Crucially, only the first of these aspects – the content – admits of any kind of direct description; both the I itself

---

[22] *Cf.* § 14.5: "Precisely the *objective unities*, therefore, are the *fundamentally determining* ones; insofar as what is subjective in consciousness is determinable at all, it is only determinable with respect to [*in Rücksicht auf*] something objective" (Natorp 1888, p. 113).
[23] See Natorp 1912a, § 2.2, pp. 24–27, and Natorp 1888, § 4.0, p. 11.

and the relation of the content to it are impossible to describe at all. Granted, reference to the content requires presupposing the second and third aspects of consciousness, but these are *presuppositions* which permit no direct description. The relation to an I is thus "an ultimate thing which, precisely as such, is no longer capable of further explanation or reduction" (Natorp, 1912a, § 2.3, p. 29).[24] The same holds for the I itself: the I which can apparently be investigated and described is not the original I, but a derivative image that reflects it (Natorp 1912a, § 2.4, pp. 30–33).[25] In a sense, there is not even consciousness of a self – not if we require the conscious I and the I of which it is conscious to be one and the same thing. Perhaps Natorp is treading dangerously close to denying the obvious fact of self-consciousness. But he is emphatic on this point. The I

> cannot, as is believed, be an object for itself; rather, one has already ceased to think of it as the I when one thinks of it as an object. And the same thing holds for *Bewusstheit*. Being-conscious [*Bewusst-sein*] means being an object for an I; this being-an-object [*Gegenstand-sein*] cannot in turn be made into an object, for such a displacement would no longer express the immediate essence of the thing. (Natorp 1912a, § 2.4, p. 33)

A field of investigation with definable components is thus available only on the side of the *content*. In trying to thematize the I and its conscious activities, psychologists inevitably find that their attempts to refer to them fall through to the content, i.e., that of which we are conscious. But now, what constitutes this content? Of what, that is, are we conscious? Only modern science gives a systematic answer to this question: we are conscious of objects standing under laws. Insofar as psychology tries to make anything else the topic of its inquiry, and especially insofar as it promises an independent grounding for modern science, it loses the only ground it has to stand on.

Natorp is quick to make the connection between his analysis of consciousness and the sad story of post-Kantian philosophy. Fichte is the "the I-philosopher κατ' ἐξοχήν" who "understood more or less everything that exists to be conjured up [*vorzuzaubern*] from out of the simple, innocuous-sounding principle that the I is the same thing that represents itself, or the identity of subject and object" (Natorp 1888, § 4.3, p. 14). Although Natorp is not (to put it mildly) offering a charitable reading of Fichte here, he is actually crediting him with an important consistency of purpose and method. If one takes seriously the idea that the objective must be primarily grounded in subjective activity, and if one then goes on to acknowledge the vast gulf separating the subjective from everything

---

24 *Cf.* Natorp 1888, § 4.2, pp. 13*sq*.
25 Again, *cf.* Natorp 1888, § 4.2, pp. 13*sq*.

objective (as Fichte *did*), such "conjuring" will be inescapable. Fichte's "titanic subjectivism" was simply the only way out of the corner into which he had painted himself: with clear insight into the inadequacy of objective language to get at the pure I, Fichte refused to import substantialist, objectivist prejudices into the subjective sphere and instead tried to build a philosophical science out of what the I *does*, its basic activity consisting in the enactment of self-consciousness. For Natorp, of course, this is impossible, but luckily Fichte's entire predicament can be avoided before it becomes so dire:

> For us, though, this entire problem of the I falls apart right here because the original definition – from which, as is always the case with the subtler metaphysical fictions, the rest consistently follows – is something we cannot admit: that the I can be one and the same thing which "represents" itself, that is, *has itself for an object*. The I is never an object, neither for another, nor – what appears to me to be the height of impossibility – for itself. (Natorp 1888, § 4.3, p. 15)

As different as the Fichtean and the psychologistic mistakes look, Natorp thinks they stem from the "same source" – the innocent-sounding proposition that the I can be an object for itself (Natorp 1888, § 5.1, pp. 15–17). We would do well to emulate Fichte (and not Cohen!) in taking the question of the subjective so seriously.[26] But we must abandon the idea of grounding the objective unities of the sciences by first gaining access to the subjective.

2 Natorp and the Early Phenomenological Movement

Natorp played a significant – and still underappreciated[27] – role in the methodological development of early phenomenology. His reception of Husserl's work began in 1901 with a review of the Prolegomena to the *Logical Investigations*. He included a critical chapter on Husserl in 1912's *Allgemeine Psychologie* and composed a substantial review essay of *Ideas I* in 1914.[28] In return, Husserl sent Adolf Reinach to Marburg in 1914 and arranged for him to review Natorp's

---

26 For a quite different interpretation of Natorp's relation to Fichte that plays up this point, see Edel 2013. But see also n. 59 below.

27 Happily, my remark here may soon sound outdated; see Kern 1964, but now also Kisiel 1993, Zahavi 2003, Luft 2011, Staiti 2013, and Dahlstrom 2015.

28 Citations will be to the second, more accessible printing of the review. See Natorp 1917–18, p. 224n for an explanation.

new book.²⁹ After Reinach was killed in the war, Husserl wasted no time in setting his next hope, the young Martin Heidegger, on Natorp's trail,³⁰ and eventually Natorp himself secured Heidegger's 1923 appointment at Marburg.³¹ Indeed, Natorp served a long and fruitful term, ceasing only with his death in 1924, as the unofficial sounding board off of which the young movement articulated its nascent self-conception.

This sounding board encouraged phenomenology finally to reckon directly with its basic methodological commitments. Given the differences between Husserl and his students that had become apparent by 1907,³² it may be hard to believe a full-fledged methodological debate had not already erupted there. But it had not. In discussing this, Lucinda Vandervort has remarked that the Göttingen students were so fixated on the business of *doing* phenomenology that they had little appetite for engaging in a methodological debate with Husserl.³³ This is, I think, correct, and is important to keep in mind as we consider the way the Natorp-Husserl(-Reinach) debate unfolded. Part of the allure of the original call to *die Sachen selbst* was its insistence on actually doing philosophy in the flesh instead of wading through a forest of academic discourse concerning how philosophy could, or ought to, be done.³⁴ Though Husserl himself was aware that he would have to confront methodological questions head-on in his upcoming work,³⁵ it was only in 1912 and 1913 that they began to take center stage.

The roots of the Natorp-Husserl encounter lie twenty-five years prior, in the analysis of consciousness (see above) in Natorp's 1888 *Einleitung*. When it comes to the pure I, at least, Husserl had originally agreed with Natorp, in the first edition of the *Logical Investigations*, both (1) that the I is presupposed in any conscious experience and (2) that it cannot be given any direct intuitive presentation. Unlike Natorp, Husserl *denies* on that basis that the pure I belongs to a theory of consciousness, its place in the latter being securable only through an intuitive presentation. We will discuss Husserl's methodology below in light of its further articulation in the *Ideas*, but note already his commitment to the-

---

29 At least this is the most likely hypothesis. See Schuhmann and Smith's plausible account in Reinach 1989, pp. 697–699.
30 See Kisiel 1993, p. 518n14.
31 See Ott 1988, pp. 122–124.
32 See the classic account in Spiegelberg 1976, pp. 168–227. But for evidence of the early sympathy of Husserl's first students with the *Ideas* itself, see Schuhmann & Smith 1985, p. 764.
33 Vandervort 1973, pp. 6*sq.*; *cf.* p. 20.
34 See Spiegelberg 1976, p. 170.
35 See Husserl to Natorp (23 Dec 1908), Husserl 1994, Hua Dok. III/5, p. 103.

orizing without "presuppositions:"[36] for Husserl, this is not just a bland call to put aside prejudices; it actually excludes, from the very start, the *inferential* access to the subjective seen by Natorp as the *only* access to the subjective. At this point, it is only and precisely the commitment to theorizing without presuppositions which keeps Husserl from agreeing completely with Natorp on the question of the I.

What is more, Husserl follows Natorp in rejecting psychology's reliance on "activities" of consciousness. Although the *Logical Investigations* is sometimes taken as a *locus classicus* for "act psychology," Husserl goes out of his way to align himself with Natorp here: "In talking of 'acts', on the other hand, we must steer clear of the word's original meaning: *all thought of activity [Betätigung] must be rigidly excluded*" (Husserl 1984, Hua XIX/1, p. 393). Since Natorp, too, could in practice hardly avoid referring to acts of consciousness, Husserl did not feel the need to differentiate himself from Natorp. Indeed, he adds an explicit, positive reference to the *Einleitung* in a footnote:

> We are in complete agreement with Natorp (*Einleitung in der Psychologie*, 1st ed., p. 21) when he objects to fully serious talk about "mental activities." [...] We too reject the "mythology of activities:" we define "acts" as intentional experiences, not as mental activities. (Husserl 1984, Hua XIX/1, p. 393n.)[37]

In the first edition of the *Logical Investigations*, then, we get something that looks like close agreement with Natorp: we can neither encounter the pure I nor understand the "acts" of psychology literally. And yet considerable differences lurk just beneath the surface. In particular, one might certainly still wonder whether talk of "intentional experiences" (rather than "mental activities") gets around the core of Natorp's objection to modern psychology. We will return to this question soon enough.

Natorp's 1901 review covers only the Prolegomena to the *Logical Investigations*. Despite conciliatory language throughout, Natorp complains not only that Husserl has misunderstood Kant (by making a sweeping attribution of psychologism to the Kantian tradition – an idea which Cohen's correction of Lange ought to have put to rest),[38] but that he "has blocked himself from the understanding of Kant that is necessary for his aims" (Natorp 1901, p. 281; translation modified). Coming from Natorp, this is a particularly serious charge: Kant's ach-

---

[36] See esp. Husserl 1984, Hua XIX/1, p. 25.
[37] See Sheredos 2017 and *cf.* Theodorou 2015, pp. 107*sq.* for deeper discussions of Husserl's remarks here.
[38] Natorp 1901, pp. 279*sq. Cf.* Cohen 1918, pp. 522*sq.*

ievement was supposed to be the shared experience of the German people that would lend all future German philosophy its decisive methodological directive.[39] For Natorp, genuine German philosophy *just is* Kantian philosophy – so long as it is understood (with Cohen) methodologically and not (with Fichte) metaphysically. Despite the seriousness of the charge, though, Natorp suspects that Husserl *is* ultimately aiming at something quite Kantian. Properly cleansed of its "psychological elements," the structure of Kant's transcendental logic "corresponds in all purity to the ideal sketched by Husserl" (Natorp 1901, p. 281). Natorp thus announces his confidence – which he would never relinquish – that Husserl would someday find his way into the Kantian fold.

Though Natorp did not review the second volume of the *Logical Investigations*, *Allgemeine Psychologie* provides some indication of his reaction to it. At first, Natorp sounds thoroughly disappointed: "In lieu of the objective grounding of cognition that was called for and promised in the first part, there ensues a 'phenomenological' grounding of cognition, which would in any case be called psychological, not logical, according to our concepts" (Natorp 1912a, § 11.11, p. 258). The underlying worry is clear: by insisting on a subjective grounding for cognition, Husserl is apparently casting his lot with Fichte, an interpretation to which Husserl himself would surely have objected.[40] But Natorp quickly reports that, on closer inspection, these initial appearances turn out to be deceiving, since "Husserl, like me, considers reflection on the subjective to be secondary, in contrast to the primary act of positing the object" (Natorp 1912a, § 11.11, p. 259). We will come back to this in a moment; for now, note that, even at this point, Natorp has convinced himself that Husserl's true aims are more transparently revealed by his practice than by his official statements of the purpose and methods of phenomenology. If Natorp is right, Husserl is, perhaps despite his own self-understanding, really on the right (Kantian, not Fichtean) side of history after all.

It is actually Husserl who, in his correspondence with Natorp following the *Logical Investigations*, generally tries to put more distance between himself and Marburg. Here the exchange from winter 1909 is especially illuminating. In a January letter, Natorp remarks that Husserl's phenomenology stands rather close to his "psychology" (Natorp to Husserl, 21 Jan 1909, Husserl 1994, Hua Dok. III/5, p. 106.), and in a long letter to Natorp two months later, Husserl offers a thought-

---

39 See esp. Natorp 1904, pp. 236 and 258–260; see below, p. 434.
40 Writing to William Hocking in 1903, Husserl refers to Fichte's "mythical and finally mystical I-metaphysics" (quoted in Hart 1995, p. 136). Like Natorp, Husserl was more sympathetic to Fichte's practical philosophy. See Seebohm 1997, p. 224.

ful interpretation of what prevents phenomenology from being assimilable to the Kantian tradition:

> From the outset, the Marburg School has another problematic and methodology. [...] At Göttingen we work with an entirely different attitude and, though we are honest idealists, we work from below, if you will. We mean that there is not only a false empiricist and psychologistic "below," but a genuine, idealistic one, from out of which one can work one's way up step by step to what is higher. (Husserl to Natorp, 18 Mar 1909, Husserl 1994, Hua Dok III/5, p. 110)[41]

For Husserl, however helpful the achievements of the sciences may be in directing our attention where to look, only the looking itself – and the faithful description of what is intuited there – can build up the basic principles of logic. In 1909 Husserl is still casting about for a way to make this bottom-up approach entirely clear; by 1913 it finds dramatic expression in his celebrated "principle of principles."

3 The Encounters of 1912–1914

In *Ideas I*, Husserl argues at some length that a rigorous, foundational philosophy can proceed only by going back to the phenomena in their barest givenness. The point of the newly introduced phenomenological reduction is to clarify the sense in which access to this field of phenomena is possible and to give a precise methodological expression of the original dictum of getting back to *die Sachen selbst*:

> But enough of erroneous theories. No conceivable theory can lead us astray when it comes to the principle of all principles: that each originally giving intuition is a legitimate source of cognition, that whatever originally presents itself to us in "intuition" ["*Intuition*"] [...] is to be taken simply as what it gives itself to be, but also only within the limits in which it gives itself there. Let us recognize indeed that each theory could itself draw its truth only, once

---

[41] *Cf.* Husserl to Jonas Cohn (15 Oct 1908): though Husserl happily concedes that the "transcendental method" may provide *indications* of the direction in which phenomenological work is to be carried out, such indications "do not even initially give us the true beginnings, the points with which the productive work can actually begin. Science is always science from below, work from the ground up to the heights; philosophical science, however, is science from the ultimate 'below,' going up to the ultimate heights – and this is no less the case in actually constructive work" (Husserl 1994, Hua Dok III/5, p. 15).

again, from original givennesses. (Husserl 1913b, § 24, p. 43*sq.*; Hua III/1, p. 51; translation modified)[42]

In practice, positive scientific cognition may proceed well enough without such a purely intuitive account of the phenomena, but its basic concepts can be secured only by reference to intuitive resources that cannot be gleaned from scientific facts themselves. The confusions and ambiguities that creep even into scientifically purified discourse can only be overcome by going back to principles afforded by pure intuition.

One might suppose that Husserl had thus announced his definitive break with Natorp. In his 1913 draft introduction for the second edition of the *Logical Investigations*, Husserl complains that even "the great and newly developed thoughts of the Marburg School and of A. Riehl concerning the Kantian critique of reason are anything but fundamental in the true sense, i.e., derived directly from the most original and clearest sources (those of pure intuition)" and that "as a result, the Kantian transcendental philosophy can neither in its original nor in its revised forms be first philosophy in the true sense" (Husserl 1913a, § 1, pp. 110*sq.*). In Husserl's mind, at least, the clarification of phenomenology afforded by the principle of principles was supposed to be an especially clear expression of the deep divide he perceived between his approach and that of the Kantians.

When we turn to the details of Husserl's new view, we can likewise see the old agreements with Natorp beginning to fall apart. In the second edition of the *Logical Investigations* of 1913, Husserl now concedes to Natorp that he has "managed to find" the pure I after all,[43] but this concession in fact only deepens the dispute: the ground of Husserl's change of heart is not a newfound agreement that what must be presupposed really can have a place in theory after all – indeed, in a marginal note in his copy of *Allgemeine Psychologie*, Husserl complains, once again, that "I cannot presuppose as necessary that which I do not *see* in its possibility"[44] – but rather a newfound *disagreement* with Natorp's insistence that the I cannot be given intuitively in the first place. Husserl now reasons as follows. If the "reduction to what is *purely* phenomenologically given"

> leaves us with no residual pure ego, then there can be no real (adequate) self-evidence attaching to the "I am." But if there is really such an adequate self-evidence – who indeed

---

42 References to *Ideas* I will be given first to the original 1913 edition, then to Schuhmann's *Husserliana* edition. *Cf.* Husserl 1913a, § 3, p. 116.
43 See Husserl 1984, Hua XIX/1, p. 374n.
44 Husserl's emphasis (underlining) in original; see Kern 1964, p. 363.

could deny it? – how can we avoid assuming a pure ego? It is precisely the ego apprehended in *carrying out* a self-evident *cogito*, and the pure carrying out *eo ipso* grasps it in phenomenological purity, and necessarily grasps it as the subject of a pure experience of the type *cogito*. (Husserl 1984, Hua XIX/1, p. 368n.)

Husserl freely admits that the necessity of this inference *guides* him to the phenomenological result in question. And yet "we intend to count the pure ego as a phenomenological datum only as far as its immediate, evidently ascertainable, essential distinctiveness and its cogivenness with pure consciousness reach" (Husserl 1913b, § 57, p. 110; Hua III/1, p. 124). Clearly, Husserl is not giving up his commitment to what is truly "given" in 1913, but he is, to be sure, expressing a certain willingness to broaden his sense of what that might mean.

Moreover, while in 1901 Husserl had shared Natorp's misgivings about references to "activities" in psychology, by 1913 he appears to be ready to reclaim a somewhat thicker sense of a mental "act."[45] Although he continues to maintain that "my original concept of act [from the *Logical Investigations*] is utterly indispensable" (Husserl 1913b, § 84, p. 170; Hua III/1, p. 190), the situation is now fundamentally altered by the fact that all such acts bear an essential reference to a possible implementation on the part of an active agent, namely, the pure I which Husserl has now managed to find. Husserl gives this insight a Kantian spin,[46] in light of which he can now draw a crucial distinction. Although he still wants to maintain, with Natorp, that the pure I "has no explicable content whatsoever" and is "in and for itself indescribable" (Husserl 1913b, § 80, p. 160; Hua III/1, p. 179), he points out that "for this reason, it provides the occasion for a variety of important descriptions of *how*, in quite particular ways, it is the ego that experiences the respective kinds or modes of experience" (Husserl 1913b, § 80, p. 161; Hua III/1, pp. 179*sq*.). While these remarks help clarify Husserl's claim to have access to a given pure I, they apparently commit him even more clearly to what Natorp was objecting to when he objected to talk of "activities of consciousness" in the first place. After all, Natorp's precise worry was that psychologists had attempted to *describe*, if not the bare I itself, then its *comportment* to its content – an impossibility if all attempted references to such comportment

---

45 See Sheredos 2017 for a much more detailed reconstruction of the logic of "activities" in the *Ideas*. It was an earlier version of Sheredos's paper that focused my attention on the key aspects of Husserl's development here.

46 "The pure ego lives itself out in a particular sense in every current *cogito*, yet all background experiences belong to it as well and it belongs to them. All of them, by virtue of belonging to the *one* stream of experience that is mine, *must* be capable of being converted into current *cogitationes* or of being included in them immanently. In Kantian language: '*The "I think" must be able to accompany all my representations*'" (Husserl 1913b, § 57, p. 109; Hua III/1, p. 123).

fall through to the content itself. Husserl, for his part, is now apparently endorsing just this possibility.

Given the direction of Natorp's subsequent review, one last wrinkle deserves our notice. In light of his sketch of the form of time-consciousness, Husserl points out that the unified stream of experience can only be reflectively grasped in the manner of a "Kantian idea," not as "a singular experience." This would seem to be a rather extraordinary concession, for Kant himself typically contrasts what is *demanded* by an idea with what can actually be *given* in experience, and Husserl is concerned precisely with the *givenness* of the stream of experience.[47] But instead of backing away from his commitment to the given, Husserl tells us that the stream "is nothing arbitrarily posited and maintained but instead an absolutely indubitable given – in a correspondingly wide sense of the word 'givenness'" (Husserl 1913b, § 83, p. 166; Hua III/1, p. 186). This should underscore how flexible Husserl's commitment to the given turns out to be.

In his review of Husserl's book, Natorp unsurprisingly shows little initial sympathy for Husserl's claims to an immediate access to self-consciousness. Husserl, Natorp allows, is perfectly correct to note that a self-giving intuitive cognition is *demanded*, or *presupposed*, by purportedly objective cognition. Natorp had been arguing just this since 1887. But "the *requirement* to exhibit pure consciousness, it appears, is being conflated with *that which can be exhibited in actual cognition*" (Natorp 1917–18, p. 238; see also pp. 240–242). Accordingly, the legitimacy of this demand cannot be taken as a requirement to *first* turn to the subjective side of experience. To fall into this mistake is, at bottom, to take the Fichtean path, no matter how much one outwardly disowns it. Evidently, Natorp has not yet put to rest his lingering worry that Husserl is not really on the right side of (post-Kantian) history after all.

For Husserl, the phenomenological reduction is supposed to secure "an intrinsically *sui generis* region of being that can indeed become the field of a new science – phenomenology" (Husserl 1913b, § 33, p. 59; Hua III/1, p. 68). While acknowledging that Husserl's recognition of this *sui generis* character of the subjective resonates strongly with his own view of the proper task of psychology, Natorp notes that

> there appears to remain between us [...] the radical difference that for Husserl pure consciousness is "absolutely" *given* (as a consequence of a simple "reduction," which actually means by the mere *omission* of the objectively positing act) and is brought to light as a self-evident "*residuum*," while my claim is that "*reconstruction*" is its own kind of task, and a difficult one, requiring its own *method*, a method which is the *exact inversion* of that of ob-

---

[47] See esp. Husserl 1913b, § 79, p. 156; Hua III/1, p. 175.

jectification and must therefore stand in the strictest *correspondence* with it and, like it, forge a *path into the infinite*. (Natorp 1917–18, p. 236; *cf.* p. 238)

To suppose that one can cut right through to pure consciousness by way of a merely negative attitudinal reversal is to underestimate – severely – the hold that objectification has over our access to the subjective. Natorp had already articulated this point clearly and forcefully in 1912:

> Husserl is reluctant – understandably – to recognize this secondary act, this thoroughly artificial objectification of the subjective as such, as absolutely dependent on the primary act of actual objectification that originally stands on its own. On his view, reflection on the subjective is, rather, only complicated by the ingrained habit of simply carrying out the primary objectifying acts and thus not reflecting on these acts themselves. The primary objectifications are familiar to us, interfering, as it were, with the secondary objectifications (of the acts of the primary objectifications) and threatening to falsify them; a special effort is required to fend off such a falsification. But Husserl thinks this is nevertheless possible in itself; thus it must also be possible to grab hold of the subjective (those acts) purely in itself. This is what I have not to this point been successful in doing. (Natorp 1912a, § 11.11, p. 259)[48]

In the *Ideas*, the phenomenological reduction gives a more precise formulation of what is necessary to overcome such an "ingrained habit," but, if anything, it only appears to strengthen Husserl's commitment to bypassing all objective constructions.

Natorp now, however, latches onto Husserl's confession that in reflection we grasp the stream of experience in the manner of a Kantian idea. Natorp's satisfaction at this point is palpable. For it turns out that the stream of experience

> can never be or become given with one single, pure glance [*Blick*] (§83), but is *intentionally* graspable in the manner of the "*limitlessness of the progress*" of the immanent intuitions; we grasp it not as a singular experience, but in the manner of the – *idea* in the Kantian sense! (Natorp 1917–18, p. 242)

Here Husserl is saying what Natorp has insisted all along he *must* say: that any attempt to get at pure consciousness can only *approach* its target. Far from affirming the intuitive givenness of either the pure I or of its comportment to its content, Husserl is rather acknowledging the unplumbable depths in which the true *logos* of the *psyche* is submerged.[49] Husserl's apparently Cartesian commitment to the given is thus unmasked as a properly chastened, critical commit-

---

[48] *Cf.* Husserl 1984, Hua XIX/1, p. 14.
[49] See Natorp 1917–18, pp. 242*sq.*; *cf.* Natorp 1912a, § 11.14, pp. 266*sq.*

ment to nothing other than the transcendental method itself! This is how Natorp answers (on Husserl's behalf) the old charge that the act of reflection, being itself a form of objectification, is inadequate to grasp the stream of experience in its subjective character.[50] For the field of phenomenology is "given" – if we insist on retaining that old, misleading expression – only as an infinite task, and its recovery is accordingly only a goal for a painstaking reconstruction.

Even in light of the *Ideas*, then, Natorp did not abandon his faith that Husserl was on a genuinely Kantian path. In spite of "a certain appearance of absolutism, incompatible with the spirit of 'critique,'" Husserl's work remains "a genuine 'critical' investigation" (Natorp 1917–18, p. 246). Indeed, Natorp finds that in the actual details of his analysis, Husserl always works from the objective side of cognition back to its subjective side, demonstrating *in practice* how superfluous the old reference to "acts" of the subject has become for phenomenology.[51] Natorp concludes:

> The task of "subjectification" (as it is roughly expressed in my terminology) unfolds itself, for Husserl as for me, basically as an "infinite task," no less than that of "objectification;" absolute (pure, that is, preobjective) *consciousness* is, no less than the absolute (pure, that is, beyond consciousness) *object*, an "*idea*" – in the Kantian sense of "limitless progression" from determination to determination. For both of us what is "absolute" is, if you will, the *method*, the *lawfulness* of the determination. (Natorp 1917–18, p. 246)

This, now, would unequivocally place Husserl on the right side of history.

Reinach's review of Natorp and his Marburg lecture make for useful points of comparison, even if our consideration of them here must be brief. Reinach had just finished the editorial work on the *Jahrbuch* in which *Ideas I* appeared and was as familiar with its content as anyone. His defense of Husserl's account of the givenness of the pure I is thus especially worth noting. Characteristically, he manages to articulate Husserl's fundamental point with great austerity and clarity:

> That it is the I itself that grasps itself, that in becoming aware of itself it is at the same time both the bearer of the grasping and the point at which it aims – in this we see not, as Natorp does, a logical difficulty, but a fact that is quite marvelous, even if it is one secured by evidence [*eine sehr wunderbare, wenn auch durch Evidenz gesicherte Tatsache*]. (Reinach 1914b, p. 318)[52]

---

50 See, e.g., Natorp 1888, § 13.3, p. 93.
51 See esp. Natorp 1917–18, pp. 244*sq*.
52 It's a striking formulation, and Reinach may be alluding to the fact that Natorp himself uses similar language in both the *Einleitung* and *Allgemeine Psychologie* in elucidating representative consciousness (which, for Natorp, is the original form of consciousness from which presentative

"Marvelous" – "even if" "secured by evidence": an especially succinct way of getting at the core of the phenomenological method. The contrast is with the transcendental method, which looks for the basis of all such "security" not in evidence, but in existing scientific and cultural facts. For Reinach, the Marburgers, for all their ingenuity, have blinded themselves to what is actually given, going so far as to deny the self-evidence of the "I am" if their theory turns out to require it.[53] In philosophy in general, as in the case of the pure I, there has to be *some* way to cut through such theoretical presuppositions right from the start. This should allow us to recognize the true force of the opening lines of Reinach's Marburg lecture of January 1914:

> I have not set myself the task of telling you what phenomenology is; rather, I would like to try to *think* with you phenomenologically. To talk about phenomenology is the most pointless thing in the world so long as we are lacking that which can first give any discourse its concrete fullness and intuitiveness: the phenomenological *way of seeing* [Blick] and the phenomenological *attitude*. (Reinach 1914a, p. 531; translation modified)

By insisting that his audience *perform* his exercises along with him,[54] Reinach showed the greatest possible appreciation for the crux of the issue dividing Göttingen from Marburg.[55]

4 Concluding Reflections

World events soon swept away whatever momentum the prewar encounter between Husserl and Natorp had gained. What was its enduring legacy and significance? Before proceeding further, a caveat may be in order. Neither Natorp nor Husserl was the type of thinker to stand pat; the methodological stakes of the prewar debate would likely have looked quite different (to each of them) a decade later. It has been suggested that further developments in Husserl's phenom-

---

consciousness is derived through an abstraction). See Natorp 1912a, § 3.10, pp. 52*sq*.; *cf.* Natorp 1888, § 7.5, pp. 41*sq*.

53 *Cf.* Natorp 1912a, § 2.4, p. 32.

54 *Cf.* Husserl's ultimately performative defense of reflection in *Ideas I:* "Here, as everywhere, skepticism loses its force if we turn from verbal argumentations to the intuition of essences, to the originally giving intuition and to the legitimacy originally attached to it [*ihr ureigenes Recht*]" (Husserl 1913b, § 79, p. 156; Hua III/1, p. 175; translation modified).

55 Denis Seron emphasizes Reinach's attitudinal conception of phenomenology, which he then contrasts with Husserl's. In my view, this puts considerably more distance between Reinach and Husserl than is really warranted. But see Seron 2015, pp. 180–182.

enology were decisively influenced by Natorp[56] and that Natorp's later investigations took him away from the position of the Marburg School altogether – and into Fichtean (and perhaps even Heideggerian) territory.[57] This paper is hardly the place to trace out and compare such claims. However much Husserl and Natorp were themselves thinkers in transition,[58] my focus is on how the stakes of the debate would have looked to the principals at the time.[59]

As we have seen, Natorp's "official" view, despite the worries pervading his evaluations of Husserl's work from 1901 to 1914, is that phenomenology's research program is – in actual execution, if not in its methodological pronouncements – a genuinely Kantian project. And of course, Husserl does say that we apprehend the stream of experience in the manner of a Kantian idea, emphasizing how unusual it may be to think of "givenness" in such a manner. We must keep in mind, however, that for Natorp a "Kantian idea" is paradigmatic of a "presupposition" or "requirement," which in Natorp's language is diametrically opposed to the idea of the "given." We can thus understand why Natorp would be so struck by Husserl's apparent concession: if "given" means for Husserl what "required" means for Natorp, then the methodological opposition between the thinkers does indeed fall apart. The difference would then be, as Natorp puts it, "almost merely terminological."[60]

Now, if, in the *Ideas*, the "givenness" of the given were just thought of as the static result of the application of a procedure (i.e., the phenomenological reduction), Natorp would have little ground for his conciliatory interpretation. But he is right to resist this picture; part of Husserl's point is that the field of phenomena is not such a mere *result*, but the always-intended, never-arrived-at goal of acts of reflection. When phenomenology stakes its claim to a secured field of

---

56 See Luft 2011, pp. 207*sq.*, and Luft 2013, p. xxxii.
57 See Edel 2002, pp. 44*sq.*, and Luft 2013, pp. xxxiii-xxxv.
58 For a strong version of this claim with regard to *Allgemeine Psychologie*, see Luft 2013, p. xxxivf.; for a strong version of this claim with regard to *Ideas I*, see Fink 1939, pp. 107*sq.*
59 Edel, e. g., tends to interpret *Allgemeine Psychologie* retrospectively from the development of Natorp's later philosophy, something I would like to refrain from doing, given my purposes. Indeed, proceeding this way leads Edel, in my view, to distort the very passages on which he stakes his interpretation. In particular, Natorp's appeal to the "immediate experience of consciousness" means something quite different from Fichte's "look at yourself"; it bears an exactly opposite methodological significance (as Natorp's note that its full independence must be conceived "always as a problem" indicates). The classical thinker whom Natorp would have recognized as the touchstone for his locution here is not Fichte, but *Schiller*, to whom he explicitly refers in a nearly identical context in his Halle lecture (Natorp 1912b, p. 201; *cf.* Natorp 1904, p. 258). In 1912, Fichte is as much Natorp's foil as he ever was. But see Edel 2003, esp. p. 43.
60 Natorp 1917–18, p. 226; *cf.* p. 246.

phenomena constituting a basis for future research, it includes an essential, ineliminable reference to a performance which is *being carried out* and which in principle always remains *still to be carried out*.

One of Natorp's persistent concerns about phenomenology was its inability to come to grips with the dynamism of cognition, its character as *fieri*. Oftentimes this takes the form of Natorp claiming that Husserl's Platonism is "incomplete," with Husserl's invocation of "essences" only an intermediate step on the way to Plato's deepest insights into the continuity of thinking (Natorp 1917–18, p. 231).[61] For Natorp, this is all of a piece with Plato's rejection of the brute givennesses that would provide principles (in Husserl's sense) for cognition. Now, Natorp, I think, is right that in the *Ideas* Husserl is laying the groundwork for a response to this charge: taking seriously the *active* side of intentional experience, as well as its mode of reflective apprehension, reveals that such "givennesses" should not be imagined as static entities standing over against an active subject whose only task is to grab hold of them. To be sure, in active reflection such givennesses come forth precisely in the mode of *being reflected upon*, but they are no less "given" for that.[62] In particular, the reference back to the reflective act does not preclude them from falling under Husserl's "wide sense of the word givenness." In this way, when Natorp demands that Husserl ascend to a higher level of Platonism and dissolve his static essences into the *fieri* of cognition, Husserl might well reply that this is precisely what his phenomenological method, with its essential reference to egoic activity, accomplishes. Husserl had already, in 1909, written to Natorp that "it seems to me as though we stand near one another, and as though it were one and the same philosophy that has been joining us, presenting its different aspects to us, and allotting us different groups of problems that nevertheless lay claim to one another" (Husserl to Natorp (18 Mar 1909), Husserl 1994, Hua Dok. III/5, p. 111). Writing to Husserl in 1914 that a true consensus is finally being reached, Natorp would appear to think that Husserl has finally made good on that claim.

At the same time, despite such professed optimism, it is not hard to imagine Natorp sitting in Reinach's audience at Marburg and wondering whether phenomenology was not, in fact, crossing over into dangerously Fichtean territory. Fichte's own insistence on the inseparability of the I's own activity from any scientific account of the I resonates strongly with the variations brought forward by both Husserl and Reinach in this context. In particular, the performative account

---

[61] See Kim 2010, pp. 99sq.
[62] I borrow this way of putting the point from Hopkins 2015.

of "finding" the pure I may find its closest traditional analogue here.[63] Is Natorp not, then, overplaying his hand a bit in laying so much weight on Husserl's invocation of the Kantian "idea?" Natorp, of course, uses this as a wedge to go back and reinterpret Husserl's methodological directives in a more Kantian light. But to employ such a strategy strictly and consistently would require a radical recasting of the project of phenomenology. After all, from Husserl and Reinach's perspective, however far we extend the relevant sense of givenness here, to collapse it into *Natorp's* conception of a demand would be to give up the bottom-up approach to philosophy altogether, against almost everything Husserl and Reinach ever stood for.[64]

Conversely, from Natorp's point of view, if we reflect on what the commitment to the bottom-up method really requires, the link to performativity – and to Fichte, or at least the version of Fichte the Marburgers were trying to banish – becomes clear. So long as we simply travel the path of merely *inferring* what is presupposed on the subjective side from what is objectively established, we are not doing phenomenology in Husserl's sense, for however much we concede that the objective unities can function as guiding clues, nothing can take the place of actually *looking*. Husserl, it seems to me, is as clear on this point in the *Ideas* as he ever was:

> Yet since all of [phenomenology's] knowledge is supposed to be descriptive, purely adapted to the immanent sphere, then inferences, all non-intuitive ways of proceeding, have merely the methodical significance of leading us to the matters [*Sachen*] that a subsequently direct discernment of essence has to bring to the level of being given. (Husserl 1913b, § 75, pp. 140*sq.*; Hua III/1, pp. 157*sq.*)

And Reinach is only pressing the same point when he insists that his Marburg audience *do* phenomenology. For both, the reference to the performance is essential precisely because the conceptual, objective clues offered by the facts of science and culture only get us so far. For Natorp, precisely this recognition that this "so far" exhausts the domain of methodologically secure philosophy is what the recovery of Kant was supposed to be all about. To reject *this* form of Kantian modesty would, indeed, send us back to Fichte.

---

[63] It has been argued on independent grounds that Husserl's development at this point roughly follows the developmental path of German idealism from Kant through Reinhold to Fichte. See Luft 2010.

[64] I am thus fundamentally in agreement with Kern, who, despite his deep appreciation of the points of contact between Husserl and Natorp, concludes that Husserl's commitment to systematically carrying out intentional analysis "from below" sets him apart from the Neokantians in a fundamental way. See Kern 1964, pp. 423*sq.*

Whatever the ultimate fate of Natorp's attempt to find common ground, I hope to have shown that the significance of his interpretation of the phenomenological movement only clearly emerges when read against the fraught historical debate over the meaning of Kant. If phenomenology was to be, or become, a living philosophy, it was crucial that it latch onto the living motives in Kant's thought. Natorp was hardly an obstinate partisan of the "historical Kant," but he was convinced that Kant held a special place in the history of German philosophy, for Kant alone had become a shared experience for the German people as a whole (Natorp 1904, p. 236). "The German nation," Natorp proclaims in a 1904 speech, "has experienced him in the true sense [*im wahren Sinne ihn erlebt hat*]. It has incorporated something of his essence into its flesh and blood" (Natorp 1904, p. 239). The recovery of true Kantianism from its partial eclipse in nineteenth-century philosophy had to be vigilantly defended if "German" philosophy was to be both an authentic philosophy for the German people and a genuinely progressive force for humanity as a whole. When Natorp alludes to the "dissipation of [Kant's] inheritance [*Erbgut*]," we should appreciate the urgency he is indicating (Natorp 1887, § 2, p. 264). It is certainly crucial to understanding why he goes so far out of his way to read his friend Husserl apparently against the grain.

Conversely, of course, for Husserl to allow his movement to be assimilated to the Kantian tradition as *Natorp* understood it threatened phenomenology's claim to be a fresh beginning. Husserl was certainly right to be wary of Natorp's olive branch, even at the cost of having to reject Kant's legacy – or at least having to lay claim to it in a fundamentally different manner. And this, in turn, is the background against which we should read the final, better-known act to this drama. When Cassirer and Heidegger debated the legacy of Kant's philosophy in Davos in 1929, many of the broad themes from the Husserl-Natorp encounter resurfaced, now transposed into the apparently merely "historical" register of Kant interpretation. Cassirer, now assuming Natorp's role, kept insisting on trying to bring Heidegger into the Kantian fold, while Heidegger insisted upon the distinctiveness of the phenomenological approach. In his own attempt to claim Kantian turf for phenomenology, Heidegger himself, I think, had learned quite a bit from the earlier encounter between the two traditions. But that is a story for another time.[65]

---

[65] Earlier, partial versions of this paper were presented at conferences for the North American Society for Early Phenomenology (Mexico City, 2015), the North American Kant Society (Atlanta, 2016), and the Society for Phenomenology and Existential Philosophy (Salt Lake City, 2016), and some important points originated as a commentary at the Husserl Circle (Chicago, 2016). I would like to thank all the audiences for their helpful questions and comments – and, even more importantly, for their encouragement in pursuing this project.

Bibliography

Beiser, Frederick (2014): *The Genesis of Neo-Kantianism, 1796–1880*. Oxford: Oxford University Press.

Cohen, Hermann (2005) [1914]: *Einleitung mit kritischem Nachtrag zur "Geschichte des Materialismus" von F.A. Lange*. Helmut Holzhey (Ed.). Hildesheim: Olms. English (partial): "The Relationship of Logic to Physics, from the Introduction, with Critical Remarks, to the Ninth Edition of Lange's *History of Materialism*". Trans. Lydia Patton. In Luft (2015a): pp. 117–136.

Cohen, Hermann (1987) [1918]: *Kants Theorie der Erfahrung*, 5th ed. (following 3rd ed. of 1918). Ed. Geert Edel. Hildesheim: Olms.

Dahlstrom, Daniel O. (2015): "Natorp's Psychology". In Nicolas de Warren & Andrea Staiti (Eds.): *New Approaches to Neo-Kantianism*. Cambridge: Cambridge University Press, pp. 240–260.

Edel, Geert (2002): "Fichte – Marburger Neukantianismus (insbesondere Natorp) und die philosophische Methode". In Detlev Pätzold & Christian Krijnen (Eds.): *Der Neukantianismus und das Erbe des deutschen Idealismus: die philosophische Methode*. Wurzburg: Königshausen & Neumann, pp. 35–48.

Edel, Geert (2013): "Zum Fichte-Bild im Marburger Neukantianismus". In: *Fichte-Studien*, vol. 37, pp. 15–32.

Edgar, Scott (2008): "Paul Natorp and the Emergence of Anti-Psychologism in the Nineteenth Century". In: *Studies in History and Philosophy of Science*, vol. 39, pp. 54–65.

Ewald, Oscar (1907): "Contemporary Philosophy in Germany (1906)". Anon. Trans. In: *Review of Metaphysics*, vol. 16, pp. 237–265.

Ewald, Oscar (1908): "German Philosophy in 1907". Anon. Trans. In: *Review of Metaphysics*, vol. 17, pp. 400–426.

Ewald, Oscar (1910): "German Philosophy in 1909". Trans. William A. Hammond. In: *Review of Metaphysics*, vol. 19, pp. 481–504.

Fink, Eugen (1939): "Vorbemerkung des Herausgebers". In Husserl (1913a): pp. 106–108. Trans.: "Eugen Fink's Editorial Remarks". In: Husserl, Edmund. *Introduction to the Logical Investigations*, pp. 13–15. Trans. Philip J. Bossert & Curtis H. Peters. The Hague: Martinus Nijhoff, 1975.

Hart, James G. (1995): "Husserl and Fichte: With Special Regard to Husserl's Lectures on 'Fichte's Ideal of Humanity'". In: *Husserl Studies*, vol. 12, pp. 135–163.

Hopkins, Burt (2015): "The 'Offence of Any and All Ready-Made Givenness': Natorp's Critique of Husserl's *Ideas for a Pure Phenomenology and Phenomenological Philosophy*". Conference given at *The Great Phenomenological Schism: Reactions to Husserl's Transcendental Idealism* (Seminario de Estudios Básicos de Fenomenología Trascendental & North American Society for Early Phenomenology). Universidad Nacional Autónoma de México. México, DF. June 5, 2015.

Husserl, Edmund (1913a): "Entwurf einer 'Vorrede' zu den "Logischen Untersuchungen". Ed. Eugen Fink. In: *Tijdschrift voor Philosophie*, vol. 1 (1939), pp. 106–133, 319–339.

Husserl, Edmund (1975): *Introduction to the Logical Investigations*. Trans. Philip J. Bossert & Curtis H. Peters. The Hague: Martinus Nijhoff.

Husserl, Edmund (1913b): *Ideen zu einer reinen Phänomenologie und phänomenologischen Philosophie: Allgemeine Einführung in die reine Phänomenologie*. Halle: Max Niemeyer. (See also Hua III/1.)

Husserl, Edmund (2014): *Ideas for a Pure Phenomenology and Phenomenological Philosophy, First Book: General Introduction to Pure Phenomenology*. Trans. Daniel O. Dahlstrom. Indianapolis, IN: Hackett.

Husserl, Edmund (1984): *Logische Untersuchungen*, vol. 2 (Hua XIX/1–2). Ed. Ursula Panzer. The Hague: Martinus Nijhoff.

Husserl, Edmund (1970): *Logical Investigations*. Trans. J.N. Findlay. London: Routledge & Kegan Paul.

Husserl, Edmund (1994): *Briefwechsel*, vol. 5: *Die Neukantianer* (Hua Dok. III/5). Ed. Elisabeth Schuhmann & Karl Schuhmann. Dordrecht: Springer.

Kern, Iso (1964): *Husserl und Kant: Eine Untersuchung über Husserls Verhältnis zu Kant und zum Neukantianismus*. The Hague: Martinus Nijhoff.

Kim, Alan (2010): *Plato in Germany: Kant – Natorp – Heidegger*. Sankt Augustin: Academia.

Kisiel, Theodore (1993): *The Genesis of Heidegger's Being and Time*. Berkeley, CA: University of California Press.

Kubalica, Tomasz (2016): "The Polemic between Leonard Nelson and Ernst Cassirer on the Critical Method in the Philosophy". In: *Folia Philosophica*, vol. 35, pp. 53–69.

Luft, Sebastian (2010): "Phenomenology as First Philosophy: A Prehistory". In Carlo Ierna, Hanne Jacobs, & Filip Mattens (Eds.): *Philosophy, Phenomenology, Sciences: Essays in Commemoration of Edmund Husserl*. Dordrecht: Springer, pp. 107–133.

Luft, Sebastian (2011): *Subjectivity and Lifeworld in Transcendental Phenomenology*. Evanston, IL: Northwestern University Press.

Luft, Sebastian (2013): "Einleitung der Herausgebers". In Natorp (1912a), pp. xi-xxxviii.

Luft, Sebastian (Ed.) (2015a): *The Neo-Kantian Reader*. London: Routledge.

Luft, Sebastian (2015b): *The Space of Culture: Towards a Neo-Kantian Philosophy of Culture (Cohen, Natorp, and Cassirer)*. Oxford: Oxford University Press.

Natorp, Paul (1887): "Über objective und subjective Begründung der Erkenntniss". In: *Philosophische Monatshefte*, vol. 23, pp. 257–286.

Natorp, Paul (1981): "On the Objective and Subjective Grounding of Knowledge". Trans. Lois Phillips & David Kol. In: *Journal of the British Society for Phenomenology*, vol. 12, pp. 245–266.

Natorp, Paul (1888): *Einleitung in der Psychologie nach kritische Methode*. Freiburg: J.C.B. Mohr.

Natorp, Paul (1901): "Zur Frage der logischen Methode: Mit Beziehung auf Edm. Husserls 'Prolegomena zur reinen Logik'". In *Kant-Studien*, vol. 6, pp. 270–283.

Natorp, Paul (1977): "On the Question of Logical Method in Relation to Edmund Husserl's *Prolegomena to Pure Logic*". Trans. J.N. Mohanty. In Mohanty, J. N. (Ed.): *Edmund Husserl's* Logical Investigations. The Hague: Martinus Nijhoff, pp. 55–66.

Natorp, Paul (1904): "Zum Gedächtnis Kants". In Joachim Kopper (Ed.): *Immanuel Kant zu ehren*. Frankfurt: Suhrkamp, 1974, pp. 236–260.

Natorp, Paul (1912a): *Allgemeine Psychologie nach kritische Methode*. Ed. Sebastian Luft. Darmstadt: WBG, 2013.

Natorp, Paul (1912b): "Kant und die Marburger Schule". In: *Kant-Studien*, vol. 17, pp. 193-221. English: "Kant and the Marburg School". Trans. Frances Bottenberg. In Luft (2015a): pp. 180-197.

Natorp, Paul (1917–18): "Husserls 'Ideen zu einer reinen Phänomenologie'". In: *Logos*, vol. 7, pp. 224–246.

Ott, Hugo (1993 [1988]): *Martin Heidegger: A Political Life*. Trans. Allan Blunden. New York, NY: Basic Books.

Reinach, Adolf (1914a): "Über Phänomenologie". In Reinach (1989), pp. 531–550.

Reinach, Adolf (2012): "Concerning Phenomenology". Trans. Dallas Willard. In *The Apriori Foundations of the Civil Law along with the Lecture "Concerning Phenomenology"*. Frankfurt: Ontos, pp. 143–165.

Reinach, Adolf (1914b): "Paul Natorp, *Allgemeine Psychologie nach kritische Methode*" (review). In Reinach (1989), pp. 313–331.

Reinach, Adolf (1989): *Sämtliche Werke*. Eds. Karl Schuhmann & Barry Smith. Munich: Philosophia.

Schuhmann, Karl & Smith, Barry (1985): "Against Idealism: Johannes Daubert vs. Husserl's *Ideas* I". In: *Review of Metaphysics*, vol. 38, pp. 763–793.

Schuhmann, Karl & Smith, Barry (1987): "Adolf Reinach: An Intellectual Biography". In: Kevin Mulligan (Ed.): *Speech Act and Sachverhalt: Reinach and the Foundations of Realist Phenomenology*. Dordrecht: Martinus Nijhoff, pp. 3–27.

Seebohm, Thomas M. (1997): "Johann Gottlieb Fichte (1762–1814)". In: Lester Embree *et al.* (Eds.): *Encyclopedia of Phenomenology*. Dordrecht: Springer, pp. 223–226.

Seron, Denis (2015): "Adolf Reinach's Philosophy of Logic". In: Bruno Leclerq, Sébastien Richard, & Denis Seron (Eds.): *Objects and Pseudo-Objects: Ontological Deserts and Jungles from Brentano to Carnap*. Berlin: Walter de Gruyter, pp. 167–182.

Sheredos, Benjamin (2017): "Act Psychology and Phenomenology: Husserl on Egoic Acts". In: *Husserl Studies*, vol. 33, pp. 191–209.

Spiegelberg, Herbert (1976): *The Phenomenological Movement: A Historical Introduction*, Vol. 1. 2nd ed. The Hague: Martinus Nijhoff.

Staiti, Andrea (2013): "The *Ideen* and Neo-Kantianism". In: Lester Embree & Thomas Nenon (Eds.). *Husserl's* Ideen. Dordrecht: Springer, pp. 71–90.

Theodorou, Panos (2015): *Husserl and Heidegger on Reduction, Primordiality, and the Categorial: Phenomenology Beyond Its Original Divide*. Cham: Springer.

Vandervort (Brettler), Lucinda Ann (1973): "The Phenomenology of Adolf Reinach: Chapters in the Theory of Knowledge and Legal Philosophy". PhD Diss. McGill University. Montréal, QC.

Zahavi, Dan (2003): "How to Investigate Subjectivity: Natorp and Heidegger on Reflection". In: *Continental Philosophy Review*, vol. 36, pp. 155–176.

Ovidiu Stanciu
"An Explosive Thought:"
Kant, Fink, and the Cosmic Concept of the World

Abstract: The task of my inquiry is to lay out the main lines of Eugen Fink's reading of Kant, focusing on his interpretation of the Transcendental Dialectic. In the first part, I explain Fink's claim that the Transcendental Dialectic represents the very heart of the Kantian project, in as much it is in this section of the first *Critique* that the question of totality (on Fink's account, the driving impetus of this work) first comes to the forefront. Secondly, I undertake an examination of Fink's argument regarding the proper outcome of the "Antinomies of Pure Reason," according to which the failure of the attempts to determine the world with "innerworldly models" is not a sufficient reason to contend that the world is merely a subjective idea. Finally, I discuss Fink's thesis concerning the construction of the "Transcendental Ideal" according to which the transition from the *omnitudo realitatis* to the *ens realissimum* is not necessary (neither objectively, nor subjectively). In this regard, Fink's project can be understood as an attempt to think the *omnitudo realitatis* for itself, prior to and independent from any realization in a being (be it a supreme one).[1]

Eugen Fink's theoretical project and, indeed, his intellectual development stand in close relation to the philosophy of Immanuel Kant. For all his early absorption in the orbit of Husserlian phenomenology and despite his latter appraisal of thinkers like Heraclitus, Hegel, or Nietzsche, it is Kant who acted as the most powerful catalyst of his philosophical undertaking, and it is from Kant's philosophy that he extracted the gist of his thought. From his early attempt to develop a "critique of phenomenological experience and cognition" and to unfold a "phenomenology of phenomenology," both under the heading of a "transcendental theory of method" (Fink 1995), to his latter inquiry aiming at unraveling a "*cosmic* concept of world" (Fink 1990, p. 33) – a concept that can be elaborated only within the framework of a "cosmic philosophy" (Kant 1781/1787, A 838/B 866;

---

[1] The Research for this paper was funded by CONICYT/FONDECYT Postdoctoral project No. 3180721 developed at the Universidad Diego Portales, Santiago de Chile.

https://doi.org/10.1515/9783110564280-020

Kant 1998, p. 694)² –, the reference to Kant played an utterly pivotal role. His first article – published in 1933 in *Kant-Studien* – already moved within such a horizon, in as much as it staged a confrontation between Husserlian phenomenology and its Neo-Kantian critics, while important sections of his latter works (such as *Alles und Nichts* and *Welt und Endlichkeit*) are entirely devoted to an exploration of Kant's conception of the world. Moreover, it is also worth recalling that he had, for a moment, in the 1930's, contemplated the possibility of writing a *Habilitation*-thesis which should have bared the title "*Weltbewusstsein und Weltganzheit. Phänomenologische Untersuchungen am Leitfaden des Kantischen Antinomienproblems*" (Fink 2008, p. 308) and that he conducted for ten years (between 1962 and 1971) a monthly seminar dedicated to a close reading of the *Critique of Pure Reason* (the recently published protocols of this seminar comprise almost two thousand pages (Fink 2011)). Thus, Fink's engagement with Kantian philosophy extends far beyond a mere exegetical level and the master of Königsberg is more than the partner of a constant philosophical dialogue. The transformation of the phenomenological inquiry into a cosmological philosophy, the breakthrough towards the question of the world as the ultimate level of analysis of the constitution of meaning and, thus, as the unique *Sache selbst* of philosophy was – on Fink's own account – accomplished under the aegis of Kant. While an unbroken overview of the emergence and development of this relation surpasses the scope of this paper, I will instead attempt to reconstruct the distinguishing marks of Fink's interpretation of the Transcendental Dialectic as it can be read in his mature works (primarily in these three central documents that are the lecture courses delivered in 1949, 1957 and 1958 and published under the titles *Welt und Endlichkeit*, *Alles und Nichts*, and *Spiel als Weltsymbol*).

Focusing on Fink's treatment of the Transcendental Dialectic will allow us both to assess the fresh horizons it opens up for a renewed understanding of Kant's work and to show how Fink's own thought emerged from a relentless meditation of the first *Critique*. From the outset, it should be noted that although Fink understands his endeavor as carrying further some key insights drawn from Kant's thought, he by no means adopts the posture of an orthodox Kantian. Quite the contrary, he attempts to bring out the undisclosed theoretical assumptions that prevented Kant from laying out the full breadth of the problem of the world – a problem he has himself been the first to acknowledge as such, for "Kant is the true discoverer of the problem of the world" (Fink 1985, p. 112).³ This double stance – positive appropriation and critical intent – comes to

---

2 *Cf.* Fink's reference to this passage in Fink 2016, p. 49.
3 When the reference is, like here, to a German edition, the English translation is mine.

vivid expression in the course of a dialogue with Heidegger. During the tenth lesson of the seminar he jointly held with Fink in 1966–67, Heidegger gives voice to his surprise with regard to the usage Fink makes of the term "cosmological," remarking that it not only deviates from the standard, naturalistic understanding of this notion, but also departs from the Greek sense of "*kosmos*." To this, Fink replies: "I do not think the cosmological from out of Heraclitus, but rather from out of Kant and from the antinomy of pure reason." And he goes on to explain what commands his adoption of this Kantian outlook (and terminology):

> [...] pure reason attempts to think the whole. The whole is a concept that is first oriented toward things. In this manner, however, we can never thoughtfully experience the gathered whole. Kant exhibits the aporias of an attempt of thought that believes itself able to think the whole on the model of a spatial thing. Because the attempt does not manage with this approach, Kant subjectivizes the whole as a subjective principle in the process of experience. (Heidegger/Fink 1979, p. 110)

As this passage makes clear, the privilege granted to the Transcendental Dialectic is motivated by the fact that in this section the question of the totality as such, the question of the whole (which Fink will straightforwardly assimilate with that of the world), edges to the forefront. Furthermore, Kant's strategy in dealing with this issue has the merit of displaying the impossibility of grasping the whole along the lines of an innerworldly totality. Therefore, the main accomplishment of the Transcendental Dialectic consists in the critique mounted against the traditional understanding of the world, against its apprehension as a "gigantic thing or of an objective system of positions" (Fink 2016, p. 69), as "a framework, a container, a gigantic vessel for manifold beings" (Fink 2016, p. 66). The *Critique of Pure Reason* is a work that breaks new ground inasmuch as it shows that the received ways of conceiving the world – according to which reason can conceptually dominate and articulate the totality of being, transforming it into an object – are fundamentally untenable. It is this point that Fink takes to be decisive in Kant's analysis, for it opens up an interpretative space where an alternative concept of world – which does not reduce it to a collection of entities – can be worked out.

However, upsetting the traditional ways of conceiving the whole, or challenging the legitimacy of this "cumulative concept of the world," is not the last word of the Transcendental Dialectic. As Fink admits towards the end of this passage, in a line that contains an implicit criticism, Kant offers a way out of this aporia, a way entailing the transformation of the concept of world, which no longer denotes the all-encompassing totality but merely a subjective principle for the organization of our experience, an *a priori* thought to which nothing can correspond. What Fink rejects under the label of "subjectivism" is the very principle of the "critical solution" Kant is advancing for dealing with the antinomies of pure reason. As he puts it in a text parallel to the one I have quoted earlier: "the exposition of the problem in Kant is more essential than his 'solution'" (Fink 2016, p. 47). Thus, the specific relevance of the Transcendental Dialectic can be brought to light only if we manage to detach the problem underlying these developments from the solution Kant gave it. On Fink's reading, Kant allows us to point out the paradoxes produced by the attempt to grasp the world with concepts stemming from our relation with innerworldly beings (in the section on the "Antinomies"), but also to unveil the mechanism elaborated by traditional metaphysics to conceal the whole under the figure of the supreme being (in the section on the "Transcendental Ideal"). And yet, after displaying this paradox and denouncing the mechanism producing it as a mere appearance, Kant goes on to assert that this appearance is necessary. Although it has no objective reality, it is still based on an irrepressible subjective penchant. Instead of following the opposite path, a path which requires us to determine the world as an existing paradox and to grasp the *omnitudo realitatis* without any reference to an *ens realissimum*, and thus to think the whole without realizing it in the figure of a supreme being, Kant accepts the necessity of such a transition and considers it to be embedded in the deep layers of subjectivity.

But is it possible to purge Kant's analysis of its "subjectivistic" outcome? Can we retain only the critical move through which it undermines the outlook prevailing within the established metaphysical tradition? If we concentrate merely on what is gained for reason in coming to understand the illusion entailed by this attempt, aren't we misconstruing the very core of Kant's strategy? As has certainly become apparent, Fink's reading of Kant is embedded in his wider project of exploring ways to think about the world which do not reduce it to an aggregate of beings or to a subjective horizon of meaning.[4] On the historical side, this project attempts to unfold a "reconstructive and apocryphal interpretation of cosmological moments in the history of metaphysics" (Franz 2010, p. 253), and thus to retrieve historical bearings for the position he is defending. Rather than questioning the Kantian accuracy of his analysis, in what follows I will seek to set down the theoretical underpinnings of his endeavor and to explore the strategy adopted by Fink in order to submit the Kantian arguments to a "coherent deformation" so that they could supply the necessary grounding for his "cosmological" undertaking. Fink's analysis is articulated around the following main theses: 1) In the first place, Fink aims at correcting a common misapprehension concerning the architecture of the first *Critique* and at showing that the Tran-

---

4 For a broader account of Fink's "cosmological philosophy," see Stanciu 2016.

scendental Dialectic represents the very heart of the Kantian project. This implies that the question of the world represents the driving impetus of this work. 2) Secondly, Fink formulates an argument regarding the proper outcome of the chapter on the "Antinomies:" we cannot legitimately infer from the failure of attempts to determine the world with "innerworldly models" that the world is merely a subjective idea. The proper result of the "Antinomy of the pure reason" is the excess of the world with regard to any innerworldly characterization. 3) Finally, Fink develops an argument concerning the construction of the "Transcendental Ideal:" the transition from the *omnitudo realitatis* to the *ens realissimum* is not necessary (neither objectively, nor subjectively). In this regard, the task Fink assumes can be understood as an attempt to think the *omnitudo realitatis* for itself, prior to and independent of any realization in a being – even if it were a supreme one.

1 The Double Orientation of the Transcendental Dialectic

The guiding conviction of Fink's interpretation of the *Critique of Pure Reason* is that Kant "represents a decisive high point in the concealed and subterranean history of the problem of the world" (Fink 2016, p. 192), which, in return, implies that the central question of Kant's critical project, the internal engine that set it in motion, is the question of the world (Fink 1990, p. 98). In what reads as a direct challenge to classical, as well as phenomenological, interpretations of Kant (including that of Heidegger),[5] Fink affirms that the focal point of the whole conceptual architecture of the first *Critique* lies in the "dramatic part of the work" (Fink 1990, p. 101), i.e. in the Transcendental Dialectic. Thus, this section should not be considered a critical appendix – added to the positive developments contained in the Aesthetic and the Analytic – aiming to display the speculative extravagances of dogmatic metaphysics and their necessary failure in successfully determining an object; nor should it be considered a necessary development whose goal is merely to curb the unbridled demands of knowledge in order to make room for faith. The Transcendental Dialectic is the theoretical site where the question of being as a whole reaches its definite formulation. Although Kant's exposition seems to follow the fault lines of *metaphysica specialis*, one should be able to recognize a unifying theme behind the threefold division into rational psychology, rational cosmology, and rational theology – that of

---

[5] For a nuanced discussion of the role Heidegger might have played in the emergence of this conception, see Lazarri 2010, p. 43.

the *Seiende im Ganzen* (Fink 1990, p. 104) for, as Kant himself admits, "the totality of conditions and the unconditioned [is] the common title of all concepts of reason" (Kant 1781/1787, A 324/B 380; Kant 1998, p. 400).[6]

According to this line of analysis, the distinction between the Aesthetic and the Analytic, on the one hand, and the Dialectic on the other, cannot be equated with the distinction between a "constructive" and a "destructive" inquiry. If this division indeed corresponds to the demarcation between the different powers of reason, Fink contends that these powers are not mere subjective faculties, but should rather be approached from the vantage point of their specific "theme," from what they give access to. Following this path will allow Fink to recast the difference between the Transcendental Analytic and the Transcendental Dialectic as the "difference between a critical ontology of the thing and a critical cosmology" (Fink 2011, p. 1270).[7]

Under the title "ontology of the thing," Fink aims to capture the core thrust of the metaphysical tradition, which not only takes its starting in the domain of the innerworldly being – cutting it off from its worldly background –, but also promotes the innerworldly being as the hallmark of being as such: "Metaphysics is the thinking which determines being in its beingness. Metaphysics focuses basically on the existing things, that is on the manifold, finite and limited beings or on things. [...] The metaphysical approach is inner-worldly" (Fink 2003, p. 166). Conceived according to this model, the world will appear as an overall entity or the sum total of existing entities. Through showing how this view necessarily engenders an inner conflict of reason, Kant dismantles the assumptions motivating it and, in the Transcendental Dialectic, already moves within the space of a "critical cosmology."

Thus, the line separating the "ontology of the thing" from the "critical cosmology" cuts across the *Critique of Pure Reason*. On this account, the success of Kant's project of emancipating himself from dogmatic metaphysics depends on his capacity to afford a real autonomy to reason, i.e. to conceive it in such a

---

[6] In one of the most challenging discussions of Fink's cosmology, Richir rejects Fink's assimilation of the Transcendental Dialectic to an exclusively "cosmological" inquiry and argues for the necessity of providing a distinct status to the question of the self and of God. Thus, on Richir's account, the inquiry Fink developed under the title *Welt und Endlichkeit* should be supplemented by further researches which could be placed under the headings: "*Selbstheit und Endlichkeit* and *Gott und Endlichkeit*" (Richir 1992, p. 114).

[7] *Cf.* also Fink 1990, p. 104. This idea is already sketched in the 1930s. *Cf.* E. Fink 2008, p. 308: "Fundamental thesis: Kant's distinction between the constitutive use of the categories and the regulative use of the Ideas is an index for a twofold phenomenological 'constitution:' object-consciousness and world-consciousness. [...] Stated differently, 'categories' are ontologic-transcendental determinations while 'Ideas' are cosmologic-transcendental determinations."

way that it not appear in a secondary position, as subjected to imperatives stemming from a different faculty, that of the understanding. Indeed, Kant forcefully stresses the autonomy of reason, showing in the "Appendix to the Transcendental Dialectic" that the transcendental ideas of reason are essential and even indispensable not only for morality, but also for the empirical investigations of nature. As M. Grier has underlined it, "with this claim, Kant moves from a 'negative' or critical project of 'limiting the pretensions to reason' to a 'positive' or 'constructive' effort to secure for reason some legitimate theoretical function" (Grier 2001, p. 3).

However, Kant remains committed to the view that the legitimacy of a rational operation is measured by the criteria of "objective validity:" the only legitimate activity of reason (in the extended sense that comprises all the faculties of the *Gemüt*) is to determine objects.[8] If, furthermore, the experience itself is reduced to the experience of objects, the prevenient whole, the backdrop against which things show themselves is expelled from the domain of what can be experienced and is converted into a subjective – yet necessary – illusion: "Kant's doctrine of the world is a doctrine about an illusion" (Fink 1990, p. 107), be it a necessary one. However, "it remains an open question [...] whether the nothing(like) [*un-dingliche*], the non-ontic being of the world can properly be captured with the term 'illusion'" (Fink 1990, p. 108).

Thus, the ontology of the thing remains the undisputed theoretical setting for Kant's enterprise and explains the subjectivistic drift of his conception. For, while Kant does acknowledge that

> the unconditional whole of all beings is not a thing, but as for him being-a-thing [*Dingsein*], being-a-substance [*Substanzsein*] constitutes the guiding model for everything that is, the whole can be nothing but a no-thing [*Un-ding*]. Kant cannot formulate in a positive manner, within the framework of its philosophy, the relation of human reason to a no-thing [*Un-ding*]. He can determine it only as a relation to something "i-real", something belonging to thought – that is, a relation having only a subjective reality, but devoid of any objective meaning". (Fink 1959, p. 113)

---

[8] From a different standpoint, yet moved by somewhat converging philosophical interests, A. Ferrarin formulates a similar description of Kant's double stance: "It is a pity that Kant did not consistently recognize and value the importance of ideas he introduced. If his concerns had been less biased (i.e. if he had not imposed the problems of the understanding's pure concepts from the Transcendental Analytic onto reason), he could have asserted more forcefully what he otherwise discovers and teaches: that is, ideas are not a failed correspondence with what can never be approximated by them, but the way reason guides, projects and produces itself. Ideas are thought's inner life and activity. They do not serve to ground an impossible possibility of objects. They are the unconditional and autonomous element in which reason produces its inner unity and pursues its ends" (Ferrarin 2015, p. 54).

Kant accepts, along with the tradition he is criticizing, that to be is to be an individual thing, to have a shape and a delimited outline, a place and duration: being belongs only to what is fragmented or splintered, and never to the whole. Or, if the totality is not a thing, if it is a no-thing (*Un-ding*), but it is still unavoidable, it has to be lodged within the depths of subjectivity as a regulative idea that we necessarily project. Surmounting this position is tantamount to overcoming the idea that the individuated thing provides the guiding thread and the theoretical model for all ontological inquiry. In effect, Fink refuses to endorse the very terms of Kant's alternative, according to which the totality has either the objective existence of a thing or the subjective existence of a regulative idea. It is precisely the attempt to brush aside this dichotomy that motivates his reading of the *Critique of Pure Reason*.

The double stance of the inquiry deployed in the Transcendental Dialectic is outlined in a passage that is worth quoting *in extenso:*

> The entire section in Kant's *Critique of Pure Reason* on the dialectic is an attempt to be finished with the *a priori* of the thought of the world, in which the exposition of the problem in Kant is more essential than his "solution." Ultimately, "world" becomes in Kant something subjective, a "regulative idea" that we cannot do without in order to guide the progress of experience, yet something that we can also never "redeem" and realize in actual experience. [...] Kant clearly recognizes [...] that the world is not a massive thing and not a massively powerful object – that the relation between the human subject and the world cannot be assessed as a relation between two beings. On the other hand, however, there is no possibility for him to conceptually determine a relation that is in play not between two innerworldly things, but rather between the innerworldly human who has an understanding of Being and the universal whole of Being. For this reason, Kant had to "subjectivize" the world, to make it into a structure of the subject that represents by means of ideas. Kant thereby closes again the problem that, in a magnificent way, he himself wrenched open. (Fink 2016, p. 48)

When placed against the broader canvas of the history of metaphysics, the Transcendental Dialectic appears to be situated at a critical juncture: repudiating a set of long-standing and still prevailing assumptions about the nature of the world, showing that its analysis in terms of an objective *series* or *nexus* necessarily fails and that the traditional problems of rational cosmology are devoid of any firm ground, Kant engages himself on a path yet untrodden by anyone. However, while registering his dissidence from the dominant metaphysical outlook, while holding firmly to the view that the world is not an object of any sort, Kant does not possess the conceptual devices necessary in order to articulate *in a positive way* the new conception which has surfaced in his analysis. Because of his implicit allegiance to the traditional equation according to which "to be" is "to be a thing," "to be an innerworldly entity," Kant must conclude that the world is marked by an "ontological deficit" (Foessel 2008, p. 60). Within such a context, the only remaining solution consists in setting forth a subjectivistic model. The consequences of the adoption of such a position are visible not only in the analysis dedicated to the "absolute whole of appearances" but also in the developments concerning the "absolute whole" the Ideal of reason represents.

2 The Explosive Thought

According to the standard reading, in the second chapter of the second book of the Transcendental Dialectic, Kant shows the contradictions that emerge when reason tries to determine the world as existing in itself. When reason falls prey to the tendency of anchoring its own requirements into the world or, more precisely, when "the subjective necessity of a certain connection of our concepts on behalf of the understanding is taken for an objective necessity, the determination of things in themselves," it raises an internal logical conflict, the result being the fact that reason annihilates or neutralizes its own cosmological productions. The solution to such a predicament consists in admitting that the world, i.e. "the absolute whole of appearances is only an idea" (Kant 1781/1787, A 328/B 384; Kant 1998, p. 402), that is, a concept to which no correspondent object can be given.

As we have already seen, Fink drives a wedge between Kant's exposition of the antinomies and the solution he offers to them. But if these two parts of his argument are not inextricably bound, one could endorse the exposition of the antinomies and still draw from it a conclusion different from the one Kant advanced. Following this train of thought, Fink argues that the positive result of the chapter devoted to the "Antinomies of pure reason" may be stated as follows:

> The world is not a thing; the whole of beings is not itself an entity [*Seiendes*]. The world cannot be grasped if we guide ourselves after the model of substance. [...] Every attempt to think the world by means of thingly representations is not just insufficient, but unavoidably lead to self-contradiction in thought. [...] The world becomes a paradox *when* the innerworldly being is set up as the measure of the world. (Fink 1990, p. 141)

In order to unfold the implications of this outcome, Fink adopts a twofold strategy. In the first place, he lays an even greater emphasis on the paradoxical, perplexing status of the world, showing how it represents an "explosive thought" (Fink 2011, p. 1679), which unsettles our rational expectations. When faced with the question of the world, reason appears to be torn asunder by opposing tendencies. Indeed, it is not surprising that the attempt to determine the "absolute whole of appearances" with concepts appropriate for grasping the innerworldy beings engenders abundant contradictions. However, this inner conflict should not be deplored, for it is a positive sign. It would be all the more problematic if the application of such concepts to the world would not produce contradictions, for in this case the world would be leveled to the status of a thing, and world and things would appear as being cut from the same cloth. Far from casting aside any attempt to conceive the world, the "Antinomies" allow us precisely to preserve its distinctiveness and thus to maintain the difference separating it from the innerworldly beings. Thus, Fink can claim that "Kant accomplishes, in a negative manner, the 'cosmological difference'; he conceives the essential difference separating the innerworldly being from the totality of the world" (Fink 1990, p. 141).[9] Or, with the sharp formulation of a manuscript from the 1930's which already discusses the chapter on the Antinomies, we may say that Kant uncovers the "a-ontic nature of the world" (*der a-ontischen Natur der Welt*) (Fink 2008, p. 227).

However, Kant does not acknowledge that the excess pertaining to the innerworldly is a positive feature of the world and interprets it in a subjectivistic framework: "Kant immediately obstructs the working out of the question of the world, inasmuch as he relocates the whole within the thought of whole, within an idea of reason and grants it only the 'reality' of a representation, which is admittedly necessary, but fundamentally 'void'" (Fink 1959, p. 99). The world as a totality preceding and exceeding all things is casted away in favor of a motivation of reason (*Vernunftmotivation*), which consists in constantly inquiring further back for the cause of a phenomenon (*cf.* Fink 2011, p. 2018). Fink can very well endorse the thesis according to which the world can be thought only by means of Ideas – that is, concepts that can never receive a proper intuitive confirmation. However, from the impossibility of any intuitive confirmation, Kant infers that the only reality the world possesses is that of the *ideatum* of an Idea. Indeed, the cosmological inquiry "concerns an object that can be given nowhere but in our thoughts, namely the absolutely unconditioned totality of the synthesis of appearances" (Kant 1781/1787, A 481/B 509; Kant 1998, p. 506). This inference rests on the implicit assumption which plays such a pivotal part in Kant's philosophy: in order for something to exist, it must align itself with the model of the thing, to subject itself to the structure of thinghood: "What is neither a thing nor a configuration of things, simply does not exist, is possesses no reality. If the whole is not a thing, it cannot exist as a whole; it must have its

---

[9] For a clear exposition of Fink's understanding of the "cosmological difference," see Nielsen/Sepp 2010.

'original place' in human reason, that is in a being capable of representing and become thus what is thought within thinking" (Fink 1959, p. 99).[10] The train of thought leading Kant to lodge the totality within the depths of reason appears to be motivated not so much by a subjectivistic penchant, inherent to his enterprise, but rather by his adherence to this ontological thesis. This subjectivism appears as the only solution for the aporias of totality only because the ontology of the thing possesses a hegemonic character within Kant's enterprise.

The second theoretical strategy adopted by Fink for handling this crucial theme consists in underlying the fact that the outcome of the "Antinomies" is paradoxical precisely because the all-encompassing whole is considered from the standpoint of the innerworldly beings. This perspective is anchored in a minute analysis of Kant's argumentative path. Fink remarks that the proper result of the first antinomy is that the world cannot be conceived – in space and time – either as finite, or as infinite. Strictly speaking, the apagogic reasoning followed by Kant proves only the non-finitude and the non-infinity of the world (Fink 1990, p. 118). The contradiction between the two theses results only if we accept that they exhaust the space of theoretical possibilities, that besides them no alternative is conceivable, that the *tertium non datur* cannot be applied in this case. However, if this assumption is removed – that is, if we show that the world cannot be subjected to the alternative of finitude and infinity, or to that of the beginning in time and of eternity –, the paradox is dissolved. It is on this theoretical path that Fink engages himself in a series of remarks added to his reconstruction of Kant's arguments. He insists that a different outlook is possible, one that would approach "innerworldy beings from the openness of the world" (Fink 1990, p. 124). Thus, for instance, inasmuch as it gives space and grants time to everything that appears, the world cannot be subjected to the principle of identity, for it is the "one space-time of *being* and at the same time the multiplicity of *beings*" (Fink 1990, p. 114). Furthermore, asking about the place the world occupies in space or its duration in time might be misleading, if we admit on the contrary that the world is "the original time [*ursprüngliche Zeit*]" and "the original space [*ursprüngliche Raum*]" (Fink 1990, p. 114). On this ground, Fink develops a conception of the world as a dynamic whole, as a "process of individuation" which gives space and grants time to everything that comes to appearance and "stamps every individuated thing into the finite contours of

---

[10] For a converging diagnosis, *cf.* Foessel 2008, p. 60: "Kant's effort to display the illusions of rational cosmology appears to be dependent on the choice of objectivity as a guiding thread: he thus confers to the world the attributes of what exceeds the power of the understanding, without acknowledging to it any authentic phenomenality."

its appearance, allocates its form, place and duration, and brings it into and removes it from presence" (Fink 2016, p. 57).

3 *Omnitudo Realitatis* Without *Ens Realissimum*

According to a long exegetical tradition, the main theoretical achievement of the section devoted to the analysis of the "Transcendental Ideal" consists in the refutation of the claims formulated by rational theology to provide a deduction of the existence of God out of pure concepts: the sublime object of rational theology is thus reduced to a mere chimera begotten by a reason insufficiently aware of its own limits. By contrast, Fink places the center of gravity of these developments at a different level: not so much in setting limits to the theological claims of reason, but rather in exposing the onto-theological structure underpinning them. The point is not so much whether the necessary existence of the *ens realissimum* can be deduced, whether we can infer its existence (or actuality) simply from its concept, but rather whether the realization of the totality in a supreme being is a compelling theoretical move. As Fink writes,

> in a deeper sense [...] Kant challenges the conception that the totality in an absolute sense (i.e. the totality of things in themselves) can in general be thought in the figure [*Bild*] of a supreme being. This is, on my account, the most important theme. Must the idea of totality merge into one thing, be it the mightiest, the most powerful, the most persistent? In doing so, aren't we attributing and annexing to a being, to an *ens*, to a substance, determinations that originally belong to the totality? (Fink 1959, pp. 100–101)

More decisive than the critique of the ontological, cosmological, and physico-theological proofs is the disclosure of the *modus procedendi* of traditional metaphysics, of the path it follows in order to forge the concept of a supreme being. Thus, the question Fink addresses is logically prior to the problem of the proofs of God's existence. Before inquiring into the pertinence of such proofs one should first examine what is entailed in the concept of God that they make use of: namely, the adoption of a specific stance with regard to the world, which Fink labels as the "reification [*Verdinglichung*] of the totality": "the significance of the Ideal of pure reason within the history of traditional metaphysics can be characterized as the speculative reification of the totality, as the theologization of the world" (Fink 1959, p. 118). The analysis carried out by Kant allows us to grasp how the Ideal of pure reason derives precisely from the "theologization" of the world, from the "reification" of the totality. In the pages where he renders the *modus procedendi* of traditional metaphysics, Kant exposes the transition it operates between the *omnitudo realitatis* (i.e. "the idea of an All of reality," Kant 1781/1787, A 575–576/B 603–604; Kant 1998, p. 555) and the *ens realissimum*, through a successive realization, hypostatization, and personification (Kant 1781/1787, A 582/B 610; Kant 1998, p. 559).

Fink insists that the concept of *omnitudo realitatis* unfolded by Kant in his discussion of the transcendental Ideal rigorously corresponds to the world, inasmuch as it encompasses not only the phenomena (as was the case for the concept of world developed in the section on the "Antinomies"), but also the things in themselves: "the *omnitudo realitatis* refers to the world in a more essential sense than the idea of the totality of phenomena, for which Kant reserves the concept of world. Isn't the world an absolute *Totum*, within which emerge not only the appearances of things but also their in-itself?" (Fink 1959, p. 107). But if the *omnitudo realitatis* captures the true meaning of the world, the Kantian attempt to uncover the roots of rational theology is tantamount to showing that the idea of a supreme being is dependent upon the idea of totality, that rational theology is tributary to an *Allheitslehre*.

This cardinal fact was overlooked by the metaphysical tradition, which not only blurred the distinction between the rational theology and the *Allheitslehre*, but also attributed to the metaphysical God characteristics proper to the totality as such: omnipresence (*All-Gegenwart*), omnipotence (*All-Macht*), omniscience (*All-Wissenheit*). In this way, "something intraworldly, even if it is of the highest order, is placed in front of the prevailing totality and conceals it […]. In the history of European philosophy this has had almost incalculable, fateful consequences and has decisively determined the onto-theological style of metaphysics" (Fink 2016, p. 196). Having brought to light the secret mechanism responsible for this distortion, Kant has set the stage for the emancipation of the cosmological inquiry from a theological tutelage.

Indeed, if we admit that the totality is the initial logical moment of any attempt at conceiving of the supreme being, it follows that, at least in principle, we could grasp it before being captured within a theological framework, before its "theological distortion" for "the God of metaphysics disguises the world" (Fink 2016, p. 64). According to Fink, it is of the highest importance that Kant considers the possibility of "liberating the concept of *omnitudo realitatis* from its reinterpretation [*Umdeutung*] as the metaphysical God" (Fink 1959, p. 119). In this way, the prevenient whole is detached from any form of realization (be it under the figure of a supreme being): its independence from the domain of the *res* is thus acknowledged. However, precisely when he discloses the possibility of grasping the totality without any ontical mask, Kant retreats from the path he has just carved.

Kant affords no ground for an autonomous doctrine of the *omnitudo realitatis*. This refusal has a double motivation: the determination of the illusion as necessary and the characterization of thinking as figurative. Kant holds that the illusion responsible for interpreting the *omnitudo realitatis*, the whole of reality, as an *ens realissimum*, as a supremely perfect being, is necessary. Fink forcefully rejects this thesis: "the human reason must think the *omnitudo realitatis* – but must it be thought by means of the fundamental concepts of speculative theology, must it necessarily be thought as *ens realissimum*, *ens summum*, *ens originarium* and *ens entium*?" (Fink 1959, p. 120). It might well be that this transition belongs only to historical metaphysics and is not an illusion grounded in the very nature of human reason: "is the interpretation of totality under the figure of a supreme being ultimately inevitable? Does this interpretation essentially belong to human reason or does it rather pertain to the historical form of Western metaphysics?" (Fink 1959, p. 114).

What are the reasons provided by Kant in support of the necessary character of this appearance? In the first place, this thesis makes it clear that metaphysics is not an arbitrary production of reason we can simply dismiss. Metaphysical doctrines have their origin not in some fallacious inferences but rather in a deep-seated and "unavoidable illusion" (Kant 1781/1787, A 422/B 450; Kant 1998, p. 467), one that, as Kant insists, is grounded in the nature of human reason. Thus, even when considered in its traditional form, metaphysics still possesses a certain legitimacy, that of a necessary errancy. But, more profoundly, insistence on the necessary character of the transcendental appearance allows Kant to maintain that thinking amounts to determining objects. For if appearance were only hypothetically necessary – that is, necessary only inasmuch as we take the ontology of the thing to be the ultimate horizon of any philosophical inquiry – and not absolutely necessary, the requirement of formulating a doctrine capable of grasping the whole before its capture by a supreme being would become unavoidable. That which does not possess a form and an outline seems to evade thinking. Speculative theology and its Kantian critique rest on the same ground and are dependent on the same type of concealment: the concealment of the totality by the God of metaphysics: "*Pan* becomes *theos:* the Kantian criticism of theology is enacted once this turn [*Umschlage*] has been accomplished and does not address the possibility of its overturn" (Fink 1959, p. 120). The rejection of this "theologically stamped ontology" (Fink 2016, p. 137) which conceives of the world as a "thinglike unity, as a system and as an architecture of lesser and greater ontologically powerful things, as a hierarchy that culminates in a highest being and descends in stages" (Fink 2016, p. 136) is possible only if we manage to call into question the ontological commitment on which it is built: the "theologization" of the world presupposes its prior "reification."

Conclusion

In the interpretation he offers to some key moments of the Transcendental Dialectic, Fink does not seek to provide an exegetically sound reconstruction of Kant's developments, but rather to seize the motive around which they revolve and to bring it to a full expression (even if this means going beyond Kant). On his account, the *Critique of Pure Reason* is a seminal work, for Kant offers compelling arguments to reject both a cumulative concept of the world (whereby "world" is equaled to be the sum of all things) and a "theologically stamped ontology." However, carrying further the fundamental thrust of Kantian philosophy means also displaying the one-sidedness of his analyses, the "operative presuppositions [*operative Voraussetzungen*]" (Fink 1990, p. 124) upon which he heavily relies. The identification of "being" with the "individuated being," with the "thing," precludes any inquiry into the world as such, which is reduced to the status of a necessary illusion. While Fink's reading of the Transcendental Dialectic is meant first and foremost to serve as a launching pad for an original philosophical project – a project aiming to resurrect the old designation and understanding of philosophy as *Weltweisheit*, world-wisdom –, it is undoubtful that such an undertaking allows for a more insightful grasp into the problematic context of Kantian philosophy and imparts a new depth to the *Critique of Pure Reason*.

Bibliography

Fink, Eugen (1959): *Alles und Nichts. Ein Umweg zur Philosophie*. The Hague: Martinus Nijhoff.
Fink, Eugen (1960): *Nietzsches Philosophie*. Stuttgart: Kohlhammer.
Fink, Eugen (1960): *Spiel als Weltsymbol*. Stuttgart: Kohlhammer.
Fink, Eugen (1985): *Einleitung in die Philosophie*. Würzburg: Königshausen und Neumann.
Fink, Eugen (1988a): *VI. Cartesianische Meditation*, Teil I: *Die Idee einer transzendentalen Methodenlehre, Husserliana Dokumente*, vol. II/1. Ed. Hans Ebeling, Jann Holl and Guy van Kerchoven. Dordrecht: Kluwer Academic Publishers.
Fink, Eugen (1988b): *VI. Cartesianische Meditation*, Teil II: *Ergänzungsband, Husserliana Dokumente*, vol. II/2. Ed. Guy van Kerchoven. Dordrecht: Kluwer Academic Publishers.
Fink, Eugen (1990): *Welt und Endlichkeit*. Würzburg: Königshausen und Neumann.
Fink, Eugen (1995): *Sixth Cartesian Meditation. The Idea of a Transcendental Theory of Method*. Trans. Ronald Bruzina. Bloomington/Indianapolis: Indiana University Press.
Fink, Eugen (2003): *Nietzsche's Philosophy*. Trans. Goetz Richter. London/New York: Continuum.

Fink, Eugen (2008): *Phänomenologische Werkstatt, Teilband 2: Die Bernauer Zeitmanuskripte, Cartesianische Meditationen und System der phänomenologischen Philosophie*, Gesamtausgabe, vol. 3.2. Ed. R. Bruzina. Freiburg/München: Karl Alber.

Fink, Eugen (2011): *Epilegomena zu Immanuel Kants Kritik der reinen Vernunft*, Gesamtausgabe, vol. 13/3. Ed. Guy van Kerckhoven. Freiburg/München: Karl Alber.

Fink, Eugen (2016): *Play as Symbol of the World*. Trans. Ian Alexander Moore and Christopher Turner. Bloomington/Indianapolis: Indiana University Press.

Heidegger, Martin, Fink, Eugen (1970): *Heraklit. Seminar Wintersemester 1966–67*. Frankfurt/Main: Vittorio Klostermann.

Heidegger, Martin, Fink, Eugen (1979): *Heraclitus Seminar. 1966–1967*. Trans. Charles H. Seibert. Tuscaloosa: University of Alabama Press.

Kant, Immanuel (1998): *Kritik der reinen Vernunft*. Hamburg: Felix Meiner.

Kant, Immanuel (1998): *The Critique of Pure Reason*. Trans. Paul Guyer and Allen W. Wood. Cambridge: Cambridge University Press.

Franz, Thomas (2010): "Weltspiel und Spielwelt. Eugen Finks symbolische Kosmologie". In: *Welt denken. Annäherungen an die Kosmologie Eugen Finks*. Eds. H.-R. Sepp and C. Nielsen. Freiburg/München: Karl Alber, pp. 250–266.

Ferrarin, Alfredo (2015): *The Powers of Pure Reason. Kant and the Idea of Cosmic Philosophy*. Chicago: The University of Chicago Press.

Foessel, Michael (2008): *Kant et l'équivoque du monde*. Paris: CNRS Editions.

Grier, Michelle (2001): *Kant's Doctrine of Transcendantal Illusion*. Cambridge: Cambridge University Press.

Lazzari, Roberto (2010): "Weltfrage und kosmologische Interpretation von Kants *Kritik der reinen Vernunft* bei Eugen Fink". In: *Welt denken. Annäherungen an die Kosmologie Eugen Finks*. Eds. H.-R. Sepp and C. Nielsen. Freiburg/München: Karl Alber, pp. 38–56.

Richir, Marc (1992): "Mondes et phénomènes". In: *Les Cahiers de Philosophie*, n° 15/16, pp. 71–88.

Sepp, Hans-Reiner, Nielsen, Cathrin (2010): "Welt bei Fink". In: *Welt denken. Annäherungen an die Kosmologie Eugen Finks*. Eds. H.-R. Sepp and C. Nielsen. Freiburg/München: Karl Alber, pp. 9–24.

Stanciu, Ovidiu (2016): "Vers une pensée du monde lui-même. Eugen Fink et les perspectives d'une philosophie cosmologique". In: *Revue philosophique de Louvain*, vol. 114, n° 4, pp. 655–682.

Yusuke Ikeda
Eugen Fink's Transcendental Phenomenology of the World

Its Proximity and Distance in Relation to Kant and the Late Husserl[1]

> "I do not think the cosmological from out of Heraclitus, but rather from out of Kant and from the antinomy of pure reason."
> Eugen Fink (Heidegger/Fink 1970, p. 178, English translation p. 110)

> "Why is there something rather than nothing?"
> Gottfried Wilhelm Leibniz

> "When we are awake, we have a common world, but when we dream, everybody has his own."
> Immanuel Kant (Kant 1905a, p. 342)

Abstract: This chapter aims to define Eugen Fink's early philosophy as a "transcendental phenomenology of the world" through illustrating Fink's philosophical relation to Kant and to the late Husserl. However, some scholars claim that Fink's philosophy is neither transcendental nor phenomenological in any sense, because his conceptions are generated from Hegelian speculative dialectic. In contrast to those views in secondary literature, this study demonstrates, on the one hand, the decisive meaning of Kant's transcendental dialectic, especially the "cosmological antinomy," for the formation of Fink's philosophy as a whole and, on the other hand, how Fink elucidates phenomenologically the problem of the pregivenness of the world by radicalizing the late Husserl's program.

Introduction

This study aims to reconstruct systematically Eugen Fink's early philosophy and to define it as a *transcendental phenomenology of the world* by shedding light, on the one hand, on his "cosmological" Kant-interpretation and, on the other, by articulating the "proximity and distance"[2] between Fink's program and that

---

[1] This study was supported by *Grants-in-Aid for Scientific Research <KAKENHI>* of the *Japan Society for the Promotion of Science* (16 J04511).
[2] The expression "proximity and distance [*Nähe und Distanz*]" is the title which Fink himself had chosen for an anthology of his phenomenological studies (see Fink 1976, pp. 323–324).

of the late Husserl. However, initially, this approach might appear incompatible with some secondary literature on Fink, such as Steven Crowell's study on Fink's *Sixth Cartesian Meditation*, according to which his philosophy could not be characterized as being transcendental-phenomenological. Two interpretative theses have been developed to support that view: (1) Fink's philosophy is not in line with a tradition of *transcendental philosophy* which was inaugurated by Kant and was transformed in Husserl's phenomenology, because its background is in Hegelian "*dialectic*"; and (2) Fink cannot be a phenomenologist insofar as his philosophical method is *not* "*descriptive*" but "*speculative*" (see Crowell 2001, cap. 13; and Moran 2007). I here consider the extent to which these hypotheses are tenable.

I do not wish, however, to concentrate on the *Sixth Cartesian Meditation* exclusively but rather to reconstruct Fink's philosophical program in the 1930s overall. This I will do by examining his other writings and some important related manuscripts in greater detail, because of the very complicated background and peculiar character of the *Sixth Cartesian Meditation*. Indeed, this work was prepared for publication as part of an intended German publication of Husserl's *Cartesian Meditations* (*cf.* Bruzina 1995), so I do not directly engage here with the complex historical question concerning the extent to which the essential claims of that work agree with Fink's thought.

First, I begin by approaching Fink's reading of Kant, which is especially dedicated to the *transcendental dialectic of pure reason*, particularly to the *cosmological antinomies* that famously treat the metaphysical problematics of the world in its totality. In doing so, it becomes apparent that Fink's metaphysical claim (concerning what he calls the "*metaphysics of Being* [Seinsmetaphysik]" or the "*problem of modalities* [Modalitätenproblem]") is generated from and an elaboration upon his interpretation of Kantian "dialectic," and that interpretation is seemingly incompatible with the Hegelian conception of it in many respects.[3] In other words, the key question posed for the first section is the following: Fink's dialectic – *Kant or Hegel*? My answer is *Kant*.

Second, I show how Fink developed the transcendental-phenomenological problem of the "pregiven world" ("pregivenness of the world"), with which the late Husserl was also struggling, that is, the question of how the world, in which we are always living, is pregiven to us. In this context, we can see clearly that the very "distance" between the two philosophers does not consist in the

---

[3] For instance, I insist, as just one of the crucial differences between Kantian and Hegelian dialectics, that Kant accentuates the *finitude of human reason* in his "transcendental dialectic," while Hegel's "speculative dialectic" is nothing other than the "*exposition of God as he is in his eternal essence before the creation of nature and of a finite spirit*" (Hegel 2010, p. 29).

point as to whether the nature of their respective methods is descriptive ("*evidenz-theoretisch*") or speculative ("*prinzipien-theoretisch*"), but rather in the differing ways in which the problem of "*enworlding* [Verweltlichung]" is elucidated by each. To support this contention, I illustrate Fink's "*phenomenology of mundanization* [Phänomenologie der Mundanisierung]" (Fink 1966, p. 9) or "*enworlding*" *in its descriptive dimension*. In contrast to the secondary literature, I contend that *Fink is a transcendental phenomenologist*, who tries to develop the Husserlian heritage in his manner.

In my conclusion, I briefly examine Fink's relation to Heidegger, insofar as their "proximity and distance" also further constitute formative background for Fink's thought.

1 Fink's "Proximity and Distance" to Kant: Fink's "Cosmological" Kant-Reading and its Meaning for his "Speculation"

Fink's Kant-interpretation could be characterized as "cosmological" because he always stresses that the key meaning of the *Critique of Pure Reason* consists in its "cosmological antinomies," that is, in Kant's discovery and antithetic formulation of the problem of the *world*. However, Fink did not hold the somewhat negative view of this work's achievement, according to which the most significant contribution of the first *Critique* culminated simply in its criticism and rejection of so-called "dogmatic metaphysics," particularly the "*cosmologia rationalis*" that involved trying to construct the world *in its full reality* from some purely speculative-logical and non-empirical principles, with Kant demonstrating that such a metaphysical adventure could never perform its task because of the *antithetic nature* of pure reason or the *finitude* of human cognition. Fink saw rather, in this "negative" achievement of Kant's "antinomies," a very "positive significance" (Fink 2008, p. 95, Z-IX, 14a), because, in providing these, Kant offers a clue to a philosophical analysis of a basic dimension on which a new kind of metaphysics must be founded: "Kant is the metaphysician who disclosed the cosmological horizon of Being" which is of decisive meaning for a formation of what Fink calls the "metaphysics of Being" (OH-III 2–4, quoted in: Bruzina 2006, p. 205). It is this "metaphysics of Being" that Fink will explore. In sum, he highly esteems Kant's "critical" or "transcendental philosophy," especially the "transcendental dialectic" of the *Critique of Pure Reason*, but also wants to reinforce a new kind of metaphysics by taking a clue from Kantian metaphysical achievement; indeed, Fink's development here seems to be "Hegelian" in a global sense, because he finds his starting point in Kant to go beyond him, exactly as Hegel did. Since the purpose of this section is to clarify whether Fink's metaphysical background owes more to Hegel or Kant, I illustrate below (1.1) Fink's cosmological Kant-interpretation as such, and I then show (1.2) how Fink develops, based on his Kantian heritage, his conception of the "metaphysics of Being."

1.1 Fink's "Proximity" to Kant: His Cosmological Kant-reading

I begin by examining a brief manuscript written in 1935 in which it is possible to trace the essential claims of Fink's cosmological Kant-reading clearly:

> Isn't it Kant's metaphysical discovery that 'being' in general is the *appearance* [*Erscheinung* in the Kantian sense], i.e., *intramundane?*
> Therefore, Kant is the metaphysician who uncovered the *cosmological horizon of Being* and, in doing so, he lifted metaphysics out of its previous focus on *problematics of a priori* (*cf.* the dispute between rationalism and empiricism, which had pervaded European metaphysics!) and *expressis verbis* located metaphysics within the global problematics of 'Being.' The pre-Kantian metaphysics = metaphysics of ideas, Kant = metaphysics of Being. Indeed, [it is] a rapture of *ontology* into a *problem of cosmology*. (OH-III 2–4, quoted in: Bruzina 2006, p. 205)

For Fink, Kant is principally a "metaphysician," because he disclosed the "cosmological horizon of Being," i.e., the apprehension of the *intramundaneity* of beings, or the ontological insight into the difference between the world as such and beings in their respective relation to the former. This result is nothing other than what Fink eventually calls in his later work the *"cosmological difference"* (Fink 1990, p. 19). Indeed, Kant argues that the world is the "absolute totality of existing things" (Kant 1781/1787, A 419/B 447; Kant 1998, p. 523) and can be *ontologically* characterized *neither* as a "thing in itself" *nor* as an "object of experience" ("appearance"): the world is rather, according to his doctrine, a *"transcendental idea"* which is a specific kind of "nothingness," i.e. an *"ens rationis"* (an "empty concept without object") (Kant 1781/1787, A 292/B 348; Kant 1998, p. 404; *cf.* Fink 1959, pp. 85–96). He claims then that the world can only be considered as a *"focus imaginarius"* (Kant 1781/1787, A 644/B 672; Kant 1998, p. 710) or as a *"heuristic fiction"* of pure reason (Kant 1781/1787, A 771/B 799; Kant 1998, p. 811), i.e. as a necessary but merely subjective and fictional idea of human reason. This is Kant's presupposition, namely, that what cannot be a "thing in itself" (or what cannot ever be "objective") must logically be "nothingness" and he interprets this outcome as a kind of subjective "fiction" (I examine this thematically later). For example, Kant demonstrates, in the famous *first antinomy*, that the world as the totality of existing things cannot be *either* finite *or* infinite, because what can be finite or infinite is not "nothingness" but an object of experience, i.e. "appearance" (see Kant 1781/1787, A 501/B 529; Kant 1998, p. 596; and Fink 1990, p. 139). Furthermore, he characterizes the world as such as a heuristic-fictive idea, whose function cannot be "constitutive" but only "regulative" for "appearances." The "cosmological idea," that is, the "absolute totality in the synthesis of appearances" (Kant 1781/1787, A 407/B 434; Kant 1998, p. 514), has a regulative function for appearances, because, in short, an appearance must be regulatively concordant with other appearances in their totality: a being can manifest *as* being meaningful if it is related to such a regulative idea of the world. Therefore, Fink claims that "Kant's metaphysical discovery" is that a "being" ("appearance") is necessarily "intramundane." Fink then denotes this metaphysical insight as the "cosmological difference" whose philosophical elucidation constitutes his "metaphysics of Being."

Since what Kant calls *cosmologia rationalis* did not mark such a difference, Fink is right to label that presupposition as an *ontological (cosmological) "indifference"* between the world and entities within-the-world (Fink 1990, p. 185). Fink characterizes the essence of such an "indifference" as the "*oblivion of the world* [Weltvergessenheit]" (see Fink 1990, pp. 16–24; and Fink 1957, pp. 40–52),[4] which had determined not only "pre-Kantian metaphysics" but also traditional "European metaphysics" in general, i.e., what he calls "metaphysics of ideas," as noted. Immersed in this "oblivion," the *cosmologia rationalis* took it for granted that the concept of the world constituted the primal principle from which one could rationally construct every entity in its respective reality. This type of *speculative a priori construction* of the world is a key characteristic of "pre-Kantian metaphysics," i.e., the "metaphysics of ideas" whose concern is nothing other than the "problematics of *a priori*." In contrast to this, Kant argues, as already mentioned, that an entity can be determined in its reality if and only if that being is an "appearance," namely, an intramundane being. In this way, Kant reveals and demonstrates the necessary metaphysical fallacy of the "metaphysics of ideas," whose representative theoretical approach was *cosmologia rationalis*. Since *cosmologia rationalis* was operating with a cosmologically indifferent conception that is a specific form of the "oblivion of the world," it was marked by a philosophical fallacy which Kant labeled

---

[4] Obviously, this "oblivion of the world" is proclaimed in consideration of and opposition to Heideggerian "oblivion of Being [*Seinsvergessenheit*]." I briefly explain the key "distance" between the two philosophers in my concluding remarks.

terminologically the "transcendental illusion." Therefore, Kant's insight into the "transcendental illusion," as expounded through the antinomies, clearly presupposes apprehension of the ontological difference between the world and the things within it ("appearance") – the "cosmological difference." Consequently, Fink concludes that the essential topic of Kant's transcendental dialectic, even his "critical philosophy" overall, is nothing other than a matter of "cosmology."[5]

Therefore, Fink interprets this insight into "cosmological difference" as the original motive which led Kant to the formation of his "transcendental philosophy," described in the celebrated slogan as a "*Copernican revolution.*" In *Welt und Endlichkeit,* Fink sets out to prove this interpretative thesis not through examining the *Critique of Pure Reason* exclusively, but also one of its antecedents intensively, the *De mundi sensibilis atque intelligibilis forma et principiis* (Fink 1990, pp. 43–87). In his *Inaugural Dissertation,* Kant designated the problematic of the world as "the crucial test of the philosopher," as far as "it is scarcely conceivable how the *inexhaustible series* of the states of the universe succeeding one another *eternally* [i.e. the world as such in its full reality] be reducible to a *whole* comprehending all changes whatsoever [i.e. the world qua object of cognition]" (Kant 1958, p. 14; Kant 1894, p. 49). For it is only possible thereby to get the "*whole of representations* [totum repraesentationis]," not the "*representation of the whole* [repraesentatio totius]" (Kant 1958, p. 10; Kant 1894, p. 47). No one can comprehend the world as such in its full reality, even if, according to Kant, the problem of the world constitutes a central topic of *metaphysica naturalis* over which argument inevitably arises (*cf.* Kant 1787, B 21–22; Kant 1998, pp. 75–77). This is why the metaphysical problem of the world must necessarily arise as a "crucial test of the philosopher." It is commonly understood that Kant's solution to this difficulty consists mainly in adopting the two following conceptions: (a) distinguishing the "sensible" and the "intelligible world" and (b) interpreting space and time not as objective but as *subjective forms of intuition,* which he calls, in various contexts, "pure intuition [*intuitus purus*]" (Kant 1958, p. 32; Kant 1894, p. 57) or an "imaginary thing [*ens imaginarium*]" (Kant 1958, p. 46; Kant 1894, p. 62). Since the original motivation for the so-called "Copernican revolution" must be found in the "crucial test of the philosopher," Fink can argue plausibly that "he [Kant] interprets the essence of the subject, subjectivity, with *world-characters* [Welt-Charakteren]" (Fink 1990, p. 72). Fink therefore understands Kant's famous "Copernican revolution" primarily within the perspective

---

[5] Kant himself stresses that the very motive or starting point of his *first Critique* consisted exactly in the problematics of the cosmological antinomy. For instance, see his famous letter to Garve (Kant 1922, pp. 257–258).

of "cosmological" problematics and interprets it as a revolutionary turn from the cosmological "indifference" ("oblivion of the world") of the "metaphysics of ideas" to the "cosmological difference" of "metaphysics of Being" (see Fink 1990, pp. 95–97). Since, as is examined here, this cosmological turn is based on Kant's core claim concerning the *finitude* of human reason, Fink also takes this claim seriously and criticizes Hegel explicitly for "*going beyond*" this Kantian insight and, therefore, having "*lost* the problem of *the world*" (Fink 1990, p. 134). In the context of the problem of the world, and eventually of the finitude of human reason, Fink is not a Hegelian, but remains loyal to Kant's key insight.

1.2 Fink's "Distance" from Kant: The "Cosmological Horizon of Being"

Even if Kant disclosed a basic dimension for a new kind of metaphysics, Fink believes that he did not sufficiently develop this program. He especially considers the Kantian "subjectivist" solution of the "crucial text of the philosopher" to be problematic. Fink argues that, unlike Kant, the world is not a merely subjective and heuristic fiction whose function must be restricted to regulative use, but is rather, as I show below, *an "actually" existing horizon whose normative rule every (real) being must obligatorily follow,*[6] that is, a horizon which he calls the "cosmological horizon of Being," or, more precisely, the "*alternation-horizon of being and illusion* [Alternationshorizont von Sein und Schein]" (Fink 1988b, p. 91). Fink understands by the latter a horizon in which, and in which only, being can manifest itself *as* being *in its respective modality* (*either* "being" *or* "illusion"). Each being *must* manifest in its respective modality, as far as it simply *is*; if an entity is *neither* "being" nor "non-being," this could be called only *chaos*. Being is necessarily amenable to this "alternation-horizon," whose rule is that a being in question must *either* be *or* not be. As demonstrated below, the *origin of the "either-or" norm is for phenomenology nothing other than the world in its "actuality* [Wirklichkeit]." Fink develops this "metaphysics of Being" not as a simple continuation of a "critique" of human cognition but as a philosophical elucidation of the "cosmological horizon of Being" in itself, without endorsing subjec-

---

6 As Crowell suggests, the concept of the "normative" is used not only "in a narrow sense, according to which a norm is an explicitly formulated rule [...] that serves as the basis for determining whether something (an action, mainly) is permissible or obligatory" but also in a "wider sense according to which a norm is anything that serves as a standard of success or failure of any kind" (Crowell 2013, p. 2). It is exactly in this "wider sense" that I use this term.

tivism of a Kantian type. What does this "metaphysics" mean precisely and how does Fink legitimate its conception philosophically?

Fink demonstrates his understanding primarily by treating what he calls the *"problem of modalities,"* that is, he interprets the world as the ultimate horizon in which and exclusively in which (real) being could manifest itself *in its modality* (Fink 1959, pp. 172–248). An entity's modality can be determined not from its ontological features or properties exclusively, but primarily and originally under the aspect of the world, to which that entity belongs. For example, a fictive entity (a Terminator or a T-1000) can be acknowledged as fictive (not actual-real), not only because of its ontological properties (a T-1000's liquid-like body or use of time travel) but also because it does not belong to the world in its actuality. To assert (or at least to dispute) that no (or almost no) time travel is likely to be compatible with the laws of physics, we need to be clear on which laws of physics we are speaking about, which will probably be the laws of physics of the actual world. If so, one of the necessary "conditions of possibility" or a better "ground [*Boden*]" for a modal statement is that we are open to the world in its modalities. This implies that *the world normatively rules the horizon of the modalities of a respective being within it*. As Fink briefly noted in 1930:

> Actuality is previous to actual things [*Die Wirklichkeit ist vor den wirklichen Dinge*]. There is actuality, not because there are actual things (not similar therefore to the case of color), but there can be actual things because there is actuality. (Fink 2008, p. 45, Z-VII, XVII/24a-b)

This "actuality" is identical with what he calls in his other writings "world-actuality [*Weltwirklichkeit*]" (see Fink 1959, pp. 198–236; and Fink 1985, p. 105).

This "world-actuality" is the specific (in a certain sense "phenomenological") aspect of the world whose traditional and Kantian definition is the "absolute totality of existing things." This claim can be developed through the following steps. First, one can ascribe "existence" or "being" to an object, if the latter is, according to Kant, "*posed* [*gesetzt*]" (Kant 1905b, p. 73). Second, if an object can be "posed," this *must be necessarily concordant with the world*, because what can be rationally "posed" must be compatible with other "posed" objects in their totality, that is, with the world as the "absolute totality of existing things." Therefore, Fink states that the world could not be philosophically apprehended sufficiently in its "structure of universal concept [*Struktur des Allgemeinbegriffs*]" but only in its own "structure of totality [*Struktur des Inbegriffs*]" (Fink 1959, pp. 193, 208–210). Third, a philosophical approach which elucidates being in its "structure of universal concept" can be characterized as the traditional "metaphysics of ideas," while "metaphysics of Being" or "cosmology" deals with the "structure of totality," which is appropriate to the world. Fourth, in what sense is "world-actuality" in its "structure of totality" "previous to" the things within it? Precise reference to "world-actuality" has always and already been accomplished if phrases used can be qualified as modal propositions, particularly alethic propositions, since *each true (or false) proposition is and must be the respectively correct (or incorrect, deceptive, falsified) description of the unique world*. Every alethic claim must follow this requirement. Fifth, therefore, it is possible to speak meaningfully about and to verify a modal statement legitimately, if and only if the world is there in the sense of "world-actuality." Husserl also posited the same thesis in a manuscript written in 1937, asserting that if there is no world, we could never even meaningfully pose a *question* as to whether an entity *is* or *is not*, because the world is the "ground-of-question [*Frage-Boden*]" (Husserl 2008, Hua XXXIX, pp. 256–257). Sixth, if there could be no meaningful question, there must be no being in the largest sense, because what can be understood as a "being" is something which respectively *either* is *or* is not and that which is *neither* "being" *nor* "non-being" appears as *chaos*. Thus, there is nothing but *chaos* if there is no world. *The Either-Or* (for example, *either* being *or* non-being) *of the being in question presupposes the existence of the world* (or "*world-actuality*"). Since the world lies at the *origin* of the "either-or," Fink is right to call it an "alternation-horizon of being and illusion"; *the world in its "structure of totality" is the normatively ultimate horizon of the respective modality* (Fink 1959, pp. 198–223).[7] Seventh, it is, of course, possible there might be no *unconditional reason* why the world exists rather than total chaos (recalling Husserl's argument concerning the "annihilation of the world"). However, it appears that the world does *de facto* exist *if* there is something (an entity in question, an object which respectively is or is not) rather than chaos.[8] The world is a fundamental *fact* which makes normatively possible the question and the respective object of it in its modality, and without which there are no entities but total chaos (*cf.* also Fink 1959, pp. 185–197): *If* there is something rather than chaos, the world must *necessarily* exist. In other words, Fink and Husserl seek an answer to the very question of why there is something rather than nothing (the famous metaphysical question of Leibniz) in the fact that *there is the world rather than chaos*. As seen, the unconditional reason why there is the

---

[7] The late Fink will develop this conception and concretize, under numerous perspectives of different modalities and "alternation," not only "being/illusion" and "true/false" but also "appearing [*Erscheinen*]," "time," "space," and "movement [*Bewegung*]." See, for example, Fink 1957, 1958, 1990.

[8] Husserlian "annihilation of the world" is not intended to support a skeptical claim but is rather a kind of thought experiment to demonstrate the absurdity of a "philosophical absolutization of the world" (Husserl 1976, Hua III/1, p. 120).

world rather than chaos could not be demonstrated philosophically (or at least phenomenologically). Thus, we can prove the existence of the world in its very specific *conditional* or *"factual necessity"* (*cf.* Tengelyi 2014, pp. 188–191). Finally, according to the Husserlian "annihilation of the world," there could be consciousness without the world (a consciousness in total *chaos*), but there cannot be any being without consciousness (Husserl 1976, Hua III/1, pp. 103–106). However, this also suggests that *a world-less consciousness or subjectivity is not a sufficient condition for being.* Since there is, at least for phenomenology, no unconditional reason why the world exists, rather than chaos, *the very source of the normative force of the "alternation-horizon" for each being must be identified with the factual-necessary existence of the world itself.* In other words, the subject as constitutive must be "enworlded" if it is to constitute a being (Fink 1966, pp. 9–16) (I treat this thematically in the second part).

Therefore, the ontological or "cosmological difference" between the world and being within it is apprehended as the *difference between the alternation-horizon of modality (or "ground-of-question") and being within it,* in Fink (and in the late Husserl). Whereas no one can comprehend the totality of things in their full reality, we are always and already referred back to the world as "alternation-horizon" if there is something, that is something meaningfully, in question. Exactly in this sense, Fink claims that the world is "previous to" each entity within it. The philosophical elucidation of this claim is identical with the formation of a "metaphysics of Being" which explores the "cosmological horizon of Being."

1.3 "Proximity and Distance" between Kant and Phenomenology in the Context of Cosmological Problematics

In this section, the "proximity and distance" between Kant and phenomenology are thematically discussed. On the one hand, the ontological claims of Fink (and Husserl) concerning the world seem to be compatible with Kantian claims, to the extent that they all share the thesis according to which *the world is not the thing in itself,* with the world becoming philosophically intelligible only in its ontological difference with "appearance" (Kant) or "intramundane being" (Fink). On the other hand, it is not possible to consider these positions identical, because their respective interpretations of "cosmological difference" are quite different. Since the world is not the "thing in itself," the former is construed as a merely subjective fiction in Kant, whereas Fink and the late Husserl claim that the world is not the "thing in itself" but is a specific kind of "horizon" ("alternation-horizon" or "ground-of-question") which factually-necessarily exists (but is unlike the existence of things within it).

Does this apparent contradiction mean that a phenomenological account of the ontological status of the world must fall victim to a "transcendental illusion," because, as with *cosmologia rationalis*, it claims that the world exists? It does not because, in contrast to *cosmologia rationalis*, phenomenology accepts that the world is not the thing in itself. As already stated, Fink and Husserl share this claim with Kant. *Mutatis mutandis*, the phenomenological concept of the world is not one of the traditional metaphysical conceptions rejected by Kant. Thus, the difference between the two philosophical positions seems more apparent than real. For example, Husserl suggests briefly that the world might be ontologically characterized as "infinity" or infinite totality in a very specific sense, that is, not as "transfinite" but as "openness" (Husserl 1952, Hua IV, p. 299). In the present context, Husserl's conception provides another argument according to which no one can comprehend the "infinity of the world" in its reality, *not* primarily because of human finitude, but *because the world is in itself "openness"* (this "openness" denotes what can be determined neither previously nor once and for all). Since such an "openness of the world" must not be chaotic, but somehow harmonious (a "chaotic openness" is likely to be a *contradictio in adjecto*, since it is virtually inconceivable without some form of meaningful orientation), phenomenology can also claim that the idea of this "openness" could *regulate* our understanding, which must also not be chaotic but harmonious; this interpretation seems to be, at least in its basic conception, not incompatible with the Kantian thesis of the regulative Idea.

However, phenomenology emphasizes that the world, as "alternation-horizon" or "ground-of-question," *exists factually-necessarily*, and this constitutes the precise "distance" between the two philosophical traditions. In other words, Husserl (implicitly) and Fink (thematically) query Kant's ontological presuppositions that: (a) what cannot be the "thing in itself" cannot *logically* exist; and therefore (b) the world is of a merely "fictional" or "subjective" nature (because Kant assumed that something must logically have either "objective" or "subjective" value) (Fink 1990, p. 142). Fink opposes these Kantian presuppositions with the following conception, namely, that what is not the "thing in itself" does not categorically have to be considered as "nothingness" whose value is merely subjective and fictional. How can this conception be given a positive formulation?

Within this context, it needs to be recalled that the phenomenological claim concerning the factual necessity of the existence of the world does not imply the existence of the absolute totality of things *in their reality* (entailing the metaphysical error of *cosmologia rationalis*), but the existence of the world qua "alternation-horizon" *in its normativity*. In other words, the very *norm* which the world, as "alternation-horizon," imposes is that the respective being in question must be *either* compatible *or* incompatible with the totality of other existing beings, that is, with the world. However, this normative rule must not be equated with the Kantian "regulative Idea" or "heuristic fiction" which involves merely subjective value, because this obligation has its *source* not primarily in subjectivity or in "pure reason" but rather in the *factual-necessary existing world in which we are involved*. This can seem problematic if one attempts to found that kind of normativity solely on the subjective-cognitive faculty since, with that presupposition, it is hard to avoid what might be called a *subjective (or anthropological) fictionalism of the world*, and the resulting skeptical position admits of no objective value, but only subjective and fictive value for any modal proposition. Such fictionalism seems counterintuitive and philosophically problematic. It is counterintuitive because modal propositions seem to have intrinsic objective value, insofar as we are always speaking about a respective being in its modality (was that all merely fiction, or my somewhat subjectively coherent dream?). It is philosophically problematic because a statement concerning a fictive world usually has no claim to alethic value.[9] If it is possible to distinguish a fictional object from a real object, whatever it may be, then one is already committed to a basic belief or "primal-doxa" that the world is not a subjective fiction but is given in its actuality (in the sense of "world-actuality"): The world is always and already pregiven as "world-actuality" in its factual necessity. In other words, an ontological claim for the existence of the world generates the "transcendental illusion" only in combination with another ontological presupposition, namely, that the world can be ontologically qualified as the thing in itself, which determines the totality of existing things in their respective reality. One must rather defend the ontological claim for the existence of the world in its own right, if the world is to be considered, as in phenomenology, in its normativity for modalities of respective being.[10]

---

9 One can meaningfully pose a question about Arnold Schwarzenegger or Robert Patrick and, if desired, verify the answer to it, but hardly about a Terminator and a T-1000. It is possible to ask a meaningful question about the film *The Terminator*, because that film is an entity or event belonging to the actual world, but not about a Terminator or a T-1000 as such.

10 More discussion than is possible here would be required to examine whether, and to what extent, from a phenomenological point of view, Kant's understanding entails this type of fictionalism. To assess this question adequately, it would be necessary to undertake a deep and systematic study on the different perceptions of transcendental idealism in Kant and in phenomenology (*cf.* for example, Loidolt 2014, Pradelle 2015), and on the different metaphysical conceptions involved in both philosophies.

This section can be summed up as follows. Kant's "Copernican revolution" or his thesis concerning the *finitude* of human reason implies and is based on an insight into an ontological distinction between the world and the things within it (Fink's "cosmological difference"). Fink considers this Kantian view metaphysical because this "cosmological difference" leads him to form a cosmologico-ontological viewpoint, namely, a metaphysical conception according to which "[world-] actuality is previous to actual things [within-the-world]." In this respect, Fink cannot easily follow Hegel's approach, which entails "going beyond Kant" and therefore is not capable of taking into account the very problem of the world. Therefore, it appears that Fink's metaphysics emerges based on his interpretation of Kant's "transcendental dialectic." If this is correct, then it is difficult to accept Crowell's claim concerning the historical value of Fink's thought: "He [Fink] drives phenomenology beyond Kant to Hegel and, alluding to Hegel's 'speculative proposition,' proposes a 'theory of the phenomenological proposition' that embraces paradox and contradiction" (Crowell 2001, p. 259). In line with this assessment, Crowell thinks that Fink fell victim to the "transcendental illusion" (Crowell 2001, p. 263). However, and on the contrary, Fink has been shown here as struggling to meet the challenge of just this type of philosophical illusion whose essence he characterizes as "oblivion of the world."

2 Fink's "Proximity and Distance" to the Late Husserl: Fink's Discovery of the World as a New Phenomenological-Descriptive Dimension

Thus far, we have examined which kind of "metaphysics" or "speculation" is at stake in Fink's thought. I have demonstrated that Fink's own "metaphysics of Being" or "cosmology" is not Hegelian, but rather is generated from Kant's insight regarding the antinomies, that is, the problem of the world. What then is Fink's "phenomenology," which needs to support and elaborate his metaphysical conception as sketched above? A clue can be found in one of his manuscripts from the early 1930s: "The question of the totality of the world [*Weltganzheit*] and, correlatively, world-consciousness [*Weltbewusstsein*] necessarily revealed using Kant's doctrine of antinomy" (Fink 2008, p. 95, Z-IX 14a, 31.8.1931). The precise "phenomenological" problem with which Fink is struggling is that of "world-consciousness." This consciousness is, according to him, correlative to the "totality of the world." The "totality of the world" or its "structure of totality" constitutes, as seen, the core metaphysical problem for Fink. In this sense, Fink's "phenomenology" is designated by his metaphysical conception according to which "(world-) actuality is previous to actual things;" this "world-actuality" is the very *horizon* or *ground of modalities* (or "ground-of-question" in Husserl's term). Since the world is such a ground of truth/falsehood, it can be assumed that the "world-consciousness" indicates a phenomenological question of *how we ourselves engage the world truthfully*. As suggested, Fink calls such a program a "phenomenology of mundanization [enworlding]," which elucidates the proper "manner of being" of the transcendental-constitutive subjectivity and the "constitution" of its "world-character" (Fink 1966, p. 9). In sum, his cosmological Kant-reading provides a so-called *"transcendental clue* [transzendentaler Leitfaden]" (see Husserl 1950, Hua I, pp. 87–88, also Fink 1966, pp. 17–18 and 172–178) *to the phenomenological analysis of the world-consciousness*. How can Fink's phenomenological program be precisely characterized?

2.1 Fink's "Proximity" to the Late Husserl: Pregivenness of the World

The thesis of a "correlation" between the totality of the world and consciousness of it recalls the Husserlian problem concerning the *pregivenness of the world* (*Vorgegebenheit der Welt*). It is necessary to note, first, that this problem refers back to the very fact of experiencing a life-world:

> The world is pregiven to us, the waking, always somehow practically interested subjects, not occasionally but always and necessarily as the universal field of all actual and possible praxis, as horizon. To live is always to live-in-certainty-of-the-world. Waking life is being awake to the world, being constantly and directly 'conscious' of the world and of oneself as living *in* the world, actually experiencing and actually effecting the certainty of the being of the world [*Seinsgewißheit der Welt*]. (Husserl 1954, Hua VI, p. 145; Husserl 1970, pp. 142–143, tr. modif.)

The factual pregivenness of the world presupposes eventually another reciprocal fact, namely, that a "waking" subject is "awake to the world" and "living" in it. The pregivenness of the world and the wakefulness of subjectivity living in it *co-belong* to each other and *co-condition* each other. In brief, subjectivity is *necessarily* "enworlded," *if* we are "waking" and "living" not in a dream or an illusion, but in the world in its certainty. Second, the world and the things within it, including human subjectivity, also co-belong to each other; things are always and can only be given to us "in such a way that we are conscious of them as things or objects within the world-horizon" (Husserl 1954, Hua VI, p. 146; Husserl 1970, p. 143). Third, this "world-horizon" must, therefore, be *ontologically* discernable from the objects within it. Husserl says, "The world [...] does not exist as an entity, as an object, but exists with such uniqueness that the plural makes no sense when applied to it. Every plural, and every singular drawn from it, presupposes the world-horizon" (Husserl 1954, Hua VI, p. 146; Husserl 1970, p. 143). The world-horizon is the ultimate horizon in which an object can be numerically distinguished from other objects, whereas this horizon itself can only be understood in its "uniqueness." Indeed, this claim is compatible with Fink's thesis on "cosmological difference." The "world-horizon" must be "unique" because this must be grasped, in Fink's words, in its "structure of totality" where "the plural makes no sense when applied to it" (*cf.* Fink 1959, pp. 211–223). Alternatively, the "actuality" or existence of a counter-world [*Gegenwelt*] or "overworld [*Überwelt*]" to which the "world-horizon" could be numerically opposed is not conceivable (Fink 1966, pp. 61–62). Last, this ontological claim necessarily requires the accomplishment of a *phenomenological* analysis of world-consciousness as such in its specific nature, because the ontologically different natures of the "world-horizon" and "something (object)" must, according to the imperative of transcendental reduction, be analyzed constitutive-phenomenologically (Husserl 1954, Hua VI, p. 146; Husserl 1970, p. 143). In other words, this ontological difference, which coincides with Fink's "cosmological difference" in its basic conception, is a *transcendental clue to a phenomenological-constitutive analysis of the "world-consciousness."* The world must be conceived in its difference from the things within it; correlatively, this "world-consciousness" must be phenomenologically elucidated in its difference from "consciousness of something." The latter can and must be analyzed in the "universal *a priori* of correlation between experienced object and manners of givenness" (Husserl 1954, Hua VI, p. 169; Husserl 1970, p. 166). A question arises as to how Husserl then analyzes "world-consciousness."

The answer to this question should be sought in *Crisis* itself, namely, in the "resolution" of what its author calls the "paradox of human subjectivity," which involves elucidating (in a transcendental, phenomenological manner) human subjectivity's proper manner of being, concerning "being a subject for the world and at the same time being an object in the world" (Husserl 1954, Hua VI, p. 182; Husserl 1970, p. 178). Since subjectivity, not only qua human subjectivity but also qua constitutive, must be "enworlded" in its manner of being, the analysis of world-consciousness refers back to this "paradox." In *Crisis*, there are two principal analytical approaches identified, namely, the transcendental-"*egological*" approach and the approach using analysis of "*intersubjectivity*" in its totality and its concreteness (Husserl 1954, Hua VI, pp. 185–193; Husserl 1970, pp. 182–190). However, another approach seems more plausible and productive, that is, through an analysis of "*wakefulness*" of subjectivity in the certainty of the existence of the world. For the fact of "wakefulness" constitutes not only the starting point of the problem of the "world-consciousness," but also, as seen, a so-called "condition of possibility" for the pregivenness of the world as such. However, Husserl himself does not treat this third way thematically.[11]

2.2 Fink's "Distance" from the Late Husserl: How we Engage the World Truthfully

It is precisely in this context that the notable "distance" of Fink from the Husserlian approach becomes evident. Fink emphasizes, contrary to Husserl, the importance of the third way (the analysis of the "wakefulness of subjectivity within-the-world") and concentrates on a phenomenological analysis of it. Why does Fink choose this third approach?

The answer is, to some extent, likely to be found in the recognition that several fundamental difficulties arise if one treats the problem of "correlation between the world and world-consciousness" using solely the first and second approaches. For example, a question arises as to how it is possible to have access phenomenologically to the issue of "*start and end*" ("birth and death") of a transcendental subjectivity, if it were necessarily presupposed that it had emerged from something "unconscious" (see Fink 2006, p. 23, Z-1 24a, p. 348, Z-VI 30a-b). Further questions arise concerning to what extent it is possible to claim that intersubjectivity or the generative community of transcendental subjectivities in its totality is constitutively correlative to the existing world as such, and what the ontological presupposition for supporting this claim might be (see Fink 2006, p. 23, Z-1 24a, p. 403, U-IV 47). These difficulties arise seemingly because Husserl operates with a presupposition according to which subjectivity qua transcendental must be *ideally* responsible for the constitution of the absolute totality of existing things *in their full reality*. If this were the case, it seems evident why Husserl claims that the world in its totality is correlative to *intersubjectivity in its full concreteness*, not just a single subjectivity, since, of course, a single subjectivity also constitutes the world in its reality, but only partially. Indeed, Fink appears to defend these basic conceptions of Husserl in the *Sixth Cartesian Meditation*, whose purpose is not primarily to develop Fink's own ideas but rather to elaborate and radicalize a Husserlian program of transcendental phenomenology under a methodic-systematic perspective, so that Fink illus-

---

[11] We can see the reason for this probably in the fact that the problem of wakefulness/sleep constitutes a "limit-problem [*Grenzproblem*]" in the late Husserl (Husserl 2014, Hua XLII, pp. 1–82).

trates formally a program of "constructive phenomenology" which considers what constitutes the "limit-problems [*Grenzprobleme*]," such as the "start and end" of transcendental subjectivity and other matters, within Husserl's framework (Fink 1988a, p. 67).

However, the tacit presupposition mentioned above is revealed, *in the light of Fink's thought*, as cosmologically problematic. As examined, Kant had already demonstrated in his *Inaugural Dissertation* that it was hardly conceivable that the world as the "inexhaustible series of the states of the universe succeeding on another eternally" could be reduced to a "*whole* comprehending all changes whatsoever"; in Husserlian terms, *the whole of intentional acts cannot be construed as the consciousness of the whole, i.e., "world-consciousness"* (*cf.* Fink 2006, p. 348, Z-VI 30a). The world-horizon is barely conceivable *as* world-horizon or, in Fink's own expression, scarcely able to be elucidated in its "*constitutive function of the horizon qua horizon,*" if one tries to apprehend world-consciousness "as an 'intentional modification [*intentionale Abwandlung*]' of an original consciousness of object" (Fink 2008, p. 32, XVII/1a). In short, the world-consciousness must be interpreted neither as a kind of intentionality in a canonical sense (that is, "consciousness of something") nor as a collection or an absolute totality of it. Since Fink takes these difficulties more seriously than Husserl, he considers and examines the problem of the world as discussed in Kant, who disclosed the "cosmological horizon of the Being," namely, the "cosmological difference." The cosmological difference must be grasped and articulated because it serves as the essential "*transcendental clue*" *to a phenomenological analysis of the world-consciousness in its difference to the "consciousness of something."* Correlatively, Fink proposes and tries to elaborate the third way, because, as examined, the wakefulness of human subjectivity constitutes the very "condition of possibility" for the pregivenness of the world (it is not possible to speak meaningfully about its pregivenness at all, if one is not "awake to" and so "living in" the world). Fink identifies this specific correlation with what he calls "primary enworlding [*primäre Verweltlichung*],"[12] which is considered the real "origin of the natural attitude" (Fink 1966, p. 11), understood conceptually in his terminology as the "*self-actualization of constitutive subjectivity in world-actualization*"

---

[12] The "primal enworlding" is the precise manner in which a subject is awake to the actual world. In contrast to this, Fink apprehends "secondary enworlding" as the manner in which a phenomenological intuition or truth could be expressed in a natural language. Since this study does not focus on this aspect of methodical problematics (which constitutes the task of the "*transcendental doctrine of method*"), but on the transcendental-constitutive problem of the pregiven world (concerning the "*transcendental doctrine of elements*"), it is not necessary to address the former aspect in this study.

(Fink 1988a, p. 49). This is how subjectivity *as* constitutive is awake to the world, which is pregiven and therefore to be analyzed constitutively. How does Fink analyze this "wakefulness" in its "enworlding" dimension?

Fink accomplishes this task by describing the phenomena of wakefulness in its multifarious modes. His descriptive analysis can be summarized as based mainly on the two following conceptions. First, he states that the various phenomena of wakefulness have the common core structure of "living-into-the-world [*In-die-Welt-Hineinleben*]" or "sinking-in [*versunken-in*]" (Fink 1966, pp. 11–12, 54–56). Second, he demonstrates descriptively that we can meaningfully differentiate between various modes of wakefulness when diverse modes of "sinking-in" are descriptively analyzed. Taking one of Fink's examples, the "pathological illusion," Fink considers that one could be so deeply immersed in (i. e., "sinking in") a world of pathological illusion that one could not be conscious of this illusion *as* pathological (Fink 1966, p. 55). Therefore, Fink is analyzing the very peculiar "*manners of givenness*" of a world of "pathological illusion," that is, modes of pathological "wakefulness" in relation to that world. In contrast to this, we are normally "awake to" *the world as actual.* We are "living into" or "sinking in" *the* world in a specific manner that cannot be identical with *a* world of pathological illusion. By descriptively analyzing such differences among several modes of "sinking-in," it is possible to obtain a "transcendental clue" to a constitutive analysis of "world-consciousness." *It is Fink's central claim that "world-consciousness" is to be analyzed in its "universal a priori of correlation" between the "world" and its diverse "manners of givenness," that is, the structure of "sinking-in" in its multifarious modes.*

Insofar as the concern here is not with the manners of givenness of *a* world but that of *the* world (wakefulness as "enworlding"), it is worth analyzing the famous characters of Don Quixote and Sancho Panza, because *they both engage with the world truthfully,* even if their respective modes of "sinking-in" are distinctly different. Don Quixote is somehow convinced that the large object in front of him must be a ferocious giant, against which he, as a knight-errant, should tilt, even though Sancho Panza expresses disagreement directly with his master on this matter. Using Fink's ideas, this scenario can be phenomenologically analyzed in the following way. While Don Quixote is "sinking in" *the* world in such a peculiar manner that a certain large object must appear as a ferocious giant rather than a windmill, Sancho Panza is "awake to" it in a way that enables him to grasp that the object in question must be a windmill rather than what his master calls a giant. After tilting against this object, it is finally revealed as a prosaic windmill for Don Quixote too. This famous scene presupposes the two following facts, namely, that both characters assume that: (a) *the world is nothing other than the precise "truth" about which they are arguing*; and (b) the world offers them, in this case, at least two alternatives involving a large object seemingly appearing *either* as a windmill *or* as a ferocious giant. This "either-or" is, as demonstrated above, the very *rule of the world*. In other words, their different modes of "sinking-in" can be apprehended as their respectively different attitudes to (or interpretations of) the unique world qua "alternation-horizon" of a specific "either-or," and this presupposes its "actuality." In this sense, the existence or "actuality" of the world ("world-actuality") is not dependent on a *subjective* interpretation of it, but on the latter's presupposing the former. Therefore, it is possible to claim that the world is the basic dimension of truth or "alternation-horizon" of truth/falsehood to which the respective subject is *de facto* awake *if* they can dispute about it in some meaningful manner. The world is and must be pregiven whose specific "manners of givenness" can be analyzed as "wakefulness" in its structure of "sinking-in." This is why it has been stressed that world-consciousness can and must be constitutively analyzed under the aspect of a "universal *a priori* of correlation" and not, therefore, between "experienced objects and manners of givenness," but rather between the "world" and the manners of "sinking in" the world.

Since, according to Husserl, a modal statement refers to and is based on intentionality as an "objectifying act" whose verifying/falsifying function is analyzed with the term "fulfillment," Fink claims that the exact transcendental-phenomenological "condition of possibility" of such "intentional acts" is the "wakefulness" qua "world-consciousness" occurring within its enworlding dimension. "World-consciousness" is not reducible to the totality of intentional acts, but offers them the very *"ground"* or *"horizon"* in which and only in which they could be constitutive for objects in their respective modality (Fink 1988b, p. 91). Based on Fink's "phenomenological" thesis, the two following claims can be made explicit: (1) the "consciousness of something" as an objectifying act is founded on world-consciousness, just as the "world" is "previous to" actual things qua "something"; (2) therefore, these two aspects must not be apprehended under one type of intentionality, but "consciousness of something" must be analyzed in a "universal *a priori* of correlation between experienced object and manners of givenness," while "world-consciousness" must be analyzed in its modes of "wakefulness" qua enworlding which could be articulated in respective "performative modes [*Vollzugsmodi*]." In sum, *"wakefulness" in its enworlding is the very manner in which one engages the world truthfully.*

In this context, two conclusions can be drawn. First, since Fink describes the world in its manner of (pre)givenness, that is, he discovers a new *phenomenologically descriptive* dimension of the world in its correlation to "world-consciousness" that is not reducible to "intentionality" or the sum of its parts, one cannot characterize his thought as purely "speculative." Rather, Fink is loyal to the phenomenological spirit. Second, since Fink's analysis of wakefulness as enworlding overcomes in a certain manner a series of difficulties intrinsic to the Husserlian approach to "world-consciousness," it is possible to claim, if wished, that Fink is "more phenomenological" than Husserl in this context. Understanding why Crowell supports an opposing view becomes easier if one considers that he only engaged with and commented on the *Sixth Cartesian Meditation*, in which Fink does not thematically undertake any *"phenomenological analysis"* of "primary enworlding." Fink concentrated in that work on the *systematic formation of phenomenological concepts*, in line with the Husserlian idea of a "phenomenology of phenomenology."

Concluding Remarks

In the first section, Fink's cosmological Kant-interpretation and its philosophical consequences in his thought were examined. This examination clarified that the real source of Fink's "speculation" is not Hegelian but Kantian "dialectic." Fink's "phenomenology of enworlding" was next illustrated. It was shown that he phenomenologically legitimates his "metaphysical" claim concerning the world by describing the phenomena of "wakefulness" in its enworlding dimension and analyzing it in its "universal *a priori* of correlation" to the pregiven world. Fink discovers the world in its correlation to "world-consciousness" as a new phenomenologically-descriptive dimension. Therefore, it appears his philosophy is not merely speculative, but genuinely phenomenological.

However, in this context, it is possible to appreciate Heidegger's profound influence on Fink's project rather than assume Fink's originality. On the one hand, I assume that Fink's analyses of the "pregivenness of the world" could be construed as a sort of continuation or phenomenological concretization of Heidegger's problem of the so-called *"transcendence of Dasein,"* which is the precise terminology under which the "condition of possibility" of the world and, correlatively, where intentionality, therefore, must be elucidated (this is one of the basic reasons why one can characterize the Heideggerian program as a specific kind of "transcendental" philosophy). Since the goal of Fink's project consists in a phenomenological elucidation of the pregivenness of the world qua *ground of intentionality*, his "proximity" to Heidegger can be acknowledged on exactly this point (see Ikeda 2015).

On the other hand, there are some noteworthy and inextinguishable differences between them. First, the Kant-interpretation strategies used by Heidegger and Fink are distinctly different. While Heidegger, globally speaking, concentrates on the "transcendental analytic of pure reason" to found each kind of cognition on so-called "transcendental imagination," the main object of Fink's Kant-interpretation is the "transcendental dialectic of pure reason" whose task is a philosophical demonstration of "transcendental illusion" in its necessity and, for Fink, metaphysical elucidation of "cosmological difference." An important "distance" results from this. Whereas Heidegger barely accounts for the core problematics of "transcendental illusion" in his framework,[13] Fink characterizes this particular fallacy of the "metaphysics of ideas" explicitly as "oblivion of the world" and contextualizes it in his thought. Second, Fink's approach intrinsically involves two further more philosophically fundamental "distances" between them. The first of these "distances" concerns their "thematic concepts," which are decisively different, namely, "Being" (Heidegger) and the "world" (Fink). Here, I suggest only that "Being" is not reducible to the "world," because the world is the "cosmological horizon of Being" in which and only in which being can manifest *as* being. For example, if a being (a woman winking at you) were revealed as non-existing (because the woman was really a wax sculpture), this being would lose entirely its "being" (the previous belief or statement concerning it would lose its truth value), whereas the world as such remains the same as before (the world does not lose its "being"). For what changes in such an "alternation" of being and non-being is not the world as such, but merely a *description* of it (*cf.* Tengelyi 2014, p. 258);[14] *whereas no being can be indifferent to such an "alternation" of its modality, the world makes possible its modalization* (*Modalisierung*). The second of these "distances" between Heidegger and Fink involves their basic understandings of "reason," which significantly differ. Heidegger attempts to found the transcendental illusion on the "internal core of the structure of *Dasein*," that is, he identifies the very origin of the world as such with *human subjectivity as Dasein*, while Fink stresses the co-belonging character of the world and subjectivity (this is the core claim of his "phenomenology of enworlding"). Correlatively, Fink considers that the source of normativity for being in its modality is to be founded not in subjectivity exclusively, as is the

---

[13] In *Davoser Disputation* Heidegger says *en passant* that he "believes" he has found the real "root of the metaphysical illusion" in the "innermost core of the structure of *Dasein*," but without any explicit justification for his statement (Heidegger 1991, GA 3, p. 281).

[14] Tengelyi explicates this difference between Being and the world based on his own reconstruction of Heidegger's "metontology," even if Heidegger himself never claimed this explicitly (Tengelyi 2014, p. 257). In this sense, it might be possible to see in this point a real "proximity" between Heidegger and Fink as well, if one could demonstrate that Fink developed an originally Heideggerian motif which his master never elaborated. However, it is in any case two very different things to allude to an idea, on the one hand and to legitimate it philosophically, on the other.

case with Kant and Heidegger, but rather in *the factual-necessary existing world* which, as "world-actuality," must be phenomenologically analyzed in its "universal *a priori* of correlation" with a subject "sinking in" the world. *This "distance" signifies consequently that the ultimate source and origin of reason, or its normativity, is conceived quite differently by the two Freiburg philosophers.*

Even if it is worthwhile studying more precisely and developing more extensively those notable "distances" between Fink and Heidegger, the results of this study have been sufficient to demonstrate the following claims: (1) Fink's thought is clearly located in a *"phenomenological"* tradition which oscillates between (the late) Husserl and Heidegger (his metaphysical period especially). (2) The main problematic of Fink's philosophy is nothing other than the *"world"* which Kant had revealed as a problematic concept for metaphysics: that is, the problem of the world through which metaphysics as such was problematized profoundly, or subjected to a Copernican revolution, so to speak. (3) This Kantian insight is, for Fink, the real origin of a philosophical tradition which has been designated as *"transcendental."* Consequently, we can plausibly characterize Fink's philosophy as a *"transcendental phenomenology of the world."*

Bibliography

Bruzina, Ronald (1995): "Translator's Introduction". In: *Sixth Cartesian Meditation, The Idea of a Transcendental Doctrine of Methode.* Bloomington/Indianapolis: Indiana University Press, pp. vii–xcii.

Bruzina, Ronald (2006): "Hinter der ausgeschriebenen Finkschen Meditation: Meontik-Pädagogik". In: *Eugen Fink Sozialphilosophie Anthropologie Kosmologie Pädagogik Methodik.* Ed. Anselm Böhmer. Würzburg: Königshausen und Neumann, pp. 193–219.

Crowell, Steven (2001): *Husserl, Heidegger, and the Space of Meaning. Paths toward Transcendental Phenomenology.* Evanston, Illinois: Northwestern University Press.

Crowell, Steven (2013): *Normativity and Phenomenology in Husserl and Heidegger.* Cambridge: Cambridge University Press.

Fink, Eugen (1957): *Zur ontologischen Frühgeschichte von Raum-Zeit-Bewegung.* The Hague: Martinus Nijhoff.

Fink, Eugen (1958): *Sein, Wahrheit, Welt. Vor-Fragen zum Problem des Phänomen-Begriff.* The Hague: Martinus Nijhoff.

Fink, Eugen (1959): *Alles und Nichts. Ein Umweg zur Philosophie.* The Hague: Martinus Nijhoff.

Fink, Eugen (1966): *Studien zur Phänomenologie 1930–1939.* The Hague: Martinus Nijhoff.

Fink, Eugen (1985): *Einleitung in die Philosophie.* Ed. Franz-Anton Schwarz. Würzburg: Königshausen und Neumann.

Fink, Eugen (1988a): *VI. Cartesianische Meditation. Teil 1. Die Idee einer transzendentalen Methodenlehre. Husserliana Dokumente*, vol. II/1. Eds. Hans Ebeling, Jann Holl & Guy van Kerckhoven. Dordrecht: Kluwer Academic Publisher.

Fink, Eugen (1988b): *VI. Cartesianische Meditation. Teil 2. Ergänzungsband. Husserliana Dokumente*, vol. II/2. Ed. Guy van Kerckhoven. Dordrecht: Kluwer Academic Publishers.

Fink, Eugen (1990): *Welt und Endlichkeit*. Ed. Franz-Anton Schwarz. Würzburg: Königshausen und Neumann.

Fink, Eugen (2006): *Phänomenologische Werkstatt Bd.1. Die Doktorarbeit und erste Assistenzjahre bei Husserl. Gesamtausgabe*, vol. 3/1. Ed. Ronald Bruzina. Freiburg/München: Karl Alber.

Fink, Eugen (2008): *Phänomenologische Werkstatt Bd.2. Die Bernauer Manuskripte Cartesianische Meditationen und System der phänomenologischen Philosophie. Gesamtausgabe*, vol. 3/2. Ed. Ronald Bruzina. Freiburg/München: Karl Alber.

Hegel, Georg Wilhelm Friedrich (2010): *The Science of Logic*. Trans. George di Giovanni. Cambridge: Cambridge University Press.

Heidegger, Martin/Fink, Eugen (1970): *Heraklit. Seminar Wintersemester 1966/1967*. Frankfurt am Main: Vittorio Klostermann.

Heidegger, Martin/Fink, Eugen (1980): *Heraclitus Seminar 1966/67*. Trans. Charles H. Seibert. Tuscaloosa: The University of Alabama Press.

Heidegger, Martin (1991): *Kant und das Problem der Metaphysik. Gesamtausgabe*, vol. 3. Ed. Friedrich-Wilhelm von Herrmann. Frankfurt am Main: Vittorio Klostermann.

Husserl, Edmund (1950): *Cartesianische Meditationen und Pariser Vorträge. Husserliana*, vol. I. Ed. Stephan Strasser. The Hague: Martinus Nijhoff.

Husserl, Edmund (1952): *Ideen zu einer reinen Phänomenologie und phänomenologischen Philosophie. Zweites Buch. Phänomenologische Untersuchungen zur Konstitution. Husserliana*, vol. IV. Ed. Marly Biemel. The Hague: Martinus Nijhoff.

Husserl, Edmund (1954): *Die Krisis der europäischen Wissenschaft und die transzendentale Phänomenologie. Eine Einleitung in die phänomenologische Philosophie. Husserliana*, vol. VI. Ed. Walter Biemel. The Hague: Martinus Nijhoff.

Husserl, Edmund (1970): *The Crisis of European Science and Transcendental Phenomenology*. Trans. David Carr. Evanston, Illinois: Northwestern University Press.

Husserl, Edmund (1976): *Ideen zu einer reinen Phänomenologie und phänomenologischen Philosophie. Erstes Buch. Allgemeine Einführung in die reine Phänomenologie. Husserliana*, vol. III/1. Ed. Karl Schuhmann. The Hague: Martinus Nijhoff.

Husserl, Edmund (2008): *Die Lebenswelt. Auslegungen der vorgegebenen Welt und ihrer Konstitution. Texte aus dem Nachlass (1916–1937). Husserliana*, vol. XXXIX. Ed. Rochus Sowa. New York: Springer.

Husserl, Edmund (2014): *Grenzprobleme der Phänomenologie. Analysen des Unbewusstseins und der Instinkte. Metaphysik. Späte Ethik. Texte aus dem Nachlass (1908–1937). Husserliana*, vol. XLII. Eds. Rochus Sowa & Thomas Vongehr. New York: Springer.

Ikeda, Yusuke (2015): "Eugen Finks Kant-Interpretation". In: *HORIZON. Studies in Phenomenology*, vol. 4, n° 2, pp. 154–185. DOI: 10.18199/2226-5260-2015-4-2-154-185.

Kant, Immanuel (1894): *Kants Inaugural Dissertation of 1770*. Trans. William J. Eckoff. New York: Columbia College

Kant, Immanuel (1905a): "Träume eines Geistersehers, erläutert durch Träume der Metaphysik". In: *Immanuel Kant Gesammelte Schriften*, vol. 2, *Vorkritische Schriften II*. Berlin: Walter de Gruyter, pp. 315–373.

Kant, Immanuel (1905b): "Der einzige mögliche Beweisgrund zu einer Demonstration des Daseins Gottes". In: *Immanuel Kant Gesammelte Schriften*, vol. 2, *Vorkritische Schriften II*. Berlin: Walter de Gruyter, pp. 63–163.

Kant, Immanuel (1922): *Kants Gesammelte Schriften*, vol. 2, *Kants Briefwechsel III: 1795–1803*. Berlin: Walter de Gruyter.

Kant, Immanuel (1958): *De mundi sensibilis atque intelligibilis forma et principiis*. Hamburg: Felix Meiner.

Kant, Immanuel (1998): *Kritik der reinen Vernunft*. Hamburg: Felix Meiner.

Loidolt, Sophie (2014): "Phenomenological Sources, Kantian Borders: An Outline of Transcendental Philosophy as Object-Guided Philosophy". In: *Phenomenology and the Transcendental*. Eds. Sara Heinäman, Mirja Hartimo, Timo Miettinen. New York, London: Routledge, pp. 190–217.

Moran, Dermot (2007): "Fink's Speculative Phenomenology: Between Constitution and Transcendence". In: *Research in Phenomenology*, vol. 37, pp. 3–31.

Pradelle, Dominique (2015): "Husserls Kritik an Kants transzendentalem Idealismus: Erörterung des phänomenologischen Idealismus". In: *HORIZON. Studies in Phenomenology*, vol. 4, n°2, pp. 25–53. DOI: 10.18199/2226-5260-2015-4-2-25-53.

Tengelyi, László (2014): *Welt und Unendlichkeit. Zum Problem der phänomenologischen Metaphysik*. Freiburg/München: Karl Alber.

Steven Crowell
Amphibian Dreams

Karsten Harries and the Phenomenology of 'Human' Reason

Abstract: What does the Kantian "transcendental turn" tell us about who we are? In his claim to "deny knowledge in order to make room for faith," some have understood Kant's achievement to have been a failed attempt to ward off nihilism, the idea that human existence is devoid of meaning. Karsten Harries argues that we can neither accept Kant's solution nor give up what it sought to reconcile: a robust affirmation of science and an equally robust insistence on our freedom. Harries argues that phenomenology – here represented by Husserl and Heidegger – cannot adequately lead us out of these antinomies, but I will argue that he underestimates the resources of transcendental phenomenology to address nihilism because he operates with a restricted concept of reason. By examining the clues Harries offers for confronting nihilism – in art, in our experience of persons, in Hans Blumenberg's notion of *Unbegrifflichkeit* – I will argue that such clues draw upon insights that belong within the scope of a transcendental phenomenology and that the concept of "human" reason they entail is not subject to the antinomies Harries attributes to transcendental philosophy.

1 Nihilism and Reason

I would like to use the opportunity presented by this volume on *Husserl, Kant, and Transcendental Phenomenology* to consider a problem that arises for the transcendental form of phenomenology that Husserl develops in the wake of Kant's insistence that rationalistic metaphysics – the purely conceptual determination of what is – leads to antinomy. Kant claimed that the original motivation for the Critical Philosophy lay in his discovery of the ineradicable conflict with itself that reason encounters when it attempts to determine the real solely on the basis of logic.[1] Husserl, in turn, developed a version of transcendental phi-

---

[1] In a letter to Christian Garve (September 21, 1798), Kant writes that "the antinomy of pure reason [...] is what first aroused me from my dogmatic slumber and drove me to the critique of reason itself, in order to resolve the scandal of ostensible contradiction of reason with itself" (Kant 1999, p. 552). Of course, Kant elsewhere attributes this original motivation to his reading of Hume, to his struggles with the Leibnizian conception of space, and so on. But in my view the antinomy of reason is philosophically speaking the most important of these.

losophy based not on the "anthropological" presupposition of two distinct "faculties" of the mind – sensibility and understanding – but on the relation between our experience of entities of whatever sort and the meaning thanks to which such entities become accessible to us.[2] Both Husserl and Heidegger differ from Kant precisely in understanding transcendental phenomenology as a "philosophical empiricism" (Heidegger 1976, p. 67, note; Heidegger 1962, p. 490) that eschews transcendental *arguments* in favor of transcendental *reflection* on experience, whereby "meaning" (*Sinn*) becomes thematic.[3] However, as we shall see, Husserl and Heidegger understand the role of reason in significantly different ways, only one of which adequately addresses the problem of nihilism.

Husserl saw transcendental phenomenology as a way of elucidating a concept of reason that could confront nihilism by reforming the "merely fact-minded sciences" of his time and by addressing "questions of the meaning or meaninglessness of the whole of [...] human existence" (Husserl 1976, Hua III/1, p. 4; Husserl 1970a, p. 6). But this project yielded a number of paradoxes, including the "paradox of human subjectivity." Husserl's efforts to resolve the paradox by means of a rational teleology seemed to demand a metaphysical extension of transcendental phenomenology, bringing with it many of the Kantian themes taken up by German Idealism, together with the problems besetting such idealism.[4] Heidegger, in contrast, rejects metaphysical teleology but does not appear to offer his own phenomenological account of reason. In a recent book, *Wahrheit: Die Architektur der Welt*, Karsten Harries, like Husserl, argues that only a new understanding of reason can address the challenge of nihilism, but he believes that both the Husserlian and the Heideggerian approach yield antinomy. Here, in contrast, I will argue that the "human" understanding of reason necessary for countering the threat of nihilism is best understood in transcendental-phenomenological terms.

Wahrheit: Die Architektur der Welt is structured around the trope of antinomy – an argument about how argument gives out, a ladder that rises toward the Ab-

---

[2] Klaus Hartmann (1988, pp. 193–219) argues that all "mixed" versions of transcendental philosophy, such as Kant's, require such an anthropological presupposition. He includes Husserl in this category, with some right, but as I will argue in the final section of the paper, Husserl's phenomenology decisively transforms the "mixed" version.

[3] Despite his criticisms of Husserl's phenomenology, Heidegger gives an appreciative interpretation of two central concepts that define Husserl's "empiricism" – namely, categorial intuition and the new sense of the *a priori* – and adopts both in his own transcendental philosophy (Heidegger 1985, pp. 47–74). For a fuller account of the overlap between the transcendental phenomenologies of Husserl and Heidegger, see Crowell 2001, and Crowell 2013.

[4] See Kern 1964.

solute only to leave us suspended there, confronting the space of which, according to the early Wittgenstein, we cannot speak. For Harries, this silence limns what we are most in need of, something that (as the later Wittgenstein might say) we must "show." We might think of such showing, in painterly terms, as a concern with the "negative space" which constitutes a figure without being figured itself. Phenomenology is the philosophical approach that takes this kind of showing seriously. It is not some epistemically privileged description of the way things are but a strategy for pointing out what is most in need of pointing out, namely, what is *inconspicuous* (*das Unscheinbare*), the negative space against which the way things are becomes conspicuous.[5]

In Heideggerian terms, the painting's figure is not static; it is the *Riss* (rift or tear) which embodies the "strife" between Earth and World (Heidegger 2003, GA 5, pp. 51–58; Heidegger 1971, pp. 62–66). That strife – the tension between the measureless and that which measures – is the inconspicuous "ground" that can be experienced, shown, in a few essential ways. One of these ways is what Harries, following Heidegger, calls "thinking." Such thinking, however, demands a new understanding of reason. Here Harries invokes Blumenberg's theory of *Unbegrifflichkeit* (non-conceptuality):[6] before there is the concept – that is, before one can talk of a cognitive "grasp" of what is – there is *metaphor* which, like the painting, incorporates the rift that allows the real to shine through (Harries 2012, p. 10). To ignore the rift-structure of thinking is to treat reason as *sui generis* and thus, as Harries argues at length, to court nihilism. In turning to those arguments my aim is both critical and constructive: critical, because I believe that the equation between reason and conceptuality ("logical space") Harries employs affords us only an *in*-human picture of reason; constructive, because it is in Harries' own reflections that we find points of departure for a more human understanding of reason, one in which reasoning itself has the structure of the rift and so does not efface the inconspicuous, but opens us to it.

2 Antinomy and the Truth of Things

As an inquiry aiming at truth, philosophy prefers positivity, "theses." But every thesis is dogged by its antithesis, its negation, and so in metaphysics, which has designs on the whole, the omnipresence of negation amounts to a continual

---

[5] Günter Figal (2015) develops many of the points that I only touch on here. In Crowell 2017, pp. 129–147, I explore the extent to which Figal's approach in *Unscheinbarkeit* cannot entirely leave transcendental phenomenology behind.
[6] See Blumenberg 1997, pp. 81–102.

oscillation between thesis and antithesis, a continual reversal of figure and ground. Is Being one or many? Is reason the law of the world or an evolutionary adaptation? Is freedom an origin or an illusion? Arguments abound on both sides, convincing so long as one is viewing one side as the figure, the other as ground. Inconspicuously sustaining this metaphysical oscillation, however, is antinomy, the "negative space" of all dialectic. Kantian transcendental philosophy thinks in *terms* of antinomy, but phenomenology attends to the figure that is delineated by antinomy itself. What is at stake in the conflict figured there is *meaning*, a philosophical *topos* that is proper neither to science (the true), nor to ethics (the good), nor to aesthetics (the beautiful). Meaning is the negative space against which the antinomy of reason appears.

A major motif of *Wahrheit* is that reason, our scientific use of concepts, builds a Tower of Babel by means of which we seek to storm the heavens, to "measure up" to the real. Kant's transcendental philosophy is born of the recognition that this project is antinomical. What Schopenhauer called the "illicit extension of the principle of sufficient reason" to the unconditioned yields the "euthanasia of pure reason" – the near-death experience of the fact that, cut loose from its foothold in sensuous intuition, reason falls into self-contradiction (Kant 1968, p. 385). Extending the principle of causality to the unconditioned, for instance, seems both to exclude a first cause – a "causality through freedom" – and to demand one. Kant's solution is agnostic: reason can get a cognitive grip only on appearances; the thing in itself lies beyond its reach.[7] As Harries reminds us, the early Nietzsche's "naturalistic" reflection on the language of science "reverts to a position that consorts very well with Kant's transcendental idealism": concepts are "metaphorical" transpositions of psycho-physical processes into the "mental" medium of universality (*Allgemeinheit*), yielding a truth that, despite its pretensions, remains human, all-too-human (Harries 2012, p. 37). "This means," Harries concludes, "that the truth sought by philosophy and science does not do justice to the truth of things" (Harries 2012, pp. 24–25).

If truth is the *adaequatio rei et intellectus*, then human intellect, in Kantian-Nietzschean terms, gets us only to appearances, things already cut to the measure of our concepts. The "truth of things," in contrast, is what things really

---

[7] Harries appears to read Kant as a two-world theorist rather than a two-aspect theorist. Here we cannot investigate this matter further, but this decisively sets him at odds with Husserl's version of phenomenological science as an "infinite task." For Harries, "the deepest ground" of such infinitude is "the incommensurability between the principle of reason [*Satz vom Grund*] and reality" (Harries 2012, p. 197). Of course, here we are concerned only with the *theoretical* use of reason. Later we will explore the way Kant's *practical* philosophy paints a quite different picture.

are, measured against the idea of them in God's creative intellect (Harries 2001, pp. 126–223). Thus Kant's transcendental solution to the antinomy of reason leaves us with a picture in which the figure of human knowledge stands out only against the negative space of "transcendence" or the "truth of things." Like the yellow urn which appears in all clarity only so long as one does not notice the black background, human knowledge loses its integrity when the background, transcendence, becomes conspicuous. With the focus on transcendence, human knowledge and reason become the nothing of negative space.

But what enables us to achieve this focus? Mustn't we somehow sense the truth of things? Kant moved in this direction with his embrace of a practical concept of noumenal freedom, and Harries makes a similar move while rejecting Kant's equation of freedom with reason. In what follows I will draw upon transcendental phenomenology to uncover an aspect of the antinomy not fully cultivated in Harries' reflections on freedom and reason. To do so, however, I must first take issue with Harries' claim that Heidegger's version of transcendental phenomenology is itself antinomical.

In *Being and Time* Heidegger introduces the notion of an "ontological difference" between Being (*Sein*) and beings (*Seiendes*): while "Being is always the Being of an entity," the "Being of entities 'is' not itself an entity" (Heidegger 1976, GA 2, pp. 12, 8; Heidegger 1962, pp. 29, 26). This notion is central to Heidegger's transcendental philosophy, but where Harries emphasizes its Kantian aspects – Being is the condition for the possibility of beings – he ignores the specifically *phenomenological* provenance of the ontological difference, which only comes into view if we "bracket" concern with the composition of and relations among beings.[8] Only thus does *meaning* come into focus: the inconspicuous space that provides access to beings *as* such. Understood phenomenologically, Heidegger's ontological difference is the difference between an entity and what it is (means) to be that entity; it is thus entirely neutral with regard to the question of the *Ding an sich*. In contrast, to assume that the way things

---

8 Harries 2012, p. 70: "In its point of departure, *Being and Time* still belongs to a transcendentally understood metaphysics indebted to Kant, as Heidegger himself emphasized." While there is certainly something right about this, Harries, like Heidegger himself, consistently obscures the way in which *Being and Time* is very *unlike* its Kantian predecessor. Most fundamentally, as Tugendhat 1970, p. 263 explained: "Heidegger no longer requires the epoché to enter the dimension of modes of givenness because, after it had been opened up by Husserl, he stands within it from the beginning." See the discussion in Crowell 2013, pp. 72–77. Only by bracketing a concern with positivity, with "beings," does the inconspicuous *meaning* of Being (*Sinn von Sein*) become philosophically salient – a salience which, as Heidegger emphasizes (1997, pp. 143*sq.*), Kant failed to interrogate.

show up for us is mere "appearance" which *must* fall short of the truth of things is dogmatic. Harries eventually arrives at a similar conclusion, but he does not think that phenomenology can get us there. Why not?

If transcendental phenomenology can, for the moment, be identified with the position Heidegger reached in *Being and Time*, Harries holds that it is subject to what he calls an "antinomy of Being" (Harries 2012, p. 10). Heidegger famously argued that "Being (not entities) is dependent upon [our] understanding of Being" (Heidegger 1976, GA 2, p. 281; Heidegger 1962, p. 255). But for Harries this poses a problem: "are there beings without Being? Doesn't Being constitute beings? What can 'Being' mean otherwise"? (Harries 2012, p. 10). Good questions, but they provoke another: What does "depends" mean here? Beings do not (for the most part) depend on human beings: they come into existence without our help, and their relations to one another do not depend on our intervention. But Being is a phenomenological concept: it is that thanks to which entities can show up "as" something and, in fortunate cases, *as* what they *in truth* are. So Being is not an entity, like DNA, or a prior cause that would explain the composition or coming to be of entities; it is the framework – in Harries' metaphor, the "architecture" – that provides us with measured (i.e., norm-responsive and so meaningful) access to such entities. Heidegger's claim that Being "depends" on the human being means that without an entity in whose being its own being is *normatively* at issue, there is no Being, no space of meaning at all.[9]

In *Being and Time* Heidegger operates with what Harries calls a "transcendental concept of Being" (Harries 2012, p. 11) and, as he rightly notes, Heidegger later embraced a "transcendent" concept of Being (*Seyn*) in which the formerly human-centric space of meaning is *not* dependent on us but is an "event" of *Seyn* itself. Harries entirely rejects Heidegger's transcendent concept of Being, with its attendant mythology of gods.[10] Instead, he tries to make room, *within* the transcendental concept of Being, for experience of the transcendent. But if we read the early Heidegger in phenomenological and not in exclusively Kantian terms, the "transcendent" is already there. We need only attend to the ground against which the antinomical dependence of Being on beings and of beings on Being is figured: the meaning that prevails.

Harries, in contrast, judges Heidegger's own transcendental philosophy in *Being and Time* a failure. One reason for this is Heidegger's supposed reliance

---

9 We will examine this sense of dependence in 5 below.
10 This is not to say that he does not recognize, and even embrace, some of the motives that led Heidegger to his transcendent concept of *Seyn*. But he concludes that "every attempt to thus name the gods [...] does violence to what surpasses comprehension. Again and again we will replace gods with golden calves" (Harries 2007, p. 91).

on "transcendental arguments" which, because they only "clarify our presuppositions," cannot "lay an unshakable foundation" for thinking; they provide no genuinely "normative conclusions," but only conditional necessity (Harries 2007, p. 83). However, if, with Husserl and Heidegger, we understand transcendental phenomenology as a "philosophical empiricism," this emphasis on transcendental *arguments* is misplaced. If Harries' Kantian understanding of transcendental philosophy seems to saddle Heidegger with an antinomy, the phenomenological alternative, freed from the traditional motivations that drove Kant, provides a better way of addressing Harries' worries about nihilism by remaining focused on the *meaning* found in experiences Harries himself draws upon in order to combat it.

3 Amphibian Dreams

Harries' assimilation of Heidegger's transcendental phenomenology to Kant's critical philosophy is thus not without serious consequences. Ignoring the Husserlian background of Heidegger's ontology makes it appear as though Heidegger's approach is one-sidedly focused on the human, all-too-human at the expense of the claims of transcendence. Kant himself avoids one-sidedness only by making room for transcendence in the form of pure practical reason. While knowledge of transcendence is ruled out, the ethical subject must "think" of itself as a "noumenal" freedom obeying an unconditional law of reason. In ethics, the meaning that was lost in the first *Critique,* when human reason was denied access to the thing in itself, is regained by a reason that governs our practical lives directly.

Harries agrees that a proper understanding of freedom is "our only possible way out of nihilism" (Harries 2012, p. 54), but Kant's own path does not get us all the way there, since it entails an unbridgeable gulf in our nature between the self as phenomenon and as noumenally free. Fichte saw the problem and argued that the two sides could be reconciled if one takes practical reason as "primary," that is, if one approaches theoretical reason (science and cognition) as *practices*, and so as products of freedom's self-legislation. Harries finds Fichte's solution unsatisfactory, since it yields yet another antinomy. While theory can be seen as a form of practice if we take its cognitive claims as the negative space against which scientific practices stand out, the roles can be reversed: if we focus on the cognitive claims themselves – on their *validity* – then practices recede into negative space and appear, within theory or science, as just more atoms in the void. Harries insists that our "concrete being-in-the-world" – phenomenologically, our *experi-*

ence – "does not allow for such a separation" of theoretical from practical reason (Harries 2012, p. 106). This is why Kant recognized the need for a *third* Critique.

But what does it mean to say that our being-in-the-world, our experience, will not let us separate these two aspects? If we can make such a judgment, must we not already view ourselves from a position where the background against which the conflict between theoretical and practical reason appears has become salient? I am arguing that the phenomenological attitude provides the perspective from which such a judgment can be made, but Harries is suspicious of phenomenology. For him, it flirts with what the medievals called the doctrine of Double Truth. Faced with the obvious assertoric conflicts between the everyday, homely language of the Bible and the scientific language of the learned Theologians, certain medieval philosophers – for instance, "Averroists such as Siger of Brabant" – argued that both might nevertheless be deemed "true" if relativized to the audience for whom such assertions were meant (Harries 2012, p. 29).[11] Harries shows how phenomenology might become caught up in such a doctrine, and why it is unacceptable, in his examination of a draft of paper by the computer scientist Drew McDermott, which struggles to square the claims of freedom with the claims of science in "existential" terms.

A very widespread view, here represented by McDermott, holds that physics provides an adequate (*angemessen*) picture of reality, one that depicts an unutterably strange world absent anything cut to the measure of the human being. In contrast, the world as we experience it, the lifeworld, is populated by things whose meanings are obvious because they are tied to freedom's existential concerns. But if physics is adequate to reality, freedom has no place; the latter is merely "an inescapable framework illusion" (Harries 2012, p. 83). How can these two notions be reconciled? For McDermott, the very *inescapability* of the framework seems to demand a doctrine of Double Truth: from the third-person point of view the world, governed by scientific reason, is an uncanny and alien place; from the first-person point of view, in contrast, it is a world of things that appear to answer to more tractable measures. The one is not reducible to the other, but reason (*in*-human reason) lies entirely on the side of the strange, while freedom lacks all reason and is forced to seek its measure, as the later Heidegger urged, in the local and historically particular, the *Heimat* of the *Volk*. But if Harries is right, our own experience precludes even the *scientist* from treating freedom as merely an inescapable framework illusion. To avoid turning antinomy into a doctrine of Double Truth, we should follow Kant and admit "a reality

---

[11] See also Harries 2001, pp. 130–131.

that transcends our knowledge" and face the fact that "our conceptual thinking will never do justice to reality" (Harries 2012, pp. 83, 73).

In his attempt at a human concept of reason that would abandon the "naive rationalism" of modernity for a "genuine rationalism" that grounds scientific *episteme* in the "despised *doxa*" of the lifeworld, Husserl, too, recognized the threat of Double Truth in the "paradox of human subjectivity" (Husserl 1976, Hua VI, p. 182; Husserl 1970a, p. 178). The human being in the lifeworld takes ordinary things, including itself, to be caught up in the causal nexus of nature, a "component part of the world" subject to the world's contingencies. In the transcendental attitude of first-person reflection, however, I recognize myself as "transcendental subjectivity," not a part of the world but something that "constitutes" the world. Thus "the subjective part of the world swallows up the whole world, and thus itself too" (Husserl 1976, Hua VI, p. 183; Husserl 1970a, pp. 179–180). This leads to attributing contradictory predicates to one and the same thing: from the pre-transcendental point of view, I am a "human being," a worldly entity, but from the transcendental point of view, "nothing human is to be found" in my subjectivity (Husserl 1976, Hua VI, p. 187; Husserl 1970a, p. 183). Such a transcendental "I" is "actually called 'I' only by equivocation" (Husserl 1976, Hua VI, p. 188; Husserl 1970a, p. 184). Husserl did not embrace the doctrine of Double Truth that is evident here, since he believed that the problem could be resolved through a historical "teleology of reason" in which "human" subjectivity would *coincide* with its transcendental vocation. But this requires a step into metaphysics of the sort that Kant's antinomy, according to Harries, rules out.

In the next section I will return to the sort of "experience" that, according to Harries, makes a doctrine of Double Truth unacceptable, but before getting to that we must consider two questions suggested by the discussion of McDermott. First, to say that physics is adequate to – *angemessen*, commensurable with – reality is not necessarily to say that it *exhausts* reality; and if that is so, then avoiding the antinomy does not seem to require embracing the idea that reality finally "transcends our knowledge" in any ultimate sense. Why can't we say, with Denis McManus following the Wittgenstein of the *Philosophical Investigations*, that the measures adopted by scientific reason "reveal what they reveal" – i.e., they are commensurable with the real – but that what they reveal may not be what is most important to us? (McManus 2012, p. 217). Harries spends a good deal of time discussing Wittgenstein, but it is the Wittgenstein of the *Tractatus Logico-Philosophicus*, the one who leaves us with a standoff between "logical space," the "limit" of what can be meaningfully asserted, and a beyond which we somehow sense but "about which we must remain silent." Why focus exclusively on this *in*-human reason? Is there no other kind?

In appealing to Wittgenstein, Harries retains his Kantian perspective. Against Hegel he argues that we can recognize a limit but that such recognition does not allow our thinking to pass beyond it. Nevertheless, against Wittgenstein's claim that "the subject does not belong to the world; rather, it is a limit of the world," Harries maintains that "this limit must be drawn back into the world" (Harries 2012, p. 111). This brings us to our second question. If, as I claim, phenomenology is the way toward such a retrieval of the self, is it condemned to a doctrine of Double Truth?

Harries writes, "we are amphibians, belonging to the earth and to the light" (Harries 2012, p. 144). Being free, we cannot find ourselves wholly within the conceptual columbarium of science, which is nevertheless an adventure of that very freedom, revealing to us the infinitely strange, "homeless" (*unheimlich*) reality encircling any homeland (*Heimat*) in which we happen to find ourselves. At the same time, we belong to the earth, are nurtured there, and can find meaning only in relation to a homeland that is familiar and measured to our bodies. "As such creatures," Karsten writes, "we dream of something that could heal this conflict [*Zwiespalt*]." But such healing cannot proceed by reducing theory to practice or by seeing practice as an inescapable framework illusion. Rather, "only a building and only a thinking that endures [*aushält*] and arbitrates [*austrägt*] this conflict can make a human dwelling possible" (Harries 2012, p. 144). I agree, and in what follows I want to offer a transcendental-phenomenological account of what this might entail. My question, then, is this: What does *reason's* homeland look like?

4 The Experience of Transcendence

The conflict in our amphibious nature leads in-human reason to antinomy. Considered absolutely, "neither a finite nor an infinite world can be conceived." Space itself is antinomical: freedom of inquiry leads to an in-human infinite space, but freedom must bind itself (Harries 2012, p. 144).[12] In the absence of an Aristotelian cosmology, freedom binds itself to a "moveable center," the lifeworld, an orderly architecture (*einräumenden Architektur*) alive to the measure of the body and its local history (Harries 2012, p. 146). As local, however, such measures cannot be conceived as final: freedom, "curiosity," delivers us once more to

---

[12] Commenting on the Davos dispute between Heidegger and Ernst Cassirer, Harries notes the latter's "fusion of infinity and totality, [...] the fusion of freedom and reason," remarking that "Heidegger calls just this fusion into question" (Harries 2007, p. 84).

the anxiety of the infinite (Harries 2012, pp. 122–125).[13] And so we try out a "deranged architecture" (*verrückte Architektur*) that would be appropriate to the uncanny: the technology that makes us masters and possessors of nature. But such building – think here of the virtual architecture of social media, or the mindless extended mind of the smart phone – only reinforces our alienation. We cannot be at home in it, and the conflict remains. The amphibian is thus torn between *Fernweh* – the desire to colonize other milieux, to grasp the whole – and *Heimweh* – the nostalgia for home, for a world cut to the measure of its finitude (Harries 2012, p. 124).

Husserl too encountered this conflict in his reflections on the lifeworld. The "embodied" transcendental subject is *necessarily* distributed, so to speak: as intersubjectivity, it is at home in specific places, "territories," and territory grounds a "homeworld" that necessarily stands in communication with the "alienworlds" of subjects beyond the territory. The norms relevant to meaning within such worlds are what is "normal" within them.[14] At the same time, however, Husserl held fast to the idea of *one* world, entailed by the "equivocally" designated "I" of transcendental subjectivity: the rational *telos* of all home- and alien-worlds. Anthony Steinbock argued that this "holdover" from Husserl's earlier "Cartesian" interpretation of phenomenological method is already surpassed by Husserl's method of "generative" phenomenology (Steinbock 1995, pp. 98–102). Harries, though, sees it as the inescapable residue of the "theological" background he finds in all transcendental philosophy from Kant to Heidegger (Harries 2007, pp. 75*sq*.).

Thus once again antinomy – this time, an antinomy of existence – figures the apparently inescapable conflict bedeviling conceptual thought. Against the negative space of the lifeworld, reason stands out as the demand for the unlimited, and the conceptual architecture of science is its monument. But the very uncanniness (*Unheimlichkeit*) of that project thereby becomes the negative space against which our amphibious need for rootedness, for human measure, stands out. If "architecture" is the metaphor for the measure of human dwelling, then the "deranged" architecture appropriate to reason is unliveable (Harries 2012, p. 142), while orderly building – which makes a place for things according to the measure of finite, historical human being – finds itself perpetually undermined by the anxiety it hopes to exclude.

Faced with the antinomy of existence, Harries turns to an insight provided by the later Heidegger: for us mortals (*die Sterblichen*), being at home can

---

[13] On curiosity (*theoretisches Neugier*), see Blumenberg 1983, Section III.
[14] See Taipale 2014.

only be thought as *return*, being on the way back home (Harries 2012, p. 125). This means that the homeland is not a place, but, like science itself, a task, something at issue in all that we do.

Can this idea help us make sense of the demand, born of worries about Wittgenstein's conception of reason, that the self be thought of not as the limit of the world but as belonging to it? What can such belonging be, if not nostalgia for a home to which we are always on the way back? Does not the very antinomical character of our being testify to our already being beyond the limit, already familiar with our amphibious nature, though in-human reason can see in it only antinomy? What allows us to think our *being in* this situation? Does not the anxious shifting between figure and ground that gives rise to nihilism *itself* stand out against a negative space which, inconspicuous though it may be, can be "shown?"

In the phenomenological attitude, such showing is not a rigorous science, not part of the in-human project of capturing reality in concepts.[15] Instead, it is an attunement to the space of meaning against which the conflict in our nature stands out. That space is equivalent neither to the homey contours of the lifeworld, nor to the logical space constructed in freedom's project of scientific curiosity. Nihilism forgets this background, while phenomenology – by attending to those experiences which show us that, and how, we belong to the world – addresses the antinomies to which such forgetting gives rise. If the in-human conceptual architecture of reason does not allow us to "say" what is thus shown, we do "give voice" to the truth of things through a kind of reason – human reason – that has abandoned the project of grounding meaning because meaning can always only be at issue in it.

In *Wahrheit*, Harries comes close to saying something similar. Though he does not embrace a phenomenological program in philosophy – holding that Husserl's "science" of first-person experience remains entangled in something like a doctrine of Double Truth, while Heidegger's phenomenological ontology leads to the antinomy of Being – Harries' approach nevertheless remains phenomenological in ascribing normative import to our experience.[16] Experience

---

[15] I cannot argue for this claim here, nor go into the vexed question of Husserl's "metaphysics." But the idea of the "truth of things" raises the metaphysical question of whether we need to conceive such things as completely "determinate" and, if so, whether phenomenology can answer such a question. For some thoughts on this issue, see Crowell 2019a. A nuanced account of Husserl's metaphysics is found in Zahavi 2018.

[16] Harries seems to think that contemporary phenomenology ought really to be understood in the terms of *Lambert's* conception of a *Logik der Erscheinung*: "So understood, phenomenology teaches us to see the human being as the measure [*Maß*] of its experiential world, which thereby

is not (or not merely) a justifying ground for conceptual cognition but the soil of a thinking that can endure and arbitrate our conflicted belonging to the world. As Harries explains it, that soil includes our ethical experience of persons,[17] the experience of the claim that the Other, as Thou, makes on us. "Of course," Harries admits, "this is a platitude,"

> but it suffices for showing that every concept of experience that reduces the experiencing human being to a thinking subject confronting a mute reality, which is just what it is and remains without meaning until this subject invests it with meaning, does not do justice to our experience of human beings and things. (Harries 2012, p. 146)

What makes this experience so significant is its second-person structure: the "I" here is not an addressor but an addressee, a "you-accusative." For phenomenology, however, all second-person experience *is* first-person: I experience *myself* as beholden to the Other, as the one addressed by a normative claim that has *prima facie* authority, a claim to which I must respond even if only by turning my back.[18] For Harries, such second-personal experience puts our amphibious nature into perspective, and by attending to *it*, rather than to the practical reason to which it is subordinated in Kant and Fichte, we can find "our only possible way out of nihilism" (Harries 2012, p. 54). "Experiencing our fellow human beings as persons" is the background *presupposition* of Kant's ethics, not already governed by freedom's rational moral law (Harries 2012, p. 146). The Other binds my freedom in a way that is not already a binding through reasons.

Such pre-conceptual "binding" can suggest a way out of nihilism because it is indigenous to meaning, the inconspicuous background against which the antinomical figure of our existence stands out. On the one hand, the experience of persons is embodied, face-to-face, not mediated by reason; it thus belongs to the lifeworld, to the "earthly" measure of our freedom. "In every human being we experience, as living reality, meaning become flesh" (Harries 2012, p. 147). On the other hand, it is not measured by my *own* body (or that of the *Volk*), but by that of the Other who touches me through a claim that cannot be located in the *Tractarian* world. The experience of persons thus lets transcendence shine through.

---

becomes an image-like appearance [*bildhaft Erscheinung*]" (Harries 2012, pp. 190–191). Behind such a view is the transformation painting underwent thanks to the theory of perspective, whereby paintings lost their medieval sense of being "metaphors of transcendence" (Harries 1968).
17 And also possibly art: "Art matters because it can open windows in the house metaphysics has built, windows to an outside for which we lack adequate words" (Harries 2009, p. 196).
18 On second-person phenomenology see Crowell 2016.

In embodiment "we experience the rift [*Riss*] in our nature" (Harries 2012, p. 147).[19] The conflict (*Zwiespalt*) is here conceptualized as what Heidegger called the "strife" (*Streit*) between Earth and World, that is, the strife "of measure and unmeasure" (Heidegger 2003, GA 5, p. 58; Heidegger 1971, p. 70). This rift-structure is invisible to those who identify reason exclusively with the conceptually adequate grasp of things.[20] The latter presents nature as immeasurably strange and calls forth an *ir*rational insistence on the authority of that particular "world" in which we happen to find ourselves. But what Harries glimpses in the experience of persons opens a path to a thinking that can "endure and arbitrate" the conflict in our nature. Freedom's being pre-conceptually bound by the Other requires what at first sight looks like a "wooden iron" (Harries 2012, p. 131): not an orderly (*einräumenden*) architecture but an *ausräumenden Architektur*, an architecture that "dismantles" the homey enclosure, opening us to that space Heidegger called the "free expanse [*freie Weite*]" (Heidegger 1995, p. 114). Such an expanse is not the infinite space of physics, nor is it the *Heimat* or homeworld; it is that openness from which human beings and things come toward us, and its architecture makes room for something like returning home *together*.

Thus Harries finds the "only possible way out of nihilism" in a *certain* phenomenology that allows us to appreciate the experience of transcendence as something other than one side of an unresolvable conceptual conflict. If Harries thinks in terms of antinomies because in-human reason demands it, thinking in terms of antinomies is not itself *antinomical thinking*. It is a painterly strategy for making the negative space of meaning stand out as something that is always at issue for us.

Perhaps I can make this more intuitive by addressing a question that Harries does not take up: If in-human reason, *Begrifflichkeit*, aims to capture reality as a whole and thereby closes us off to what transcends our concepts, might the experience of persons point toward a phenomenological understanding of reason that belongs to the rift-structure of our nature and which does not let the two sides fall apart into a nihilistic antinomy between reason and meaning?

---

[19] "That which first of all and for the most part always binds our freedom already is our shadow-casting body" (Harries 2012, p. 146).
[20] The rift-structure is an analogue of Husserl's "paradox of human subjectivity." But unlike Husserl, Harries does not think that the paradox can be resolved through a metaphysical teleology of reason. The rift is phenomenologically fundamental.

5 Human Reason as Reason-Giving

The beginning of an answer is found in Harries' reflections on the transition from a centered pre-Copernican world to the centerless, measureless universe of the modern world. The Cartesian project of creating an ersatz center by means of method – whereby we "begin with the simplest and most easily known objects" and ascend to the more complex by "supposing some order even among objects that have no natural order of precedence" (Descartes 1985, p. 120) – makes us "masters and possessors of nature" but leaves us inhabiting the world of what Heidegger called "technology" – not a homeland but a wasteland of faceless, meaningless stuff (resources, *Bestand*).[21] Here Harries asks the decisive question: Is technological building and thinking a *necessary* consequence of our freedom? Is the loss of center only a *loss*? (Harries 2012, p. 157). What if, instead, it teaches us something about our situation that is concealed both by the idea of a fixed cosmological center which would establish the "proper" place of things, and by the idea of an ersatz center keyed to the in-human reason of techno-science?

To show the positive yield of losing a fixed normative orientation, Harries turns to the Wittgenstein of the *Philosophical Investigations*. For Wittgenstein, philosophical questions have the form "I have lost my way," and Harries generalizes this insight: "Is not such losing one's way the presupposition of every really free decision?" (Harries 2012, p. 157). To be placed before a decision is to stand at a fork in the road, where the very meaning (*Richtungssinn*) of the path one has been following comes into question. Philosophy, in this sense, is not one among many practices in which we occasionally engage; rather, it is a synechdoche for our own kind of being. Heidegger's definition in *Being and Time* captures this: human being is not a substance with fixed properties, nor is it the autonomous freedom of self-consciousness with its practically rational legislation; rather, it is "a being in whose very Being that being is an *issue* for it" (Heidegger 1976, GA 2, p. 16; Heidegger 1962, p. 32).

To say that my being is always at issue is to say that what it *means* for me to be is a question, and remains one. Never a thesis, any answer to it has the form of an interpretation – that is, a decision – which cannot be derived from a further conceptual ground.[22] Though meaning is a normative concept, and so something that involves a measure of success or failure which must be in play in my deci-

---

[21] Heidegger 1977. For some discussion of the phenomenological aspects of Heidegger's essay, see Crowell 2019b.
[22] Derrida 2008, pp. 25–29 offers keen analysis of this situation, which he calls the "aporia of responsibility."

sion, this measure is not a matter for *episteme*, but for *phronesis*, "judgment." Existing is the task I face when, having lost my way, I have to judge how it is best to go on. Meaning is thus always at issue in what I do; that's what makes meaning meaning.

Harries rightly sees this as the deep point of Kant's third *Critique*, but I think Hannah Arendt has expressed the matter most directly. The nihilism of the modern technological world reflects "an innate incapacity to understand the distinction between utility and meaningfulness, which we express linguistically by distinguishing between 'in order to' and 'for the sake of'." Such incapacity, she continues, "generates meaninglessness." Utility is determined by the work (*ergon*) to be brought about; acting for the sake of something, in contrast, has meaning in view and can refer to no such end. "Meaning," as Arendt notes, "must be permanent and lose nothing of its character, whether it is achieved or, rather, found by man or fails man and is missed by him" (Arendt 1998, pp. 154–155).

Here Arendt only makes explicit what is entailed in Heidegger's definition of the human being as that being in whose being that very being is always at issue. For Heidegger, too, following Aristotle, this definition is cashed out in terms of acting for the sake of something. The "utility" of work – my doing X with Y in order to bring about Z – rests upon an inconspicuous ground: I can try to make something only if I simultaneously try to *be* something, act for the sake of some "possibility" for being (Heidegger 1962, p. 116). Success in the matter of building a house can be measured by the result, the *ergon*; but what it is that a person is doing (say, building a house) can be determined only by reference to what that person is trying to be – in this case, a carpenter. And the measure of being a good carpenter is not exhausted by the result I achieve, the house. What it means to be a carpenter is at issue in my trying to be one. In Nietzschean terms, the difference between trying to do something and trying to be something is the difference between technical *skill* and existential *style*.

Phenomenologically, then, being a carpenter or a father is "essentially" *trying* to be one, and success is not measured by what results from what I do. Rather, the measure of fatherhood, what it means to be a father, is itself part of what is at stake in the trying, at issue in every moment of it. Of course, my trying is typically guided by the norms of fatherhood in my culture, by "what one does" (Heidegger 1976, GA 2; Heidegger 1962, pp. 163–168). Everyone knows how fathers are supposed to conduct themselves. But to take such norms as fixed and grounded measures is to mistake utility for meaning; and to absolutize them is to embrace one side of the antinomy of existence, to mistake local rootedness for the whole of my being. Treating the norms of fatherhood as technical recipes, however, is not sustainable; the freedom that it denies can break through in our experience of what Heidegger calls *Angst* (Heidegger 1976, GA 2, pp. 244–253; Heidegger 1962, pp. 228–235). In anxiety, cultural norms show themselves as inert sociological facts whose putative normativity depends on my commitment to them, that is, on my "care" about living up to them. In commitment, what it means to be a self finds its ontological measure – namely, *authenticity* as taking responsibility for the normative force of the norms in play in whatever it is that I am trying to be.[23] Being a father is thus always deciding how it is *best* to go on, what is best in the matter of fatherhood.

This has led to the charge that Heidegger's position is decisionistic: Whatever I choose to do is normatively authoritative. But this gets everything wrong. The issue here is not the *authority* of the norms, but their *meaning*. We may approach this point in Kantian terms. In the flow of everyday life I experience the "grounds" of my conduct, the social norms of being a father, almost as though they were causes. In this respect, their motivational force is much like the natural predispositions of my being that Kant calls "inclinations" (Kant 1964, p. 65). But in anxiety such natural and social inclinations can lose their grip, appearing as normatively inert possibilities. According to Heidegger, this experience provides phenomenological evidence that my existence does not merely include the possibility of choice but *is* choice from the ground up. I am not grounded except insofar as I *take over being* a ground (Heidegger 1976, GA 2, p. 378; Heidegger 1962, p. 330). As Harries puts it, any attempt to overcome the groundlessness of meaning "makes us deaf to the claim [*Anspruch*], blocks our access to its transcendence in which everything that gives our life meaning has its ground, a ground which, according to its essence, does not permit of being conceived or mastered" (Harries 2012, p. 198).

To "take over" being a ground is necessarily to stand toward my inclinations as toward potentially justifying *reasons* for which I am responsible. In my culture, fatherhood might entail norms of distance, reserve, and breadwinning, but there is no recipe for being a father, and I may come to feel that it is better to be emotionally involved with my children and leave the breadwinning to others. This judgment about what is best is, with a nod to Plato, what a genuine reason *is*.[24] When I decide to act in this way, I come to exemplify a normative conception of fatherhood, but this exemplarity does not amount to establishing the authority of the conception I embrace. Thus, this is no decisionism: my commitment does not make a norm authoritative; it is a response to a claim that yields a

---

[23] See Haugeland 1998, esp. pp. 340–343. The topics touched on in the present section of this paper are developed and defended in more detail in Crowell (2013, esp. Parts III and IV).
[24] Heidegger 2004, GA 9, pp. 160–161; Heidegger 1998, pp. 124–125 makes this connection to Plato explicit.

reason, a claim whose authority cannot be rationally grounded because it is that whereby anything at all can take on the character of a (normative) reason.

This is the structure of what I am calling "human" reason, a reason that can be understood neither as logical space nor as practical legislation. Still, this provides only part of an answer to nihilism, since it seems to leave us with a kind of solipsism in which the very notion of a normative reason – something that is valid for others – can get no purchase.

This kind of solipsism is, however, entirely foreign to Heidegger's phenomenological account of our existence. While each of us alone must take responsibility for what it means to be whatever it is that one is trying to be, one is never alone; I am essentially with others. Therefore, my responsibility (*Verantwortlichkeit*) for the normative force granted to or withheld from the givens of my situation, their status as justifying reasons, is also always answerability *to* the other, and potentially all others, for what I say and do. Reason is originally reason-*giving*. It is what I owe to the Other, an intentional implication of what Harries called the "experience of persons." To say that such an experience is "meaning become flesh" is to say that meaning is always at issue in a dialogical situation that we occupy together.

The concept of reason as reason-giving contrasts with the sort of reason – the logical space of concepts and their inferential relations – that figures in Harries' diagnosis of nihilism. However, such calculative reason, cut loose from the measures of our being, is not really reasoning at all; it is what Hannah Arendt calls "a function of the brain," a natural facility in which we have already been outstripped by our computing devices (Arendt 1998, p. 322). In contrast, Harries' claim that the experience of persons binds me in a way that is not already a binding through reasons – that "without the mediation of the body the claim [*Anspruch*] of reason remains empty and powerless" (Harries 2012, p. 146) – points us toward the homeland of reason itself. To be normatively bound by the Other prior to reasons is to be answerable *to* the other for what I say and do – that is, to owe them an account of why I think it is best to go on as I do.

Human reason, then, reason-giving, stands on neither side of the antinomy of existence: it is neither the exclusive preserve of a scientific project that uproots us from all homelands, nor does it embrace the authority of whatever home we happen to occupy. Thus it does not exacerbate the conflict (*Zwiespalt*) that threatens to tear the amphibian asunder but belongs to the rift that holds Earth and World together in their tension. Thinking of reason in this human way accomplishes what Harries calls for: a thinking that "endures" and "arbitrates" the conflict by refusing to identify reason with the logic of concepts and the figure of antinomy to which logic gives rise. Such thinking can perceive the traces of the play of metaphor that reason bears within it. If "I have lost my way" is the "presupposition of every really free decision," and if acting for the sake of something always involves such freedom, then to act for the sake of being something is to put what binds me – for instance, the measure at stake in my commitment to fatherhood – into play in trying to be one. Seen in this way, my decision can be said to constitute my self *within* the world as a metaphor for what I am trying to be. In exemplifying what I take to be best in the matter of fatherhood, I embody the *metaphor* "I am a father." There is no room in this locution for the "am" of conceptual identity.[25]

Thus it is not surprising that Harries returns, finally, to a kind of anthropocentrism – or better, a "post-postmodern geo-centrism" (Harries 2012, p. 176)[26] – which he, following Hans Blumenberg, calls "astro-noetics" (Harries 2012, p. 166).[27] Nothing in science's centerless and groundless picture of the world compels us to conclude that "the human being cannot and may not stand at the center of its own interests" (Harries 2012, p. 161). True, this center cannot be conceptually contained and defined; but, as what concerns us in the meaning that prevails, it is at issue in what we do. If "astronomy" stands for a thinking that strives to grasp the whole uncanny cosmos in which we find ourselves, and "astro-nautics" represents the attempt to colonize and explore such a cosmos with the in-human reason of techno-science, "astro-noetics" is concerned "not so much with extending our knowledge, but with pondering [*bedenken*] the essence and value of such research activity," with "what meaning it has" to engage in such exploration (Harries 2012, pp. 167–168). This recalls McManus's suggestion that the conceptuality of physics is not, as Nietzsche thought, nothing but metaphor; it is commensurable (*angemessen*) with reality but does not exhaust it. Physics measures what it measures, but it is up to us to think what the meaning and value of such research is. In the end, Harries, with Blumenberg, can say that "there is no alternative to human reason" (Harries 2012, p. 171).

6 Transcendental Empiricism Again

I have argued that Heidegger's transcendental-phenomenological analysis of acting for the sake of being something shows what human reason *is* and should not

---

[25] This is well expressed by Sartre's paradoxical description of the for-itself as "being what it is not and not being what it is" (Sartre 1956, p. 113).
[26] Husserl himself considered a similar idea. See Husserl 1940, pp. 307–325.
[27] See Blumenberg 1997b.

be assimilated to the antinomies of Kantian transcendental philosophy. Since it does not treat reason as an independent faculty whose form commits it to a principle of *sufficient* reason, the phenomenology of human reason as reason-giving avoids the antinomy to which that principle gives rise. Though Harries does not embrace the epithet "phenomenology" for his thinking, his attention to the experiences in which the inconspicuous meaning of what is becomes conspicuous – for instance, the experience of the other person's claim on us – is phenomenological. But can this sort of phenomenology still be called *transcendental*? In conclusion, I will sketch an answer to this question.

At the outset we noted a key point of difference between Kantian and phenomenological transcendental philosophy: while the former employs a transcendental *deduction*, an argument that purports to establish a priori conditions of possibility of experience, the latter employs a transcendental *reduction*, a reflection that brackets our ordinary concern with beings to focus on the meaning that makes experience of beings *as* beings possible. Transcendental phenomenology is thus a kind of empiricism. As Heidegger put it:

> But to disclose the *a priori* is not to make an "*a-prioristic*" construction. Edmund Husserl has not only enabled us to understand once more the meaning of any genuine philosophical empiricism; he has also given us the necessary tools. "*A-priorism*" is the method of every scientific philosophy which understands itself. There is nothing constructivistic about it. (Heidegger 1976, GA 2, p. 67, note; Heidegger 1962, p. 490)

But isn't the very idea of a transcendental empiricism a wooden iron?

The term "empiricism" here signifies, above all, that transcendental phenomenology is not a search for "ultimate grounds," not an epistemic foundationalism in the traditional sense.[28] Its notion of the *a priori* is not an epistemic principle but the target of an inquiry that attends to the meaning that is "always already" there when we experience entities of any sort.[29] Despite this reference to "our" experience, transcendental phenomenology does not depend on the sort of "anthropological presupposition" that Klaus Hartmann identified in Kant's critical philosophy. It does not start with a conception of the human being as an animal endowed with both sensibility and reason, as though these were known quantities; rather, it elucidates "that *a priori* basis which must be visible before the question of 'what man is' can be discussed philosophically" (Heidegger 1976, GA 2, p. 60; Heidegger 1962, p. 71). We have seen that for

---

28 This does not mean that it has nothing to contribute to epistemological discussions of foundationalism. See, for instance, Drummond 1990 and Berghofer 2018.

29 Heidegger calls it a "*perfect* tense *apriori* which characterizes the kind of Being belonging to *Dasein* itself" (Heidegger 1962, p. 117).

both Husserl and Heidegger this basis consists in norm-responsiveness: meaning depends on measure, and so intentional directedness toward beings *as* beings depends on sensitivity to measure *as* measure. It is this capacity, and not some anthropological presupposition, that grounds the transcendental character of phenomenology.

In revisions to the Introduction to Volume II of his *Logical Investigations*, written after his transcendental turn, Husserl emphasized the difference between phenomenological empiricism and traditional foundationalism:

> On our view, theory of knowledge, properly described, is no theory. It is not science in the pointed sense of an explanatorily unified theoretical whole. [...] The theory of knowledge has nothing to explain in this theoretical sense, it neither constructs deductive theories nor falls under any. [...] Its aim is not to *explain* knowledge in the psychological or psychophysical sense as a *factual* occurrence in objective nature, but to *shed light* on the *Idea* of knowledge in its constitutive elements and laws. (Husserl 1984, Hua XIX/1, pp. 26–27; Husserl 1970b, p. 178)

Extended to the phenomenological project as a whole, and in contrast to Kantian transcendental philosophy, this sort of "clarification" yields a *conditional* concept of the *a priori*. As Tugendhat noted, because phenomenology is a descriptive enterprise – that is, "does not seek to ground [truth] *a priori* in the essence of experience in general or in the ego" – it does not possess the means "to demonstrate that a particular form of experience is necessary and universal." Rather, "there is an open plurality of experiential possibilities, and these alone, not experience in general, have necessary structures" (Tugendhat 1970, p. 181). For a phenomenological transcendental philosophy, then, we can say that *if* experiences of such and such a sort are given, then these and those normative conditions must already be in play; but there is no argument that there *must* be such experiences, or that all experience whatsoever must exhibit these normative forms.

A phenomenological transcendental philosophy, therefore, avoids the two main objections that, according to Harries, undermine all transcendental philosophy: that the transcendental subject is a remnant of the theological idea of God as the ground of the world, and that transcendental arguments can only clarify our presuppositions but cannot establish any genuinely normative conclusions. The second objection is nothing but a re-statement of Husserl's position, if by clarifying our "presuppositions" one understands a reflection on the normative order already, and *necessarily*, at work in any one of the "plurality of experiential possibilities" we find ourselves in. It is simply not part of phenomenology's mission to use transcendental arguments to justify the norms or measures that order such experiences; it seeks only to *disclose* them.

For the same reason, phenomenology's recourse to the first-person standpoint, its reference to the "transcendental" subject who is engaged in phenomenological reflection, has nothing to do with providing an ultimate ground of the world in a metaphysical sense. In exploring the normative constitution of things – that is, in clarifying the way that meaning allows things to show up *as* the things they in truth are – phenomenology reveals how such showing up is founded on a correlational *a priori* that necessarily includes a norm-responsive subject. But as Tugendhat remarks, "founding does not mean grounding" (Tugendhat 1970, p. 182). Transcendental phenomenology clarifies how the truth of things can show itself in experience; it does not purport to ground such truth in a "theological" subject that could stand surety for the ultimate rationality of things.

We may summarize these points by saying that phenomenology is transcendental because it clarifies how anything that we experience as transcendent can *be* experienced by us precisely *as* transcendent. Whether it be the sort of transcendence exhibited by ordinary things, their "reality," or the sort exhibited by the other person's ethical claim on me – or indeed, the transcendence of the gods or God, the "holy" – transcendence must show itself within *some* normative order of meaning for which I who experience it am responsible. Reason, too, is a kind of transcendence constituted in this way, not a principle that might compel phenomenological inquiry into antinomy.

Human reason, therefore, cannot be identified with conceptuality (*Begrifflichkeit*), a potential theory of everything; rather, it is a possibility arising from the norm-responsiveness that is necessary for any experience of meaning at all. Meaning *precedes* reason and is founded on "care," a kind of being for whom what it means to be is necessarily at issue. So conceived, reason belongs to the rift-structure (being-at-issue) that characterizes any relation to measure. Transcendental empiricism neither aims at, nor provides, an ultimate measure for the truth of things because it is not concerned with things, but with meaning.

If phenomenology is an infinite task – as it must be, since its "conditional" *a priori* is open to new forms of experience – it remains transcendental in its commitment to clarifying the transcendence that necessarily informs any such experience. It is not metaphysically necessary that there be meaning, that there be an "ontological difference" or a distinction between intentional content and psychological content. But if meaning is somehow there, then so is its transcendental condition: a subject who can care about the truth of things because it has already *measured itself* against what is best in trying to be whatever it is trying to be. And since being a philosopher, a thinker, is something for the sake of which one can act, the *project* of philosophy is the thinker's commitment to the task of thinking. Finally, if philosophical thinking is fundamentally concerned with meaning, "transcendental phenomenology" is the name for what is at stake in what it means to be a thinking being.

Of course, other thinkers will have different views about what the measure or meaning of philosophical practice is. A transcendental empiricism has no knock-down arguments to refute such views. Like all empiricism, transcendental phenomenology is fallible. Nevertheless, it is a cognitive enterprise and so remains beholden to reasons. This means that while transcendental phenomenology adopts a first-person stance and bears "radical self-responsibility" (Husserl) for the *Evidenz* it achieves there, it does so always in a dialogical space where I am answerable, accountable, to others for what I think. The phenomenological claim that meaning presupposes care is a move in the game of giving and asking for reasons; thus one may be called upon to offer reasons. What one offers may well generate other queries, demanding other offerings, but this does not presuppose that a *sufficient* reason can be given. The dialogical, "human" concept of reason thus has an advantage over the "principle" of reason, since it follows from the essential nature of thinking's "object," the meaning that prevails.

Thus, even if transcendental-phenomenological empiricism provides no "ultimate" cognitive ground, it has the virtue that its own elucidation of what a ground or reason *is* does not contradict its own possibility. As Emil Lask pointed out, Kant's transcendental philosophy fails precisely on this point: "In Kant's theory of categories there is no room for the categorial forms of his own speculation, and thus the critic of theoretical reason denies the logical conditions of his own critique of reason" (Lask 2003, p. 216).[30] Karsten Harries extends this judgment to any philosophical approach that takes reason as a principle governing a logical space of concepts. The supposed "autonomy" of reason leads to antinomy. Transcendental phenomenology, in contrast, focuses on the negative space that allows antinomy to stand out, the meaning that inconspicuously sustains all experience of the transcendent, including the transcendence that belongs, pre-eminently, to our own "finite" thinking. But here finitude cannot be thought of as the negation of the infinite. Finitude is the *positive* term; the infinite is at issue in the finite, "empirical," measure-taking that thinks it.

Bibliography

Arendt, Hannah (1998): *The Human Condition*. Trans. Margaret Canavan. Chicago: The University of Chicago Press.

---

[30] See the discussion in Crowell 2001, pp. 76–92.

Berghofer, Philipp (2018): "Why Husserl is a Moderate Foundationalist". In: *Husserl Studies*, vol. 34, n° 1, pp. 1–23.
Blumenberg, Hans (1983): *The Legitimacy of the Modern Age*. Trans. Robert M. Wallace. Cambridge: The MIT Press.
Blumenberg, Hans (1997a): "Prospects for a Theory of Non-Conceptuality". In: *Shipwreck With Spectator*. Trans. Steven Rendall. Cambridge: The MIT Press, pp. 81–102.
Blumenberg, Hans (1997b): *Die Vollzähligkeit der Sterne*. Frankfurt: Suhrkamp.
Crowell, Steven (2001): *Husserl, Heidegger, and the Space of Meaning: Paths Toward Transcendental Phenomenology*. Evanston: Northwestern University Press.
Crowell, Steven (2013): *Normativity and Phenomenology in Husserl and Heidegger*. Cambridge: Cambridge University Press.
Crowell, Steven (2016): "Second-Person Phenomenology". In: *The Phenomenology of Sociality: Discovering the "We"*. Eds. Thomas Szanto and Dermot Moran. London: Routledge, pp. 70–89.
Crowell, Steven (2017): "Interiors: The Space of Meaning and the Great Indoors". In: *Raum Erfahren. Epistemologische, ethische und aesthetische Zugänge*. Eds. D. Espinet, T. Keiling, and N. Mirkovic. Tübingen: Mohr Siebeck, pp. 129–147.
Crowell, Steven (2019a): "Determinable Indeterminacy: A Note on the Phenomenology of Horizons". In: *The Significance of Indeterminacy*. Eds. Greg Moss et al. New York and London, Routledge, pp. 127–147.
Crowell, Steven (2019b): "The Challenge of Heidegger's Approach to Technology: A Phenomenological Reading". In: *Heidegger on Technology*. Eds. Adam Wendland, Christos Hadjioannou, and Christopher Merwin. London: Routledge.
Derrida, Jacques (2008): *The Gift of Death*. Trans. David Wills. Chicago: The University of Chicago Press.
Descartes, Rene (1985): *Discourse on the Method*. In: *The Philosophical Writings of Descartes*, Vol. I. Eds. John Cottingham, Robert Stoothoff, and Dugald Murdoch. Cambridge: Cambridge University Press.
Drummond, John (1990): *Husserlian Intentionality and Non-Foundational Realism*. Dordrecht: Kluwer Academic Publishers.
Figal, Günter (2015): *Unscheinbarkeit. Der Raum der Phänomenologie*. Tübingen: Mohr Siebeck.
Harries, Karsten (1968): *The Meaning of Modern Art*, Evanston: Northwestern University Press.
Harries, Karsten (2001): *Infinity and Perspective*. Cambridge, MA: The MIT Press.
Harries, Karsten (2007): "The Descent of the 'Logos'". In: *Transcendental Heidegger*. Eds. Steven Crowell and Jeff Malpas. Stanford: Stanford University Press, pp. 88–92.
Harries, Karsten (2009): *Art Matters: A Critical Commentary on Heidegger's "The Origin of the Work of Art"*. Dordrecht: Springer.
Harries, Karsten (2012): *Wahrheit: Die Architektur der Welt*. München: Wilhelm Fink Verlag.
Hartmann, Klaus (1988): "On Taking the Transcendental Turn". In: *Studies in Foundational Philosophy*. Amsterdam: Editions Rodopi, pp. 193–219.
Haugeland, John (1998): "Truth and Rule-Following". In: *Having Thought. Essays in the Metaphysics of Mind*. Cambridge, MA: Harvard University Press, pp. 305–361.
Heidegger, Martin (1962): *Being and Time*. Trans. John Macquarrie and Edward Robinson. New York: Harper & Row.

Heidegger, Martin (1971): "The Origin of the Work of Art". In: *Poetry, Language, Thought*. Trans. Albert Hofstadter. New York: Harper & Row, pp. 15–88.
Heidegger, Martin (1976): *Sein und Zeit. Gesamtausgabe*, vol. 2. Ed. Friedrich-Wilhelm von Herrmann. Frankfurt: Vittorio Klostermann.
Heidegger, Martin (1977): "The Question Concerning Technology". In: *The Question Concerning Technology and other Essays*. Trans. William Lovett. New York: Harper & Row, pp. 3–35.
Heidegger, Martin (1995): *Feldweg-Gespräche (1944–45). Gesamtausgabe*, vol. 77. Ed. Ingrid Schüßler. Frankfurt: Vittorio Klostermann.
Heidegger, Martin (1997): *Kant and the Problem of Metaphysics*. Trans. Richard Taft. Bloomington: Indiana University Press.
Heidegger, Martin (1998): "On the Essence of Ground". In: *Pathmarks*. Trans. William McNeill. Cambridge: Cambridge University Press, pp. 97–135.
Heidegger, Martin (2003): *Holzwege. Gesamtausgabe*, vol. 5. Ed. Friedrich-Wilhelm von Herrmann. Frankfurt: Vittorio Klostermann.
Heidegger, Martin (2004): *Wegmarken. Gesamtausgabe*, vol. 9. Ed. Friedrich Wilhelm von Herrmann. Frankfurt: Vittorio Klostermann.
Husserl, Edmund (1940): "Grundlegende Untersuchungen zur phänomenologischen Ursprung der Räumlichkeit der Natur". In: *Philosophical Essays in Memory of Edmund Husserl*. Ed. Marvin Farber. Cambridge: Harvard University Press, pp. 307–325.
Husserl, Edmund (1970a): *The Crisis of European Sciences and Transcendental Phenomenology*. Trans. David Carr. Evanston: Northwestern University Press.
Husserl, Edmund (1970b): *Logical Investigations, Volume I*. Trans. J. N. Findlay. London: Routledge and Keegan Paul.
Husserl, Edmund (1976): *Die Krisis der europäischen Wissenschaften und die transzendentale Phänomenologie. Eine Einleitung in die phänomenologische Philosophie. Husserliana*, vol. VI. The Hague: Martinus Nijhoff.
Husserl, Edmund (1984): *Logische Untersuchungen. Zweiter Band. Erster Teil: Untersuchungen zur Phänomenologie und Theorie der Erkenntnis. Husserliana*, vol. XIX/1. Ed. Ursula Panzer. The Hague: Martinus Nijhoff.
Kant, Immanuel (1964): *Groundwork of the Metaphysics of Morals*. Trans. H. J. Paton. New York: Harper & Row.
Kant, Immanuel (1968): *Critique of Pure Reason*. Trans. Norman Kemp Smith. London: MacMillan.
Kant, Immanuel (1999): *Correspondence*. Trans. Arnulf Zweig. Cambridge: Cambridge University Press.
Kern, Iso (1964): *Husserl und Kant*. The Hague: Martinus Nijhoff.
Lask, Emil (2003): *Die Logik der Philosophie und die Kategorienlehre*. In: *Sämtliche Werke*. Jena: Dietrich Schegelmann Reprintverlag.
McManus, Denis (2012): *Heidegger and the Measure of Truth*. Oxford: Oxford University Press.
Sartre, Jean-Paul (1956): *Being and Nothingness*. Trans. Hazel Barnes. New York: Washington Square Press.
Steinbock, Anthony (1995): *Home and Beyond: Generative Phenomenology After Husserl*. Evanston: Northwestern University Press.

Taipale, Joona (2014): *Phenomenology and Embodiment: Husserl and the Constitution of Subjectivity.* Evanston: Northwestern University Press.
Tugendhat, Ernst (1970): *Der Wahrheitsbegriff bei Husserl und Heidegger.* Berlin: Walter de Gruyter.
Zahavi, Dan (2018): *Husserl's Legacy. Phenomenology, Metaphysics, and Transcendental Philosophy.* Oxford: Oxford University Press.

Natalie Depraz
Husserlian Phenomenology in the Light of Microphenomenology[1]

Abstract: This chapter seeks to place itself in the lineage of the Husserlian transcendental gesture, which operates the epoché of pregiven positive contents, and to reveal the subjectivation inherent in objectivation. Now, such a becoming aware was taken up again by the recent discipline of microphenomenology, which questions anew what is called subjectivity by placing once more the subject at the core of the living experience, but more acutely this time, of his singular *hic et nunc* real life, and by proposing a rigorous fine-tuned description of its specific lived experiences. What does it borrow from Husserlian phenomenology, how it establishes its difference, what does the prefix "micro" mean? This is the first step of the presentation. On this basis I will come back to some aspects of the complex situation of phenomenology as a science describing the structures of lived experience in its relationship to the psychologies of introspection (Titchener's and Külpe's), and particularly the example of attention, which is situated at their crossroads. This will enable me to testify to the intimate bond between phenomenology and psychology. In a third stage, I will return to the project of microphenomenology, in relation to Varela's research program on the naturalization of phenomenology.

Introduction

Husserlian phenomenology can be seen as a transcendental philosophy of a new genre compared to Kant's critical philosophy. From one transcendental philosophy to another, one moves from the formal conditions of the possibility of experience, which themselves cannot be experienced by the subject, to a transcendental experience thanks to which the subject constitutes the intentional meaning of given objects. But whether one or the other transcendental is concerned, it is still the subject who is placed at the center of the knowledge of objects and who is their carrier. In one case, the subjective structures of knowledge are *a priori* forms, which are independent of experience and are applied to it, whereas in the other, these structures can be experienced by the subject insofar as they are intuitively given. Yet, in both transcendental philosophies, the subject

---

[1] Translated from French by Yves Millou and revised by Scott Davidson.

is the provider of meaning for the object, i.e. for the empirical data which are straightaway invested with meaning.

So it is from this function of a meaning-giving subject, who is invested with such a function, that Husserl can deliver a critical and genealogical diagnosis of the sciences. Their unfolding in History goes hand in hand – according to his reading – with the forgetting of "the enigma of subjectivity" (Husserl 1934–1937; Husserl 1954; Husserl 1970). One therefore notes the covering over of the first *Faktum* according to which science occurs only when a subject performs science, and this blindness has contributed to an exclusive precedence ceded to science's positive results. This objectivation process, while valid in itself, becomes a concern as soon as it adds to itself a blindness, which would be inherent in the scientific task, in which the subject becomes absent to herself. Identified as early as Husserl's *Philosophy as Rigorous Science* in 1910 (Husserl 1911/1965) through the term "naturalism" and the expression "the naturalization of consciousness," this idea extends in the 1930s, in *The Crisis of European Sciences and Transcendental Phenomenology*, to a historical-critical archeology of scientific objectivism. This diagnosis confers to the phenomenologist the function of a discerning subject, which belongs to the practitioner of an epoché viz. the reflexive suspension of unquestioned positive contents. Upon practicing such an epoché, the phenomenologist sharpens her discerning skills and opens up the possibility for the scientist to become aware of her actions, whereas as a rule her standard tendency and thematic attitude consists most of the time in producing positive results without realizing that such results are the outcome of a subject who has a structural influence on them, and who is, at an even deeper level, an essential part of obtaining them. It is from this transcendental attitude, understood in an operative way as the practice, from moment to moment, of an epoché of the operations producing scientific results, that the phenomenological subject may "found" scientific practices by "discovering" their objectifying tendency and by uncovering the subjective operations which are constitutive of the objectivation process.

In this contribution, I wish to place myself in the lineage of such a radical transcendental gesture, which is at the core of the enigma of a subjectivity that constantly operates the epoché of pregiven positive contents, and reveals, from this self-aware attitude, the subjectivation inherent in objectivation. Indeed, the recent discipline of microphenomenology proposes to implement an epoché of unquestioned contents that are active not only in sciences now called cognitive but which also (although specifically) remain unquestioned by the founding of phenomenology itself. It does this by re-questioning what is called subjectivity, i.e. by placing once more the subject at the core of the living experience of her singular *hic et nunc* real life, and then by proposing a rigorous and fine-tuned description of this subject's specific lived experiences.

I thus propose to start from the following analogy: microphenomenology stands in relation to Husserlian phenomenology in the same way as the latter used to stand vis-à-vis positive sciences and, in this circumstance, towards psychology, especially experimental psychology. We shall see, nevertheless, that this analogy isn't completely unambiguous. On the one hand, if microphenomenology, like Husserlian phenomenology, questions the positivity and the objectifying, third-person approach of the experimental sciences – essentially, today, the neuroscientific and psychological sciences –, it has constitutive internal links with these sciences. This wasn't the case for Husserlian phenomenology, even if, as we shall see later with the example of attention, its links are more deeply internal than is often said. On the other hand, microphenomenology today is far from claiming the status of a general ontology which would found regions of scientificity, as was the case for Husserlian phenomenology. But that probably isn't its objective, at least at this stage, which, for now, is more fundamentally methodological.

So my proposition in this contribution will be more modest. It will introduce some arguments to show how the discipline of microphenomenology can play the role of a critical instance method for the transcendental discernment of a phenomenology which indeed had defended in its own time the necessary uncovering of a subject who had been covered over by scientific objectifications, but which didn't go any further than positing it without actually achieving it.

But first, one has to make clear what microphenomenology is: what it borrows from Husserlian phenomenology, how it places itself within its filiation and establishes its difference. What exactly does the prefix "micro" mean? This will be the first step of my inquiry. On this basis I will then, in a second step, come back to some aspects of the complex situation of phenomenology as a science describing the structures of lived experience in its relationship to the various psychologies of introspection, and especially the emblematic example of attention, which is situated at their crossroads. This will enable us to testify, in the act, to the intimate bond between phenomenology and psychology. In a third stage, I will return to the project of microphenomenology, this time from my own proposal, which is to confer it with the status of a dimension – a transcendental one – of a possible overhaul of Husserlian phenomenology, and this through an epoché carried out on the subject herself.

1 Microphenomenology

The birth of microphenomenology is a recent one. The term was coined some years ago, in the Spring of 2016, during talks held by researchers belonging to the Paris Husserl-Archives (Claire Petitmengin, Michel Bitbol, Dominique Pradelle and myself), and Pierre Vermersch, a psychologist trained in Jean Piaget's theories, and founder in the early 1980s of the technique of the explicitation interview (*entretien d'explicitation*), now called the microphenomenological interview, which he began within the frame of his research into organizational psychology as early as 1976 (Vermersch 1994/2004/2011).

Starting from everyday professional or personal activities and their distinction into time-sequences, in which the subject performs successfully what she performs, and knows how she performs it (disassemble a microprocessor, go to the baker's to get some bread), P. Vermersch's question was the following: *how* does the subject do what she does? And as a corollary, is she capable of describing the manner in which she goes about doing what she does? Indeed, if one asks somebody how she's done what she's done, most of the time one gets an answer which supplies her *representation* of what she has done, much more than *how she effectively went about* doing what she has done. I linger on the starting point of P. Vermersch's interrogation since, as a researcher in psychology, he underlines the core of what will become his specific practice of describing a subject's preconscious experience, which he will term *"pré-réflexive,"* or *"implicite,"* and which will lead him to set up an interview technique aimed at enabling this subject to "make explicit" (*"expliciter"*) her manner of doing what she does with a great degree of fineness and precision, a rarely reached "granularity" (*granularité*) as he himself puts it.

It is in the middle of the nineties, more precisely in 1993, that Vermersch encountered the texts of Husserl's phenomenology, especially his *Ideas Pertaining to a Pure Phenomenology I* (1913) (Husserl 1982), then in the following years, his writings of the twenties: *Analyses Concerning Passive and Active Synthesis* (1918–1926) (Husserl 2001), which belong to the Husserlian period of genetic phenomenology, but also the earlier Course given by Husserl in the Winter semester of 1904–1905 entitled *On the Phenomenology of Inner Time-Consciousness* (1893–1917) (Husserl 1990). He thus discovers the fertility of the Husserlian concepts of intentional lived experiences, reflexive acts, attentional shifts, awakening intentions, passive retentional processes, and the passive pregiven field of consciousness. In these concepts, Pierre Vermersch sees operations of consciousness, acts one can carry out, and which help to make more accurate the description of the various acts and procedures which I achieve when I do something. While adopting these concepts for their operational and descriptive value, Vermersch parts with Husserl's philosophical position, especially his transcendental idealism and foundational ontology (Vermersch 2012). Thus the epoché, the emblematic method of the suspension of positive unquestioned contents, is understood less as a principle of theoretical justification of knowledge than as a practical operation, producing a reexamined experience which is free from presuppositions. In the mid-1990s, my own rereading of Husserlian phenomenology, understood as a practice of experiential effectuation of the epoché, a rereading which then identified itself as "transcendental empiricism" (Depraz 2001), met Vermersch's work on the explicitation of lived singular *hic et nunc* experience of a given subject. It gave rise, during five years between 1996 and 2001, to continuous and intense exchanges between P. Vermersch, F. J. Varela, and myself, that led to the publication of a work written by six hands: *On Becoming Aware. A Pragmatics of Experiencing*. (Depraz, Varela, Vermersch, 2003/2011a).

The understanding of transcendental phenomenology as a transcendental empiricism refers indeed to Husserl's innermost claim (against Kant) of the validity of the "transcendental experience" of the subject. It involves taking seriously the concreteness and effectiveness of the transcendental attitude and the genuine experimentation of the transcendental epoché. Thus, transcendental empiricism intends to do justice to transcendental phenomenology in its genuine meaning (Szilasi 1959/2011; Depraz 2001, 2011b; Rölli 2003/2012).

Through the technique of the microphenomenological explicitation interview, one enables the subject to gain a more fine-tuned access to singular lived experiences, which are often covered over by generic representations. Typically, if I ask how you woke up this morning, and you answer me that in general, the alarm clock wakes you up, you are describing the usual structure of your wake-up reality, or your own spontaneous representation of this morning's waking-up. According to P. Vermersch, you would be describing a "class of lived experiences," but not your lived and unique experience of that particular morning: in other words, the formulation of this morning's experience is in fact the implicit and sedimented result of a multiplicity of experiences. This is the type of description which one reads in the analyses of phenomenological philosophers when they refer to a situation. For example, in § 27 of his *Ideas I*, Husserl writes: "I can let my attention wander away from the writing table which was just now seen and noticed, out through the unseen parts of the room which are behind my back, to the veranda, into the garden, to the children in the arbor, etc." (Husserl 1982, Hua III/1, p. 51). In spite of the fact that the statement is in the present tense, contains a deictic ("this desk"), and is carried by an I situated in a concrete and familiar living space, all indicators of an embodied speech ("*prise de parole incarnée*" in Vermersch's words), the example remains generic and the description structural. In fact, the indicator of the structural generality of the experience consists in the mode of possibility which begins the description: "I *can* let my attention wander..." Husserl might well have lived this experience dozens of times; he is in fact reproducing for us a structural experience of attentional displacement, which we can enter, of course, which we can even carry out for ourselves, in accordance with an imaginary mode of transposition of the phenomenological level of possibility inherent in the Husserlian proposition. Nevertheless, this attentional experience has nothing singular about it, and so, as a consequence, the description remains general.

On the contrary, getting back to my own example, I suggest that you return to the precise moment when you woke up this morning and describe the microprocess of emerging into consciousness which was your awakening. By inviting you to go back precisely to that moment, I will get a fine-tuned description of your experience of that moment. First, describe the context: your lying position, what sort of room are you in (airy or close), the lighting, the heat; go back to the precise moment when the alarm-clock rings, or perhaps you wake up before it rings, how you feel, what sort of emotional or cognitive state is yours – how about your possible internal orientation movements in space, the speed (or absence of it) with which you recognize the environment, whether you are in a hotel room or anywhere other than your usual environment.

In short, the explicitation interview, recently rebaptized as 'microphenomenology,' is a fine-tuned description technique of micro-processes both bodily (feelings, kinesthesis, proprioception, cardiac) and internal (cognitive, attentional, emotional, imaging) of a singular moment lived by a subject at a given time and in a given space. Placing themselves in the wake of the Husserlian discipline of the description of lived moments of consciousness, P. Vermersch and later Claire Petitmengin (Petitmengin 2017), whose specific purpose was to situate the microphenomenological interview on a theoretical scientific ground of research, chose a singular and fine-tuned description which, compared to Husserl's approach, shifts the descriptive focus in two ways: 1. The lived experience is singular, content-laden, not generic and structural; 2. The granularity level of the description is reinforced, which gives rise to fine-tuned micro-sequences, to the detailed emergence of lived processes and the highlighting of (quasi) synchronic moments of experience (Depraz 2014a).

2 Introspection and Psychophysics: The Ambiguous Situation of Husserlian Phenomenology in the Light of the Example of Attention

I am now going to situate microphenomenology in relation to Husserlian phenomenology by placing it, using the example of attention, in the context of the historical debate between introspection and psychophysics.

Methodologically, microphenomenology belongs to the framework of "first person" approaches: the subject is defined as an embodied and situated instance, in a relation of intimate contact with herself, able to refer to herself by the effective exploration of her lived experiences most of the time through the "second person" mediation of an interviewer who accompanies the microphenomenological process of the implicit, unacknowledged, pre-conscious dimensions of the lived experience. Before adopting the term "microphenomenology," which refers to the fine-tuned granular level of description *and* the phenomenological philosophy dimension of the discipline, P. Vermersch had used the expression "psycho-phenomenology" (Vermersch 1996; Depraz, Varela, Vermersch 2003/2011a) in order to underline his adoption of Husserlian phenomenology as intentional and eidetic "phenomenological psychology" and to place his research in the framework of a reciprocal renewal of the relations between psychology and phenomenology. Thus, Vermersch proposes a historical genealogy of the technique of the microphenomenological interview (Vermersch 1999; 2009). Some psychologists like W. Wundt, O. Külpe, and E. Titchener, who were Husserl's contemporaries, called "introspection" (*Selbstbeobachtung*) the internal movement of contact with one's lived experience. Vermersch traces back such an inner move and provides a finer description of this very moment where the subject is accompanied by the interviewer in order for her to contact a singular lived moment of her experience. Such an experiential contact is called in French *"mise en évocation"*: thanks to "how" questions, the subject is able to "come back" to the singular lived moment of her experience and to "be there" again in a very intense and concrete way.

Now, in the very long *excursus* from § 79 of *Ideas I* entitled "Critical *excursus*. Phenomenology and the difficulties of 'Self-observation,'" Husserl allies himself with the Munich introspection psychologist Th. Lipps, who strongly influenced him. He reconsiders both the possibility of the access to my immediate lived experience in the face of H. J. Watt's skepticism *and* limits this access by playing the principle of intuition against the primacy of reflection, which is regularly charged with the recurring criticism of the deformation-alteration of lived experience under reflection (Husserl 1982, Hua III/1, § 79, pp. 181–183). I shall not go back here to the various historical forms of introspection in psychology, whether experimental-psychophysiological with Fechner and Wundt, internal-psychic with Lipps and Külpe, which I have expounded elsewhere (Depraz 2014a), or the critical discussion led by Husserl in this very long *Excursus*, which I have already discussed at length (Depraz 2008). Here I simply wish to indicate that Husserl's reasonings in this paragraph are directly connected to his transcendental position: the philosopher, in his concern with the critical demarcation of scientific disciplines and, in particular, with "empirical psychology," contrasts the lived truth of the principle of intuition, presented in § 24 of *Ideas I*, with the skepticism which is characteristic of experimental psychology. According to the argument concerning the "deformation" or the alteration of the lived experience, as soon as one observes it from the point of view of reflection, such a psychology bars any access to the subject's immediate lived experience. Now, what we have here is a transcendental reaffirmation of the originary immediate intuitive access to the subject's lived experience, contra empirical behavioristic psychology which still today sees in it nothing but a "black box."

The proposal of P. Vermersch, in the wake of Husserl's principle of intuition, is to rehabilitate introspection as a method of access to the singular lived experience of a given subject. To do this, he implements the technique of "*évocation*" we mentioned above, where the subject reinvests in detail her experience of a singular moment by being there again (I see the room where I wake up this morning, I feel the flavor of the sheets, I perceive the morning light under my still closed eyelids), then produces a description of the segments, levels, and micro-phases of her experience (of this precise moment of awakening). Thus, in the face of the Neowattian skeptic's argument that only swears by observable behavioral (today neuronal) traces, Vermersch moves to the practical plane of producing a description of a singular moment of the lived experience of a given subject.

We now understand better the configuration of the different historical psychologies in which Husserlian phenomenology is situated and what precursory role it can play in a contemporary discussion that opposes approaches in the first and third person (with its internal limits, linked in particular to the situation of phenomenology at the level of the possibility, in accordance with Husserl's mathematical anchoring and his parallel staging of the imagination in the eidetic variation method, which is an opening of possibilities).[2] It isn't my intention

---

[2] I shall come back towards the end of this article to the status of Husserl's eidetic variation, its resumption and difference in the framework of a microphenomenological analysis.

within this contribution to produce a detailed inventory of contemporary phenomenological psychologies, beyond the well-known Husserlian critique of psychologism. This one, which we know better now, is only the tip of the iceberg of psychology. It really concerns only the targeted stakes of the psychological (moreover atomistic) foundation of logic, which was the only critical entry into psychology for phenomenologists for decades and which blocked the possibility of a thorough investigation of the internal relationship with contemporary psychologies of phenomenology, with which Husserl was in contact throughout the constitution of phenomenology.[3] What emerges from our rapid treatment of the issues raised in *Ideas I* by § 79 on phenomenology in relation to introspection is that Husserl is clearly in search of a method that will allow a rigorous observation of the internal experiences of the subject, contrarywise to a physiological psychology that seeks to measure quantitatively the sensory intensity and temporality of attentional states, as was the case of G. Fechner and W. Wundt. The principle of Husserl's method lies in the "principle of principles" of intuition. From this point of view, Husserl is closer to psychologists such as Th. Lipps, O. Külpe, or even E. Titchener, who, as we will see, strive to describe the modalities and qualitative psychic processes of attention.

Indeed, W. Wundt in his 1896 *Grundriß der Psychologie* (Wundt 1896; on Wundt's experimental "objectifying" introspection, see Friedrich 2008) and E. Titchener in his 1908 *Lectures on the Elementary Psychology of Feeling and Attention* (Titchener 1908, Flajoliet 2010) propose experiments and hypotheses that identify the criteria of indirect (i.e. physiological) measurements of attention: on the one hand, the intensity of the sensation *via* the increase of its clarity, on the other hand, the intermittent rhythm of its maintenance. To the contrary, Th. Lipps, as early as his *Grundzüge psychischen Lebens* in 1883 (Lipps 1883/ 2018), and O. Külpe in his *Grundriß der Psychologie* in 1893 (Külpe 1893), focus on the direct apprehension of attention (through introspection), especially through its internal psychic degrees and fluctuations.

I would like to clarify these two aspects of attention – sensory clarity and temporal dynamics – which are at the heart of the experiments and epistemological propositions of Husserl's contemporary psychologists, with the aim of bringing out the intimate relationship between the phenomenologist and certain introspective psychologies of his time. Other aspects, such as reaction time and attentional anticipation (pre-attention), or attentional plurality-division are also very present in psychologists like C. Stumpf and W. James. But Husserl's

---

[3] A well-documented inventory has been recently released under the responsibility of Maria Gyemant (Gyemant 2014).

phenomenal and descriptive position is in fact determined more in relation with the first two aspects, the sensory and the temporal.

I will not restate here all the details of Wundt's, Titchener's and Külpe's positions and analyses on these two aspects, which I have broached at length in *Attention and Vigilance* (Depraz 2014b). But I will synthesize the epistemological debate based on specific experiments in the following way: according to Wundt's and Titchener's elementarist approach, "sensory clarity," a Wundtian concept, is the source of attention. Thus, when I see clearly the figures on my iPhone indicating the time I have left to write this contribution, I am *attentive* to these figures (Wundt 1874/2008; Titchener 1908, p. 182 on "sensible clearness;" also Titchener 1912, p. 490, n. 9). "Subjective sharpness" comes from the intensity of the sensory stimulus. As a result, the properties of attention merge with the attributes of elemental sensation, and give rise to a unique concept of *attensity*. But how can one define the feeling of clarity if it is identified with physical intensity? Indeed, the intensity of clarity as a criterion of attention was commonplace within the psychology of the time, and its meaning is first physical. The "first law" of attention, namely of the attentional process, will be the increase of sensory clarity. Titchener thus names eight conditions for such an increase, which are all stages of the process: 1) the *intensity* of the stimulus-origin that triggers attention; 2) *the shape and quality of the stimulus:* a vision that is not focal but felt as insistent can hold my attention; 3) *repetition:* gradual awakening of my attention by a *summation* of *stimuli*; 4) *stimulus movement*, which can facilitate our attention; 5) *novelty, rarity, weirdness* of the *stimulus*, which strikes the attention, this *stimulus*, isolated, being not yet inscribed in the associative chains of the mind; 6) *associative connections:* a sensation is all the more noticed as the subject prepares to welcome it by the existence in his mind of *associative connections* where sensations have already been incorporated by habit; 7) *accommodation of sense organs:* this is the main condition. Without sensory accommodation, attention does not follow; 8) *absence or disappearance* of a stimulus, a factor of attraction of attention. Certain conditions (1, 4, 5, 8) describe the properties of sensation that trigger the awakening of attention, namely, the initial moment of the process; others (2, 3, 6, 7) refer to sequences that identify later, less specific, more continuous phases, which support the unfolding of the attentional process: insistence, repetition, habit, accommodation. However, this emphasis on sensory intensity as a criterion of attention does not lead Titchener to insist on attentional (voluntary) reinforcement or even psychic control. Instead, he chooses the opposite position: attention appears when the intense physical stimulus (trigger, mobile, novelty) whose intensity, insistent at first, has become familiar by accommodation, repetition, and habit, ends up unnoticed. This is where the attentional process spontaneously begins to move: attention appears when sensation disappears. These different phases of emergence of attention provide an original description of the attention process, anchored in the sensation and its gradual erasure, which ultimately contributes to its de-physicalization (Titchener 1908, pp. 288–289, 300). Without mentioning the English psychologist, especially in Appendix XIII of the Lessons on *Perception and Attention* in 1904–1905, which also refers to Wundt's, Külpe's, Pillsbury's, and Ribot's works, Husserl obviously studies these laws and the phases of this process. His conception of attention results from a complex of conditions, which are not only related to the objective property of sensory intensity, nor to the adaptive behavioral capacity of the subject, but to her internal experience, her psychic disposition: these conditions are articulated together as "*conditions of remarkableness*" or "conditions favoring the activity of noticing." Thus, in his Lessons on *Perception and Attention*, especially in § 22, he rejects the first elementary summation: his schema of association describes the synthetic structure of attentional experience; second, he also refuses to consider the clarification of sensation as a criterion of attention: he criticizes the "differences of clarity," which are according to him attributable to the external context (Husserl 2004, Hua XXXVIII, §§ 21–23, p. 88, and § 22, p. 94). In short, we can now answer the initial question: is the strength of a stimulus responsible for the quality of attention? No, in any case not exclusively: other conditions, lived, bodily, and internal are necessary. On this point, Husserl will be closer to Külpe, who focuses on describing attention as a global transversal modal act of the subject, than Titchener and *a fortiori* Wundt, both of whom defend a mental atomism.

In 1904, Külpe presented a task at the Congress of Psychology in Berlin: the subject receives a directive, adapts herself to it with a particular conscious disposition (*Bewußtseinsanlage*), namely, by elaborating a strategy or a rule of action that produces a specific adjustment (*Einstellung*). In this specific case, the objective is to measure her ability to pay attention to the traits that characterize a perceived object: the number of letters, their color, their location, their shape. Her attention reveals itself to be selective: she retains certain traits of the percept and disregards the others. Her attention is motivated by the proposed framework (including the instruction to focus on certain traits), which puts into question the hypothesis of an immediate effect of an external *stimulus* (the object) that would affect it punctually. Thus, the effects of the *set* (*Einstellung*) on the attentional capacity of the subject stand in opposition to any atomistic understanding. As early as 1893, in his master book *Grundriß der Psychologie* (Külpe 1893/1895), attention is presented as a "state of consciousness," identified following Leibniz as "apperception" or "internal perception" and accessible through introspection. Claiming the "introspective method" as a direct method of observation and investigation, he enumerates three of its criteria: 1) the self-observing subject must be attentive; 2) she must be impartial; 3) she must be able to correctly describe what she feels. The "experimental method" here will be nothing more than a complement to introspection. Attention is a modal act, irreducible to the sum of its sensory traits and transversal to them. We are dealing here with a qualitative and global perspective, which considers attention as an internal activity (*innere Tätigkeit*) yet non-disjointed from the sensory contents that present it. Thus Külpe dismisses both Wundt and Titchener's elementarist empiricism and their atomistic method of sensory association, as well as the rationalist conception of attention as a Leibnizian act of mental apperception at the same time endorsed by Wundt (Külpe 1893, pp. 440–442; Külpe 1895, pp. 425–431). Külpe turns out to be close to the Husserlian conception of attention in the Lessons on *Perception and Attention* in 1904–1905 and in § 92 of *Ideas I* in particular, which present attention as a processing aid act backed by and modulating every intentional act, awakened by sensory resonance without ever being dependent on it.

The contrasting perspectives of Titchener and Külpe from their common Wundtian horizon therefore allow us to situate the Husserlian approach to attention in relation to the epistemological framework of the psychology of form. In effect, Wundt's two students present a polarization (elementary act/global act) which in a certain way overlaps with the complexity of the Husserlian position, which itself starts with simple perceptual acts of visual focus but proceeds to a critique of associationism in the name of the eidetic ideality of lived experience.

More briefly, I would like to mention a second aspect of attention, which concerns its mode of temporal maintenance. Wundt defines the rhythm of attention from his intermittence function: "Attention is [according to its essence] an intermittent function," he writes in his *Grundzüge der physiologischen Psychologie* (Wundt 1874/2008, p. 266; Titchener 1908, p. 276), while Titchener, like Külpe, defines it as fluctuations (*Fluktuationen*) or oscillations (*Schwankungen*) (Titchener 1908, pp. 266sq.; Külpe 1893, §§ 73–76). The law formulated by Wundt reads as follows: "between the apperception of two successive representations, there is always an interval of time [*Zwischenzeit*] in which, to be clearly seen, the first has already sunk too far, and the other has not been sufficiently enhanced" (Titchener 1908, p. 263). Wundt therefore thinks that there is an "interval" of darkness between two clear representations succeeding each other: attentional time is "intermittent." Titchener interprets this difference in terms of variation and does not conclude with an "intermittence" of attention. He writes clearly about this: "instability is not discontinuity" (Titchener 1908, p. 264). According to him, the phenomenon that deserves analysis is that of "waves of apperception," "fluctuations of attention" (*Apperceptionswellen*). For his part, when Külpe approaches the "internal conditions" of attention, he invokes the "disposition of mind" (*geistige Disposition*) of the subject as a determining factor of the quality of attention, which acts on sensory intensity and feeling: it is the internal attentional oscillations (*Schwankungen der Aufmerksamkeit*) which have an influence on the intensity of the sensations, not the opposite. Now the origin of these fluctuations lies in the central sensitivity, this central sensitive state of the subject impulsing attention, not in the sensory *stimuli*, in which he is opposed to Titchener, who favors its peripheral sensory conditions. A line runs through the descriptions of Titchener, Külpe, and Husserl: a dynamic of fluctuations, called *Fluktuationen, Schwankungen,* or *Wandlungen* in § 92 of *Ideas I*, and which respond to a similar concern for the qualification of attentional time as a continuous rhythm, as opposed to the dual mechanical alternation of intermittence.

Thus, as the case of attention shows abundantly, transcendental phenomenology genuinely benefits from empirical analyses by taking a stand against an elementarist epistemology in favor of an introspective internal and Gestaltist epistemology. From this connection between transcendental and empirical analyses, it emerges that the Husserlian methodological transcendental schemata also draw their strength from their ability to be informed by the richness of such Gestaltist psychological analysis.

It is therefore difficult simply to stick to the schema of a transcendental foundation of empirical psychology, associated with the criticism of psychologism. More precisely: transcendental phenomenology draws resources at once experiential, methodological, and descriptive from certain psychological propositions of the time. This is apparent from the detailed examination of the lectures on *Perception and Attention*, where the description of the attentional quality of the perceptive and affective acts of the subject is nourished and enriched by the psychologies of attention that Husserl has studied, and in particular here that of O. Külpe, as evidenced by the Appendix II of the *Lectures*. Hence, again, the understanding of transcendental phenomenology as a transcendental empiricism: thanks to a modified understanding of empiricism (not atomist, but Gestaltist), we see how the transcendental attitude of the subject becomes a genuine experiential one (and not only a formal one).

3 The Microphenomenological Subject: A Transcendental Eidetic Instance "in First Person"

After this immersion of the transcendental phenomenology of attention into certain propositions of the empirical psychology of Külpian introspection, I would now like to show, finally, how microphenomenology, a contemporary method of the disciplined psychology of introspection, in particular makes it possible to sharpen Husserl's transcendental-empiricist critical diagnosis of science by shifting the focus of subjectivity and lived experience.

To situate this hypothesis, I will briefly return to what was called the "naturalization of phenomenology" more than twenty years ago, on the occasion of a 1995 Conference in Bordeaux, crystallized by the book *Naturalizing Phenomenology* co-edited by J. Petitot, F. J. Varela, B. Pachoux, and J.-M. Roy (Petitot, Varela, Pachoux, Roy 1999/2001). This scientific approach to phenomenology has been sometimes interpreted as a return to empiricism, to the positivity of experience, and as an impeachment of the transcendental, in a sort of mirror image of the Husserlian critique of psychologism and naturalism. Two scientific phenomenological paradigms have emerged: neurophenomenology (with F. J. Varela), which proposes to implement mutual generative constraints between the neuro-empirical data and the subjective experiences and their description, and psychophenomenology (with P. Vermersch), which proposes a singularized and granular experience approach of the subject and its description. Both may have been seen by some as empirical phenomenologies that have given up the transcendental structuring of experience.

In my opinion, this is not the case. Of course, the transcendental here at stake should not be taken as a foundational ontology of positivity, but rather as an operation of the epoché of unquestioned contents. In an article entitled "The Naturalization of the Phenomenology as the Transcendence of Nature," published in the No. 5 of the Journal for Phenomenology *Alter*, Varela defines "naturalization" as a "phenomenalization" (Varela 1997). Also, in the first footnote of his 1999 article, "The Specious Present," Varela explicitly states that naturalizing phenomenology and phenomenalizing cognitive science go hand in hand (Varela 1999). This critical remark with regard to an "empiricizing" misunderstanding of naturalization paves the way for the "how" of the phenomenon, that is to say, for a subject practicing the epoché on herself. This echoes precisely the Husserlian requirement, as early as 1923–1924 in his *First Philosophy* lecture, of a critical epoché of transcendental naivety; it also echoes precisely Husserl's concern for a deepening of the path of the reduction through psychology, according to a "double reduction" (Husserl 1923–24; Husserl 1956; Husserl 1990).[4] Microphenomenology, by presenting itself in turn as the science of a single object,

---

4 Regarding the highlighting of the importance of the path through psychology and the genetic phenomenology to which it is related, which notably describes the temporal process of passive emergence of the lived experiences of consciousness, see Depraz 1995, second section.

has the subject, at one and the same time, both to pursue the objective of Husserlian phenomenology and to radicalize the epoché by making it bear on the subject herself, still naive in her general and structural lived experiences. On the opposite side of the spectrum, the first-person microphenomenological subject is anchored in her real lived experiences, given here and now. She is characterized by a critical discernment which results from a relation concretely established to a situated experience, and not to its representation, nor simply to its possibility.

In this respect, and this should not be surprising, a homologous relationship of filiation, differentiation, and re-interrogation is at stake concerning the reductive method of eidetic variation. Here too, as with the transcendental epoché, microphenomenology allows a new kind of illumination on Husserlian phenomenology.

The Husserlian eidetic invariant, being given *a priori*, and the invariant derived from the experimental inductive method, are commonly opposed. With such a distinction, the Gordian knot of the eidetic seems decided from the outset. The *eidos* of the lived experience being given *a priori*, it does not have to be established at the end of a procedure. But Husserl defines eidetics as a process of variation at the end of which the invariant essence of a lived experience is extracted. It is not a principle independent of experience, in the Kantian sense (as we know), but a dynamic of constitution in the mode of an integral which retains in itself, in its very constitution, the intuitioned potential of lived experience. In short, the dynamic phenomenological structure of the *a priori* constitutes here in itself an experiential component. Moreover, in accordance with this dynamic sense of the *a priori*, the process of variation is a progressive discrimination between the accidental and the essential in the series of traits of a lived experience. This means that if the invariant is not established at the end of an induction which starts from the facts alone, it is still part of a dynamic where the structure of the lived experience is co-constructed as a result of a double movement, of intuitive bodily nourishment and of formalization.

This is where the method of microphenomenological explicitation, which also contradicts the experimental inductive method through which we obtain constants by eliminating the non-significant variables, and which is anchored in the initial condition of the choice of a singular experience, can find its place at the very heart of Husserlian eidetic variation. The latter is indeed unique because it takes into consideration, at the heart of the constitution of the *eidos*, the singularity of all the facts, which are retained in it as the irreducible fabric of the concreteness of experience and integrated into the structure of the lived experience, which remains weighted with incarnation through this very process.

Thus, even though Husserl did not explicitly formulate the need for a reference to a singular experience, nor did he produce or establish specific and detailed examples, the eidetic method contains in itself the possibility of the experiential microphenomenological method. This real possibility is perhaps an opportunity for phenomenology. As an unsuspected resource not seen in eidetics, it adopts its proper mode as a phenomenology assuming and achieving its demand for a return to the singular experience, and thus makes it possible to engage a microphenomenological analysis capable of generating dynamic invariants of the singular experience, according to a double generative movement of back-and-forth between structural *a priori* categories and categorical heuristic emergences in direct contact with situated experiences (Depraz, Gyemant, Desmidt 2017).

Bibliography

Depraz, Natalie (1995): *Transcendance et incarnation. L'intersubjectivité comme altérité à soi chez E. Husserl*. Paris: Vrin.
Depraz, Natalie (2001): *Lucidité du corps. De l'empirisme transcendantal en phénoménologie*. Dordrecht: Kluwer Academic Publishers.
Depraz, Natalie (2008): *Lire Husserl en phénoménologue. Les Idées directrices...* I. Paris: Presses universitaires de France-CNED.
Depraz, Natalie, Varela, Francisco and Vermersch, Pierre (2003): *On Becoming Aware: A Pragmatics of Experiencing*, Boston/Amsterdam/New York: Benjamins Press.
Depraz, Natalie, Varela, Francisco and Vermersch, Pierre (2011): *A l'épreuve de l'expérience. Pour une pratique phénoménologique*. Bucharest: Zeta Books.
Depraz, Natalie (2011): "L'empirisme transcendantal: de Husserl à Deleuze". In: *Revue germanique internationale*, n° 13, pp. 125–148.
Depraz, Natalie (2014a): "Husserl, psychologue?" In: M. Gyemant (Ed.): *Psychologie et psychologisme*. Paris: Vrin.
Depraz, Natalie (2014b): *Attention et vigilance. A la croisée de la phénoménologie et des sciences cognitives*. Paris: Presses universitaires de France.
Depraz, Natalie, Gyemant, Maria, Desmidt, Thomas (2017): "A First-Person Analysis Using Third Person-Data as a Generative Method. A Case Study of Surprise in Depression". In: *Constructivist Foundations*, vol. 12, n° 2, Neurophenomenology, pp. 192–218.
Gyemant, Maria (Ed.) (2014): *Psychologie et psychologisme*. Paris: Vrin.
Flajoliet, Alain (2010): *Lectures on the Elementary Psychology of Feeling and Attention* by E. B. Titchener. *Alter. Revue de phénoménologie*, vol. 8: *L'attention*.
Friedrich, Janette (2008): "La psychologie de la pensée de l'école de Würzburg – Analyse d'un cas de marginalisation". In: *L'Homme et la société*, vol. 167–168–169, n° 1–2–3, pp 251–278.
Husserl, Edmund (2004): *Wahrnehmung und Aufmerksamkeit* 1904–1905. *Husserliana*, vol. XXXVIII. Ed. Thomas Vongehr and Regula Giuliani. Dordrecht: Kluwer Academic

Publishers (French translation of Part I by Natalie Depraz under the title *Phénoménologie de l'attention*, Paris, Vrin, 2009).

Husserl, Edmund (1990): *On the Phenomenology of the Consciousness of Internal Time (1893–1917)*. Trans. John Brough. Dordrecht: Kluwer Academic Publishers.

Husserl, Edmund (1965): *Philosophy as Rigorous Science* (1911). Trans. in *Phenomenology and the Crisis of Philosophy*. Ed. S. J. Quentin Lauer. New York: Harper & Row.

Husserl, Edmund (1982): *Ideas Pertaining to a Pure Phenomenology and to a Phenomenological Philosophy – First Book: General Introduction to a Pure Phenomenology (1913)*. Trans. Fred Kersten. The Hague: Martinus Nijhoff.

Husserl, Edmund (2001): *Analyses Concerning Passive and Active Synthesis. Logic on Transcendental Logic (1918–1926)*. Trans. Anthony Steinbock. Heidelberg: Springer.

Husserl, Edmund (1956): *Erste Philosophie, 2. Teil: Theorie der phänomenologischen Reduktion (1923–1924). Husserliana*, vol. VIII. Ed. Rudolf Boehm. The Hague: Martinus Nijhoff.

Husserl, Edmund (1970): *The Crisis of European Sciences and Transcendental Phenomenology*. Trans. David Carr. Evanston: Northwestern University Press.

Külpe, Oswald (1893): *Grundriß der Psychologie: Auf experimenteller Grundlage dargestellt*, Leipzig: Wilhelm Engelman.

Külpe, Oswald (1895): *Outlines of Psychology, Based Upon the Results of Experimental Investigation*. Trans. E. B. Titchener. London: Macmillan.

Lipps, Theodor (1883): *Grundtatsachen des Seelenlebens*. Bonn: Verlag M. Cohen und Sohn, chapter VII. (French transl. Maria Gyemant, revised by Natalie Depraz and Mildred Galland, publ. HAL Archives, in connection with the bumper issue *Theodor Lipps, Revue de métaphysique et de morale*, ed. N. Depraz and M. Galland, 2018).

Petitmengin, Claire (2017): website: https://www.microphenomenology.com/seminars#!

Petitot, Jean, Varela, Francisco J., Pachoud, Bernard and Roy, Jean-Michel (Eds.) (1999): *Naturalizing Phenomenology. Issues in Contemporary Phenomenology and Cognitive Science*. Stanford: Stanford University Press.

Rölli, Marc (2003/2012): *Gilles Deleuze. Philosophie des transzendentalen Empirizismus*. Vienna: Turia.

Szilasi, Wilhelm (1959/2011): *Einführung in die Phänomenologie Edmund Husserls*. Tübingen: Niemeyer.

Titchener, Edward Bradford (1908): *Lectures on the Elementary Psychology of Feeling and Attention*. New York: Mc Millan.

Titchener, Edward Bradford (1912): "The Schema of Introspection". In: *The American Journal of Psychology*, vol. 23, n° 4, pp. 485–508.

Varela, Francisco J. (1997): "The Naturalization of the Phenomenology as the Transcendence of Nature". In: *Alter. Revue de phénoménologie*, n° 5.

Varela, Francisco J. (1999): "The Specious Present: A Neurophenomenology of Time Consciousness". In: Jean Petitot, Francisco J. Varela, Bernard Pachoud, Jean-Michel Roy (Eds.): *Naturalizing Phenomenology. Issues in Contemporary Phenomenology and Cognitive Science*. Stanford: Stanford University Press, pp. 266–314.

Vermersch, Pierre (1994/2004/2011): *L'entretien d'explicitation*, Paris, ESF (1st edition 1994, 4th enlarged edition 2004, 7th edition 2011). See GREX website (Groupe de Recherche sur l'Explicitation: http://www.grex2.com/#tabs-2)

Vermersch, Pierre (1996): "*Pour une psycho-phénoménologie*". In: *Expliciter*, vol. 13, pp. 1–6.

Vermersch, Pierre (1999): "Introspection as Practice". In: Francisco J. Varela & Jonathan Shear (Eds.): *The View from Within, Journal of Consciousness Studies*, pp. 17–43.
Vermersch, Pierre (2009): "Describing the Practice of Introspection". In: Claire Petitmengin (Ed.): *Ten Years of Viewing from Within: the Legacy of Francisco Varela, Journal of Consciousness Studies*. Exeter, Imprint Academic, pp. 20–58.
Vermersch, Pierre (2012): *Explicitation et phénoménologie*. Paris: Presses universitaires de France.
Wundt, Wilhelm (1896): *Grundriß der Psychologie*. Leipzig: Wilhelm Engelmann.
Wundt, Wilhelm (1874/1902): *Grundzüge der physiologischen Psychologie*, 2 Bände, Leipzig: W. Engelmann.

Index of Persons

Albrecht, Gustav 144
Allison, Henry 128, 164, 168, 172
Arendt, Hannah 494, 496
Aristotle 28, 60, 215, 287, 494
Augustine 113
Augustus 152
Avenarius, Richard 236

Baumgarten, Alexander Gottlieb 3, 42–44, 148–150, 154, 156
Benoist, Jocelyn 32, 190f., 207
Berkeley, George 166–168, 288, 290
Bernet, Rudolf 137, 219f.
Blumenberg, Hans 4, 101f., 104, 107, 119–121, 266, 479, 481, 489, 497
Boehm, Rudolf 225
Bontadini, Gustavo 288
Brandt, Reinhard 102–104
Brentano, Franz 10, 73, 199, 207, 275, 292–294, 300, 368
Breuer, Irene 8, 213, 220, 223, 225
Bruzina, Ronald 323, 456–458

Cairns, Dorion 266
Calogero, Guido 287f.
Calov, Abraham 3, 42f.
Cassirer, Ernst 13, 259, 412, 434, 488
Castoriadis, Cornelius 41
Cavaillès, Jean 60, 66, 75
Cohen, Alix 5, 13, 96–98, 113, 127–130, 140, 269, 370, 411–418, 420, 422f.
Cohen, Hermann 5, 13, 96–98, 113, 127–130, 140, 269, 370, 411–418, 420, 422f.
Copernic 379–380, 391–407
Corneille, Pierre 152
Croce, Benedetto 279
Crowell, Steven 1, 14f., 47–49, 309–313, 320, 322, 324f., 456, 461, 467, 474, 479–481, 483, 490f., 493, 495, 501

Deleuze, Gilles 23
Depraz, Natalie 15f., 23, 144, 505, 509–512, 514, 518, 520

Desanti, Jean-Toussaint 154, 396
Descartes, René 7, 25, 69f., 84, 87, 89, 166–168, 174–177, 183, 190, 237, 288, 290, 292, 493
Dilthey, Wilhelm 115, 119
Don Quixote 472
Doyon, Maxime 319
Drummond, John 49, 164, 177, 498

Eberhard, Johann August 89, 92, 171
Edel, Geert 412, 420, 431
Elsenhans, Theodor 32
Engelland, Chad 1
Epicurus 159, 376
Erdmann, Benno 8, 241, 244f.
Ewald, Oscar 411

Fabbianelli, Faustino 1
Ferrarin, Alfredo 289, 296f., 445
Fichte, Johann Gottlieb 13, 128, 236, 269, 399, 403, 405, 411–416, 419f., 423, 431–433, 485, 491
Fink, Eugen 13f., 120, 160, 345, 395, 431, 439–453, 455–465, 467–476
Flajoliet, Alain 513
Foessel, Michael 447, 449
Foucault, Michel 3, 5, 41, 57, 60, 64–67, 69f., 78, 102, 104, 110, 113, 118
Friedrich, Janette 513
Fries, Jakob Friedrich 109

Gardner, Sebastian 1
Geniusas, Saulius 143–145
Gentile, Giovanni 288
Grandjean, Antoine 4, 7, 16, 38, 86, 189
Grier, Michelle 445
Grist, Matthew 1
Gurwitsch, Aron 397
Guyer, Paul 163, 166, 171f., 174, 339, 342
Gyemant, Maria 513, 520

Harder, Yves-Jean 154
Harries, Karsten 14f., 479–499, 501

Index of Persons

Hartenstein, Gustav 143, 145
Hartimo, Mirja 1
Hartmann, Eduard von 411, 480, 498
Heffernan, George 215
Hegel, Georg Wilhelm Friedrich 5, 14, 127–130, 140, 391, 398, 411, 439, 456, 458, 461, 467, 488
Heidegger, Martin 5, 13–15, 58, 96–98, 101, 114f., 120, 127–130, 132, 140, 160f., 392, 398, 404, 407, 421, 434, 441, 443, 455, 457, 474–476, 479–481, 483–486, 488–490, 492–499
Heinämaa, Sara 1, 304, 324
Held, Klaus 6, 128, 139, 219
Henry, Michel 24, 266
Heraclites 160
Herbart, Johann Friedrich 59, 416
Hering, Jean 146
Herz, Marcus 25–27, 30, 103, 105, 118
Hinske, Norbert 42–44
Hoeltzel, Steven 1
Honenberger, Phillip 1
Housset, Emmanuel 38, 206
Hugo, Zachary 303f., 321f.
Hume, David 63, 71, 84f., 131, 197, 235, 243, 265, 288–291, 294, 297–299, 306, 308, 328, 359, 367, 374f., 479

Ikeda, Yusuke 14, 455, 474

Jacobs, Hanne 155, 324

Kassis, Raymond 8, 16, 235, 240, 243f.
Kern, Iso 6, 34, 76, 117, 128, 134, 137, 145, 213, 217, 219–221, 265, 282, 294f., 304, 420, 425, 433, 480
Kerszberg, Pierre 237
Kim, Halla 1, 432
Külpe, Oswald 16, 505, 511–517

Landgrebe, Ludwig 218f., 226
Leibniz, Gottfried Wilhelm 31, 60, 87–89, 96, 140, 145, 156, 160, 206, 237, 455, 463, 515
Levinas, Emmanuel 58, 399, 405, 407
Lipps, Theodor 8, 16, 241–245, 250, 511–513

Locke, John 67, 288, 290, 305, 308
Lohmar, Dieter 134, 137
Loidolt, Sophie 327, 466
Longuenesse, Béatrice 312
Louden, Robert 103, 108
Lucretius 158
Luft, Sebastian 1, 164, 304, 345, 413, 420, 431, 433

Malabou, Catherine 406
Marbach, Eduard 6f., 128, 193f., 196, 198, 200, 205, 208, 219f., 229
Marburg school 96–98, 411–412, 414, 416, 424–425, 431
Marion, Jean-Luc 399
Marosán, Bence Péter 117
Martin, Gottfried 42
McManus, Denis 487, 497
Meier, Georg Friedrich 150, 154, 157–159
Merleau-Ponty, Maurice 114, 122
Miettinen, Timo 1
Misch, Georg 119
Mohanty, Jitendra Nath 1, 304, 309, 313, 317
Montaigne, Michel de 158
Moran Dermot 1, 47, 49, 236, 456
Moreau, Joseph 90–92
Musil, Robert 396

Natorp, Paul 13, 198, 208, 411–434
Nelson, Leonard 412
Nenon, Thomas 304, 306, 309, 327
Newton, Isaac 416
Nietzsche, Friedrich 439, 482, 497

Petitmengin, Claire 508, 510
Petitot, Jean 518
Plaass, Peter 336–338, 342
Plato 28, 96, 279–286, 290f., 295, 299, 432, 495
Port-Royal Logic 66
Pradelle, Dominique 11–13, 35, 57, 59f., 64f., 67, 70, 84, 86, 98, 206, 261f., 265, 269, 275, 293, 359, 367, 378, 391f., 394–401, 466, 508

Reinach, Adolf 13, 370, 420f., 429f., 432f.
Renaut, Alain 102

Richir, Marc 391f., 406, 444
Rickert, Heinrich 133, 238, 411
Rölli, Marc 509
Romano, Claude 392
Römpp, Georg 251

Sartre, Jean-Paul 397, 497
Scanlon, John 120
Scheler, Max 48, 115, 242
Schelling, Friedrich Wilhelm 128, 236, 269
Schiller, Friedrich 431
Schmidt, Claudia 42, 104
Schnell, Alexander 12f., 16, 391, 405–407
Schopenhauer, Arthur 9, 259f., 265–270, 275, 482
Schubert-Soldern, Richard von 240
Schuhmann, Karl 240, 266, 421, 425
Sepp, Hans-Reiner 448
Serban, Claudia 1, 4f., 85, 101, 259
Sextus-Empiricus 235, 255
Smith, Kemp 45, 73, 164, 166, 177, 421
Socrates 283, 286
Sommer, Christian 266
Sowa, Rochus 144f.
Staiti, Andrea 1, 420
Stanciu, Ovidiu 14, 439, 442
Stumpf, Carl 73, 370, 513

Summa, Michela 260, 263, 266, 297
Szilasi, Wilhelm 509

Taguchi, Shigeru 224f.
Tengelyi, László 8, 222f., 225, 464, 475
Titchener, Edward Bradford 16, 505, 511, 513–517
Tugendhat, Ernst 404f., 483, 499f.

Vandewalle, Bernard 104
Vanzo, Alberto 88
Varela, Francisco 505, 509, 511, 518
Vermersch, Pierre 15, 508–512, 518
Vongehr, Thomas 134, 144

Walton, Robert 322
West Coast phenomenology 177–179
Wilson, Holly 108
Wittgenstein, Ludwig 23, 76, 481, 487f., 490, 493
Wolff, Christian 25, 31, 42, 44
Woods, Allen 45, 48
Wundt, Wilhelm 16, 511–516

Zahavi, Dan 1, 32, 164, 174, 177, 239, 420, 490

Subject Index

Abnormality 316, 318
Absolute 6, 13, 36, 44, 51, 57–59, 66f., 69, 74, 90, 92, 152, 165, 175f., 179, 182, 204, 209f., 217, 219–222, 224–226, 229f., 237, 251, 253, 287, 322, 355, 363–365, 380, 383, 385, 394, 398, 405, 414, 429, 447f., 450f., 458f., 462, 465, 470f., 481
Actionality 191f., 198, 204
Actuality 8, 88, 93, 183, 216–220, 222, 308, 450, 461f., 466–469, 473
– World-actuality 462f., 466, 468, 473, 476
Aesthetic 9, 111, 238, 259–266, 269–272, 274f., 346, 348, 354, 367, 374, 443f., 482
– Transcendental aesthetic 1, 9, 29f., 97f., 130, 259–266, 269–275, 336, 339f.
Analogy 6, 77, 136, 157, 194, 241f., 244f., 288, 290, 308, 363, 372, 377, 382, 507
– Reasoning by analogy 241–243, 245
Analytic 9f., 58, 78, 86, 95, 107, 113f., 130, 260–262, 264–266, 269–273, 275, 320, 337, 374, 381f., 443f.
– Transcendental analytic 6, 10, 24, 259, 261f., 264f., 269, 273, 444f., 475
Anger 152f., 241, 244
Animality 143f., 324, 384
Anomy 144
Anonymity 6, 13, 127, 138–141, 398–401
Anthropology 3–6, 16, 57, 60, 65–67, 70, 101–105, 107f., 110–119, 121f., 131, 143, 145, 147, 149, 152–156, 158–160, 266, 342
– Anthropologism 4, 16, 65, 83, 92, 99, 101, 109, 114–116, 121, 130f., 260f., 362, 378, 396, 401
Anti-Copernican revolution 11f., 394f., 397f.
Antinomy 12, 15, 97, 441, 443, 449, 455, 459f., 467, 479–490, 492, 494, 496, 498, 500f.
– Cosmological antinomies 456f.
Anti-realism 163f.

Apodictic 11, 138, 213, 217–219, 221–225, 247, 249–251, 334, 336–338, 340f., 344, 347–349, 353, 355, 396
A posteriori 63f., 66, 71, 75f., 87, 179, 369, 371, 375
Apperception 28, 111f., 116, 127, 129, 137, 140, 241, 244–248, 296–298, 385, 394, 403, 515f.
– Apperception by analogy 243
– Transcendental apperception 5f., 127f., 130, 134f., 137–141, 396f.
A priori 2–4, 12, 15f., 24f., 27–29, 57, 60, 62–64, 66f., 70–72, 74–76, 78, 83f., 86–89, 92, 94–96, 106, 108f., 131f., 173, 179, 183, 189, 215, 217, 220, 223, 227f., 249f., 252f., 261, 263, 266, 269–271, 273, 275, 279, 289, 295–297, 304–306, 308, 312, 314f., 318f., 322, 324, 336–339, 341f., 348, 353, 359f., 364, 368–372, 375, 378–380, 382, 391f., 396, 398, 401, 403–405, 414, 441, 446, 458f., 469, 472–474, 476, 480, 498–500, 505, 519f.
– A priori correlation 165, 181–183
– Contingent a priori 309, 313, 315, 317, 321
– Material a priori 3, 60, 62f., 72–74, 77, 271, 309, 315, 368, 371
– Synthetic a priori 11, 62, 270–272
Atomism 515
Autonomy 327, 365, 383, 385, 444f., 501

Being 1, 3f., 8–10, 14f., 24, 26, 31f., 36f., 41–52, 60–64, 72–76, 84–86, 88–97, 99, 102–104, 108, 110–122, 131, 136, 138, 140, 144–150, 152, 158–160, 167, 174f., 177f., 181, 190, 192, 196, 201–204, 214, 219–225, 228, 230, 236–238, 241, 246–253, 271, 279–292, 294–300, 310, 319, 324, 327, 346, 360, 362–373, 375, 378–385, 391, 393–395, 397–400, 407, 413, 419, 427, 439, 441–

453, 456–459, 461–464, 466, 468f., 471, 475, 482–501
– Being in itself   236, 284
– Being otherwise   249f., 252
– Oblivion of Being   459
Biology   11, 113, 180, 340–342, 352, 356
Birth   6, 35, 143–147, 149f., 159f., 252, 281, 300, 305, 315, 470, 508
Body (*Leib*)   16, 41, 48, 92, 115, 147–154, 157f., 202f., 241f., 244, 246, 248, 263, 265f., 289f., 318–320, 325, 334, 351, 355, 384, 462, 488, 491f., 496
Borderline   6, 149, 155
– Borderline case   6, 143f., 147, 149f., 152, 155, 159–161
– Borderline phenomena   143f.

Categories   5, 10, 24, 28, 46, 48, 50, 60, 64, 66–72, 75, 85–89, 96f., 106, 127, 129f., 132, 135, 139f., 170f., 267f., 271f., 289, 295, 298, 306, 312, 336, 370, 378, 392, 396f., 401–405, 407, 444, 501, 520
– Material categories   271
Causality   9, 171, 259–261, 263f., 266–270, 275, 289, 305f., 362, 370, 383f., 482
Chemistry   11, 340–342, 350–352, 356
Childhood   103, 143f.
Claim (*Anspruch*)   495f., 500f.,
Cogito   176, 190–192, 194, 198, 201, 204f., 208, 216, 218, 227, 236f., 247, 252f., 288, 293, 393, 426
– *Cogitatum*   236–239, 241, 253
Commitment   3, 13, 41f., 47–49, 52, 58, 495, 497, 500
Consciousness   7, 9, 13, 33–35, 61, 63–65, 67, 69, 72f., 75–78, 91–94, 105, 111f., 121, 131f., 137, 155–158, 163–165, 167, 175, 177–183, 189–194, 196–200, 202f., 205–210, 214f., 217, 224, 226, 230f., 235–237, 240–242, 244–246, 250, 262, 272f., 275, 292–294, 296–298, 310f., 313, 325, 335, 340, 346–348, 354, 361, 366–369, 372, 380f., 383f., 393–397, 399–406, 415–419,
421f., 426–431, 444, 464, 467–469, 471, 473, 506, 508, 510, 515, 518
– Loss of consciousness   144f., 153, 157f., 160
– Self-consciousness   6, 103, 111f., 167, 241, 298, 412, 419f., 427, 493
Constitution   6, 9, 13f., 36, 38, 41f., 48, 51, 61f., 65, 75, 85, 93, 102, 132, 135, 137–139, 143, 145–147, 150f., 154, 159, 171, 177, 179, 196, 203, 205f., 209, 221, 236, 239, 246, 248, 262–266, 270, 272f., 275, 298f., 309f., 312, 314–319, 321, 325f., 347, 360, 369f., 378, 391, 393f., 397f., 404f., 407f., 440, 444, 468, 470, 500, 513, 519
Construction   59, 67, 70, 77, 109, 133, 148f., 307f., 341, 395, 401, 405–407, 428, 439, 443, 459, 498
– Constructive phenomenology   471
Contingency   89, 213f., 221, 224–227, 231, 238, 311
– Contingent   8, 10f., 63, 65, 73, 76, 89, 203, 213, 217–219, 223–228, 238, 284, 306, 311, 313–315, 317, 319, 325f., 329, 370, 379
Contradiction   6, 43, 63, 70, 73f., 96, 110, 166, 181, 210, 248, 262, 374, 447–449, 465, 467, 479, 482
Copernican revolution   12f., 35, 57, 66, 69, 359f., 378f., 391f., 394f., 400, 407, 412, 460, 467, 476
Core   5, 8, 43, 61, 64, 101, 165, 213, 225–229, 231, 306, 336, 339, 341f., 344, 375, 401, 411, 422, 430, 442, 444, 461, 467, 472, 475, 505f., 508
Cosmology   443f., 446, 449, 458, 460, 462, 467, 488
– Cosmological   14, 359, 361f., 383f., 440–442, 444, 447f., 450f., 455, 457–461, 464, 468, 471, 474f., 493
– Cosmological difference   14, 448, 458–461, 464, 467, 469, 471, 475
Counter-sense   163, 165

Dasein 115, 140, 160, 324, 474 f., 498
Death 6, 143–145, 149 f., 152–155, 157–161, 221, 225, 315, 343, 391, 411, 421, 470, 482
Deduction 5, 10, 70, 129–136, 140 f., 176, 244 f., 289, 294–298, 305 f., 370, 401, 403, 405, 450
– Transcendental deduction 5, 13, 15, 28, 62, 71, 127–130, 132–135, 137, 140, 236, 281, 295, 298 f., 305, 310, 378, 401–404, 407, 412, 498
Description 6 f., 14–16, 43, 47, 57 f., 61 f., 67, 73, 75, 77 f., 103, 105, 107, 111 f., 144, 168, 195, 197, 217, 262–264, 273 f., 285, 294 f., 310 f., 316, 320, 323 f., 335, 393, 395, 418 f., 424, 426, 445, 463, 475, 481, 497, 505, 507–512, 515, 517 f.
Dialectic 14, 29, 106, 288, 316, 444, 446, 455 f., 474, 482
– Transcendental dialectic 14, 396, 439–447, 453, 455–457, 460, 467, 475
Discernment 12, 366, 368, 381 f., 433, 507, 519
Drive 6, 10, 87, 127, 138–141, 194, 199, 222, 293, 304, 315–317, 319–323, 326, 353, 447, 467

Ecstasy 145
Ego 3, 5–9, 16, 35, 51, 69 f., 72, 77, 90, 93, 106, 115 f., 120, 143, 146–152, 154 f., 157, 159 f., 175 f., 181, 189–210, 213 f., 216–222, 224–231, 235–240, 242 f., 245–253, 272, 288–292, 298, 380, 384 f., 396 f., 401, 425 f., 499
– Mundane I 308, 320
– Transcendental I 119–121, 219, 229, 308
Eidos, eidetic 8, 68, 213 f., 216–219, 226–228, 249 f., 252, 273, 400, 519
Empathy 8, 147, 199, 227, 235, 239, 241–244, 246 f., 249, 251 f., 324
Empiricism 15, 76 f., 83, 85, 87, 198, 401 f., 458, 480, 485, 498 f., 501, 516–518
– Transcendental empiricism 15 f., 23, 497 f., 500 f., 509, 517
Epicureanism 159, 376
Epigenesis of pure reason 4, 83 f., 86

Epoché 3, 36 f., 41 f., 47, 49–52, 93 f., 116, 201, 208 f., 237, 248, 350, 393, 483, 505–507, 509, 518 f.
Essence 8, 33, 43–45, 47–49, 64, 68, 84, 90, 95, 108, 132, 175, 191–193, 195, 208 f., 213–215, 217–219, 222, 226–231, 246, 250, 252, 261, 268, 271, 280, 284, 308 f., 360, 371 f., 380–382, 384, 397 f., 400, 419, 430, 432–434, 456, 459 f., 467, 495, 497, 499, 516, 519
Ethics 1, 3, 9, 11 f., 41 f., 50, 152, 159, 327, 359–364, 366, 368, 372, 377 f., 482, 485, 491
– Ethical decision 375 f.
– Ethical insight 368, 382
Evidence 26, 28, 33, 36, 59, 93, 108 f., 165, 175, 183, 204, 210, 219–221, 224 f., 243, 247, 250, 260, 273, 283, 308, 310, 322, 324, 327 f., 334, 336, 344–347, 349 f., 352 f., 356, 360, 366–368, 371 f., 374 f., 391, 393, 396, 405, 421, 425, 429 f., 495
Experience 3 f., 7–9, 11, 13, 15 f., 27, 32–35, 41, 46 f., 58, 62–64, 67–69, 71 f., 74–77, 84–89, 94, 99, 103, 108, 110–112, 118, 129, 133–135, 139, 143–145, 147–154, 156–158, 160, 164, 166, 168–171, 173, 177–179, 181, 190–202, 204 f., 207–209, 215, 217, 220–225, 227, 230, 235 f., 240 f., 243–246, 259, 262–269, 272–275, 293–295, 305 f., 308–310, 312, 314 f., 317–319, 324, 326–328, 334 f., 337 f., 340–342, 346, 350–354, 361, 369 f., 379 f., 382–385, 394–397, 401–405, 407, 414, 418, 421–423, 426–429, 431 f., 434, 439, 441, 445 f., 458 f., 479 f., 482, 484–488, 490–492, 495 f., 498–501, 505, 507–512, 515 f., 518–520
– External experience 5, 107 f., 111, 241
– Internal experience 7, 107, 110, 112, 513, 515
– Possible experience 6, 62 f., 65, 70 f., 165, 169 f., 174, 179, 181, 183, 261, 267, 323, 398
– Self-experience 8, 107, 111, 201, 204

Subject Index

Facility 151, 496
Fact 9, 11, 67, 71, 72, 74f., 85–89, 95, 108f., 119f., 131, 133, 146, 150, 210, 213–226, 250f., 260, 305f., 328f., 363f., 366, 370, 380, 398, 413f., 418f., 429, 463, 468–470, 472, 480, 519
– Facticity 4, 8f., 85f., 89f., 108, 114, 120, 138, 213, 218–223, 225, 370, 396
– Factuality 363f.
– Matters of fact 63, 71, 214–217, 224, 363
– Primal facts 8, 213f., 220–227, 231
Faculty 29f., 65, 90f., 112, 129, 149, 151–153, 155f., 160, 172, 184, 261, 264, 266–268, 296f., 361, 366, 369, 371f., 375, 382, 445, 466, 498
– Faculties 3f., 44, 49, 57, 59f., 64, 66f., 70–72, 75–77, 83–85, 90, 95, 109, 131, 143, 145, 261, 295, 360, 369–371, 378, 392, 395–398, 402, 444f., 480
Feeling 12, 41, 111f., 190, 222, 243f., 361f., 367f., 371f., 374–379, 381f., 384, 510, 513f., 517
Fiction 112f., 288–290, 382, 396, 420, 458, 464, 466
– Heuristic fiction 458, 461, 466
Figurativity 404
Finitude 4, 12, 16, 38, 83f., 92–95, 97, 99, 121, 378–382, 449, 456f., 461, 465, 467, 489, 501
– Finite 4, 12, 66, 71, 86, 91–93, 95, 102, 108, 121, 359f., 364, 366, 370, 378–383, 396f., 444, 449, 456, 459, 488f., 501
First philosophy 8, 130, 213–215, 220f., 344, 347, 425, 518
Flow 7, 41, 49f., 52, 156, 193–199, 205f., 208, 287, 495
Formalism 135, 321, 372f.
Foundation 1f., 8f., 11, 16, 26f., 31, 33, 45, 48, 65, 78, 84, 103, 114, 144, 153, 175, 198f., 213f., 220, 223, 237, 259, 272, 333, 335–338, 340f., 349, 359–362, 371, 374–377, 382, 391, 397, 401, 417, 485, 513, 517
Freedom 32, 97, 153, 192, 227, 231, 327, 361f., 383–385, 479, 482f., 485f., 488, 490–494, 497

Fulfillment 68, 117, 139, 246, 288, 307, 326, 367, 381, 473

Generativity 315, 391, 406, 408
Geography 334f., 338, 354
Gestalt 73, 284
Given 3, 8–13, 15, 30, 34, 42, 44–46, 48, 50, 59, 62–64, 67f., 71–73, 75, 77, 89f., 106f., 112, 136, 138f., 143, 168, 171, 174f., 178f., 189–192, 195, 204, 207, 213f., 219–226, 229, 235f., 241, 245–249, 262–265, 272f., 281, 295, 297, 305, 310, 316–320, 324, 328, 335f., 340f., 346, 350–353, 361, 366, 368, 370f., 374f., 380, 383, 385, 393., 398, 403–405, 417f., 421, 425–433, 447f., 466., 468, 496, 499, 501, 505, 509f., 512, 519.
– Givenness 3, 9, 13, 16, 59, 61, 71, 93, 95, 189, 204, 220, 222, 226–228, 246, 261, 263, 272–274, 282f., 298, 319, 327, 360, 366f., 380, 382, 398, 424f., 427–429, 431–433, 469, 472f., 483
Given 3, 8–13, 15, 30, 34, 42, 44–46, 48, 50, 59, 62–64, 67f., 71–73, 75, 77, 89f., 106f., 112, 136, 138f., 143, 168, 171, 174f., 178f., 189–192, 195, 204, 207, 213f., 219–226, 229, 235f., 241, 245–249, 262–265, 272f., 281, 295, 297, 305, 310, 316–320, 324, 328, 335f., 340f., 346, 350–353, 361, 366, 368, 370f., 374f., 380, 383, 385, 393., 398, 403–405, 417f., 421, 425–433, 447f., 466., 468, 496, 499, 501, 505, 509f., 512, 519.
– Givenness 3, 9, 13, 16, 59, 61, 71, 93, 95, 189, 204, 220, 222, 226–228, 246, 261, 263, 272–274, 282f., 298, 319, 327, 360, 366f., 380, 382, 398, 424f., 427–429, 431–433, 469, 472f., 483
– Pregiven 14, 89, 115, 320, 350–352, 385, 391, 393, 407, 456, 466, 468, 471–474, 505f., 508
– Pregivenness 14, 116, 222, 272, 455f., 468, 470f., 474

God   12, 26f., 31, 87, 89, 108, 144, 223, 363, 380–382, 444, 450–452, 456, 483f., 499f.
Good   31, 152, 363, 365–368, 375, 377, 381f., 494
Grammar   73
Ground   7f., 10, 23–25, 27f., 31, 33–35, 61, 77, 86, 89, 92, 98, 102, 114, 116, 131, 141, 159, 163, 182, 198, 210, 213, 215–217, 220–227, 248, 272, 290, 305f., 308, 311, 316–318, 327f., 334f., 340, 348, 350f., 354, 368, 372–374, 377, 382, 385, 396, 413, 415–417, 419, 424f., 431, 433f., 441, 445f., 449, 451f., 462–465, 468, 473f., 481f., 484, 487, 489–491, 493–495, 498–501, 510

Habitus   136, 138, 151, 154, 205
– Habituality   151, 229–230, 320
Hallucination   170, 328
Health   150f., 221
History   9f., 14, 23, 35, 42, 57, 65, 78, 95f., 111, 113, 136, 204–206, 221, 229–231, 236, 259, 272, 279–283, 287f., 290f., 299f., 307, 416, 423, 427, 429, 434, 442f., 446, 450f., 488, 506
Homeworld   489, 492
Horror   153, 158
Human   2, 4, 14f., 25, 32, 38, 41, 44–52, 59f., 64–68, 71f., 75, 78, 84–86, 88–90, 92, 95, 99, 102–122, 129–131, 140, 144–147, 149, 152, 154, 158, 163, 165, 168, 173f., 184, 190, 197, 201, 203f., 214, 221, 225, 230, 235, 261, 281, 296f., 310, 312–315, 317, 320f., 325, 327, 329, 341f., 346, 348f., 362f., 367, 369, 378–380, 383f., 394, 413, 445f., 449, 452, 456–458, 461, 465, 467–469, 471, 475, 479–494, 496–498, 500f.
– Humanity   3, 5, 41, 50f., 101, 114, 117, 119, 121, 280, 374, 434
Hylē   138–140, 222–223, 309, 372,

Idea   4–8, 10, 13f., 25, 31–33, 35f., 43f., 50, 57, 62–66, 70f., 73f., 77f., 83, 85, 88, 90, 92f., 95f., 101, 104, 110–113, 115f., 120, 127f., 132, 134–137, 139, 144f., 149f., 158f., 163, 165, 167f., 170, 175, 178–182, 189f., 193, 196, 201, 204f., 213f., 216, 219f., 223, 227, 229, 235, 237f., 242, 244, 263, 265, 269–272, 279, 282–288, 290–292, 300, 303f., 307f., 310, 313, 316f., 319, 327, 347, 359, 361f., 366, 370, 374, 383–385, 392–394, 396, 398–401, 404, 406, 419–422, 424–433, 439, 443–448, 450f., 458f., 465, 470, 472, 474f., 479, 483, 487, 489f., 493, 497–499, 506, 508f., 511–513, 516f.
– Regulative Idea   385, 446, 459, 465f.
Idealism   1, 6f., 36, 58f., 78, 91f., 95, 97, 107, 111, 163f., 166–168, 170, 177f., 183, 200f., 208, 235, 288, 338, 363, 391, 393, 396, 399, 407, 412, 433, 480
– Phenomenological idealism   218, 391
– Skeptical idealism   6, 163, 166, 183f.
– Transcendental idealism   2, 5–7, 36, 163–165, 167–172, 174f., 179, 183f., 236, 333f., 337f., 349, 391–393, 398, 466, 482, 509
Illusion   69, 94, 113, 159, 170, 239f., 280, 397, 442, 445, 449, 451–453, 461, 463, 467f., 472, 475, 482, 486, 488
– Transcendental illusion   45, 69, 235, 460, 465–467, 475
Image   46, 48f., 66, 92, 156, 244–246, 249f., 333, 419, 491, 518
Imagination   45f., 49, 91, 97f., 129f., 155f., 183, 191, 296f., 360, 392, 401–404, 406, 475, 512
– Synthesis of imagination   295–297
Immanence   7, 57, 76, 91, 93–95, 182, 189, 196, 199–201, 203, 237, 240, 295
Imperative   2f., 23, 38, 71, 239, 379–382, 445, 469
– Categorical imperativeness   379
Inconspicuous (*das Unscheinbare*)   481, 483, 490f., 494, 498
Inebriation   145
Innatism   86–89

Instinct   10, 138 f., 243 f., 304, 315, 322–325, 367
– Drive   6, 10, 127, 138–141, 222, 304, 315–323, 326, 353
Intellect   2, 4, 7, 9 f., 12, 23, 26, 28–31, 34, 37, 41 f., 44, 47 f., 50, 57, 60–62, 64–68, 70 f., 75 f., 84, 87–89, 97, 102–104, 108, 119, 129 f., 132–134, 136, 138, 140 f., 166, 170–174, 181 f., 235, 243, 260 f., 264 f., 267–269, 280, 284, 287–289, 295, 298 f., 303–305, 307–309, 311, 314, 323, 325, 328, 334, 342, 344 f., 347–350, 353–356, 360 f., 365, 370, 375, 378 f., 382, 391 f., 395, 402–404, 412, 415 f., 422 f., 434, 440 f., 445–449, 453, 462, 465 f., 474 f., 480–485, 492, 509, 515, 517
– *Intellectus archetypus*   64, 83, 95
– *Intellectus ectypus*   64
Intentionality   6 f., 10, 14, 60, 62–64, 69, 77, 127, 139–141, 164, 192, 222, 229, 235, 237, 239, 291–293, 300, 397, 471, 473 f.
– Intentional connection   291–294, 300
– Intentional content   69, 292, 500
– Intentional object   10, 64, 68, 174, 177, 229, 292–294, 300, 360
– Intentional relation   10, 393
Interiority   69, 78, 90, 110 f., 251
Intersubjectivity   1, 37, 139, 147, 199, 203, 213, 221 f., 235, 238, 247, 406, 469 f., 489
Introspection   15, 106, 111, 505, 507, 511–513, 515–518
Intuition   3, 9, 12, 16, 45 f., 59, 61–63, 67 f., 71, 77, 86, 88–93, 97, 107, 128–130, 132 f., 139, 171–173, 175, 182 f., 208 f., 214–216, 241, 259 f., 262, 264, 267–269, 274 f., 289, 296 f., 308, 324, 339, 341 f., 353, 360, 366–369, 371 f., 379–381, 383 f., 398, 401–404, 406, 417, 424, 428, 430, 460, 471, 480, 482, 511–513
– Eidetic intuition   63, 71, 75, 214, 370–372
– Empirical intuition   214, 267–269, 275, 339, 342
– Pure intuition   97 f., 129, 262, 271, 297, 352, 402, 425, 460
Intuitive   3, 9, 13, 59, 62, 70 f., 106, 109, 131–133, 172, 182, 207 f., 237, 251, 261–265, 267–270, 272–275, 308, 347, 366 f., 384, 396, 400, 402, 405, 421, 425, 427 f., 433, 448, 492, 512, 519
Irrationality   213 f., 221, 231

Joy   153, 191, 202, 241
Judgment   11, 27, 35, 44, 65, 67 f., 75, 87, 94, 112, 129, 135 f., 140, 153, 191, 215, 218, 309, 312, 320, 337, 339, 363 f., 367 f., 486, 494 f., 501
Justificatory responsibility (*Rechtfertigung*)   327 f.

Knowledge   2, 4, 10 f., 24 f., 27–34, 36, 38, 41–43, 47, 51, 57, 59 f., 62, 64–66, 68 f., 71, 74, 78, 83–86, 88–90, 92, 97 f., 104, 106–108, 110, 112 f., 115, 117–119, 129, 132, 143, 166, 171, 215, 240, 265, 267, 270, 281, 283, 290, 292, 303, 305–307, 312, 314–320, 333 f., 336–338, 341–345, 347–349, 351–356, 365, 368, 370 f., 379 f., 392, 394 f., 401–405, 407, 433, 443, 479, 483, 485, 487, 497, 499, 505, 509
– Intuitive knowledge   267
– Self-knowledge   2, 25, 104, 106 f., 112

Law   8, 11, 27 f., 63, 65–67, 72–74, 84, 87, 103, 107 f., 131, 136, 150, 153, 181, 196, 216, 218–220, 229, 266–268, 288, 296, 318–321, 339 f., 342, 346, 349, 362–366, 370–376, 379–384, 398, 401, 404, 407, 412–419, 462, 482, 485, 491, 499, 514–516
– Practical law   369, 372 f., 375, 380
Legality   12, 84 f., 103, 319, 364, 370, 372, 397, 401 f., 404 f., 407
Limit   6, 11, 23, 26 f., 29, 31, 34, 66, 72, 88, 92 f., 118, 136, 144 f., 149, 151, 160, 173, 182, 203, 213, 221, 237, 247, 272, 296, 304, 315, 324, 350 f., 363, 377 f., 404, 406, 424, 450, 470 f., 487 f., 490, 511 f.

Logic 1f., 9, 27, 29, 31–34, 36, 44, 60f., 66f., 73, 75f., 78, 96–98, 111f., 129, 176, 182, 259f., 265, 270–272, 275, 305, 311, 321, 363f., 371, 374, 406, 415, 424, 426, 479, 496, 513
– Formal logic   60, 62, 73, 75, 180f., 215, 270, 272
– Genetic logic   272
– Real logic   9, 259, 270–272
– Transcendental logic   9, 44, 86, 97f., 239, 259f., 265, 270–273, 275, 315, 423
– World-logic   259, 272f.

Meaning 1–3, 7, 14f., 23–26, 29f., 33–38, 41f., 44–50, 52, 74, 84, 86, 88, 90–92, 94f., 98, 101f., 105f., 108f., 115, 121, 130, 144–150, 152, 154f., 159, 165, 172–174, 179–181, 189, 191, 201, 203, 206, 216, 221, 223, 231, 240, 247, 249, 261, 268, 273, 281, 283, 287, 292, 294f., 300, 308f., 347, 351f., 355, 359–361, 363, 367, 375, 383, 385, 392–394, 397–400, 404–406, 422, 434, 440, 442, 445, 451, 455, 457, 479f., 482–486, 488–501, 505f., 509, 514
Measure   327, 447, 481f., 486–497, 499–501, 513, 515
Mechanism   10f., 285, 303–306, 309, 311–317, 319, 321–326, 328f., 383, 442, 451
Mereology   57, 63, 72f.
Metaphor   87, 149, 152, 160, 193f., 481, 484, 489, 491, 497
Metaphysics   2, 8, 16, 23, 25–27, 29–32, 42–44, 58, 60, 62, 66, 87, 95, 97, 145, 151–154, 159, 176, 213–216, 220–226, 339, 364, 376, 407, 413, 423, 442–444, 446, 450–452, 457–459, 461f., 467, 476, 479, 481, 483, 487, 490f.
– Metaphysics of Being (*Seinsmetaphysik*)   457–459, 461f., 464, 467
– Metaphysics of Ideas (*Ideenmetaphysik*)   458f., 461f., 475
– Phenomenological metaphysics   8, 16, 213f., 220f., 223f., 226, 231
Method   8, 15, 23, 26, 29, 32–34, 36f., 60–62, 64, 69, 73, 78, 115, 131–133, 165, 175, 198, 204, 209, 213, 215f., 259, 290, 324, 333, 335f., 342, 345, 349, 354, 379, 382, 392f., 395, 399, 406f., 413, 418f., 423, 427, 429f., 432f., 439, 456f., 471, 489, 493, 498, 507, 509, 512f., 515f., 518–520
– Transcendental method   253, 391, 407, 411, 424, 429f.
Microphenomenology   15, 505–508, 510f., 518f.
Mind   4, 6, 45f., 49–51, 60, 66, 69, 76, 78, 83, 86f., 89, 91f., 94, 112, 115, 117, 134, 165, 168, 170, 176, 179–181, 191, 202–204, 235, 242, 268, 271, 285f., 294, 323, 333, 348, 375, 403, 412, 415f., 421, 425, 431, 480, 489, 514, 516
– Mental activity   66, 76, 412, 415f.,, 422, 426
Modality   366, 461–464, 466, 473, 475
Monad   51f., 120, 147, 160, 206, 220, 229, 250, 314
Mundane,   11, 14, 105, 116, 308, 320, 458
– Mundanization   457, 468

Naturalism   4, 10, 16, 83, 85f., 89f., 105, 288, 290, 309f., 324, 506, 518
– Natural attitude   3, 37f., 49, 65, 69f., 93, 115, 119, 121, 146, 168, 190f., 201, 203, 206, 350, 394, 400, 471
– Naturalization   4, 11, 15f., 70, 83, 105, 505f., 518
– Naturalize   69, 83, 115
Necessity   1, 3–5, 10, 12, 31, 48, 50f., 62–64, 67f., 71f., 74–76, 87, 94, 99, 101, 108f., 112f., 115, 131, 151, 173f., 181, 183, 193, 196, 204, 214, 217–220, 224f., 227f., 238, 247, 287, 289, 309, 313–315, 317, 319–321, 338, 340, 362, 369–372, 375, 379–381, 391, 395, 402, 405, 414, 426, 442, 444, 447, 464–466, 475, 485
Nihilism   479–481, 485, 490–492, 494, 496
Nonsense   77, 119, 180, 244
Norm   6, 10, 12, 15, 67, 83, 133, 165, 168, 170, 179, 183, 217, 265, 303, 305, 309–314, 317f., 321f., 325–329, 363f., 366,

368f., 392, 400, 461, 465, 484, 489, 494f., 499f.
– Ethical norm   359f., 364, 366f., 372
– Normative assessment   305, 312
– Normative claim   312f., 491
– Normativity   11, 67, 305, 319, 322, 391, 407, 465f., 475f., 495
Normality   152, 154, 316, 318f., 326
Noumenon   31, 64, 163–165, 171–174, 180, 183, 238

Object   3, 6f., 12f., 15, 23–29, 32, 41–43, 45, 48f., 57–59, 61–64, 67–70, 72–75, 77, 84–92, 95–98, 106–108, 111f., 118, 129, 131f., 135f., 139, 148f., 159, 163–172, 174, 177–184, 189, 191f., 194–197, 200, 207–210, 214f., 217f., 226f., 231, 239–241, 247, 249, 261, 265–274, 282f., 292, 294–299, 306, 309f., 312, 314f., 319f., 328, 334, 336, 339–341, 346, 348, 350, 352, 359–361, 364f., 367–370, 372, 374f., 378–380, 382f., 391–394, 396–404, 406f., 413, 415, 419f., 422f., 429, 441, 443–448, 450, 452, 458–460, 462f., 466, 468f., 471–473, 475, 493, 501, 505f., 515, 518
– Objectifying act   210, 428, 473
– Objectivism   176, 288, 506
– Objectivity   7, 59, 70, 75, 84–86, 88, 96, 130–132, 134f., 139, 141, 164, 180, 208, 236, 238, 247, 265, 289, 314f., 317f., 322, 326, 369, 391, 407, 412, 415, 417, 449
Observation   61f., 65, 111, 158, 266, 271, 284f., 320, 337f., 347, 353, 364, 513, 515
– Self-observation   111, 511
Ontology   3, 30, 44, 48, 59f., 70, 73, 76, 93–95, 97, 180, 220, 222f., 227, 262, 264, 270f., 399, 452f., 458, 485, 490, 507, 509, 518
– Formal ontology   60, 180, 223
– Ontological difference   460, 464, 469, 483, 500
– Ontology of the thing   14, 444f., 449, 452
Openness   90, 99, 136, 213f., 226–228, 230f., 449, 465, 492

Optimality   318, 321
Origin   33, 49, 67, 86, 88, 95, 98, 138, 141, 219, 222, 279–283, 287, 290, 299, 359f., 366, 368–371, 375, 392, 398, 407, 452, 461, 463, 471, 475f., 482, 514, 517
Other   8, 50, 52, 85, 140, 145, 147, 203, 220, 226–230, 235f., 238–253, 265, 313, 325, 466, 491f., 496, 498, 500f.
Other   8, 50, 52, 85, 140, 145, 147, 203, 220, 226–230, 235f., 238–253, 265, 313, 325, 466, 491f., 496, 498, 500f.
– Otherness   4f., 8, 16, 90, 203, 235

Paradox   15, 38, 91, 96, 110, 119, 140, 202, 245, 381, 442, 447, 449, 467, 469, 480, 487, 492
Participation   17, 49, 229, 239, 285
Perception   34, 46f., 77, 109, 147–149, 166f., 169f., 180, 191, 201, 207–209, 239, 242f., 250, 268, 273, 295, 297f., 305, 312, 317, 319, 326, 328, 346f., 353, 361, 367, 370, 384, 396, 466, 515–517
Person   33, 71, 103, 112, 117–120, 143, 154, 158, 190f., 203, 206f., 224, 227–230, 289, 305, 310f., 313, 323, 367, 373, 397, 479, 486f., 490–492, 494, 496, 498, 500f., 507, 511f., 517, 519
Phantom   248, 250, 262–264
Phenomenon   27, 30, 35, 48, 58, 61, 64, 67, 73, 93f., 113, 147, 155, 164, 200, 241, 244, 247, 249, 252, 346, 348, 383, 406f., 448, 485, 516, 518
– Phenomenalization   405–407, 518
– Phenomenology of phenomenology   439, 474
– Neurophenomenology   518
Phronesis   494
Physics   11, 38, 290, 319, 333, 335–342, 351–354, 370, 462, 486f., 492, 497
Plasticity   406f.
Positivism   416
– Logical positivism   76
Possibility   2, 8, 11, 15, 23f., 27–33, 36, 41, 43, 48, 57, 59f., 65f., 70, 72, 74f., 85–88, 94, 97, 103, 106, 120, 133f., 147f., 155, 157f., 163, 165, 169, 171–175,

180–184, 213, 217f., 220, 222, 228, 230f., 235f., 244, 248–252, 269, 272, 280, 282, 292, 303–305, 312, 314–320, 325, 333, 337f., 341f., 350, 363, 367, 370f., 373–375, 378, 383, 385, 392, 395–397, 400, 403, 412–414, 425, 427, 440, 445f., 451f., 462, 470f., 473f., 483, 494f., 498, 500f., 505f., 510–513, 519f.
– Possibilization   407
– Real possibility   171, 173, 182, 520
Potentiality   88, 228, 252, 317, 323, 325
– System of potentialities   323, 325f., 329
Principle   7, 11, 14, 24f., 28–30, 43, 58, 61–64, 70f., 73f., 84, 86f., 93, 96, 107, 109, 129f., 133, 176, 180, 193, 196–199, 203, 208, 215–218, 227f., 237, 246, 261, 266, 281, 290, 293, 295, 306, 308, 335–343, 349, 352, 355, 359–363, 365–367, 369, 371f., 375–380, 382f., 385, 401, 404, 406f., 411, 414, 419, 424f., 432, 441f., 449, 451, 457, 459, 482, 498, 500f., 509, 511–513, 519
– Principle of principles   61, 63, 65, 70f., 77, 424f., 513
– Principle of sufficient reason   270, 482, 498
Psychology   2, 4f., 11, 13, 15f., 32–34, 60, 66, 73, 76, 84, 102, 105–113, 116, 145f., 148–150, 154–157, 159, 179, 198, 240, 242, 244, 300, 310f., 349f., 354, 364, 415f., 418f., 422f., 426f., 443, 505, 507f., 511–518
– Act psychology   422
– Experimental psychology   507, 512
– Psychologism   3f., 57–61, 64f., 83f., 89, 99, 107, 109, 112, 115, 130, 202, 311, 349, 401, 414, 416, 422, 513, 517f.

Quality   3, 46, 49, 170, 195, 199, 346, 377, 514f., 517

Realism   6f., 78, 163–167, 174, 178, 183, 360, 362, 391, 399f., 407
– Empirical realism   163, 165, 169–171, 184
– Transcendental realism   7, 163–165, 168–171, 174f., 180, 183, 202, 236

Reality   7, 36, 41–43, 47f., 59, 91–96, 146, 159, 163f., 166, 168–171, 173f., 178f., 182–184, 202, 204, 215–217, 220f., 223, 230, 236, 262–264, 266, 269, 271–273, 280f., 343, 348, 354, 393, 403f., 442, 445, 448, 451f., 457, 459f., 464–466, 470, 482, 486–488, 490–492, 497, 500, 509
– Empirical reality   93, 269, 275
– Ens realissimum   44, 439, 442f., 450–452
– Omnitudo realitatis   439, 442f., 450–452
Reason   2f., 5, 9, 12, 14f., 24, 26–31, 33, 38, 42, 47, 66f., 75, 83, 87, 89f., 97f., 102, 104f., 107, 109f., 112, 115f., 129f., 132, 134, 144, 149, 158f., 166f., 169–171, 183, 193, 195f., 225, 227, 235, 237, 239, 242, 245, 248, 260, 265, 268, 270, 281, 288, 292, 294, 299, 305, 307f., 321f., 327, 329, 335–338, 340f., 343, 346, 349, 352, 354f., 359f., 362f., 365–369, 371–376, 378f., 381–385, 392, 394, 398, 401, 418, 425f., 439–450, 452f., 455–458, 460f., 463f., 466f., 470, 474–476, 479–493, 495–498, 500f.
– Practical reason   359f., 362, 365f., 368, 372, 375, 378, 485f., 491
Reduction   2f., 5, 34–37, 41f., 47, 49, 60f., 63f., 66–68, 71–73, 77, 84, 93, 98, 112, 115, 118f., 121, 131–134, 136f., 146, 159, 178, 192, 201, 203, 206f., 235–237, 239, 247–249, 253, 268, 289–291, 297, 311, 379, 393, 419, 424f., 427f., 431, 518
– Transcendental reduction   15, 33, 35, 37f., 68f., 77, 116, 121, 146, 159, 236f., 239f., 248f., 469, 498
Reflection   7, 15, 28, 34, 63, 65, 90, 102, 104, 108, 110, 113, 116, 120, 137, 152, 189, 192, 204, 207–210, 213, 218, 220, 223, 226, 229, 253, 327, 380, 391, 393–396, 401, 404–406, 423, 428–432, 480–483, 487, 489, 493, 498–500, 511f.
Reification   14, 202, 450, 452
Renewal   15, 327, 511

Repetition   5, 16, 102, 104, 110, 118, 316 f., 319, 326, 411, 514
Resemblance   58, 78, 241
Retention   139, 209 f.
Rift (*Riss*)   481, 492, 496, 500

Schema   45–47, 50, 248, 515, 517
– Schematism   45, 129 f., 295
Science   1 f., 8 f., 11, 26 f., 29–34, 37 f., 43, 58, 60, 65–67, 69, 75–77, 84, 86, 97, 104 f., 107, 109, 113–120, 122, 131, 133, 170, 175 f., 180, 189, 203, 214–217, 220, 223, 231, 237, 259, 265 f., 270–275, 280–282, 288 f., 312, 326, 333–345, 347–356, 365, 412 f., 416–420, 424, 427, 433, 455, 479 f., 482, 485 f., 488–490, 493, 497, 499, 505–507, 518
– World of science   273
Selfhood   214, 229, 239, 244, 249
Sensation   30 f., 46, 69, 148, 150, 153–158, 230, 262, 267 f., 317, 513–515, 517
– Sense data   67 f., 76 f., 346, 417
Sensibility   9, 12, 26, 30 f., 47, 57, 64 f., 68, 70 f., 76, 88, 106, 129, 132, 134, 168, 170–174, 222 f., 260 f., 264 f., 267–269, 274, 284, 288, 298, 312, 360 f., 369–371, 378 f., 381 f., 384 f., 392, 402 f., 480, 498
Sociology   117, 342
Solipsism   8 f., 59, 164, 235, 238–240, 242, 247, 251–253, 318, 496
Soul   26 f., 67, 70, 107, 112, 120, 147, 150, 155–157, 168, 170, 202, 288, 290, 308, 381, 417
Space   9, 15, 30, 35, 51 f., 88–92, 96 f., 111, 132, 152, 166, 169, 173, 179 f., 200, 222, 226, 237, 241, 259, 261–263, 266, 268 f., 271, 275, 290, 328, 336, 339–341, 352, 378, 396, 413, 441, 444, 449, 460, 463, 479, 481–485, 487–490, 492, 496, 501, 509 f.
Structure   2, 4, 6, 8 f., 13, 23, 30 f., 36, 51, 57, 63–66, 68, 72, 75–77, 83–86, 88–90, 95, 109, 131, 134, 139, 144, 148, 152, 156, 160, 163, 170, 173, 183, 189, 213, 216, 218–223, 225 f., 238, 241, 247–249, 260–263, 266, 270, 272, 275, 306 f., 318, 321, 326, 334 f., 344, 346–348, 350, 352, 354, 359 f., 366 f., 369–371, 378–380, 382, 396–398, 400 f., 405, 412, 414, 423, 446, 448, 450, 462 f., 467, 469, 472 f., 475, 481, 491 f., 496, 499 f., 505, 507, 509, 515, 519
– Regulative structure   359 f., 380
Subjectivity   1–3, 5–7, 10, 13, 15 f., 23, 31, 35–38, 51, 75, 83, 85, 90, 94 f., 99, 108, 114 f., 119–121, 130–134, 139, 141, 144, 176, 178 f., 190, 198–201, 216, 224, 226, 235, 238 f., 253, 272, 306–310, 313–316, 320 f., 325, 359 f., 369 f., 384 f., 393–395, 397 f., 417, 442, 446, 460, 464, 466, 468–472, 475, 480, 487, 489, 492, 505 f., 518
– Concrete subjectivity   306–309, 312, 318
– Subjectivism   85, 90, 288, 412–413, 415, 420, 441
Substantiality   194, 263 f., 269 f.
Sympathy   167, 241–245, 421, 427
Synthesis   9 f., 45 f., 83, 92, 97, 129 f., 132, 136, 156 f., 198 f., 262, 269, 275, 279–281, 285–287, 289, 291–296, 298–301, 306, 401–404, 448, 459, 508
– Passive synthesis   299, 313
– Synthesis of apprehension   295 f., 401
– Synthesis of identification   300, 316
– Synthesis of recognition   295–297, 401
– Synthesis of reproduction   295 f., 401
– *Synthesis speciosa*   294, 403
– Synthetic   27 f., 45, 62, 65, 73, 75, 78, 127, 129, 170, 174, 183, 196, 198, 261 f., 264, 286 f., 291, 294–296, 298, 306, 337 f., 396, 403, 515
– Transcendental synthesis   401 f.
System   23, 25, 27, 29–31, 43, 45, 52, 65, 74, 76, 86 f., 102, 137, 215, 250 f., 293, 299 f., 313 f., 319, 321, 323, 334, 353, 383, 441, 452
– Systematicity   11, 334 f., 337, 347

Teleology   10, 144, 221, 223, 316, 319 f., 480, 487, 492
Thing-in-itself   72, 97

Time 1, 3, 6, 8f., 30–32, 35f., 44, 46, 48–52, 72f., 88f., 92, 95–98, 102, 106f., 109, 111f., 114, 121, 130, 132, 136–138, 143, 145–147, 149, 152, 154, 165, 171, 173f., 176, 179f., 183f., 195, 197f., 204–206, 209, 216–219, 222, 226, 235, 239–241, 244–250, 259, 261–264, 266, 268–271, 274f., 283, 299, 305, 308, 311, 317f., 325–328, 339, 341, 350, 372, 378, 396, 402f., 406, 421, 429, 431f., 434, 449, 460, 462f., 469, 480, 483f., 487–489, 493, 505–508, 510f., 513f., 516f., 519
– Consciousness 128, 135, 137, 141, 222, 427
– Constitution 6, 127f., 137f.
– Temporality 49, 129f., 138, 140, 196–198, 205, 209, 262, 407, 513
– Temporalization 5f., 51, 127f., 140, 315
Transcendence 7, 35, 38, 70, 85, 90–95, 97, 182, 189, 196, 200f., 203f., 237f., 246, 310, 474, 483, 485, 488, 491f., 495, 500f., 518
Truth 3, 11, 47, 49, 61f., 65, 67, 77, 86f., 89f., 101, 119, 160, 170, 179, 183, 215f., 271, 283, 285, 310–312, 316–319, 322, 326f., 336, 338, 340, 347, 349, 355, 359, 361, 364, 368, 371f., 380, 382, 404, 424, 468, 471–473, 475, 481–484, 490, 499f., 512
– Double truth 15, 486–488, 490

Uncanny (*unheimlich*) 486, 489, 497
Unity 7–9, 28, 42–44, 48–51, 72, 76f., 84, 97f., 107, 127, 129, 135f., 138, 140, 171, 180, 196–200, 202, 206, 208, 215, 227, 230, 235–239, 245, 247f., 251–253, 262, 264, 273, 281, 288, 292, 296–299, 317f., 321, 323, 396, 401–406, 413–415, 417f., 445, 452

Validity 10–12, 47f., 50, 65, 67f., 84, 106, 108, 116, 130, 133, 136, 138, 181f., 210, 239f., 303, 305f., 308, 310, 313, 321f., 327, 343–345, 347–349, 351, 353, 355f., 360, 362–364, 366f., 369–371, 373, 378, 382, 384, 393f., 399, 485, 509
– Objective validity 265, 362, 395, 402f., 415f., 445
Variation 77, 183, 217, 219, 222, 225, 245–247, 249f., 252f., 282f., 292, 309, 326, 432, 516, 519
– Eidetic variation 8, 62, 71–73, 76, 213f., 216f., 219f., 223, 226–228, 231, 370, 382, 512, 519
– Self-variation 8

Wakefulness 468–474
World 2, 7–9, 11, 13f., 16, 23, 26f., 31, 34–38, 41f., 47–49, 51, 58, 68f., 74, 76f., 92f., 95, 106, 110f., 113–120, 133, 135f., 138f., 141, 146–152, 154, 156f., 159f., 163–169, 173–183, 190, 201–203, 206, 213f., 216, 218–225, 227–231, 235–239, 241, 245, 247f., 251, 253, 259, 262, 264–268, 270, 272–275, 279, 284f., 288–291, 309f., 312–319, 323–326, 333–338, 341f., 345–356, 379, 393–395, 399, 407, 411, 430, 439–453, 455–476, 481f., 485–494, 496f., 499f.
– Aesthetic world 273f.
– Enworlding 457, 468, 471–475
– Innerworldly 439, 441–444, 446–449
– Lifeworld 3, 11, 350–356, 486–491
– Oblivion of the world 459, 461, 467, 475
– World-consciousness 14, 444, 467–474

www.ingramcontent.com/pod-product-compliance
Lightning Source LLC
Chambersburg PA
CBHW031748220426
43662CB00007B/315